BUSINESS STATISTICS

# BUSINESS STATISTICS

## MICK SILVER

*Professor of Business Statistics,*
*University of Wales College of Cardiff*

## McGRAW-HILL BOOK COMPANY

**London** · New York · St Louis · San Francisco · Auckland · Bogotá · Caracas
Lisbon · Madrid · Mexico · Milan · Montreal · New Delhi · Panama · Paris
San Juan · São Paulo · Singapore · Sydney · Tokyo · Toronto

Published by
McGRAW-HILL Book Company Europe
Shoppenhangers Road, Maidenhead, Berkshire, SL6 2QL, England
Telephone 0628 23432
Fax 0628 770224

**British Library Cataloguing in Publication Data**

Silver, M. S.
  Business Statistics
  I. Title
  519.5

  ISBN 0–07–707445–9

**Library of Congress Cataloging in Publication Data**

Silver, M. S.
  Business statistics / Mick Silver.
    p.   cm.
  Includes bibliographical references and index.
  ISBN 0–07–707445–9
  1. Commercial statistics.   I. Title.
  HF1017.S527   1992
  519.5–dc20      92–7384 CIP

  34 HWV 943

Typeset by Vision Typesetting, Manchester
and printed and bound in Great Britain by BPCC Hazell Books Ltd. Member of BPCC Ltd

# CONTENTS

# ACKNOWLEDGEMENTS

This book reflects some of my teaching in the quantitative area to undergraduate first year management/business students and MBA students at Aston University's Management Centre, Bath University's School of Management and now Cardiff Business School, University of Wales College of Cardiff. Only naturally my teaching, and thus this book, has benefited from student feedback. A feature of the book is the reference at the end of each chapter to appropriate commands on Lotus 1-2-3 and Minitab software as well as summaries of the commands in Appendices 2 and 3. Both Lotus 1-2-3 and Minitab are registered trademarks and I am grateful to Lotus Development (UK) Ltd and Minitab Inc. for permission to reproduce summaries of the commands from their publications. The Monopolies and Mergers Commission gave permission for the reproduction of a section of their report on *The Supply of Beer* in Chapter 1, this being permitted under Crown Copyright. The *Journal of the Royal Statistical Society* gave permission for three diagrams from Cleveland and McGill (1987) to be reproduced in Chapter 3. *The Economist* allowed reproduction of one of their charts in Chapter 3, and the *Biometrika* trustees gave permission to reproduce the table in Appendix 4.

The appendices contain a number of statistical tables which, unless otherwise stated, were reproduced from Z. W. Kmietowicz and Y. Yannoulis (1988) *Statistical Tables for Economics, Business and Social Studies*. This excellent publication contains many additional tables to those given in the appendices and I am grateful to the Longman UK Group for permission to reproduce the tables in the appendices.

I am most grateful to Mike Brigden, University of Bath, for his painstaking reading of the manuscript and many suggestions from which the book has benefited. I would also like to thank Gerald Harbour (UWCC) for his comments on Chapter 7. My thanks go to Stacy Vallis and Sarah Ingram for their excellent secretarial assistance. And finally to Bernice for her love and support.

To my brother Leon

# INTRODUCTION

*Business Statistics* is concerned with the application of statistical methods to management and business-related areas. I have written this book with MBA and first-year undergraduate management/business students in mind, though its coverage embraces the syllabuses of a wide range of qualifications. The book is also intended to be of use to practising managers wishing to extend the use of statistical methods in their work. The concern of this book is *not* with mathematical derivations and proofs. Only minimal mathematical skills are required and Appendix 1 provides a test (with answers) to see if you possess these skills (and more) and, if not, provides instruction in this area. After reading this introduction you should turn to Appendix 1, undertake the test and, if necessary, find out where and why you went wrong. You will then be better placed to start the book.

The book is concerned with the application of statistical methods: it is not just about applying formulae, but about understanding the assumptions and principles of the methods and interpreting the results in an applied, problem-orientated context. If your perception of a good statistics text is one that solely and clearly explains how to calculate several measures, this book will be disappointing, and rightfully so. What you will discover from the book is that a proper use of the methods requires a good understanding of the principles behind them and the assumptions implicit within them. The calculation of the measures is an almost trivial part of the exercise, especially given the developments in computing hardware and software. This is not to say that you should have no experience of undertaking such calculations, for they can help you identify the principles upon which the measures are based. Indeed, Chapter 13 of this book comprises exercises for each chapter accompanied by worked examples. Exercises are also provided at the end of each chapter, though they are without answers. Should you require further worked examples you can refer to Spiegel (1988) and Kazmier (1988); it is emphasized that *doing* exercises is the best way of learning. However, such texts are insufficient by themselves. To use (and indeed choose) an appropriate method we must be able to question assumptions and interpret results in the context of the particular problem we are concerned with.

The subject should be broached with enthusiasm: it is a powerful, fascinating, applied area of critical importance. It is powerful because its rigorous mathematical basis provides the means by which new insights can be derived, and the conclusions of others challenged over a wide range of important applications. It introduces new concepts or frameworks for thinking, opening up facets of problems. It is fascinating at a personal level with discoveries being tied to the statistical skills of the analyst, identifying patterns and relationships that may have major policy implications. It will become apparent from the chapters that follow that the subject matter is of critical importance to a range of functional areas including marketing, operations, human resource management, finance and strategy. More generally it is about how to handle numerical information in business. Much information comes in this form (and can be collected by you): if you cannot handle it, you miss out on what is happening. With the revolution in information technology (IT) generating vast quantities of numerical data and easy-to-use software to facilitate the analysis, an inability to handle all of this leaves you sorely disadvantaged. Indeed the principles and methods considered in this book apply to social, environmental, economic and scientific issues and should help make you more able to handle the issues at stake in these areas, and thus be a better informed person.

The book makes little demand in terms of mathematical ability, concepts being explained and developed on an intuitive level. Yet it is not a basic text. At times it may cover material in far greater depth than required by your course. But this is when a basic treatment of the subject would leave you ill-placed to use the methods. The power of statistical software and spreadsheets has broadened what might practically be done, and this book responds to such developments. Nonetheless students should bear in mind that at times the book may cover a subject in more detail than your lecturer. Chapter 7 has potential for this, though the material may well come into its own later in life if you use these methods.

Spreadsheets have become a widely adopted management tool and relevant commands for the use of *Lotus 1-2-3* can be found towards the end of each chapter. In addition the statistical package *Minitab* is most suitable for techniques covered here and quite easy to use. Again relevant commands are at the end of each chapter and summaries of commands are in Appendices 2 and 3 for Minitab and Lotus 1-2-3 respectively. It is stressed that the commands and outlines given are intended to support you, and assume you have received some introduction to the software.

The starting point is obtaining data: you can use data collected by someone else or collect your own. In Chapter 1 a variety of sources of data are outlined along with a consideration of potential sources of error to judge the suitability of the data. All too often the results of surveys are quoted to us as if they were the absolute truth, be they surveys by competitors on relative merits of products, unions on the views of the workforce, or other managers on plant performance. It is necessary to be able to identify sources of error in such surveys if we are to challenge (or validate) the results. Alternatively you may wish to collect data yourself in order to confirm, deny or try to understand some issue. Details of how to conduct surveys are provided in Chapter 2. Even if you hire an outside agency to do such work, an understanding of survey methodology is useful to help you ensure that their methodology is sound.

Once you have results it is necessary to present them clearly. It is no use undertaking expensive research if the results are poorly communicated. Chapter 3 provides guidelines for drawing up tables, graphs and other pictorial devices, as well as showing how different presentational techniques can mislead the user.

In Chapter 4 we turn to the need to summarize information. The IT revolution in particular means large datasets are generated by and for organizations. These may include information on each purchase via the cash register of a supermarket (Electronic Point of Sale—EPOS) linked to the characteristics of the purchasers through a store credit card, or information on employee databases, or from the continuous monitoring of production and quality, or from surveys of customers or your workforce, and much more. To understand all of this we need to summarize the data via frequency tables (and their graphical counterparts—histograms) and by summary measures such as averages. There are several measures of 'the average', each reflecting a different facet of central tendency suitable for different purposes. But there are other dimensions to the data such as dispersion, skewness and kurtosis. Monitoring just the average is like being colour blind, unable to appreciate that something else is occurring because you are not monitoring it.

When we monitor financial flows over time it is often not sufficient to know, for example, that the value of goods produced has increased by 5 per cent between one year and another. It may be that the prices of such goods on average have increased by 10 per cent and the volume produced actually fallen. Index number are concerned with the decomposition of value changes into their price and quantity components. Their application at the organizational level is discussed and details are provided of the Retail Prices Index (prices of retail goods and services) as an example of an application at national level. Index numbers are described in Chapter 5.

So far the concern has been with describing variation in data on a single variable, say sales performance between salespersons, or price changes over time. However, often our concern is with the association between variables: whether, and if so, the extent to which advertising expenditure is related to sales, hours worked to productivity, sex to pay or whatever. Chapter 6 covers measures of association between variables and emphasizes the need to take account of the assumptions behind these methods and the care needed in the interpretation of the results. Chapter 7 extends this work to building regression models of the relationships to yield further insights. All too often it is assumed or pronounced that something is related to, or caused by, something else with little attempt to go to the empirical world to see if there is at least a mathematical association. Regression models are one approach to forecasting. If, for example, we can model how sales is related over time to the variables of price, advertising expenditure, disposable income, etc., then by considering future scenarios of those variables we can derive an estimate for future sales from the model of the relationship.

Yet changes in sales, for example, need not be analysed with respect to other variables, because the sale of a product may 'naturally' have its own patterns—trend, seasonal or cyclical fluctuations. Time series analysis in Chapter 8 enables us to identify the extent to which changes in a variable relate to each of these components. These methods are used, for example, for the seasonally adjusted unemployment figures, often cited to prevent us mistaking, for example, a month-on-month decrease for a fall in the trend, when it might be a mainly seasonal fluctuation. Time series methods are also used in forecasting, there being a range of methods to add to and complement the regression-based forecasting tools.

In Chapter 9 we move on to probability: there are few things that occur with certainty in management and important decisions have often to take into account probabilities of events occurring. Probabilities are not always known: sometimes they are based on past experiences, or theory or even a subjective judgement. In all cases the laws of probability can be applied and it is much better that these probabilities are combined properly by these laws in decision making. Decision trees, as a specific management tool, are considered in this context. Chapter 10 moves on to probability distributions where the different outcomes of 'experiments' can be assigned probabilities. Experiments may include a salesperson cold calling customers with the probabilities of 0, 1, 2, etc. successes per day being evaluated simply from knowing the number of calls in a day and the overall probability of a success. Certain types of situations in life follow these experimental patterns, allowing us to deduce whole ranges of probabilities from only a little information.

The next two chapters take us into a quite different set of problems. Here we consider data from random samples and are concerned with how to interpret the results, bearing in mind that data from small samples will be less reliable in some sense than data from large samples. Confidence intervals are described in Chapter 11 as a means by which we can estimate the required characteristic of the population, with (other things being equal) more 'error' associated with results from small samples than large ones. The principles are also used for the determination of sample size in surveys and in Chapter 12 for testing claims made on the basis of samples of data. In both of these chapters the application to quality control is highlighted.

Exercises are provided at the end of each chapter. Chapter 13 contains exercises, and their worked answers, for each chapter. The necessity of undertaking exercises as part of your course cannot be overemphasized. There is a sense in which much of this text (and your lectures) can be followed without picking up the real skills that arise from the *doing* of data analysis. If this is left to assessed coursework and examinations it is much too late, and there will be a certain floundering while you attempt for the first time to apply concepts to a different context, to arrange data, to use a calculator or computer, to try to identify what the assumptions mean or to interpret results in an unfamiliar context. It is essential that you do exercises as you proceed along the course.

Appendix 1 provides a basic outline of algebraic/arithmetical tools; Appendices 2 and 3 provide summaries of commands for the statistical packages Minitab and the spreadsheet Lotus 1-2-3. Statistical tables make up the rest of the appendices.

There is of course more to life than numerical information. Often we enrich our understanding of issues through studying them from more than one perspective and using more than one analytical approach. It is quite limiting to believe that only numerical information and the results of statistical analysis can be treated as facts. However, there is also cause for concern if we are unable to undertake quantitative analysis well or are fooled by so-called facts and figures which are the result of improper and misleading collection, analysis, and presentation of numerical data. We now begin a task that should equip you with skills that will be useful throughout your life, in business and more generally: i.e. the ability to handle numerical information well.

# ONE

## DATA: ITS SOURCES AND USES

# OBTAINING DATA: SECONDARY SOURCES

Much of this book is concerned with how to handle data; yet our first task must be to obtain or collect data. Two sources exist: we use data collected by someone else (secondary sources) or we collect the data ourselves (primary sources). Once collected and analysed the results are often treated as facts, yet the process of collection (never mind analysis) may have encompassed a multitude of errors and biases which once appreciated may destroy or damage the validity of the results. If secondary sources are used it is necessary to be aware of all potential types of errors and biases. We can then challenge the results, or at least be aware of the direction and approximate margins of error and bias associated with them, so that they are treated with the respect they deserve. If primary sources are used, our aim is to keep to a minimum such errors and biases in the collection of the data.

This chapter examines secondary sources of data and potential sources of error or bias to look out for. Chapter 2 is concerned with how to collect data yourself (primary sources), including the use of appropriate computer software for analysis.

## SECONDARY SOURCES

If information is power, a knowledge of secondary sources is a gateway to such power. It allows for better informed decision making, cheaply and speedily. In meetings it means that you are better prepared to support your case, or challenge other people's views with data. It may also save expensive data collection from primary sources if appropriate data are available from secondary sources. However with secondary sources the definitions used, scope, coverage, frequency (how often), timeliness (up-to-date), level of disaggregation (detail) and accuracy (including sample size, how representative the sample is, bias in questions asked) may all be inappropriate for your needs, having been designed for a different or general purpose. When using data from another source you have to check if they are suitable for your purpose. Even this checking will need a critical approach. The published headings and definitions may be quite limited, or technically correct within the sense used by civil servants, but no one else. The figures may include estimates or omit salient groups, or the method of compilation may be changed, harming comparisons with previously issued figures. Thus, whenever you use data from secondary sources, check how accurate and appropriate they are for your purpose; if they are inappropriate your time has not been wasted, you will at least be able to challenge other people who have not gone to the effort of checking. Secondary sources include: official statistics, non-official statistics and in-company statistics.

## Official statistics

This is the term given to statistics prepared by and large by government (funded) agencies which generally follow, at least in principle, internationally accepted guidelines. Different international agencies have responsibility for agreeing standards on different areas. For example, the International Monetary Fund's responsibilities include Government Finance and Balance of Payments statistics; the United Nations (UN) Statistical Office is responsible for National Accounts Statistics and the UN's International Labour Office for consumer price indices. By following agreed standards international comparisons are thus possible and the statistics have a certain validity, at least in principle. An independent or government statistical office (in the UK it is the Government Statistical Services—GSS) is responsible for the supply of each country's statistics. Public confidence in the quality of such statistics is important, especially with respect to the independence of the statistical office. The author has worked in countries where inflation (Consumer Price Indices) figures are generally considered to be manipulated by the government statistical agency to understate the problems of the country, and where the Department of Industry record impressive (and untrue) increases in production from industries they have poured money into, to prove the success of their policies. Even in the UK doubts have been raised about public confidence in official statistics in the face of conflicting GDP estimates and regular redefinitions of unemployment statistics. (For a discussion, see Hibbert, 1990.) Since the Conservative government came to office in 1979 the official definition of unemployment has changed *thirty* times (at the time of writing) with all but one of these changes resulting in a fall in unemployment—though to be fair 'only' seven of the changes had an effect of any significance. Nonetheless, UK official statistics are of a high quality and generally respected.

The Central Statistical Office (CSO) is responsible for the vast majority of official statistics in the UK, having in 1989 taken over responsibility for the Family Expenditure Survey and Consumer Price Index from the Department of Employment, work of the Business Statistics Office also now coming under its wing. Exceptions include the Office of Population Censuses and Surveys (OPCS) whose responsibilities include the Population Census, and statistical work in government departments (e.g. Departments of Energy, Environment, Education and Science, Welsh Office, Home Office, Inland Revenue) though statistics from such bodies are included in some CSO publications, e.g. *Annual Abstract* and *Monthly Digest of Statistics*.

Official statistics provide a wealth of well-prepared information including: expenditure patterns (*Family Expenditure Survey* (*FES*)); earnings, employment, unemployment, stoppages and hours worked (*Employment Gazette*); detailed import and export statistics (*Overseas Trade Statistics of the UK*); social characteristics (*Social Trends*); a host of economic series (*Economic Trends*); energy statistics (*Digest of Energy Statistics*); key financial indicators (*Financial Statistics*); detailed information on the characteristics of business in specific industries (*Report on Census of Production/Business Monitor*–including price index numbers for current cost accounting); estimates of the population and its social and economic characteristics by region, useful for marketing (*Population Census*); regional differences for key series (*Regional Trends*) and much much more.

The information can be highly detailed—for example, the FES (Central Statistical Office, 1990) will tell you that in 1988 the average weekly expenditure on ice cream by a 'one man, one woman, one child family' earning less than £280 per week was 18p, compared with the 45p on average by such families earning £450 or more per week. The CSO publishes (on behalf of the GSS) each year the *Guide to Official Statistics* (CSO, annual (a)) as well as a (at the time of writing free) small booklet available from the CSO, Great George Street, London SW1P 3AQ (071-270-6363/4), entitled *Government Statistics*: *A Brief Guide to Sources*. This lists major publications along with telephone numbers of departments responsible for a particular set of data. The methods used to collect the data are well documented in the publications (and/or references to details on sources and methods given). The CSO will take calls/letters with more specific enquiries: it is not unknown for more disaggregated unpublished data to be available for a charge. The *Annual Abstract of Statistics* (CSO, monthly) and *Social Trends* (CSO, annual (c)) provide a good selection of many important economic and social variables. There is even a hotline for up-to-date data on the retail prices index (0839-338-337), trade figures (338), balance of payments (339), producer prices (342), retail sales (343) and more; and a free 'United Kingdom in Figures' pocket-sized leaflet. Public reference/college/polytechnic/university libraries will have copies of many of these publications, and there are also specialized public reference libraries, for example at the Export Market Information Centre, 1–9 Victoria Street, London SW1H 1X9.

**Non-official statistics**

If all of the above were not enough, private and quasi-governmental organizations have stepped in to fill the gaps in the market for information. For example, if you want information on a particular consumer market, *Mintel* produce a number of regular reports and studies; reports on industrial sectors are produced by, among others, The Economist Group, the Financial Times Business Information Service, and National Economic Development Office (NEDO). Information provided by the Registrar of Companies (in electronic form) on Profit and Loss Accounts, Balance Sheets and Company Reports are adapted to provide performance ratios for industries as well as profiles of individual companies by, for example, The Extel Group, ICC (Business Ratio Reports) and Datastream. Much of this is available as on-line information services, as well as hard copy, there also being a number of more specialized or limited yearbooks and directories such as Dun and Bradstreet's *Who Owns Whom* and *The Times Top 1000* (companies).

How do you find out about it all? Ball (1989), Business Information Associates (1990), British Overseas Trade Board (annuals) and more generally Vernon (1984) are good starting points, though more directly a trade association or professional institution (e.g. British Institute of Management, Market Research Society) may be of help. Your organization may subscribe (in hard or soft copy) to some sources, though teletext and major commercial or business school libraries are alternative sources.

**In-company data**

In many (usually) large organizations vast amounts of data are collected and analysed, of which managers in some departments are unaware, or the data are in an inappropriate form or are analysed using software quite inflexible for other people's needs. Data may be quite detailed and vast, for example sales in a store of a particular product from Electronic Point of Sale (EPOS)—i.e. recording each actual purchase, quantity, time and date, price—may be matched to the characteristic of the purchasers via their store credit card. Detailed data are also available on labour force, production, stocks, purchases, etc. If the nature of the data or software used are inadequate to extract the required information there is a long-term need to reconsider the organization's Management Information System. Often if the data-processing software and/or hardware is not up to meeting your immediate needs without costly modification, a short-term solution is to generate a representative sample of data from the organization's database which can be entered onto your personal computer (PC) for analysis using more appropriate software. In the author's experience it is not unusual for managers to be quite unaware of the existence or potential use of data routinely collected in other parts of the organization.

## POTENTIAL SOURCES OF ERROR AND BIAS

In using secondary sources you have cheap and speedy access to information, but you must be able to check for errors and biases. This applies to official and non-official sources as well as to results from surveys undertaken by competitors 'proving' the superiority of their product, or samples of raw materials tested for quality, or surveys of employee morale in your plant compared with others, or whatever. All too often statistics are quoted from secondary sources/other people's surveys and we do not know whether to believe the figures or not. What should we look out for? We shall consider four types of error:

1. Sampling error
2. Response error
3. Non-response error
4. Design error

After reading these sections you should feel confident in your ability to identify possible problems in data given to you as 'facts'. A case study will follow as a practice example.

### Sampling error

This arises whenever results are based on a sample as opposed to the population. For example, if a sample of one individual was randomly selected and a question put as to 'whether they have or have not smoked any cigarettes in the last year' to which the truthful reply was 'have not', we might conclude that 100 per cent of the population did not smoke. If we imagined the same exercise concurrently undertaken for a sample of two individuals the result might still be 100 per cent, while for a sample of three, one individual might have smoked, i.e. the smoking pattern of the UK population has 'shifted' so that 33 per cent now smoke; but a sample of four might find that 50 per cent have smoked, and a new sample of five could possibly take us to 20 per cent. These widely fluctuating results are due to sampling error and are purely due to the fact we are basing our results on a sample rather than the population. Sampling error decreases (not proportionately) as sample size increases. It is measurable in the form of a probable error margin: for a sample size of three (selected by a process akin to drawing names out of a hat) which yields a sample result of 33 per cent, the error margin would be such that there is a 95 per cent chance that the percentage of 'smokers' in the population fell in the margin 0 to 86 per cent. This is not very accurate, but what do you expect from a sample size of three? The principles and practice of estimating these margins are considered in Chapter 11. Thus, for any results *based on a sample*, find out the sample size and use the techniques in Chapter 11 to determine the sampling error. Sample sizes of 250 can lead to results (with 95 per cent confidence) for percentages with sampling errors of over $\pm 6$ per cent. I have seen senior managers become alarmed at 2 per cent falls in market shares using sample panel data of around this sample size.

### Response error

This is the difference between the true value and the actual response recorded and applies both to surveys based on samples or the whole population (e.g. where all items produced are automatically tested for quality). It can take many forms, can be quite substantial and is generally not easily measured. Our concern is with *systematic* response error: *non-systematic* response error will have some positive errors, some negative, cancelling out overall. An example of systematic response error is the response to a question concerning income which may be systematically (but not exclusively) overstated to impress the interviewers. Sources of response error are numerous and specific to individual studies. They arise from the whole context of the way information is collected: for personal interviews, for example, this would include not just the phrasing of the questionnaire, but the whole interviewer–interviewee interaction (Chisnall, 1986, Ch. 15).

Response errors can be large: three-quarters of the general public and over half of the lawyers surveyed in a US study expressed an opinion (other than 'don't know') on the performance of the *non-existent* National Bureau of Consumer Complaints (Hawkins and Coney, 1981); 53 per cent of respondents had heard of the Taft–Johnson–Pepper Bill on Veterans' Housing and 33 per cent recalled voting last December in the special election for their state representatives when neither the Bill nor election existed (cited in Owen and Jones, 1982). Consider the implications for surveys of intentions-to-buy new luxury products, awareness of health and safety legislation, etc. Respondents consciously or unconsciously give incorrect answers for a variety of reasons: lack of information, imperfect recall of events, a desire to impress or conform to his or her perception of what response the interviewer would like. Insights into such errors should be gained by consideration of all aspects of the data collection process. These include the place of questioning (e.g. postal ballot on strike action versus 'show of hands' at workplace), the sponsors of the survey (e.g. surveys by government bodies suspected of passing information to the poll tax registrar, or Inland Revenue), the personal characteristics (e.g. age and sex) of the interviewer and the phrasing, order, form, etc., of the questionnaire. These last points will be considered in Chapter 2 under questionnaire design.

The problem with response error is that it might be substantial, but each survey has its own characteristics and it is difficult to quantify the error except to 'suspect' it is high, low or whatever. There are a number of ways of checking for response error (Moser and Kalton, 1985, Ch. 10), none of which is perfect or applies to all situations. They include consistency checks within the questionnaire (asking the same question in different ways) and where possible re-interviewing a sample of respondents, using better trained interviewers (such as supervisors) paid by the hour (not interview) and checking their results against the original results for these respondents.

It is not always easy to judge response error: for example, Collins and Sykes (1987) compared two surveys on social attitudes. In one, data were collected by dual mode (229 telephone, 170 face-to-face: 399 respondents) and in the other, all face-to-face (1569 respondents). Both surveys covered people with similar characteristics and were broadly comparable, the same questionnaire being used. Questions included: 'Most frequently read daily morning paper (at least 3 times a week)'; 'Which social class would you say you belong to?' Views as to 'whether there is a lot, little or hardly any racial prejudice in Britain against Asians'. Do *you* think the (part) telephone versus face-to-face context would yield different replies in the different surveys? Think about it, before reading on.

The problem with evaluating response errors is the subjective component. We might argue that over the phone there is not the same need to impress or conform and different answers would result; however, for these and other straightforward questions similar results did ensue. For example, dual mode : face-to-face results were 16:17 per cent respectively for the Sun, 24:24 per cent middle class (though poor was 5:3 per cent, working 40:47 per cent and upper working 29:24 per cent) and 'a lot of prejudice' 54:56 per cent. Differences do generally exist however for mail versus face-to-face data collection.

### Non-response error

Non-response error may apply to studies of the whole population or a sample. The sample size may be large with little sampling error and no response errors might exist; however, if the number of respondents refusing to answer is high and their (pertinent) characteristics/views are different from respondents, non-response error will need to be considered. Thus the first thing to do is to find out about the response rate.

This may be hidden for some questions by being high for the survey, but low for 'awkward' questions, only the overall response rate being quoted. For some methods of selecting respondents (quota sampling) the interviewer selects the respondents in line with certain controls—for example, proportions of respondents of different age groups and sex. There may not be a count of the number of people who refused to stop and answer the questions, the interviewer simply asking others until their quota is filled. As such we have difficulty estimating non-response error since we are not always told the number who did not respond. With random sampling, unlike quota sampling, we have a list of those to be surveyed and thus a knowledge of those who refused. We can also follow up the refusals to learn something of their characteristics and/or views.

Non-response error cannot generally be eliminated by increasing the number of people surveyed to make up for the non-respondents. We might do this to ensure that our sampling error is not too high, but non-response error may remain. The error arises if the views of non-respondents differ from respondents, and the extent of the error depends on the response rate and the extent to which the views differ. For example, a mail survey on whether companies undertook any formal management training found 6.6 per cent of the 1000 + employee (large companies) respondents did not train, but in the follow-up of large non-respondents the corresponding figure was 22.6 per cent (Silver, 1989). It is not surprising that the Hite Report (1988) on female sexuality in the US made interesting reading, given that the 4500 respondents from the around 100 000 women's groups contacted were those more open about their personal life. And non-response error may not always be cured by determining the demographic characteristics (e.g. number of children, sex, etc.) of the non-respondents, and giving respondents with such characteristics proportionately more weight in the results. The sorts of people who do not reply may well have different views than their demographically equivalent counterparts. For example, in a survey on reactions to promotions for Heinz products the non-respondents were followed up, and while found to be demographically similar to respondents, had quite different responses to their reaction to the promotion: e.g. 36 per cent of respondents changed their purchasing while non-respondents were less affected by the promotion at 52 per cent (Drake, 1987).

### Design error

In our final type of error all those contacted may respond, but there is something in the manner of the selection of the sample to be contacted that makes it unrepresentative of the population.

To select a sample we first need a comprehensive list of all members of the population—a *sampling frame*. From this list the sample is selected. Design error might arise because of inadequacies (a) in the sampling frame or (b) in the method of selecting the sample from the frame.

Consider, for example, the use of the telephone directory as a sampling frame for market research on dishwashers; it is most suitable as 98 per cent of households owning a dishwasher have a telephone. However, for a survey on households who live in rented accommodation, only 59 per cent of such households have telephones—and those with telephones are likely to be better off, less transient and older (Collins and Sykes, 1987). Unless we ask what frame was used for a survey, we do not know if it is adequate or otherwise. Surveys of managers' interest/ability/awareness of the latest fad in management thinking may use as a sampling frame the list of members of the British Institute of Management—the people who join such an institute being the very same people who would want to keep up with such things and thus be unrepresentative, giving biased results. Some designs have implicit frames: a survey based on interviewing people on a Monday afternoon in the City Centre has as its implicit frame those around at that time and place, who may not be representative of the population.

As regards the *selection from the frame* each individual unit should have the same probability of selection. If, for example, the frame was individuals by each region listed in turn starting with London and the South East and our selection of the sample of 400 was by choosing the first 400, we would have an unrepresentative sample, all from London.

*In summary, when evaluating results*, aside from errors due to inappropriate methods of analysis discussed in later chapters, *find out how the data were collected*, paying attention to the following.

1. If a sample, the size of the sample and (using Chapter 11) the sampling error.
2. The questionnaire and whole context in which the data were collected in an attempt to identify response error.
3. The response rate and extent to which non-respondents were likely to have different results to respondents.
4. If a sample, the adequacy of the sampling frame and method by which the sample is selected from the frame.

An example might help: presented below is an extract from the *Report on the Supply of Beer in the UK* by the Monopolies and Mergers Commission (1989, pp. 433–437). The paragraph numbers refer to the original report. In their defence the Brewers' Society (which owns many public houses) commissioned three surveys among which was one concerned with how British public houses stood up against their foreign counterparts. The Commission described the survey and its validity. Both are included here. Try to evaluate this survey before looking at the Commission's 'comment on survey'. Not all issues are considered here, but it provides an insight into how results from surveys might be challenged. This is followed in Chapter 2 by a look at primary sources, to which some readers may wish to turn directly.

**INTRODUCTION**

15. The Brewers' Society provided the Commission with the results of a study it had commissioned. The study was carried out on behalf of the Society by Neilsen Consumer Research in January 1988 and was intended to identify the relative consumer preference between United Kingdom public houses and on-licences in some parts of the world. The commission were informed in advance of The Brewers' Society intention and were not therefore consulted on the form of the study, the places at which it was carried out or the questions that were asked.

**SAMPLE**

16. Three samples were constructed:

(a) A sample of 827 foreign visitors to Britain (American, German, French, Italian, Belgian/Dutch, Spanish). All were interviewed at Heathrow Airport (87 per cent were male).
(b) A sample of 661 British travellers abroad interviewed at Heathrow Airport and at Dover (96 per cent were male).
(c) A sample of 509 United Kingdom public house users who had been on holiday to a Mediterranean resort in the last 12 months. These were all male and under the age of 35.

17. All those taking part claimed to have an impression of both British public houses and bars in their own country and, in the case of the holiday-makers, holiday bars.

## STRUCTURE OF THE SURVEY

18. The survey was carried out between 13 and 25 January 1988 and all respondents were asked whether they preferred British public houses or continental bars or their own national bars as appropriate. They were asked to give voluntary reasons as to why they had given their preference and were then asked a series of direct questions of preference on different aspects of the public house/bar offering. Finally, they were asked to rate British public houses and bars on a good value scale.

## MAIN FINDINGS

19. The Brewers' Society believes that the results of this study indicated the following findings:

(a) There was considerable conformity in the way people perceived British public houses in respect of continental or foreign bars, whether this was done through the eyes of British travellers, British Mediterranean holiday-makers or foreign visitors to Britain.

(b) On a straight question of preference all three major groups preferred British public houses. Amongst British travellers 62% claimed to prefer British public houses whilst 28% claimed to prefer continental bars. Amongst foreign visitors 48% claimed to prefer British public houses and 27% bars in their own country. Amongst British holiday-makers to Mediterranean resorts 56% claimed to prefer British public houses and 41% to prefer their holiday bars.

(c) More British travellers rated British public houses 'extremely' or 'very good' value (38%) than they did continental bars (30%) and more foreign visitors rated British public houses 'extremely' or 'very good' value (50%) than bars in their own country (34%).

(d) Greatest preference for British public houses was expressed by Americans (66% for public houses, 17% for own bars) followed by the French (57% for British public houses, 16% for own bars) and Germans (54% for British public houses, 21% for own bars). Italians were somewhat less committed though more claimed to prefer British public houses (44%) than their own bars (29%). The Belgian/Dutch group were evenly split with similar numbers claiming to prefer British public houses (38%) to their own bars (36%). Spanish visitors expressed a clear preference for their own bars (40%) compared with British public houses (29%).

(e) The primary reason for preferring British public houses was their atmosphere, selected voluntarily by 35% of all British travellers and 33% of all foreign visitors.

(f) There were some differences in the character of the perception of British public houses versus 'continental bars or bars from own country'. The character of the perception was, according to The Brewers' Society, the particular blend of aspects that made it up, many of which were not very important in their own right. When only salient reasons were analysed (i.e. those reasons the respondent volunteered for preference of one type of outlet over the other) British public houses were preferred for four out of the five reasons for which significant differences emerged: better atmosphere, style/character/comfort, family/friends, better bar drinks. Foreign bars scored higher on better hours (the survey took place before recent changes in opening hours in United Kingdom on-licensed premises).

(g) Detailed questioning on preference of different aspects of public houses/bars showed quite big differences between British public houses and continental bars but those differences were similar for British travellers and foreign visitors. Both British travellers and foreign visitors agreed that British public houses were seen to be better for draught beer range, the atmosphere, comfort, agreeableness, friendliness and games facilities. There were no differences between public houses and continental bars in respect of cleanliness but continental bars were preferred for cheapness of drink and food. On two aspects that were asked about, the better drinks range and better bottled beer range, the two groups perceived the outlets differently with foreign visitors perceiving their own bars to be better while British travellers believed public houses to be better for bottled beer range and did not perceive a difference between British public houses and continental bars for drinks range.

(h) Drinks prices were clearly seen by foreign visitors and British travellers alike to be cheaper in continental/own bars. The Brewers' Society suggested it was important to note that even though British public houses were seen as being less cheap for drinks than other bars, they were also seen as giving a better value for money.

(i) British holiday-makers to Mediterranean resorts were more likely to prefer holiday bars to British public houses than were British travellers abroad, although more of them still preferred British public houses.

**Before reading on try to find fault with the way the survey was conducted.**

## COMMENT ON SURVEY [by the Commission]

21. The Society told us that samples were selected with regard to costs and practicalities. We observed that no attempt had been made to take a representative sample of the relevant populations. The great majority of those questioned were

male and in the case of the Mediterranean holiday-makers all were under 35. The Society said that men, in general terms, were the people who most frequently bought beer in public houses. The survey did not ensure that the foreign bars experienced by British respondents were distributed across countries and outlet types in the same way as the 'home' bars of foreign respondents. The Brewers' Society argued that the Commission's comments showed a misconception of the philosophy, theory and practice of sampling. It explained that the survey did not attempt to sample the universe of the populations of the countries surveyed; the universe from which the respondents had to be drawn was people in the world who had experience of United Kingdom public houses and bars in other countries, i.e. that universe must be a subset of the universe of international travellers. For the purpose of testing the particular hypothesis under consideration the Society said that it did not matter in which other country people had their experience. It further explained that demographic variables such as age, class and sex were unlikely to influence perception of relative preference to a significant degree. In particular, it was argued that the uniformity of the responses across the different samples suggested that these demographic variables did not have an effect which was greater than the overall preference for the United Kingdom public house. Furthermore, it did not matter whether the nature of bars experienced by British travellers was the same as foreign visitors' experiences showed that British pubs were preferred by many different groups. If their experience was not comparable then this indicated that the preference for British public houses transcended the detailed nature of the experience.

22. We do not accept that demographic variables such as age, class and sex are unlikely to influence perceptions of relative preference. It is highly plausible that women, for example, have a very different perception of the atmosphere and facilities of a British public house from men. Again, if the sample of foreign visitors is biased towards business travellers (as may be the case with interviews carried out at Heathrow Airport in January) the outlets they will have visited in the United Kingdom are likely to have had a high representation of hotel bars and city centre public houses. Perceptions of public houses in other areas might have been very different. Nor do we think it irrelevant that British holiday-makers were comparing Mediterranean coastal bars, particularly in Greece and Spain, with their own public houses. They might have had a different view had they visited bars in New York, Paris or Rome. Despite the Society's arguments, we remain of the view that the construction of the sample makes it unsafe to place any weight on the results of the survey.

23. Moreover, since all the interviews were conducted in Britain, there was a strong danger of bias through interviewees thinking that the interviewer was hoping to hear a response favourable to British public houses. The Society replied that professional market research companies, using trained interviewers, structured their surveys in such a way that interviewer bias did not affect the results. In any event, responses to questions where the respondents had to explain their preference without interview suggestions showed remarkable uniformity. We remain of the view that it is impossible to remove bias entirely from a survey conducted in this way. We are, for instance, left to speculate on what would have been the result if the sample of male British under-35s had been interviewed by a Spanish interviewer at Palma de Mallorca Airport.

# EXERCISES

**1-1** Using official statistics determine the average weekly expenditure per household on toilet paper by one-parent families in the UK in 1988.

**1-2** The National Readership Survey collects data on the readership patterns of over 200 national and regional newspapers and magazines and the characteristics (e.g. age, social class, sex, etc.) of their readers, to aid those advertising via this medium to target their adverts effectively. The questionnaire is 21 pages long and undertaken by personal interviews conducted with a randomly selected sample of adults aged 15+ selected from the Electoral Register. Around 27 000 successful interviews are carried out every year from an original sample of 40 000 individuals. On the basis of this information identify potential sources of error and give some judgement as to their extent. (Information is from Smith, 1987.)

# OBTAINING DATA: PRIMARY SOURCES

## PRIMARY SOURCES

What if secondary sources are unavailable or inadequate? If resources permit we have to collect the data ourselves. Sometimes the whole population will be surveyed, for example views on the course of all MBA students registered in 1991/1992 at a particular university; in other cases cost and/or time constraints—or the destructive nature of survey, e.g. testing television screens for pressure at which they break—means we have to take a representative sample. There is much to every individual survey that is particular to that survey and only general guidelines can be given here, incorporating the points raised in the previous section on sources of error. We are not evaluating other secondary sources for error; we are minimizing error for our survey. A brief account will be given here, but see Moser and Kalton (1981) for further details.

### Alternative approaches

Alternative approaches to primary data collection include:

1. *Observation*—participative or otherwise, in which we record behaviour or information, such as sex of purchaser in a store, exhibits in a museum attracting most attention, idle time in a manufacturing plant. Hidden cameras can help facilitate such matters and were used to estimate the (full-face watching) audience for advertising on the outside of London buses (Day and Dunn, 1969).
2. *Experimentation*—for example, recording the quality of goods produced by a machine in a day, modifying the machine (treatment), and then recording the results. A control group (another identical machine) should be tested alongside without treatment. If the treatment occurred at the start of the afternoon the group control should show differences between morning and afternoon, which might otherwise be taken to be the effect of the machine. In Japan statistically based methods are widely used in production using (albeit not perfect, but easily applied) experimental designs and statistical approaches to quality control and productivity improvement (as derived by Taguchi and Deming—see Deming (1986) and Barker (1990)). Such techniques are also used to assess the effect of such treatments as advertising, promotions, pricing, or product modifications on sales. Where several treatments are involved (e.g. change

in price, packaging, location in store, etc.) more complex Latin square designs are required. Sources of error and a range of designs are given in Tull and Hawkins (1987, Ch. 5). In some cases an actual experiment is not conducted, but we treat the present situation as if it were caused by an experiment. For example, we may consider those employees who have stayed with the firm, and those who have left, and look back to identify the characteristics of stayers and leavers. This is known as an *ex post facto* study.

3. *Questionnaires*—either mail, post, personal, leave and collect, telephone, or individual small group discussions.

4. *Documentary sources*—while a great deal of data held on individuals is confidential, it is possible to gain information from other sources for special use or to complement questionnaires. For example, an answer to questions to employees may be linked to the personnel database. Silver (1989) used information from Companies House on individual companies to link to responses to a questionnaire from companies, some questions being duplicated for validation.

Chisnall (1986, Ch. 2) emphasizes the value of using more than one approach to data collection. Each method will have its own source of error, and viewing the area of study from different angles makes you aware of the various biases in each approach, which can but help to enlighten. It must be emphasized that our concern here is with quantitative data collection. There is much of value in life not susceptible to the measurement devices considered here and a variety of qualitative research methods exist. These approaches to data collection are more flexible and responsive to the interviewee. The data often refer to what people's lives, experiences and interactions mean to them in their own terms and are extensively used in market research (see Sykes, 1990).

## STAGES IN A SURVEY

1. Aims and objectives.
2. Sampling frames.
3. Sample design.
4. Sample size.
5. Methods of collecting data.
6. Questionnaire design.
7. Using computers.
8. Initial Data Analysis
9. Methods of presentation.

The above stages mainly relate to a questionnaire-based sample survey, though similar principles can be derived for other approaches. The order is not so important since many stages are interrelated. The exception is that the starting point must be the formulation of aims and objectives since all other stages relate to this: sample size and design are concerned with the 'accuracy' of the results, which is determined in the aims and objectives; method of collecting data is dictated by cost and type of questions; questionnaire design is concerned with the hypotheses to be tested; analysis of the issues at stake is determined by aims and objectives; and for the presentation, i.e. who is to use the results, we have to go back to aims and objectives.

Stages 1 to 9 are interrelated, examples including cost and accuracy dictating sample size (but efficient sample designs can attain the same sampling error via a smaller sample); the sample design is affected by the availability of sampling frames, some designs being appropriate when sampling frames are costly to generate or don't exist; the method of analysis may be constrained by the sample size or questionnaire design; the method of collecting data may be determined by the questionnaire design or sampling frame; and the method of presentation may be influenced by the method of analysis. In practice, rather than make hard and fast decisions at each stage of the above list, our approach is one of trial and error, considering and reconsidering each stage as we progress. Nonetheless we examine here each stage in turn.

### Aims and objectives

The starting point is a clear statement of the purpose of the survey, including the population under study, period, issues of concern and hypotheses (i.e. specific formulations of ideas you wish to test empirically). The general aims must lead to specific hypotheses in order that the questions asked correspond with what is to be tested. It is all too easy to end up providing the right answer to the wrong question, because of poorly formulated aims and objectives. You may not always be aware of all the issues and so discussions with experts, ordinary workers and users will help in formulating the issues worth studying. For example, in the market research for the UK 'naughty-but-nice' cream cake campaign, the Milk Marketing Board had their own ideas on factors likely to influence cream cake consumption, but still used the help of qualitative focus groups. In these, small groups of women (main purchasers) were paid to discuss their feelings about fresh cream cakes, the results being noted by an unobtrusive researcher and incorporated into a large-scale survey for testing.

The qualitative research 'found' heavy consumption patterns moving away from family treat (as found in their previous research) to adult, personal self-indulgence, the pleasurable rather than functional properties being the most motivating:

> 'We sometimes have one each later on in the evening when the children have gone to bed. It's frightfully mean!'

> 'I always feel a bit wicked when I'm having anything luxurious. I think that's part of the pleasure really.'

The qualitative results led to additional questions being put on the questionnaire for the quantitative (1250 'housewives') study which confirmed the above, leading to the naughty-but-nice campaign (Dickens, 1987).

An eye has then to be kept on the measuring instruments and methods of analysis available in order that hypotheses are formulated in a realistic way. For example, IQ is not universally accepted as a good approximation or 'proxy' for intelligence. We often forget that we are using a limited proxy variable as a measuring instrument. There was a time when changes in production in the service/government sectors of the UK economy were measured using changes in employment as a proxy indicator because of the difficulty in measuring production. Others then used these same figures to discover that labour productivity (changes in 'production' divided by change in employment) was constant over time in these sectors! Our hypotheses also have to be formulated in a realistic way such that not only are suitable measurement instruments available, but the methods of data collection and analysis can help test the hypotheses. For example, ice-cream manufacturers may formulate hypotheses about the recent (at the time of writing) very hot summers being due to global warming, but the small available sample size of hot summers makes it difficult to test the hypothesis.

### Sampling frames

There are often a range of alternative frames available each with its own defects and relative cost and convenience advantages. For consumers these include the items detailed below.

**Telephone directory**    Around 78 per cent of households in Britain have telephones; those without mainly comprising the elderly, young people living apart from parents, unemployed and those reliant on benefits. For luxury products (e.g. a compact disc player) these people may be outside the 'scope' of the survey, while for other more basic products their omission is more critical. In addition, there are those unlisted by request (ex-directory) comprising 12 per cent of those with telephones, bringing the percentage of households accessible to $(1-0.12)78=69$ per cent. Also there are those who have moved, or errors in entries in the directories, reducing the effective coverage to around 60 per cent. Random digit dialling (RDD), involving by-passing the directory and dialling digits at 'random' to contact the unlisted and avoid the need for a directory, is common in the US, much less so in the UK, and is quite sophisticated in design (Collins and Sykes, 1987).

**Electoral register**    This lists persons who have registered to vote. Every October information is sought from each household as to who is eligible to vote. A new register is compiled which is published the following February, by which time it is four months out of date. As the year progesses the information on people living in the area becomes more out of date. By the time the next register is published we are dealing with information that is 16 months old. Those eligible include those who are 18 years or more between each February to the period in question, who are British subjects (including Commonwealth citizens) or citizens of the Irish Republic resident at the given address. The registers are not computerized; they provide names, addresses and, via the name, a good indication of sex and, via the address, the number of adults in a household and, via comparison between registers, the propensity to change address. In spite of the problem of the timeliness of the register the coverage is much superior to that of the telephone directory, at the end of the register's life being 95.6 per cent. However, the missing 4.4 per cent are biased against ethnic minorities and movers (Wilson and Elliott, 1987). It seems likely that the electoral register will become less reliable in certain areas as those defaulting on the 'Poll Tax' (poor and young)—and its replacement—become reluctant to register.

**Postcode address system**    This is a comprehensive list of addresses created by the Post Office based on postcodes. Great Britain is divided into approximately 119 areas (NW), 2700 districts (NW10 4), 1 284 852 postcodes (NW10 4HA) and 21 828 957 delivery points (addresses), on average 17 delivery points per address. A random selection of postcodes, then of all addresses in each selected postcode can form a frame for Britain. Addresses (postcodes) have been grouped (using data from such sources as the Population Census, County Court Judgements and the Electoral Role) into a number of types. For example, CCN Systems provide MOSAIC which divides addresses into 58 types (e.g. 'highest income and status areas', 'newish family housing') based on socio-economic data which allow surveys (and junk mail) to be directed to specific 'types'. The junk mail you receive is tailored to the characteristics of your area, though much of this is based on data from the Population Census which is carried out every ten years. While the postcode system covers empty and non-existent addresses (about 12 per cent), it is quite comprehensive in that 98 per cent of addresses that exist are included (Wilson and Elliott, 1987). It is used in many surveys by the OPCS, by the CSO for the Family Expenditure Survey, as well as for direct mail marketing.

**Community charge (Poll Tax) register**    Councils are required by law to publish the address, surname and initials only of all people (adults) on their register and make it open to public inspection. Applications can be made by individuals to have their names omitted if the inclusion of their names puts them at risk of violence. At the time of writing (though this may change) the 'can't pay–won't pay' lobby was strong enough to make the register quite unsuitable as a frame—though there were regional variations in this. Local government tax systems create sampling frames, but too little is known at present to ensure the reliable permanence of any new system.

**Specialized lists**  Rather than requesting a frame for the population at large, your target population may be a small subset of the population, possibly the rich, or those active in certain sports. A number of organizations keep lists of consumers with specific interests willing to receive mail. Companies such as Lifestyles, through the response to detailed questionnaires by people who want to be informed of product developments (receive junk mail) build up substantial lists of people with details on their lifestyles and their specific area of interest. Such people may not of course be representative of the target population at large; they are people who are interested in receiving direct mail and thus have a heightened product awareness or responsiveness to promotions. Alternatively, mailing lists relating to certain bodies (e.g. membership of organizations, people registering warranties on white goods) are sold to those with an interest in surveying similar groups. Those who have sold lists of their customers range from Butlins (holidays) to Bejams (freezer purchased)—(Durlacher, intermittent).

The above are, of course, related to sampling frames of individuals/households. In some cases our enquiry is about the household and the sampling frame must be a list of households—the sampling unit being a household. For other purposes our sampling unit comprises individuals. Here, if a suitable frame does not exist for individuals we can use a frame for households, selecting at random a member from each household after asking how many people are in the household and who they are. A range of frames for surveying companies are discussed in Silver (1989). If suitable frames are expensive, or not available, an alternative is to choose a sample design that does not require a frame (see quota sampling below).

## Sample design

The sample design is the means by which the units of interest are selected for the survey. A random design gives every unit a fixed probability of selection. To achieve this we need a frame. There are several methods of random selection, including:

**Simple random sampling**  This is similar in principle to putting each unit (e.g. each person's name) from the frame on a piece of paper, dropping them in a big hat, shaking it very well and picking the required sample size blindfolded. Random number tables or generators on computers make this more practical, especially if the frame is computerized—the computer generates the random numbers which are matched to those on the frame and the units selected. Each unit has an equal chance of being selected.

**Systematic (quasi) random sampling**  If we have a frame of $N$ units (say $N = 5000$) and require a sample of size $n$ (say $n = 250$), then we divide $N$ by $n$, i.e. $N/n = 5000/250 = 20$ and select at random a number between 1 and 20, e.g. 7. The first unit selected is the 7th on the list, the next $(20 + 7 =)$ 27th, then $(27 + 20 =)$ 47th, 67th, 87th, ..., 4987th—in all, 250 units. The method is particularly practical if the units are on a card index or computer printout with a constant number of units on each page. Selection involves counting the cards or choosing, for example, the second name from the end of every other page. A simple routine can be written to programme a computer to select such a sample from a computer database. In addition if, for example, the units are people ordered by region, a 'stratification' effect will occur with larger regions naturally having near proportionate larger samples. A similar effect would be a survey of users of a Safari Park: every, say, 20th person would

**Table 2-1**  Age and sex structure of the UK population in 1988 in millions of people (and per cent of population*)

| Age band (years) | Males | Females | Both sexes† |
|---|---|---|---|
| Under 16 | 5.9 (10.3) | 5.6  (9.8) | 11.5  (20.1) |
| 16–39 | 10.3 (18.0) | 10.1 (17.7) | 20.4  (35.7) |
| 40–64 | 8.0 (14.0) | 8.2 (14.4) | 16.2  (28.4) |
| 65–79 | 2.9  (5.1) | 3.9  (6.8) | 6.9  (12.1) |
| 80 and over | 0.6  (1.1) | 1.4  (2.5) | 2.0   (3.5) |
| All ages† | 27.8 (48.7) | 29.3 (51.3) | 57.1 (100.0) |

*Figures in parentheses are percentages.
†Subtotals and totals may differ from the sum of the components due to rounding.
*Source*: Central Statistical Office (1990) *Social Trends*, Vol. 20, HMSO, London, Table 1.2.

rightly give you a larger sample when usage was more intense and dissatisfaction possibly greater. However, the way units are ordered may lead to bias: for example, if the frame is ordered male, female, male, female, etc., a systematic design will lead to only males or only females.

**Stratified random sampling**  Table 2-1 shows data on the age and sex breakdown of the UK population. Using simple random sampling does not guarantee that the sample is going to be representative of the population in relation to these (or other) variables. By chance (as discussed in Chapter 11) we might over-represent 'under 16 year olds', or whatever. For example, with stratified random sampling using proportionate allocation, a sample of $n = 1000$ would be identified as being composed of $(5.9/57.1)1000 = 103$ boys 'under 16', 98 girls 'under 16', 180 '16–39 years old' females, yet only 177 '16–39 males', etc. The sampling frame will be divided by age and sex, and appropriately sized samples randomly chosen (say using simple random sampling) from each 'strata'. For a given sample size this leads to less sampling error than simple random sampling since we control for error due to unrepresentative sample strata sizes, though there will remain error from sampling within strata.

The variables used for stratification need not be sex and age, but must be pertinent to the subject of the survey *and* must exist on the sampling frame in order that frames for each strata can be compiled. Allocation of the sample size need not be proportional among strata: for example if we are interested in the weight (as a component of quality) of goods produced from three production lines, we may stratify by 'line used' and 'time of day—am : pm'. One line, from observation and prior knowledge, may be producing goods of a consistent weight, so a smaller than proportionate sized sample can be generated from this line since the results are fairly consistent. Larger samples can be taken from strata where more variability is suspected (Neyman allocation). As long as the results for average weight are proportioned according to the population proportions, we have less sampling error for a given sample size than proportional allocation. In addition, the allocation may take account of the costs of sampling from any one strata (e.g. if strata are regions): this leads to more sampling error than proportional allocations, but also to cost savings which *may* offset this. In general, stratified random sampling is more efficient than simple random sampling, but requires a more comprehensive frame to allocate the units by strata. The more variability in results between strata, the more efficient the design.

**Multistage random sampling**  Suppose we required a random sample of 1000 university students for personal interviewing. We would need a sampling frame of all such students and would probably send interviewers to each university, which is a costly and time-consuming business. Alternatively, we might select at random—possibly using stratification by type/region of university—10 primary sampling units (PSUs), in this case universities. The selection would be with probability proportionate to size (PPS). We would take the first university with, say, 11 000 students as 1 ... 11 000; the next with, say, 5000 students as 11 001 ... 16 000, etc., up to, say, 250 000 as the assumed total. To select 10 universities with PPS we generate 10 random numbers between 1 and 250 000 and find which university they belong to. Larger universities have a proportionately larger chance of selection. As a second stage, from each university (PSU) chosen we might select at random—again possibly with stratification—100 students. Note, we would only need to interview at, and have frames for, 10 universities thus saving travel and administrative costs. You may wonder why equal sized samples are drawn from each university when, at first instinct, larger samples should be drawn from larger universities. Since, at the primary stage, universities were selected with probability proportionate to size, the selection at this final stage must be of equal size if we are to maintain equal probability of selection of each student (see Moser and Kalton, 1985, Ch. 5).

With regard to the number of PSUs and secondary units to choose, at one extreme we could select one university and 'sample' everyone from that source (Cluster sampling). At the other extreme we could select all universities, sampling only a few students from each. If the PSUs have different pertinent characteristics, serious errors would arise from taking a small number of PSUs and resources should be concentrated on increasing the number of PSUs. However, if each PSU has very similar pertinent characteristics, the cost advantages of multistage sampling are better realized. Multistage sampling can extend to more than the two stages considered here and is less efficient than simple random sampling for a given sample size, though it generates cost savings. It is particularly useful when personal interviews/observation is required over large geographical areas and/or where sampling frames are expensive to compile

**Quota sampling**   This is *not* random and each unit does not have the same probability of selection. Its main advantages are that it does *not* require a sampling frame (though one is implicit in its use) and it is relatively cheap and quick to use. Because of this it is widely employed in market research and political opinion polling where time/cost is often of the essence. This need not of course justify its use *if* the results are misleading. Consider a survey on perceptions of different makes of cars within a price band. Say a sample of $n = 1000$ is required. First, we find data on the population for related variables as with stratification, say age and sex as in Table 2-1. Assume (so we can relate the example to Table 2-1) that our concern is only with those 16 years and over—a population of 45.6 million. Samples of $(10.3/45.6)1000 = 226$ males, '16–39 years'; $(10.1/45.6)1000 = 221$ females, '16–39'; 175 males '40–64 years', etc., would be required. Interviewers are given quotas, say, of 50 to interview in a given day composed of $(10.3/45.6)50 = 11$ males '16–39'; $(10.1/45.6)50 = 11$ females '16–39'; 9 males '40–64', etc., so that the quotas for all interviewers together make up the required samples. In *stratified sampling*, random methods (e.g. random number tables) are used to select each, for example, young female, from the frame: in *quota sampling* the interviewer selects the sample by judging and confirming via question (for age or whatever) the characteristics of the units. If you have wondered why you pass an interviewer in the street and are not asked to participate, it may be because your characteristics are not part of the interviewer's quota, or have been filled. The resulting sample is often claimed to be 'representative'. It is controlled and representative with respect to the quota controls (in our example, age and sex), but it may be totally unrepresentative with regard to other things that matter. The variables used as 'controls' should (1) be available on an up-to-date basis for the population, (2) be easy for the interviewer to classify, (3) be closely related to the subject matter of the survey and (4) be kept to a reasonable number so as not to produce too many cells (Tull and Hawkins, 1987).

Potential problems with quota sampling include:

1. The implicit sampling frame for a street interview comprises those on the street at that time. A mix of types of areas, days and times of interviewing is necessary. Workers in manufacturing will be under-represented, while those unemployed or employed in distribution, construction, transport and public services will be over-represented. The question that needs to be asked is: 'Are men and women with certain characteristics and "lifestyles" more likely to be found in the areas used for surveying and if so are they likely to have different views on cars?'
2. The individuals are selected by the interviewer. However, people not in a hurry or 'safer' looking people may be chosen. 'Socio-economic group' is sometimes used as a control with the interviewer judging the group to which individuals belong and asking some (by necessity biased) qualifying questions to ascertain if they belong to the quota.
3. Extremes of the quota are avoided as interviewers select individuals in the middle of the (e.g. age) band to save wasting time.
4. Non-response (those who refuse to answer) rates are not always collected and we have little insight into non-response bias.
5. It is difficult to validate the work: with random sampling the selection of individual names and addresses is random and there can be a follow-up to check if the interview took place and whether it was correctly completed. This is very problematic with quota sampling: addresses are rarely given to people with clipboards.

All is of course not (always) lost with quota sampling. For each survey you must think about the sort of bias that may arise and by interviewer training, quota controls including a variety of places and times of interviewing, attempt to minimize the bias. However, it should only be employed when resources/timeliness or availability of frame dictate, and then after careful examination of the potential types of bias and control mechanisms possible, the results being interpreted alongside caveats as to these possible sources of bias. Naturally when organizations employ market research companies to undertake such 'representative' surveys, the caveats are often left out of the final report.

In all cases it is worth not just thinking of the technical issues, but the whole context in which the data are collected. For example, a traffic census involves selecting a random sample of cars and a particular route to identify traffic density, journey patterns, etc. A radio announcement warning drivers to avoid the census because of delays to traffic would not help matters (reported in *News and Notes*, Royal Statistical Society, March 1991).

## Sample size

Determination of sample size, as discussed earlier, depends on the required error margin (sampling error), the confidence (in probabilistic terms) you require in the real result being included within the error margin, the variability in the data and the sample design used—some designs being more efficient than others. *In Chapter 11 we outline the theory and practice of determining sample size.* However, it is worth noting here that different sample sizes may be necessary for different questions (due to different error margins/confidence required and variability in the response for different questions). It is sometimes possible for larger samples to be taken, which include certain clusters of questions that require more accuracy and can be analysed with respect to each other. In addition, results are often disaggregated by, for example, region and sex. It is no use determining that a sample size of 1000 is required for all individuals, only to require the same level of accuracy for results broken down into smaller groups for each region or whatever. Such disaggregated results will, by necessity, be derived from smaller samples and thus, other things being equal, will have a larger sampling error. It is clearly necessary to think about the analysis to be undertaken before considering questions of sample size.

## Methods of collecting data

We referred previously to observation, experiments and questionnaires as methods of collecting data. Here we shall look into questionnaires in more detail, but see Tull and Hawkins (1987) for information on collecting data via observation and experiments. For questionnaires, a variety of methods are available including personal interview, telephone, mail, leave-and-collect or combinations of these, such as initial contact by mail with follow-up by telephone/personal interview. Factors determining choice include:

1. *Cost*   Mail and telephone (with regional locations) are cheaper than interviews.
2. *Speed*   Telephone (depending on number of interviews) is quickest.
3. *Bias*   Discussed above under response error.
4. *Help provided*   Further prompting/help with questions best for personal interviews and (as with Population Census) leave-and-collect where questionnaire is left, later collected and checked before leaving.
5. *Corroboration and aids*   Least by mail and telephone; personal interviews allows physical aids—e.g. which packaging is preferred or colour for toy (show three toys). Personal interviews also allow some corroboration, for example, interviewing at the house allows some insights into wealth and lifestyle.

## Questionnaire design

Some insights have been provided into questionnaire design under the discussion of response error above, and in practice each questionnaire has its own specific design problems. However, some general points can be made.

There is much to be gained from a pilot survey to test your questionnaire. The questionnaire might be administered to at least 20 respondents of varying characteristics, after which their responses should be reconsidered, with their help, to ascertain areas of ambiguity, etc.

Questions may be 'open-ended' or 'coded', the former not restricting the respondent's answer, the latter providing a number of coded options (including 'other'). Their respective merits depend on the aims of the study and needs of analysis; *if* desired the results of open-ended questions can be coded into different categories so that an enumeration of different responses is available, though we lose qualitative information in doing so. We might for example have:

1. 'Are you willing to accept the latest pay offer by the company?'
   ☐ Yes    ☐ No [coded]
2. 'If "No", why not?' [open ended].

The interviewer might suggest a list of possible reasons, or simply code your answer into available slots, or write as much as possible for later coding. This last option allows for some useful 'quotes' to flesh out and enrich the quantitative results, but requires subsequent effort in coding. In *some* circumstances it might be argued that the (rotated) list is better since it gives reasons that respondents might not have thought of, their answers therefore being better informed. Against this is the influencing of the respondent by the very suggestion of particular answers. The choice depends on the purpose of the survey. Schuman and Presser (1979) found quite marked differences in results from the two approaches.

The following are general guidelines on questionnaire design.

1. Give a letter of introduction accompanying the questionnaire (or if face-to-face, a verbal introduction) clearly and briefly explaining by whom and why the survey is being undertaken, stressing its importance, confidentiality, what (and by when) to do with the completed questionnaire, who you may contact if you require further information, the need for completion by the respondent to ensure a representative sample, and so forth. Incentives such as advance summaries of the findings (say, for surveys of companies) may help. The aim is to minimize non-response, and this is your 'chat-up'. At the end there should of course be a 'thank you'.
2. Use clear layout and instructions to help and encourage commitment from the respondents and facilitate coding and data entry of the results onto (computer) disk or tape.
3. Each question should be examined (for wording, inclusion and response format) in terms of its ability to satisfy the aims and objectives and test the hypotheses of the survey. Long questionnaires unrelated to the respondent's area of interest run the risk of high non-response or response error.
4. The phrasing of questions constitutes a rich source of error, details being provided in Moser and Kalton (1985) and Kalton and Schuman (1982).

   - Be short and use simple language (replace 'Ascertain the duration . . .' with 'How long . . . '), though in some cases long simple questions are useful to give the respondent time to marshal his or her thoughts (Cannell et al., 1981).
   - Avoid ambiguities; Chisnall (1986, p. 111) cites the possibility of the question on sources of job information (expecting newspaper, job centre, etc.): 'How did you find your last job?' yielding 'Very interesting and enjoyable'.
   - Take account of the ability of the respondent to answer them accurately: houseperson on spouse's income; memory losses and 'telescoping' (bringing forward in time something that occurred some time ago, e.g. 'When did you last purchase . . .?') are common problems (Sudman et al., 1984)
   - Do not lead the respondent towards a particular answer or make unwarranted assumptions ('Do you think DIY stores should be open on Sunday—our Lord's day of rest?').
   - Take account of social conventions, be they questions that are personal, embarrassing or reflect on prestige (e.g. age, drinking, sex, wealth). See Moser and Kalton (1985, Ch. 3) on methods for minimizing such bias.
   - Bear in mind the order in which questions are asked, providing a logical sequence and ensuring that bias is not introduced: an episode of 'Yes Minister' illustrated how quite different responses arose when a question on the desirability of nuclear weapons was preceded by a series of questions on 'the need to protect loved ones' as opposed to those on 'the futility of war'—see Chisnall (1986) and Kalton et al. (1978) for actual examples.
   - Ensure that several questions are not hidden in one, making it confusing to answer (and analyse the results of) or that the question over-simplifies the issue. 'Do you think environmental issues are more important than third world issues?'
       □ Yes     □ No
   - Avoid hypothetical questions: surveys on, for example, 'intentions to buy' a new product are usually misleading.
   - Make it clear whether your requirement from the survey is a general view or a personal view ('Do you think it is a good idea to . . .?' versus 'Would you . . .?').
   - Be clear on periodical queries ('How often do you . . .?' may be replaced by 'How many times in the last month have you . . .?'—even the latter is likely to be answered in terms of usual practice rather than actual in last month).

- Be careful of acquiescence bias—the tendency of respondents to agree with the interviewer. Kalton and Schuman (1982) cite the example of two statements in comparable (US) surveys:

  (a) '*Individuals* are more to blame than *social conditions* for crime and lawlessness in this country.'

  (b) '*Social conditions* are more to blame than *individuals* for crime and lawlessness in this country.'

  Options in both cases were 'agree' or 'disagree'. The percentage answering 'agree' to (a) should equal those answering 'disagree' to (b), but acquiescence bias led to 59.6 per cent to agree with (a) and 43.2 per cent to disagree with (b).

5. Beware of response errors that may arise due to the characteristics of the interviewer; for example, responses by males to predominantly female and middle-aged interviewers may be those perceived as being 'acceptable' to such people, or designed to impress the interviewer or those the respondent is accompanied by. The opinions and expectations of interviewers may also lead to response error; for example, answers may have to be coded or interpreted into predetermined possibilities by the interviewer. In such a case borderline responses may be coded according to the interviewer's prejudices, or expectations of what the respondent's reply is likely to be from his or her characteristics (e.g. sex, age) or replies to earlier questions. It may just be that the interviewer has perceptions as to what the overall results should be (or the sponsor wants) and will bias the recoded results accordingly to do an 'acceptable' job. Well-trained and appropriately chosen interviewers are essential to surveys, as is the context of the survey. Think how the characteristics (age, sex, dress) of an interviewer might affect adolescents' response to a questionnaire on drug use administered in a school playground.

6. Include some questions that allow you to validate the representativeness of your sample against accurate external data, and where possible cross-validate answers to questions of particular interest by asking them later in a different form.

7. Pilot (or pre-test) your questionnaire by recourse to at least 20 respondents and discuss with them areas of potential confusion (Hunt *et al.*, 1982).

## USING COMPUTERS

Data collection is followed by the assigning of a name to each variable, and codes and labels to possible outcomes from each variable, and its entry onto the computer. For example, a variable of interest might be 'Which store did you last purchase a record/cassette/CD from?': the name 'STORE' might be assigned to the variable and responses labels and codes: OURPRICE—1, WHS—2, BOOTS—3, . . ., OTHER—6, NOTAPPLI—7, DKNOW—8. The precise manner/format of the entry may be dictated by the requirements of the statistical package envisaged for use in the analysis. The fixed column(s) (for each variable) format of Table 2-2 is quite acceptable to most statistical packages. Once the data have been coded and entered, we have to check for errors; then undertake some initial data analysis, and, if necessary, further analysis.

The analysis of anything but the most trivial of datasets should be undertaken using a computer. There are a number of general statistical software or 'packages' designed for the statistical analysis of survey data (and/or data collected over time). The first stage is data entry: Table 2-2 illustrates entry for the statistical package SPSS. The first questionnaire is number 0001; columns 5–6 are the age of the respondent (35 years); column 7, the sex (1 = female); column 8, the response to 'Which morning national newspaper do you usually read?' (3 = *Daily Mirror*). The second row is respondent number 2, who is 28 years old, male (0 = male) and reads the *Daily Mail* (= 2). All questions are given a code for each answer and the coded results accordingly entered. In Table 2-2 less than 80 columns are completed; had more than 80 been completed, column 5 would have indicated the continuation, i.e. row 1—00011, row 2—00012, i.e. second 'line' of 0001. Sometimes

**Table 2-2**  Data entry

| 1 | 2 | 3 | 4 | 5 | 6 | 7 | 8 | ... | 75 | 76 | 77 | 78 | 79 | 80 |
|---|---|---|---|---|---|---|---|-----|----|----|----|----|----|----|
| 0 | 0 | 0 | 1 | 3 | 5 | 1 | 3 | | | | | | | |
| 0 | 0 | 0 | 2 | 2 | 8 | 0 | 2 | | | | | | | |
| ⋮ | | | | | | | | | | | | | | |

the results are written from the questionnaire onto 'coding sheets' similar to Table 2-2, and then typed from the sheets onto disk. However, well-designed questionnaires should allow entry directly from the questionnaire to disk (e.g. see Day, 1987, appendices), the package sometimes taking over the format automatically, prompting for the first row of data, second row, etc. An increasing trend is for interviewers to enter responses electronically via hand-held devices.

The package will allow you to label which columns contain what information (column 7 = sex; 0 = male, 1 = female); the analysis can then proceed. The simple instruction on SPSS: FREQUENCY SEX, PAPER will generate the number and percentage of males, females; number and percentage who read each newspaper. DESCRIPTIVES AGE will calculate all sorts of summary measures (see Chapter 4) such as the average age, dispersion of ages, maximum and minimum age. If you want to relate the answers of one question to another, CROSSTAB PAPER BY SEX will provide a table of different newspapers read (columns) for each sex (rows). And there is much more: from tables and graphs to complex multivariate analysis via simple commands (though understanding their principles and interpreting the results is a little more difficult).

SPSS is one of two major statistical packages to which the majority of universities, polytechnics and colleges of higher education will have access, Minitab being another. There are versions for mainframes (SPSSX) and Personal Computers (PCs) (SPSS-PC +). There are books, user guides and reference manuals (Minitab: Ryan *et al.*, 1985; Bond and Scott, 1988; Miller, 1988; Minitab, 1989—SPSS: Frude, 1987; SPSS, 1988; Norusis, 1985, 1987, 1988a, b, c) on how to use them, though you will need advice from your lecturer on how to register on the mainframe or gain access to PCs, and how to use the computer's operating system to enter 'the world of the package in question'. SPSS is tailor-made for survey analysis; Minitab is more limited in this respect though it has better facilities for time series analysis. While SPSS is not difficult to learn, Minitab is remarkably simple. Consider the following (underlined commands for Minitab only will be those entered by you—the rest is prompted by 'the computer'; after each line you press the 'enter' key).

```
MTB  > READ C1-C3
DATA > 35 1 3
DATA > 28 0 2
DATA > END
MTB  > NAME C1 'AGE', C2 'SEX', C3 'PAPER'
MTB  > DESCRIBE 'AGE'
MTB  > TABLE 'SEX' 'PAPER'
MTB  > TABLE 'PAPER' BY 'SEX'
MTB  > STOP
```

This undertakes on Minitab the same analysis described above for SPSS. The 'naming' is not even essential, the commands being possible in terms of column numbers (e.g. DESCRIBE C1).

To generate 100 random numbers in ascending order between 0 and 10 000 using Minitab:

```
MTB  > RANDOM 100 C1;
SUBC > INTEGER 1 TO 10000.
MTB  > SORT C1 PUT IN C2
MTB  > PRINT C2
```

There are specialized packages for particular types of analysis such as forecasting, graphics, databases, econometrics. However, of popular and increasing use in business by managers are spreadsheets. There are several versions, the discussion in this text relating to Lotus 1-2-3, though 'clones' such as Quattro Pro by Borland exist which replicate Lotus 1-2-3. While the description here will be of Lotus 1-2-3 version 3.1, it will be characterized in two dimensions.

Spreadsheets are neither specifically designed nor suitable for survey analysis, but provide many useful features for data analysis in general. The spreadsheet appears on screen as a very large matrix or table of (numbered) rows and lettered (columns). Data (and text) are entered directly into each cell by typing the number then pressing the 'enter' key or moving the cursor to another cell via the 'arrow' keys. Pressing the '/' key takes you to the menu. Operations can be undertaken on rows, columns or blocks of data. For example, graphs, bar charts, pie charts can be drawn for entered data; an array of functions exists for statistics such as averages, mathematical transformations and financial operations (e.g. discounting). Simulation facilities characterize the spreadsheets, for example the effect on a calculated average of changing a number in a cell can be shown automatically, so 'what if?' type questions can be easily answered. The spreadsheet can be 'programmed' to perform a range of operations, and routine calculations entered for one cell can be copied for vast numbers of cells, and much more (see Ross, 1987; Gorham, 1990; Judge, 1990).

This text is *not* an introduction to any of the packages, though reference will be made at the end of many chapters to appropriate Lotus 1-2-3 and Minitab commands. A brief reference to Minitab commands is given in Appendix 2 (shortened forms are allowed and used above) and Lotus 1-2-3 in Appendix 3.

## INITIAL DATA ANALYSIS

Analysis starts with Initial Data Analysis (IDA), which is followed, if necessary, by the use of more formal techniques and tests. IDA includes processing the data into a suitable form for analysis, checking the quality of the data and the calculation of simple descriptive statistics, as well as the use of graphical devices. All of this is to get a 'feel' for the data—their structure and patterns—to help judge and improve their quality, indicate whether assumptions of subsequent, more sophisticated forms of analysis are likely to be met, and maybe help formulate models or even suggest hypotheses of interest. The importance of IDA has only recently been stressed by, for example, Chatfield (1985, 1988a) following work by Tukey (1977). IDA involves assessing the *structure* of the data, which includes an examination of the sample size, number of variables and the measurement of these variables. For example, data from a survey of employees on job satisfaction may be found to have a small sample size and a large number of questions asked, thus not allowing a detailed breakdown by age group, department, sex, etc. Some variables might be measured inappropriately, e.g. age in years and months (25 years 6 months) when for analysis we want 25.5 years. As part of the structure of the data we should note the scale of measurement used for each variable, this being (as will be reiterated in Chapter 6) crucial to the choice of statistical method adopted. Some methods are appropriate only for variables measured on specific types of scales.

It is in our assigning of codes to the outcome of a variable that the question of 'scales of measurements' to be used is raised. We can distinguish between data measured on different scales (see Table 2-3): a *ratio scale*, for example 'age', has a hierarchy in that one value on the scale (e.g. 20 years) can be said to be higher than another (e.g. 19 years), and the difference between successive (integer) values are the same—the difference between 19 and 20 years is the same as between 40 and 41 years. An *interval scale* has the same characteristics as the ratio, except that the value zero is arbitrary (as in temperature, measured in Celsius or Fahrenheit). Fortunately, for practical purposes here we shall treat ratio and interval scales alike and use the term 'interval' to mean interval or ratio.

**Table 2-3** Characteristics of different scales of measurement

|  | Has a hierarchy | Difference between successive (integer) values are equal |
|---|---|---|
| Ratio/Interval | ✓ | ✓ |
| Ordinal | ✓ | × |
| Nominal | × | × |

An *ordinal or ranked scale* has a hierarchy, but differences between successive values are not equal. For example, opinions on customer service may be rated and entered on the computer as: 1, very good; 2, good; 3, neither good nor bad; 4, bad; 5, very bad. There is a hierarchy (5 is worse than 1), but can we say the difference between 3 and 2 is the same as that between 1 and 2? It is the same numerically, but is this numerical representation valid? Some researchers say the advantages of using it outweigh any errors, while others are (rightly) more careful. There are more clear-cut cases such as ascribing numerical values to the ranking of applicants from an interview: 1, best; 2, next best; 3, third best; etc. The difference between first and second may well be quite minimal, while that between second and third substantial; the numerical codes do not show this.

Finally, a nominal or classificatory scale has no hierarchy at all. The variable 'sex' or 'region currently living in' have possible outcomes which may vary between individuals, but we do not generally assign a hierarchy to these outcomes. Having distinguished between different scales you may wonder why we bother. It is to warn us from the start not to use certain techniques on certain variables: calculating the average by summing all values and dividing by the number of such values is fine for 'age' to compute the average age; but the average 'sex', 'paper read' or 'region' makes little sense and the average opinion score may be misleading. The average ranking of the quality of the applicants will always be the same for the same number interviewed. The average as portrayed here can only be calculated from data on a ratio or interval scale. Similar considerations will be examined in Chapter 6. IDA would include a consideration of the scales used for different variables and the implications for subsequent analysis.

Having considered under IDA the structure of our data, we now look to its *quality*. Here our concern is with examining the data to identify if there are any extreme values or outliers. Great care is needed in the treatment of *outliers*. For example, data on 'time spent by customers waiting in a queue' may in general contain values between 5 and 10 minutes. A few values of around 50 minutes may be transcription errors of '5.0' appearing as '50' or may be genuine extreme waiting periods. An all too enthusiastic exclusion of outliers as errors may obscure very real problems. Naturally the detection of outliers should be followed by a procedure to check if they are genuine or errors. Errors may be revealed by consistency checks (e.g. age (if under 17 years) and number of cars owned), defining 'credible ranges', tracing the questionnaire and respondent. If extreme values cannot be ruled as errors or otherwise, Chatfield (1988a) suggests running the analysis with their inclusion and exclusion, and if the results differ greatly treat them with caution. What is not always apparent is that even if outliers are genuine and not mistakes, the decision to include or exclude them depends on their origins *and* the purpose of the analysis. For our example on waiting times, if the few outliers were caused by a bomb threat, then they should be removed from any analysis of the efficiency of the system since such systems should not be designed to cope with such rare events. However, if they arose as a natural by-product of the system and the purpose of the system was to provide a 'good' service to *all* customers, then it is critical that the outliers are not simply disposed of. Their discovery should make us ask questions as to why they have arisen, and help us formulate/discover vital areas of interest.

Care is also necessary in the treatment of *non-response* while non-response bias was discussed earlier for the questionnaire, here our concern is with non-response to particular questions, i.e. *missing values*. Similar issues of course apply, and where the missing value rate is high and characteristics or views of non-respondents are likely to differ from respondents, there will be bias. Missing values must be separately coded (preferably not with a number) and excluded from the analysis. Statistical software generally have routines for achieving this. However, care must be taken to ensure that 'don't know', 'not applicable', 'indifferent', or 'none' are not treated as missing values.

IDA further includes the *initial statistical analysis* of the data. This takes the form of the calculation of summary measures such as the proportion of respondents giving a particular answer, the average age, range of ages, etc., as well as some graphical devices that help to illuminate the features of the data, all of this being outlined in Chapter 4. IDA is not limited to the description of the features of one variable, but embraces methods such as scatter diagrams (Chapter 6) and data reduction methods such as principal components analysis, cluster analysis and multidimensional scaling which can provide a simplified picture of quite large datasets (Manly, 1986). The techniques discussed in Chapters 4 and 6 are quite valid in their own right and might be sufficient for some analyses (see Velleman and Hoaglin, 1981): but for questions requiring more sophisticated methods they should only act as a starting point.

IDA is useful for exploring data, helping in data description, identification if assumptions required by subsequent techniques are likely to be met, and the formulation of statistical models and derivation of hypotheses. However, we must be careful to avoid a process referred to as 'data mining'. Our approach is to start with theories about business-related variables and collect and analyse data to see if our ideas hold up in the real (empirical) world. Good research is theory-driven. However, if we come across a pattern or feature of the data in our IDA that is of great importance to the real world, and we can see a good reason for its occurrence (even though we did not think of it before), it would be unwise to neglect it. We often tell the story as if we had thought up the theory ourselves and tested it. Yet data will by chance possess patterns and there is a danger, having found a chance pattern, of thinking of some not too outrageous theory to justify it and then announcing that 'discovery' to the world. Using data to help generate theories (referred to as grounded theory) is well established in qualitative research (Glaser and Strauss, 1967). The problem of data mining, however, remains.

Having undertaken IDA we move (if necessary) to more formal analysis and tests and a number of techniques are outlined in this book. Chatfield (1988a) provides a problem-orientated introduction to methods not covered here. Naturally, thought should have been given to the methods to be used prior to collection of data in order to ensure that the data meet the method's requirements in terms of, for example, sample size and scale of measurement used (see Chapter 6).

### Methods of presentation

Having come along the route of collecting and analysing your data, the need now is to communicate your results effectively, bearing in mind the accuracy with which they are portrayed and the audience at whom they are directed. This book contains a mixture of text, graphics and tables to (hopefully) help you learn statistics. The language used in the text and clarity of graphics and tables will (again hopefully) be appropriate to your needs. When you communicate results you may have a variety of media available: printed reports, overheads, slides, video, computer, television, posters, black/white board or whatever is possible and relevant. Within these media, pictures, text, graphics, tables, speeches and music may be used to present accurately the desired information in an attractive form to the audience in mind. The next chapter is concerned with the use of tabular, graphical and pictorial approaches to presenting numerical information.

## EXERCISES

**2-1** Widgets are manufactured by your company to customers' very tight specifications. Unfortunately you do not possess the technology to continuously monitor the quality of widgets produced, so you rely on taking random samples. You only have resources to test about 500 from the 10 000 produced each day by three machines, these machines being responsible in turn for 60, 30 and 10 per cent of production. You suspect quality variations exist between the 3-hour morning 'shift' and the 4-hour afternoon 'shift', and that in the first hour of every day the product quality variation is twice that of production generally. How would you go about formulating a sample design for the selection of a random sample of 500 widgets a day?

**2-2** The Shirt Shop has 100 branches distributed across the UK. You wish to administer a short questionnaire to a sample of those entering the shop. One purpose of the survey is to determine the proportion of shoppers who made a purchase; the other is to seek their views on the relative merits of the store *vis-à-vis* competitors. Design a method for selecting a random sample of shoppers to the Shirt Shop. Bear in mind that during the lunch hour each store is particularly busy and the cost of sending interviewers to all 100 branches is prohibitive. State any assumptions made (e.g. concerning geographical distribution of stores) for your design.

**2-3** As a paint manufacturer you have developed a new range of paints and want consumers' views on the attractiveness of different colour schemes. The present method of achieving this is via a 'hall test' in Bath, Avon, whereby shoppers who fit quota controls of age (3 bands) and sex are asked into the hall to judge the relative merits of the paints in return for a small gift. The controls are such that the sample will reflect the age (16 plus) and sex distribution of the UK as a whole. What weaknesses and merits are there in this scheme? Suggest an alternative design drawing attention to its relative merits.

**2-4** Mr Cubitt, the manager of a local squash club known as Newton Sports Centre, is anxious to collect some information about the type of person who uses his club. In particular he wishes to know age, sex, frequency of play, length of game of users and their preference with regard to possible new facilities such as a car park, a bar, coaching or a shop. He has asked his sons, both of whom are studying management at a local college, to design a questionnaire that could be issued to people attending the Centre. Mr Cubitt intends that the door-keeper should give a copy of the questionnaire, together with an introductory letter from himself, to each person entering the Centre and that they should be asked to put the completed questionnaire in a box as they leave. Each of his sons has produced a questionnaire (see A and B) and Mr Cubitt is wondering whether to use either of them or to design a questionnaire himself. Compare and contrast these questionnaires, drawing attention to how you would formulate an appropriate questionnaire.

---

**QUESTIONNAIRE A**

**Instruction**   Please tick relevant box

1. Are you male or female? ........................

2. How old are you?

   0–15 years  ☐      30–40 years  ☐
   15–25 years  ☐      40+          ☐
   25–30 years  ☐

3. How often do you come to the Centre?
   ..............................................

4. How long do you spend on a court on average?
   ..............................................

5. If you had to choose between the following, which do you think is the most important for the Centre to provide?

   Car                                Don't
   park      Coaching    Bar          know
   ☐         ☐           ☐            ☐

---

**QUESTIONNAIRE B**

1. Are you male or female? .........................

2. How old are you? ................................

3. Do you usually play squash:
   once a week?                ☐
   twice a week?               ☐
   more than twice a week?  ☐

4. How long do you usually take over a game?
   0–5 minutes            ☐
   6–10 minutes           ☐
   10 minutes or over   ☐

5. What other facilities would you most like the Centre to provide (e.g. bar, coaching, car parking, a shop)?
   ..............................................
   ..............................................
   ..............................................

Many thanks for your help. Please put this questionnaire, when complete, in the box at the exit.

# PRESENTING NUMERICAL INFORMATION

It is difficult to overstate the importance of properly presenting the numerical results of your work. No matter what effort and cost has gone into the collection of data, and no matter how sophisticated the analysis, if the results of the work are not communicated to their audience in a manner that allows the pertinent issues to be identified, the study will fail. Good presentation allows the user to discern the salient information quite easily to the required level of detail. It also helps the analyst: you may collect and analyse data, yet your results must be in a form that allows *you* to identify what you have found, quite apart from communicating these findings to your audience.

Often vast quantities of numbers are collected and first we have to summarize the data before presenting them. Methods of summarizing data are considered in the next chapter, as are further methods of presentation (including frequency tables, histograms, ogives, box plots, stem-and-leaf charts) more suitable for data requiring summarizing. Here we look at two types of approaches to presenting numbers: charts (including graphs, bar charts, pie charts, etc.) and tables.

## CHOICE BETWEEN CHARTS AND TABLES

The choice between charts (of different forms) and tables depends upon the effectiveness with which they accurately communicate the information and the receptiveness of the audience to the format. This lesson even applies to the extent and form of the numbers represented by the graph or in the table. There is an adage in advertising: 'No one ever got poor by underestimating the intelligence of the audience.' It is important in presenting numerical information to remember many people have trouble assimilating such information. A survey by the Office of Fair Trading into the views of credit users as to what was meant by APR (annual percentage rate) included the identification of the meaning of '40 per cent'. A choice between 'one in 25', 'a quarter', 'one in 40' and 'four in ten' was given with only 53 per cent getting it right. Even when the answer was posed a second time as a choice between '40 in every 100', 'one fortieth', '40 in every 1000' and 'multiplied by 40', only 69 per cent chose the correct answer. Out of this second set of answers only 45 per cent of readers of the *Sun* 'newspaper' chose '40 in every 100'. (Reproduced from *The Times* in the Royal Statistical Society's *News and Notes*, 17(2), October 1990.) In some cases it is well worth piloting any graph or table in different forms among a small sample of the potential audience to

ensure that they get the message. What you consider a simple and clear presentation may not be received as such.

As regards the choice between charts and tables consider the Isobar in Fig. 3-16 as an alternative to a table of the figures: both accurately communicate the required information, but if we want to attract the attention of a more general audience to the data, and to highlight its characteristics, the isobar is more suitable. In a technical report to a technical audience an isobar might be deemed inappropriate. Alternatively, the graph in Fig. 3-6 attractively highlights the trend (or lack or it), but is not as accurate as a table of numbers. You must decide which will be attractive and suitable for your audience to convey the relevant point(s). However, generally speaking, charts are good for quantitative comparisons, for example, over time or for relationships where the information is directed towards general audiences and where the attractiveness of the report is important, while tables are better for communicating specific numerical amounts to technical audiences. Tables are especially appropriate when data are to be put down for future reference so that a future user of the data can decide on an appropriate format. Data stored in electronic form suitable for reading by general statistical and spreadsheet software are particularly useful for reference purposes since the user can readily generate charts and tables as required (Ehrenberg, 1978).

It is easy to dismiss presentation as being unimportant or self-evident compared with analysing the data. But remember, managers spend much of their time communicating information to others and information poorly presented, and thus poorly communicated, can at best waste information, and at worst mislead. We start with charts.

## DESIGNING GOOD CHARTS

Good charts are judged according to how well they represent the patterns in the data and how clearly they tell the story intended of them to the audience in question. In presenting a chart you are conveying information in an easier-to-read format than the numbers. Badly drawn charts, intentionally or otherwise, may confuse and mislead. Before considering some general principles for good charts, we look at a number of types of charts.

### Graphs

Figure 3-1 shows the growth in sales volume of XYZ's two models of their product between 1991 and 1992. The visual impression, via the rising slopes, is one of gradual increases in sales volumes. If you need a more impressive representation, Fig. 3-2 shows a graph based on the same data with steeper slopes.

Graphs are extremely valuable for showing patterns over time which the eye would have difficulty in tracing from a table of numbers. However, the visual impression of the slope is dictated by the scales used on the axes. You might ask: why should graphs be used at all when the visual impression of their slope is so affected by the scaling? The answer is that they still provide us with a representation of fluctuations, growth, falls, turning points, etc. However, they should be read by looking at the scales on the axes as well as the shape. Since the visual impression of the rate of change is in part dependent on the scale used on the axes, it follows that axes need to be precisely labelled as to their units of measurement.

Figure 3-2 shows sales of model A to be increasing at a faster rate than B. In Fig. 3-1 the differential slopes are not so apparent. There is a question as to the *shape* of the graph which best facilitates such comparisons. It can be shown that if we take the angle of the slope for the first line (model A), add it to the slope of the second line (model B) and take the average, then when the

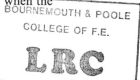

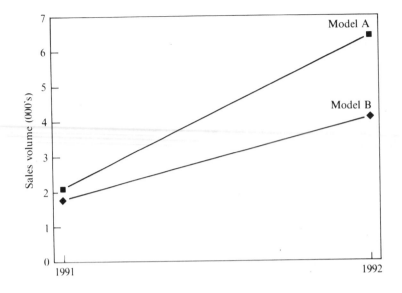

**Figure 3-1** Sales volume XYZ Ltd: models A and B

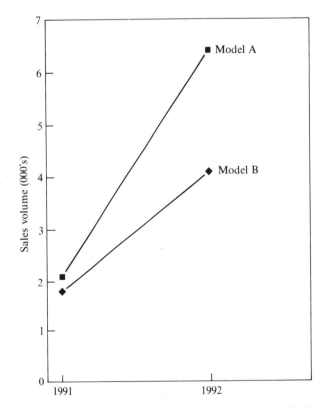

**Figure 3-2** Sales volume XYZ Ltd: models A and B

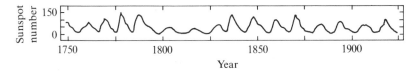

**Figure 3-3** Sunspot activity: example 1
*Source*: Cleveland and McGill (1987)

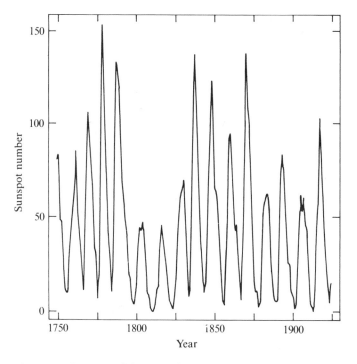

**Figure 3-4** Sunspot activity: example 2
*Source*: Cleveland and McGill (1987)

average (called the mid-angle orientation) is around 45° our ability to judge the differential slopes is maximized (Cleveland and McGill, 1987). We choose our scales to achieve a mid-angle orientation of 45° (or −45° if applicable). [Remember angles are derived by dividing the vertical height by the width, and looking up the value in tables of tangents—or alternatively by using a protractor.] The mid-angle orientation in Fig. 3-1 is just under 20° while that in Fig. 3-2 is just under 50°, the latter reflecting the quite different growth rates much better (model A: 205 per cent; model B: 128 per cent).

If there are fluctuations in the data it is as well to consider the shape (mid-angle orientation) of the graph in terms of individual adjacent pairs of slopes; focusing on an adjacent pair of positive and a pair of negative slopes of 'average' (median—see Chapter 4) size. We would want the mid-angle orientation to be (plus or minus) 45° *for these pairs*, not for the whole graph. Compare Figs 3-3 and 3-4 on sunspot activity between 1750 and 1925, reproduced from Cleveland and McGill (1987). Figure 3-3 shows that sunspot numbers rise more rapidly than they fall; the mid-angle orientation is 45° in this figure for a pair of adjacent slopes, while in Fig. 3-4 we no longer see the more rapid rise than fall because the shape for adjacent slopes is all wrong.

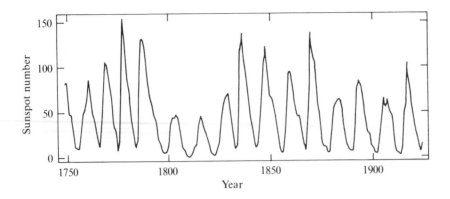

**Figure 3-5** Sunspot activity: example 3
*Source*: Cleveland and McGill (1987)

More than one shape may be used. An interest in the maximum sunspot activity would mean drawing a line between two successive (typical or average) peak values and drawing the graph so that the increase (or decline) in this line is 45° (−45°), as in Fig. 3-5 on the same sunspot data, allowing the peak-to-peak changes to be better assessed. All of this may suggest to the reader either a lot of work or an ability to 'fix' the impression given by the data. In the former case graphics facilities such as those on spreadsheets or specialized graphics software allow us to experiment and these are being developed to facilitate a high level of interaction in different formulations. As regards the 'fixing', we have seen that different scales may provide different impressions. Rather than choose an arbitrary scale we choose scales which improve the audience's chances of detecting, and properly understanding, the patterns and behaviour of the data.

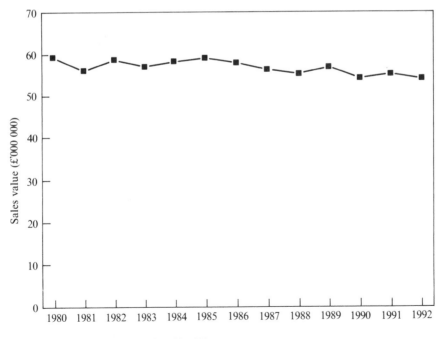

**Figure 3-6** Sales value ABC Ltd, 1980–1992

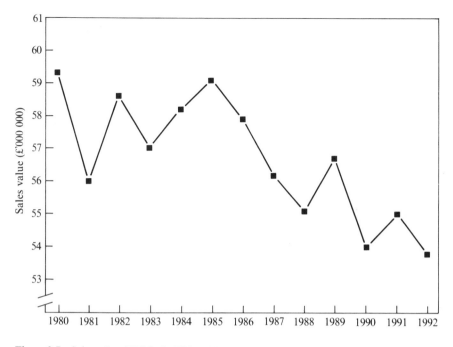

**Figure 3-7**  Sales value ABC Ltd, 1980–1992

A common phenomenon with graphs is a break in one or both of the axes. Consider Fig. 3-6, which tells us that sales in this case are relatively stable, the fluctuations being only slight. Often there is a misplaced embarrassment about the blank space in the body of the graph and the scale may be broken as in Fig. 3-7 to 'highlight' the pattern. Using the same numbers as in Fig. 3-6, we now have falling and fluctuating sales. Breaking an axis acts like a telescope, and while it allows us to identify more clearly the pattern the graph takes, we must remember it is out of porportion to the overall picture. Graphs with breaks in axes should thus be interpreted carefully and used, if at all, to identify patterns and not changes in relative magnitudes.

A comparison of the two lines in Figs 3-1 and 3-2 succeeded because both variables were roughly the same size. But what if the graphs take up quite different ranges of values? One solution is to change the numbers into index numbers with a common starting point (reference period) of 100, with each graph showing changes from this. For example, if we matched temperature (20, 25, 30°C) against ice-cream sales (6, 8, 12 million) the temperature data would be 100, $(25/20)100 = 125$, $(30/20)100 = 150$ and ice-cream sales 100, $(8/6)100 = 133$, $(12/6)100 = 200$; i.e. both plotted on the same scale (see Chapter 5 for further details). Alternatively, Fig. 3-8 shows how three different variables are 'plotted' each with its own axes and scales.

Sometimes our interest is not with how a variable—for example, unemployment or retail prices—changes annually, but with its annual *rate of change*. Here, instead of using the actual figures, we take logarithms of these figures (using logarithmic tables or **log** on our pocket calculators), as in Table 3-1. The actual data show a doubling of sales every year; logarithms show the same increase each year, i.e. the same rate of change, increasing by 0.301 each year. The graph of the annual rate of increase would be a straight line. For example, given monthly figures on inflation we might be interested in the (month-on-month) rate of increase and monitor a graph of the logarithm of inflation, and not the index or level. Note with Table 3-1 the antilogarithm of

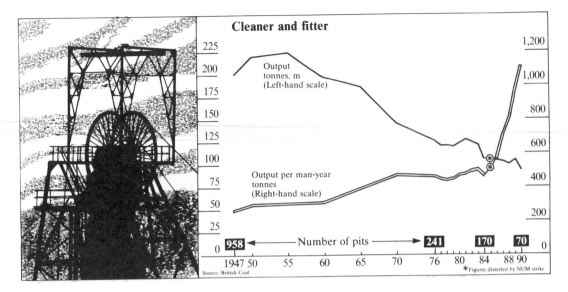

**Figure 3-8** A cleaner and fitter Britain
*Source*: *The Economist*, 14 July 1990

**Table 3-1** Fictitious data on sales of Gizmos, worldwide 1988 to 1991

| Year | Number sold (millions) | Logarithm (to base 10) of number sold |
|------|------------------------|----------------------------------------|
| 1988 | 2 | 0.301 |
| 1989 | 4 | 0.602 |
| 1990 | 8 | 0.903 |
| 1991 | 16 | 1.204 |

0.301 ($10^x$ on your calculator) is equal to 2—a doubling of the figures or 100 per cent increase per annum. Thus, plotting the logarithm of a variable is useful to show the pattern of the rate of change of that variable.

### Bar charts

Bar charts allow comparisons to be shown between different groups, such as the income of workers in different regions. They can also be used like graphs to monitor changes over time. In this they are most effective when only a small number of periods are to be compared, though thin bars (or spike graphs using lines) can be used if such charts are to be plotted over a large number of periods. Figure 3.9 shows monthly data on UK unemployment rates. It can be argued that a graph is inappropriate because the data relate not to the whole of the month, but to a single day in each month on which the unemployed are counted. The bar chart or spike graph thus more honestly represents the data not as a flow (as in a conventional graph), but as a series of points over time. In spite of this argument conventional graphs are to be preferred since the purpose of the chart is to facilitate the identification of the pattern of the changes over time, and if joining the points helps to do so, all well and good. Thus graphs are generally preferred to bar charts for displaying changes over time when there are a large number of periods (as in Fig. 3-9) or when the desired visual impression is a flow of data.

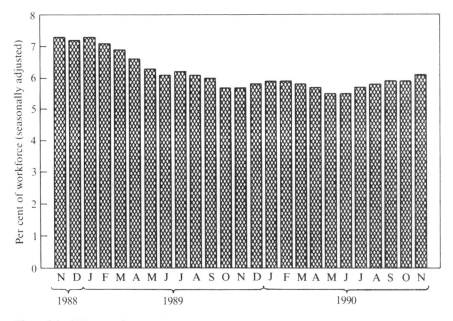

**Figure 3-9**   UK unemployment rates
*Data source*: Department of Employment, *Employment Gazette*, January 1991

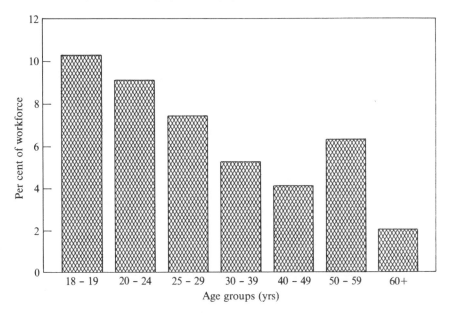

**Figure 3-10**   UK unemployment rates by age groups, October 1990
*Data source*: Department of Employment, *Employment Gazette*, January 1991

Bar charts need not be confined to the showing of changes over time periods, but are more generally used for changes across categories such as age groups in Fig. 3-10. Bar charts may also be used to show how variables are interrelated, such as the unemployment rate, age band, and sex as in Fig. 3-11. It is usually the case that the charts will be illustrating a point made in the text of an article or report, or orally in a presentation. In such cases the title of the figure might relate to the

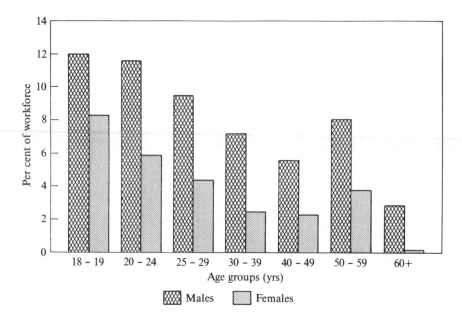

**Figure 3-11**   UK unemployment rates by age groups and sex, October 1990
*Data source*: Department of Employment, *Employment Gazette*, January 1991

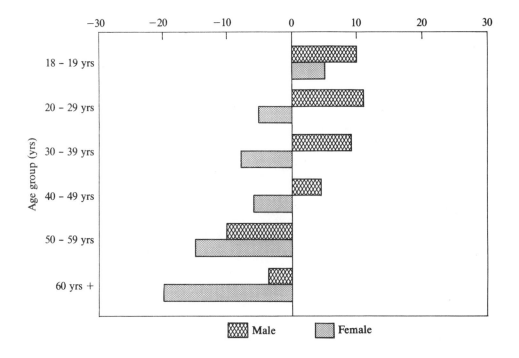

**Figure 3-12**   Percentage change in numbers unemployed, by sex, October 1989 to 1990
*Data source*: Department of Employment, *Employment Gazette*, January 1991

point being made. For example, Fig. 3-10 might be titled 'Unemployment trap'. Figure 3-11 might illustrate the lower rates of unemployment for females and how the differentials vary in different age bands. As pointed out in Chapter 1, care is needed in the interpretation of statistics from secondary sources. Unemployment statistics relate to those registered, which in turn is affected by the entitlement to benefits, which in turn acts against women.

Two-directional (two-way or bilateral) bar charts allow positive and negative values to be highlighted, for example, profit and loss, or, as in Fig. 3-12, the percentage change in the numbers of unemployed between October 1989 and 1990 for males and females of different age bands. Things seem to be getting worse for the younger men, though the number of 18 to 19 year olds who are unemployed is increasing irrespective of sex. Note how the horizontal bar chart (Fig. 3-12) allows more room for titles for each bar and more bars to be included.

The composition of the total measurement, changes in the total, and comparisons in the relative importance of the constituent elements of the total can be shown by a stacked (component) bar chart. Figure 3-13 shows the total number of unemployed made up according to the age bands that constitute the total. This is done for males and females for comparison. We can see that the total number of females unemployed is much less than that for males, and also undertake comparisons for different age bands. Notice how 18 to 19 year olds make up a fairly small proportion (the band including only 2 years and not 10 years and has a higher provision of training schemes) and how the size of this group is not dissimilar for males and females even though the size of males unemployed is much greater in all other age groups. This would reflect couples starting families in their twenties, the female not continuing with paid employment and not registering as unemployed actively seeking work. [Compare the differential unemployment rates for males and females in Fig. 3-11 for the 18 to 19 years band and the 20 to 24 years band.] It is not easy to compare the size of individual bands across sexes in Fig. 3-13. If we were not interested in the changing total across sexes, but only

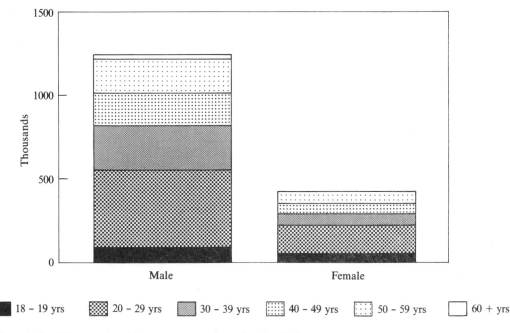

**Figure 3-13**  UK unemployed by age groups and sex, October 1990
*Data source*: Department of Employment, *Employment Gazette*, January 1991

the relative number of unemployed in each age band, we might use 'percentage unemployed in an age band out of total unemployed' calculated for each sex, the stacked bar charts in Fig. 3-13 thus becoming the same size (100 per cent).

The size of the bar chart depends on such factors as the importance of the point to be illustrated, the media used, and the prominence given to text as opposed to graphs. However, Weber's law should be borne in mind, which tells us that to determine the relative lengths of two lines (bars), we need look at the ratio of the lengths and not at their overall size. Our ability to detect a difference in two lines of length 6 mm and 6.1 mm is the same as between 60 mm and 61 mm (Cleveland and McGill, 1985). A small bar chart can make the point as well as a large one.

### Pie charts

Pie charts are an alternative to bar charts for showing the composition of a total. Two or three pies alongside each other are often drawn to illustrate the changing composition (Fig. 3-14). For a pie chart the 360° of each circle is divided up according to the relative contribution of each element as in Fig. 3-14; slices should be ordered in decreasing size. Alternatively, they may be ordered in the natural scale of the variable as in Fig. 3-14, starting anticlockwise at 3 o'clock. If the purpose of the pie chart is to highlight the contribution of a single category, that slice of the pie might be slightly lifted for visual impact. Note that the size of the pies in Fig. 3-14 are the same even though the absolute number of male and female unemployed differs. The pies could have been drawn so that their relative sizes (areas) represented the different total amounts. However, this is *not* advised; most people cannot evaluate the relative areas of different sized circles accurately (Meihofer, 1973). Indeed Cleveland and McGill (1985) show that judgements as to the relative magnitude of quantities are better perceived in terms of their relative lengths than angles in the pie chart, and bar charts thus convey information more accurately than pie charts. Pie and bar charts should in any event include data on the percentage contribution (and/or quantity) alongside or in each wedge or bar. Unless there is a strong argument for the aesthetic appeal of pie charts, which over-rides the loss in the accuracy of their perception of the data, you should stick to bar charts.

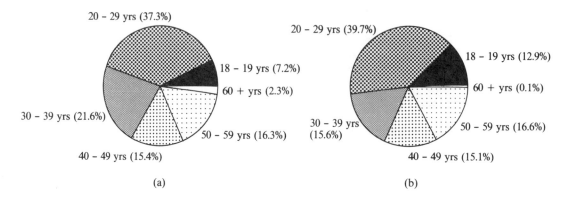

(a)                                         (b)

**Figure 3-14** Percent of total UK unemployed by age groups, male and female, October 1990
*Data source*: Department of Employment, *Employment Gazette*, January 1991

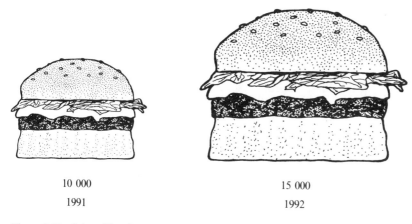

|             |             |
|-------------|-------------|
| 10 000      | 15 000      |
| 1991        | 1992        |

**Figure 3-15**  Sales of hamburgers

## The Magic Lantern Technique

Figure 3-15 shows an impressive growth in sales of hamburgers; sales have increased by 50 per cent between 1991 and 1992. The height of the hamburger in 1992 is 50 per cent higher than that in 1991. However, to maintain the shape of the hamburger we have also to increase its width by 50 per cent. Thus the area increases, over and above the increase in the height, by 125 per cent in this case, and it is the area that the eye focuses on in the comparison. Such comparisons are referred to in Moroney (1965) as the Magic Lantern Technique; they create an illusion by giving a larger visual impact to an increase (or greater fall) than in fact occurred.

## Isobars

These powerful pictorial devices increase the appeal or attractiveness of a chart. They are essentially horizontal bar charts with symbols used to designate a given number of units. For, example, a picture of a hamburger could signify 250 burgers sold (Fig. 3-16). The symbols should be self-explanatory, with it being clear how many units each symbol represent (fractions of symbols being used where appropriate).

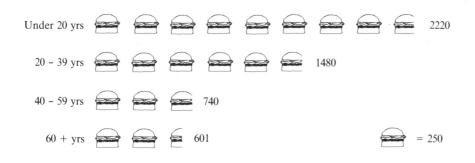

**Figure 3-16**  Number of hamburgers purchased by age group, ABC Burger Bar, January 1992

### Statistical maps

Often our concern is with variation over a geographical area, and a map of the area on which the information is placed—for example, regional unemployment rates—is one way of conveying such information. It is particularly useful when a part of the exercise includes showing how regions are located with respect to each other. The approaches can be classified into three forms (see Dickinson, 1977, for details) displaying quantitative data at:

- specific points
- within a given area
- along a line.

Unemployment rates in London, Birmingham, Cardiff, Edinburgh, Leeds, etc., are figures to be represented at different *points* on the map. Aside from the actual data, you could represent the figures by using appropriately sized dots, each dot equal to a certain number of unemployed, or instead of dots, bars, squares, circles, spheres, cubes or whatever. Instead of having more dots to represent more unemployed we could have a graduated range of symbols (growing larger to signify more). If we wanted to represent more than one variable for each point, pie diagrams or stacked bars (of different sizes if necessary) could represent the relative mix of, say, unemployed persons of different age bands.

The data may not refer to geographical points but to geographical *areas*, such as unemployment rates in the South East, North West, etc. The above techniques could be used though the visual impression is that the unemployment rate is equally distributed within the geographical area. Since more disaggregated data are available we could split the country into finer divisions, but then there is less room on the map for the symbols and the size of the dots for each region, or the number of dots representing each percentage point unemployed, has to become smaller. Alternatively, we could forsake dots for shading or colours in a number of different hues, each of which representing (from a scale) different unemployment rates. Indeed, the very intensity of the shading can be regulated to the scale of the variable. Our concern with areas of different sizes requires our measures to be expressed relative to the size of the area, as densities, such as *percentage* unemployed rate, births per thousand people, etc. A final method for areas, which is not instantly apparent to the general user, uses isolines, as represented for example on ordnance survey maps showing the height of land (see Dickinson, 1977, p. 58).

Finally, maps may have quantities displayed *along a line*. This is generally used for road traffic where the thickness of the road on a map corresponds to the traffic intensity. It might also be used to depict a company's trading flow, nationally or internationally.

### General points

We shall come across further graphical techniques in other chapters; in particular the histogram, ogive, stem-and-leaf, box plots in Chapter 4, the scatter diagram in Chapter 6 and use of graphs for time series in Chapter 8. However, there are some general points on charts that should be borne in mind when using any of the above techniques (see also Schmid, 1985, Tufte, 1983 and Huff, 1965).

- Words have a role to play alongside charts, as Chapman and Mahon (1986, p. 2) note: 'A table or chart without accompanying verbal [or written] commentary is like a silent film: it may be excellently planned and executed, but without words to highlight the important points, indicate general patterns and state the message explicitly, only a few dedicated souls will really understand it.' Guidance on writing reports and plain English is beyond the scope of this book (and possibly this author) and Gowers (1973) and Fletcher (1983) are recommended.

- Unless space is at a premium two simple charts make the desired points better than a single cluttered one.
- Horizontal grid lines can be superimposed across a graph to help read-off values of the graph at particular points from the $Y$-axis.
- For charts aimed at a non-technical audience, use your imagination to think of graphical inserts, eye-catching (sub) titles or text pointing to certain parts of the chart to make it more user-friendly.
- Clearly title the chart, making sure the units of measurement, geographical coverage, time period covered, definitions of variables and source of data are clearly labelled somewhere. If there is more than one chart, each should be numbered for ease of reference.
- If some readers might require accurate figures, include these in the body of bar charts or on the top of the bars, at the end of a row of symbols in an isobar, in or at the end of a slice of the pie.
- Wherever possible, lines and sections of pies or bars should be labelled directly on the graph, and not by use of a key or legend which requires the eye to move constantly between chart and key (Culbertson and Powers, 1959).
- Use differential shading, colours (unless the report is to be photocopied in black and white), hatching and symbols to differentiate between different slices of pies, stacks of bar charts, lines on line graphs, etc.
- In any comparison of trends over time, ask yourself why you are starting the graph at that particular time period. Starting at different periods can yield quite different impressions and as a general rule it is good practice to include at least one turning point (if they exist).

## DESIGNING A GOOD TABLE

The principles outlined here are for tables designed to demonstrate information to an audience, not tables for future reference for which slightly different principles apply (see Chapman, 1986).

- Tables should be titled and, if more than one, numbered for easy reference; the title should explain in simple, brief words the data contained and how they have been classified, geographical and time coverage and units of measurement. The units and coverage may take the form of a secondary title in a smaller typeface. Alternatively, a 'punchy' title conveying the main message of the table may be used, in which case the above information must be clearly identified elsewhere in the table.
- Since titles and column and row headings should be kept brief, footnotes may be used to elaborate on definitions, highlight unusual observations, etc. However, lengthy footnotes should be avoided, their role being to prevent misunderstanding or misinterpretation of data and to elaborate on headings, but not to distract attention from the table.
- The full source of the data should always be given (usually at the bottom of the table) so that users can trace the origin of the data.
- Capital letters are usually only used for the initial letter of the first word in a row or column heading.
- If there are several rows of figures, horizontal lines or spaces every four or five rows helps the eye run along the row.
- Decide on how precise your figures should be. How many decimal places, the extent to which integers should be rounded—for example, should your data be units, hundreds, thousands, etc. As a general rule, round numbers to two effective units unless you have reason to believe greater accuracy is required. Two effective units would be to round: 151, 191, 203, 241, 287, 344 to 150,

190, 200, 240, 290, 340. The reason is that it is easier for the user of the table to compare and do mental arithmetic on rounded figures at this level (Ehrenberg, 1975 and 1977).

- Give row and column totals or averages or any summary calculations that you believe the user will probably be interested in, such as percentage changes over time or proportionate shares. This is especially useful if data are required at a level of accuracy over and above two effective figures. If this crowds out a table ask yourself what the user is interested in: a table of data, a table of the results of these calculations, or both.
- Put the numbers to be most often compared next to each other in columns rather than rows—the eye reads down columns more easily than across rows (Wright and Fox, 1970).
- Where possible put large numbers at the top of the table—for example, if you were giving data by region, put the region with the largest figures as the first row, etc.
- In the text, give a summary in words of the main points of the table. A well-designed table should allow the patterns and exceptions referred to in the text to be immediately apparent.
- In general, don't use tables to show broad trends or relationships. Charts are much better.

For a step-by-step improvement of a badly designed table, see Chapter 1 of Ehrenberg (1975).

## USING COMPUTERS

### Minitab

Charts on Minitab are limited to relatively poor quality plots and methods for displaying frequency distributions (which are considered in the next chapter).

```
MTB > TSPLOT C1
```

Provides a plot of the data in C1 against the integers 1, 2, 3, etc., on the horizontal axis. It is primarily for use for time series plots where the 1, 2, 3, etc., represents increasing periods of time. Starting points and new scales (e.g. 4, 6, 8, 10, etc.) can be imposed via subcommands:

```
MTB  > TSPLOT C1;
SUBC > INCREMENT=2;
SUBC > START=4.
```

TSPLOT uses as symbols for successive points on the graph the values 1, 2, 3, ..., 8, 9, 0, 1, 2, etc. If, for example, we had monthly data it would be useful if the same symbol represented the same month, in order that seasonal patterns are apparent. This is achieved by:

```
MTB > TSPLOT PERIOD=12 C1
```

where, if we started at January = 1, the letters A and B would take over for November and December, starting again at January = 1.

For TSPLOT and the following plot commands the height and width of the plot can be adjusted by, for example:

```
MTB > HEIGHT=20 (lines)
MTB > WIDTH=60 (spaces)
```

the only exception being TSPLOT for which WIDTH does not apply. Alternatives are PLOT, MPLOT and LPLOT. Their scales and starting points can be altered, in this case for a simple scatter PLOT of one variable against another, by the subcommands:

```
MTB  > PLOT C1 VS C2;
SUBC > XINCREMENT=1;
```

```
SUBC > XSTART=0 [END AT 20];
SUBC > YINCREMENT=0;
SUBC > YSTART=0 [END AT 100].
```

Should it be required that more than one time series be plotted on the same graph use:

```
MTB > MPLOT C2 VS C1 & C3 VS C1 & C4 VS C1.
```

This will produce three plots for each of C2, C3 and C4 against a common C1 on the horizontal axis which may be entered as 1, 2, 3, etc., or 1981, 1982, 1983, etc., or whatever time-based numerical sequence is appropriate. The symbols A, B and C will be used respectively for the data plotted in C2, C3 and C4 to distinguish the different series. Alternatively

```
MTB > LPLOT C1 VS C2 USING TAGS IN C3
```

allows data in C1 to be plotted against C2 on the horizontal axis; however, we can choose the symbols for any of the points based on the correspondence:

$$\dots \quad -4 \quad -3 \quad -2 \quad -1 \quad 0 \quad 1 \quad 2 \quad 3 \quad 4 \dots 25 \quad 26 \quad 27$$
$$\quad V \quad W \quad X \quad Y \quad Z \quad A \quad B \quad C \quad D \dots X \quad Y \quad Z$$

Thus, starting with January, if we wanted all the summer months (May, June, July) to be separately identified, we would read into C3 (starting at January):

$$1\ 1\ 1\ 1\ 2\ 2\ 2\ 1\ 1\ 1\ 1\ 1\ 1\ 1\ 1\ 2\ 2\ 2\ 1\ 1\ 1, \text{etc.,}$$

yielding 'A's for non-summer and 'B's for summer months.

For scatter diagrams of one variable against another we have PLOT C1 VS C2, though this is discussed in Chapter 5.

We discussed in this chapter how to present data in tables; Minitab has a facility for generating the figures for such a presentation. If, for example, C1 contains data on the sex of customers and C2 on their age group:

```
MTB > TABLE C1 C2
```

provides a table with sex (C1) as rows and age group (C2) as columns, with the elements of the table being the number of customers of each sex and age group. Subcommands of COUNTS, ROWPERCENT, COLPERCENT, TOTPERCENT allow the inclusion for each sex and age group in the table, the percentage for a particular sex (row), or age group (column) or all customers (total).

Alternatively we might be interested in the purchases (in C3) of customers of different sexes and age groups; the average (MEAN) purchases of each category of customer is provided by:

```
MTB  > TABLE C1 C2;
SUBC > MEAN C3.
```

As well as the mean, further summary statistics discussed in the next chapter can be provided by a similar use of subcommands: MEDIAN, STDEV (standard deviations), MAXIMUM, MINIMUM, N, NMISS (number of missing values), STATS (N, MEAN and STDEV), DATA (prints all data values for each cell).

LAYOUT provides more flexibility in the layout of tables allowing, for example, two variables C1 and C2 in the rows and different summary measures in the columns.

```
MTB  > TABLE C1 C2;        The first number after layout show how
SUBC > STATS C3;           many variables are used for row headings,
SUBC > LAYOUT 2,0.         the second for column headings.
```

For three or more classifying variables separate tables are generated for each classification (e.g. alcoholic drinks, food) of the additional variable (e.g. type of purchase), though with the help of LAYOUT, they can be combined into a single table.

### Lotus 1-2-3

Lotus is particularly useful for drawing up tables since it allows both text (labels) and numbers (values) to be entered directly onto the worksheet. You would simply enter in A1 the title of the table and it would stretch across the first row into B1, C1, D1, etc., depending on its length. Column titles, row titles, sources and notes can all be entered and the numerical values then entered into the appropriate cell corresponding to a particular row and column title—for example, 754 respondents were female (first column) and 'light users' (first row) of your product. The added value of using a spreadsheet instead of a word processor is that it allows a variety of calculations, formats and simulations to be undertaken. For example, a copy of the table can be drawn up, /Copy, and the figures converted to percentages by undertaking the calculation (preceded by a plus) in one cell, and copying it for all others. If we want the entries to two decimal places, /Range Format Fixed provides the means. Totals, averages, etc. (see next chapter) can be inserted in the table using the statistical function @ commands, e.g. @AVG(A2..A50) yields the average (mean) of the values entered in column A rows 2 to 50.

The /Graph Type command provides a good range of graphical representations of a relatively high quality. These include line graphs, bar charts, scatter diagrams (XY), stacked bar charts, pie diagrams, HLCO (High–Low–Close–Open, used for opening/closing prices of stocks), and mixtures. /Graph Options includes titles: (two lines for a) title and (a line each for the) axes, data-labels, legends, formats, grids, scales, colour, with 'Advanced' options allowing variable colours (e.g. for lines on a graph), hatches, text (in different fonts, sizes and colours). For example, /Graph Option Scales allows scales for the variables on the $X$ and $Y$ axes (or two $Y$ axes, on the left and right) to be deduced from the data automatically, or allows the user to choose the highest and lowest values manually or if required (for example) every other scale indicator to be skipped, or the user to decide on the scale indicator (hundreds, thousands, etc.), or to operate in logarithmic scales, or to specify the width of the scale entries on the $X$-axis, and more. Of particular use is the ability to view the graph as you build it up. /Graph View allows you to see the graph; if you are not satisfied with some feature simply return to the command concerning it, change your choice, and using the ESC (escape) button, move back to the view facility to admire the changed graph.

To start a graph enter (for example) 6 numbers into each of A1..A6 and B1..B6. In C1..C6 enter 1987, 1988, ..., 1992. Then use /Graph Type to arrive at your choice of graph and choose Line (for a line graph). Now choose X (press enter) and moving the cursor to C1, anchor it (by typing a period (full stop)) and move the cursor down to C6 highlighting the range C1..C6 for the $X$-axis; press enter. For A enter the data in A1..A6 and for B enter the data in B1..B6 in a similar manner; press View (or F10) to see what you have achieved (which should be two lines on a graph). Try some of the options, e.g. Options Format Graph Area [to return up the command structure use ESC]. Experimenting and reference to the 'help' [F1] command or manual should help you master the possibilities. /Graph Name allows you to work with any number of graphs during a session; /Graph Name Create saves it for future use in Lotus. Once a graph has a name it can be retrieved along with its settings for display, change, deletion and via /Graph Name Table you can provide a table of all graphs created and their details, though remember to save and call up the worksheet of data to which the graph relates. For saving for use outside of Lotus use /Graph Save; for example, many word processing packages (e.g. Word5 and 5.5) allow Lotus graphs to be incorporated onto a page of text.

## EXERCISE

A supervisor in a machine room has reports weekly on output from two machines (A and B) for the morning and afternoon shifts. The report compares the current week with the preceding week and thus takes the following form (weeks are numbered from 1 to 52 each year):

| Report | | Output |
|---|---|---|
| Machine A | 1 (am) | 68.433 |
| | (pm) | 75.962 |
| Machine A | 2 (am) | 74.34 |
| | (pm) | 82.75 |
| Machine B | 1 (am) | 28.394 |
| | (pm) | 34 |
| Machine B | 2 (am) | 32.49 |
| | (pm) | 39.375 |

(a) Reformulate this table in a manner that facilitates the understanding of the patterns of output.
(b) Comment on the patterns in the data.
(c) Using appropriate chart(s) present the data.
(d) What other information would you feel appropriate and how would you use it in your reformulated table and chart(s)? Use fictitious information to illustrate this.

# SUMMARIZING DATA

In the previous chapter we looked at methods of presenting data. However, if for example we collected data from a random sample of 4000 individuals on the number of cigarettes smoked per week, we would get 4000 separate figures. Without summarizing this information it would be difficult to describe their smoking patterns. In addition, if the survey was repeated in a subsequent year, it would be difficult to identify how smoking patterns had changed by comparing one list of 4000 figures with another. Alternatively, we may wish to look at data on wages, age or whatever of all employees in a firm or industry. Again it is difficult to have a meaningful discussion based on several sheets of pages listing the raw data. This is not to say lists of data are never of use: the list of examination marks for each student is of use because we want to identify the mark each student gains. However, if we want to talk about the overall pattern of marks we may need to summarize the data.

Our concern is thus with methods of summarizing observations on a variable such that the pertinent characteristics of the variables become discernible. Since the mind has difficulty in coping with, for example, the 4000 separate figures on cigarette consumption, we must summarize these data into a smaller set of figures with which we can cope without losing too many of the characteristics of the data. Two methods are considered: (i) grouping the data and (ii) the use of summary measures.

## GROUPING THE DATA

### The frequency table

Consider the first two columns of Table 4-1 (the rest will be considered later in this chapter). This is a *frequency table* of the inflation rates of 106 countries. Instead of listing the 106 separate figures we have summarized the data in a convenient form by identifying a succession of mutually exclusive ranges of values or *class intervals* within which inflation rates may fall, and then counted the *frequency* with which the data (countries) fall into each class interval. Thus seven countries had negative inflation rates down to − 5 per cent (i.e. falling prices); 35 countries of zero to just under 5 per cent, and so forth. We can clearly see the pattern of inflation rates from the frequency table with most countries having positive rates in the 0 to 15 per cent range (though around one-third of all

**Table 4-1**  Annual percentage rates of inflation for 106 countries

| Class interval | Frequency $f_i$ | Mid-point $X_i$ | $f_iX_i$ | $f_iX_i^2$ | Cumulative frequency $F$ |
|---|---|---|---|---|---|
| −5 to under  0 | 7 | −2.5 | 17.5 | 43.75 | 7 |
| 0 to under  5 | 35 | 2.5 | 87.5 | 218.75 | 42 |
| 5 to under 10 | 24 | 7.5 | 180.0 | 1 350.00 | 66 |
| 10 to under 15 | 11 | 12.5 | 137.5 | 1 718.75 | 77 |
| 15 to under 20 | 8 | 17.5 | 140.0 | 2 450.00 | 85 |
| 20 to under 25 | 3 | 22.5 | 67.5 | 1 518.75 | 88 |
| 25 to under 30 | 3 | 27.5 | 82.5 | 2 268.75 | 91 |
| 30 to under 35 | 2 | 32.5 | 65.0 | 2 112.50 | 93 |
| 35 to under 40 | 3 | 37.5 | 112.5 | 4 218.75 | 96 |
| 40 to under 100 | 5 | 70.0 | 350.0 | 245 000.00 | 101 |
| 100 or more* | 5 | 2 606.0 | 13 030.0 | 33 956 180.00 | 106 |
| All countries | 106 | | 14 235.0 | 34 217 080.00 | |

*The highest value is Bolivia with an annual inflation rate of 11 748 per cent per annum. The mid-point for the last class interval is thus 5824; however, it is more accurate to use the arithmetic mean of the five observations (or a guesstimate of it), which is in fact 2606 per cent per annum. Had the mid-point of 5824 been used the mean inflation rate would have been 286.1 per cent per annum as opposed to 134.3.

(a)  For countries excluded see Table 4-5, footnote *.

(b)  The columns headed $f_iX_i$ and $f_iX_i^2$ will be referred to later in this chapter.

*Source*: International Monetary Fund, *database* 1986; also available from IMF, *International Financial Statistics*, Washington DC: IMF.

countries are in the 0 to 5 per cent range). However, there are a small number of countries with very high annual inflation rates; five countries with 100 per cent or more. It should be emphasized that this data set contains an unusual number of awkward features which will stretch the methods described in this chapter to the limit. It has been deliberately chosen for this purpose, but fortunately most data sets are better behaved.

We could construct a similar table for our 4000 individuals with the number of individuals smoking no cigarettes a week, 1 to under 5, 5 to under 10, 10 to under 15, etc. Care must be taken in constructing frequency tables since inappropriate class intervals may well mislead the users:

1. Class intervals should not overlap. If, for example, our variable can only take whole numbers (is discrete) as with cigarette consumption, we might use 0; 0.5 to 4.5; 4.5 to 9.5, etc. *or* 0; 1 to under 5; 5 to under 10, etc. Both methods achieve the same purpose.
2. Class intervals must be representative in the sense that the average (mean) of the values within an interval should approximate to the mid-point of the interval. A firm, for example, which pays most of its workers £15 000 p.a. should not have as its range £15 000 to £20 000 since this would mislead the user.
3. Class intervals should not obscure relevant ranges of variation. For example, for our cigarette consumption the range 0 to 5 cigarettes not only obscures the interesting information as to the number smoking no cigarettes, but also probably misleads for reasons given in the above point.
4. Class intervals should be of even size unless particular attention needs to be devoted to a specific narrow range of values (e.g. no cigarettes) and/or there are so few values in a range that it can be aggregated with other class intervals with similar characteristics (see upper interval of Table 4-1).

5. The number of class intervals used should be a trade-off between the amount of detail required and the ease with which the user can assimilate the data. The 11 intervals in Table 4.1 allows the reader to identify the appropriate patterns and the creation of, say, an additional 10 intervals of 5 per cent width for each country with 40 per cent or more inflation would make the table less easy to read, without adding much more useful information. There are in many statistical packages (e.g. Minitab and SPSS) routines for automatically creating frequency tables. It is advisable to start with a large number of intervals to identify where observations lie, and then use your judgement based on the needs of the study to group the results into a smaller set of intervals, rather than relying on such routines.

The frequency table thus succeeds in the task of taking hundreds, thousands, tens of thousands or more of separate observations on a variable and allowing the characteristics of the variable to be identified. The frequency tables in Exercises 4-3 and 4-4, at the end of this chapter, show how comparisons can be made where more than one set of frequencies are included, though Table 4-1 could show a new set of frequencies for each year to indicate how the distribution has altered. Note that we could detect changes in the whole pattern, or in the way the frequencies are distributed across the class intervals—not only if the central cluster changes but also if any deviation occurs at the extremes or in any pertinent range.

Finally, our concern in some situations is not with the frequency, i.e. how many observations lie in an interval, but with the cumulative frequency ($F$), i.e. how many observations lie above (or below a value. The final column of Table 4-1 shows the 'less than' cumulative frequencies indicating how many countries have inflation rates less than the upper boundary of each class interval (e.g. 91 countries with rates less than 30 per cent). We can also devise 'more than' cumulative frequencies showing how many countries have rates more than the lower boundary of each class interval, or calculate either of these in relative or percentage terms.

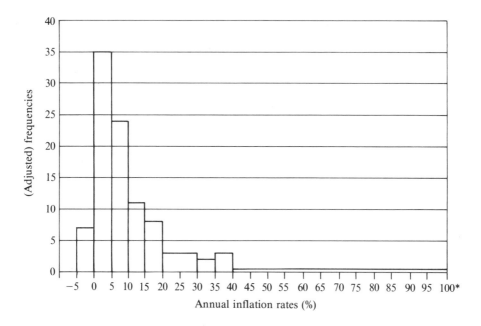

**Figure 4-1**   Histogram: inflation rates
        *5 countries had rates over 100 per cent

## The histogram

We noted in the previous chapter that for some purposes graphical/pictorial methods of presenting information are preferable to tabular ones. The histogram is simply the graphical equivalent of the frequency table. On the $X$-axis are the lower values of each class interval. On the $Y$-axis are the frequencies that correspond to the class intervals. The histogram should display the information in the frequency table; e.g. from Table 4-1 to Fig. 4-1: in the interval $-5$ to 0 per cent p.a. inflation (class intervals on $X$-axis, Fig. 4-1) there were 7 countries (frequencies on $Y$-axis); 0 to 5 per cent, 35 countries, etc. Note that:

- The histogram is ambiguous on the border of the class intervals unless we note the fact that the block '0 to 5' does not include 5 but does include 0, i.e. is 0 to under 5.
- The height of the block for the wider class interval 40 to 100 per cent is *not* 5 countries but 0.42. Had a height of 5 been used across this interval the impression would have been that there were 5 countries with inflation rates between 40 and 45 per cent, a further 5 countries with rates between 45 and 50 per cent continuing up to 95 to 100 per cent. Since the width of this class interval is 12 times the width of the other intervals, we divide the frequency by 12 (5/12) to arrive at 0.42. Thus, if a class interval is $x$ times the size of the 'standard' class interval we divide its frequency by $x$, where $x$ may be more or less than 1. In this way the *area* under the respective bars of the histogram correspond to the frequencies.
- Finally, the last class interval has no end value. One alternative is to guess at an end value and continue as above. In our case it is so large that we pass this information on to the reader by way of a note on the histogram.

## The polygon

The polygon is a 'smoothed' version of the histogram, constructed by joining together the mid-points of the top of each block in the histogram. Figure 4-2 is constructed using

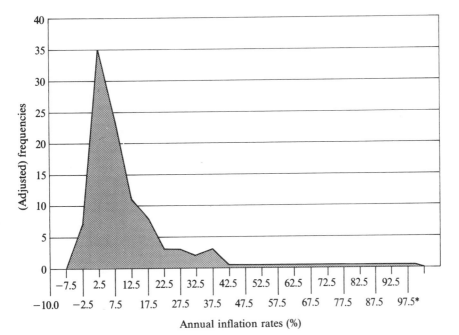

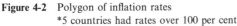

**Figure 4-2**  Polygon of inflation rates
    *5 countries had rates over 100 per cent

/Graph/Type/Area in Lotus 1-2-3; it is the area above different ranges of inflation rates (as is the case with the histogram) that reflects the frequencies.

### The stem-and-leaf diagram

Stem-and-leaf diagrams allow us to identify the individual values of each observation while at the same time providing a pictorial representation akin to a histogram so that characteristics of the data's distribution can also be discerned. For example, *suppose* the annual percentage inflation rates for 15 countries on a specific continent were:

5   12   8   14   25   15   12   21   32   11   11   15   23   41   18

The stem is the first or 'leading' digit representing units of tens (5 is 05); the leaf is the last or 'trailing' digit representing units of one. The possible stem values are placed in a vertical line, and the successive leaf values are placed alongside their corresponding stem:

| | |
|---|---|
| 0 | 5  8 |
| 1 | 1  1  2  2  4  5  5  8 |
| 2 | 1  3  5 |
| 3 | 2 |
| 4 | 1 |
| Stems | Leaves |

The first row is 05 and 08, the next row is 11, 11, 12, etc., and we can see from the width of the leaves (frequency of occurrence being the length of the row) that by far most countries on this continent have inflation rates in the interval 10 to 20 per cent. Not only do we see the pattern, but we see the actual values. Sometimes stems are stretched over two lines with leaves 0 to 4 on the first line (often marked '.') and 5 to 9 on the second line. This is equivalent to choosing the width of the class interval. In other cases (e.g. Minitab) the depth of a stem is given alongside the stem, showing the number of leaves on that stem or cumulated up or down from the nearest edge of the diagram. Other formulations are given in Hoaglin *et al.* (1983). The stem-and-leaf is a clever device since it solves the problem of trying to see a pattern in the data, not by losing information in the grouping of class intervals, but by laying out *all* the data in a grouped form that reveals the patterns.

### The Ogive

In the above discussion of the frequency table we noted that our concern might be with the cumulative frequencies: how many/what proportion of observations are more/less than a given value? Figure 4-3 shows the 'less than' type ogive, which is the graphical equivalent of the cumulative frequency in Table 4-1. The cumulative frequency ($F$) in Table 4-1 is plotted ($Y$-axis) against the upper value of the class interval ($X$-axis). We can read off from the graph how many countries had inflation rates less than a given number. It can alternatively be constructed using cumulative relative frequencies, with each frequency divided by the total frequency to show the proportion of countries with less than a given inflation rate. The less steep the graph, the smaller the number of countries in that range. 'More than' type ogives are derived by plotting the cumulative frequency (in a descending order) against the lower value of the class interval, i.e. 106 countries had a rate more than $-0.5$ per cent, 98 countries more than 0 per cent, etc.

Several ogives can be plotted on a given graph with, for example, each ogive showing inflation rates for different categories of countries, e.g. industrialized, newly industrialized, less developed; alternatively, an ogive could be constructed for each year to show how the distribution of inflation rates has changed over time.

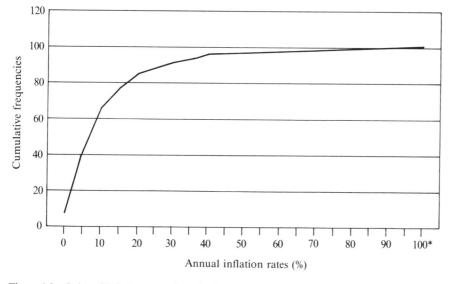

**Figure 4-3**  Ogive of inflation rates: 'less-than' type
*5 countries had rates over 100 per cent

## SUMMARY MEASURES

Grouping data is one way of summarizing those data. An alternative approach is the use of summary measures, i.e. measures that encapsulate a particular facet of the data. For example, if a student was asked what the marks of, say, 200 students in statistics were like, then rather than read them out he or she might give an estimate of the average, or the range. The average would reflect in a single figure what we call the 'central tendency' of the data, and the range the 'dispersion'. There are other facets to data such as 'skewness' and 'kurtosis', and there are different concepts of a facet reflected in particular measures. For example, we shall outline four different measures (concepts) of central tendency all concerned with the 'average', some being more useful for different purposes. In many cases more than one measure will be of interest. The need for all of these different measures arises from our problem: we are summarizing perhaps thousands of pieces of information in a few measures. If the measure only reflects one facet of the data—for example, central tendency—then this is all we find out about. For example, we may collect data on consumption of a new chocolate bar and analyse this by sex, finding average consumption to be the same for each sex. We would conclude that there is no difference in consumption patterns between sexes. But female consumption may be much more dispersed, being more extreme on either sides than that of males. If we don't measure and compare dispersion by sex, we don't find out about it.

All of this, of course, assumes fairly large data sets. If our data comprised 10 or 20 figures we can get an idea of its characteristics by looking down the figures. However, vast amounts of data flow into many organizations on stocks, sales, orders, purchases, production, etc. Much of the data are received, stored and exchanged between computers. If you only programme the computer to generate a limited range of summary measures, all you will find out about is what the measures tell you. Some summary measures are outlined below: proportions, totals, central tendency, dispersion, skewness and kurtosis.

## Proportions

A simple summary measure is the proportion: the proportion of individuals smoking no cigarettes out of the 4000 surveyed provides us with useful information in the form of a single figure. While it takes the form of a single measure it arises out of the grouping of data into a frequency table and is simply the relative frequency for a particular value or class interval.

## Totals

We may find the total amount of cigarettes purchased, and since our data are derived from a random sample of individuals, we proportion this figure up by the size of the relevant population to the sample in order to provide an estimate of the total potential market. One purpose of collecting the 4000 pieces of data on cigarette consumption was to summarize the information by finding the total consumption.

## Central tendency

More commonly referred to as 'averages' these measures take a number of forms.

**The arithmetic mean**    The arithmetic mean (hereafter referred to as 'the mean' though there is a geometric mean, to be discussed later) is what we commonly think of as the average. The mean time taken to produce a good is found by summing the time taken to produce all the goods and dividing by the number of goods. We shall look at a formula for calculating this in somewhat tedious detail since it provides us with an opportunity to introduce some notation necessary for further calculations. Consider the data in Table 4-2 relating to two clerks in a building society. This shows the actual time taken to 'process' ten customers. We wish to summarize the characteristics of each variable. Some of these are obvious if we look at the data; however, we are mainly concerned with the principles of the calculations and these are best examined via a small data set.

Consider clerk A: the variable is 'time taken to process a customer', which we shall call '$X$' for $i = 1, 2, \ldots, n$ customers; $n$ is equal to 10 since we have 10 observed values or observations on $X$. Thus $X_1$ is the observed value for customer 1 (i.e. 1.1), $X_2$ for customer 2 (i.e. 0.7), $\ldots$, $X_{10}$ for

**Table 4-2**   Time taken to process customers in a building society (time in minutes)

| Clerk A ($X_i$) | Clerk B ($Y_i$) | $X_i^2$ | $Y_i^2$ | $|X_i - \bar{X}|$ | $|Y_i - \bar{Y}|$ |
|---|---|---|---|---|---|
| 1.1 | 0.8 | 1.21 | 0.64 | 0.18 | 0.94 |
| 0.7 | 1.8 | 0.49 | 3.24 | 0.58 | 0.06 |
| 0.8 | 1.1 | 0.64 | 1.21 | 0.48 | 0.64 |
| 2.2 | 0.8 | 4.84 | 0.64 | 0.92 | 0.94 |
| 1.5 | 0.9 | 2.25 | 0.81 | 0.22 | 0.84 |
| 0.9 | 4.0 | 0.81 | 16.00 | 0.38 | 2.26 |
| 1.8 | 1.0 | 3.24 | 1.00 | 0.52 | 0.74 |
| 1.3 | 2.4 | 1.69 | 5.76 | 0.02 | 0.66 |
| 1.5 | 3.8 | 2.25 | 14.44 | 0.22 | 2.06 |
| 1.0 | 0.8 | 1.00 | 1.00 | 0.28 | 0.94 |
| 12.8 $= \Sigma X_i$ | 17.4 $= \Sigma Y_i$ | 18.42 $= \Sigma X_i^2$ | 44.38 $= \Sigma Y_i^2$ | 3.80 $= \Sigma|X_i - \bar{X}|$ | 10.08 $= \Sigma|Y_i - \bar{Y}|$ |

customer 10 (i.e. 1.0). We use the symbol $\Sigma$ (capital (upper case) sigma) to denote summation. We want to add up all the observed values or observations for clerk A, i.e.

$$\sum_{i=1}^{n=10} X_i$$

read as sigma (sum) from $i(=1)$ to $n(=10)$ all of the values of $X_i$, i.e. $X_1 + X_2 + X_3, \ldots, X_{10}$. Thus

$$\sum_{i=1}^{10} X_i = 1.1 + 0.7 + 0.8 + 2.2 + 1.5 + 0.9 + 1.8 + 1.3 + 1.5 + 1.0 = 12.8$$

The arithmetic mean of $X$ is denoted by $\bar{X}$ (pronounced $X$-bar) where:

$$\bar{X} = \frac{\sum_{i=1}^{n} X_i}{n} = \frac{12.8}{10} = 1.28 \text{ minutes} \qquad (4\text{-}1)$$

All we have done is to add up all the figures and divide the total by the number of figures; the notation only serves to confuse here. However, it is introduced here because it is to be used extensively later, so it is worth the effort here. An alternative formulation of the mean is given by:

$$\bar{X} = \frac{\Sigma f_i X_i}{\Sigma f_i} \qquad (4\text{-}2)$$

This is useful if we have $X_1$ and/or $X_2$, $X_3$, etc., occurring many times. For example, in 400 batches of 20 manufactured goods the number of defectives in each batch might be distributed as shown in Table 4-3. Thus in 200 batches there were no defective goods, 100 batches had 1 defective good, and so forth. To calculate the mean using Eq. (4-1) we would add together 0, 200 times; 1, 100 times; 2, 50 times; 3, 25 times; and 4, 25 times and total the lot. It is easier to multiply the frequency by its corresponding $X$ to yield $f_i X_i$, and sum these values to yield $\Sigma f_i X_i$. This is divided by the total frequency to yield the mean, i.e.

$$\bar{X} = \frac{\Sigma f_i X_i}{\Sigma f_i} = \frac{375}{400} = 0.9375 \text{ defectives}$$

An alternative formulation of the arithmetic mean is the *trimmed mean* whereby the highest and lowest 5 per cent of observations are removed from the data and the mean calculated from the remaining 90 per cent of observations, thus militating against the influence of extreme values.

**Table 4-3**

| Number of defective goods, $X_i$ | Number of batches, $f_i$ | $f_i X_i$ | $f_i X_i^2$ |
|---|---|---|---|
| 0 | 200 | 0 | 0 |
| 1 | 100 | 100 | 100 |
| 2 | 50 | 100 | 200 |
| 3 | 25 | 75 | 225 |
| 4 | 25 | 100 | 400 |
| | 400 $= \Sigma f_i$ | 375 $= \Sigma f_i X_i$ | 925 $= \Sigma f_i X_i^2$ |

**The median** (*Md*)    The median is an alternative concept of central tendency and is the value of the middle observation when all observations are ranked in order of magnitude. The middle observation is the $(n+1)/2$th observation. For example, the median wage of university academics can be envisaged by considering all academics lined up in a very large field, the highest earners at one end and the lowest earners at the other. You ask them to file past you, and ask the person half-way along the queue to state how much he or she earns. Thus, for clerk A the ranked data are:

$$0.7; \ 0.8; \ 0.9; \ 1.0; \ 1.1; \ 1.3; \ 1.5; \ 1.5; \ 1.8; \ 2.2$$

The middle observation is the $(n+1)/2$th $= (10+1)/2$th $= 5.5$th, i.e. mid-way between the 5th and 6th observation; $X_5 = 1.1$ and $X_6 = 1.3$. The median can be taken to be mid-way between these values, i.e. $(1.1+1.3)/2 = 1.2$ minutes.

[*N.B.* if there was an odd number of observations the median would *not* lie between two figures, e.g. if $N = 11$ the median is the value of the $(11+1)/2 = 6$th observation.]

**The mode** (*Mo*)    The mode is the value of the observation with the highest frequency; or the value occurring most often. In some circumstances there is one (or even more) value which occurs much more often than others, and this is especially likely for discrete data that have a limited range of values. For example, female shoe sizes may well have a distinct mode, while shoe sizes for males and females may well have two modes (bi-modal). It is often helpful to talk of a distribution as having more than one mode even if the frequencies of each mode are not identical. All we are saying is that one or two (or more) observations have very high frequencies and a mean or median would yield a single value and not reflect this important feature. For continuous data the observations can take a large range of values and the mode may be considered (as we shall discuss later) in terms of intervals of values. For clerk A there is a mode of 1.5 minutes, though its frequency is not much higher (two values) than all others, and thus the measure is not of great value here.

**The geometric mean** (*Gm*)    The geometric mean is arrived at by multiplying together the values of each observation and taking the *n*th root of the result. Mathematically this is represented as:

$$Gm = \left( \prod_{i=1}^{n} X_i \right)^{1/n}$$

$$= (1.1 \times 0.7 \times 0.8 \times 2.2 \times 1.5 \times 0.9 \times 1.8 \times 1.3 \times 1.5 \times 1.0)^{1/10} \qquad (4\text{-}3)$$

$$= (6.4216152)^{1/10} = 1.204 \text{ minutes}$$

The geometric mean is particularly useful for measuring the average rate of change of a variable over time. For example, if sales increased annually over the last five years by 5, 6, 4, 3 and 8 per cent respectively, the geometric mean of

$$\left( 1 + \frac{X_i}{100} \right) = (1.05 \times 1.06 \times 1.04 \times 1.03 \times 1.08)^{1/5} = 1.05186 \ (5.186 \text{ per cent})$$

If we multiplied sales at the start of the initial period, say £20 000, by this average growth for each of five years, i.e. $20\,000(1.05186)^5 = £25\,752.50$, this equals the sales values at the end of the five years. This is the same as

$$20\,000(1.05)(1.06)(1.04)(1.03)(1.08) = £25\,752.50$$

which is the way it should be. The other measures considered here do not possess this useful property.

**Table 4-4**   Summary measures for building society clerks. (Time taken to process customers (minutes))

|  | Clerk A | Clerk B |
|---|---|---|
| *Measures of central tendency* | | |
| Arithmetic mean | 1.28 | 1.74 |
| Median | 1.20 | 1.05 |
| Mode | 1.5 | 0.8 |
| Geometric mean | 1.20 | 1.42 |
| *Measures of dispersion* | | |
| Standard deviation | 0.45 | 1.19 |
| Mean absolute deviation | 0.38 | 1.0 |
| The range | 1.5 (0.7 to 2.2) | 3.2 (0.8 to 4.0) |
| The semi-interquartile range | 0.35 (0.875 to 1.575) | 0.975 (0.8 to 2.75) |
| Coefficient of variation | 0.35 | 0.68 |
| *Measures of skewness* | | |
| Pearson's coefficient | 0.53 | 1.74 |
| Bowley's coefficient | 0.14 | 1.49 |
| Third moment | 0.61 | 1.00 |
| *Measures of kurtosis* | | |
| Fourth moment | 2.11 | 2.37 |

**On choice of measure of central tendency**   There are yet further measures of central tendency, for example the harmonic mean, though the above are sufficient for just about all purposes. Before examining which is appropriate for use when asked 'What is the average?', it is worth noting that they can give quite different results, as shown for clerk B in Table 4-4, an average time of as little as 0.8 minutes (mode) or as much as 1.74 minutes (mean).

Table 4.5 provides an even more glaring demonstration of the power of the statistician. We want the average rate of inflation, based on the individual values for the 106 countries, we derive from Table 4-5; this yields at first an annual world inflation rate of 134 *per cent*, i.e. prices more than double. For the 'weighted' results in our calculations we do not treat small and large countries as equally important and give proportionately more weight in the calculation (using share in world GDP over the last three years) to countries producing more. Smaller economies with higher inflation have thus less weight in the calculation, reducing world inflation at a stroke to 11.1 per cent. We might remove Bolivia as an atypical 'outlier' or use the geometric mean (as used by the IMF for their report, *World Economic Outlook*) which reduces the impact of extreme values, or the median or mode. All of the measures can be justified—world inflation can almost be of whatever order you want it to be. It should be emphasized again that this is a highly unusual set of data. Fortunately, in most cases the differences between alternative measures are less marked.

Choice of measure depends primarily on purpose. The arithmetic mean is influenced by extreme values on one side, with a few extremely high values pulling it up and low ones pulling it down. The median and mode are not affected by such values. For example, the salaries of 20 workers may be £12 000 per annum, while the 21st is £80 000. The median and mode are unaffected by the extreme value; however, the means are affected, the geometric mean less so than its arithmetic counterpart. For the purpose of finding out the salaries offered by the company the median and mode are more representative. However, for the purpose of computing total salary paid by multiplying the average by the number of workers, we need to include the extreme value. The geometric mean is a compromise—it gives some weight to extreme values, but not as much as the arithmetic mean. The UK official statistics on average earnings use the median, since they do not want extreme values to

**Table 4-5** Measures of central tendency of annual inflation rates, 1986—all countries*

|  | Percentage |
| --- | --- |
| *Arithmetic means* |  |
| Unweighted | 134.0 |
| Weighted | 11.1 |
| Without Bolivia |  |
|   unweighted | 22.2 |
|   weighted | 8.2 |
| *Geometric means* |  |
| Unweighted | 21.3 |
| Weighted | 6.4 |
| Without Bolivia |  |
|   unweighted | 15.9 |
|   weighted | 6.3 |
| *Median*† | 6.8 |
| *Mode*† | 3.6 |

*These countries were not included due to lack of data: Afghanistan, China, Grenada, Guadeloupe, Guyana, Iraq, Libya, Mauritania, Reunion, Sudan, Suriname, Syria, Tanzania, The Congo, The Gambia, The Maldives, The Arab Republic of Yemen, Trinidad and Tobago, Uganda and Zaire.

†These are, of course, unweighted; a weighted median and mode would have frequencies for each observation equivalent to their weights, though the meaning of such measures would be less than clear.

influence the figures. In Table 4-5 for some types of economic analysis we would want Bolivia included since our theories are concerned with the implications of extreme economic conditions, though, since it is a small economy, we might want its effect to be reduced in proportion to its size, i.e. weighted. For others the median might be appropriate since we want to monitor—treating all countries equally, irrespective of size—what happens to a typical country measured as one half-way along the inflation queue. The diversity of measures help us formulate our theories better by making us ask which is appropriate. Trade union officials might argue for the modal salary since their concern is with what most workers earn. The employers would incorporate extreme values if they are on the high side since they have to pay them. Often more than one measure is appropriate since, as we shall see later, the differences between the measures are revealing. The power of the methods is that by their very choice they force us to refine our ideas about what is important to our study, and then apply the appropriate technique. So we pass the buck; we do not tell you which is 'the best' since this would not meet all needs. Which measure is appropriate must be considered by the users in the context of their study for their purposes.

We noted in the first chapter that different variables will be measured on different scales of measurement: ratio, interval, ordinal, or nominal. Variables measured on ordinal or nominal scales should not generally use the geometric or arithmetic mean for reasons given in Chapter 2. The mode can be applied to all scales as long as it suits the purpose of the study, and the median can be applied to variables measured on ordinal scales, but of course not nominal scales since we cannot rank observations on nominal scales as there is no hierarchy.

## Dispersion

Consider the following two sets of data:

(I)    2    4    6    8    10
(II)    4    5    6    7    8

In each case the mean and median is 6. If we only had these measures of central tendency then we could only conclude that there was no difference between the data for (I) and (II). However, the data for (I) differ from (II) in that they are more dispersed. For many situations dispersion is a characteristic of data of practical importance. For example, with earnings we are concerned with how they are dispersed as well as the average; increases in the average may be welcome, but increases in the dispersion may not be so welcome. The dispersion of ages of a workforce has implications for planning personnel; the dispersion in the quality of goods produced is of concern to quality control.

Whenever data are given on averages for a variable it is not usually an unprofitable exercise to ask yourself whether the dispersion is important for the issue under consideration. If so, the question is then: How do we measure it?

**The standard deviation**   The standard deviation, denoted by $s$, is based on subtracting each individual value from the arithmetic mean. For example, with data set (I) above, the mean $(\bar{X})=6$; the first value is 2, therefore $2-6=-4$; the second value is 4, therefore $4-6=-2$, etc. The more distant the values are from the mean, the more dispersed and the higher the result of this calculation. Therefore, at first sight a good indicator of dispersion is to sum these differences to get the total dispersion:

$$\Sigma(X_i-\bar{X}).$$

This is the result of summing the differences between each value and the mean, i.e. for data (I):

$$(-4)+(-2)+(0)+(2)+(4)=0$$

Unfortunately the result will always be zero since positive values will always cancel with negative values. One solution is to square the results of each calculation since a 'minus' multiplied by a 'minus' yields a plus: i.e.

$$\Sigma(X_i-\bar{X})^2=(-4)^2+(-2)^2+(0)^2+(2)^2+(4)^2=40$$

However, if we wanted to compare the dispersion of two data sets of different sizes the larger one will have additional terms to add to its measure of dispersion and thus unfairly influence the comparison: we want an average measure of dispersion, so we divide by the number of observations. Even then our measure is not appropriate since, when we squared each difference, we boosted the magnitude of the differences. To return the measure back to its original units we take the square root, giving us the following formula for the standard deviation:

$$s=\sqrt{\frac{\Sigma(X_i-\bar{X})^2}{n}}=\sqrt{\frac{40}{5}}=2.828 \qquad\qquad (4\text{-}4)$$

If the square root is not taken the expression is called the *variance*, i.e. $s^2$, and this is often a more convenient formulation for work in subsequent chapters. Note that in our notation we have not shown the range above and below the $\Sigma$ sign; when this is not shown, or the subscript $i$ for $X$, it is assumed all values of $X_i$ are summed.

For data set (II) above:

$$s = \sqrt{\frac{(4-6)^2 + (5-6)^2 + (6-6)^2 + (7-6)^2 + (8-6)^2}{5}}$$

$$= \sqrt{2} = 1.414$$

An examination of datasets (I) and (II) show the former to be twice as dispersed as the latter, which is reflected in the measure. The measure also takes account of each individual value and is thus affected by extreme values. If the last figure in data set (II) had been 100 instead of 8, then we would have obtained $\bar{X} = 24.4$ and $s = 37.8$. Note that in the comparison between data sets (I) and (II) we could say that (I) was twice as dispersed as (II) since each value was proportionately larger or smaller. Yet this interpretation is not generally valid (though often used). When we changed the end value in data set (I) to 100, $s$ increased by (37.8/1.416), nearly 27-fold, but this was mainly due to one figure, the other figures remaining quite close together. In practice, all we might know is that, for example, $s$ has increased by a given per cent, which may or may not be due to extreme values. It is often wise also to use other measures of dispersion (see below) that are less sensitive to extreme values.

Equation (4-4) was useful for explaining the concept of $s$, dispersion being defined in terms of the differences between individual values and the mean: the further away from their mean, the more dispersed the data. However, in practice it is generally easier to compute $s$ using the mathematically equivalent formula:

$$s = \sqrt{\frac{\Sigma X^2}{n} - \left(\frac{\Sigma X}{n}\right)^2} \qquad (4\text{-}5)$$

$\Sigma X^2$ is each individual $X$ squared, and the results summed; $n$ is the number of observations and $\Sigma X/n$ is of course the arithmetic mean ($\bar{X}$) from Eq. (4-1). [For $(\Sigma X/n)^2$ we sum each individual value of $X$, divide by $n$ and *then square the result*. For $\Sigma X^2$ we square each value of $X$ as we go along and *then sum them*.] They are quite different calculations as illustrated in Table 4-2. Using Eq. (4-5) for clerk A:

$$s = \sqrt{\frac{18.42}{10} - \left(\frac{12.8}{10}\right)^2} = 0.451 \text{ minutes}$$

For clerk B a similar calculation yields 1.19 minutes. The larger standard deviation for clerk B can be seen to emerge from the figures in Table 4-2, the two customers requiring 3.8 and 4.0 minutes respectively, pushing up the value of $\Sigma X^2$ and thus $s$ quite dramatically. The squaring of the terms leads to a feature of $s$, being strongly influenced by extreme values.

When we discussed the calculation of the mean we noted that if many observations had the same value it facilitated calculations if the data were arranged as a frequency table with, instead of class intervals for $X$, the actual values being used along with the frequency with which they occurred. The formulae equivalent to Eqs (4-4) and (4-5) become:

$$s = \sqrt{\frac{\Sigma f(X - \bar{X})^2}{\Sigma f}} = \sqrt{\frac{\Sigma f X^2}{\Sigma f} - \left(\frac{\Sigma f X}{\Sigma f}\right)^2} \qquad (4\text{-}6)$$

Note that $\Sigma f X^2$ is each individual $X$ squared, then multiplied by its corresponding $f$; or equivalently $fX$ multiplied by its corresponding $X$, and then summed. Looking back at Table 4-3 on defective goods for the arithmetic mean, the standard deviation would be:

$$s = \sqrt{\frac{925}{400} - \left(\frac{375}{400}\right)^2} = 1.197 \text{ defectives}$$

We have seen how to interpret $s$ to see if one data set has values more dispersed than another. But what if we were interested in simply describing a mass of figures for one variable in terms of central tendency and dispersion? We may find, for example, the arithmetic mean life (continuous play on a 'standard' cassette 'boom box') of a large sample of batteries tested to be 8 hours with a standard deviation of 1 hour. What does this mean? It is not unusual for values of $s$ to be quoted without being understood.

We interpret a standard deviation by use of one of two rules. Figure 4.4 shows the frequency distribution, a histogram, which is described as 'symmetrical'—the average is 8 hours but a good number (frequency) of batteries have lives a little above 8, and a correspondingly good number have lives a little below 8. Only a few are well above the mean, but again only a correspondingly few are well below it. To be described as 'symmetrical' the distribution to the right-hand side of the mean is the mirror image of the left. We can also describe the distribution in Fig. 4-4 as bell-shaped, the smooth line through the mid-points of the peaks of the bars is shaped like a bell. Many frequency distributions take this form; consider the marks of a very large number of students taking an examination. A few will be very high, a corresponding few very low, with most around the middle or mean of the distribution. In practice, frequency distributions are not exactly symmetrical or bell-shaped. It is enough for our purpose that they are approximately so.

Thus, to interpret $s$ we must thus ask in theory (or if we have data, in practice) whether the distribution is roughly symmetrical and bell-shaped? If this is likely, as in this case the *empirical rule* is that the interval:

$$\bar{X} \mp s \quad \text{contains approximately 68 per cent of all observations}$$
$$\bar{X} \mp 2s \quad \text{contains approximately 95 per cent of all observations}$$
$$\bar{X} \mp 3s \quad \text{contains approximately all observations}$$

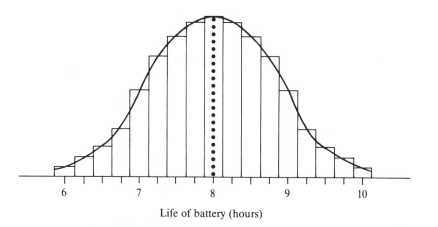

Life of battery (hours)

**Figure 4-4**   Distribution of life of battery

For example, let us take the middle statement, if $s = 1$, then

$\bar{X} \mp 2s$    contains approximately 95 per cent of all observations
$\therefore$      $8 \mp 2(1)$ hours contains approximately 95 per cent of all observations
$\therefore$      6 to 10 hours contains approximately 95 per cent of all observations

This gives us a good idea of dispersion: 95 per cent of batteries will last between 6 and 10 hours. If $s = 0.1$ instead of 1, i.e. less dispersion, then 95 per cent of batteries will last between $(8 \mp 2(0.1)) = 7.8$ and 8.2 hours—much less dispersed. We can choose any (or we could construct more—see Chapter 10) of the three statements to help us think about dispersion. For clerk A in Table 4.2 using data in Table 4.3, 95 per cent of customers take between $1.28 \mp 2(0.45)$, i.e. 0.38 and 2.18 minutes to process an order—a look at the original data show this to be a reasonable statement about their dispersion—but then we assumed a bell-shaped distribution, which was not perfectly valid. What if the distribution is unlikely to be symmetrical or bell-shaped? Here we apply the *simple rule*:

*For any set of numbers, essentially 90 per cent of their values will lie between plus or minus 3 standard deviations of the mean of the values.*

So, first decide if the distribution is likely to be bell-shaped, then choose and apply the appropriate rule. It is quite likely that, for example, your examiner will have the mean and standard deviation mark for your course available at the Examination Board; for quantitative subjects the standard deviation might be quite high at, *for example*, $s = 10$ for $\bar{X} = 55$, while more qualitative subjects might be $s = 5$ for $\bar{X} = 55$. If we assume bell-shaped distributions for the quantitative course, 95 per cent of marks lie within the range 35 to 75 per cent, while for the qualitative course 95 per cent of marks lie within the range 45 to 65 per cent: the standard deviations tell us about the dispersion of marks.

So far all is well; we know how to calculate $s$ and interpret the results. Unfortunately, an additional complication is necessary. It concerns whether you look at your data as belonging to a population or a sample. We might consider the data on the time taken by clerk B to be a random sample of the population of all of his or her times. Or we might be interested only in what happened on those 10 occasions for some reason. In the former case we calculate a sample mean denoted by $\bar{X}$; in the latter case a population mean denoted by $\mu$ (pronounced mu). Fortunately the formulae are the same. We have treated here all data as sample data and used $\bar{X}$, some other statistic books use $\mu$. The importance of the distinction is developed in Chapter 11 so it is of little concern for now, it being just a matter of notation. However, the formula for the sample standard deviation ($s$) differs from that of the population standard deviation ($\sigma$, lower case sigma). Our formula for $s$ is that of the population standard deviation, i.e. $\sigma$. To be consistent and to treat the data as from a sample we should use

$$s_{n-1} = \sqrt{\frac{n}{(n-1)} s^2}$$

which is the formula for the standard deviation with the sum of squared differences divided by $(n-1)$ instead of $n$. On an intuitive level this is because if we take a sample of values we are unlikely to include the extreme values and the dispersion will be less. By dividing by $(n-1)$ instead of $n$ we increase the dispersion compensating for the omission of extreme values, thus rendering $s_{n-1}$ as a better estimate of $\sigma$. If all values are population values there is no need to compensate and we calculate $s = \sigma$. Indeed, for large $n$ there is very little difference between the formulae. The reason for dividing by $(n-1)$ is related to a concept concerned with the *degrees of freedom* of an expression, which will be considered later in this book. So to choose whether to use $s_{n-1}$ or $s = \sigma$, ask yourself if the values you are considering are representative of some larger group (use $s_{n-1}$) or are you solely interested in those values, so that your conclusions will relate to them alone, and will not be applied to draw wider conclusions (use $s = \sigma$).

**Mean absolute deviation**   In deriving a measure of dispersion ($s$) based on the total of the differences between each value and the mean, we had to square these differences to stop positive and negative values from cancelling each other out in the total. As an alternative formulation, instead of squaring the difference between each value and the mean, make it positive; simply call it positive irrespective of its sign. We call this the *modulus* of an expression and it is denoted by two perpendicular lines surrounding the expression. A measure using this is the *mean absolute deviation* (MAD), i.e.

$$\text{MAD} = \frac{\Sigma |X_i - \bar{X}|}{n} \qquad (4\text{-}7)$$

For clerk A, where $\bar{X} = 1.28$ from Table 4-2, $\Sigma |X_i - \bar{X}| = 3.8$ and $\text{MAD} = 3.8/10 = 0.38$; for clerk B where $\bar{Y} = 1.74$; $\Sigma |Y_i - \bar{Y}| = 10.08$ and $\text{MAD} = 10.08/10 = 1.008$ minutes.

MAD is quite easy to interpret: the average deviation each customer had from the mean (irrespective of whether it was positive or negative) was, for clerk A, 0.38 minutes. However, we shall see from subsequent chapters that we make much use of $s$ as our measure of dispersion since MAD, unlike $s$, is not easy to handle mathematically. This is not to argue against its use for descriptive purposes, except insofar that the more common usage of $s$ will mean (at least in theory) greater familiarity with its properties, and less suspicion at its introduction.

**The range**   The above measures of dispersion have been based on using the difference between the values of individual observations and the mean: values further from the mean imply more dispersion. The range is the difference between the maximum and minimum values:

$$\text{Range} = \text{Maximum} - \text{Minimum} \qquad (4\text{-}8)$$

The larger the difference, the more dispersed the values of observations. For our example of time taken to process customers for clerk A, the range is $2.2 - 0.7 = 1.5$; for clerk B, $4.0 - 0.8 = 3.2$, reflecting greater dispersion. A problem with the range is that its value is determined by only the highest and lowest value, and if these are exceptionally high or low they will give a misleading impression. For example, of 100 sales representatives, 98 each bring in exactly 50 orders per month, one brings in no orders and the other, 120 orders. The range would show a wide dispersion when, in practice for the vast majority of salespeople there is no deviation in the number of orders achieved. Nonetheless, there are many situations in which the concept of dispersion concerning us is the spread of values actually attained. In such cases our measure of dispersion may not be the single-valued range, but the two figures for the maximum and minimum: we are interested in the highest and lowest. A prospective employee may be interested in the dispersion of bonuses achieved in a job; the extremes are *for this purpose* of interest.

When comparing the range for different sets of data it may be important to ensure that the two sets of data have the same number of observations. If you compare data on 'late arrival to work' for males and females, with samples of 10 females and 100 males, your conclusion may not hold since increasing the 10 females to 100 will no doubt increase the range even though the real level of variability is the same. The point applies to box plots considered later.

**Semi-interquartile range**   A deficiency of the range is, for some purposes, its reliance on its two extreme defining values. A measure that maintains the properties of the range without this disadvantage is the semi-interquartile (SIQ) range, given by:

$$(Q_3 - Q_1)/2 \qquad (4\text{-}9)$$

where $Q_1$ is the first quartile and $Q_3$ is the third quartile.

When we calculated the median we ranked all observations in order of magnitude and took the value of the observation in the middle of the rank. Here we rank the observations from lowest to highest, but $Q_1$ is the value of the observation one-quarter of the way along the queue or ranking, and $Q_3$ the value of the observation three-quarters of the way along. (See Fig. 4-5.) The range $Q_1$ to $Q_3$ encloses the values of the middle 50 per cent of observations. The SIQ converts this to a single figure. The higher the range of values within which the middle 50 per cent of observations lie, the more dispersed are the data. For example, in income distribution $Q_1$ would be the annual income of someone in the UK 25 per cent up the income league; $Q_3$ someone 75 per cent of the way. As (half) the difference between the incomes widens—the semi-interquartile range—the more dispersed is income in the country becoming. Note that unlike the range it is not affected by the extreme values of the very rich and very poor, which may be regarded as atypical.

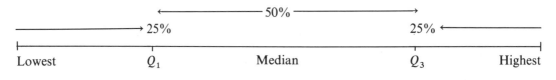

**Figure 4-5** Quartile range

For our calculation of the median we determined the value of the middle observation along the ranked observations. We explained that there is a need to use $(n+1)/2$. For similar reasons, for $Q_1$ —the first quartile—use $(n+1)/4$. For clerk A in Table 4-2, $Q_1$ is given by the value of the $(n+1)/4$th customer $= (10+1)/4 = 2.75$th. Consider the ranking for clerk A of these data in the earlier discussion on the median; 0.8 is the second value, 0.9 the third; the 2.75th value is three-quarters of the way between the second and third value, i.e. 0.875. For $Q_3$ we want the value of the $3(n+1)/4$th customer: i.e. $3(10+1)/4 = 8.25$th. This is a quarter of the way between the 8th and 9th value, i.e. between 1.5 and 1.8, i.e. $1.5 + 0.25(1.8 - 1.5) = 1.575$. The semi-interquartile range is $(1.575 - 0.875)/2 = 0.35$. A similar calculation for clerk B can be shown to yield $(2.75 - 0.8)/2 = 0.975$.

It is worth noting that, first, the interquartile range is often of more use than the single-valued SIQ. With the former we can see, for example, for income over time, what happens to the earnings of the $Q_1$ and $Q_3$ individuals. The single-valued SIQ may show the difference to be increasing. But observing $Q_1$ and $Q_3$ will show if this is because $Q_3$ is becoming better off, $Q_1$ is becoming worse off, or a combination of these. Second, there is nothing sacrosanct about using the middle 50 per cent. The interpercentile range based on $(n+1)/10$ and $9(n+1)/10$ encompasses the middle 90 per cent. It is for the user to determine where the likely cut-offs of extreme value will be.

**The coefficient of variation**   We have had two broad measures of dispersion: one based on deviations from the mean, the other on ranges. Yet these are all concepts of *absolute* dispersion. Consider the prices charged for a 'cream tea' in five different cafés in a tourist village several years ago: 90p, 95p, £1, £1.05 and £1.10. Over the years all prices doubled, i.e.

$$£0.90 \rightarrow £1.80$$
$$£0.95 \rightarrow £1.90$$

$$£1.00 \rightarrow £2.00$$
$$£1.05 \rightarrow £2.10$$
$$£1.10 \rightarrow £2.20$$

The standard deviation several years ago is £0.0707, which increases to £0.1414, i.e. the dispersion of the figures doubles (as measured by the standard deviation and range). This is proper, for in an absolute sense the difference between each value and the mean is now twice what it was—the figures are more dispersed from the mean. However, there is a *relative* concept of dispersion that would argue that no change in dispersion has occurred. Customers who have adjusted to the new average price would see a difference of, at most, 40p between the new prices charged while previously it was 20p. But the 40p relative to an average of £2.00 may be equivalent in their minds to 20p relative to an average of £1.00. The coefficient of variation (C.V.) is given by:

$$\text{C.V.} = s/\bar{X} \qquad (4\text{-}10)$$

For the two sets of prices it is the same, i.e. $0.0707/1 = 0.1414/2$. When we compare the dispersion of two or more sets of data with different means it is necessary to ask which concept of dispersion is more applicable to the problem at hand: relative or absolute. If it is the former, the coefficient of variation should be used. It is often used for measuring changes in dispersion *over time* where the mean may be moving upwards or downwards.

**On choice of measure of dispersion**  The principles governing choice of measure of dispersion are in many ways similar to those discussed for central tendency. The standard deviation and MAD take into account the values of all observations and are thus affected by extreme values. If this is the purpose, such measures are appropriate. They should not, however, be applied to data measured on ordinal or nominal scales (see Chapter 2). The semi-interquartile range is designed so as not to be influenced by extreme values and is to be used when this is desirable. It is not surprising that when the arithmetic mean is used as a measure of central tendency, the standard deviation is its accompanying measures of dispersion, and the median is accompanied by the semi-interquartile range. Also, when comparing dispersion of different sets of data, it is necessary to consider whether a relative or absolute concept is required, the former requiring the coefficient of variation and the latter the standard deviation. As with central tendency, more than one measure can throw insights on the data. For example, if we look at the range and semi-interquartile range for A and B in Table 4-4, we see that time taken for B is over twice as dispersed as A by the range, while the semi-interquartile range shows dispersion to be nearly three times more. This suggests (if we look at the range bands in parentheses) that the difference in the dispersion of time taken for A and B is much less marked for the top and bottom 25 per cent than for the middle 50 per cent.

## Skewness

We might at this stage feel that given 4000 separate figures on weekly cigarette consumption from a random sample of individuals in the UK we could happily calculate means, medians, standard deviations, ranges, etc., and confidently comment on the characteristics of cigarette consumption in the UK. We might separate the figures into male and female smokers or whatever and see how their averages and dispersions differed. But there is more we can glean from the data by way of summary measures. For example, two distributions may have the same mean and standard deviation and we may conclude they are the same in these respects, but their skewness may differ. Skewness is concerned with the degree of lack of symmetry to the distribution.

Consider the histogram in Fig. 4-6(a); the $X$-axis shows values of the variable, and the $Y$-axis the frequency with which each value occurs. The symmetric distribution might, for example, represent the number of keying-in errors per day for entering data onto a database. There will be an average number of daily errors, say 20, but on some days there will be a very high number, say 24, while on a roughly equal number of days there will be a correspondingly smaller number, say 16. The mean is equal to the mode, which is equal to the median, since any extremely high values (for the mean) are counterbalanced by extremely low values. The mode is the value of the observation with the highest frequency and the median is half-way along the distribution since the number of observations to its left is equal to those to its right.

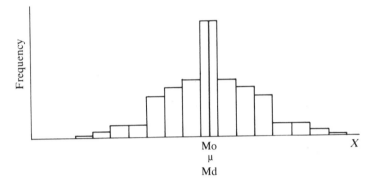

(a) A symmetric distribution

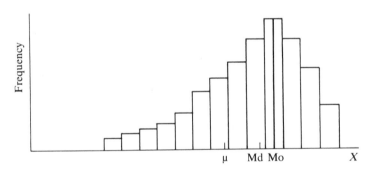

(b) Distribution skewed to the left (negative)

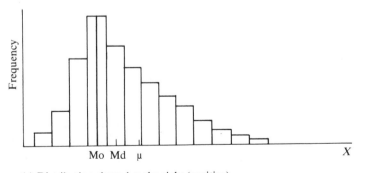

(c) Distribution skewed to the right (positive)

**Figure 4-6**  Skewness of distribution

The negatively skewed distribution (Fig. 4-6(b)) has a long tail to the left with relatively few observations taking very low values; this is not matched by observations taking very high values to the right. Note that the extremely low values pull the mean away from the mode and median with the mean < median < mode. Alternatively, the positively skewed distribution (Fig. 4-6(c)) has its tail to the right with the mean > median > mode. As an example, data on earnings are often positively skewed with the mean pulled up by a few very high earners. The age distribution of workers may be negatively skewed *if* a lot of workers were taken on when young, when the factory was set up, and stayed in the job leaving a bulge of older workers alongside a few younger recruits. The skewness of such a distribution has implications for planning human resources, especially with regard to training. Central tendency and dispersion tell us the location and spread of the distribution. Skewness gives us a picture of its shape. Measures of skewness include:

**Pearson's coefficient**   This is given by:

$$3(\text{Mean} - \text{Median})/\text{Standard deviation} \tag{4-11}$$

Since Fig. 4-6 shows that skewness of a distribution leads to different values for the measures of central tendency, it is not surprising that the differences between these measures are used to measure it. The multiplication of the difference by 3 and the division by the standard deviation is used to form a scale for the measure: the result generally lies in the range $-3$ to $+3$ with 0 being symmetric and $-3$ and $+3$ the extremes of negative and positive skewness. Using the results in Table 4-2 for clerk A we have $3(1.28 - 1.20)/0.45 = 0.53$, i.e. a positive skewness reflecting a relatively small number of customers taking a very long time not counterbalanced by a small number taking a corresponding very short time. The positive skewness is more marked for clerk B at 1.74.

**Bowley's coefficient**   Skewed distributions also lead to differences in the positions of the quartiles relative to the median, as measured by:

$$2(Q_3 + Q_1 - 2\,\text{Median})/(Q_3 - Q_1) \tag{4-12}$$

For clerk A we have (Table 4.4):

$$2[(1.575 + 0.875) - 2(1.20)]/(1.575 - 0.875) = 0.143$$

showing on a range of generally $-2$ to $+2$ (zero: symmetric) a positive skew. For clerk B the equivalent figure was again higher at 1.487. Note that Bowley's does not take account of the value of all observations, using only the median and the quartiles. It is less sensitive to extreme values than Pearson's which, via the mean, takes account of all values.

**Third moment**   The third moment is based on all values of $X_i$, given by

$$\frac{\Sigma(X_i - \bar{X})^3/n}{s^3} \tag{4-13}$$

The third moment can take quite high or low, positive or negative, values but is zero for a completely symmetric distribution. It is possible for skewed distribution to also give a value of zero, so the measure is not totally reliable.

## Kurtosis

Skewness does not tell us all there is to know about the shape of a distribution. Two distributions may, for example, be symmetrical with the same mean and dispersion, but differ with respect to

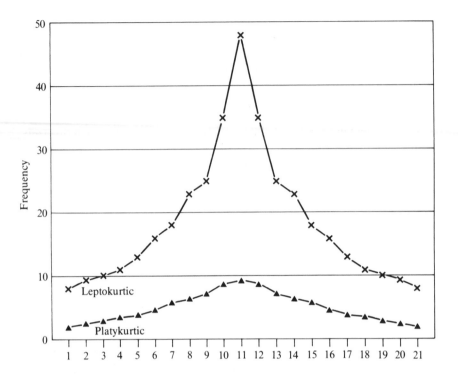

**Figure 4-7** Kurtosis

how 'peaked' they are. Figure 4-7 shows a peaked (leptokurtic) and fairly flat (platykurtic) distribution (an intermediate one is mesokurtic).

For the leptokurtic distribution there is a rapid fall-off in the frequency as we move away from the mean. The peakedness of a distribution is not always of interest, but suggests a clustering around the mean (e.g. for overtime hours worked, which may be a socially acceptable level) with a rapid fall-off in frequency around it. It is measured (somewhat imperfectly) by the fourth moment:

$$\Sigma (X_i - \bar{X})^4 / ns^4 \quad \text{if greater than 3 it is leptokurtic} \qquad (4\text{-}14)$$
$$\text{if less than 3 it is platykurtic}$$

For our data on clerks, Table 4-4 shows leptokurtic distributions.

### Box plots

So far four different dimensions of the data—central tendency, dispersion, skewness and kurtosis—have been discussed. A graphical device that captures some of these properties is the box plot. In its simplest form (Fig. 4-8) the edges of the box are (ascending from left to right) the lower and upper quartiles; a line is placed in the box for the median, and extending from either side of the box are *whiskers*; the line extending to the left as far as the minimum value and to the right as far as the maximum value. For example, using Table 4.4 for the time taken to process a customer, for clerk A the box is drawn in Fig. 4.8 with $Q_1$ and $Q_3$ (0.875 and 1.575) defining its boundaries and the median, 1.20 within it. The maximum and minimum are 2.2 and 0.7 respectively. The plots tell us a lot about the two distributions: there is not much difference in the median time taken for A and

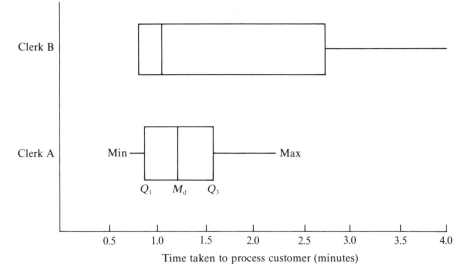

**Figure 4-8**  Box plots of time taken by clerks

B (B is slightly quicker), but the time taken by B is very much more dispersed and positively skewed with a few customers taking a disproportionately longer time. There is very little dispersion in the time taken for the quickest 50% of B's customers, each of whom are processed under little more than one minute. However, after that it is downhill, there being a few on whom B takes an exceptionally long time. For A the median is in the middle of the box and whiskers are of similar magnitude on either side pointing to a symmetrical distribution. Of course the sample sizes are small for the purpose of illustration and it would be difficult to make generalized statements about the two clerks from such small sample as discussed in Chapters 11 and 12. However, the data serve to illustrate the principles of the methods.

It was mentioned above that Fig. 4-8 illustrated a simple form of the box plot. To complicate matters the terminology and measures used vary a little. Tukey (1977) uses *Hinges*, similar to $Q_1$ and $Q_3$, with *H-spread* being similar to the interquartile range. A *step* is defined as 1.5 times the H-Spread. An *inner fence* is one step beyond the hinges; an *outer fence* is two steps beyond the hinges. The point of all of this is that instead of the whiskers extending to the maximum and minimum, they may extend to the inner fence with observations lying between the inner and outer fence being marked with, for example, an asterisk, and those outside the outer fence with, for example, a zero. This helps identify possible outliers. Minitab produces results akin to this, as shown and explained in the answers to questions on this subject in Chapter 13.

## SUMMARY MEASURES ILLUSTRATED

Table 4-6 shows summary measures of prices of different styles of girls' sweaters sold in stores in Birmingham, UK, in 1986. The prices relate to styles of sweaters, so that a sweater of a given style, even though it may be available in several colours, is regarded as one price observation. Given the summary measures alone, we judge the central tendency of the prices, the dispersion and shape of the distribution. The mean shows that Benetton, Next and Miss Selfridge clearly have much higher

**Table 4-6**   Summary measures of prices of girls' sweaters in Birmingham stores. (Values in pounds sterling)

| Store | Mean | Median | Range | Standard deviation | Coefficient of variation |
|---|---|---|---|---|---|
| Now (7)* | 13.70 | 13.99 | 11.99–14.99 | 1.03 | 0.075 |
| Next (27) | 20.88 | 19.99 | 14.99–26.99 | 3.47 | 0.166 |
| Chelsea Girl (34) | 12.52 | 12.49 | 3.99–17.99 | 2.68 | 0.214 |
| Benetton (10) | 32.10 | 32.40 | 18.90–48.90 | 10.10 | 0.315 |
| Miss Selfridge (18) | 17.55 | 16.99 | 12.99–24.99 | 2.85 | 0.162 |
| C&A (20) | 12.59 | 12.49 | 7.99–16.99 | 2.92 | 0.232 |
| Top Shop (30) | 14.16 | 13.49 | 5.99–24.99 | 4.31 | 0.304 |

*Figures in parentheses are the number of styles available in each store.

average prices than the other stores. The mean and median prices are also quite similar for all stores, which is surprising. This suggests a symmetrical distribution. You would have expected stores to either have a few very expensive sweaters to 'upgrade' the image of the store and 'skim off' customers willing to pay the extra—a positively skewed distribution. Alternatively, a few lower priced goods as 'loss leaders' might have been apparent—a negatively skewed distribution.

If stores were operating both policies we might be left with something broadly symmetrical, but with a high dispersion. If the dispersion is low the stores are simply finding their price range and keeping to it: the stores do not give particular emphasis to relatively high- or low-priced sweaters. The range shows the maximum and minimum values with, for example, Benetton starting where C&A finishes. The standard deviation shows the dispersion of prices, Now pricing over a narrow range while Benetton's prices are much more dispersed. A value of 1.03 for Now can be interpreted as virtually all price points will lie within plus or minus $3(1.03) = £3.09$ of the mean (£13.70). The small standard deviation reflects little dispersion in prices charged by a store.

The coefficient of variation is of interest here. For Benetton, for example, a couple of pounds difference in price between styles is of little importance relative to their mean of £32.10. However, a similar difference for Top Shop reflects in a relative sense a greater dispersion in their prices. Compare the standard deviations and coefficient of variation for these stores. In an absolute sense Benetton's prices are very dispersed. However, relative to their different means their prices have a similar dispersion. With a few summary figures we gain insights into the characteristics of a distribution of many figures.

Note that these data refer to styles of sweater offered and it must not be thought that the results would necessarily apply to the prices of sweaters actually sold. Because different styles sell in different quantities, the results from Electronic Point of Sale (EPOS) data would be likely to differ from those given in Table 4-6.

## SUMMARY MEASURES REVISITED: GROUPED DATA

So far our concern has been with ungrouped data: the actual observations for each variable were used to calculate the summary measures. However, it is sometimes the case (when using secondary sources) that we don't have access to the raw data, though this is always preferable, but to a frequency table of grouped data, i.e. the data have been grouped into class intervals with associated frequencies.

We now consider how to rework our preceding measures if our starting point is grouped data. Consider the data in Table 4-1 on percentage annual inflation rates for 106 countries. In order to calculate the mean and standard deviation (and MAD and third and fourth moments) we need to assume the mid-points of the class intervals are the means of the values in each class interval, and form another column in Table 4-1 comprising these mid-points. We thus have seven countries with an annual inflation rate of $-2.5$ per cent, 35 countries with an annual inflation rate of 2.5 per cent, and so forth. Now we simply use Eqs (4-2) and (4-6) for the mean and standard deviation respectively, i.e.

$$\bar{X} = \frac{\Sigma fX}{\Sigma f} = \frac{14\,235}{106} = 134.3 \text{ per cent p.a.}$$

$$s = \sqrt{\frac{\Sigma fX^2}{\Sigma f} - \left(\frac{\Sigma fX}{\Sigma f}\right)^2} = \sqrt{\frac{34\,217\,080}{106} - \left(\frac{14\,235}{106}\right)^2} = 552.06 \text{ per cent p.a.}$$

Note first that the very high value of $s$ is strongly influenced by the extreme values. Second, the mean gives a value very similar to that in Table 4-5, calculated using ungrouped data. This is only because the mid-points for the class intervals accurately reflected the mean of values within the intervals. The footnote to Table 4-1 illustrates how a bad choice of intervals can lead to errors in the estimated mean. In general, if ungrouped data are available, use them. If you have to guess the mid-point of an open-ended class interval, experiment with plausible values to give the user an indication of the reliability of the measure.

So far we have used grouped data for the mean and standard deviation, though similar principles apply for MAD and the moments. What about the median, quartiles and mode? Table 4-1 already has our observations ranked in order of magnitude and this aids the calculation of the median and quartiles. For the median we first identify the median class interval: the median observation is the $(n+1)/2$th $= (106+1)/2 = 53.5$th. The class interval that contains this value is '5 to under 10', as can be seen by following the cumulative frequency $(F)$ column in Table 4-1. This shows 42 countries with less than 5 per cent inflation, 66 countries with less than 10 per cent; so the median class interval is 5 to under 10 per cent since the 53.5th country lies here. A crude estimate of the median is the mid-point of the interval, 7.5 per cent per annum. However, if the median were the 43rd country it would only just be included in the interval, and the mid-point would overstate the value. Alternatively, if the median were the 65th country, it would have a value near the end of the interval and the mid-point would understate the median. We need a mechanism that will allocate to the median a value that depends on its relative penetration into its class interval. Such a mechanism is

$$M_d = L_m + C_m \left[ \frac{(n+1)/2 - F_{m-1}}{f_m} \right] \tag{4-15}$$

where $L_m$, $C_m$ and $f_m$ are the lower boundary, width and frequency of the median class interval respectively, $n$ the number of observations and $F_{m-1}$ the cumulative frequency of the interval *before* the median class interval, i.e.

$$M_d = 5 + 5 \left[ \frac{107/2 - 42}{24} \right] = 7.40 \text{ per cent p.a.}$$

[*N.B.* First evaluate the expression in square brackets, multiply the result by 5 and then add this to (the first) 5.]

Quartiles are evaluated on a similar basis: we first find the appropriate quartile class interval and then adapt Eq. (4-15) using, instead of $(n+1)/2$, $(n+1)/4$ for $Q_1$ and $3(n+1)/4$ for $Q_3$, yielding for our example $Q_1 = 2.79$ and $Q_3 = 16.56$.

A grouped equivalent of the mode leads to a conceptual problem. An approach adopted in some texts is to look for the class interval with the highest frequency, the range with the most observations. If all intervals are the same width, or if wider intervals do not have the highest frequency, there is some meaning to calculating the mode. The modal inflation rate is the range 0 to under 5 per cent since the highest number of countries have inflation rates in this range. Adjustments similar in principle to Eq. (4-15) are sometimes suggested to ascertain where in the class interval the mode best lies. In some cases there is little meaning in this. Where the variable can only take on whole number (integer) values, or is *discrete*—that is, the values are countable, e.g. 0, 0.5, 1.0, 1.5, 2.0 . . .—we can think of modal values within class intervals. The number of persons attending a cinema each night is countable. On most nights there may be between 100 and 125 persons. Yet if the variable is *continuous*, e.g. height, it is not countable and a modal value makes no sense. Height is not countable since if you take 2 metres, the next values are 2.00001 metres, 2.00002 metres; but even this is wrong, as you have neglected 2.000001 metres. This is all impossible and so is a modal value because all observed values on a continuous scale will, if measured accurately, have a frequency of 1. However, in practice we may take measurements up to 1 decimal place, so it might be that most men are 1.7 metres tall, but here we are really using an interval of 1.65 to under 1.75, with 1.8 being 1.75 to under 1.85, etc. Thus, in practice, for ungrouped discrete variables, a single-value mode can be determined. For grouped data (discrete or continuous) and continuous variables not grouped, the mode should be considered as an interval. Yet even the consideration of a modal class interval is fraught with difficulties. Had we grouped the data on inflation in 10 per cent intervals, we would then have $7 + 35 = 42$ countries with rates of $-5$ to under 5, $24 + 11 = 35$ countries with rates of 5 to under 15 etc. The modal class interval is the one with the highest frequency, i.e. $-5$ to under 5; different from the 0 to under 5 per cent determined above.

This is not to say the mode should not be calculated for grouped data—it is useful as an indicator of where most observations are clustering. However, for grouped data it should be defined as a range (as opposed to single value) and care has to be exercised in its interpretation. In our example on inflation rates there are other ways class intervals can be formed that will yield other modal intervals—nonetheless there will remain a clustering of points around the 0 to under 10 per cent (and more probably 0 to under 5 per cent) range, and this is worth pointing out.

## USING COMPUTERS

### Minitab

```
MTB > HISTOGRAM C1
```

This provides a histogram of the raw data in column C1 along with the frequencies of values falling within each interval (frequency table). Minitab automatically chooses intervals, though subcommands of INCREMENT for the width of the intervals) and START for the first and END (optional) for the last interval can allow the user to design the histogram/table, e.g.

```
MTB  > HISTOGRAM C1;        Produces a histogram/frequency table which starts at a mid-point of 5, has intervals of width 5,
SUBC > INCREMENT=5;         and ends at a mid-point of 50.
SUBC > START= 5  END= 50.
```

If, say, for classificatory data a frequency table is required for the values in a column without grouping, then TALLY C1 provides this, though the subcommand ALL also yields percentages, cumulative counts and cumulative percentages useful for ogives. Alternatively, an ogive can be drawn from ungrouped data by first sorting the data (SORT), putting the smallest first, then generating a new column of figures (GENERATE) $1, 2, 3, \ldots, n$ where $n$ is the number of observations and plotting (PLOT) the generated numbers on the vertical axis against the sorted data; e.g. for 50 observations:

```
MTB > SORT C1,put into C2
MTB > GENERATE 50 C3
MTB > PLOT C3 VS C2
```

A stem-and-leaf display of data in C1 is given by

```
MTB  > STEM-AND-LEAF C1;
SUBC > INCREMENT = 5.
```

where the (optional) increment subcommand specifies the increment from one stem to the next.

```
MTB > BOXPLOTS C1-C3
```

provides box plots of the data in each of C1, C2 and C3 for comparison.
   For summary measures of data in C1:

```
MTB > DESCRIBE C1
```

prints the number of observations (N), arithmetic mean (MEAN), MEDIAN, 5 per cent trimmed mean (first the data are sorted then the smallest and largest 5 per cent of observations are trimmed, the arithmetic mean being calculated for the remaining 90 per cent, TRMEAN), standard deviation (STDEV), standard error of the mean (SEMEAN—see Chapters 10 and 11), MINimum and MAXimum values, upper ($Q_3$) and lower ($Q_1$) quartiles and the number of missing values (NMISS). The measures can be requested and stored individually, e.g. MEAN C1 [put in K], along with the total: SUM C1 [put in K]; sum of squares: SSQ C1 [put in K] and the count (N + NMISS): COUNT C1 [put in K]; measures of skewness and kurtosis can be derived using LET commands and some of the preceding statistics. Summary measures on rows require the prefix R, e.g. for the means for each row of data in columns 1–5:

```
MTB > RMEAN C1-C5, put in C6
```

In the last section of the preceding chapter we noted how the command TABLES with appropriate subcommands can be used to generate summary measures for a variable classified by further variables, the example used being mean purchases by sex and age group of customers. Often our concern is to calculate summary measures for a variable such as income (C1) by subgroups of another variable, e.g. age group (C2), sex (C3).

```
MTB  > TABLE C2 C3;
SUBC > STATS C1.
```

## Lotus 1-2-3

A frequency distribution of the column of ($X_i$) data is derived using /Data Distribution. This requests the range for the data (e.g. A1..A100), then to set up a single column bin range in ascending order—say to the right of the data:

| BIN | FREQUENCY |
|-----|-----------|
| 200 | 6 |
| 400 | 24 |
| 600 | 56 |
|     | 5 |

The first range is $X_i \leqslant 200$; the next, $200 < X_i \leqslant 400$; the third, $400 < X_i \leqslant 600$; and the (implicit) last, $X_i > 600$. The frequencies are then generated to the right of the bin range: e.g. 5 observations had values greater than 600. /Data Fill creates a bin range with equal intervals.

Lotus 1-2-3 can be used for histograms, polygons and ogives. It can be used to generate (see below) the summary measures (median, etc.) necessary to draw box plots and the graphics facilities can be used to plot symbols from these measures, the rest being drawn in by hand. A particular problem is that with bar charts the bars are detached from each other, while the continuous scale of the histograms requires that they be connected. For histograms with limited numbers and equal sized intervals, individual components of a clustered bar graph can be used. An outline of the graphics facilities was given in the previous chapter.

Lotus 1-2-3 has a range of @ functions that can be used to generate summary measures, or as part of a formula. For example, by entering @AVG(5,10,15) the arithmetic mean of these numbers, 10, is generated. More usually data would be in a column, say A1 to A100:

@AVG(A1..A100)    Calculates the arithmetic mean of the values
@MAX(A1..A100)    Finds the maximum value
@MIN(A1..A100)    Finds the minimum value
@STD(A1..A100)    Calculates the standard deviation
@STDS(A1..A100)   Calculates the sample deviation (Chapter 10)
@SUM(A1..A100)    Sums the values

If a single entry, say A100, is changed the summary measures would also change. As such we can see how sensitive our results are to outliers.

The above list is not exhaustive; many of the measures included in this chapter are not available, though Lotus 1-2-3 has a range of facilities that allows us to determine these measures. For example, for the median we first sort the data in ascending order using /Data Sort; then we need to count how many values are in the range; @COUNT(A1..A100) will tell us there are 100 observations. We want the value of the $(100+1)/2 = 50.5$th observation. Using /Data Fill set up in B1 to B100 a list of numbers starting from zero for B1 to 99 for B100. Then @CHOOSE(B49,A1..A100) will yield the value of the 50th observation and @CHOOSE(B50,A1..A100) the value of the 51st, which can then be averaged.

Of particular use in statistics is the ability to copy calculations.

| A | A | B | C | D |
|---|---|---|---|---|
| 1 | $X$ | $f$ | $fX$ | ABSDEV |
| 2 | 2 | 3 | 6 | 3 |
| 3 | 4 | 12 | 48 | 1 |
| 4 | 6 | 14 | 84 | 1 |
| 5 | 8 | 2 | 16 | 3 |
| 6 | | | 154 | 2 |

For example, A2..A5 contains four observations on a variable $X$ and B2..B5 the corresponding frequencies; if we enter $+A2*B2$ into C2 we get $2 \times 3 = 6$. [Note that the '+' before A2 is necessary for the following operation.] /COPY allows you to copy the calculation *from*: C2 *to*: the other cells, i.e. C3..C5. We specify C3..C5 when the *to*: prompt appears by moving the cursor to the top of the desired range (C3), entering a period (.) or colon (:) to anchor the cursor, and then moving the cursor down to highlight the desired range followed by pressing 'enter'. In C6 we might put @SUM(C2..C5) to give us $\Sigma fX$. Alternatively @SUMPRODUCT(A2..A5,B2..B5) would give us the sum of the corresponding products $= 154$.

A range of mathematical functions exist including:

@SQRT(A1)   Calculates the square root of the value in A1
@ABS(A1)    Calculates the absolute value of the value in A1
@LN(A1)     Calculates the natural logarithm of the value in A1
@LOG(A1)    Calculates the common logarithm of the value in A1.

For example, to calculate the mean absolute deviation (Eq. (4-7)) of the values in A2..A5, we enter in D2: @ABS(A2–(@AVG$A$2..$A$5))), and copy this down to D5 using /COPY. MAD is given in D6 by @AVG(D2..D5)=2. The dollar signs ($) hold A2 and A5 constant when using /COPY.

It must be stressed that Lotus 1-2-3 is not a statistical package and does not generate the summary statistics with the ease of Minitab. However, it has many other useful facilities and the functions given above are but a limited selection. With a little thought it is not too difficult to undertake a wide range of statistical exercises.

## EXERCISES

**4-1** The following data are the hardback publishers' prices of 24 popular management books '... for today's business professionals' as marketed for Executive World in the *Sunday Times Magazine* (1990). Using a frequency table, and then the arithmetic mean, median, mode range, standard deviation and a measure of skewness summarize the characteristics of these data.

| £ | £ | £ | £ | £ |
|---|---|---|---|---|
| 17.95 | 16.95 | 45.00 | 14.95 | 17.95 |
| 14.95 | 9.95 | 15.00 | 14.95 | 30.00 |
| 15.00 | 10.95 | 14.95 | 8.95 | 9.95 |
| 12.95 | 14.95 | 15.00 | 9.95 | 12.95 |
| 12.95 | 19.92 | 12.95 | 13.95 | |

**4-2** A study of number of hours worked overtime (including evenings and weekends) over the last year in a large plant yielded the following measures given in the table.

| | | Age | | |
|---|---|---|---|---|
| Sex | | Under 30 years | 30 to under 45 years | 45 years and more |
| Male: | mean | 400 | 350 | 280 |
| | median | 350 | 275 | 300 |
| | std. dev. | 80 | 100 | 140 |
| Female: | mean | 180 | 200 | 150 |
| | median | 200 | 220 | 140 |
| | std. dev. | 80 | 90 | 70 |

Discuss these findings.

**4-3** The following table shows average gross weekly earnings for full-time male and female workers in Great Britain, 1989.
(a) Calculate the mean and median earnings for (i) male and (ii) female employees.
(b) Calculate the standard deviation for earnings for males and females.
(c) Interpret the results in (a) and (b) explaining clearly the information provided by the measures, any assumptions made, and the usefulness or otherwise of such measures in comparing earnings of male and female employees.

| Average gross weekly earnings† | Number of full-time employees in sample (thousands)* | |
| --- | --- | --- |
| | Males | Females |
| under £150 | 13.7 | 19.8 |
| £150 to under £200 | 17.5 | 10.8 |
| £200 to under £250 | 17.1 | 6.3 |
| £250 to under £300 | 13.2 | 3.9 |
| £300 and over | 23.6 | 3.5 |
| Total | 85.1 | 44.3 |

*Derived from the new earning survey, the figures being based on random samples of over 44 000 and 85 000 female and male employees respectively.
†Gross earnings before deductions for tax, insurance, etc. Includes wages and salaries, overtime pay, bonuses, commission, etc., but excludes the value of benefits in kind.
*Source*: Central Statistical Office, *New Earnings Survey 1989*, London: HMSO, 1990.

**4-4** In marketing concerts of different types it is useful to know something of the ages of people attending different types of concerts. The *General Household Survey 1987* provides the information given in the following table. It shows, for example, that out of the representative sample of nearly 20 000 adults surveyed, 42 people in the age band 16–19 attended in the last month a jazz, blues, etc., concert.
(a) Determine the mean and median age of those attending (i) jazz, blues, soul and reggae concerts and (ii) classical music concerts.
(b) Determine the standard deviation of the ages of those attending (i) jazz, blues, soul and reggae concerts and (ii) classical music concerts.
(c) Comment on your findings in (a) and (b).

| Age band | Number from sample attending in the 4 weeks before interview* | |
| --- | --- | --- |
| | Jazz, blues, soul and reggae concerts | Classical music concerts |
| 16–19 | 42 | 28 |
| 20–24 | 91 | 18 |
| 25–29 | 73 | 37 |
| 30–44 | 103 | 103 |
| 45–60 | 41 | 124 |
| 60 and over | 0† | 260 |

*Figures are derived from the *General Household Survey 1987* which involved interviews of 19 529 people selected on a random basis. The above data are in response to a question on the number of these types of concerts attended in the 4 weeks before the interview. The figures include those attending both jazz, blues, etc., and classical music concerts.
†Negligible number.
*Source*: Office of Population Censuses and Surveys, *General Household Survey 1987*, London: HMSO, 1989.

**4-5** Twenty applicants were interviewed for a job. Ten were male and ten female. They undertook a test on their technical skills for the work. The percentage scores for each of the applicants were as follows:

Males:    50  55  60  48  62  51  66  57  59  58
Females:  43  72  69  45  68  65  40  66  62  63

(a) Calculate the mean and median score for (i) male and (ii) female applicants.
(b) Calculate the standard deviation and coefficient of skewness of the score for (i) male and (ii) female applicants.
(c) Using your results from (a) and (b), compare the performance of male and female applicants.

**4-6** Expenditure per person from till receipts on a given day in a staff canteen are given as follows (all data in £s):

| | | | | | | | | | | | |
|---|---|---|---|---|---|---|---|---|---|---|---|
| 0.8 | 1.2 | 1.0 | 1.15 | 0.9 | 0.2 | 0.2 | 0.2 | 0.75 | 0.82 | 0.8 | 0.9 |
| 0.86 | 1.4 | 1.15 | 1.0 | 0.8 | 0.2 | 1.1 | 0.2 | 0.9 | 1.2 | 0.2 | 0.8 |
| 1.4 | 1.3 | 1.2 | 2.8 | 1.2 | 1.5 | 0.9 | 0.8 | 0.8 | 0.8 | 0.1 | 0.65 |
| 0.4 | 1.1 | 1.3 | 1.4 | 1.8 | 0.4 | 0.2 | 0.2 | 0.2 | 1.3 | 1.1 | 1.0 |
| 1.3 | 0.6 | 1.2 | 0.8 | 0.8 | 1.1 | 0.8 | 1.4 | 3.6 | 2.4 | 0.2 | 0.2 |

(a) Summarize the data using a stem-and-leaf diagram and a histogram. How do the two methods compare?

(b) Calculate appropriate summary measure for the data and compare the effectiveness of such measures with the diagrams in part (a) for describing the features of the data.

# INDEX NUMBERS

Index numbers are primarily concerned with the decomposition of *changes* in money values over time into their price and physical quantity components. For example, a manufacturer may quote the initially impressive result that company sales increased by 50 per cent in 1993 compared with 1992. However, if the prices of goods produced by the manufacturer increased (on average) by 60 per cent, the physical quantity of goods sold would in fact have fallen. Thus a need exists to decompose the change in the money value of sales into changes in the price of goods sold and changes in the quantity of goods sold. Similarly we may determine changes in the *money values* of goods and services consumed by an individual, goods and services purchased by an organization, goods and services exported and imported by a country, shares sold on the stock market, primary products purchased from less-developed countries, government expenditure on education, labour costs and so forth. Yet changes in these money values may stem from variations in *price* and/or *quantity* of goods and services consumed, purchased, sold, exported, imported, etc., and index numbers provide a means by which the price and quantity components of such changes can be separately identified. For example, a 10 per cent pay (value) increase would be most unsatisfactory if the prices of goods and services consumed over the relevant period increased on average by 15 per cent, implying a fall in the physical quantity of goods and services that may be purchased.

Index numbers pervade official economic statistics where the natural question to be put to any change in the value of a country's consumption, production, exports, imports, etc., is how much is due to price and quantity (or volume) changes. The national accounts of a country are given at both constant and current prices, the latter being in terms of money values, the former at a given period's prices to reflect only 'quantity' changes in production or whatever (Stuvel, 1986; United Nations, 1979; Silver and Mahdavy, 1989). There are international guidelines on the construction of price and quantity indices for such accounts (United Nations, 1977, 1979). We shall look later at one index used in economic analysis—the Retail Prices Index, measuring changes in the prices of goods and services consumed.

Index numbers also have their place in industry. It is not enough to know that sales value has increased by, for example, 50 per cent without knowing how much is due to increases (decreases) in quantity produced and how much by prices. Labour productivity measures should relate changes in the *quantity* produced to labour input, otherwise productivity might rise not because of any additional effort or efficiency, but because of increasing prices. Price indices for goods and services bought-in compared to those sold are also of interest, for differential input/output price changes

**Table 5-1** Data of prices, quantities and values of flowers and chocolates

|  | 1992 | | | 1993 | | | 1994 | | |
|---|---|---|---|---|---|---|---|---|---|
|  | Price (£) | Quantity (No.) | Value (£) | Price (£) | Quantity (No.) | Value (£) | Price (£) | Quantity (No). | Value (£) |
| Flowers | 4.00 | 1000 | 4000 | 5.00 | 900 | 4500 | 4.80 | 1500 | 7200 |
| Chocolates | 4.00 | 500 | 2000 | 3.50 | 1000 | 3500 | 4.00 | 550 | 2200 |
|  |  |  | 6000 |  |  | 8000 |  |  | 9400 |

affect profits. The multiplicity of goods and services bought-in and sold beg a need for index numbers if we are to examine *overall* price and quantity changes. First we look at their construction.

## THE CONSTRUCTION OF INDEX NUMBERS

In this section we explain some different index number formulae and their rationale using the data in Table 5-1 on the prices and quantities of flowers and chocolates sold. We start with a one commodity 'simple' index number to illustrate some basic principles. However, index numbers come into their own when we want the overall or aggregate price and quantity changes of many products. We only use two products for simplicity of exposition, though the principles and methods apply to any extension of this. The Laspeyres relatives formula is considered first, this being available in two forms, relatives and aggregative. Both yield the same answers, the choice being a matter of preference. For each of these two forms formulae are available for both price and quantity indices. We then look at the Paasche formula, though we emphasize the aggregative form here, again for price *and* quantity index numbers. Fisher's 'ideal' formula, the Tornqvist formula and the process of chaining will then be discussed. The formulae are given in Table 5-2 for reference.

### Simple index numbers

Consider in Table 5-1 the sales of flowers alone. Between 1992 and 1993 the value of flowers sold increased from £4000 to £4500. However, this increase stemmed partly from a change in the price and partly from a change in the quantity of flowers sold. In index number work a base period is chosen and ascribed an arbitrary value (usually 100.0). The period chosen to be the base period is usually the first period for which data are available or a period for which no 'abnormal' prices and/or quantities of goods or services are purchased or sold. If a value of 100.0 is ascribed to the base year, 1992, the index of the *value* of flowers sold in 1993, compared with 1992 is:

$$(4500/4000)100 = 112.5$$

Similarly, the index of the value of flowers sold in 1994 compared with the base year 1992 is:

$$(7200/4000)100 = 180.0$$

The index for the value of flowers sold may be summarized as:

| Year | 1992 | 1993 | 1994 |
|---|---|---|---|
| Index | 100.0 | 112.5 | 180.0 |

**Table 5-2**  Some index number formulae

| Formulae | Price | | Quantity | |
|---|---|---|---|---|
| Laspeyres | *Relatives* | *Aggregative* | *Relatives* | *Aggregative* |
| | $\dfrac{\Sigma P_b Q_b (P_c/P_b)}{\Sigma P_b Q_b} \times 100 = \dfrac{\Sigma P_c Q_b}{\Sigma P_b Q_b} \times 100$ | | $\dfrac{\Sigma P_b Q_b (Q_c/Q_b)}{\Sigma P_b Q_b} \times 100 = \dfrac{\Sigma P_b Q_c}{\Sigma P_b Q_b} \times 100$ | |
| Paasche | *Relatives* | *Aggregative* | *Relatives* | *Aggregative* |
| | $\dfrac{\Sigma P_c Q_c}{\Sigma P_c Q_c (P_b/P_c)} \times 100 = \dfrac{\Sigma P_c Q_c}{\Sigma P_b Q_c} \times 100$ | | $\dfrac{\Sigma P_c Q_c}{\Sigma P_c Q_c (Q_b/Q_c)} \times 100 = \dfrac{\Sigma P_c Q_c}{\Sigma P_c Q_b} \times 100$ | |
| Fisher's 'ideal' | *Aggregative* | | *Aggregative* | |
| | $\sqrt{\dfrac{\Sigma P_c Q_b}{\Sigma P_b Q_b} \times \dfrac{\Sigma P_c Q_c}{\Sigma P_b Q_c}} \times 100$ | | $\sqrt{\dfrac{\Sigma P_b Q_c}{\Sigma P_b Q_b} \times \dfrac{\Sigma P_c Q_c}{\Sigma P_c Q_b}} \times 100$ | |
| Tornqvist | *Relatives* | | *Relatives* | |
| | $\exp[\Sigma 0.5(W_b + W_c)\ln(P_c/P_b)] \times 100$ | | $\exp[\Sigma 0.5(W_b + W_c)\ln(Q_c/Q_b)] \times 100$ | |
| | where  $W_c = \dfrac{P_c W_c}{\Sigma P_c Q_c}$  and  $W_b = \dfrac{P_b Q_b}{\Sigma P_b Q_b}$ | | where  $W_c = \dfrac{P_c Q_c}{\Sigma P_c Q_c}$  and  $W_b = \dfrac{P_b Q_b}{\Sigma P_b Q_b}$ | |

*Notation*: $P_b$ and $P_c$ are prices in the base and current period respectively and $Q_b$ and $Q_c$ are quantities in the base and current period respectively, the summation extending over all goods and services within the scope of the index.


Note the indices are expressed by reference to an arbitrary 1992 (base) value of 100.0. Between 1992 and 1993 the value of flowers sold increased by 12.5 per cent, between 1992 and 1994 by 80 per cent and between 1993 and 1994 [(180.0/112.5)100 = 160.0] by 60 per cent.

   To decompose these value changes into their price and quantity components we calculate price indices from Table 5-1 using a similar procedure to that adopted for value, i.e.

| Year | 1992 | 1993 | 1994 |
|---|---|---|---|
| Index | 100.0 | 125.0* | 120.0† |

*(5.0/4.0)100    †(4.8/4.0)100

Similarly, for quantities

| Year | 1992 | 1993 | 1994 |
|---|---|---|---|
| Index | 100.0 | 90.0* | 150.0† |

*(900/1000)100    †(1500/1000)100

Thus we have a story: the value of flowers sold may have increased by 12.5 per cent between 1992 and 1993, but this was achieved only through an increase in price of 25 per cent, the physical quantity actually sold *falling* by 10 per cent. However, in 1994, compared with 1992, value increased by 80 per cent, achieved by a combination of a 20 per cent increase in price (though 4 per cent fall compared with 1993) and 50 per cent increase in quantity.

   Since the value of goods consumed or purchased ($V$) is equal to the price ($P$) multiplied by the quantity ($Q$) of the goods, the index of the value of goods consumed or purchased ($IV$) is equal to the index for prices ($IP$) multiplied by the index for quantities ($IQ$). Thus given only two of the price, quantity or value indices, the third may be deducted. For example, the indices for value and price may be known. Since:

$$IP \times IQ = IV \qquad \therefore \; IQ = \frac{IV}{IP}$$

Thus, if the value of earnings increased by 8 per cent and the prices of goods and services purchased by them (as represented by the Retail Prices Index) increased by 10 per cent, the quantity index or real income changes by $(108/110)100 = 98.2$, i.e. a *fall* of 1.8 per cent.

### Weighted index numbers

At this stage the reader may be somewhat confused as to why index numbers are so prolific, since the previous information could have been arrived at directly from Table 5-1. We have only formalized a relatively simple and intuitively plausible procedure. Index numbers come into their own when we wish to measure the overall change in the prices and quantities of more than one product. The Retail Prices Index, for example, summarizes in one set of figures the changes in prices of around 350 products sold to consumers over time. The Index of Industrial Production attempts to reflect changes in real (physical) production over time for all products produced by the industrial sector into one set of figures, built up from some 700 'activity indicators' (Central Statistical Office, 1989).

Consider the data given in Table 5-1. The change in the overall *quantity* of goods sold between 1992 and 1994 may, at first sight, be evaluated by adding together the physical quantity of goods sold, first, for 1992 and, second, for 1993 and then dividing the former into the latter and multiplying the result by 100 to yield an index, that is:

$$\left[ \frac{900 + 1000}{1000 + 500} \right] 100 = 126.7$$

However, such a procedure is likely to lead to error since the calculation assumes that one bunch of flowers is equally important as one box of chocolate. Furthermore, the result is determined by the units in which the goods are measured. The error involved in this method may be further illustrated by considering a country that produces one nuclear submarine and 100 packets of jelly-babies in period 0; and 10 nuclear submarines and 50 packets of jelly-babies in period 1. The above method would yield a *fall* in the quantity of goods produced of 40.6 per cent between period 0 and 1 since it treats a single nuclear submarine as being equally important as a packet of jelly-babies, which, at least in terms of the relative price the market puts on these goods, is not correct.

An alternative procedure would be to consider the sum of the relative changes in the quantity consumed of each individual product. Thus the index for the quantity of products consumed in 1993 compared with 1992 is equal to:

$$\left[ \frac{900}{1000} + \frac{1000}{500} \right] 100 = 290.0$$

This method is also invalid since first, as the number of products in both periods increase, so too will the index irrespective of whether the quantity of the products sold (or produced) is increasing. Second, while the method does not suffer from the problem of being affected by the units in which quantity is measured, it also attaches in the calculation equal importance to both goods. Table 5.1 shows the value of flowers sold to be much higher than that of chocolate. However, the above method may yield a 'satisfactory' solution if we incorporate into the calculation an indicator of the relative importance of each product. One such indicator is the relative value of each product to the value of total sales.

**Laspeyres relatives**   The change in the quantity of flowers sold between 1992 and 1993 is given by (900/1000)—the relative; the importance or *weight* ascribed to this increase is the share flowers have in total sales value, i.e. 4000/6000. The quantity change of chocolates is (1000/500) and their weight (2000/6000). Laspeyres (weighted relatives) uses as its weights the proportionate importance of each good *in the base period*, i.e.

$$I_{92,\,93} = \left[ \frac{4000(900/1000)}{6000} + \frac{2000(1000/500)}{6000} \right] 100$$

$$= \left[ \frac{4000(900/1000) + 2000(1000/500)}{6000} \right] 100 = 126.7$$

Note how the method correctly ascribes proportionately more weight to the quantity increase for flowers than chocolates, because of its greater importance in terms of sales value. For 1992 compared with 1994:

$$I_{92,\,94} = \left[ \frac{4000(1500/1000) + 2000(550/500)}{6000} \right] 100 = 136.7$$

Note how base period weights are applied throughout the index, as if the importance in the base year was valid for all years. The index is:

| Year | 1992 | 1993 | 1994 |
|------|------|------|------|
| Index | 100.0 | 126.7 | 136.7 |

The above method is the Laspeyres relatives *quantity* index and is referred to as a base-weighted index number since the weights ascribed to changes in quantities sold, consumed (or produced)—these changes are called quantity relatives—are always those pertaining to the base period. The formula for the Laspeyres quantity index is given by:

$$I_{b,\,c} = \frac{\Sigma P_b Q_b (Q_c / Q_b)}{\Sigma P_b Q_b} \times 100$$

$$= \frac{\Sigma V_b (Q_c / Q_b)}{\Sigma V_b} \times 100 \tag{5-1}$$

where $P$, $Q$ and $V$ are price, quantity and value respectively; the subscripts $b$ and $c$ refer to the base and current periods, respectively, the index measuring quantity changes between a current period $c$ and a base period $b$ and the summation extends over different products. It can be looked at as a weighted arithmetic mean of quantity changes; using Eq. (4-2) the frequencies $(f_i)$ reflect the value weights and the $X_i$ the quantity changes.

For similar reasons to those outlined above, the Laspeyres relatives *price* index uses the relative values of individual goods sold, consumed or purchased as weights. These weights are applied to the change in the prices of goods sold, consumed or purchased, i.e. the price relatives. Thus the Laspeyres relatives price index is given by:

$$I_{b,c} = \frac{\Sigma P_b Q_b (P_c/P_b)}{\Sigma P_b Q_b} \times 100$$

$$= \frac{\Sigma V_b (P_c/P_b)}{\Sigma V_b} \times 100 \tag{5-2}$$

Again the weights applied always relate to the relative importance of products in the base period, a characteristic of the Laspeyres index. The Laspeyres relatives *price* index, using data in Table 5-1, is given by:

$$I_{92,93} = \left[ \frac{4000(5.00/4.00) + 2000(3.50/4.00)}{6000} \right] 100 = 112.5$$

$$I_{92,94} = \left[ \frac{4000(4.80/4.00) + 2000(4.00/4.00)}{6000} \right] 100 = 113.3$$

| Year | 1992 | 1993 | 1994 |
|------|------|------|------|
| Index | 100.0 | 112.5 | 113.3 |

The corresponding *value* index is:

| Year | 1992 | 1993 | 1994 |
|------|------|------|------|
| Index | 100.0 | 133.3* | 156.7† |

*(8000/6000)100    †(9400/6000)100

Thus for 1993 compared with 1992 the value of overall sales increased by 33 per cent mainly due to a quantity increase of 26.7 per cent but helped along by a price increase of 12.5 per cent. The sales value increase of 56.7 per cent in 1994, compared with 1992, again was primarily due to an overall quantity increase of 36.7 per cent, accompanied by a 13.3 per cent price increase.

Note we have something of an inconsistency here: Price index × Quantity index (with adjustments for the 100s) do not give us a value index, e.g. 1992:1993, $(112.5 \times 126.7)/100 = 142.5 \neq 133.3$. We shall return to this later.

**Laspeyres aggregative**   Both Laspeyres aggregative and relatives give the same result. They are simply different ways of approaching the same problem and readers may use whichever they prefer.

The Laspeyres aggregative *quantity* index is best derived by first considering the value index between the base period $b$ and a current period $c$, given by:

$$\frac{\Sigma P_c Q_c}{\Sigma P_b Q_b} \times 100 \tag{5-3}$$

While this formula may measure changes in the value of goods sold between periods $b$ and $c$, our purpose is to identify the change in the physical quantity of goods sold. As such, if the term $P_c$ in the numerator is changed to $P_b$, then the quantity sold in period $c$, valued at prices in period $b$ in the numerator, is compared with the quantity sold in period $b$, at prices in period $b$ in the denominator (or the total value of production). The Laspeyres aggregative quantity formula thus holds prices constant in the base period in order to allow changes in the quantity of goods consumed to be identified.

The Laspeyres aggregative quantity index is given by:

$$\frac{\Sigma P_b Q_c}{\Sigma P_b Q_b} \times 100 \tag{5-4}$$

The Laspeyres aggregative quantity index is equal to the Laspeyres relatives quantity index, that is:

$$\frac{\Sigma P_b Q_c}{\Sigma P_b Q_b} \times 100 = \frac{\Sigma P_b Q_b (Q_c/Q_b)}{\Sigma P_b Q_b} \times 100 \qquad (5\text{-}5)$$

since the $Q_b$'s in the numerator on the right-hand side cancel (for example, $6 \times (5(3/5)) = 6 \times 3$).

Similarly, the Laspeyres aggregative *price* index is derived from the value index given in formula (5-3). In order to isolate the effect of price changes, quantities are held constant (being a Laspeyres index) at base period $b$ values. Thus, $Q_c$ in the numerator of formula (5-3) is converted to $Q_b$ to yield the Laspeyres aggregative price index formula:

$$\frac{\Sigma P_c Q_b}{\Sigma P_b Q_b} \times 100 \qquad (5\text{-}6)$$

The Laspeyres relatives price index (Eq. (5-2)) can be identified as being equal to the Laspeyres aggregative price index (formula (5-6)).

Applying data given in Table 5-1 to the Laspeyres aggregative *price* index (formula (5-6)) for comparison between prices:

$$I_{92,\,93} = \left[ \frac{5.00(1000) + 3.50(500)}{6000} \right] 100 = 112.5$$

Note that $\Sigma P_b Q_b$ is the total ($\Sigma$ over products) value ($P \times Q$) in the base period.

$$I_{92,\,94} = \left[ \frac{4.80(1000) + 4.00(500)}{6000} \right] 100 = 113.3$$

For quantity indices using formula (5-4):

$$I_{92,\,93} = \left[ \frac{4.00(900) + 4.00(1000)}{6000} \right] 100 = 126.7$$

$$I_{92,\,94} = \left[ \frac{4.00(1500) + 4.00(550)}{6000} \right] 100 = 136.7$$

The figures are identical to those generated for the relatives method, choice being a matter of personal preference.

**Paasche aggregative**  While Laspeyres maintains base period weights throughout the index, Paasche uses current period weights. Consider again the comparison between the total value of goods consumed (produced) in the current period with that in the base period:

$$\frac{\Sigma P_c Q_c}{\Sigma P_b Q_b} \times 100 \qquad (5\text{-}7)$$

and, for a price index, adjust formula (5-7) so that only changes in price are registered by the measure, that is the quantities are held constant. However, in this instance the quantities will be held constant at current period levels (unlike the Laspeyres formula which utilized constant base period levels). The Paasche current period weighted aggregative *price* index is given by:

$$\frac{\Sigma P_c Q_c}{\Sigma P_b Q_c} \times 100 \qquad (5\text{-}8)$$

For a Paasche aggregative *quantity* index, again consider formula (5-7). We want to hold the prices constant in the comparison and, as it is a current period weighted index, we shall hold them constant at current period prices, i.e.

$$\frac{\Sigma P_c Q_c}{\Sigma P_c Q_b} \times 100 \tag{5-9}$$

Using formula (5-8) for prices:

$$I_{92, 93} = \left[\frac{8000}{4.00(900) + 4.00(1000)}\right] 100 = 105.3$$

$$I_{92, 94} = \left[\frac{9400}{4.00(1500) + 4.00(550)}\right] 100 = 114.6$$

and formula (5-9) for quantities:

$$I_{92, 93} = \left[\frac{8000}{5.00(1000) + 3.50(500)}\right] 100 = 118.5$$

$$I_{92, 94} = \left[\frac{9400}{4.80(1000) + 4.00(500)}\right] 100 = 138.2$$

Note that a Paasche relatives form is given in Table 5-2, which gives equivalent answers to Paasche aggregative.

Table 5-3 summarizes the results, and quite marked differences can be identified for 1992 : 1993 comparisons. We shall look at the choice of method later; for now we draw attention to a property of Laspeyres and Paasche, i.e.

$$Q_{\text{Laspeyres}} \times P_{\text{Paasche}} = \text{Value} \tag{5-10}$$

or

$$Q_{\text{Paasche}} \times P_{\text{Laspeyres}} = \text{Value} \tag{5-11}$$

**Table 5-3**  Results of indices for flowers and chocolates

| Formulae | 1992 | 1993 | 1994 |
|---|---|---|---|
| *Price* | | | |
| Laspeyres | 100.0 | 112.5 | 113.3 |
| Paasche | 100.0 | 105.3 | 114.6 |
| Fisher's 'ideal' | 100.0 | 108.8 | 113.9 |
| Tornqvist | 100.0 | 108.9 | 114.0 |
| Chained: Laspeyres | 100.0 | 112.5 | 117.0 |
|        Fisher's 'ideal' | 100.0 | 108.8 | 112.9 |
| *Quantity* | | | |
| Laspeyres | 100.0 | 126.7 | 136.7 |
| Paasche | 100.0 | 118.5 | 138.2 |
| Fisher's 'ideal' | 100.0 | 122.5 | 137.4 |
| Tornqvist | 100.0 | 122.4 | 137.4 |
| Chained: Laspeyres | 100.0 | 126.7 | 149.3 |
|        Fisher's 'ideal' | 100.0 | 122.5 | 141.3 |
| *Value* | 100.0 | 133.3 | 156.7 |

i.e. a Laspeyres quantity index times a Paasche price index gives a value index (or vice versa) after adjusting for the 100s. From Table 5-3 for 1992:1993, using Eq. (5-10):

$$(126.7 \times 105.3)/100 = 133.4 = 133.3 \ (= 8000/6000)$$
(the slight difference due to rounding errors)

Thus, for example, we use the index for the prices of construction materials to 'deflate' (divide into) changes in the value of construction materials used on site to obtain an estimate of quantity changes in those materials. Then, if the price index is Laspeyres the quantity index will come out as Paasche. This property of $P \times Q = V$ is known as the 'factor reversal test'. Laspeyres and Paasche satisfy it together, but not individually.

As we shall see later, it is difficult to choose between Laspeyres and Paasche so we have a number of 'compromise' formulae using 'averages' of base and current period weights. We shall consider two: Fisher's 'ideal' and Tornqvist.

**Fisher's 'ideal' index**   This is given as the geometric mean of Laspeyres and Paasche, i.e. $\sqrt{\text{La} \times \text{Pa}}$. For example, for a price comparison between 1992:1993, Fisher's 'ideal' is $\sqrt{112.5 \times 105.3} = 108.8$, the remaining results being given in Table 5-3.

**Tornqvist (or Translog)**   An index that is becoming increasingly familiar in economic analysis is given for a price index, by:

$$\exp[\Sigma 0.5(w_b + w_c)\ln(P_c/P_b)] \times 100 \tag{5-12}$$

where 'exp' is the exponent of the expression following it, i.e. 'e' to the power of the expression, and $w_b$ and $w_c$ are the relative value share, weights, of each product in the base and current period respectively. The formula for a quantity index is arrived at by substituting $Q$'s for the $P$'s in Eq. (5-12).

Thus, comparing 1992 with 1993 we have a price index of:

$$\exp\left[0.5\left(\frac{4000}{6000} + \frac{4500}{8000}\right)\ln\left(\frac{5.00}{4.00}\right) + 0.5\left(\frac{2000}{6000} + \frac{3500}{8000}\right)\ln\left(\frac{3.50}{4.00}\right)\right]100$$

$$= \exp[(0.615)0.223 + (0.385)(-0.1335)]100 = 108.9$$

i.e. a similar figure to that from Fisher's 'ideal' index, as is usually the case.

**The chained-base method**   This is not so much a formula, more an approach that can be applied to any of the above index number formulae. Rather than comparing the base period directly with the current period, we do so via a series of links multiplied successively together. For example, an index comparing 1990 with 1995 is given (though appropriate adjustment for the 100s are needed) by

$$I_{90,95} = I_{90,91} \times I_{91,92} \times I_{92,93} \times I_{93,94} \times I_{94,95} \tag{5-13}$$

If the index is chained Laspeyres, $I_{90,91}$ compares 1990 with 1991 using 1990 weights; $I_{91,92}$ compares 1991 with 1992 using 1991 weights, and so on. The weights of the index are recomputed to reflect the changing importance of the products over time. A chained Fisher's 'ideal' would be calculated in a similar manner, but using this formula for each link.

Thus, a chained Laspeyres price index for 1992:1993 is the same as an ordinary or 'fixed based' Laspeyres, i.e. it is the first link. The chained Laspeyres (relatives) for 1992:1994 is:

$$I_{92,94} = I_{92,93} \times I_{93,94}$$

$$= 112.5 \times \left[ \frac{4500(4.80/5.00) + 3500(4.00/3.50)}{8000} \right]$$

$$= 112.5 \times 1.040 = 117.0$$

other results are given in Table 5-3.

As with the measures of central tendency in the previous chapter we are now faced with an embarrassing number of different results in Table 5-3. The changes in quantity between 1992 and 1994 could be shown to have increased by as 'little' as 36.7 per cent or by as much as 49.3 per cent. We must now turn to the question: Which formula is appropriate?

## ON CHOICE OF FORMULA

### 'Fixed' base formulae

If we are comparing retail prices in 1988 with 1993 it is difficult to say whether the weights in 1988 or 1993 are more appropriate. There is at first sight a sense in which the 1993 weights are more up to date. However, we are simply considering with Paasche how prices of a 1993 basket of goods and services changes over the period, and if this basket happens to contain more goods and services (than in 1988) that have had relatively low price increases, should this mean inflation is lower? It is lower for a 1993 basket compared with a 1988 one: but in 1988 we were not using a 1993 basket. It is very difficult to say that only the 1993 basket is relevant. The difference between Laspeyres and Paasche can be substantial (see Table 5-3 and Fowler, 1970) with Laspeyres price indices—given a negative association between price and quantity—being above Paasche prices, with the positions being reversed for quantity indices (see Allen (1975) for more details on this relationship). The large potential gap between Laspeyres and Paasche and the difficulty in choosing between them argue for compromise solutions such as Fisher's 'ideal' and Tornqvist.

There are a number of criteria for choice of formula, which increases the complexity of the matter. There is an axiomatic approach setting out a number of mathematical properties that a good formula ought to have. These include the factor reversal test: Price × Quality = Value. We have seen Laspeyres and Paasche jointly satisfy this test, but not individually. Fisher's 'ideal' satisfies this test, and in fact was termed 'ideal' on its ability to satisfy tests – though it has its faults, failing the transitivity test: that $I_{a,c} = I_{a,b} \times I_{b,c}$. This is hardly surprising since these two tests are inconsistent in that a formula cannot pass both tests. Such inconsistencies militate against the 'passing of tests' as a sole criterion governing choice (see Eichhorn and Vveller (1983) for details of tests).

An alternative approach is from economic theory which has shown that a 'true' price index, which measures the cost of maintaining consumer's standards of living based on the utility derived from purchases, must lie between Laspeyres and Paasche. This argues for Fisher's 'ideal' and Tornqvist, both of which use some form of average of current and base period weights. Economic theory further supports these formulae since they are 'superlative'. While this concept is outside the scope of our text, it is worth mentioning that 'superlative' indices correspond to a wide range of (flexible) functional forms of—in the case of price indices—the underlying utility functions. We buy goods for the utility they provide and economists make assumptions about the functional form of the utility relationship. It is fitting that our index number formulae reflect quite flexible functional forms (see Silver, 1984). These flexible functional forms are used in econometric work and require less restrictions on the relationships considered.

Often more pragmatic considerations are of concern. Laspeyres requires weights for only the base period, making it easier to calculate. For a consumer (retail) prices index, for example, the weights are derived from (expensive) surveys of household spending. Laspeyres is also easy to understand—changes in the prices (quantities) of a fixed (base period) basket of goods and services. While the constant fixed weights lead to bias, the direction of the bias (assuming price and quantities are negatively related) is known. Laspeyres suffers from a substitution bias in that consumers facing products with relatively high price increases will substitute away from these products, thus lessening the impact of inflation. Laspeyres, with its fixed weights, does not reveal this, overstating the price increases actually faced.

However, for many firms data on the prices and quantities of their inputs and outputs should be available and, if computerized, the more complex calculations of Fisher's 'ideal' and Tornqvist are of no consequence. In general, they are to be preferred to Laspeyres and Paasche unless a quite specific question is asked in terms of price or quantity changes of a (base *or* current period) *fixed* basket of goods and services. The results from Fisher's 'ideal' and Tornqvist are generally very similar.

### To chain or not to chain?

Laspeyres, Paasche, Fisher's 'ideal' and Tornqvist may all be chained: their 'fixed' base form keeps them in the world of comparative statics. We compare, for example, 1988 with 1993 and are not interested in what happens between these periods. Chained indices are 'path dependent'. They are concerned with 'dynamic' analysis being affected by the path that prices (quantities) follow over the periods 1988 and 1993. Users have to establish whether the question needing answered is a dynamic or a comparative static one. If workers are concerned with retail prices between the years they have lived through, the intervening years and price changes have affected their livelihood. They may want a chained index, for it represents price changes *over* the period. Yet if management want to know the changes in quantities produced in 1993 compared with what happened specifically five years ago, i.e. 1988, then chaining is inappropriate.

Chaining has a number of problems. Unlike Laspeyres it is not consistent in aggregation. For example, a chain index for quantities of toys produced may show a higher figure than for the two component subindices of 'electronic' and 'non-electronic' toys. It does not happen often, but is confusing when it does. A further problem is that when relative prices and quantities oscillate or 'bounce', e.g. due to seasonal variations, chain indices drift outside the fixed base Laspeyres and Paasche interval to an extent that appears unwarranted (see Szulc, 1983). However, chain indices are representative in the sense that as purchase or production (weights) patterns change, these new weights are reflected in the measure. They also allow new products and new improved data to be readily included since, as soon as they are available for two successive periods, they can be included fully in a link. They are transitive, but do not satisfy the factor reversal test. They have had some theoretical support in that they generally lie within the Laspeyres and Paasche interval and approximate an index derived in theory, which has been called the Divisia index (Forsyth and Fowler, 1981). They may not always add up very well (not consistent in aggregation), unlike fixed base Laspeyres, but they are more likely to add up to a figure that is closer to being correct than Laspeyres.

As should now be apparent, 'choice of formula' is not an easy matter and provided above are an outline of the issues at stake, as opposed to a few easy-to-understand homilies. If computation and data are not a severe limitation, a starting point is to calculate Laspeyres and Paasche and see if the gap is large. If the gap is acceptable, then Fisher's 'ideal' or Tornqvist can be used; if the gap is unacceptable, then the fact that different weighting systems can lead to major discrepancies is of

**Table 5-4**  Index of Industrial Production, 1983 to 1989

|  | All production industries | | |
|---|---|---|---|
|  | 1980 = 100.0 | 1985 = 100.0 | 1980 = 100.0 |
| 1983 | 103.3 |  | 103.3 |
| 1984 | 106.7 |  | 106.7 |
| 1985 | 110.7 | 100.0 | 110.7 |
| 1986 |  | 102.1 | 113.0 [= 110.7(102.1/100)] |
| 1987 |  | 105.8 | 117.1 [= 110.7(105.8/100)] |
| 1988 |  | 109.6 | 121.3 [= 110.7(109.6/100)] |
| 1989 |  | 110.5 | 122.3 [= 110.7(110.5/100)] |

*Source*: Central Statistical Office, *Economic Trends*, HMSO, various issues; figures given above may not correspond with figures in subsequent issues since the index is revised in the light of more reliable data.

interest in itself, reflecting high variability in relative price and quantity changes and a strong association between them, leading to major changes in consumption (production) patterns. The decision to chain must depend in part on purpose, bearing in mind the other considerations raised.

### Shifting the base

One final point on chained indices is worth making. In the UK the index of industrial production uses a fixed base Laspeyres formula. The Central Statistical Office stops the index every five years, and starts again at 100.0 with a new set of weights since they do not wish the weights to become unrepresentative. This is common practice for a range of index numbers in all countries. Table 5-4 illustrates the position for the UK index of industrial production: note that to find a single series of figures extending from 1980 to 1989 we have to shift the series to a common base. In Table 5-4 we have used 1980 = 100.0, and thus have a single series for which the weights are changed every five years. Even when fixed base indices are used, it is difficult to keep your nerve and hold old, unrepresentative weights constant for a long period. It seems that the distinction between fixed base and chain base indices are not so marked: chained indices reweight every period (every year in our example); fixed base indices reweight when the compilers lose their nerve in the face of obviously unrepresentative weights, and have the resources to update them.

The effect of rebasing may not always be large since, if price changes are similar for products, the changing of weights will not affect the index. However, generally we expect rebasing to reduce the estimate of output changes. Production increases at a higher rate where relative prices (and thus weights) fall. Rebasing thus gives less prominence than hitherto to those goods experiencing large production increases. For example, the output-based estimate of Gross Domestic Product (at constant prices) showed the UK's physical production to increase by 16.0 per cent between 1983 and 1987, using 1980 weights. Yet with the weights rebased to 1985, the statisticians cut the growth rate for this period to 14.6 per cent (Bryant and Daniel, 1989).

## AN 'OFFICIAL' INDEX: THE RETAIL PRICES INDEX

### What it includes

All countries have consumer price indices, some more reliable than others, some quite out of date, but all concerned with measuring overall price changes. They are used to measure 'inflation' and thus are important for macro-economic policy. They are also used in wage determination, saving schemes, project appraisal, for uprating State benefits and pensions—in fact, anywhere the effects of inflation have to be borne in mind. International guidelines are produced by the International Labour Office (1992—annual) on their construction, though the methods advocated are not universally adopted.

The United Kingdom's Retail Prices Index (RPI) measures the overall change in the prices of things people buy, including services like travel and entertainment and goods from shops. Savings (including pension contributions and the capital element of mortgages) are excluded being treated as deferred expenditure. Life assurance and national insurance contributions are also excluded, as is income tax, though VAT (being part of the price we pay) and the Poll Tax (community charge—being payment for local government services) are included. There exists an index, the TPI, which excludes the effects of indirect taxes (VAT). This was devised when the move from direct taxes (income tax—not included in the RPI) to indirect tax was causing the RPI to increase further than was believed warranted (Flaxen, 1980). It is an index we hear little of now.

### The cost of shelter

Included in the index is the price changes of housing or 'shelter'. This comprises rent, repairs, rate (community charge) and water charges, owner-occupier's insurance and ground rent and mortgage interest payments. Note that only mortgage interest payments, and not capital gains or losses, are included for owner-occupied housing. However, such gains or losses are obviously to the benefit or detriment of the owner of the accommodation, as argued by Fry and Pashardes (1986). Yet it can also be argued that such gains or losses are not part of consumption but wealth or deferred expenditure and, as is current practice, should be excluded. Given the extent of such gains and losses there is much controversy surrounding how we measure changes in the price of shelter. Governments fight inflation by raising interest rates to squeeze demand. But mortgage interest payments are part of the RPI. There is thus an (albeit once off) increase in the RPI by way of mortgage interest payments, thus increasing the very thing they want to keep down. Furthermore, this increase fuels inflation via higher wage demands. In response to this, the government has drawn attention to a measure of inflation which conveniently strips out the awkward mortgage interest payments to show the 'underlying' rate as opposed to the normal RPI all-items (newspaper) 'headline' rate. Such an index is included in monthly CSO press releases and variants of it exist. For example, at the time of writing we have one published by the Institute of Fiscal Studies and *The Sunday Times* which excludes mortgage interest payments and the 'Poll Tax'. The argument used is that the inclusion of mortgage interest rates creates unfair comparisons with European countries, since such countries by and large use changes in rents or an estimate of rents to represent changes in the cost of shelter. However, the UK is unusual in Europe in that around two-thirds of UK householders are owner-occupiers paying interest on mortgages. In Europe owner-occupation is much less and mortgages tend to be fixed rate or subject to less frequent change. High mortgage rates are part and parcel of the cost of living in the UK and thus should be included. In any event to totally exclude interest rates will be of little help. In the latter half of the 1980s almost every European country saw the shelter component (based on rents) of the index increase at a faster rate than the overall index. By taking out the shelter component (mortgage interest payments), UK rates would appear lower than they should be relative to what is happening in Europe (see Department of Employment, 1975, and Fry and Pashardes, 1986).

### Level of detail provided

Figures for the RPI go back to 1914 (see Department of Employment, 1987a) though the index then was very imperfect and restrictive, concentrating on basics such as bread, potatoes, clothing materials and miscellaneous items—for example, lamp oil and candles were also included. Monthly indices are published in the Central Statistical Office's *Employment Gazette* with longer series in CSO's *Economic Trends* (in particular the annual supplements). The *Employment Gazette* publishes results for 11 major categories of expenditure: food, alcoholic drink, tobacco, housing, fuel and light, durable household goods, clothing and footwear, transport and vehicles, services, meals out and other miscellaneous goods. Various issues provide even more detail, for around 80 subgroups (e.g. fresh fruit) and for around 80 well-defined food items (e.g. bananas). Responsibility for the index lies, since 31 July 1989, with the Central Statistical Office (CSO) who took it over from the Department of Employment. The index is calculated on a monthly basis using Laspeyres, but the weights are revised (chained) each January, for the subsequent 12 months. Bearing in mind the Laspeyres relatives formula, there are two parts to be considered: the weights and price relatives (changes).

**The weights**    The weights are taken from the annual *Family Expenditure Surveys* (FES) (see Department of Employment (1988) and Kemsley *et al.* (1980) for details) for which over 7000 households each year are interviewed and requested to keep a diary of their expenditure for a two-week period, the interviews/diary-keeping being spread evenly over the year in question. The year extends from June to the following June to allow analysis of results in time for the January reweighting. Thus the weights used in any year are, on average, one year out of date. Fry and Pashardes (1986) show this to have introduced at worst a 0.8 percentage point error over the period 1974 to 1984. Not all households asked to take part in the FES agreed, and an approximate 30 per cent non-response rate tended to under-represent households without children, self-employed, older, with many cars, lower rateable values, and less (for male) and more (for female) qualified heads of households. These may well have quite different expenditure patterns than the population under study. Response errors for alcohol and tobacco are compensated for by using other sources of data. Excluded from the weights are the 4 per cent of households with the highest incomes and pensioner households mainly dependent on State benefits in order that 'typical' expenditure patterns are represented. Separate quarterly price indices (excluding housing) are published for pensioner households, though, surprisingly, there is little difference in the resulting indices (see Carruthers *et al.*, 1980).

**Price changes**    Data on prices are collected on almost 600 goods and services, each considered to be representative of similar items in the group; for example, price changes of glasses of whisky, vodka, gin and wine, and bottles of whisky, vodka, gin, brandy, vermouth, sherry and various imported wines, are considered to be representative of 'all spirits and liqueurs, fortified and non-fortified wines'. For each representative good or service a large number of price quotations in different parts of the country (more than 180 towns) over different types of shops are collected by civil servants from the unemployment benefits office. Thus, it is claimed that around 175 000 price quotations (e.g. around 800 for sugar) are collected. A report on the practice showed that 'only' about 95 000 are collected with prices in new towns under-represented (Comptroller and Auditor General, 1990), though the Central Statistical Office reacted to the report by seeking to remedy matters.

Average prices are then calculated for each representative item as sold in a type of shop (co-operative, multiple or independent) in a given region (12 regions), and compared with the average price in the preceding January to form the (36) price relatives for each item. Care is exercised in the definition of the products to ensure that like is compared with like, though changes in quality mean this is not always the case. Adjustments for quality changes are made where practical (see United Nations (1977, 1979) and Deaton and Muellbauer (1980) for some methods) though the potential for bias due to ignoring quality changes or inappropriate adjustments is great, and it is likely that the RPI is overstating price changes because of this.

The weights are combined with the price relatives to form the index, which is published approximately 4 to 6 weeks after the price data are collected. In its entirety it is not an unimpressive venture. The weights or relative importance of each price change are revised annually and are based on detailed diaries of spending by a random sample of around 7000 households. Prices charged for around 600 representative items are collected by region and type of store requiring, in principle, 175 000 monthly quotations. The results are compiled and published in just over a month from the period to which the price data relate. (For further details on the index, see Department of Employment (1987b) and Fry and Pashardes (1986).)

Two final points are worth bearing in mind. First, the RPI may be presented in the media in a number of forms. Often it takes the form of the percentage change in (for example) May of the current year compared with May of the previous year. The aim is to derive for the current point in time (May of the current year) the annual rate comparing 'like with like', so seasonal influences are minimized. Alternatively, you might require the annual changes for one year compared with another; or the average index for the year compared with that for the preceding year. Then there are monthly changes: the rate of change for this month compared with the preceding month, thus including seasonal effects.

Secondly, the index is an overall measure and, as Moore (1990) argues, its presentation and composition must inevitably be a compromise since it cannot itself represent price changes for each individual household and serve all possible uses at the same time. If anything, this argues for a range of indices for different regions (as supplied by private organizations) or for particular income groups or whatever. As noted before, the CSO does publish indices for pensioner households. However, there will always remain a need for *the* RPI as the overall measure of price changes.


## USING COMPUTERS

A company may, for example, have several hundred different types of baby food with lines for specific ages, different courses (main/desert), different meals for each course, different sizes for each meal and types of packaging. For each of these products we require figures for two of the three items of (average) 'price', 'quantity' and 'value' since the third can always be deduced from any two. All of this should be computerized (if not this is your first task) and your problem will be to decide whether the formula for the index numbers are best written within the existing system, or whether these data can be input in a form that can be read by Minitab or Lotus 1-2-3.


### Minitab

Since the calculations involve columns of data, each row being a product, the LET statements can be used to calculate the indices, as shown below:

```
MTB > LET K1=(SUM('WEIGHT'*('PRICE 1'/'PRICE 0')))/SUM('WEIGHT'))*100
```


### Lotus 1-2-3

For Lotus 1-2-3 we might derive a Laspeyres price index by first putting the value weights for each of the 200 products in rows A2 to A201; the first period's prices would be rows B2 to B201, the next period's C2 to C201, etc. In B250 we would type the weights times the price change for the first product:

```
+(A2*C2/B2)
```

which would then be copied for all products:

```
/C
B250..B250
B251..B449
```

In, say, A460 we would enter 100.0 for the index for period 0; in B460 the index for the first period would be:

```
(@SUM(B250..B449)/@SUM(A2..A201))*100.
```

## EXERCISES

**5-1** Given below is the average earnings index for all employees in manufacturing industries which measures the change in the money *value* of average earnings from January 1989 to December 1989. Also given is the all-items Retail Prices Index for the same period. Derive a series for this period for *real* average earnings, showing changes in the quantities of goods and services consumed from average earnings.

(*N.B.* The two indices have different base periods and it may be useful to shift their bases to a common reference point of January 1989 = 100.0.)

| | 1989 | | | | | | | | | | | |
|---|---|---|---|---|---|---|---|---|---|---|---|---|
| | Jan. | Feb. | Mar. | Apr. | May | June | July | Aug. | Sept. | Oct. | Nov. | Dec. |
| Average earnings (1988 = 100) | 104.2 | 105.0 | 105.7 | 107.8 | 108.0 | 109.4 | 110.3 | 108.3 | 109.5 | 110.6 | 112.2 | 113.9 |
| Retail Prices Index (1987 = 100) | 111.0 | 111.8 | 112.3 | 114.3 | 115.0 | 115.4 | 115.5 | 115.8 | 116.6 | 117.5 | 118.5 | 118.8 |

*Source*: Department of Employment, *Employment Gazette*, vol. 98, no. 3, March 1990.

**5-2** You are given the following information concerning a factory which produces only two products: brand A and brand B cigarettes.

| Product | 1989 | | | 1990 | | | 1991 | | | 1992 | | |
|---|---|---|---|---|---|---|---|---|---|---|---|---|
| | P | Q | V | P | Q | V | P | Q | V | P | Q | V |
| Brand A | 0.25 | 1.5 | 375 | 0.30 | 1.4 | 420 | 0.45 | 1.3 | 585 | 0.50 | 1.3 | 650 |
| Brand B | 0.35 | 0.4 | 140 | 0.45 | 0.5 | 225 | 0.55 | 0.5 | 275 | 0.60 | 0.4 | 240 |
| Total | | | 515 | | | 645 | | | 860 | | | 890 |

In the table, $P$ is the ex-factory price per packet (£), $Q$ is the number of packets produced (millions) and $V$ is the value of production (£000) (*N.B.* 1 million = 1 000 000). Compile:

(a) Laspeyres index of production for the years 1985 to 1988 inclusive.
(b) Laspeyres index of prices for the years 1985 to 1988 inclusive.

**5-3** A factory manufactures three products: combined harvesters, tractors and rubber ducks. The following data show the prices ($P$), physical quantities produced ($Q$), and value of output ($V = PQ$) for each of the products in 1990, 1991 and 1992. ($V$ is shown in £000's, $P$ in £s and $Q$ in units.)

| Product | 1990 | | | 1991 | | | 1992 | | |
|---|---|---|---|---|---|---|---|---|---|
| | $P$ | $Q$ | $V$ | $P$ | $Q$ | $V$ | $P$ | $Q$ | $V$ |
| Combined harvester | 100 000 | 5 | 500 | 120 000 | 4 | 480 | 150 000 | 1 | 150 |
| Tractor | 15 000 | 3 | 45 | 17 500 | 10 | 175 | 17 500 | 20 | 350 |
| Rubber duck | 1 | 1 000 | 1 | 0.5 | 10 000 | 5 | 0.3 | 50 000 | 15 |
| Total | | | 546 | | | 660 | | | 515 |

(a) Calculate the Laspeyres price index for this factory for the years 1990 to 1992 inclusive.

(b) Calculate the Paasche (aggregative) price index for the factory for the years 1990 to 1992 inclusive.

(c) Compare your two answers and calculate alternative formulae which make use of base *and* current period weights in year upon year comparisons. Which formulae do you think are appropriate?

# MEASURES OF ASSOCIATION

Chapter 4 was concerned with summarizing the observations on a variable. For example, our variable might be the number of chocolate bars consumed by UK households. We might determine the arithmetic mean number of bars consumed per household along with the standard deviation. While such information is useful in establishing the extent of the market and variability in consumption patterns, it gives no insights into which, if any, other variables are associated with variability in household consumption of chocolate bars. It might be the case that variation in household consumption of chocolate bars is associated with variation in the number of persons in the household, the disposable income of the household, proportion of children living in the household, take-up-rate of school lunches, region lived in, exposure to advertising and so forth. Understanding variability in household chocolate bar consumption rests not only with its description, valuable as this may be, but also in establishing the other variables to which it is related, and the strength and nature of the relationship. The analysis of the relationships between variables is central to effective policy making. For example, a relationship between wastage rates (employees leaving an organization) and length of service is an important element in successful manpower planning. Alternatively, variation in sales over time may be associated with variation over time in the relative price of the product along with variation in advertising expenditure. An understanding of the strength and nature of the association between sales and relative price changes is essential in determining pricing strategies. Similarly, the effectiveness of advertising expenditure is determined by examining how its variation has been associated with variations in sales.

Our life should thus not be confined to describing the variables around us, but should extend to analysing the relationships between these variables. It is almost as if the previous chapters have only been concerned with answering each clue in a crossword puzzle, without appreciating that there is an interdependency between the solutions to the clue, and if we ignore this interdependency we reduce our effectiveness in dealing with the crossword of business and economic life.

This chapter is divided into three parts and examines in turn association between variables measured on three different scales.

| Scale | Measure |
|---|---|
| (a) Interval/ratio | Product moment correlation coefficient |
| (b) Ordinal | Spearman's correlation and brief reference to Somer's delta, Kendall's tau and Goodman and Kruskal's gamma |
| (c) Nominal | Cramer's $V$ (chi-squared) and Guttman's lambda |

In part (a) we consider the product moment correlation coefficient which requires an interval/ratio scale of measurement for the variables considered. The distinction between these scales has been mentioned in Chapter 2 but is reiterated later in this context. The discussion of the product moment correlation coefficient remains the cornerstone of this chapter since many general principles which apply to measures in other parts of the chapter are considered here. It may be that your course only considers the product moment correlation coefficient, in which case this part is self-contained. In some courses on statistics measures of association based on ordinal and nominal scales are considered separately later, so you may return to parts (b) and (c). They are all part of the single problem-orientated task: determining if an association exists between two variables, and, if so, its nature and strength.

## MEASURES OF ASSOCIATION: INTERVAL/RATIO SCALE

The product moment correlation coefficient, also known as Pearson's correlation coefficient (hereafter referred to as 'the correlation coefficient') is a means by which the nature and extent of an association between two variables can be discovered. We shall consider the need to examine theory, data and look at the assumptions implicit in the method, before considering the calculation, why it works, and how to interpret the results. Consider the data in Table 6-1 and a possible association between regional variation in the possession of freezers and household income. We do not simply undertake the calculation and get a result. You have to ask yourself why you expect a relationship (*theory*) and, if so, the nature of the relationship (positive or negative, or possibly both). You also have to know something of the quality of the *data* used and the scales of measurement, use of a *scatter diagram* to identify outliers and the linearity of the data. All of this is how we start.

**Table 6-1**  Ownership of freezers and household income for UK regions 1984–1985*

| Region | Average weekly household income (£) | Percentage of households having deep freezers† |
|---|---|---|
| North | 170.4 | 57 |
| Yorkshire and Humberside | 179.1 | 56 |
| East Midlands | 203.2 | 65 |
| East Anglia | 204.8 | 71 |
| South East | 248.0 | 70 |
| South West | 208.8 | 70 |
| West Midlands | 192.4 | 58 |
| North West | 183.2 | 60 |
| Wales | 187.1 | 63 |
| Scotland | 198.3 | 51 |
| Northern Ireland | 172.9 | 43 |

*Average of figures for each year.
†Includes 'fridge-freezers' as 'deep-freezers'.
*Source*: Central Statistical Office, *Regional Trends 22, 1987 Edition*, London: HMSO, 1988.

**Getting started**

**Theory**   Before calculating the correlation coefficient we must have some idea of the theory (or to challenge an association—the lack of theory) as to why an association exists.

- *Dependency*   Theory should allow us to hypothesize the dependency of the relationship. We consider a relationship between two variables and wish to consider which variable depends on which. We would hypothesize that regional variation in possession of freezers is dependent on regional variation in income; we would not talk of regional income variations arising because of variation in possession of freezers. The dependent (criterion, endogenous) variable is labelled $Y$ (possession of freezer) and the independent (predictor, explanatory, controlled or exogenous) variable $X$ (income). In some cases it is more difficult: for the data in Exercise 6-1 we need to consider whether increases in readership of the *Sun* newspaper arises from increases in alcohol consumption, or vice versa. The choice of $Y$ and $X$ does not affect the calculation of the correlation coefficient, but helps aid interpretation of the results and is important for the work in the next chapter.

- *Nature* (sign) *and strength of association*   Theory should tell us whether the association is expected to be positive (high values of $Y$ associated with high values of $X$—low $Y$, low $X$) or negative (high $Y$, low $X$—low $Y$, high $X$). High income levels lead to high freezer possession and low incomes with low freezer possession—a positive association in this case. It may not be strong, since purchases may not be from income, but (more so in some regions) from credit or savings. Also, major outgoings on other items may be higher in one region than in another (e.g. mortgage repayments). Regional variations in attitudes to freezer ownerships or different demographic profiles (age of householders, number of people in household) may affect the desire to buy, as may variation in the prices, promotion, distribution, or choice/nature of products available in different regions. We would expect a positive relationship, but not a very strong one.

- *Causation*   Theory may suggest that variation in one variable (income) causes variation in another (freezer possession); the correlation coefficient does not prove it, it simply shows that a mathematical association of the correct sign exists. If the world does behave in the way theory predicts we have not determined an unassailable truth or finding. The association may be compatible with other theories, some unthought of. The same dilemma applies to the sciences which have seen their fair share of 'laws' and 'facts' come and go. Yet theory corroborated by empirical evidence gives us a good basis for believing we have discovered something. Yet we must always be careful. The association may be spurious—i.e. it may have occurred by chance. We may select by chance an unusual sample of values that do not display an association when one exists, or do display one that does not exist. Yule (1971) 'discovered' that Church of England marriages between 1866 and 1921 were strongly and positively related to the mortality rate. Alternatively, third (or more) variable effects may mislead us. We might have a theory that more storks cause more births. Regional data from Sweden on storks nesting and birth rates happen to confirm this (via the correlation coefficient); we have a theory and proof (Scott, 1979). But the third variable is of course chimney stacks—urban areas have more stacks, higher birth rates and storks nest on stacks, and thus the association. Fisher (1960) cites the apparently true story of peasants of a province of Russia observing a strong association between the number of doctors in a given area (sent by the government to stem a cholera epidemic) and the incidence of cholera; the peasants murdered all the doctors. As a final example, it is undeniable that average earnings of women in the UK are much lower than those of men. But this should not be claimed as proof of their relative ability—there are a host of other variables operating in favour of men and against women in this respect. The message is: get the theory of association right before attempting to measure it to prove something.

**Data**  Having outlined what we expect in theory, we move to the empirical world of data to see if it is borne out. Our concern is that there may in reality be an association, but inadequacy of the data prevents us from identifying it.

- *Reliability*  Here, as in Chapter 1, we consider the sources of error in the data—sampling error, response error, non-response error and design error—to see if the data are reliable. We know little here of how the data in Table 6-1 were collected, though the two variables come from different surveys which may have different coverages. If our data were very poor we might discover no association, not because an association did not exist, but because the data collected to measure it were not reliable. Thus, always check the reliability of data.

- *Proxy variable*  Often what we want to measure as a theoretical concept is difficult in practice (for example, changes in the physical volume of output, including quality of service, provided by a hospital). Proxy variables are indicators of this; a very poor proxy being the number of occupied bed-hours. IQ has been used as a proxy for intelligence. In our example the expected strength of the empirical relationship between income and possession of freezers is weakened because fridge-freezers are defined as freezers and no account is taken of the quality of freezers (the South East may have a higher income and better quality of freezers—but only 'possession' is considered by the data).

- *Aggregation*  Our study is concerned with explaining *regional* variation in freezer possession by recourse to regional variation in income. Quite different findings may arise from a study for variations in possession of freezers for the UK over time, against variation in income for the UK over time, or by individuals within a region. We need to establish in theory what level of aggregation is required for a particular purpose, and use the appropriate data.

- *Scales of measurements*  The use of the correlation coefficient requires data to be measured on an interval or ratio scale. If data are not measured on either of these scales, alternative measures considered later should be used. An interval scale has a hierarchy with equal differences between successive values; for example, age lies on a ratio scale—the difference in years between a 20 and 21 year old being the same as that between an 80 and 81 year old (though it may not feel it). For practical purposes, ratio scales are treated as being similar to interval scales, the only difference being that the latter does not have a natural origin. An ordinal (or ranked) scale has a hierarchy, but the differences between successive values are not constant. For example, a human resource manager may examine if academic qualifications are associated with some aspect of performance. These may be ranked in order of a Master's degree > a Bachelor's degree > a GCE 'A' level > a GCSE, but the differences between these qualifications are not, however, equal. Some may ascribe the values of 1, 2, 3 and 4 respectively to these qualifications, but this would still not make the differences equal in reality. All that would be done would be to impose on the variable a scale that bears no relation to the reality of the differences. The final scale is the nominal—by name—(or classificationary) scale, which has no hierarchy, simply assigning cases to pigeon-holes on the basis of whether they do or do not possess a characteristic. The sex of an individual is measured on a nominal scale, as is the region in which the individual lives, or his or her religious beliefs. Thus a decision is necessary for our example on incomes and freezers as to whether the scales of measurement used are interval (or ratio) so that we can proceed. In both cases there are natural hierarchies and the differences in successive values are the same—the difference between an income of £220 and £230 is the same as that between £280 and £290. A more elegant theory would say that at higher income levels the utility received from £10 is different from that at lower incomes, but we leave this aside for our purposes. For freezer possession the difference between 20 and 21 per cent possession is the same as the difference between 80 and 81 per cent, 1 per cent in each case on an interval scale. Had one variable been on an interval scale and the other on an ordinal (ranked scale), one approach would be to transform the interval scale to an ordinal one and apply a technique more appropriate to ordinal scales. The matter is far from straightforward since we lose information in such transformations; methods based on interval scales called parametric methods are more 'power efficient' but may require restrictive assumptions. (For further details on all of this, see Gaito (1980).)

In summary: examine the data to be used to test your theory, unreliable data/use of proxy variables may temper the strength of the relationship expected—you may end up with a weak association only because of the poor data used. Consider if the aggregation of the data is suitable for your theory and that interval or ratio scales of measurement are used for the correlation coefficient.

**Scatter diagrams** (outliers and linearity) The scatter diagram helps identify whether outliers are present in the data, and whether the overall pattern of the data is linear. Both are important considerations in the use of the correlation coefficient.

The scatter diagram is simply a plot of one variable against another. We take possession of freezer as the dependent variable on the $Y$-axis and income as the independent variable on the $X$-axis. [Where neither variable can be judged dependent or independent, the choice of axis is arbitrary.] The pairs of observations are plotted on the diagram as shown in Fig. 6-1. For example, for the North, $X = 170.4$ and $Y = 57$ and the single cross representing this point is labelled 'North'. Other points are similarly derived, though without labels.

Observations whose unusual values temper or obscure underlying patterns in the data are outliers. Their treatment depends on why they occur. We could 'discover' relationships when none exists by enthusiastically removing awkward values by calling them outliers. This is not acceptable. For example, removing the South East (top right of Fig. 6-1) would certainly improve the pattern—that area being a little out on a limb—but its existence is part of the evidence that regional variations in income do not fully reflect regional variation in freezer possession. If they arise from a one-off unusual phenomena, or from a group of observations whose values are influenced by a third variable, then they should be removed. For example, if there was civil war in Wales in the year in question, we would probably exclude it from the analysis. Often scatter diagrams reveal patterns and prompts which help develop theory.

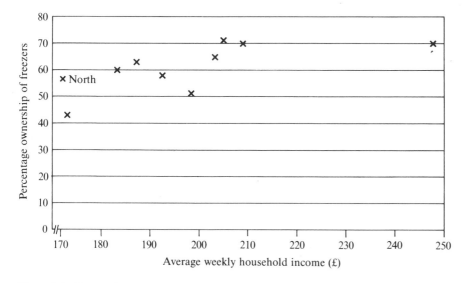

**Figure 6-1** Scatter diagram of freezer ownership by income for UK regions

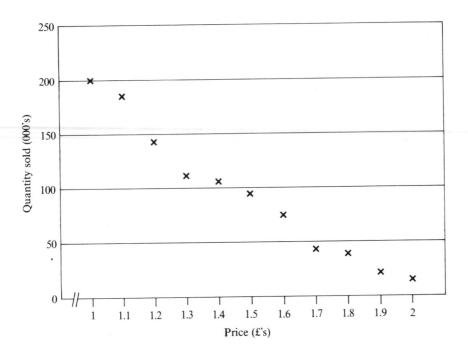

**Figure 6-2**  Scatter diagram: negative association—sales and price

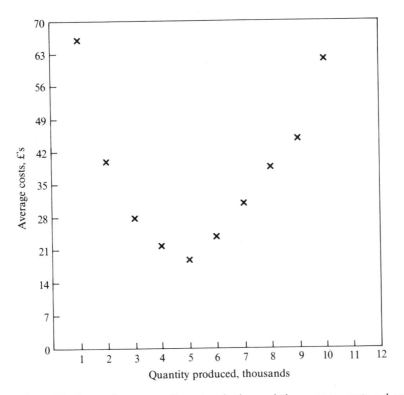

**Figure 6-3**  Scatter diagram: non-linear (quadratic association—average costs and quantity produced)

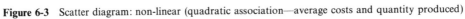

A second function of scatter diagrams concerns the fact that the correlation coefficient assumes an underlying linear association, i.e. that the pattern apparent from the data can be best replicated by a straight line. The scatter diagram can help with ascertaining the validity of this. The scatter diagram not only helps us to identify whether the relationship is roughly linear, but also, if it is linear, whether the slope of the line is positive or negative. A negative slope is depicted in Fig. 6-2 and here high values of $Y$ are associated with low values of $X$ and vice versa, as would be the case were $Y$ sales and $X$ price. Figure 6-1 depicts a positive linear association (high $Y$ with high $X$; low $Y$ with low $X$). Relationships need not always be linear. Figure 6-3 shows a relationship between average cost and quantity produced which takes a non-linear (quadratic) form. As quantity produced increases, economies of scale move in and average cost decreases. However, with further increases in quantity produced the organization becomes so large and bureaucratic that average costs rise. There is a relationship between average costs and quantity produced—but it is not a linear one.

At this point it may be thought that the scatter diagram is sufficient. We can learn from Fig. 6-1 about the nature of the relationship (linear with positive slope) and its strength. If the points fell on a straight line (as in Fig. 6-4), instead of around it, we could then use the linear model to explain *perfectly* the variation in freezer possession by variation in income. For example, a £5 increase in income in a region would lead to a known (depending on the slope) increase in the percentage of households possessing freezers. As the points spread away from the line the relationship becomes weaker, as in the case of Fig. 6-1. In Fig. 6-5 there is no discernible relationship. Thus, one might ask, why not use judgement, taking the spread of the points away from the line to be an indicator of the strength of the relationship? First, as was found in Chapter 3, the visual spread of points will be

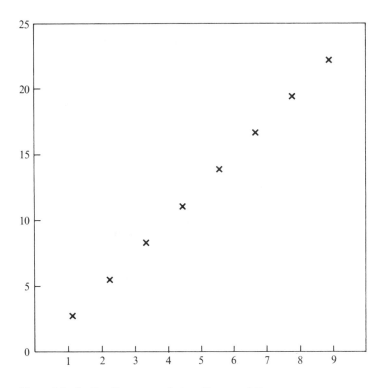

**Figure 6-4**  Scatter diagram: perfect positive association

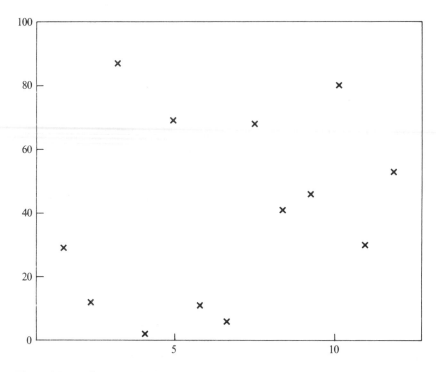

**Figure 6-5** No linear association

determined by the scale chosen for the graph. Second, the eye will be judging the overall dispersion of points from an imagined line (in this case) which best represents the underlying relationship. There may be some difficulty balancing points with large dispersion against those with smaller dispersion. Third, a bad initial judgement on where the line lies would lead one to suspect a weaker relationship than really exists. Much better that a properly constituted measure be derived to put the analysis on an objective, rather than subjective, basis. The measures may have their defects, but at least these, unlike the subjective bias of an individual, will be known.

Given a problem—be it to test if an association between two variables exists or to challenge the conclusions of someone who has calculated a correlation coefficient to prove an association exists—you first need to say in *theory* why you think there is an association, examine the quality of the *data* used and *scales of measurement*, and construct a *scatter diagram* to see if the relationship is linear or if outliers exist. Then we can proceed.

We now turn our attention to the calculation of the correlation coefficient (denoted by $r$); the result has two components: the sign and the numerical value. The sign tells us whether any association is positive or negative, the numerical value denotes the strength ranging from 0 (no linear association) to 1 (perfect linear association). A value of $r = -0.8$ shows a strong negative association.

### How do we calculate $r$?

The formula for $r$ is usually given in two (algebraically equivalent) forms shown by Eqs (6-1) and (6-2), the former being more helpful in explaining why it works, and the latter being easier to calculate (though this may not be immediately apparent). Both give the same answers.

$$r = \frac{\Sigma(X - \bar{X})(Y - \bar{Y})/n}{\sqrt{\Sigma(X - \bar{X})^2/n}\sqrt{\Sigma(Y - \bar{Y})^2/n}} \tag{6-1}$$

$$= \frac{n\Sigma XY - \Sigma X \Sigma Y}{\sqrt{[n\Sigma X^2 - (\Sigma X)^2][n\Sigma Y^2 - (\Sigma Y)^2]}} \tag{6-2}$$

Equation (6-2) is quite straightforward to apply. The sigma ($\Sigma$) sign denotes that we sum the results of each calculation across regions. Thus $\Sigma X$ in Table 6-2 is simply the sum of each individual $X$-value = 2148.2; similarly $\Sigma Y = 664$. $\Sigma XY$ is the sum of each individual $X$ multiplied by its corresponding $Y$. Thus for the first region in Table 6-2, we see that North has a value for $XY$ of $170.4 \times 57 = 9712.8$. Similar calculations are undertaken for other regions; the sum of these products being equal to 130 953.7. $\Sigma X^2$ is equal to 424 251.4, which is the sum of each individual $X$ multiplied by itself (squared). Similarly, $\Sigma Y^2$ is equal to 40 834, which is the sum of each individual $Y$ multiplied by itself. $n$ is the number of *pairs* of observations, which is equal to 11, and by substituting these values into Eq. (6-2) we end up with:

$$r = \frac{11(130\,953.7) - (2148.2)(664)}{\sqrt{[11(424\,251.4) - (2148.2)^2][11(40\,834) - (664)^2]}}$$

$$= \frac{1\,440\,490.7 - 1\,426\,404.8}{\sqrt{[52\,002.16][8278]}}$$

$$= +0.68, \quad \text{i.e. a fairly strong positive association}$$

Note that $\Sigma XY$ is generally not equal to $\Sigma X \Sigma Y$—the former being each individual $X$ multiplied by its corresponding $Y$, the products then being summed; the latter is the sum of all the $X$'s multiplied by the sum of all the $Y$'s.

Needless to say, Eq. (6-1) could have been used for the calculation and would have yielded exactly the same results; however, subtracting each value of $X$ and $Y$ from their respective means is more laborious than the above process. Many pocket calculators have built-in facilities for calculating $\Sigma X$ and $\Sigma X^2$ and in some cases $r$ itself.

**Table 6-2**  Ownership of freezers and household income for UK regions 1984–1985

| Region | $X$ | $Y$ | $XY$ | $X^2$ | $Y^2$ |
|---|---|---|---|---|---|
| North | 170.4 | 57 | 9 712.8 | 29 036.16 | 3 249 |
| Yorkshire and Humberside | 179.1 | 56 | 10 029.6 | 32 076.81 | 3 136 |
| East Midlands | 203.2 | 65 | 13 208.0 | 41 290.24 | 4 225 |
| East Anglia | 204.8 | 71 | 14 540.8 | 41 943.04 | 5 041 |
| South West | 208.8 | 70 | 14 616.0 | 43 597.44 | 4 900 |
| South East | 248.0 | 70 | 17 360.0 | 61 504.00 | 4 900 |
| West Midlands | 192.4 | 58 | 11 159.2 | 37 017.76 | 3 364 |
| North West | 183.2 | 60 | 10 992.0 | 33 562.24 | 3 600 |
| Wales | 187.1 | 63 | 11 787.3 | 35 006.41 | 3 969 |
| Scotland | 198.3 | 51 | 10 113.3 | 39 322.89 | 2 601 |
| Northern Ireland | 172.9 | 43 | 7 434.7 | 29 894.41 | 1 849 |
| Total ($\Sigma$) | 2 148.2 | 664 | 130 953.7 | 424 251.4 | 40 834 |

### Why does the formula for $r$ work?

The denominator (bottom line) to Eq. (6-1) is the standard deviation of $X$ multiplied by the standard deviation of $Y$ using the formula given in Chapter 4 (Eq. (4-4)). The numerator (top line) is called the covariance. The respective standard deviations show how $X$ and $Y$ vary from their respective means. The covariance is concerned with the simultaneous variation of $X$ and $Y$ about their means. From Table 6-2 the mean of the regional incomes is $\Sigma X/n = 2148.2/11 = 195.29$ and the mean of the regional percentage of households possessing freezers is $664/11 = 60.36$ per cent. The North has an $X$-value of 170.4; $(X - \bar{X})$ for the North is $(170.4 - 195.29) = -24.89$. The $Y$-value for the North is 57; $(Y - \bar{Y}) = (57 - 60.36) = -3.36$. Thus the covariance term for this region is

$$(X - \bar{X})(Y - \bar{Y}) = -24.89(-3.36) = +83.63$$

The North is below regional averages on freezer possession *and* income (negatives) but positive on the covariance; so how does this covariance help?

Consider Fig. 6-6; the $Y$ and $X$ axes are freezer possession and income, and the horizontal dotted line represents the mean value of 195.29 for $X$ and the vertical dotted line the mean value of 60.36 for $Y$. The North can be seen to lie in quadrant 4, being below average on both axes. All points in this quadrant will have a positive covariance as the negative deviation from $\bar{X}$ is multiplied by a negative deviation from $\bar{Y}$, to yield a positive product. The South East is above both of these mean values in quadrant 2. At $Y = 70$ it is above $\bar{Y}$ and at $X = 248$ it is above $\bar{X}$. Its contribution to the covariance is positive

$$\{(248.0 - 195.29)(70 - 60.36) = 508.12\}$$

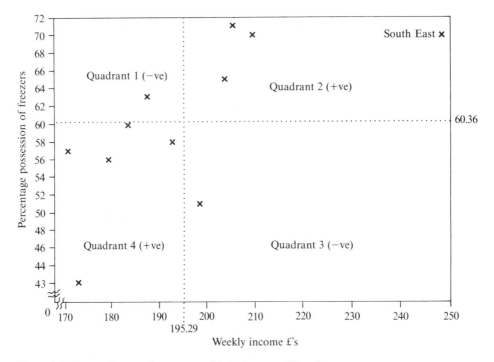

**Figure 6-6**   Scatter diagram: freezer ownership by income, UK regions

as are all points in this quadrant, being the product of two positive values. Observations falling in quadrants 2 and 4 will have positive contributions to the covariance.

However, observations falling in quadrants 1 and 3 will have negative contributions to the covariance. For quadrant 1: $(X - \bar{X})$ will be negative and $(Y - \bar{Y})$ will be positive—the product being negative. Similarly, for quadrant 3, the product will be negative with positive $(X - \bar{X})$ and negative $(Y - \bar{Y})$. The scatter of points in Fig. 6-6 fall predominantly in quadrants 2 and 4, which are both positive, yielding when summed, $\Sigma(X - \bar{X})(Y - \bar{Y})$, a positive covariance. Had the points dominated quadrants 1 and 3, the covariance would have been negative reflecting a negative underlying slope to the relationship. In Fig. 6-6 the relationship is positive since the negative contribution to the covariance of the few regions in quadrants 1 and 3 is more than outweighed by the positive ones in quadrants 2 and 4. Since the standard deviations are always positive the sign of the covariance holds for the correlation coefficient in Eq. (6-1). Thus the sign of the covariance tells us about the nature of the relationship, positive or negative.

The magnitude of the covariance is the key to finding out about the strength of the relationship. In a perfect positive linear relationship all points lie on a straight line which must pass through the means thus allowing no points in quadrants 1 and 3 to detract from the covariance. Figure 6-5 showed no linear association between $X$ and $Y$, with points in all four quadrants, the positive and negative contributions to the covariance term for each region amalgamating to yield a figure close to zero. The covariance by itself is not an appropriate measure of association since its value depends upon the units of measurement used for each variable. For example, a similar exercise conducted 10 years ago would have shown smaller figures for both $X$ and $Y$ and thus a smaller dispersion from their respective means and a smaller covariance. However, the strength of the relationship may well be the same then as now. We need to adjust the covariance for the dispersion in the $X$ and $Y$ variables to bring it to a standard scale. This is achieved by dividing the covariance by both the standard deviation for $X$ and $Y$ as shown in Eq. (6-1). Thus the smaller covariance for $X$ and $Y$ 10 years ago would be deflated (divided) by the smaller standard deviations holding in those years to yield an appropriate measure. The covariance also involves division by the sample size, $n$, in Eq. (6-1) since otherwise the size of the covariance would increase as more points were considered. Since the strength of the relationship should not depend on the number of observations, we divide by $n$ to give an average figure for the covariance. Equation (6-1) provides a measure of the linear association between $X$ and $Y$; the sign denoting the nature of the relationship (positive or negative) and the numerical value the strength of the relationship: 0 denoting no linear association and 1 perfect linear association. (For a formal demonstration of this see Maddala (1977), p. 71.)

**Interpreting the result for $r$**

- The sign of $r$ tells you if a positive or negative relationship exists.
- The value between 0 and 1 tells you the strength of the association: 0 is no linear association; 1 is perfect linear association.
- Finally, it is necessary to determine if the difference between the result and zero (no linear association) is statistically significant (at a given level) or otherwise. It is to this point that we direct the remainder of this section.

At first sight there is no apparent reason why the strength and sign are not sufficient to give a result—the problem arises when we are dealing with a random sample of data as opposed to the population of all values. For example, if our concern was with whether an association existed between age and number of chocolate bars consumed in a year, we would take a random sample of individuals, collect the appropriate data and calculate the correlation coefficient. But because the data are from a sample, a test of statistical significance is required. In statistical analysis in economics and business we take data and results for one period as the basis of policy action in another and thus consider the data as a sample. It is common to treat, for example, the $n = 11$ regions as if they were a sample from a population of the results from many years. The logic is not perfect since subsequent years may have different degrees of association, but this is borne in mind when applying the results. We thus treat the data in Table 6-1 as if they formed a random sample.

Results based on data from a random sample also have associated sampling errors. Sampling error was discussed in Chapter 1 and arises simply because we are concerned with a sample. A result based on a random sample of 50 pairs of observations is, other things being equal, more reliable than one based on a random sample of 5 observations. This is because larger sampling errors are associated with a small sample of 5. The extent of the sampling errors can be measured, with certain caveats.

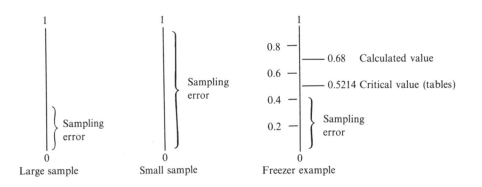

**Figure 6-7** Principle of sampling error

Figure 6-7 illustrates the principle. The value of $r$ ranges (ignoring signs) from 0 to 1. Yet, since our result is based on a random sample, it will in part contain a sampling error. For example, if there was no association between 'size of head' and 'IQ of adults', and we took a random sample of 10 adults and calculated $r$, it is possible by chance that we would include some with a large head who happen to have a high IQ, and vice versa. The correlation coefficient might be moderately high, but this is due to sampling error; it is not real. Had we taken a very large sample, a much broader and fairer representation of head sizes and IQ would arise to swamp the few results creating the misleading impression. We can, however, in some sense measure sampling error. It will be less for larger samples. So, given information on the size of the sample and other factors discussed below, we can say how much of the range 0 to 1 is made up of possible sampling error. We require our calculated value of $r$ to be in addition to the part of the range of 0 to 1 that might be attributed to sampling error. If this is the case, we say the difference between 0 (no linear association) and the calculated value of $r$ is statistically significant at some level; by statistically significant we mean in addition to that due to sampling error.

Thus, the calculated value of $r$ must be over and above that part of the range of 0 (no linear association) to 1 (perfect linear association) that is attributable to sampling error. For large samples there are smaller errors, the task is not so great; for small samples the threshold can be very high reflecting the increased sampling errors. Thus, for any problem the test we use is to determine the threshold or 'critical value' over which $r$ must exceed before the difference between zero (no linear association) and the calculated value can be proclaimed 'statistically significant'; i.e. due to a real association, over and above the sampling errors. This test process is by no means certain. One source of error is that, in truth, there may be no linear association, but our test reveals one. In the very formulation of the test and determination of the threshold level the probability of this occurring is specified. You may see studies concluding that the difference between $r$ and zero is statistically significant at the 5 per cent (or 1 per cent or 0.1 per cent or whatever) *significance level*. This reflects the probability of our establishing via the test that an association exist when one does not. The term 'statistical significance' only has a meaning if a level is attached since a lower level (probability of error) leads to higher thresholds for the tests. So how do we find the threshold level?

- *Step 1*    Determine an acceptable significance level depending on what risk is acceptable for the purpose of the study—say 5 per cent (0.05). This is commonly accepted in the social sciences and, at least for this chapter, you can take this as given.
- *Step 2*    Determine the degrees of freedom $v = n - 2$, for our freezer example $v = 11 - 2 = 9$. This is straightforward; the critical value depends on the size of the sample and the number of restrictions operating on a test. For this purpose there are two. You simply calculate $v = n - 2$.
- *Step 3*    Determine if it is a one-tailed or a two-tailed test: in a one-tailed test the association is positive or negative, not both; in a two-tailed test the association can be both positive and negative.

At the start of this chapter we decided in theory whether we expected the association to be positive (high $Y$, high $X$, low $Y$, low $X$) or negative (high $Y$, low $X$, low $Y$, high $X$). We decided it was positive, a high income leading to a high proportion of freezer ownership; it could not be negative, there is no reason why high income regions would have lower proportions of freezer ownership. This is a one-tailed test. The decision as to its being one- or two-tailed must be made independently of what the data reveal. In our example it was difficult to imagine *in theory* a negative association, so we have a one-tailed test. If, for example, we looked at 'number of books purchased by students' against 'final examination mark' it might be positive (extra books mean you learn more/more interested) *or* negative (weak students buy more books in panic and confuse themselves); this would be a two-tailed test.

- *Step 4*    Using Table 6-3, the figures in the body of the table give the critical (or threshold) value. If the calculated value (ignoring the +ve or −ve sign) is greater than this critical value the difference between the calculated value and zero (no linear association) is statistically significant; we have found an association. The column headed $\alpha = 0.05$ is a 5 per cent level of significance, as is the column $\alpha = 0.025$, the former being for one-tailed and the latter with the 0.05 divided between two-tails at 0.025 each. We can now choose the appropriate column, i.e. one-tailed 5 per cent for our freezer example is the sixth from the right. The rows are headed by $v$ which equals $11 - 2 = 9$; the critical value from the tables is 0.5214. Since our calculated value is $r = 0.68$ which exceeds 0.5214 we can say the difference between $r = 0.68$ and zero is statistically significant at the 5 per cent level. There is an association that is not due to sampling error at this level.

The procedure for testing for statistical significance is thus quite straightforward; it applies equally to negative correlations (we ignore the sign). Much of the theory upon which it is based is considered in Chapters 11 and 12. But the procedure is quite straightforward; the principle of why the test is needed and what it does is understandable on an intuitive level. So we should now feel confident of our being able to interpret results for a correlation coefficient. Interpretation of the correlation coefficient now includes the sign, strength and statistical significance.

To test your understanding and make an important point, not always appreciated by seasoned

**Table 6-3**  Significance of correlation coefficient, when $\rho=0$

Values of $r$ significant at $\alpha$ (one-tail) and $2\alpha$ (two-tail) levels for different number of degrees of freedom ($v=n-2$) where $n=$ number of observations in the sample. Example: If $|r|\geqslant0.4438$ when $v=18$, $H_0$ that $\rho=0$ may be rejected at 5 per cent level of significance ($2\alpha=0.05$). When testing partial correlation coefficient, $v=n-k-2$, where $k=$ number of variables held constant, e.g. for $r_{12.3}$, $k=1$.

| $v$ | $\alpha=0.25$ $2\alpha=0.5$ | $\alpha=0.15$ $2\alpha=0.3$ | $\alpha=0.1$ $2\alpha=0.2$ | $\alpha=0.05$ $2\alpha=0.1$ | $\alpha=0.025$ $2\alpha=0.05$ | $\alpha=0.01$ $2\alpha=0.02$ | $\alpha=0.005$ $2\alpha=0.01$ | $\alpha=0.001$ $2\alpha=0.002$ | $\alpha=0.0005$ $2\alpha=0.001$ |
|---|---|---|---|---|---|---|---|---|---|
| 1 | .7071 | .8910 | .9511 | .9877 | .9969 | .9995 | .9999 | 1.0000 | 1.0000 |
| 2 | .5000 | .7000 | .8000 | .9000 | .9500 | .9800 | .9900 | .9980 | .9990 |
| 3 | .4040 | .5851 | .6870 | .8054 | .8783 | .9343 | .9587 | .9859 | .9911 |
| 4 | .3473 | .5112 | .6084 | .7293 | .8114 | .8822 | .9172 | .9633 | .9741 |
| 5 | .3091 | .4592 | .5509 | .6694 | .7545 | .8329 | .8745 | .9350 | .9509 |
| 6 | .2811 | .4202 | .5067 | .6215 | .7067 | .7887 | .8343 | .9049 | .9249 |
| 7 | .2596 | .3896 | .4716 | .5822 | .6664 | .7498 | .7977 | .8751 | .8983 |
| 8 | .2423 | .3648 | .4428 | .5494 | .6319 | .7155 | .7646 | .8467 | .8721 |
| 9 | .2281 | .3442 | .4187 | .5214 | .6021 | .6851 | .7348 | .8199 | .8470 |
| 10 | .2161 | .3267 | .3981 | .4973 | .5760 | .6581 | .7079 | .7950 | .8233 |
| 11 | .2058 | .3116 | .3802 | .4762 | .5529 | .6339 | .6835 | .7717 | .8010 |
| 12 | .1968 | .2984 | .3646 | .4575 | .5324 | .6120 | .6614 | .7501 | .7800 |
| 13 | .1890 | .2868 | .3507 | .4409 | .5140 | .5923 | .6411 | .7301 | .7604 |
| 14 | .1820 | .2764 | .3383 | .4259 | .4973 | .5742 | .6226 | .7114 | .7419 |
| 15 | .1757 | .2671 | .3271 | .4124 | .4821 | .5577 | .6055 | .6940 | .7247 |
| 16 | .1700 | .2587 | .3170 | .4000 | .4683 | .5425 | .5897 | .6777 | .7084 |
| 17 | .1649 | .2510 | .3077 | .3887 | .4555 | .5285 | .5751 | .6624 | .6932 |
| 18 | .1602 | .2439 | .2992 | .3783 | .4438 | .5155 | .5614 | .6481 | .6788 |
| 19 | .1558 | .2375 | .2914 | .3687 | .4329 | .5034 | .5487 | .6346 | .6652 |
| 20 | .1518 | .2315 | .2841 | .3598 | .4227 | .4921 | .5368 | .6219 | .6524 |
| 21 | .1481 | .2259 | .2774 | .3515 | .4132 | .4815 | .5256 | .6099 | .6402 |
| 22 | .1447 | .2207 | .2711 | .3438 | .4044 | .4716 | .5151 | .5986 | .6287 |
| 23 | .1415 | .2159 | .2653 | .3365 | .3961 | .4622 | .5052 | .5879 | .6178 |
| 24 | .1384 | .2113 | .2598 | .3297 | .3882 | .4534 | .4958 | .5776 | .6074 |
| 25 | .1356 | .2071 | .2546 | .3233 | .3809 | .4451 | .4869 | .5679 | .5974 |
| 26 | .1330 | .2031 | .2497 | .3172 | .3739 | .4372 | .4785 | .5587 | .5880 |
| 27 | .1305 | .1993 | .2451 | .3115 | .3673 | .4297 | .4705 | .5499 | .5790 |
| 28 | .1281 | .1957 | .2407 | .3061 | .3610 | .4226 | .4629 | .5415 | .5703 |
| 29 | .1258 | .1923 | .2366 | .3009 | .3550 | .4158 | .4556 | .5334 | .5620 |
| 30 | .1237 | .1891 | .2327 | .2960 | .3494 | .4093 | .4487 | .5257 | .5541 |
| 35 | .1144 | .1751 | .2156 | .2746 | .3246 | .3810 | .4182 | .4916 | .5189 |
| 40 | .1070 | .1638 | .2018 | .2573 | .3044 | .3578 | .3932 | .4633 | .4896 |
| 45 | .1008 | .1544 | .1903 | .2429 | .2876 | .3384 | .3721 | .4394 | .4647 |
| 50 | .0956 | .1465 | .1806 | .2306 | .2732 | .3218 | .3542 | .4188 | .4432 |
| 60 | .0873 | .1338 | .1650 | .2108 | .2500 | .2948 | .3248 | .3850 | .4079 |
| 70 | .0808 | .1238 | .1528 | .1954 | .2319 | .2737 | .3017 | .3583 | .3798 |
| 80 | .0755 | .1158 | .1430 | .1829 | .2172 | .2565 | .2830 | .3364 | .3568 |
| 90 | .0712 | .1092 | .1348 | .1726 | .2050 | .2422 | .2673 | .3181 | .3375 |
| 100 | .0675 | .1036 | .1279 | .1638 | .1946 | .2301 | .2540 | .3025 | .3211 |
| 120 | .0616 | .0946 | .1168 | .1496 | .1779 | .2104 | .2324 | .2771 | .2943 |
| 150 | .0551 | .0846 | .1045 | .1339 | .1593 | .1886 | .2083 | .2488 | .2643 |
| 200 | .0477 | .0733 | .0905 | .1161 | .1381 | .1636 | .1809 | .2162 | .2298 |
| 300 | .0390 | .0598 | .0740 | .0948 | .1129 | .1338 | .1480 | .1771 | .1884 |
| 500 | .0302 | .0463 | .0573 | .0735 | .0875 | .1038 | .1149 | .1376 | .1464 |

Reproduced from Z. W. Kmietowicz and Y. Yannoulis (1988), *Statistical Tables for Economic, Business and Social Studies*, Harlow: Longman, reproduced with permission.

researchers, consider the following. If the difference between the calculated value and zero was found to be statistically significant, the next question to ask is whether the association is strong or weak. For large sample sizes the sampling error associated with $r$ is very small and thus a quite weak association (low calculated value of $r$) may be statistically significant. The lesson is: do not always be impressed with claims of having found statistically significant associations. If they come from large samples, it may be that the association is very weak. For small samples, sampling errors are large. The warning is: do not be impressed with claims of large values of $r$ from small samples; they may be due to sampling errors, so test if they are statistically significant and, if so, do not conclude that a high value automatically denotes a strong relationship. If, for example, 0.9 of the scale is due to sampling errors, a value of 0.95 may not be anything to write home about.

## MEASURES OF ASSOCIATION: ORDINAL SCALE

A critical assumption of the product moment correlation coefficient, as identified above, was that either an interval or ratio scale was the basis of the measurement of any of the variables. If one or more of the variables is measured on an ordinal scale and the errors might be expected to be serious if the values were used as an interval, then an alternative measure must be utilized. A measure that is tailor-made for situations when the scale of at least one of the variables involved is ordinal, is Spearman's correlation coefficient.

### Its derivation from $r$

Consider the data given in Table 6-4 on 10 applications for a job. The second column of the table provides the ranking in descending order of merit of the interviewer's judgement on personal qualities such as communication skills, personality and so forth. The next column in the table is the score each candidate received on a written test relating to technical ability, or in the case of candidates D and G, lack of it. Our interest lies in whether technical skills are associated with the interviewer's judgement of what we shall call 'personal skills', and if there is an association, the extent or strength of it.

Note that we have to lose information by converting the scores on technical skills from an interval scale to an ordinal scale given in column 4. This is because Spearman's coefficient requires an ordinal scale for both variables. Such loss of information should be borne in mind when choosing between the product moment and Spearman's correlation coefficient (denoted by $r$ and $r_S$ respectively). When the scales for both variables are ordinal this consideration does not, of course, arise.

Readers who have followed the discussion of the product moment correlation coefficient should have no problems interpreting the results from this measure, since Spearman's coefficient is derived from it; the interpretation of $r$ being similar to that for $r_S$. With both measures the sign denotes the nature of the relationship—positive or negative association—and the numerical value denotes the extent of the association ranging from 0 to 1 as with $r$.

### Calculation of Spearman's correlation coefficient

Spearman's correlation coefficient is given by:

$$r_S = 1 - [6\,\Sigma D_i^2/(n^3 - n)]   \tag{6-3}$$

where $D_i = V_i - X_i$ and $n$ is the number of pairs of observations. (Some texts give different formulae

**Table 6-4** Data on personal and technical skills of candidates

| Candidate | Personal skills, rank $Y$ | Technical skills, score (%) | Technical skills, rank $X$ | $D = Y - X$ | $D^2$ | Interviewer 2 person skills, rank $Z$ |
|---|---|---|---|---|---|---|
| A | 1 | 29 | 6 | $-5$ | 25 | 1.5 |
| B | 2 | 12 | 7 | $-5$ | 25 | 1.5 |
| C | 3 | 87 | 1 | 2 | 4 | 9 |
| D | 4 | 2 | 10 | $-6$ | 36 | 7 |
| E | 5 | 68 | 3 | 2 | 4 | 9 |
| F | 6 | 11 | 8 | $-2$ | 4 | 6 |
| G | 7 | 6 | 9 | $-2$ | 4 | 4 |
| H | 8 | 69 | 2 | 6 | 36 | 5 |
| I | 9 | 41 | 5 | 4 | 16 | 9 |
| J | 10 | 46 | 4 | 6 | 36 | 3 |
| Total | | | | | 190 | |

(e.g. Meddis, 1984, p. 273) though they are mathematically equivalent.) Applying Eq. (6-3) to the data in Table 6-4 requires, first, the calculation of each individual $D_i$, i.e. the difference between each $Y_i$ and its corresponding $X_i$ (after ranking any interval scale) as shown in the column of the table. Second, each individual difference $D_i$ is squared; the sixth column of the table. Third, the squared differences are summed to yield $\Sigma D_i^2 = 190$.

### Interpreting $r_S$

The result of $-0.15$ is very close to zero, demonstrating that there is only a weak association. [This was expected since the values ascribed to $Y$ in Table 6-4 were 1 to 10 and those for the scores for $X$ were taken from the first 10 rows, first two columns of random number tables.] If we treat the 10 applicants as a random sample of all applicants, we should query that since the value of $-0.15$ was close to zero, was the difference due to sampling errors, or, if not, did it reveal evidence that some association existed, albeit a very weak one? The test for statistical significance follows a similar approach to that of the product moment correlation coefficient. The table in Appendix 4 provides the critical values: for $n = 10$ and a 5 per cent (0.05) significance level (two-tailed), the critical value is 0.6346. The calculated value of 0.15 is less than this and we thus do not, at a 5 per cent level, have a statistically significant association.

However, Appendix 4 only helps for $n \leqslant 30$; when $n > 30$ an alternative procedure applies to the test statistic (though when more than 25 per cent of the observations are tied a correction is needed—see Lehmann (1975), Sec. 7.3). The critical value for a two-tailed test at a 5 per cent level is given by $1.96/\sqrt{(n-1)}$ while for a one-tailed test it is $1.64/\sqrt{(n-1)}$.

### Linearity assumption relaxed for $r_S$

Note that a departure for our interpretation of $r_S$ from that of $r$ is that the assumption of linearity can be slightly relaxed. Spearman's correlation coefficient can be applied to functional forms which are monotonically increasing (or decreasing). That is, those in which $Y$ rises (or falls) consistently with $X$—a linear function has this property; a quadratic function does not, as it turns at a peak or trough; an exponential function is non-linear, yet $Y$-values monotonically increase with increases in $X$, but not proportionally so. In the case of an exponential relationship the fact that, for example, the highest value of $Y$ has a much greater divergence from the previous point on the scatter diagram than would be warranted by a linear relationship, is of no consequence for $r_s$, since the point would be ranked as number 1 on both $X$ and $Y$ and as a zero difference in the calculation, as is right and proper for a perfect ordinal association. However, were $r$ applied to an exponential form the bending of the curve away from the linear form would wrongly suggest a weakness in the relationship, as opposed to the method's inability to track an exponential form.

## Dealing with ties

Consider again Table 6-4; the final column gives data for the views of a second interviewer on the personal skills of the candidates. We are testing whether a significant association exists between the rankings of these interviewers and if it does we are interested in the strength of the association. Note that candidates C, E and I tie for last place while candidates A and B tie for first place. Note also that the ranking given is the mean of the tied positions (e.g. tied first for A and B is $(1+2)/2 = 1.5$; similarly, tied last place is $(8+9+10)/3 = 9$). The value for $r_s$ using these averages for tied values is $r_s = 1 - [6(128.5)/990] = 0.22$, which is a weak positive association. Since $0.22 < 0.6364$ (two-tailed, 5 per cent significance level) we cannot on the basis of the data say that there is a significant association between the rankings of the two interviewers at a 5 per cent level. The company should be concerned that the two interviewers have quite different conceptions as to their perception of personal skills.

## Ties and ordered contingency tables

If the number of tied values is very large, Spearman's coefficient should not be used, but either Goodman and Kruskal's gamma, Kendall's tau or Somer's delta may be applicable. Consider the results of a survey on a city's consumers whereby their views on a product—good (1), indifferent (2), bad (3)—are related to the age of the consumer as given by four unequal bands: young (16–24 years) 1, middle (25–39) 2, older (40–64) 3, senior citizen (65 plus) 4. The views of 500 consumers may be summarized as in Table 6-5. Such a table is referred to as a contingency table and since there is an order or hierarchy to each variable it is an ordered contingency table. Now both variables are ordinal, and indeed we could use Spearman's correlation coefficient with $n = 500$; consumer 1 might have age $X = 1$ and views $Y = 1$ young : good) as would 19 other tied values. And for $X = 4$ and $Y = 1$ (senior : good) we have 90 tied values. Yet the variables are ordinal, they have an hierarchy, but the difference between successive values of each age band or view cannot be said to be the same. While it is outside of the scope of this book to describe the calculation and interpretation of gamma, tau and delta (see Kendall (1962), Chs 3 and 4, for details), it is necessary to point out that in such cases with many ties Spearman's correlation would give distorted results. Somer's delta is particularly applicable if one variable can be categorized as the dependent variable of interest, to be explained by the other. The data in Table 6-5 would fit such a requirement since views depend on age, not age on views. However, such measures do not pick up non-monotonic associations.

**Table 6-5**  Age bands and views in survey of a product

| Age band (years) | Views on product | | |
| | 1 (Good) | 2 (Indifferent) | 3 (Bad) |
| --- | --- | --- | --- |
| (1) 16–24 | 20 | 35 | 45 |
| (2) 25–39 | 35 | 60 | 20 |
| (3) 40–64 | 60 | 40 | 20 |
| (4) 65 and over | 90 | 50 | 25 |

## MEASURES OF ASSOCIATION: NOMINAL SCALE

A relatively large number of measures of association exist for variables measured on a nominal scale. Here the values of the variable have no hierarchy and the difference between successive values are not equal.

Consider the sales of a make of video recorder (hereafter 'video') for which a one-year warranty is given as part of the sales price. The videos may be manufactured at any one of four plants. It is of interest to ask whether the reliability of the videos, as represented by a repair in the first year being undertaken or not under the warranty, is independent of the plant of origin. Table 6-6 provides illustrative data, the figures in the body of the table (ignoring for now those in parentheses) being the number of videos in a category from a random sample of videos monitored over the last year.

Note the layout of the data, with the classifications of one variable (plant) serving as rows, while that of the other (repair) serves as columns. Such a layout is a contingency table, a fairly obvious format, which shall be used throughout this section. Since there are four outcomes or categories or classifications for the rows of the table, and two for the columns this is a $4 \times 2$ (the '$\times$' is read as 'by') contingency table, containing eight cells or possible combinations of the two variables. The focus of this section will be on ascertaining whether the two variables are independent of each other, and if not, measuring the strength of their 'association'. Two by two contingency tables (e.g. 'sex of respondent' against 'whether or not they have recently purchased a particular product') have particular problems associated with them. As such, attention will first be focused on larger tables than these.

**Table 6-6**  Repairs under warranty and plant of origin for video recorders whether repaired under warranty

| Plant | Repaired | Not-repaired | Total |
| --- | --- | --- | --- |
| A | 20 (17.11) | 90 (92.89) | 110 |
| B | 4 (11.51) | 70 (62.49) | 74 |
| C | 6 (10.27) | 60 (55.73) | 66 |
| D | 12 ( 3.11) | 8 (16.89) | 20 |
| Total | 42 | 228 | 270 |

**Testing the statistical significance: the chi-squared test—principles and calculation**

**Tables other than 2 × 2 tables**    In many practical problems there is a need to establish the existence of an association, and, if one is demonstrated, its strength and nature, for cases when either or both of the variables have more than two outcomes. For example, views on canteen facilities (very good, good, neither good nor bad, bad, very bad) against the employee's sex; or the location of company (region registered office is located) against whether it is operating or not five years hence.

Table 6-6 shows a 4 × 2 contingency table on repairs being undertaken by plant. The technique outlined below is appropriate for a $r \times c$ contingency table when $r$ and/or $c$ is greater than 2; however, with an appropriate correction it can also be applied, as will be shown later, to the 2 × 2 case. The test of statistical significance is the chi-squared ($\chi^2$) test and associated measure of strength of any association include the contingency coefficient, phi coefficient and Cramer's $V$.

In Table 6-6 the figures in the body, or each cell, of the table (ignoring the total) show the number of observed values ($O_i$) associated with each cell, when there are $i = 1, \ldots, 8$ cells. For example, there were 20 videos in the first plant requiring a repair, cell $i = 1$ so, $O_1 = 20$. The first step in the analysis is to calculate for each cell the corresponding expected values ($E_i$). These values show the number of observations we would expect in each cell *if the two variables were independent*. The calculation of these expected values is quite straightforward, being:

$$E_i = (\text{Row total} \times \text{Column total})/\text{Grand total} \tag{6-4}$$

Thus the expected value for the cell corresponding to 'Plant A: repair' is $(110 \times 42)/270 = 17.11$ on the assumption that 'plant' and 'whether repaired or not' (reliability) are independent of each other. While the reason why this works can be found in greater detail in the basic probability laws discussed in Chapter 9, the following should suffice. The probability of a video selected at random being from plant 1 is the total number of such videos from plant 1 (the row total) divided by the total number of all videos (grand total). The probability of a video selected at random having repairs required is equal to the total number of such videos (column total) divided by the total number of all videos (grand total). Probability laws show (Chapter 9) that if the two variables, plant and reliability, are independent the probability of both outcomes occurring—i.e. 'Plant 1: repair necessary'—is given by multiplying these probabilities together, i.e.

$$(\text{Row total}/\text{Grand total}) \times (\text{Column total}/\text{Grand total}) \tag{6-5}$$

However, we want the expected number of values in the cell, not the probability; thus the probability given by product (6-5) is multiplied by the total number of observations (the grand total) to yield Eq. (6-4).

The figures in parentheses in Table 6-6 are the expected values for each cell calculated using Eq. (6-4). The rows and columns of the expected values should be summed to see if they correspond (rounding errors apart) to the row and column totals of Table 6-6 as a check against arithmetical errors. The differences between the number of videos observed in a category, and the number expected if no relationship existed, is crucial to the test of independence. If the variables are independent, observed and expected values would be broadly similar.

The chi-squared statistic ($\chi^2$) is based upon these differences, being given by:

$$\chi^2 = \Sigma(O_i - E_i)^2/E_i \tag{6-6}$$

The larger the differences between $O_i$ and $E_i$, the higher the value of $\chi^2$. For our example we compile Table 6-7 with, for each cell, the observed and expected values from Table 6-6 and the difference between the two. Since we do not want positive and negative differences to cancel—since both represent departures from independence— we square the differences and then divide by the

**Table 6-7**  Calculation of chi-squared

| $O_i$ | $E_i$ | $O_i - E_i$ | $(O_i - E_i)^2 / E_i$ |
|---|---|---|---|
| 20 | 17.11 | 2.89 | $(\ 2.89)^2 / 17.11 = \ 0.488$ |
| 4 | 11.51 | $-7.51$ | $(-7.51)^2 / 11.51 = \ 4.900$ |
| 6 | 10.27 | $-4.27$ | $(-4.27)^2 / 10.27 = \ 1.775$ |
| 12 | 3.11 | 8.89 | $(\ 8.89)^2 / \ 3.11 = 25.412$ |
| 90 | 92.89 | $-2.89$ | $(-2.89)^2 / 92.89 = \ 0.090$ |
| 70 | 62.49 | 7.51 | $(\ 7.51)^2 / 62.49 = \ 0.903$ |
| 60 | 55.73 | 4.27 | $(\ 4.27)^2 / 55.73 = \ 0.327$ |
| 8 | 16.89 | $-8.89$ | $(-8.89)^2 / 16.89 = \ 4.679$ |
|  |  | Total | $38.574 = \chi^2$ |

respective expected values to show the relative differences (column 4). This final column is then summed to yield 38.574 as required by Eq. (6-6).

Before moving on to the interpretation of this result the adjustment to the above formula for the $2 \times 2$ case will be considered.

**The 2 × 2 case**  The $2 \times 2$ case requires a modification—Yates's continuity correction—to the chi-squared formula. Much of the rationale for the correction stems from the corrected version of chi-squared's correspondence to another test, Fisher's 'exact' test. However, both the corrected version of $\chi^2$ and Fisher's 'exact' test are not without their critics and numerous alternative tests have been proposed (see Upton (1982) for a critical analysis and a listing of 22 tests and comparative results on 17 tests). Indeed, many statistics texts (e.g. Meddis, 1984, p. 109) do not provide details of Fisher's 'exact' test and Yates' correction because of these concerns. The issues are quite complex and beyond the scope of this text. However, readers encountering warnings in other texts against these measures should take heart from a defence by Frank Yates in Yates (1984).

Yates' correction for continuity is applied to the calculation of $\chi^2$ and involves finding $(O_i - E_i)$ for each cell as before, calling the differences positive irrespective of the sign (i.e. taking the modulus denoted by two vertical lines surrounding the expression) and subtracting a value of 0.5 from this figure. The result for each cell is squared, divided by the expected value for each cell and then summed across cells, i.e.

$$\chi^2 = \Sigma [|(O_i - E_i)| - 0.5]^2 / E_i \qquad (6\text{-}7)$$

Had the data in Table 6-6 been only for plants A and B with a sample of 184 videos—a $2 \times 2$ table—we would have Table 6-8 with $\chi^2 = 5.285$; quite different from $\chi^2 = 6.362$ without the correction.

**Table 6-8**  Calculation of chi-squared $2 \times 2$ table

| $O_i$ | $E_i$ | $[|(O_i - E_i)| - 0.5]$ | $[|(O_i - E_i)| - 0.5]^2 / E_i$ |
|---|---|---|---|
| 20 | 14.35 | 5.15 | 1.848 |
| 4 | 9.65 | 5.15 | 2.748 |
| 90 | 95.65 | 5.15 | 0.277 |
| 70 | 64.35 | 5.15 | 0.412 |
| Total |  |  | $5.285 = \chi^2$ |

## Interpretation of results: statistical significance

We move now to the interpretation of the results which follows the same principles with or without Yates' correction. We shall do this by way of the example relating to videos in Tables 6-6 and 6-7. The calculated value of $\chi^2$ was 38.574. There are two issues of concern to us. The first is whether the variable 'repair of videos' is independent of the variable 'plant of origin', or whether the difference between observed and expected is due to sampling errors. Second, the strength of the association.

If the variables are independent then $\chi^2$ will be zero and we need to determine whether the difference between zero and our calculated value—i.e. between what we observe and what we would expect if they were independent—is in addition to that attributable to sampling errors at a given significance level. Thus, we shall first be concerned with finding a critical value for $\chi^2$. Consider the statistical tables for the chi-squared distribution in Appendix 5. Note that the rows show differing degrees of freedom. We proceed as follows:

- *Step 1* We determine the degree of freedom for our problem by the formula:

$$\text{Degrees of freedom} = (r-1)(c-1)$$

  where $r$ is the number of rows in the contingency table and $c$ is the number of columns. Thus, for our $4 \times 2$ table the degrees of freedom $= (4-1)(2-1) = 3$.
- *Step 2* We establish the significance level (probability of rejecting independence when the variables are independent) and take this to be 0.05 or a 5 per cent level. The level chosen depends on the context and the implications of such an error; however, it is usual in the social sciences to establish a 5 per cent level.
- *Step 3* The critical value of $\chi^2$ from tables is at the intersection of the appropriate degrees of freedom ($= 3$) and significance level ($= 0.05$) in Appendix 5, i.e. 7.81 for our example.
- *Step 4* We compare the calculated value (Table 6-7) with the critical value from Appendix 5, and if the calculated value exceeds the critical value (in this case it does: 38.574 is greater than 7.81) we reject the hypothesis of independence at the 5 per cent level. Reliability of videos is not independent of plant of origin at the 5 per cent level.

## Some possible problem areas

Before we move on to consider how strong the relationship is, it is necessary to consider a number of assumptions employed in the analysis. First, the data must be the observed values of a random sample of independently selected cases. The test considers the likelihood of departures from independence occurring by chance and, as such, the selection of data considered must arise from an exercise where each case has the same probability of selection. Selection of one video for the sample must have no effect on the probability of selection of another. Note also that we used the observed values in the contingency table, the test not being valid for a contingency table made up of percentages. It is also assumed that the expected values are not too small. Different books (and warning messages in statistical software) contain different ideas as to what we mean by 'too small', but Lawal (1980) suggests that when the smallest expected value generated is 3 or more, the $\chi^2$ test may be used. In other cases Lawal suggests that a geometric mean of small expected values is used in tables provided in Lawal (1980). Alternatively, if the expected values are too small, one possibility is to combine rows or columns of the contingency table. However, this must be borne in mind in the interpretation of the results. A result may show, for example, that age is independent of whether a particular television programme was ever seen. This might be simply because the members in the sample over 50 years, who generally do not watch it, were grouped with the 30–45 who are great fans, while the under-30s are mixed. Therefore, when measuring variations in a variable, bear in mind that grouping the classes may subsume the relationship.

### Interpreting the nature of the 'association' and its strength

It is further worth noting that the result of the test does not tell us anything about the relationship. For example, its 'direction' in terms of whether particular values of one variable (e.g. plant A, B, C or D) have proportionately more faults than expected. It is often of interest to compile contingency tables showing the deviations of $O_i$ and $E_i$ for each cell or the contribution of each cell to the $\chi^2$ statistic, or some standardized formulation to acquire further insights. There are a number of measures of the strength of any 'association' available based on the $\chi^2$ statistic. One such measure is Cramer's $V$.

**Cramer's $V$**  Cramer's $V$ has a maximum value of 1 and a minimum of zero, the latter denoting independence. It has an advantage over a frequently cited measure, the contingency coefficient, of having a maximum value which does not depend on the dimensions of the contingency table. It is given by:

$$\text{Cramer's } V = \sqrt{\frac{\chi^2}{n(m-1)}} \tag{6-8}$$

where $n$ is the number of observations and $m$ the minimum number of rows ($r$) or columns ($c$). Since, in our example, $r=4$ and $c=2$:

$$\text{Cramer's } V = \sqrt{\frac{38.574}{270(2-1)}} = 0.378$$

Thus, from the chi-squared test we found the difference between our calculated value and a value resulting from independence of the two variables to be statistically significant at the 5 per cent level, and from Cramer's $V$ that it was only a small departure from independence, which is weak. It is stressed that had they *not* been statistically significant, there would have been no point in continuing with a measure of strength of association. Alternatively, had the difference been statistically significant and had a large sample been used, it would have been *essential* to establish the strength of association. This is because very slight statistically significant departures from independence, which are for all practical purposes meaningless, can be achieved from large samples.

It is also worth noting that the measures of association (contingency coefficient and Cramer's $V$) do not have readily identifiable meanings. They simply reflect departures from independence which we take to be a concept of association. There are measures based on more valid concepts of association, and because they measure different things it is quite possible that for one measure the association between variables A and B as compared with C and D will be the stronger, while for a different measure it will be the weaker. While it is undoubtedly best in principle to match the purpose of what we want to measure with the principle behind each measure, it is more likely in practice, albeit wrongly so, that a 'favourite' measure will be used or that several measures that have been generated by a statistical package will be available. In the latter case it is worth examining those measures that give a different picture to the rest and ask why this should be so for the problem/purpose at hand. Upton (1982), page 21, advises that measures based on the $\chi^2$ statistic should not be recommended since they lack any probabilistic interpretation, being simply departures from independence. Yet such departures are a concept of association, though the limitations should be borne in mind. A measure whose rationale is based on predictive/probabilistic interpretation is Guttman's lambda ($\lambda$).

**Guttman's lambda**  The basis of this measure is the ability to predict values of one variable given a value of the other variable. The stronger the association the better should be the predictive ability.

Consider the example of the association between plant of origin and reliability in Table 6-6. Suppose a video is drawn at random and we wish to determine whether it is likely to need repair or not. If we know the plant it came from and if there is an association between plant of origin and reliability, then our prediction of whether the video will need repair or not need a repair should be better given this information than if we know nothing about the video. Lambda is a measure based on the increase in the probability of correctly guessing whether the video will need repair or not that arises from knowing its plant origin, against not knowing. If origin of plant and reliability were perfectly associated then the probability of correctly guessing whether the video was reliable or not, given a knowledge of its plant of origin, will be 1 (certainty). To confuse matters it should be noted that there are three measures of lambda, $\lambda$, $\lambda_a$ and $\lambda_b$. We shall deal with $\lambda_b$ first.

If we wished to predict whether a video will need repair or not, and we knew it was manufactured in plant A, then our prediction based on the most likely outcome would be 'not repaired', since from Table 6-6 it can be seen that 90 as against 20 videos did not need repair. Similarly, if the video was manufactured in plant B we would predict it would not need repair since 70 videos, as against only 4 videos, did not need repair. For a video from plant C the prediction would be the same. However, for plant D the prediction would be 'needs repair' since 12 as against 8 did require repair. The principle is quite straightforward; given the plant of origin we predict whether it will need repair or not on the modal value, the most likely possibility.

If we had no information on plant of origin we would predict on the modal value again, by asking whether there were more repairs or non-repairs overall. In this case, from the row 'Total' of Table 6-6 we would predict that a video would not need repair—228 against 42. Now $\lambda_b$ is based on increased effectiveness of predicting the column headings (repair/not repair)—denoted by $b$—from the row headings (plant)—denoted by $a$—as opposed to just using the totals. It is given by:

$$\lambda_b = \frac{(M_1 + M_2 + \ldots M_a) - T_b}{n - T_b} \tag{6-9}$$

where $M_1, M_2, \ldots, M_a$ are the largest (most likely) frequencies (entries) in each of the $a$ rows and $T_b$ the largest of the column $b$ totals, $n$ being the sample size, i.e.:

$$\lambda_b = \frac{(90 + 70 + 60 + 12) - 228}{270 - 228}$$

$$= \frac{4}{42} = 0.095$$

$\lambda_b$ lies between 0 (independent) and 1 (perfect predictive power). The higher the value of $\lambda_b$ the better the variable in columns $b$ can be predicted by the variable in rows $a$—it has an interpretation throughout its range. For our example the two variables are near independent in this predictive sense. It is only the increased predictive power from the relatively small plant that keeps us from zero.

The statistic $\lambda_a$ is used if we wished our measure to be based on the effectiveness of predicting the values of the variable in rows $a$ from values of the variable in columns $b$. Clearly, in the current example, a measure based on predicting plant of origin on the bases of reliability ($\lambda_a$) is not as sensible as one based on predicting reliability from plant ($\lambda_b$). However, were we to go ahead:

$$\lambda_a = \frac{(M_1 + M_2 + \ldots + M_b) - T_a}{n - T_a} \tag{6-10}$$

where $M_1, \ldots, M_b$ are the largest frequency in each of the $b$ columns and $T_a$ the largest frequency of the row totals. Thus,

$$\lambda_a = \frac{(20+90)-110}{270-110}$$

$$= \frac{0}{160} = 0$$

Note that the results from $\lambda_a$ and $\lambda_b$ can differ and thus the importance of establishing in theory prior to the analysis, whether a measure based on predicting variable $X$ from $Y$, is more appropriate than one based on predicting $Y$ from $X$. Knowing the plant of origin marginally helped us to predict whether a repair was likely for a video (than no knowledge of the plant), while knowing if a video needed repair or not did not help us predict the plant of origin (compared with no knowledge of whether a repair was necessary). If it is difficult to distinguish from theory which is appropriate, a compromise is one which assumes that, for half the cases, we are interested in predictions of a form inherent in $\lambda_a$, and for the other half, $\lambda_b$. If the fraction immediately prior to the answer of each of $\lambda_a$ and $\lambda_b$ is examined, we see that $\lambda$ is derived from these, i.e.:

$$\lambda = \frac{0+4}{160+42} = \frac{4}{202} = 0.02$$

that is, we sum the numerators of Eqs (6-9) and (6-10) and divide this by the sum of the denominators of these equations. There will of course be sampling errors attached to these measures; this can be ascertained, but is beyond the scope of this book. Readers are referred to Upton (1982, p. 31) for details of confidence intervals (see Chapter 12).

## CONCLUSIONS

In summary, this chapter has not only considered quite a few measures, though these are far from exhaustive, but has tried to emphasize the care necessary in employing such measures. This area of study requires skilled practitioners, not people simply wanting to apply formulae to get answers. Answers depend on formulating questions well, applying theory, using reliable data, exploring the data, being aware of the assumptions implicit in methods and knowing what the measure is doing and asking whether it is appropriate for your purposes. Decisions based on identifying whether the empirical world accords with some theory can be important; thus the measures deserve care and attention. The chapter also provides the weapons with which to challenge the views and policies of others by seeing if the relationships and associations behind their views and policies can be supported by data.

## USING COMPUTERS

### Minitab

As noted in the last section of Chapter 2

MTB > PLOT C1 VS C2

with its associated subcommands, provides scatter diagrams of the variables in C1 and C2. If you think a third categorical variable (e.g. sex) may have an effect on the relationship, then LPLOT (discussed in Chapter 2), with tags for male and female, will help to show if the relationship in the scatter diagram is influenced by sex; if it is, sex may be entered as a dummy variable in regression analysis, as discussed in the next chapter.

For PLOT, asterisks (*) are used to represent individual points, although if two or more (up to 10) coincide, the number of points coinciding are used; a plus sign is used ( + ) to show 10 or more values coinciding.

```
MTB > CORR C1 C2
```

provides the product moment correlation coefficient for variables with data in C1 and C2; if more than two columns follow the CORR command a matrix of correlation coefficients is presented showing all possible correlations between the columns mentioned.

For Spearman's correlation there is no separate command; however, if one variable is on an interval scale it can be ranked using

```
MTB > RANK C1, PUT IN C2.
```

The above CORRelation command on the ranked columns yields Spearman's coefficient.

```
MTB  > READ C1-C3
DATA > 35 42 90
DATA > 86 25 13
DATA > END
MTB  > CHISQUARE C1-C3
```

will calculate chi-squared on the $2 \times 3$ contingency table in C1–C3, producing observed and expected values, degrees of freedom and the number of cells with expected values less than 5. If your data have not been formed into a contingency table, then for a chi-squared on raw data use:

```
MTB  > TABLE C1 C2;
SUBC > CHISQUARE 3.
```

The '3' prompts the observed, expected and standardized residual in each cell; the subcommand LAYOUT cannot be used here; for a $2 \times 2$, Yates' correction is NOT applied.


## Lotus 1-2-3

/Data Regression will undertake a regression analysis on data in two columns, prompting you for the range of the $X$-variable, $Y$-variable and an output space for the results. The details of the regression analysis are provided in the next chapter; however, for now it is sufficient to know that the R-squared computed is the square of the product moment correlation coefficient, the coefficient thus being derived by taking the square root of it.

Alternatively, given a column of $X$-values and another column of $Y$-values, the multiplication of $X$ in the first cell by its corresponding $Y$, i.e. $+(A1*B1)$ in C1, generates $XY$ for the first pair of values. This can be copied for subsequent observations: /Copy and @SUM(C1..C10) (assuming 10 observations) would yield $\Sigma XY$. Similar calculations would yield $\Sigma X^2$ and $\Sigma Y^2$.

If you have two columns of data with a label describing each column at the head, you can sort the data in one column (say $Y$) in descending order using /Data Sort. The ordered $Y$-values can be converted into 1, 2, 3, . . ., etc., using /Data Fill. If you then repeat this sort operation sorting the $X$-values and carrying along the $Y$-values, then /Data Fill on the $X$-values will generate their ranking. This should allow you to calculate Spearman's formula without undue effort using, for example, /Data Regression on the ranks. Readers are referred to the manual for the details of the /Data Sort command.

Given a contingency table the expected values can readily be generated using the formula given and summed using the @SUM function. Chi-squared follows from the formula given in this chapter. If you have raw data, a contingency table can be formed using /Data Table 3; alternatively

/Data Query Extract allows you to extract a column of data that has particular characteristics (e.g. 'female', 'born north of Watford') from which @COUNT(D1..D10) will count the observed number of such people if they are listed in (D1..D10). Both of these data commands require reference to the 'help' facility or a manual/text as their implementation is not immediately obvious.

## EXERCISES

**6-1** Using the data given in the table below, determine whether regional variations in the percentage of the population who read the *Sun* newspaper is associated with variations in the regional average expenditure on alcohol. Your work should include:

(a) Drawing a scatter diagram.
(b) Calculating the product moment correlation coefficient.
(c) A brief interpretation of the results, paying particular attention to the implicit assumptions of the method and the theoretical basis, if any, of the findings.

| Region | Percentage readership of the *Sun** | Average household income† (£ p.w.) | Average expenditure on alcohol‡ (%) |
|---|---|---|---|
| North Yorks and Humberside | 23 | 175.7 | 5.5 |
| East and West Midlands | 31 | 197.2 | 4.9 |
| East Anglia and South East including Greater London | 29 | 243.0 | 4.3 |
| South West and Wales | 26 | 199.9 | 4.6 |
| North West | 20 | 183.2 | 5.5 |
| Scotland | 18 | 198.3 | 5.6 |

*Percentage of adults (15 or over) who read a national daily, reading the *Sun*, July 1985–1986.
†Average weekly household income includes benefits and investment income; average 1984 and 1985.
‡Average weekly expenditure on alcoholic drinks as a percentage of total weekly expenditure, average of 1984 and 1985.
*Source*: Central Statistical Office, *Regional Trends, 22, 1987 edition*, London: HMSO, 1988.

[*Note*: The data on average household income is reserved for an exercise in the next chapter.]

**6-2** You have recently purchased 10 trucks and find some variability in the miles per gallon (mpg) recorded. Since the trucks are driven on similar routes you suspect that it is in part due to the way they are driven by different drivers, as well as the fact that they carry loads of different weights. You have data on the trucks for a similar run and a record of the loads they carried. Is there an association between miles per gallon and load carried by trucks, and if so how strong is it?

| Truck | Y (mpg) | X (lb) |
|---|---|---|
| 1 | 18.33 | 2800 |
| 2 | 15.91 | 3700 |
| 3 | 16.37 | 3600 |
| 4 | 17.50 | 3200 |
| 5 | 15.52 | 4100 |
| 6 | 18.85 | 2600 |
| 7 | 16.97 | 3600 |
| 8 | 16.45 | 3400 |
| 9 | 16.51 | 3800 |
| 10 | 17.88 | 2700 |

**6-3** The following data show the results of a market research investigation based on a random sample of 550 consumers. Our interest lies in whether the product usage is independent of the region in which the consumer lives. Is it?

| Region | Product usage in given week | | |
| | Not at all | Once | More than once |
| --- | --- | --- | --- |
| North | 20 | 40 | 60 |
| Midlands | 60 | 35 | 35 |
| South | 100 | 60 | 20 |
| Scotland | 10 | 15 | 10 |
| Wales | 25 | 30 | 30 |

**6-4** In order to drive unaccompanied in Great Britain it is necessary to pass a driving test, there being no limit to the number of attempts at the test allowed. The government office responsible for such tests needs to estimate the number of applicants in order that they can recruit and train staff to supervise tests, or if there is a fall-off in applicants, to plan for wastage of staff. One theory is that the number of applications received is related to average earnings, the growth of which is shown by the index in the table. Does the evidence support this theory?

Average earnings index and applicants for driving test, 1982–1988, Great Britain

| Year | Average earnings index (1985 = 100)* | Applications received for driving tests† |
| --- | --- | --- |
| 1982 | 80.2 | 1891.6 |
| 1983 | 87.0 | 1917.0 |
| 1984 | 92.2 | 1955.7 |
| 1985 | 100.0 | 1935.2 |
| 1986 | 107.9 | 1968.7 |
| 1987 | 116.3 | 1990.4 |
| 1988 | 126.4 | 2241.4 |

   *Figures for average earnings are gross before deductions. Generally they exclude the value of earnings in kind but include wages and salaries, overtime, bonuses, commissions, etc.
   †Irrespective of whether the tests are for the first time or not.
   *Source*: Central Statistical Office, *Annual Abstract of Statistics 1990*, London: HMSO.

**6-5** Preferences in elections for a worker's representative from a random sample of 100 workers are given below for two candidates by the sex of the worker. Comment on whether preferences are independent of sex.

| | Candidate A | Candidate B |
| --- | --- | --- |
| Sex: Male | 15 | 30 |
| Female | 35 | 20 |

**6-6** You have sent eight different forms of packaging for a new product to your MD and he has designated the order of preference he believes is most likely to sell (1 = most preferred, 8 = least preferred). The following day you receive the results from the test marketing on a representative panel of consumers. What can you say about the MD's judgement?

| Packaging | MD's preference | Test marketing preference |
| --- | --- | --- |
| A | 2 | 3 |
| B | 1 | 2 |
| C | 3 | 4 |
| D | 4 | 1 |
| E | 4 | 5 |
| F | 6 | 6 |
| G | 8 | 8 |
| H | 7 | 6 |

# REGRESSION ANALYSIS

In the last chapter we studied in some depth measures of association. Here we have a similar concern, the association between variables, except we develop it further in two respects. First we learn how to build statistical models of relationships to better understand their features. Second, we extend the models to consider their use in forecasting for non-linear relationships and multiple regression, as opposed to bivariate relationships (between only two variables) considered previously. Finally, we draw attention to the need for caution in using the technique and sources of potential errors. It is stressed that the second and final part are quite advanced and may be beyond your syllabus. Our primary concern will be with parametric methods appropriate for variables measured on interval or ratio scales. This is not to say that non-parametric methods do not exist for this purpose, it is just that they are outside the scope of this text and reference may be made to Sprent (1990) or Neave and Worthington (1988) for details.

## WHAT IS REGRESSION ABOUT?

Consider Fig. 7-1: it is the scatter diagram of the relationship between regional percentage ownership of freezers and average income, as discussed in Chapter 6. Our aim is to superimpose on the scatter diagram a line which best fits or represents the underlying relationship. Line I is probably the best guess at this. Now, as we are aware from the mathematical Appendix 1, the equation of a straight line relationship between two variables, $Y$ and $X$, is given by:

$$Y = a + bX \qquad (7\text{-}1)$$

where $a$ and $b$ are constants or numbers, $Y$ is 'freezer ownership' and $X$ is 'average weekly income'. The constant $a$ is known as the intercept, being the value of $Y$ where the line intercepts the $Y$-axis, i.e. the value of $Y$ where $X = 0$. From line I the intercept takes a negative value of $Y$. The value of $b$ is the slope coefficient of the line; this is the (change in $Y$)/(change in $X$), denoted by $\Delta Y/\Delta X$, where the $\Delta$ (delta) sign is shorthand for 'change in'. This is shown in 'close up' in Fig. 7-2. For line I, the slope coefficient has been measured as a change in $X$ ($\Delta X = 220 - 200 = 20$) divided into the corresponding change in $Y$ ($\Delta Y = 70 - 62.5 = 7.5$). The slope coefficient is $7.5/20 = 0.375$. The slope would be the same irrespective of the 'range' taken for $\Delta X$ since one property of a straight line is that its slope is constant throughout its range. Any line can be represented by particular values of $a$ and $b$.

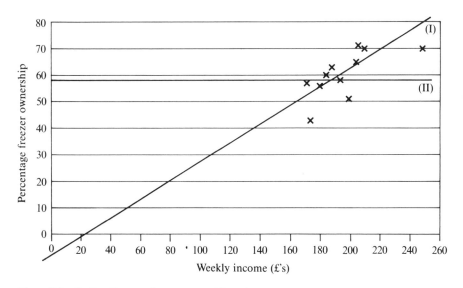

**Figure 7-1**   Scatter diagram: freezer ownership vs income

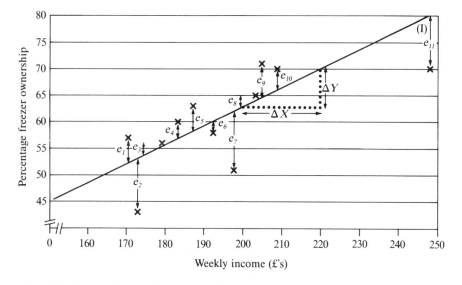

**Figure 7-2**   Scatter diagram: freezer ownership vs income

Regression is about finding the equation of the line (values of $a$ and $b$) that best represents the pattern of the data. We do this because if the line captures the features of the data, it acts as a model (albeit imperfect) of the data, grounded in and reflecting the characteristics of the data. The values of $a$ and $b$ tell us about the line, and thus about the data. By substituting values of $X$ into the equation we predict values of $Y$, based on the real life data upon which the model is grounded.

The values of $a$ and $b$ are of particular interest. Consider (1) the relationship between sales ($Y$) and advertising expenditure ($X$); $a$ is the intercept, the value of $Y$ when $X = 0$, i.e. the value of sales if there was no advertising expenditure; or (2) between total cost ($Y$) and quantity produced ($X$); $a$ is the value of total costs if nothing was produced, i.e. fixed costs. As the value of $a$ is predicted at the extreme of the relationship, it is not always useful. For example, in our freezer example 'percentage regional freezer ownership' would be negative (see Fig. 7-1) if 'average weekly household income' were zero.

The value of $b$ is the slope—for our sales and advertising example, the change in sales ($Y$) that results from a unit change in advertising expenditure ($X$) (if advertising expenditure were measured in thousands of pounds). Now $b$ would yield the value of sales resulting from a £1000 increase in advertising expenditure, i.e. the effectiveness of advertising expenditure. For our total cost example it is the change in total costs resulting from a unit change in quantity produced ($X$)—the marginal cost, which is an important concept for decision making. Economic theory tells us that decisions should be based upon what happens at the margin, not the average. Average sales per sales representative, for example, may be high in an area, but the area may have reached saturation point as far as sales representatives are concerned and the marginal sales (from adding another one representative) may be quite different to the average. As a final example compare $C = 10 + 0.95I$ with $C = 100 + 0.75I$, $C$ being household consumption expenditure and $I$ disposable income. The first of these 'consumption functions' might be for a developing country where $a$ is very low: when income is zero (autonomous) consumption expenditure may be from subsistence farming, dissaving, stealing, borrowing. The change in consumption expenditure arising from a change in income ($b$, the marginal propensity to consume, the driving force of Keynesian economics) is very high. When you have little, most additional income is spent, not saved. Since savings equal investment, there is a vicious circle. Because developing countries are poor, little additional income is saved and invested, thus perpetuating the poverty. Contrast this with a developed country where $a$ is relatively high from social security benefits, using savings, borrowing, etc., and $b$ is lower allowing more saving and investment and thus growth from any increase in income. The point of all this is that determining the $a$ and $b$ of a relationship tells us useful things about the real world relationships between the relevant $Y$ and $X$ variables.

Note the choice of which variable is labelled $Y$, and which $X$; unlike correlation analysis this is of critical importance here. A regression of $Y$ 'on' $X$ yields different predictions and coefficients to one of $X$ 'on' $Y$. The $Y$ and $X$ variables will be called 'endogenous' and 'exogenous' respectively since $Y$ is within the system we wish to know about, while $X$ is outside it, being used to explain any variation in $Y$. More often they are known as 'dependent' and 'independent' variables, respectively, since $Y$ depends on $X$ for its values. The $Y$-variable is the one we shall now explain—it is what concerns us and we look to other variables by which we might explain variations in $Y$. For example, the amount we consume ($Y$) can be explained by how much we earn ($X$). Unfortunately, the transpose does not work; scores in an examination ($Y$) may be related to age ($X$), but we cannot and would not want to explain age variations in terms of scores in an examination.

Determining the values of $a$ and $b$ are thus useful for analysis and for predictions. However, guesses of the 'best fit' line—such as that for Fig. 7-1—in order to derive these values are singularly inadequate for such an important decision-making tool.

## THE LEAST SQUARES CRITERION

We need a good objective basis for determining the equation of the line that best fits the data. In guessing line I in Figs 7-1 and 7-2 an attempt was made to ensure that the total vertical distance between points above the line were cancelled by those below the line. Thus, if $e_1$ is the vertical distance between the first point and the line (see Fig. 7-2), $e_2$ between the second point and the line, etc., we want $\Sigma e_i = 0$, the sum of the positive differences above the line cancelling with the negative ones below it. More formally, if the actual $Y$-value of a point is $Y_i$, and its corresponding $X$-value $X_i$, then the predicted values from the line are $\hat{Y}_i = a + bX_i$, and the sum of the errors is

$$\Sigma e_i = \Sigma(Y_i - \hat{Y}_i) = 0 \qquad (7\text{-}2)$$

[In our notation the 'hat' above the $\hat{Y}$ denotes a predicted value of $Y$.]

Now this is a reasonable criterion at first sight, but if we look at line II on Fig. 7-1 we see that it may come close to satisfying the criterion. Obviously line I is better than II in the sense that they both come close to satisfying Eq. (7-2), but line I 'hugs' the points closer. For this closeness we want the total difference between the points and the line to be a minimum. The total difference is $\Sigma e_i$, but then negative and positive differences cancel to yield zero, so this provides no idea of how close all points are in total. Therefore, we square the differences (as we did for $s$ in Chapter 4) to make them all positive. This gives us our least squares criterion:

Minimize
$$\Sigma e_i^2 = \Sigma(Y_i - \hat{Y}_i)^2 \quad \text{is the least squares criterion} \qquad (7\text{-}3)$$

where $\hat{Y}_i = a + bX_i$.

Our criterion is such that the line of best fit minimizes the sum of the squared vertical differences between each point and the line. We should note that we are estimating the equation

$$Y_i = a + bX_i + e_i \qquad (7\text{-}4)$$

where $e_i$ is the error term, i.e. $e_i = (Y_i - \hat{Y})$.

The expression $a + bX_i$ will not generally perfectly yield actual $Y$ values since the line approximates the shape of the relationship as we saw in Fig. 7-2, the $e_i$ being the vertical differences between the actual $Y_i$-values and those predicted by the line, $\hat{Y}_i$.

## METHOD

We now have to consider how we get from our criterion to estimates of $a$ and $b$. A knowledge of the calculus is useful here and while Gauss formulated the derivation when he was only 17, we shall leave it to the annex of this chapter for those 'without the time' to solve Eq. (7-3) for values of $a$ and $b$. The resulting equations give the values of $a$ and $b$ based on the least squares criterion, i.e.

$$\left. \begin{aligned} b &= \frac{n\Sigma XY - \Sigma X\,\Sigma Y}{n\Sigma X^2 - (\Sigma X)^2} \\[2em] a &= \frac{\Sigma Y - b\Sigma X}{n} = \bar{Y} - b\bar{X} \end{aligned} \right\} \qquad (7\text{-}5)$$

Consider the data on freezers and average earnings used in the previous chapter in Table 6-2. It follows that

$$b = \frac{11(130\,953.7) - (2148.2)664}{11(424\,251.4) - (2148.2)^2} = \frac{14\,085.9}{52\,002.16} = 0.27087$$

$$a = \frac{664 - 0.27087(2148.2)}{11} = 7.465$$

i.e. $\hat{Y} = 7.465 + 0.27X$.

We have considered the interpretation of $a$ and $b$ above. Here $a$ is not so meaningful but the value of $b$ is the change in percentage freezer ownership (0.27) arising from a one unit ($X$ is measured in £'s per week) change in average weekly income. Note that the values of $a$ and $b$ differ from those for the 'best fit' line in Figs 7-1 and 7-2. This line was a guess at the line of best fit and the figures for $a$ and $b$ are poor estimates compared with those from the regression equation.

We can provide predictions of $Y$ for given values of $X$; for example, if a region had its average earnings at £210 per week, predicted percentage ownership of freezers would be:

$$\hat{Y} = a + bX$$
$$= 7.465 + 0.27(210) = 64.2 \text{ per cent}$$

The reliability of the forecast will depend in part on the strength of the association and there is no use even undertaking the analysis unless there is a reasonably high and statistically significant relationship between $Y$ and $X$. Thus, our first step is to look at the correlation coefficient before proceeding with regression. More usually we look at the *coefficient of determination*, $R^2 = r^2$, i.e. the correlation coefficient squared, in this case $(0.68)^2 = 0.4624$. It shows that the proportion of variation in $Y$ explained by the model is 0.4624 or 46.24 per cent. Thus $(100.0 - 46.24) = 53.8$ per cent of regional variation in ownership of freezers is explained by factors other than the linear relationship found by our model. It can be shown mathematically that

$$R^2 = \left[ 1 - \frac{\Sigma(Y_i - \hat{Y}_i)^2}{\Sigma(Y_i - \bar{Y})^2} \right] \tag{7-6}$$

is unexplained variation as a proportion of total variation, deducted from 1 to yield explained variation as a proportion of total variation.

We learned in the previous chapter that it is not enough to know that the relationship is strong, since a strong relationship may not be statistically significant due to small sample sizes. We must also test for statistical significance. However, in doing so we must also bear in mind that statistical significance does not imply that the relationship is strong, since in large samples the sampling error can be very small. While we can do this for $r$, the correlation coefficient, we are interested here in whether the difference of $a$ and/or $b$ from zero is statistically significant. It should be pointed out that what follows in this chapter develops the subject to a level that may be beyond that required for the course. However, it requires no further mathematical knowledge, the applied side being emphasized, and may even be of some interest.

We wish to test whether the difference between our calculated $b$ and zero is statistically significant; that is, the difference is in addition to that attributable to sampling error at, say, a 5 per cent significance level. If $b$ were equal to zero, a change in $X$ would have no effect on $Y$. To undertake this test we first calculate the *standard error of the slope coefficient* ($b$) given by:

$$\text{SE}_b = \left[ \sqrt{\Sigma(Y_i - \hat{Y}_i)^2/(n-2)} \right] \Big/ \sqrt{\Sigma(X_i - \bar{X})^2} \tag{7-7}$$

To test if the slope coefficient is statistically significant we calculate:

$$t = b/\text{SE}_b \tag{7-8}$$

For example, using the data in Table 6-2 and from Eq.(7-5), $b = 0.27087/0.09765 = 2.77$. (A further illustration with details of this calculation is given in the next section.) We then compare this calculated $t$-value with a value of $t$ from the tables in Appendix 6. This value from tables is derived by:

1. Deciding on an appropriate level of significance, say 5 per cent.
2. Deciding whether to use a one-tailed or two-tailed test as outlined in the previous chapter. If a

one-tailed test is used the column headed 0.05 is chosen; for a two-tailed test use the column headed 0.025.
3. Determining the degrees of freedom, i.e. $v = n - 2$ in the rows of the $t$-table; the intersection of the appropriate column and row yields the $t$-value from the table.
4. If the calculated $t$-value from Eq. (7-8) (ignoring the sign) is greater than the $t$ value from the table, the slope coefficient is statistically significant at a 5 per cent level. In our case the calculated $t$-value was 2.77, the value from tables with $(n - 2) = 11 - 2 = 9$ degrees of freedom is 1.8331 (one-tail); the difference between the slope coefficient and zero is statistically significant at a 5 per cent level.

We can now estimate a regression equation and derive $a$ and $b$, which are useful for decision making and prediction. We can ascertain the strength of the relationship via $R^2$, and test if the slope coefficient is statistically significant in order to ascertain how much faith (if any) we should have in the results.

## FURTHER DEVELOPMENTS

Having covered the estimates for a basic model we consider here some developments: forecasting, non-linearity and multiple regression.

### Forecasting

Consider the data in Table 7-1 and in Fig. 7-3 on sales and price. The manager wishes to predict sales in a future period, but knows that any prediction has to take account of the price that will be charged due to the close association between the two variables. Regression is thus an appropriate tool since not only does it take account of the association, but allows the manager to predict sales from a range of price scenarios, thus aiding decision making.

$$b = \frac{10(4557.71) - 44.5(1053.1)}{10(198.85) - (44.5)^2} = -155.861$$

$$a = [1053.1 - (-155.861)(44.5)]/10 = 798.89$$

[Note how rounding the calculations in Table 7-1 to one decimal place would affect the results: $b = -146.97$ and $a = -548.69$—try rounding $\Sigma XY, \Sigma X, \Sigma Y$ and $\Sigma X^2$ to no decimal places and see the effect.]

We can test the statistical significance of the slope coefficient using Eqs (7-7) and (7-8). From Table 7-1:

$$SE_b = \left[\sqrt{3054.67/(10-2)}\right] \Big/ \sqrt{0.825} = 21.51$$

$$t = -155.86/21.51 = -7.24$$

The $t$-value from Appendix 6 at a 5 per cent level of significance using a one-tailed test (we only expect a negative association), with $v = 8$ degrees of freedom, is 1.86. Since (ignoring the sign) 'calculated-$t$' exceeds '$t$-from-tables' ($7.24 > 1.86$) the difference between zero and the coefficient for $X$ at the 5 per cent level is statistically significant, being over and above that expected from sampling errors at this level.

Our (ex-ante) forecast of sales when price falls to £3.90 is

$$\hat{Y} = 798.89 - 155.861(3.9) = 191.032$$

**Table 7-1** Data on sales quantity and price

| Quantity sold (000's) $Y_i$ | Price (£) $X_i$ | $X_iY_i$ | $X_i^2$ | $Y_i^2$ | $\hat{Y}_i$ | $(Y_i - \hat{Y}_i)^2$ | $(X_i - \bar{X})^2$ |
|---|---|---|---|---|---|---|---|
| 50.0 | 4.9 | 245.00 | 24.01 | 2 500.00 | 35.17 | 219.90 | 0.2025 |
| 68.4 | 4.8 | 328.32 | 23.04 | 4 678.56 | 50.76 | 311.27 | 0.1225 |
| 65.3 | 4.7 | 306.91 | 22.09 | 4 264.09 | 66.34 | 1.09 | 0.0625 |
| 69.0 | 4.6 | 317.40 | 21.16 | 4 761.00 | 81.93 | 167.17 | 0.0225 |
| 82.3 | 4.5 | 370.35 | 20.25 | 6 773.29 | 97.52 | 231.51 | 0.0025 |
| 109.1 | 4.4 | 480.04 | 19.36 | 11 902.81 | 113.10 | 16.01 | 0.0025 |
| 99.9 | 4.3 | 429.57 | 18.49 | 9 980.01 | 128.69 | 828.73 | 0.0225 |
| 128.6 | 4.2 | 540.12 | 17.64 | 16 537.96 | 144.27 | 245.67 | 0.0625 |
| 180.0 | 4.1 | 738.00 | 16.81 | 32 400.00 | 159.86 | 405.62 | 0.1225 |
| 200.5 | 4.0 | 802.00 | 16.00 | 40 200.25 | 175.45 | 627.70 | 0.2025 |
| 1 053.1 | 44.5 | 4 557.71 | 198.85 | 133 998.00 | 1 053.09 | 3 054.67 | 0.8250 |

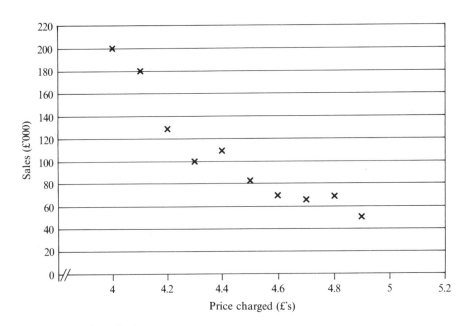

**Figure 7-3** Sales and price

or, since the data are in thousands, 191 032. Predictions (ex-post) for existing values of $X_i$ are given under $\hat{Y}_i$ in Table 7-1. Note that we are on happier ground predicting values of $Y$ from values falling within the range for which the regression was undertaken, e.g. when $X = 4.63$, $\hat{Y} = 77.25$. Predictions for $X$-values outside the range, e.g. when $X = 3.9$, obviously require the assumption that the relationship continues to hold for these values.

**Prediction intervals for forecast values**   All is well and good in that we have a sales forecast that takes into account the effect of price changes. However, how reliable is this forecast? One indicator is the strength of the relationship. The correlation coefficient for these data is 0.9315, which is strong and statistically significant at the 5 per cent level (see Chapter 6). So too is the slope coefficient; a unit (£1) increase in price decreases quantity sold by nearly 156 000—the difference between the coefficient and zero being statistically significant at the 5 per cent level. Yet the accuracy of our forecast should also depend on how far the value of $X$ used for the prediction is away from the centre of the data range used to calculate the regression. There is likely to be more error associated with a prediction based on $X=£1$ than one based on $X=£3.90$. In addition, the larger the $n$ or sample size used, the more 'accuracy' is expected. It is possible to devise what are known as confidence intervals for a predicted value—giving an upper and lower bound to the forecast—which takes these factors into account. The formula is given by

$$\hat{Y} \mp t.s \sqrt{\frac{1}{n} + \frac{(X^* - \bar{X})^2}{\Sigma(X_i - \bar{X})^2}} \tag{7-9}$$

where $\hat{Y}$ is the predicted value, 191.032 for $X=£5$ in our example; $t$ is a value from the $t$ tables which reflects how much confidence we have that (if the exercise was repeated many times, other things being equal) the result will fall in our interval. To ascertain its value you need to (i) decide on the confidence required, say 95 per cent, and (ii) turn to the tables in Appendix 6 and find the figure corresponding to the intersection of $(1-0.95)/2=0.025$ in the column headings and $v=n-2=10-2=8$ in the row headings—at their intersection is 2.306 (the rationale for this is explained in Chapter 11). The term $s$ is the standard error of the regression, given by $\sqrt{\Sigma(Y_i - \hat{Y}_i)^2/(n-2)}$. This is the discrepancy between actual and predicted values and thus the strength of the relationship. The first term in Eq.(7-9) under the square root is concerned with the number of observations ($n$)—the higher $n$, the wider the interval. The final term is concerned with the distance the value of $X^*$ used for prediction is from the centre (mean) of the ($X$) data. Applying formula (7-9) to the data in Table 7-1 for $X^*=£3.90$ we have:

$$191.032 \mp 2.306 \sqrt{\frac{3054.673}{(10-2)}} \sqrt{\frac{1}{10} + \frac{(3.90-4.45)^2}{0.825}}$$

$$191.032 \mp 2.306(19.54)(0.6831)$$

$$191.032 \mp 30.780$$

i.e. we are 95 per cent confident that (given the formula holds when $X^*=£3.90$) predicted sales lie in the interval 160.252 to 221.812. The interval need not contain the actual result: first, we are only 95 per cent confident and, second, we rely on the model of the relationship holding outside the range of which it was estimated, £4 to £4.90. Yet we don't disallow any use of judgement to adapt the forecast on the basis of new information—the model takes into account some factors, leaving you to adjust it for others, e.g. changes in fashion.

You might come across formula (7-9) in the form

$$\hat{Y} \mp t.s \sqrt{1 + \frac{1}{n} + \frac{(X^* - \bar{X})^2}{\Sigma(X_i - \bar{X})^2}} \tag{7-10}$$

Formula (7-9) is often referred to as a confidence interval for the *mean* of $Y$ given a specific value of $X$, while formula (7-10) yields a prediction interval for an *individual value* of $Y$ given a specific value of $X$, the latter being wider than the former. For example, if in costing haulage expenses we regressed 'annual repair bill' on 'miles travelled' for our trucks and then wanted to predict the *mean* repair bill for trucks travelling a given mileage, our confidence interval would be calculated using formula (7-9). However, for predicting the repair bill of an individual truck, we also have the 'inter-truck variation' to take into account, and formula (7-10) holds.

128   BUSINESS STATISTICS

**Table 7-2**   Regression output from Minitab using data in Table 7-1

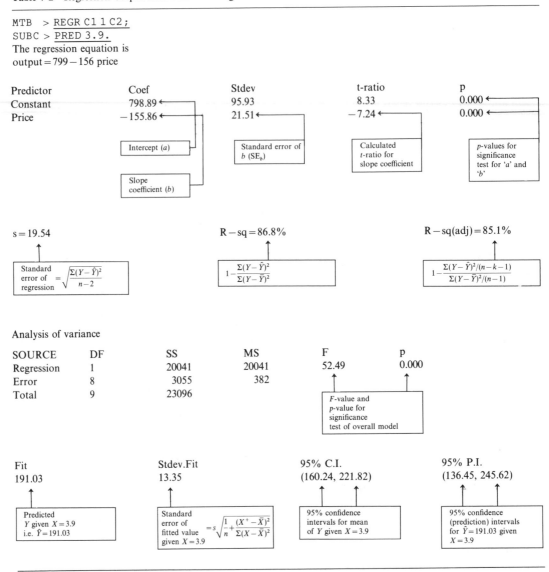

```
MTB  > REGR C1 1 C2;
SUBC > PRED 3.9.
```
The regression equation is
output = 799 − 156 price

| Predictor | Coef | Stdev | t-ratio | p |
|---|---|---|---|---|
| Constant | 798.89 | 95.93 | 8.33 | 0.000 |
| Price | −155.86 | 21.51 | −7.24 | 0.000 |

Intercept (a)

Slope coefficient (b)

Standard error of b (SE_b)

Calculated t-ratio for slope coefficient

p-values for significance test for 'a' and 'b'

$s = 19.54$

$R-sq = 86.8\%$

$R-sq(adj) = 85.1\%$

Standard error of regression $= \sqrt{\dfrac{\Sigma(Y-\hat{Y})^2}{n-2}}$

$1 - \dfrac{\Sigma(Y-\hat{Y})^2}{\Sigma(Y-\bar{Y})^2}$

$1 - \dfrac{\Sigma(Y-\hat{Y})^2/(n-k-1)}{\Sigma(Y-\bar{Y})^2/(n-1)}$

Analysis of variance

| SOURCE | DF | SS | MS | F | p |
|---|---|---|---|---|---|
| Regression | 1 | 20041 | 20041 | 52.49 | 0.000 |
| Error | 8 | 3055 | 382 | | |
| Total | 9 | 23096 | | | |

F-value and p-value for significance test of overall model

| Fit | Stdev.Fit | 95% C.I. | 95% P.I. |
|---|---|---|---|
| 191.03 | 13.35 | (160.24, 221.82) | (136.45, 245.62) |

Predicted Y given X=3.9 i.e. $\hat{Y}=191.03$

Standard error of fitted value given X=3.9 $=s\sqrt{\dfrac{1}{n}+\dfrac{(X^+-\bar{X})^2}{\Sigma(X-\bar{X})^2}}$

95% confidence intervals for mean of Y given X=3.9

95% confidence (prediction) intervals for $\hat{Y}=191.03$ given X=3.9

Finally, in calculating the regression we have given equal weight or importance to each point on the scatter diagram in determining the equation of the line. However, if, for example, the data in Table 7-1 were for different time periods, the first pair of observations being the most recent, the next pair the next most recent and so forth, there may be a case for giving more weight to the more recent observations. Details of such a method—discounted least squares—are given in Gilchrist (1976, Ch. 6).

It is useful to illustrate the output relating to regression for Minitab here. Table 7-2 shows the regression equation for the data in Table 7-1 calculated above. The coefficients *a* and *b* are given—in this case *b* is the coefficient for price along with the associated standard errors and *t*-ratios. The latter are to be compared to values of *t* from tables to undertake significance tests on the coefficients. For convenience the $p$-values save us the effort of undertaking this test procedure: if the $p$-value is more than 0.05 we conclude the difference between the coefficient and zero is not statistically significant at a 5 per cent level. In this case the $p$-values are so low they round to 0.000, the difference between the coefficients and zero in this case being statistically significant at the 5 per cent level. The value of $s$ is the standard error of the regression, also referred to as the root mean squared error (RMSE) and is one indicator of how well the model's ex-post predictions stand up.

The coefficient of determination is given by $R$-squared ($R^2$) and its adjusted version is particularly applicable when there are more than one (say $k$) exogenous (independent) variables and a relatively small sample size. The analysis of variance via its $p$-value allows us to test whether the explanatory power of the model as a whole is statistically significant.

The final two lines arise from the use of the prediction subcommand and provide the prediction (fitted value) for $X = 3.9$ (Fit), the standard error of the fit (Stdev) which is the result of calculating everything to the right of $t$ in Eq.(7-9). Confidence intervals (formula (7-9)) and prediction intervals (formula (7-10)) follow.

## Non-linear relationships

So far the analysis has been confined to linear relationships; but what if the relationship is non-linear? Linear models imposed on non-linear relationships will lead to errors, the extent of the errors depending on the deviation of the data from the linear form. If the relationship is non-linear we can still use linear regression as long as we are able to transform the non-linear data to linear form, apply linear regression, and then reinterpret the coefficients $a$ and $b$ back into their non-linear form. To do this we need to know the non-linear form the data are taking, and which appropriate transformation to use. We discussed a few non-linear functional forms in the mathematical Appendix 1. Others are given in Fig. 7-4 with their mathematical counterparts in Table 7-3.

Consider the first equation: this may take a number of shapes depending on the values of $b$, as illustrated in Fig. 7-4. If we thought $Y$ increased by only relatively small amounts for a unit increase in $X$, when $X$ was small, but as $X$ took on larger values the increases in $Y$, from unit increases in $X$, became larger and larger, then something like Fig. 7-4(b) is being described. This is common for compounded growth over time, e.g. when interest is compounded or a spiral of inflation takes off. The scatter diagram helps to confirm these theoretical suspicions and there are 'curve fitting' software that will test a host of functional forms to see which provides the highest $R^2$—one is provided with Lewis (1989). If we think this functional form is appropriate we have to transform it into a linear form. Using logarithms to the base $e$, denoted by 'ln' (see mathematical Appendix 1):

$$Y = aX^b, \qquad \ln Y = \ln a + b \ln X$$

that is, (7-11)

$$Y^* = a^* + bX^*$$

where $Y^* = \ln Y$, $a^* = \ln a$, and $X^* = \ln X$. That is, we first form two new columns of data, $Y^*$ and $X^*$; we apply linear regression on this linear form $Y^* = a^* + bX^*$ to yield $a^*$ and $b$; $b$ is in the required form, the antilog of $a^*$ has to be taken to convert it to $a$, i.e. exponent ($a^*$).

The data in Fig. 7-3 can be seen to have a little more in common with Fig. 7-4(c) than the linear form imposed upon it. If we used ln $Y$ instead of $Y$ and log $X$ instead of $X$ and continued as in Eq.(7-5) we get values of $a^* = 14.23926$ and $b = -6.4921$, i.e. $b < 0$ as expected. To derive $a$ we want the antilog of $a^*$, i.e. $e^{14.23926} = 1\,527\,678.77$. Our model is thus:

$$Y = aX^b = 1\,527\,678.77X^{-6.4921}$$

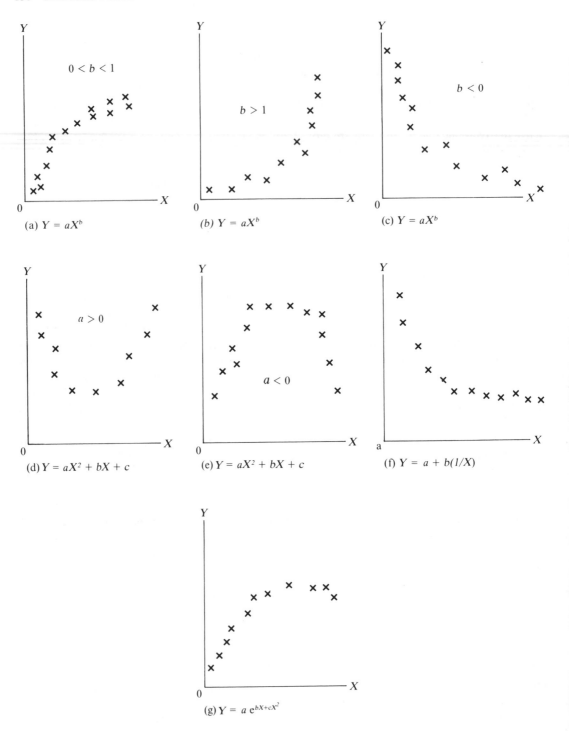

Figure 7-4   Some functional forms

**Table 7.3** Some functional forms and transformations

| Functional form | Transformation | |
|---|---|---|
| (1) $Y = aX^b$ | $Y^* = a^* + bX^*$ | where $Y^* = \ln Y$ |
| | | $a^* = \ln a$ |
| | | $X^* = \ln X$ |
| (2) $Y = a + bX + cX^2$ | $Y = a + bX + cX^*$ | where $X^* = X^2$ |
| (3) $Y = a + b(1/X)$ | $Y = a + bX^*$ | where $X^* = 1/X$ |
| (4) $Y = a e^{bX} + cX^2$ | $Y^* = a^* + bX + cX^*$ | where $Y^* = \ln Y$ |
| | | $a^* = \ln a$ |
| | | $X^* = X^2$ |

The $R^2 = 0.9482$ is slightly better than the linear model ($R^2 = 0.8677$), the difference being not too great since, as is apparent from Fig. 7-3, the departure from linearity is not substantial. However, the linear model fails to incorporate the increase in the slope as $X$ falls to its lower values: thus the forecast for sales when price is £3.90 would be underestimated using the linear model, which gave us 191 032. Using the new form:

$$Y = 1\,527\,678.77(3.9)^{-6.49208} = 1\,527\,678.77(0.00014546592) = 222.225$$

i.e. sales of 222.225. A glance at Fig. 7-3 shows this to be a much more reasonable prediction.

Some further functional forms and transformations were given in Fig. 7-4 and Table 7-3. It is stressed that theory as to the form of the relationship should guide the choice of functional form followed by an examination of the scatter diagram. For example, the relationship between average costs and quantity produced may take a quadratic form, as in Fig. 7-4(d) with average costs ($Y$) at first decreasing with economies of scales as quantity produced ($X$) increases; however, as production becomes increasingly large, complex and bureaucratic decreasing returns to scale arise with average cost rising. Note that the transformation Table 7-3(2) requires $Y$ to be regressed on two exogenous variables, i.e. $X$ and $X^*$ ($= X^2$). This requires the use of multiple regression, to which we turn in the next section.

The reciprocal relationship in Fig. 7-4(f) and Table 7-3(3) was once used to depict the relationship between the percentage change in wages ($Y$) and the rate of unemployment ($X$)—the Phillips curve. The logarithmic parabola—Fig. 7-4(g) and Table 7-3(4)—might reflect the relationship between earnings ($Y$) and age ($X$) of manual workers with overtime falling off after a certain age. Theories not only exist as to whether two variables are related, but also as to the form of the relationship, and this is critical to correct modelling.

## Multiple regression

So far our concern has been with bivariate regression: $Y$ (the endogenous or dependent variable) is regressed on a single exogenous (or independent) variable $X$. However, in practice the thing we want to explain, $Y$, is often related to a number of exogenous (independent) variables. Sales variations, for example, may be related to variation in price, advertising expenditure, seasons, number, size and location of distribution outlets, quality of the product, disposable income, fashion, in some cases weather and so forth. Thus instead of $\hat{Y} = a + bX$ we have

$$\hat{Y} = a + b_1 X_1 + b_2 X_2 + b_3 X_3 + \ldots + b_n X_n \tag{7-12}$$

where $X_1, \ldots, X_n$ are the exogenous (independent) variable and $b_1, \ldots, b_n$ are their are respective coefficients and $e$. Our job now is to estimate not just $a$ and $b$, but $a, b_1, b_2, b_3, \ldots, b_n$. This is quite

**Table 7-4** Data on car registrations and related variables

|  | New cars reg.* Y | Real income index† INC | Real consumer credit index‡ CRED | GDP constant prices** GDP | Price of motoring exp/all index†† PRICE | Unemployment rate percent‡‡ UNEMP |
|---|---|---|---|---|---|---|
| 1985: Q1 | 150.2 | 98.9 | 100.00 | 1331 | 106.68 | 11.2 |
| Q2 | 150.2 | 99.7 | 94.16 | 1349 | 101.36 | 11.3 |
| Q3 | 151.3 | 100.2 | 108.47 | 1351 | 101.96 | 11.3 |
| Q4 | 157.4 | 101.2 | 99.08 | 1352 | 103.20 | 11.3 |
| 1986: Q1 | 152.3 | 101.5 | 105.45 | 1371 | 101.56 | 11.1 |
| Q2 | 158.3 | 104.8 | 111.75 | 1385 | 98.61 | 11.2 |
| Q3 | 157.6 | 104.8 | 143.19 | 1399 | 99.30 | 11.2 |
| Q4 | 160.9 | 108.8 | 77.34 | 1410 | 99.75 | 11.0 |
| 1987: Q1 | 159.4 | 105.1 | 116.45 | 1420 | 100.39 | 10.7 |
| Q2 | 162.5 | 106.7 | 166.47 | 1441 | 100.79 | 10.6 |
| Q3 | 172.6 | 108.0 | 146.27 | 1463 | 102.63 | 10.1 |
| Q4 | 178.3 | 110.0 | 156.39 | 1478 | 101.99 | 9.5 |
| 1988: Q1 | 177.8 | 111.8 | 138.04 | 1495 | 101.49 | 8.9 |
| Q2 | 180.5 | 111.4 | 145.88 | 1501 | 101.18 | 8.5 |
| Q3 | 193.0 | 113.3 | 193.68 | 1519 | 101.68 | 8.0 |
| Q4 | 184.8 | 116.3 | 102.60 | 1524 | 100.09 | 7.6 |
| 1989: Q1 | 193.9 | 117.0 | 128.18 | 1536 | 99.46 | 7.0 |
| Q2 | 197.6 | 117.8 | 154.48 | 1537 | 100.02 | 6.6 |
| Q3 | 186.0 | 118.0 | 154.93 | 1544 | 99.18 | 6.3 |

*New registrations of cars, thousands: DKBY (codes in these notes refer to CSO references for the series).

†Real personal disposable income at 1985 prices (1985 = 100); deflated by implicit consumer's expenditure deflator: CFAF.

‡Real total outstanding consumer credit at 1985 prices (1985: Q1 = 100); deflated by implicit consumer's expenditure deflator: AIKM, CFAF, AIIL.

**Gross domestic product (average estimate) at factor cost and constant 1985 prices, million pounds: CAQC.

††Retail prices index for motoring expenditure (purchase, maintenance, petrol and oil, tax and insurance) divided by all items, RPI (Jan. 1987 = 100): FRAG. Department of Employment, *Employment Gazette*.

‡‡Percentage of workforce (in employment and unemployed claimants) unemployed excluding students registered during vacation. Figures are seasonally adjusted and allow for changes in coverage of definitions due to changes in benefit regulations—see *Employment Gazette*, Dec. 1988: BCJE.

*Source*: Central Statistical Office, *Economic Trends*, Nos. 407, 423 and 436, Sept. 1987, Jan. 1989 and Feb. 1990, London: HMSO; Dept. of Employment, *Employment Gazette*, 95, 7 July 1987, 96, 6 June 1988 and 98, 3 March 1990, London: HMSO.

arduous even for two exogenous variables (though see Croxton *et al.*, 1968, for formulae) and, in practice, we generally use computers for multiple regression. Minitab, as will be explained later, can easily cope with multiple regression and the spreadsheet package Lotus 1-2-3 also has such a facility. We shall illustrate the principles of multiple regression and interpretation of the results by way of an example.

Consider the data in Table 7-4. We wish to explain (quarterly) variations in the number of cars registered in Britain—NCRB—over the period 1985 to 1990 by recourse to variations in: income, adjusted for inflation (INC); consumer credit, adjusted for inflation (CRED); the total quantity of production of the economy, to reflect cars purchased by businesses (GDP); the price (cost) of motoring relative to the cost of other consumer goods (PRICE); and the unemployment rate (UNEMP). We would expect the richer the population, or the more purchasing power they have through credit, the more cars would be registered, i.e. the signs of the slope coefficients for INC and

**Table 7-5** Regression output

| | | | | | |
|---|---|---|---|---|---|
| Constant | − 141.227 | | | | |
| Std Err of Y Est | 3.894177 | | | | |
| R Squared | 0.958322 | | | | |
| No of Observations | 19 | | | | |
| Degrees of Freedom | 13 | | | | |
| X Coefficient(s) | 1.472498 | 0.064107 | 0.033625 | 1.145415 | − 2.16644 |
| Std Err of Coef | 1.021117 | 0.051349 | 0.085441 | 0.689546 | 1.749454 |

CRED would be positive. The more industry produced (GDP), the more cars might be registered yielding a positive coefficient on GDP, though a negative coefficient might arise if more sales representatives were hired due to flagging demand. If the price of cars increased relative to other goods, we would expect a negative coefficient on PRICE reflecting less sales and registrations. Finally, falls in UNEMP might reflect the economy moving out of a recession and more confidence in putting money into consumer durables such as cars. We have theories as to whether and how some variables might affect car registrations; we have collected data in Table 7-4 from existing sources to test the theory empirically (for further details on such models, see Evans (1969, Ch. 6)) and we shall use Lotus 1-2-3 to regress $Y$ on all of the exogenous variables as a block (using Data Regression)—see page 139 on Lotus 1-2-3—to provide a single model of the form given in Eq. (7-12). The output is reproduced in Table 7-5 and shows the model to be:

```
NCRB=-141.23+1.47INC+0.06CRED+0.03GDP+1.15PRICE-2.17UNEMP
```

where $a$ is the 'constant' and the $b$ slope coefficients for each variable in turn are given by the $X$-coefficient(s) in the order they appeared when entering the data. Note that $R^2$ ($R$ squared) shows that the 95.8 per cent of variation in car registration is explained by the model. The coefficient on INC, for example, shows that a change in the index of income of 1 will increase car registrations by 1.47 (thousands). But how do we know the relationship is statistically significant? The standard error for each $X$-coefficient given in the computer output in Table 7-5 allows us to undertake the appropriate test: we divide the coefficient by the standard error to yield the calculated $t$-values. The value from tables for a one-tailed test at 5 per cent for $v = 13$ is 1.771. The order of the variables is the same as in Table 7-4. For income we thus have $1.4725/1.0211 = 1.442$, i.e. the difference between the coefficient and zero (no relationship) is less than 1.771, i.e. *not* statistically significant at the 5 per cent level. Repeating the exercise we find *none* of the coefficients to have a statistically significant difference from zero (no effect). Yet the $R^2$ is high. This is all somewhat surprising.

## THE NEED FOR CAUTION

This exercise illustrates first the power of the technique. Those concerned with marketing products need to know how sensitive their sales are to price, income or whatever and the models allow this to be undertaken. Forecasting car registrations is the result of simulation, as different scenarios of income, price, GDP or whatever figures are fed into the model to see the effect on car registrations. Yet while in some cases quite robust regression models *may* result from relatively inexperienced users, it is the case with regression that considerable skill may be required since a host of assumptions are implicit in the method. This section refers to more advanced facets of the method, and while you should be aware of the potential problems, a detailed knowledge is not part of this basic course. What is particularly unfortunate is that the method can be applied by unskilled users without their being aware that quite serious errors are often being committed. Software like Lotus 1-2-3 do not help matters as they do not contain sufficient 'test statistics' for the user to check what is wrong. Econometric software such as PC-GIVE, TSP or RATS are much more appropriate for serious work. Some of the problems to watch out for include:

- *Multicollinearity* If the exogenous (independent) variables are themselves correlated with each other, the coefficients and tests may be misleading. Predicted values will still be unbiased, though we assume the multicollinearity is stable (Silver and Goode, 1990). An effect of multicollinearity is that $R^2$ is often high while the coefficients are not statistically significant. This is because the variation shared by the (say) two multicollinear variables is not properly used for the estimate of the coefficient as we do not know whether the variation in $Y$ is due to the variation in the first or second exogenous variable. However, the joint variation is included in $R^2$ and for prediction, the results for these being valid, but not the coefficients and their significance tests. Since most of the exogenous variables in our examples are increasing (decreasing) over time it is likely that they are collinear, and this in part explains our poor test results.
- *Co-integration* One effect of this is that spurious associations resulting in high $R^2$ can result when variables are related to their own past values, as would happen with a trend over time, but unrelated to each other (Granger and Newbold, 1974). (Co-integration need not be spurious, but be a feature of models that has meaning in the theory of why variables are related.)

Both of the above points suggest in this case 'removal' of the trend from all the variables. If we take each value away from its preceding value (first differences)—e.g. for $Y$: $150.2 - 150.2 = 0$; $151.3 - 150.2 = 1.1$, etc.—we remove the trend [try it with $1, 2, 3, 4, 5, \ldots$]. Table 7-6 shows the new data and Table 7-7 the results which, although they have a lower $R^2$, are more sensible. The problem of multicollinearity has been removed with the previous correlation coefficients for INC with GDP and INC with UNEMP being 0.98 and $-0.94$ respectively, now with differenced data they are 0.15 and 0.003 respectively. In Table 7-7 the $t$-values on coefficients INC (2.093673/0.984282) and CRED (0.097297/0.047098) are 2.13 and 2.06 respectively. If we look at the $t$-tables in Appendix 6, the row shows the degrees of freedom given in Table 7-7 as 12 $(n - k - 1)$—our $n$ is now 18, due to differencing we lose an observation; if we test at a 5 per cent level using (see Chapter 6) a one-tailed test, the column heading is 0.05 and $t$ has to be greater than 1.782 from the tables, which it is. Had a two-tailed test been used (column headed 0.025) the results would not be statistically significant at a 5 per cent level since $t$ has to exceed 2.179. As noted in Chapter 6, before undertaking the tests great care is necessary to decide in theory if both positive and negative associations are possible (two-tailed) or if only positive or negative is possible (one-tailed).

Thus our investigation shows variations in the rate of change in car registration to be affected by income and credit expansion. For GDP, PRICE and UNEMP there is no statistically significant relationship at the 5 per cent level. The initial curious results were due to multicollinearity, which we cured (in this case) by taking first differences.

- *Heteroscedasticity* Here an assumption of the method is that the variance of the residuals (errors) is constant; heteroscedasticity occurs when this assumption is broken. For example, if we regressed consumption on disposable income, we might expect those who earn more consume more; but at higher levels of income the dispersion or variance of the residuals will be greater as richer people deviate more from expected patterns, acting on whims. A scatter diagram of the errors against the exogenous variable (income) to which the higher errors are considered to be related, should be undertaken and if a pattern is revealed, e.g. higher absolute residuals for higher income, we have good reason to expect heteroscedasticity, which may render tests of significance misleading.

**Table 7-6** Data transformed to first differences

| | Y | INC | CRED | GDP | PRICE | UNEMP |
|---|---|---|---|---|---|---|
| | | | First differences in | | | |
| 1985: Q1 | | | | | | |
| Q2 | 0 | 0.8 | −5.84 | 18 | −5.32 | 0.1 |
| Q3 | 1.1 | 0.5 | 14.31 | 2 | 0.60 | 0 |
| Q4 | 6.1 | 1 | −9.38 | 1 | 1.24 | 0 |
| 1986: Q1 | −5.1 | 0.3 | 6.37 | 19 | −1.64 | −0.2 |
| Q2 | 6 | 3.3 | 6.30 | 14 | −2.95 | 0.1 |
| Q3 | −0.7 | 0 | 31.45 | 14 | 0.69 | 0 |
| Q4 | 3.3 | 4 | −65.85 | 11 | 0.45 | −0.2 |
| 1987: Q1 | −1.5 | −3.7 | 39.11 | 10 | 0.64 | −0.3 |
| Q2 | 3.1 | 1.6 | 50.01 | 21 | 0.41 | −0.1 |
| Q3 | 10.1 | 1.3 | −20.20 | 22 | 1.84 | −0.5 |
| Q4 | 5.7 | 2 | 10.12 | 15 | −0.64 | −0.6 |
| 1988: Q1 | −0.5 | 1.8 | −18.35 | 17 | −0.50 | −0.6 |
| Q2 | 2.7 | −0.4 | 7.84 | 6 | −0.31 | −0.4 |
| Q3 | 12.5 | 1.9 | 47.80 | 18 | 0.49 | −0.5 |
| Q4 | −8.2 | 3 | −91.08 | 5 | −1.58 | −0.4 |
| 1989: Q1 | 9.1 | 0.7 | 25.58 | 12 | −0.63 | −0.6 |
| Q2 | 3.7 | 0.8 | 26.30 | 1 | 0.55 | −0.4 |
| Q3 | −11.6 | 0.2 | 0.45 | 7 | −0.84 | −0.3 |
| Q4 | | | | | | |

**Table 7-7** Regression output: first differences

| | | | | | |
|---|---|---|---|---|---|
| Constant | −1.93479 | | | | |
| Std Err of Y Est | 5.440702 | | | | |
| R Squared | 0.452722 | | | | |
| No of Observations | 18 | | | | |
| Degrees of Freedom | 12 | | | | |
| X Coefficient(s) | 2.093673 | 0.097297 | 0.087891 | 1.065681 | −2.97284 |
| Std Err of Coef | 0.984282 | 0.047098 | 0.217338 | 0.887218 | 5.888981 |

- *Omitted or included variable bias* Leaving out pertinent variables or including ones with no relationship may bias the results. The effect of the bias depends on the extent to which omitted or wrongly included variables are multicollinear with those included. If we omit related relevant variables our coefficients will be wrong and tests of significance conservative (less likely to find the difference between coefficient and zero statistically significant). As regards inclusion of irrelevant variables, this also leads to conservative significance tests, though our estimates of the coefficients are not biased.
- *Simultaneous equation bias* Here variation in the endogenous variable is determined by the simultaneous interaction of several relationships. For example, increases in car registrations over time may in part be 'explained by' increases in consumer credit to finance the purchases. Yet an equation to explain the increase in consumer credit might include the number of cars registered. Another example is in macro-economics, where consumption depends on income; income equals expenditure which in turn is made up of consumption, investment and government expenditure, and we build up vast models like crossword puzzles where the

equations interact. This is why we use the terms endogenous and exogenous variables instead of dependent and independent, because what is independent in one equation (e.g. income) is dependent in another. Exogenous means it is determined outside the system of equations, endogenous implies there is a relationship in the system that explains it. The *slimmed down* version of the Treasury econometric model, for example, is made up of 524 variables of which 400 are endogenous with about 300 determined by 88 behavioural equations (Mellis *et al.*, 1989). When we have more than one interrelated relationship it is sometimes possible to express them as a 'reduced-form' and use the methods outlined. However, we may not be able to derive the coefficients of the original model (structural parameters). Alternatively, we can estimate the model as a system simultaneously using more sophisticated estimation procedures. All of this is fairly complex. The warning is that if the work you are undertaking looks as if it is one equation which belongs to a system of equations, we may have a problem. In an example for cars, we have in theory equations for the quantities demanded and supplied, and price can be looked at as the result of the interaction of demand *and* supply equations. We cannot always separately identify the two equations. All we may have is price and quantity purchased data. Variation in these data may have resulted from a number of factors, including shifts in the supply curve across a given demand curve (Fig. 7-5(a)) or shifts in a demand curve along a given supply curve (Fig. 7-5(b)) or a combination of these (Fig. 7-5(c)). The equilibrium points (denoted by circles), which are all we would observe, may trace out the demand or supply curve or neither; with only data on price and quantity we cannot identify the separate parameters of the supply and demand curve. For

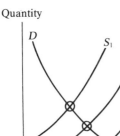
(a)

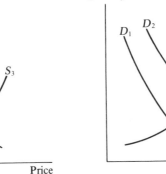
(b)

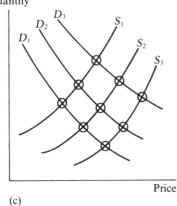
(c)

**Figure 7-5**  Interaction of supply and demand

simultaneous equation models, we not only need to be aware of the estimation procedures for the models, but must also have sufficient data to identify all the structural parameters.

- *Stability* We assume that the coefficients are the same for the whole time period. The 'Chow' test allows us to test that the model as a whole is the same if we split the data in half. If the model is unstable we can test which coefficients are unstable and even incorporate varying coefficients into the model.

- *Interval/ratio scale* We assume that the endogenous (dependent) variable is measured on an interval/ratio scale. If it is on a nominal scale (dichotomous, e.g. why people buy or do not buy a product regressed on age, sex, income, etc.) or multinomial scale (e.g. in which region, of several, does a person live) probit or logit models are appropriate. For multiple regression and logit/probit models if the exogenous (independent) variables are not on an interval/ratio scale, dummy variables are used. For example, sex is given by the variable $X_1 = 1$ for male and $X_2 = 0$ for female; or for seasonal effects $X_2 = 1$ for $Q_1$, $X_2 = 0$ for other quarters gives the seasonal effect of the first quarter. Other dummies for other quarters may be included, but if a constant is in the model only three quarterly dummies in total should be used. Some of the variation in car registrations may be due to seasonal influences. If we include such dummies, the $R^2$ increases from 0.45 to 0.49 (using the differenced model) but none of the variables (including the dummies) is statistically significant. One explanation is that the seasonal dummy variables do not explain the seasonal variation in car registrations since such variation is already explained by seasonality in existing independent variables. Indeed, the seasonal dummies might together be collinear with one or more of the independent of exogenous variables.

- *Autocorrelation* If the exogenous variables explain variations in $Y$, the resulting error should be randomly distributed. Autocorrelation refers to a pattern in the residuals whereby, for example, the value of a residual (e.g. for 1989 : Q4) is related to its preceding value (1989 : Q3), etc. This is first-order autocorrelation in the residuals and is tested by the Durbin–Watson statistic *not* given at the time of writing by Lotus 1-2-3—a serious omission. The non-random pattern might be due to the imposition of a linear model on a non-linear relationship or the omission of a variable, or seasonal patterns or prolonged effects of 'shocks' (e.g. a strike). Autocorrelation may result in invalid tests for statistical significance and unduly high $R^2$.

- *Linearity* This was discussed above and methods to cope with non-linear functional forms were outlined. For example, it might be that INC, CRED and PRICE are not additive effects on car registration, but compound together multiplicatively, i.e. $Y = a\text{INC}^{b_1}\text{CRED}^{b_2}\text{PRICE}^{b_3}$; therefore, $\ln Y = \ln a + b_1 \ln \text{INC} + b_2 \ln \text{CRED} + b_3 \ln \text{PRICE}$. However, in our case this does little to improve the estimated model in terms of the $R^2$.

- *Lags* So far we have assumed that a variation in $Y$ is affected by a variation in $X$ in the same period. However, the effect of, for example, advertising on sales is not just with the current period; if advertising dropped to zero, sales may still be kept relatively high due to the affects of advertising in previous periods lingering in the consumers' memories. Similarly, decisions to invest in, say, property depend not only on current interest rates, return from alternative investments, etc., in the present period, but how these have evolved over past periods. Thus $Y$ in the current period may be regressed on $X$ in the current period, $X$ with a one-period lag, $X$ with a two-period lag, etc. In practice a distributed lag model allows us to incorporate many lagged values of $X$ in a simple model. Expectations models are a development of this whereby, for example, desired consumption is related to expected wealth rather than current income, with expected wealth being based on a distributed lag model of past income, i.e. we have a model of expectations based on past values of data. Thus, for example, purchases of cars may depend on expected prices of petrol with expectations being a function (distributed lag) of past prices of petrol.

The problems referred to above are the subject of econometrics, which takes the technique of multiple regression many stages further than that found in texts on introductory statistics. While the subject developed via a concern with (generally) macro-economic relationships and models, the principles also apply to models at the firm level for decision making. Even introductory econometrics texts cannot be classified as 'light reading', though Kennedy (1985) is a remarkably readable attempt; others include Maddala (1977), Koutsoyiannis (1977) and Wallace and Silver (1988). The means of testing for and dealing with the aforementioned issues are beyond an introductory course. However, when we need to forecast, and what we want to forecast, is related to other variables and these other variables may change their values substantially; or when we want to identify the extent to which different variables affect sales or whatever, regression provides the means to achieve this. It is unfortunate that such a powerful technique can involve such complexities. It may be easier, as in many statistic books, to just introduce the basic concepts so as to not put students off the use of the technique. However, students need to be warned that what they apply may not always give the right answer and there is more to this technique than the initial formulae provided. This is not to say that models estimated by you will be wrong. They may be fine; it is only that you would not have tested your models (and the sparse output from, for example, Lotus 1-2-3 does not help here) for potential problems (which may be curable). The above warning points need to be considered in regression analysis, for any of them can seriously damage your model.

## USING COMPUTERS

### Minitab

If the data in the first and second columns of Table 7-1 are read into C1 and C2 respectively, the output in Table 7-2 results from the command:

```
MTB  > REGR C1 1 C2;
SUBC > PRED 3.9.
```

The subcommand is only used to generate the last two rows of the output for the confidence and prediction intervals for a forecast when $X = 3.9$. The first command is to regress $Y$ in C1 on 1 predictor (exogenous variable) in C2. Multiple regression may be undertaken (for three predictors) by simply entering:

```
MTB > REGR CI 3 C3 C4 C5
```

A number of options exist:

```
MTB  > REGR C1 3 C2, C3, C4, C5, C6;
SUBC > NOCONSTANT;
SUBC > WEIGHTS C7;
SUBC > MSE K1;
SUBC > COEF C8;
SUBC > RESID C9.
```

In turn: the additional inclusion of C5 and C6 in the REGR puts standardized residuals in C5 and fitted values in C6; the NOCONSTANT estimates a regression without an intercept, in theory we sometimes have reason to believe $a = 0$, and thus force the model to behave like this; we referred previously to the possibility in forecasting to give more weight to more recent values—exponentially declining weights, for example, could be put in C7; the Mean Squared Error (MSE) of the regression could always be put in K1, COEFficients can be put in C8 to use LET statements which include them; we already have our RESIDuals in C5, but we put them in C9 via this subcommand in case they were not included in the REGR command.

Minitab also contains a stepwise regression facility:

```
MTB > STEPWISE C1 C2 C3 C5-C25
```

will run a stepwise regression on $Y$ in C1 against all the exogenous variables subsequently listed. Given the large number of exogenous variables, stepwise constructs a regression equation by including at the first step the exogenous variable most highly correlated with $Y$, then as a second step the variable that next explains the most variation in $Y$ not explained by the first one included, etc. There are a large number of subcommands relating to different procedures for stepwise, and criteria for stopping the stepwise. It is not uncommon for researchers to collect a large number of variables that they think may affect the $Y$-variable of interest and use stepwise to pick out the main influences. A preferable approach is to use theory as to what really is important and data reduction techniques to which meaning can be ascribed. Stepwise is particularly sensitive to problems of multicollinearity and should generally be avoided.

### Lotus 1-2-3

/Data Regression leads to a menu of six commands:

1. Independent—specify the column(s) of $X$ for your exogenous variable. For multiple regression all your columns of independent variables should have been entered alongside each other (if not MOVE them); anchor and include the full block of independent variables.
2. Dependent—enter the appropriate column.
3. Output—find a space (the dimensions can be gleaned from Table 7-5) and enter the block (or move the cursor to the top left-hand corner of the desired space and press ENTER).
4. $Y$ Intercept—forces the intercept to be zero ($a=0$) as discussed above for Minitab under NOCONSTANT.
5. Go—undertakes the regression analysis, dumping the results in the output block specified.
6. Reset—returns regression menu values specified by you to their default settings.
7. Quit—leaves this menu.

For simulation, changing an entry for the $Y$ or $X$ values will not affect the regression results until you re-use the Go command.

### EXERCISES

**7-1** Determine the values of $a$ and $b$ for the regression equation $Y=a+bX$ for the following set of data *without* undertaking any calculations [hint: graph the relationship].

| X | Y |
|---|---|
| 0 | 5 |
| 1 | 4 |
| 2 | 3 |
| 3 | 2 |
| 4 | 1 |

**7-2** Consider the data sets given in the exercises at the end of Chapter 6. Which of these have the appropriate scale of measurement (interval/ratio) for regression analysis to be used?

**7-3** For each exercise at the end of Chapter 6, *in turn*, for which both variables are measured on an interval or ratio scale:

(a) Briefly outline the theory as to why the two variables are related, state which should be labelled $Y$ and which $X$, and say whether a one-tailed test of significance for the slope coefficient would be appropriate and, if information exists, give your perception of the quality of the data.

(b) Having confirmed in your answers to the relevant exercises in Chapter 6 that the relationship is linear, estimate where appropriate the linear regression equation.

(c) Determine $R^2$ and test whether the difference between the slope coefficient and zero is statistically significant.

(d) Interpret all your results.

**7-4** Using the regression equation determined in Question 7-1 above, provide a forecast when $X = 5$, determine confidence intervals for this forecast and comment on your results.

**7-5** You are given information on the percentage market share, price as a percentage of competitor's average price and advertising expenditure as a percentage of competitor's average price for a specific line of cat food for the last eight years.

|  | Market share (%) | Relative price* | Relative advertising* |
|---|---|---|---|
| 1985 | 30 | 89 | 110 |
| 1986 | 31 | 85 | 115 |
| 1987 | 30.5 | 86.5 | 120 |
| 1988 | 29 | 92 | 114 |
| 1989 | 29.5 | 90 | 112 |
| 1990 | 28.5 | 102 | 115 |
| 1991 | 28 | 115 | 116 |
| 1992 | 26 | 125 | 114 |

*Figures show your price/advertising divided by the average for your competitors, the result being multiplied by 100. A value of 100 denotes your price/advertising is the same as the average for your competitors.

Using appropriate software, calculate a multiple regression equation to explain variations in market share. Interpret your answer especially with regard to tests of statistical significance for the slope coefficient. By appropriate transformations identify whether a non-linear functional form better fits the data (according to the highest $R$-squared criterion) than a linear one. Compare your result with a regression which ignores the variable for relative advertising.

## ANNEX

Derivation of $a$ and $b$ in $Y = a + bX + e$ using least squares criterion.

The difference between an actual value of $Y$ and a predicted value $\bar{Y}$, where $\hat{Y} = a + bX$, is given by $Y - (a + bX)$. To minimize the total squared deviations between $Y$ and $\hat{Y}$:

Minimize $\Sigma(Y - a - bX)^2$.

Now

$$\frac{\delta}{\delta a}\Sigma(Y - a - bX)^2 = -2\Sigma(Y - a - bX) = 0 \qquad \text{(i)}$$

and

$$\frac{\delta}{\delta b}\Sigma(Y - a - bX)^2 = -2\Sigma X(Y - a - bX) = 0 \qquad \text{(ii)}$$

(i) simplifies to

$$2\Sigma Y = 2na + 2b\,\Sigma X$$
$$\Sigma Y = na + b\,\Sigma X$$

(ii) simplifies to

$$2\,\Sigma XY = 2a\,\Sigma X + 2b\,\Sigma X^2$$
$$\Sigma XY = a\,\Sigma X + b\,\Sigma X^2$$

For the normal equations

$$\Sigma Y = na + b\,\Sigma X \qquad\qquad\qquad \text{(i)}$$
$$\Sigma XY = a\,\Sigma X + b\,\Sigma X^2 \qquad\qquad\qquad \text{(ii)}$$

multiplication of (i) by $(\Sigma X)/n$ and subtraction from (ii) leaves

$$\Sigma XY = a\,\Sigma X + b\,\Sigma X^2$$

i.e. Eq. (i) $\times \Sigma X/n$ is $(\Sigma X\,\Sigma Y)/n = a\Sigma X + (b(\Sigma X)^2/n$

Eq. (ii) $-$ Eq. (i)* is $\Sigma XY - (\Sigma X\,\Sigma Y)/n = b\Sigma X^2 - (b(\Sigma X)^2/n$

$$\frac{n\,\Sigma XY - \Sigma X\,\Sigma Y}{n}$$

Multiplying both sides by $n$ we obtain

$$n\,\Sigma XY - \Sigma X\,\Sigma Y = nb\,\Sigma X^2 - b(\Sigma X)^2$$
$$n\,\Sigma XY - \Sigma X\,\Sigma Y = b[n\,\Sigma X^2 - (\Sigma X)^2]$$

so that

$$\frac{n\,\Sigma XY - \Sigma X\,\Sigma Y}{n\,\Sigma X^2 - (\Sigma X)^2} = b$$

Finally rearrangement of (i) given that $b$ has been found enables $a$ to be calculated:

$$a = \frac{\Sigma Y - b\,\Sigma X}{n}$$

# TIME SERIES ANALYSIS AND FORECASTING

In much of business and economic analysis there is a particular concern with how a variable changes over time. We are interested in whether a variable, be it profits, costs, sales, advertising expenditure, exports, prices or whatever, has a rising or falling or stationary (horizontal) trend or long-term movement over time. In addition, there may be seasonal effects, or in the longer term, cyclical patterns. And of course there will be some random fluctuations or 'noise' unexplained by the cycle, trend or seasonality.

In order to help understand the movements of the variable over time we need to decompose its movements into these components: cyclical, trend, seasonal and random—a process referred to as the 'classical decomposition of a time series'. Figure 8-1 and Table 8-1 show the value of consumers' expenditure on cars, motor cycles and allied vehicles in the UK between the last quarter of 1984 and the third quarter of 1989. The graph clearly shows a rising trend, though there

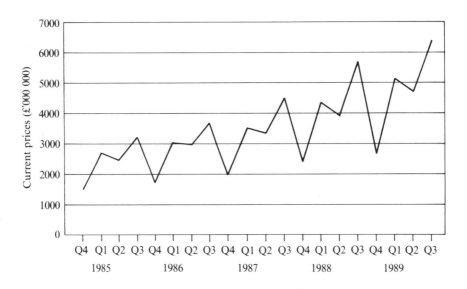

**Figure 8-1** Expenditure on cars, motor cycles, etc.: current prices

**Table 8-1**  Consumers' expenditure on cars, motor cycles and other vehicles (£ million at current and 1985 prices)

| | Expenditure on cars, etc. Prices: | | Moving average | Centred moving average, trend | De-trended series | Seasonal component | Random component |
|---|---|---|---|---|---|---|---|
| | Current | 1985 | | | | | |
| 1984:Q4 | 1498 | 1527 | | | | | |
| 1985:Q1 | 2716 | 2697 | | | | | |
| | | | 2412.79 | | | | |
| Q2 | 2472 | 2358 | | 2424.95 | 0.9725 | 0.9932 | 0.9791 |
| | | | 2437.11 | | | | |
| Q3 | 3235 | 3069 | | 2448.97 | 1.2532 | 1.2745 | 0.9833 |
| | | | 2460.82 | | | | |
| Q4 | 1720 | 1625 | | 2501.35 | 0.6495 | 0.6348 | 1.0230 |
| | | | 2541.87 | | | | |
| 1986:Q1 | 3038 | 2792 | | 2567.83 | 1.0871 | 1.0975 | 0.9906 |
| | | | 2593.80 | | | | |
| Q2 | 2980 | 2682 | | 2606.86 | 1.0290 | 0.9932 | 1.0360 |
| | | | 2619.91 | | | | |
| Q3 | 3706 | 3277 | | 2657.09 | 1.2332 | 1.2745 | 0.9676 |
| | | | 2694.26 | | | | |
| Q4 | 1963 | 1729 | | 2719.59 | 0.6358 | 0.6348 | 1.0014 |
| | | | 2744.92 | | | | |
| 1987:Q1 | 3528 | 3089 | | 2806.59 | 1.1006 | 1.0975 | 1.0029 |
| | | | 2868.25 | | | | |
| Q2 | 3349 | 2885 | | 2897.12 | 0.9958 | 0.9932 | 1.0026 |
| | | | 2926.00 | | | | |
| Q3 | 4506 | 3770 | | 2963.75 | 1.2720 | 1.2745 | 0.9981 |
| | | | 3001.50 | | | | |
| Q4 | 2406 | 1960 | | 3022.75 | 0.6484 | 0.6348 | 1.0214 |
| | | | 3044.00 | | | | |
| 1988:Q1 | 4337 | 3391 | | 3104.25 | 1.0924 | 1.0975 | 0.9954 |
| | | | 3164.50 | | | | |
| Q2 | 3931 | 3055 | | 3163.38 | 0.9657 | 0.9932 | 0.9724 |
| | | | 3162.25 | | | | |
| Q3 | 5692 | 4252 | | 3197.38 | 1.3298 | 1.2745 | 1.0434 |
| | | | 3232.50 | | | | |
| Q4 | 2665 | 1951 | | 3273.88 | 0.5959 | 0.6348 | 0.9387 |
| | | | 3315.25 | | | | |
| 1989:Q1 | 5148 | 3672 | | 3338.50 | 1.0999 | 1.0975 | 1.0022 |
| | | | 3361.75 | | | | |
| Q2 | 4713 | 3386 | | | | | |
| Q3 | 6381 | 4438 | | | | | |

*Source*: Central Statistical Office, *Monthly Digest of Statistics*, Nos 504 and 530, Dec. 1987 and Feb. 1990, respectively.

is also a distinct seasonal pattern. The period is too short to expect cyclical economic fluctuations (booms and slumps) to be apparent. The seasonal pattern shows higher values (than expected from the trend) in the third quarter (Q3), coinciding with new annual registration letters on registration plates, which 'show-off' the vehicle as being new. This is followed by lower values in the fourth quarter, rising again in the first quarter (though not to the heights of the previous peak, and then falling off slightly in the second quarter in preparation for the new registrations.

For planning production it is essential to be aware of any strong seasonal patterns to ensure that the supply of materials, labour and capital are sufficient to meet these fluctuating demands, or if the items are not perishable and the costs of storage relatively low (as for example, with Christmas cards) to plan production and the accumulation of stocks around the year. Retailers must also be aware of seasonal patterns to militate against being left with unwanted stocks, not having sufficient goods to meet demand, etc. In some industries seasonal patterns are very marked as with, for example, electricity generation.

Our example will consider quarterly seasonal patterns though similar principles will apply to monthly patterns, daily, hourly or even finer divisions as, for example, the electricity and water industries having to plan and cope with sudden needs for hot water during the television advertisements between soap operas.

Our interest in time series is not just with seasonality, but also extends to the trend. From Table 8-1 we can see that expenditure increased from £4713 million to £6381 million between the second and third quarter of 1989. But how much of this 35 per cent increase was due to seasonal fluctuations, and how much was a genuine increase in the trend of expenditure? It might be the case that the normal *seasonal* effect between these periods is a 30 per cent increase, so the 35 per cent increase which everyone might have been congratulating each other on, was obscuring a less than impressive growth.

## CLASSICAL DECOMPOSITION

Our task is thus to separate the series into its constituent elements, for these data: trend, seasonal and random components. We shall ignore cyclical patterns because of the brevity of the series, though this requires only a relatively simple extension of the method (see Wilson and Keating, 1990, Ch. 6). We shall use as our example the data in Table 8-1 on expenditure on vehicles. However, we learned in Chapter 5 that this will be affected by movements in prices *and* quantity purchased. We shall thus use from Table 8-1 a series measured at constant prices, having deflated

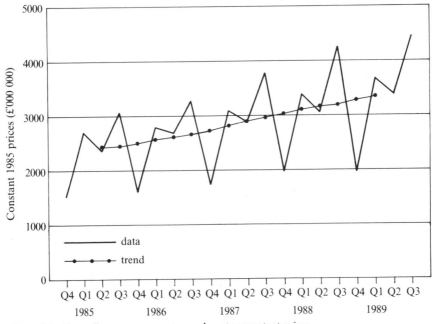

**Figure 8-2** Expenditure on cars, motor cycles, etc.: constant prices

the current price (value) series by a price index for vehicles to yield a series which holds prices constant at 1985 levels—i.e. reflects changes in the quantity of vehicles purchased. These data are given in graphic form in Fig. 8-2 and reveal a less marked trend, but a similar seasonal pattern.

## The model

Our first task is to specify a model showing the form by which the elements make up the data. Two models are considered: the *additive model*, whereby the trend in period $t$ $(T_t)$ *plus* the seasonal *plus* random components in period $t$ $(S_t$ and $R_t$ respectively), make up the data $(X_t)$, i.e.

$$X_t = T_t + S_t + R_t \tag{8-1}$$

In contrast, the *multiplicative model* is given by

$$X_t = T_t \times S_t \times R_t \tag{8-2}$$

Figure 8-3 maps out these two models. Both show increasing trends with seasonal fluctuations. The *amplitude* of the seasonality is the vertical distance between the peak and slump of the seasonal 'cycle' in each year. Note that in the additive model the amplitude remains the same even though

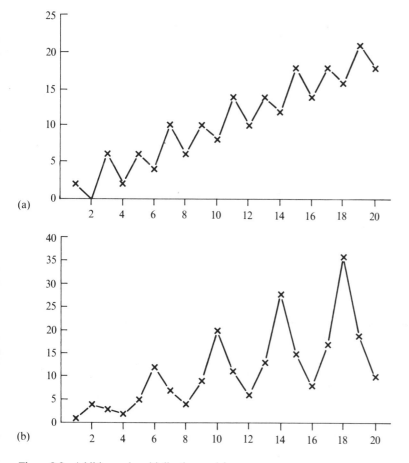

(a)

(b)

**Figure 8-3**  Additive and multiplicative models

the trend is increasing, while in the multiplicative model the amplitude increases (here) with the increasing trend. We should ask ourselves in theory, for each application, which model is appropriate. If our sales of motor vehicles is greater in 1989 than in 1985, we would expect the absolute magnitude of any quarterly rise or fall in 1989 from the trend to be higher than its counterpart in 1985—thus, a multiplicative model. Alternatively, a bingo hall, for example, *might* have a weekly 'seasonal' fluctuations with Saturday night always filled to capacity and Monday night closed. There may be an upward or downward trend on other occasions, but if we plotted sales on a daily basis the amplitude of the Saturday and Monday variation would remain constant—an additive model. There are of course other models including mixed additive and multiplicative ones, though these are outside the scope of this text (see Majani, 1983).

### The trend

First we have to derive the trend ($T_t$). We shall use *moving averages* to achieve this, as applied to data in Table 8-1 on expenditure on motor vehicles at constant 1985 prices (second column of figures) and Fig. 8-2. The first four observations suffer from seasonal effects, being raised above the trend in Q1 and Q3, and falling below it in Q2 and Q4. An average (mean) of these four figures will not suffer from seasonality since the higher seasonal effects will be counterbalanced by the lower ones. The first figure of the third column of figures in Table 8-1 (moving average) is:

$$(1527 + 2697 + 2358 + 3069)/4 = 2412.79$$

we now drop the first figure (1527) and include the next figure of data (1625) to form a new average:

$$(2697 + 2358 + 3069 + 1625)/4 = 2437.11$$

Note that we dropped here a Q4 figure, and picked up a new Q4 figure, so we still averaged over Q1, Q2, Q3 and Q4. For our next average we drop 1985:Q1, but pick up 1986:Q1:

$$(2358 + 3069 + 1625 + 2792)/4 = 2460.82$$

Now, the 1986 figures are on average higher than 1985, but as the moving average 'invades' 1986, the moving average will increase; the higher 1986:Q1 figure is substituted for its lower 1985:Q1 counterpart. The further we move into 1986, the larger the moving average, thus replicating the increasing trend. The trend need not be linear; if, for example, there was an increase in 1986 compared with 1985, but the 1987 figures were the same as in 1986, the trend would flatten out, as what is dropped in 1987 is replaced by the same number in 1986, a non-linear trend being mapped out over 1985 to 1987.

Our estimate of the trend is not complete since, as should be apparent from Table 8-1, the moving average figures do not correspond to a precise time period, 2412.79 for example being half-way between 1985:Q1 and 1985:Q2. The fourth column of figures—centred moving average—takes an average (mean) of the moving average figures (in 1985) lying between Q1 and Q2, and between Q2 and Q3 to yield the Q2 figure of:

$$(2412.79 + 2437.11) = 2424.95$$

which is a trend figure. This has been graphed on Fig. 8-2. We have used in our calculations a *four-point* moving average embracing four figures. Because the 'pointage' was an even number there was a need to centre the figures. This is not necessary when the pointage is an odd number. For monthly data we might have used a 12-point moving average, though we should not automatically assume the pointage follows the divisions of the year, though it is usually the case. To determine the pointage, first consider in theory how the data might fluctuate around the trend.

We have discussed above reasons why quarterly data on car registrations might be expected to have such a quarterly pattern. Then confirm the theory via a graph by counting the number of data points from (and including) a peak up to (but not including) when a similar peak occurs (at which the seasonal pattern has been completed). In Fig. 8-2 this should be 4.

Our trend (fourth column of figures in Table 8-1) does not have figures for all periods, having lost two figures at the start and end. Generally for an $n$-point moving average we lose $n/2$ points at the start and end. Note that our trend does not incorporate random fluctuations since, by definition, these are high in some periods, low in others with no particular sequential pattern. The averaging will thus in principle remove such effects.

An alternative procedure for deriving the trend is to use regression (Chapter 7). Our $Y$-variable is the series; the $X$-variable is 'time' with $1984:Q4 = 1$, $1985:Q1 = 2$, $1985:Q2 = 3$, etc. The trend is derived by first estimating the regression of $Y$ on 'time', which yields:

$$Y = 2029.521 + 81.0218(\text{time}) \qquad R^2 = 0.33$$
$$\phantom{Y = } (2.88) \qquad (2.96)$$

We do not expect a good fit since the seasonal variations around the line will by definition adversely affect the fit. The trend values result from, for $1984:Q4$, substituting time $= 1$ in the above equation to yield $2110.543$ and similarly for $1985:Q1$ time $= 2$ to yield $2191.565$, etc., for all trend values. The method does not suffer from the disadvantage of losing any start or end points and this, as we shall see later in the chapter, is an advantage for forecasting purposes. However, if the trend is non-linear we need to improve the fit by using specific functional forms (e.g. exponential) as outlined in the previous chapter, while moving averages will itself follow any twists and turns in the trend. For simply decomposing a series to determine the trend, the simplicity and lack of assumptions as to functional form for moving averages has much to commend it over regression. However, where the trend is linear, or follows a pattern easily transformed into a linear form, regression is quite suitable for the decomposition of a time series and is particularly suitable, as will be illustrated, for forecasting. Having determined the trend, we now move to deriving the seasonal components.

**The seasonal components**

Figure 8-2 shows the amplitude increasing with the trend, thus reflecting a multiplicative model. We start by removing the trend (centred moving average) from the data by division (in an additive model it would be by subtraction) to yield the seasonal *and* random components, i.e.

$$X_t = T_t \times S_t \times R_t$$
$$X_t/T_t = S_t \times R_t \qquad (8\text{-}3)$$

The third column from the end of Table 8-1 provides the results, e.g. for $1985:Q2$, $2358/2424.95 = 0.9725$. We take these *de-trended* figures and rearrange them in a new format in Table 8-2. Here all the figures for a particular quarter are in the same column. Now these figures comprise both seasonal and random effects (Eq. (8-3)). Because it is a multiplicative model the effects are given as a proportion of 1; e.g. for $1985:Q3$ there was a 25.32 per cent seasonal and random fluctuation above the trend, while for $1985:Q2$ there was a $(1 - 0.9725 = 0.0275) = 2.75$ per cent fluctuation below the trend. If we find the mean of all the Q1 fluctuations this will produce the average seasonal fluctuation in Q1 and in doing so we lose the random fluctuations. This is because we argue that the seasonal effect, for example, is 1.095 in Q1 (the mean) and the differences between each of the four Q1 figures and 1.095 are due to random variations. Since, by definition, they are random they are higher than 1.095 in one year, lower in another, but the average should

**Table 8-2** Seasonal effects

| Year | Quarters | | | |
| | Q1 | Q2 | Q3 | Q4 |
|---|---|---|---|---|
| 1985 | | 0.9725 | 1.2532 | 0.6495 |
| 1986 | 1.0871 | 1.0290 | 1.2332 | 0.6358 |
| 1987 | 1.1006 | 0.9958 | 1.2720 | 0.6484 |
| 1988 | 1.0924 | 0.9657 | 1.3298 | 0.5959 |
| 1989 | 1.0999 | | | |
| Mean | 1.0950 | 0.9907 | 1.2721 | 0.6324  Total = 3.9902 |
| Adjusted mean* | 1.0975 | 0.9932 | 1.2745 | 0.6348  Total = 4.0000 |

*Adjusted mean = mean + (4 − 3.9902)/4.

cancel out the randomness leaving pure seasonality. Needless to say, the more years for which we have data (assuming the seasonal effect is stable) the 'purer' will be our seasonal estimate.

A similar procedure is adopted in Table 8-2 for all quarters and the seasonal means are summed to yield 3.9902. However, the seasonal effects should counterbalance over the year leaving a total effect of 4 (or average of 1). Our seasonal estimates are slightly in error since they only sum to 3.9902. We do not know which season(s) is 'light' and by how much, and thus distribute the missing 4 − 3.9902 = 0.0098 evenly (0.0098/4 = 0.00245) over the mean (seasonal) components to yield the adjusted means. These go back into Table 8-1 (second last column) as the seasonal component for each period. Thus in 1989 : Q1 the seasonality effect is a 9.75 per cent increase above the trend. The trend was 3338.50, this being pushed up (multiplied) by a seasonal component of 1.0975 to yield 3664.004.

**The random components**

It follows from Eq. (8-2) that since we have determined $T_t$ and $S_t$ we can now find $R_t$ as:

$$X_t/(T_t \times S_t) = R_t \qquad (8\text{-}4)$$

Alternatively, the de-trended series is $(S_t \times R_t)$ and this can be divided by $S_t$ to yield $R_t$, as given in the final column of Table 8-1. Figure 8-4 is a 'close up' of Fig. 8-2 for 1986 : Q1 to 1986 : Q3. We can identify how, for example, in 1986 : Q3, the actual data falls short of what the expected seasonal figure should be (the cross), the difference being due to random variations. For 1986 : Q2 the data point is above the predicted seasonal figure, which is in any event only just below the trend.

The random components are of interest for two reasons. First, their magnitude: the figures in the final column of Table 8-1 are very close to 1, reflecting a relatively small random effect. Thus the seasonal and trend components 'explain' much of the variation in the data. Second, there should be no pattern in the random component. If, for example, the random component was steadily increasing, then the component would not be random, suggesting an inappropriate model (say, additive when it should be multiplicative) or something wrong with the trend estimates.

**Using classical decomposition**

Classical decomposition is useful in both planning and forecasting. If demand, for example, is seasonal it is useful to know the extent of the seasonality. Table 8-1 shows, for example, demand to be 27 per cent over and above the trend in Q3. Production may be increased and stored in other

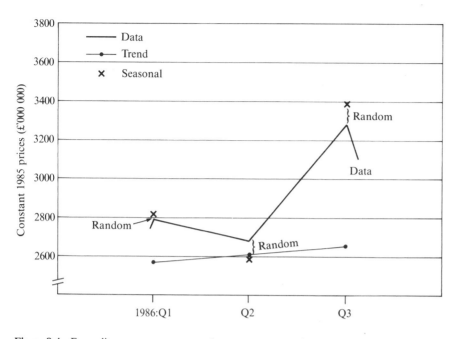

**Figure 8-4**   Expenditure on cars, motor cycles, etc.: constant prices

periods if the good is not perishable and storage costs relatively low. Alternatively, additional temporary capital or labour may be hired, or production contracted-out or 'synchromarketing' adopted to reshape the seasonal pattern into a more manageable regular form. Often in planning, classical decomposition is used simply to disentangle the trend from seasonal patterns so that the overall performance can be better identified.

For forecasting, trend extrapolation is often adopted. First we need to identify the trend; then extrapolate it into the future, and then add (or for a multiplicative model—multiply) back the seasonal patterns. The use of moving averages to determine the trend is particularly problematic in this instance since, for our four-point moving average, we lose the two end-points making, for example, the extrapolation of the trend in Fig. 8-2 into the future (1989:Q4) require trend estimates for 1989:Q2 and Q3. For forecasting purposes we adopt the alternative method of estimating the trend using regression mentioned earlier. The resulting regression equation was:

$$Y = 2029.521 + 81.0218(\text{time})$$

For the future, time = 21, the trend will be

$$2029.521 + 81.0218(21) = 3730.979$$

Since period 21 is the fourth quarter of 1989 we use Table 8-2 to adjust the predicted trend for the predicted seasonal downswing, i.e. $3730.979(0.6348) = £2368.425$ million. It should be borne in mind that we have used a linear model, which is quite reasonable given the pattern in Fig. 8-2. However, had a non-linear pattern been apparent an appropriate transformation would have been necessary, as discussed in the previous chapter.

Many time series of official statistics (e.g. industrial production, average earnings, unemployment) are available 'seasonably adjusted' since the statistical office assumes the user will wish to distinguish seasonal fluctuations from trends. These adjustments are based on the X-11 method, a computer-based user-controlled seasonal adjustment program developed by the US Bureau of the Census (Shiskin *et al.*, 1967). The method is based on classical decomposition with a choice between additive and multiplicative models, though it also includes trading-day and length-of-month adjustments (if some months include more trading days or are longer than others), user-controlled adjustments for extreme values, choice of pointage of moving averages and a set of diagnostic tests to determine the adequacy of the models used. A number of problems exist with the method—see Auerbach and Rutner (1978) and Raveh (1984)—though it has proved quite robust. However, more generally when using classical decomposition or results from the Census X-11 method you should bear the following in mind.

- The definition/coverage of the series should be consistent or adjustments made. The seasonally adjusted UK unemployment statistics, for example, as at December 1988, included adjustments for seven changes in coverage deemed to have significantly affected the series (Department of Employment, 1988).
- If two variables are seasonally adjusted with different procedures, it may create a relationship when previously none existed, or blur one which existed (Wallis, 1974).
- Different components of the series may have different seasonal patterns; for example, the 'unemployed' will contain 'unemployed school leavers' and 'long-term unemployed', and in some cases separate seasonal adjustments should be applied to the individual disaggregated elements.
- The method is not robust against abrupt changes in the trend of a series, even if the seasonal pattern is unchanged.
- Results from the Census X-11 method can be improved by updating seasonal adjustments as soon as new data are available, as opposed to once a year, or by augmenting the (monthly) series with 12 forecasts (see Kenny and Durbin, 1982).

## FORECASTING METHODS AND SOME GENERAL POINTS ON FORECASTING

The outline given here is relatively brief, given the range and relative complexity of some of the methods available. However, appropriate references and a flavour of the methods and issues at stake are provided.

### Univariate methods

Univariate forecasting methods are those based on only utilizing a time series of the variable we wish to forecast. We may, for example, have data on sales of a product over time and wish, using this data, to estimate what sales will be in a future period. In this chapter we have already looked at one method, *trend extrapolation*, whereby the variable is regressed on 'time', and a future time period substituted for $X$ in the regression equation to yield a predicted value for the variable. We can apply the principles of this chapter to adjust the forecast for seasonal variations, or directly incorporate seasonality into regression models by including 'dummy variables' and lag structures as discussed in the previous chapter. In addition we might apply the principles of the previous chapter to develop confidence intervals for the forecast. If we expect the pattern over time to be non-linear, appropriate transformations can be made to the data and a non-linear function estimated, as discussed in the previous chapter. Software which applies a range of transformations to the data to apply the non-linear form which best fits the data (according to the highest $R^2$) is available (see Lewis, 1989). However, care should be exercised; the fact that, for example, sales are rising at an increasing rate and a form such as in Fig. 7-4(b) best fits the data, does not mean that sales will continue to rise in this way indefinitely, and Fig. 7.4(g) might be a more realistic description to take account of the inevitable market saturation (Meade, 1984).

An alternative approach is via a range of *smoothing techniques*. We have seen a fairly crude smoothing technique in our use of moving averages to determine the trend. Exponential smoothing (exponentially weighted moving averages), while smoothing the data, gives less (exponentially declining) weight to past observations than more recent observations. It also has the feature of being self-correcting in that forecast values are regulated by changing them in the opposite direction of errors in the preceding period. Exponential smoothing can be applied if there is a strong trend (Holt's double parameter), or a seasonal pattern (Holt–Winters' triple parameter). These also give more emphasis to recent trend and seasonal patterns than older ones and provide self-correcting forecasts of the trend and seasonal components (see Gardner, 1985).

The Box–Jenkins approach is based on ARIMA model-building: ARIMA models include autoregressive (AR) models whereby the variable is related to its own previous values, moving average (MA) models whereby the variable is related to past forecasts errors and the need to integrate (I) the results since our starting point is to remove the trend by differencing the data. The methodology is by no means simple; the principles upon which it is based are not of simply extrapolating trends, but looking for relationships within the series and errors generated. The Box–Jenkins approach involves (a) differencing the data to remove the trend, (b) formulating an ARMA model, (c) estimating the model's parameters, (d) diagnostic checking—which if unsatisfactory lead to formulating a different ARMA model (see O'Donovan, 1983) and (e) integrating the results to derive the forecast inclusive of the trend.

## Multivariate methods

These usually involve building multiple regression models of the type discussed in the previous chapter. Sales of a product, for example, might be a function of disposable income, price of the product relative to a competitor's price, price relative to the Retail Prices Index, advertising expenditure, number of distribution outlets and so forth. Forecasts of sales require scenarios of future pricing, advertising, distribution, income levels and managers may put forth a number of options to see the effect on sales.

## Judgemental methods

A range of judgemental or qualitative techniques exist that are particularly useful for forecasting sales of new products. These are outside the scope of this text but include Delphi techniques, surveys of salesforce/buyer's intentions, S-curves, experimental marketing (see Wright and Ayton, 1987).

## Choice of methods

There is much scope for integrating the above approaches and formal models exist which include features of these approaches, such as multivariate ARIMA models. Combining the results from different procedures can yield gains in accuracy (Bunn, 1989; Winkler and Makridakis, 1983). As a principle, an awareness of the assumptions implicit in a model is critical to its proper use. Judgement may then be used to adjust the model for factors not included in it, and for the effects of any assumptions of the method unlikely to be met. Quite simple models can be quite effective since they properly incorporate what can be measured, leaving the user to adjust the forecast using judgement for what cannot. Computer-generated forecasts have in some organizations an unwarranted sanctity. It is always necessary to learn more about the model the computer is using to be aware of the principles upon which the forecasts are based, and not to be afraid to use judgement to adjust the results if necessary.

Issues to be considered in choice of method include: uses to which the forecast will be put, the time horizon of the forecast, the number/cost of forecasts required (automatic computer-generated or requiring human intervention), expertise of analyst and user, periodicity, compatibility with existing planning systems (level of disaggregation, planning horizons, accuracy), statistical properties of the series (e.g. seasonality or whether it is related to other variables) and number of past observations.

It generally follows that if the variable to be forecast is strongly related to other variables that are likely to change unduly, a multi variate model as opposed to a univariate model is required. As regards univariate models, simpler models (e.g. Holt–Winters) have been found to perform as well as more complex ones (Box–Jenkins), and have the advantage of being easier to explain, thus making it more likely that managers might adjust the results for factors not included in the model, since they are aware of what is included. Where there is a need for a large number of regular forecasts, automatic computer-generated forecasts may be necessary and smoothing techniques may be more applicable than multiple regression and ARIMA models which benefit more from human intervention in the model building. Some methods, e.g. regression, are preferable for medium or long-term forecasts, while others, e.g. smoothing techniques, are only suitable for short-term forecasting.

There are many organizational factors that are conducive to forecasts actually being used, such as the need to involve managers who are to use the forecasts in the model development. This is to avoid the 'greenhouse syndrome' under which models taken from their rarified hothouse atmosphere wilt and die when exposed to the chilly winds of the management process (Jenkins, 1982; Schultz, 1984). Some methods are better for some purposes. There have been a number of 'competitions' to see which methods generally perform better for over 1000 series (see Mahmoud, 1984; Makridakis *et al.*, 1984). However, in practice the specific features of your series and uses to which it is to be put should be given more weight than the broad generalizations emanating from such 'competitions'. Attention should also be given to combining the forecasts from methods likely to encapsulate different, pertinent features of the data. For a review of choice of methods see Makridakis (1986) and Chatfield (1988b); for a more detailed account of the techniques see Makridakis *et al.* (1980) and Wilson and Keating (1990).

## USING COMPUTERS

### Minitab

Minitab does not contain a command for classical decomposition, but it can be carried out as follows (Bond and Scott, 1988). TSPLOT C1 provides a plot of the series in C1, though it helps if you join the points by hand. The trend can be generated as the predicted values using the regression command to estimate the equation of $Y$ on a time trend (Chapter 7), and a LET command to generate from the equation the predicted values. A non-linear formulation might be appropriate here. Alternatively, the method of moving averages can be used via the LAG command and row totals. For example, the following commands generate from data in C1 a moving average in C2 and centred moving average in C3, which is moved up in C4 to correspond to the appropriate row for the original data in C1.

**Table 8-3**

| Row | C1 | C6 | C7 | C8 | C2 | C9 | C3 | C4 |
|-----|----|----|----|----|----|----|----|----|
| 1 | 6 | * | * | * | * | * | * | * |
| 2 | 7 | 6 | * | * | * | * | * | * |
| 3 | 9 | 7 | 6 | * | * | * | * | 10.250 |
| 4 | 13 | 9 | 7 | 6 | 8.75 | * | * | 13.375 |
| 5 | 18 | 13 | 9 | 7 | 11.75 | 8.75 | 10.250 | 17.000 |
| 6 | 20 | 18 | 13 | 9 | 15.00 | 11.75 | 13.375 | 21.500 |
| 7 | 25 | 20 | 18 | 13 | 19.00 | 15.00 | 17.000 | 27.625 |
| 8 | 33 | 25 | 20 | 18 | 24.00 | 19.00 | 21.500 | 35.500 |
| 9 | 47 | 33 | 25 | 20 | 31.25 | 24.00 | 27.625 | 45.375 |
| 10 | 54 | 47 | 33 | 25 | 39.75 | 31.25 | 35.500 | 58.375 |
| 11 | 70 | 54 | 47 | 33 | 51.00 | 39.75 | 45.375 | * |
| 12 | 92 | 70 | 54 | 47 | 65.75 | 51.00 | 58.375 | * |

```
MTB > LAG 1 C1 C6
MTB > LAG 2 C1 C7
MTB > LAG 3 C1 C8
MTB > LET C2=(C1+C6+C7+C8)/4
MTB > LAG 1 C2 C9
MTB > LET C3=(C9+C2)/2
MTB > COPY C3 C4
MTB > DELETE ROWS 1 AND 2 C4
MTB > LET C4(11)='*'
MTB > LET C4(12)='*'
MTB > PRINT C1 C6 C7 C8 C2 C9 C3 C4
```

The output from this last print command is given in Table 8-3.

To determine the seasonal component we follow the commands listed below. We first (for a multiplicative model) derive the de-trended series in C10; in C11 we set 3 lots of identifiers 1, 2, 3, 4 to represent the four quarters; remove rows in C10 and C11 with missing values, and insert in C12, C13, C14 and C15 the data for each respective quarter using the UNSTACK command. The means of each of these columns are the seasonal effects which we set into C5.

```
MTB  > LET C10=C1/C4
MTB  > SET C11
DATA > 3(1:4)
DATA > END
MTB  > DELETE ROWS 1,2,11,12 FROM C10 C11
MTB  > UNSTACK C10 INTO C15 C16 C17 C18;
SUBC > SUBSCRIPTS IN C11.
MTB  > MEAN C15 K1
   MEAN=1.0473
MTB  > MEAN C16 K2
   MEAN=0.92764
MTB  > MEAN C17 K3
   MEAN=0.89151
MTB  > MEAN C18 K4
   MEAN=0.95077
MTB  > SET C5
DATA > 3(K1,K2,K3,K4)
DATA > END
MTB  > PRINT C10 C11 C15-C18 C5
```

The output from this print command is given in Table 8-4.

**Table 8-4**

| Row | C10 | C11 | C15 | C16 | C17 | C18 | C5 |
|-----|---------|----|---------|----------|----------|----------|---------|
| 1 | 0.87805 | 3 | 1.05882 | 0.930233 | 0.878049 | 0.971963 | 1.04732 |
| 2 | 0.97196 | 4 | 1.03581 | 0.925054 | 0.904977 | 0.929577 | 0.92764 |
| 3 | 1.05882 | 1 | | | | | 0.89151 |
| 4 | 0.93023 | 2 | | | | | 0.95077 |
| 5 | 0.90498 | 3 | | | | | 1.04732 |
| 6 | 0.92958 | 4 | | | | | 0.92764 |
| 7 | 1.03581 | 1 | | | | | 0.89151 |
| 8 | 0.92505 | 2 | | | | | 0.95077 |
| 9 | | | | | | | 1.04732 |
| 10 | | | | | | | 0.92764 |
| 11 | | | | | | | 0.89151 |
| 12 | | | | | | | 0.95077 |

Smoothing techniques can be derived on Minitab using LET and LAG commands.

Multivariate forecasting using regression can be undertaken on Minitab using the commands outlined at the end of the last chapter. The subcommand PREDICT is particularly useful since it generates for an individual (e.g. future) value of $X_i$, the associated predicted value of $Y$ along with prediction and confidence intervals. For multiple regression the PREDICT subcommand is followed by an individual value of each of the exogenous (independent) variables.

Minitab also has ARIMA commands, which can be used to generate forecasts. However, this is beyond the scope of this text.

### Lotus 1-2-3

There is no facility for classical decomposition on Lotus 1-2-3, though as with Minitab the results can easily be generated. For example, for a series in the columns A1 to A20 using a four-point moving average, the centred moving average (trend) corresponding to the value in A3 may be put into B3 via: $+(@\text{AVG}(A1..A4)+@\text{AVG}(A2..A5))/2$. All subsequent values (with the rightful exception of the last two) of the trend can be derived by using the /Copy command to copy this calculation down for trend values in B4 to B18. The generation of de-trended values in C3 to C18 is a simple numerical operation and the setting up of a table to derive the seasonal components can be undertaken either (for a short series) by entering or copying interspersed de-trended values or using /Data Query Extract via a column containing 1, 2, 3, 4, 1, 2, 3, 4, etc., to act as a criterion.

Lotus 1-2-3 has the advantage over Minitab in its much better graphics facilities. Regression facilities are also available, as outlined at the end of the previous chapter. Lotus 1-2-3 is an inapplicable tool for Box–Jenkins forecasting methods. Smoothing techniques can be written onto Lotus 1-2-3. There are 'add ons' to Lotus 1-2-3 designed to provide forecasts from a range of techniques using a Lotus 1-2-3 environment; 4CAST is one such package.

### EXERCISE

**1** Prescriptions dispensed in England and Wales by NHS are given below in thousands. Decompose the series into its trend, seasonal and random components and provide forecasts for 1991:Q4.

| 1987 | 1988 | | | | 1989 | | | |
|------|------|------|------|------|------|------|------|------|
| Q4 | Q1 | Q2 | Q3 | Q4 | Q1 | Q2 | Q3 | Q4 |
| 94071 | 95388 | 90655 | 90819 | 96737 | 92309 | 95105 | 91863 | 100339 |

| 1990 | | | | 1991 | | |
|------|------|------|------|------|------|------|
| Q1 | Q2 | Q3 | Q4 | Q1 | Q2 | Q3 |
| 97120 | 96404 | 94506 | 100769 | 100054 | 99604 | 100991 |

*Source*: CSO, Monthly Digest of Statistics, No 553, Jan. 1992, London: HMSO.

# PROBABILITY

In the world of business, as in life in general, there is much that goes on whose outcome is not certain. In holding views and taking action on such matters we require estimates as to the extent of the uncertainty. Our concern may be with the degree of certainty of making a sale, there being a traffic jam on the way to the airport, the car breaking down, a pay offer being accepted, a power cut, a virus being on some software just handed to you, a manufactured good being defective, and so forth. Fortunately there are rules of probability to guide us in their use, a use that will extend throughout the next few chapters reflecting the importance of this area.

## PROBABILITY DEFINED

We start probability by considering what is called an *experiment* which is usually a well-defined action having a defined set of outcomes. Rolling a die (singular of dice) would be an experiment, as would seeing if a fault occurs in a BMW in its first year. The *sample space* is the set of all possible outcomes of the experiment: for a die it is 1, 2, 3, 4, 5, 6; for the BMW it is 'a fault' or 'no fault'. We may be interested in specific outcomes or combinations of outcomes, i.e. parts of the sample space that we shall call an *event*. Obtaining a 5 or a 6 might be an event, as may be no fault developing in the BMW. There are three concepts or ways of considering probability (see Chung, 1979).

### Classical or *a priori* concept

If all the outcomes in the sample space are *mutually exclusive*—that is, they cannot occur simultaneously—and are equally likely (as in the example of a perfect die) we can define:

$$\text{Probability of an event} = \frac{\text{Number of outcomes of an experiment favourable to the event}}{\text{Total number of outcomes of the experiment}} \quad (9\text{-}1)$$

Thus, for every roll of a die, the probability of event $A$ occurring, where $A$ is obtaining a 5 or a 6, is $2/6 = 0.3333$. This is denoted by $P(A)$. This is NOT $P$ multiplied by $A$. In our notation $P(A) = 0.3333$. Note that the measure requires no actual experiment; it is based on the theory that each outcome is equally likely and mutually exclusive—there are 6 possible outcomes of which 2 define the event of interest. A probability of zero means that it is impossible for the event to occur; a probability of one means that it is certain: thus, $0 \leqslant P(A) \leqslant 1$. Since the outcomes for the BMW cannot in theory be considered to be equally likely, we have difficulty in applying this concept to the BMW example.

### Relative frequency or empirical approach

Here we actually undertake and repeat the experiment a large number of times, keeping track of the relative frequency with which the event occurs. For our example of the die, where 5 and 6 are called 'successes', we would toss it once obtaining for example a 2, i.e. 0 successes out of 1 throw (0/1); then again and obtain a 5, i.e. 1 success out of 2 throws (1/2); a 3, (1/3); a 6, (2/4); a 1, (2/5); a 6, (3/6), etc. The process continues a large number of times until the relative frequency settles down. The approach can sometimes upset theory: W. F. R. Weldon threw a die 49 152 times, and of these 25 145 yielded a 4, 5 or 6 suggesting a biased die (cited in Kendall and Stuart, 1969).

$$\text{Probability of an event} = \frac{\substack{\text{Number of times event is the outcome of an} \\ \text{experiment repeated a very large number of times}}}{\text{Total number of repetitions of the experiment}} \qquad (9\text{-}2)$$

The approach does not require possible outcomes to be equally likely and can be applied to the BMW example where (hopefully) this is not the case. Collecting records of reported (and confirmed) faults under the warranty for a large number of year-old cars approximates repetition of the experiment. The total number of reported faults in the first year over the total number of cars sold in that year would give an estimate of the probability of a reported fault.

### Subjective probability

Unlike the other two objective approaches, probability is defined here based on subjective judgements; that is, as:

$$\text{Probability} = \text{Degree of belief in the occurrence of the event} \qquad (9\text{-}3)$$

It is simply someone's personal view on the probability of an event occurring.

It is not worth delving too deeply into these differing approaches. In practice we need to feel confident that our theory is good if using Eq. (9-1), or for (9-2) that the empirical experiments conducted are valid for their use (e.g. if conducted in the past the results hold for the future) and for Eq. (9-3) have some (albeit subjective) idea of the expertise of the person making the estimate and the margin of error involved (though see Subjective estimates on page 162 below). It is worth pointing out that $P(A) = 0$ means that $A$ is 'impossible in theory' by the classical approach, $A$ 'has not occurred' in experiment for the relative frequency approach and 'we do not believe $A$ can occur' for the subjective approach. Having defined probability in different ways we now go on to treat them the same, irrespective of their origins.

The rules of probability apply to probabilities derived from the different approaches. Often a lot is made of the lack of objectivity of subjective approaches. However, in business there is uncertainty, and decisions have to be made. Better they are made by properly applying probability rules to the subjective probabilities of managers, than in the absence of such rules. Of interest, it is now recognized in the theory of chaos that random behaviour may arise from quite simple, deterministic equations and, while this is beyond the scope of this text, it suggests that the division between 'objective' and 'subjective' probability is more blurred than first thought (Durbin, 1987; Stewart, 1989; Bartlett, 1990). However, for our purposes, in any application you should just ask yourself how much faith you have in the probability estimates irrespective of their origin, and bear this in mind in reporting the results.

## SOME RULES OF PROBABILITY: ADDITION AND MULTIPLICATION

From our definitions for the classical and empirical approaches:

$$0 \leqslant P(A) \leqslant 1 \qquad (9\text{-}4)$$

Subjective probabilities must also satisfy (9-4) in order to be valid.

### Addition rule (OR)

Here our concern is with the probability of an event OR another event occurring. For example a credit company may lend money on very generous terms but with short payback periods, the sting being that quite punitive rates of interest are charged if payments are late. The company classifies borrowers as 'bad' if they either default on the loan altogether and cannot be traced (event $A$), or pay regularly on time thus not incurring the high interest rates (event $B$). Our rule is:

$$P(A \text{ or } B) = P(A) + P(B) \qquad (9\text{-}5)$$

Assume $P(A) = 0.1$ and $P(B) = 0.6$; the probability a borrower is 'bad' is $0.1 + 0.6 = 0.7$. Note that in some statistics books $P(A \text{ or } B)$ will be written as $P(A \cup B)$ where $\cup$ is called the union (of event $A$ with $B$).

   We assume in this *specific rule of addition* (Eq. (9-5)) that the events are *mutually exclusive*; that is, an outcome can only be one of $A$ or $B$, not both. If they are not mutually exclusive the *general rule of addition* holds:

$$P(A \text{ or } B) = P(A) + P(B) - P(A \text{ and } B) \qquad (9\text{-}6)$$

For example, if membership of a professional body required an MBA (event $A$) or three years senior management experience (event $B$), some applicants might have both (they are not mutually exclusive). The Venn diagram in Fig. 9-1 is useful here; if the area $A$ denotes all managers with MBAs, and $B$ managers with the required experience (the relative size of the areas not intending to reflect this accurately) then to apply Eq. (9-5) and add the separate areas of $A$ and $B$ (as a proportion of the total area) would double-count the shaded area $A$ and $B$. Thus we subtract the

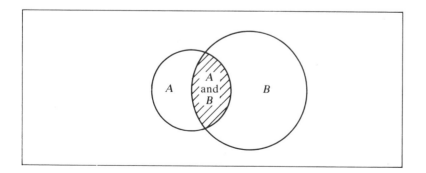

**Figure 9-1**  Venn diagram

intersection of $A$ and $B$ in Eq. (9-6). Thus, if (using fictitious figures) there were 3 million managers in the UK of whom 20 000 had MBAs and 40 000 had three years management experience including 5000 who had both, then by Eq. (9-6):

$$P(A \text{ or } B) = (20\,000/3\,000\,000) + (40\,000/3\,000\,000) - (5000/3\,000\,000)$$
$$= 0.00667 + 0.01333 - 0.00167 = 0.01833$$

In this case we can see the result another way. There are 55 000 managers who have at least one of the qualifications and 55 000/3 000 000 is equal to 0.01833.

Note that in some books $P(A \text{ and } B)$ is denoted by $P(A \cap B)$ where $\cap$ is called the intersection. If no managers with three years senior management experience had an MBA, the two events would be mutually exclusive and there would be no need to subtract $P(A \text{ and } B)$; Eq. (9-5) would hold.

**Multiplication rule (AND)**

Here our concern is with the probability that $A$ AND $B$ occur.

$$P(A \text{ and } B) = P(A) \times P(B) \tag{9-7}$$

This *specific rule of multiplication* assumes $A$ and $B$ to be *independent*, i.e. knowing that the outcome $A$ has occurred does not affect the probability of $B$ occurring. For example, the probability that a good is defective AND gets lost in the post requires the application of Eq. (9-7) since they are independent. Knowing a good is defective tells us nothing about the probability of its being lost.

However, whether you have an MBA might be related to your experience in senior management either by providing a means to obtain the position, or if not in senior management, the prompt to study for one. If $A$ and $B$ are *not* independent the *general rule of multiplication* holds:

$$P(A \text{ and } B) = P(A) \times P(B|A) \tag{9-8}$$

$P(B|A)$ is the *conditional probability* that $B$ will occur *given* (on condition) *that* $A$ has already occurred. In our example this is equivalent to the probability that a manager will have three years senior experience, given he or she has an MBA. Thus we take all of our managers with MBAs, and find out the probability of their having three years senior management experience, i.e. $P(B|A) = 5000/20\,000 = 0.25$.

We know $P(A) = 0.00667$, therefore:

$$P(A \text{ and } B) = 0.00667 \times 0.25 = 0.00167$$

which is much smaller than $P(A \text{ or } B)$. We would in this case of course have derived this directly from 5000/3 000 000 but it is nice to test whether the formula works.

Note how we combine probabilities (even subjective ones) in everyday decisions, but often do not do this rigorously. The rules of probability allow this. Consider a further example: you sell boxes of 20 items from a street stall in which four items are broken, the broken items being randomly distributed in each box. A punter checks two; what is the probability of *both* being found to be not broken? If $A$ is 'the first item selected is not broken' and $B$ 'the second item selected is not broken', the application of Eq. (9-8) gives:

$$P(A \text{ and } B) = (16/20) \times (15/19) = 0.632$$

These rules can be extended to more than two events. It is worth noting that if $\bar{A}$ is event $A$ not occurring then by Eq. (9-5):

$$P(A) + P(\bar{A}) = 1 \tag{9-9}$$

## TREE DIAGRAMS AND DECISION TREES

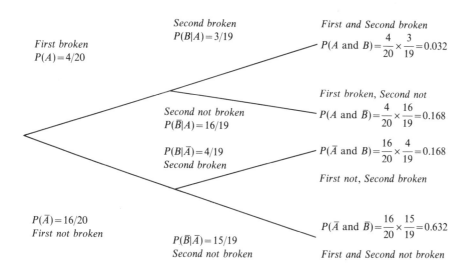

where $A$ is first item being broken and $\bar{A}$ first item not broken, $B$ is second item broken and $\bar{B}$ second item not broken and, for example, $P(B|\bar{A})$ is the probability of the second item being broken *given* the first item was not broken.

**Figure 9-2**   Tree diagram: broken items

Tree diagrams are often helpful for plotting out different outcomes and their associated probabilities. Figure 9-2 shows the tree diagram for the above example. It is read from left to right. Each branch represents an event and the probability is given of this event occurring on the assumption that all events prior to it on the tree have occurred. All branches that emanate from a point must be mutually exclusive and cover all possible outcomes. This allows all the probabilities emanating from one point to sum to 1, certainty. Note that aside from the first set of branches all others are conditional probabilities. As we journey along the tree every probability is conditional on our having been along preceding branches. Finally, at the end of the branches we have joint probabilities: the result of multiplying together all the probabilities along the branches that led to that end. We arrive at them through multiplication since they are the probabilities of the first event *and* second event of that particular path occurring. If we sum the joint probabilities we get 1 since these joint probabilities together encompass all possible outcomes (and addition is outcome $A$ or $B$ occurring).

The tree not only helps by listing relevant and useful probabilities, but drawing it up also helps in formulating the problem. If you can see problems involving probabilities as sequences of events with different outcomes, the tree is a means to help you map out the problem. Consider a second example: 8000 students taking for the first time a professional examination; there are a number of taught courses available with little to differentiate them. A course run by Getuthru Ltd is taken by 2000 students and, for the first time, the figures in Table 9-1 are available.

**Table 9-1**   Success rates using Getuthru

| Result at first sitting | Take Getuthru | Not take Getuthru | Total |
|---|---|---|---|
| Pass | 1500 | 4200 | 5700 |
| Fail | 500 | 1800 | 2300 |
| Total | 2000 | 6000 | 8000 |

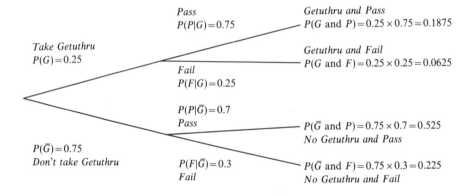

where $G$ is taking Getuthru and $\bar{G}$ not taking Getuthru; $P$ is passing and $F$ failing $(=\bar{P})$.

**Figure 9-3**   Tree diagram: Getuthru

The tree diagram in Fig. 9-3 can be seen to be composed of the taking of Getuthru and whether or not the student passes. There are only four possible outcomes in this case, one of which is that they will take Getuthru ($G$) *and* Pass ($P$). To arrive at the probability of this route we use Eq. (9-8):

$$P(G \text{ and } P) = P(G) \times P(P|G)$$

$P(G)$ is the first branch of Fig. 9-3 and from Table 9-1 is equal to $2000/8000 = 0.25$; $P(P|G)$ is the conditional probability of passing, given the course has been taken, and is $1500/2000 = 0.75$. Thus $P(G \text{ and } P) = 0.25(0.75) = 0.1875$.

Since $P(P|G) = 0.75$ and $P(P|\bar{G}) = 0.7$, Getuthru Ltd seems to help get you through.

There is a second use of tree diagrams which can help with decision making. Here our concern is with evaluating alternative courses of action, identifying their respective pay-offs, the probabilities of their occurring and deciding on which course of action to take. The appropriate technique is a *decision tree*. We extend the above example.

For example, let us now assume that a correspondence course was taken by all students and, in addition, there was the single option of a Getuthru taught course to supplement the correspondence course, but this was at an extra cost of £2000 in fees. We assume for simplicity that it is rare to fail the second sitting irrespective of the type of preparation for the first sitting. However, the pay-off for passing in the first sitting is an additional £10000 on a salary of £20000—is it worth taking the course? The pay-offs for each outcome (less fees where applicable) are given in Fig. 9-4,

which is a decision tree. For example, the pay-off to take Getuthru and pa[ss]
less £2000 costs = £28 000.

There are conventions governing the drawing of decision trees. We dist[inguish]
and *events*. Actions are represented by branches from squares, the squares
*nodes*. Events that occur because of these actions are represented by br[anches]
circles being known as *event nodes*. Probabilities are recorded on e[ach]
probabilities on each branch emanating from a particular event node must
the probabilities of all possible (mutually exclusive) outcomes. Figure 9-[4]
from the decision node we can either take Getuthru or not as our action.
pass or fail with their associated probabilities (decision trees only have p[------]
event branches). The pay-offs are at the end. Having drawn the decision tree, how do we use it? The
very drawing of it helps identify the salient aspects, but we want to make decisions, in this case do
we take Getuthru? It depends of course on the pay-off, but we do not know what this will be for
certain, only probabilities and related pay-offs.

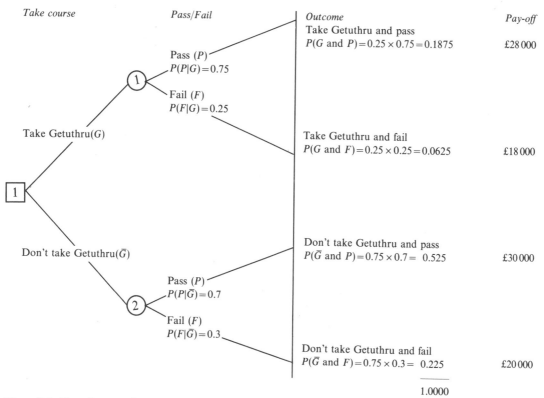

**Figure 9-4**   Tree diagram of success rates

To consider whether it is worth taking Getuthru we work backwards on the tree diagram, from
right to left, calculating expected monetary values (EMV) for each 'node' of the tree. EMV is given
by the sum of each pay-off times its associated probability. For event node 1 we have

$$0.75(28\,000) + 0.25(18\,000) = £25\,500$$

node 1 is the decision to take the course and the expected monetary value is based on the babilities and pay-offs of the different possible results. Similarly, EMV for event node 2 is:

$$0.7(30\,000) + 0.3(20\,000) = £27\,000$$

Since this is higher than £25 500 we advise people not to take the course. Note that no single individual will actually have a pay-off of £25 500 or £27 000—it is what would happen on average from many people taking or not taking the course and some individuals (those who take and pass) will do better than others (those who do not take and fail). However, as an overall indicator of the worth of the course it is useful. The use of tree diagrams is also useful for sensitivity analysis, especially if the probabilities are subjective. We can substitute higher and lower estimates of the probabilities to see how sensitive our answer is to such estimates. Some problems involve estimates based on imperfect information and we could re-run calculations on the basis of full information if we were sure of the outcome, and derive the monetary value of the information (see Anderson *et al.* (1987) for further details).

## BAYES' THEOREM

Here we consider how new information can help us to revise our probabilities and shed insights into the effectiveness of the information. We start with *prior probabilities* (e.g. the likelihood of a product being successfully launched) and add new information (e.g. a test report by consultants on whether it will be successful). The new information is not perfect (in the sense that a report that a successful launch will take place is no guarantee that the launch will be successful). If this were the case we would have no problem. Yet we may know the *conditional probability* (the probability of the launch being successful given a favourable report). The prior probability and conditional probability (new information) can be applied in Bayes' theorem to yield *posterior probabilities* (the probability of the product being accepted, given a favourable report). Note that we could also evaluate via Bayes' theorem the posterior probability of the product being successful given an unfavourable report—the two posterior probabilities allowing us to comment on the effectiveness of the consultants' reports.

Consider an interest in finding out the probability that a book will be a 'success'. We may know that for this type of book 60 per cent are successes—i.e. if the book is a success $(A_1)$, $P(A_1) = 0.6$; if the book is a failure $(A_2)$, $P(A_2) = 0.4$. We may ask: Is there any new information, perhaps from the nature of the book or from test marketing, we can use to help us predict $P(A_1)$ and $P(A_2)$ more accurately? Thus the initial value, $P(A_1) = 0.6$, is a *prior probability* to which we add new information, then apply Bayes' theorem to yield improved estimates (*posterior* or *revised probabilities*). The new information may be a market research company which test markets books by sending them to a panel of experts. These experts send their predictions to the company, who determine a consensus view, ask those with deviant views to justify them, send the panel the justification in case anyone wants to change his or her view (possibly leading to a new consensus and thus a new round) and finally gives a thumbs up or down on the book's prospects (Delphi technique—see Saren and Brownlie (1983)).

Now this market research company is adding new information: assume that, from past experience, there is a probability of 0.8 that this company will predict a book to be a success (event $B$) and be right, i.e. $P(B|A_1) = 0.8$. There is also a probability of 0.3 that the company will predict the book to be a success, and be wrong, i.e. $P(B|A_2) = 0.3$.

Remember, we have a prior probability of $P(A_1) = 0.6$; but if we can evaluate $P(A_1|B)$ this revised posterior probability provides better information about the book being a success: it is the probability of success given a successful test market—it includes new information.

The evaluation of $P(A_1|B)$ may seem straightforward since we have come across conditional probabilities above.

Using Eq. (9-8) we can derive:

$$P(A_1|B) = P(A_1 \text{ and } B)/P(B) \tag{9-10}$$

We do not know $P(A_1 \text{ and } B)$ from the information in the question, but since, from (9-8),

$$P(A_1 \text{ and } B) = P(A_1) \times P(B|A_1) \tag{9-11}$$

we have from Eqs (9-10) and (9-11):

$$P(A_1|B) = P(A_1) \times P(B|A_1)/P(B) \tag{9-12}$$

We also do not know $P(B)$, the probability the market research company will predict a success. However, a tree diagram (Fig. 9-5) can help us. Note that the tree diagram looks wrong. A logical flow of information would be the test results followed by the market success or failure. However, for this type of problem the conditional probabilities given ($P(B|A_1)$ and $P(B|A_2)$) require the test results to follow the market success or failure. We are told the probability of the test being favourable, given the product is a success/failure.

$P(B)$ is determined as $\{P(A_1 \text{ and } B) + P(A_2 \text{ and } B)\}$, i.e. probability of success and favourable report *or* probability of failure and a favourable report equals probability of a favourable report as should be apparent from Fig. 9-5. Thus, from Eq. (9-12):

$$P(A_1|B) = \frac{P(A_1) \times P(B|A_1)}{P(A_1 \text{ and } B) + P(A_2 \text{ and } B)} \tag{9-13}$$

and using Eq. (9-11) in the denominator of Eq. (9-13)

$$P(A_1|B) = \frac{P(A_1) \times P(B|A_1)}{P(A_1) \times P(B|A_1) + P(A_2) \times P(B|A_2)} \quad \text{Bayes' theorem} \tag{9-14}$$

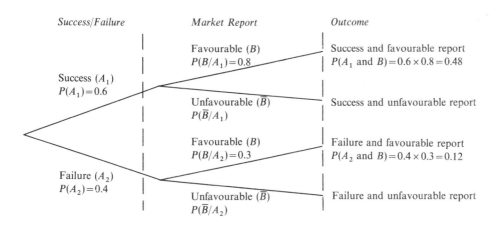

Figure 9-5   Tree diagram illustrating Bayes' theorem

For our example, from Fig. 9-5:

$$P(A_1|B) = \frac{0.6(0.8)}{0.48 + 0.12} = 0.8$$

Our prior probability of a success $P(A_1)$ was 0.6; on the basis of new information (a favourable test result) and the application of Bayes' theorem we determine a revised, posterior probability of 0.8.

As a further example of Bayes' theorem the probability that a customer will pay by credit card $(A_1)$ is 0.2 as opposed to 'cash' (cash or cheque) $(A_2)$, which is 0.8. The store makes less money from credit sales since they have to pay a commission to the card firm which they do not pass on by way of a higher price. You have two separate departments, food and drink; by analysing payment records you find that 30 per cent of credit card payments and 25 per cent of cash payments are for drink. A customer has just purchased some drink. What is the probability that payment will be by card?

We can revise our prior probability of $P(A_1) = 0.2$ by use of the new information on type of purchase and application of Bayes' theorem to yield our posterior probability of $P(A_1|B)$, where $B$ is the purchase of drink. Using Eq. (9-14)

$$P(A_1|B) = \frac{P(A_1) \times P(B|A_1)}{P(A_1) \times P(B|A_1) + P(A_2) \times P(B|A_2)}$$

$$= \frac{0.2(0.3)}{0.2(0.3) + 0.8(0.25)} = 0.4615$$

Equation (9-14) can be extended to cover more than two (mutually exclusive) events.

The more general application of Bayes' theorem is not without controversy, and the issues involved are beyond the scope of this book and not altogether straightforward. However, the methods and formulae considered here are uncontroversial and mathematically correct.

We now have a number of ways of manipulating probabilities to aid decision making. However, it is worth returning to the definition of probabilities where our concern was with the number of favourable outcomes over all possible outcomes. This involved counting outcomes, and this is not always as straightforward as it may seem. We thus leave this chapter with a section on counting.

## COUNTING

To evaluate probabilities under the *a priori* or relative frequency concept we need to be able to count. We need to count the total number of possible outcomes, and the number of favourable outcomes. This is not always as easy as it seems. One type of problem involves multiple choices: for example, a retailer sells boxed shirts and ties made up of five different shirts and two different ties; how many different sets (assuming all matches are possible) can be sold? The answer is to multiply 5 by 2 = 10. If, in addition, there were three types of braces, then we would have $5 \times 2 \times 3 = 30$ possible sets (see figure 9-6):

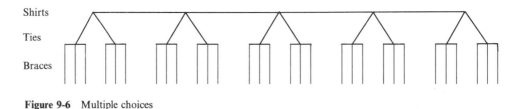

**Figure 9-6**   Multiple choices

If only one set of braces, shirt and tie was red, the probability of picking an all-red set would be $1/30 = 0.033$. Our interest is also with determining the number of arrangements, sequences and orderings that things may take. One type of ordering is a *permutation*. For example, in a competition with six finalists, how many different ways can a winner and second place be selected? First we enumerate all possibilities:

| | | | | | |
|---|---|---|---|---|---|
| ~~11~~ | 21 | 31 | 41 | 51 | 61 |
| 12 | ~~22~~ | 32 | 42 | 52 | 62 |
| 13 | 23 | ~~33~~ | 43 | 53 | 63 |
| 14 | 24 | 34 | ~~44~~ | 54 | 64 |
| 15 | 25 | 35 | 45 | ~~55~~ | 65 |
| 16 | 26 | 36 | 46 | 56 | ~~66~~ |

'51' denotes finalist number 5 first, and finalist number 1 coming second. Note '51' differs from '15', the latter being finalist number 1 coming first and finalist number 5 coming second. The crossed out numbers are ineligible: no finalist can come first *and* second. We thus have 30 ways of ordering 2 from 6 if things are treated as different outcomes when they take different orders (as with '51' and '15'). To be called a permutation it is necessary that when things take different orders they are treated as different outcomes. All of this is well and good for simple examples, but what of the different permutations that can arise for first, second and third place out of six finalists? A formula is required. The permutation formula is:

$$_nP_r = \frac{n!}{(n-r)!} \tag{9-15}$$

which yields for us the number of permutations of $n$ distinct things taken $r$ at a time. The exclamation marks (!) need to be explained: they are called factorial signs and are simply shorthand: $n! = n(n-1)(n-2)\ldots 1$; $4! = 4 \times 3 \times 2 \times 1 = 24$. Note that $0! = 1!$; calculators may have factorial signs on them allowing direct calculations, or even $_nP_r$ itself. Thus, using Eq. (9-15) for our problem we have $n = 6$ to be taken $r = 3$ at a time where the order is important:

$$_6P_3 = \frac{6!}{(6-3)!} = \frac{6!}{3!} = \frac{6 \times 5 \times 4}{1} = 120$$

Note that 3! is part of 6! and can be used to cancel out part of the numerator, e.g. $20!/19! = 20$.

If we had eight letters of the alphabet ABCDEFGH and we wanted to know how many ways to choose two from eight the answer is $_8P_2 = 8!/(8-2)! = 56$. However, it must be stressed that this holds only if the order matters, in this case AB is a different selection to BA. If the order is irrelevant we are concerned with **combinations**.

The number of combinations of a distinct object taken $r$ at a time is:

$$_nC_r = \frac{n!}{(n-r)!r!} \tag{9-16}$$

For example, if you were asked to form teams of two people from a group of 20, the total number of possible teams is:

$$_{20}C_2 = \frac{20!}{(20-2)!2!} = \frac{20!}{18!2!} = \frac{20 \times 19}{2 \times 1} = 190$$

Note that the order is unimportant: a team of Jack and Jill is the same as one of Jill and Jack. This if a team is picked at random, the probability of Jack and Jill forming the team is $1/190 = 0.005$

(assuming that only one Jack and one Jill are available). If we take our example of choosing two letters from eight, and if the order of the letters does not matter—i.e. *AB* is the same as *BA*—then the number of combinations is:

$$_8C_2 = 8!/(8-2)!2! = 8!/(6! \times 2!) = 28$$

## SOME FINAL POINTS

In applying probabilities a number of points are worth making since incorrect predictions are a rich source of error (see Moore, 1990).

- *Unlikely events are often misinterpreted*  If you are told that the probability is one in a million that one of the products from your production process is lethal, do not ignore the problem as you may produce millions of products per week. Even if you produce only 100 products per week this does not mean you have $(1\,000\,000/(100 \times 52)) = 192$ years to go under current production methods before the lethal product is produced; it may be produced that day. In meeting people we often express surprise at coincidences, but given the number of people we meet it is not surprising. In business life coincidences are often ascribed to be the results of conspiracies, which may (or may not) be the case.
- *Subjective estimates of probabilities may be biased*  Individuals commonly believe they are more certain on issues than they are. They are influenced by the ease with which relevant information can be recalled from memory (e.g. probabilities of airplane crashes occurring are deemed higher than justified, because their high media profile allows us to readily recall their occurrence). Individuals also have difficulty revising probabilities given additional information, some placing more weight on new information (than justified by Bayes' theorem) and others concentrating virtually exclusively on the original information. Also, individuals do not generally recognize that probabilities based on large samples are less variable than those based on small samples (e.g. if 2 per cent of entries in your bank account are wrong it is more likely that a sample of 20 entries will have 4 per cent wrong (be more variable—contain more extreme results) than a sample of 100 entries would have 4 per cent wrong).
- *Interpretation of probabilities*  Independent events should be recognized as such. The probability of an unbiased coin being a head on the fourth toss, even if we know it has been a head on the first three tosses, is still 0.5. If you have been unlucky and you know the trials are independent, you should not allow your probabilities to be influenced by your history. It is also necessary to apply the appropriate probability. It may be that there is a probability of 0.9 a student will pass his or her exam in this subject, but if you failed the continuous assessment (or studied 'A' level mathematics or whatever) the relevant probability for you may be quite different.

## EXERCISES

**9-1** (a) Provide examples of two events which are (i) mutually exclusive and (ii) independent.
(b) Of the total production in a normal day, 1200 products are faulted. The faults are classified as Type A and Type B and it is possible for a product to suffer from both. If the product suffers from A or B it goes for repair. If it suffers from both A and B it is destroyed. On a normal day 600 products have fault A, 800 have fault B, but 200 of these products have faults A and B. What is the probability of a faulty product picked at random being destroyed?

**9-2** You have just marketed a machine and the R&D division now informs you that they have discovered a flaw in the design. The machines are sold so that they can be used in only one of three modes, A, B and C, and 20 per cent of machines are sold in mode A. A warning light is faulty in 1 out of every 100 machines. The machines contain two thermostats, I and II. If the machine is used in mode A, and has a faulty warning light, and either thermostat I or thermostat II independently fail (2 per cent and 5 per cent likelihood respectively) then the machine might explode, endangering life. Your MD thinks it best to keep quiet because it is unlikely to happen with only 10 000 machines on the market. What do you think?

**9-3** The warranty for a car allows free repairs if there is a fault in the first two years or under 20 000 miles. A make of car has been on the market for four years now and from the 1000 cars sold in the first six months, 200 have had faults repaired under the two-year criterion, 100 under the first 20 000 miles criterion, but 50 of the cars qualified under both criteria. What is the probability of a repair being claimed under the warranty? In what way is the question ambiguous?

**9-4** The following chart shows whether or not graduate applicants of each sex were asked to an interview for a large corporation.

|  | Male | Female |
| --- | --- | --- |
| Invited to interview | 20 | 5 |
| Not invited to interview | 130 | 45 |

Determine the probability of (i) a male and (ii) a female being invited to an interview. Assume now that being invited to an interview and being female are independent events. How would this affect your answer to (ii) and what interpretation might be given to any such effect?

**9-5** You are about to sell to a new client. You know from bitter experience that 8 per cent of clients default on payment. You hire a company that briefly surveys possible clients and gives you an estimate of the likelihood of the client defaulting, in this case 20 per cent. However, the company does not always get it right, and their advice is not always followed. Via your own and other people's experience, you believe that 70 per cent of clients who they think will default actually will, and 20 per cent of clients who they believe will default, will not. What is the probability your new clients will not default?

**9-6** You have a choice of jobs, one in Australia and one in the UK. You want to work out the (expected) income from each job over a four-year period to help you choose. Thus, all income figures are projections over the next four years and appropriately discounted to present-day values. The UK job will give you £90 000 irrespective of how well you do, the career plan being laid out. The Australian job gives an option to leave after a year to their UK branch. Irrespective of whether you stay or go to their UK branch, you are considered after a year-and-a-half for promotion to their 'fast track' career development. There is a probability of 0.2 that you might feel less than enamoured with Australia and want to leave after a year. In such a case your income (including the period in Australia) will be £75 000, or if you are put into the 'fast track' category, £95 000—the probability of being put into this category being 0.65. If you stayed the income would be £85 000 or £130 000, the latter if you were put into the 'fast track', though the probability of this is 0.75 in Australia (for someone from the UK). Assume that currency conversion rates will not disturb the sums and that the figures take account of the different cost of living (i.e. adjusted for purchasing power parity). Using decision trees, what should you do?

# PROBABILITY DISTRIBUTIONS

## PROBABILITY DISTRIBUTIONS: THEIR NATURE

Consider the following three problems:

- *Problem I*   A salesperson is given 20 addresses to call on each day. The household at each address has responded to a mail shot expressing an interest in having a salesperson call to discuss the product. The salesperson's experience is that a sale is made at 1-in-10 households. What is the probability that 5 sales will be made in a given day?
- *Problem II*   A type of photocopier has a paper jam on average once every 2000 copies. What is the probability there will be more than two jams in a 2000 copy run?
- *Problem III*   The (arithmetic) mean life (continuous play on a specific cassette player) of a make and type of battery is 20 hours with a standard deviation of 0.5 hours. What is the probability a battery will last no more than 21 hours?

In Problem I the *random variable* of interest is the 'number of sales per day'. We refer to it as a random variable since the outcome in any one day is uncertain and may be considered to be dependent on chance. The 'number of jams in 2000 copies' (Problem II) and 'life of a battery' (Problem III) are also random variables. Associated with each possible value of the random variable in Problem I is a probability, and the concern of the problem is with the probability that the random variable, denoted by $X$, takes the value of 5, i.e. $P(X = 5)$. A probability distribution (also called a frequency function) maps out how probabilities are distributed over all possible values of the random variable.

Figure 10-1 (and the first two columns of Table 10-1) show how the distribution might look with, on the horizontal axis, $X$ taking values ranging from 0 to 20 sales in a day, and the associated probabilities on the vertical axis. The probability of five sales in a day is 0.0319; very small. The probability distribution can be seen in this case to be positively skewed, with the probabilities of $X$ taking values higher than five quite minimal.

Similarly, probability distributions might be drawn up for the 'number of jams in 2000 copies' with associated probabilities for each value of $X$ (though these will become very small for even relatively low values of $X$). Similarly, for Problem III, we can find the probabilities of a battery lasting for specific (non-overlapping and exhaustive) ranges of $X$ (e.g. $0 \leqslant X < 1$ hour; $1 \leqslant X < 2$ hours; etc.) in a manner akin to the histograms of Chapter 4. Often we consider (cumulative)

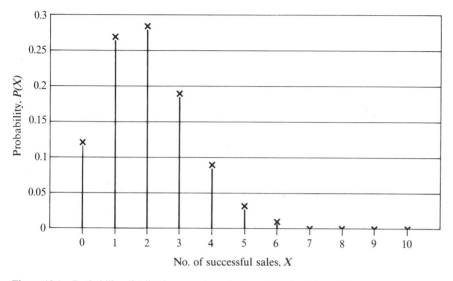

**Figure 10.1**  Probability distribution: number of successful sales (binomial)

distribution functions which, instead of mapping out values of $X$ and their associated probabilities, map out the probabilities of $X$ taking a particular value along with all values cumulated up to it; much like the less-than type ogive in Chapter 4.

It should be apparent that being able to evaluate the probability that a random variable takes a particular value (or range of values) is useful for planning purposes. In our examples it helps the salesperson to evaluate the expected variability of bonuses, and the manufacturer of copiers and batteries the performance of their products. However, in order to derive these valuable distributions it might seem we need to observe sales performances for a long period to identify the relative frequency (probability) with which different sales figures (values of $X$) emerge. The

**Table 10-1**  Probability distribution (binomial) of number of successful sales

| Number of successful sales, $X$ | Probability binomial (20, 0.1) $P(X)$ | $X \times P(X)$ | $(X - \mu)^2 P(X)$ |
|---|---|---|---|
| 0 | 0.1216 | 0 | 0.4865 |
| 1 | 0.2701 | 0.2701 | 0.2702 |
| 2 | 0.2852 | 0.5704 | 0.0000 |
| 3 | 0.1901 | 0.5703 | 0.1900 |
| 4 | 0.0898 | 0.3592 | 0.3591 |
| 5 | 0.0319 | 0.1595 | 0.2871 |
| 6 | 0.0089 | 0.0534 | 0.1424 |
| 7 | 0.0020 | 0.0140 | 0.0500 |
| 8 | 0.0003 | 0.0024 | 0.0108 |
| 9 | 0.0001 | 0.0009 | 0.0049 |
| 10* | 0.0000 | 0.0000 | 0.0000 |
|  | 1.0000 | 2.0002 | 1.8010 |

*Values of $X$ for 11 to 20 are not given since the associated probabilities are very small.

problem with this is, first, by the time the data are collected they might be out of date. And, second, it is not helpful for 'what if?' questions: for example, if the overall proportion of successes (Problem I) increased to 1 in 8, how would the distribution change? These difficulties can be overcome by expressing the distribution in a mathematical form which we can build into more complicated models of business-related behaviour.

The magic of probability distributions is that, given limited information (for example, in Problem I on the overall proportion of successes and number of contact addresses), the probability of $X$ taking any value or range of values can be generated. All we have to do is identify which of a number of 'standard' probability distributions might describe the problem situation, then identify the particular information or parameters that the particular distribution requires to generate the individual probabilities, and finally generate the probabilities. We shall look at three standard distributions that cover a range of useful situations, namely the binomial, Poisson and normal distributions. Before doing so we have to consider the measurement of our random variable.

## CONTINUOUS AND DISCRETE RANDOM VARIABLES

It is necessary to distinguish between two crude classifications of our random variables. *Discrete random variables* can take on only a finite number of values, such as the integers (whole numbers) 0 to 20 inclusive in Problem I (or an infinite sequence as long as the values are arranged in a *countable* definite order). Examples include the number of people in a queue, the number of eggs arriving broken at a supermarket from cartons packed in lots of 36, the expenditure on soft drinks per month by different households. Note that in this last case discrete random variables need not take integer or whole numbers (e.g. £2.15) but are discrete because they are limited, in this case, to two decimal places. We cannot have £2.153—we can count up the possible values which, as we shall see, is not possible in principle for continuous random variables.

*Continuous random variables* can in theory take on any value in a range or interval. For example, the life of the battery can take on any value within the interval of a physically possible life. The number that comes after zero cannot be 0.00001 second, because a smaller number is 0.000001 second, and this is no use because a smaller one is 0.0000001 second, and this is no use for there must exist an even smaller number. We cannot count the values the variable might take. Each time we try to start, the existence of an even smaller number stops us. In practice, the number of values are limited by the accuracy of measuring devices. These may be to the nearest minute, second, half-second, etc. However, even were we able to subdivide the possible life of batteries into a very large number of ranges of values by splitting time into very small bits, we would be left with very few observations (and low probabilities) for each value of $X$. To find out that there is an extremely small probability of a battery lasting *exactly* 19 hours 4 minutes 6.071943587 seconds is less than useful. In practice, our continuous random variables are measured at a meaningful level of accuracy, even though in theory they may take any value in the interval. Examples of continuous random variables include height of students, weight of a product, distance travelled by delivery vans in a year. Probability distributions involving continuous random variables cannot be drawn with the values of the random variable on the $X$-axis and corresponding probabilities on the $Y$-axis, as in the discrete case, since the probabilities will always be infinitesimal. Instead, for distributions of continuous random variables it is the area under the curve over the relevant range of values of the random variable that the probabilities represent. Probability distributions involving continuous random variables are described by a *probability density function*.

## SOME PROPERTIES OF PROBABILITY DISTRIBUTIONS

First, probabilities associated with individual values of $X$ cannot be negative or greater than 1 since this has no meaning. We saw in the previous chapter that $0 \leqslant P(X) \leqslant 1$. Second, the sum of the probabilities of all possible values of $X$ must equal 1, e.g. by summing (the addition rule) we are saying, for Problem I for example, either $X = 0$ or $X = 1$ or $X = 2 \ldots X = 20$; i.e. there is a probability of 1 (certainty) that one of the mutually exclusive outcomes will occur.

Thus for the discrete case:

$$\sum_{-\infty}^{+\infty} P(X) = 1 \tag{10-1}$$

In practice, the range of possible values will not generally go from minus infinity $(-\infty)$ to plus infinity $(+\infty)$, the range only being stipulated here for completeness. For continuous distributions readers with a knowledge of the calculus will appreciate that $f(X)$ describes the curve of the probability density function:

$$\int_{-\infty}^{+\infty} f(X)\, dX = 1 \tag{10-2}$$

The integral sign ($\int$) embraces (in theory) all possible values from minus infinity to plus infinity $(-\infty$ to $+\infty)$ and sums the probabilities by evaluating the total area under the curve. The area above any range of values denotes the probability of that range of values occurring. You may ask why don't we just sum the individual probabilities as in the discrete case. However, you must remember in principle that the random variable $X$ may take an infinite number of possible values with an infinite number of associated probabilities, and summing these is slightly problematic. This is why integral calculus helps out. For our purpose there is no need to know how to integrate, but only why the integral sign has appeared.

For probability density functions it is the area under the curve corresponding to a range of values for $X$ that yields the probability of that range of values occurring. Thus:

$$\int_{a}^{b} f(X)\, dX = P(a < X < b) \tag{10-3}$$

Probability distributions such as the one in Fig. 10-1 have an average (mean) value for $X$ as well as a standard deviation and variance. The mean or *expected value* of $X$ is defined by:

$$E[X] = \begin{cases} \displaystyle\sum_{-\infty}^{+\infty} XP(X) & \text{discrete random variable} \\[4ex] \displaystyle\int_{-\infty}^{+\infty} Xf(X)\, dX & \text{continuous random variable} \end{cases} \tag{10-4}$$

For example, in Problem I if we multiplied each value of $X$ by its associated probability in Table 10-1, and summed the results we would get $E[X]$. This is equal to approximately 2. Expected values need not correspond to actual possible results in the same way that the average size of a family might be 2.4 children. Expected values may be considered as averages in that the probabilities serve as relative frequencies in the formula for the mean, i.e. $\bar{X}=\Sigma fX/\Sigma f$

$$\Sigma\left(\frac{f}{\Sigma f}\right)X$$

where $f/\Sigma f$ is the relative frequency or probability. It is a weighted average where the weights are the probabilities, giving relatively more emphasis to outcomes of the random variable with relatively high probabilities. We also denote $E[X]$ by the symbol $\mu$ (pronounced 'mu'). This is used in the next chapter as the mean of the population of all values of a variable. We use it here because the probability distribution covers all outcomes and $E[X]$ is, as just noted, an arithmetic mean.

The variance of a probability distribution can also be considered in a similar manner and provides a measure of the dispersion of the values of a random variable. The variance is denoted by the symbol $\sigma^2$ (pronounced sigma (squared)—the lower-case version of the Greek letter for $s$) and is defined by:

$$\sigma^2 = \begin{cases} \sum_{-\infty}^{+\infty} (X-\mu)^2 P(X) & \text{discrete random variables} \\ \\ \int_{-\infty}^{+\infty} (X-\mu)^2 f(X) & \text{continuous random variables} \end{cases} \tag{10-5}$$

The standard deviations are the square roots of these expressions. Table 10-1 shows the expected value of the number of sales per day to be 2.0002 with a standard deviation $\sqrt{1.801}=1.342$. The mean and standard deviations are interpreted along similar lines to those explained in Chapter 4.

Thus, to summarize, probability distributions show the distribution of probabilities associated with values or ranges of a random variable. For discrete random variables the probabilities sum to 1, and for continuous random variables the equivalent of this is the area under the probability density function being equal to 1. The distributions naturally have means and variances that are calculated as shown above. For particular situations we can judge the form the probability distribution is likely to take, and we shall now consider some of these forms.

## SOME PROBABILITY DISTRIBUTIONS

We are now in a position to consider some standard probability distributions and their application. Each probability distribution is applied to a particular situation. The trick is, first, to know that a problem requires the application of a probability distribution; because, to solve the problem, the probability that a (random) variable takes a specific value or range of values has to be evaluated. Second, we must determine which of the standard probability distributions applies to the problem situation. We shall deal with three distributions (types of situations) though there are more, as outlined in Kendall and Stuart (1969). However, the three situations considered here apply to a wide range of problems. Finally, you simply have to know how to evaluate the probabilities using the parameters required by each distribution.

## The binomial distribution

**When to apply it**  The binomial situation applies when we have an experiment (or trial) repeated a number of times and there are only two possible outcomes to the experiment. We shall call the possible outcomes 'success' and 'failure'. Also, the result or outcome of any experiment should not influence that of another—each should be independent. The parameters, or information requirements, for the distributions are $n$ (the number of times the experiment is conducted) and $p$ (the probability of 'success' at each trial). Since trials are identical and independent, $p$ is the same. Since the number of successes will be countable, it applies to discrete random variables.

An example is the tossing of a coin (say) 50 times: $n = 50$, $p = 0.5$ (say obtaining a head). Each time the coin is tossed the experiment is repeated. The results of the experiments are independent of each other; obtaining a head on one throw does not affect the probability of doing so on another. From just knowing $n$ and $p$ we can generate the full probability distribution, i.e. the probabilities of obtaining $0, 1, 2, 3, \ldots, 50$ heads. How does this occur? It is as if in certain situations there are 'laws' of how things must happen. We are more used to deterministic scientific 'laws' of causality than laws of probability. Yet in all fields of science (especially genetics), probability laws are used to explain matters. Einstein's belief that God does not roll dice has fallen on deaf ears as physicists apply the laws of probability to explain the behaviour of atomic particles. The distributions can also be applied to business-related areas.

Consider Problem I: each visit can be regarded as a repeated experiment with two outcomes: 'sale' or 'no sale'. The outcomes are not strictly independent in that failure to sell may affect the salesperson's 'patter'; but overall the problem may be defined by the binomial with $n = 20$ and $p = 0.1$.

Alternatively consider boxes of 40 items ($n = 40$) with, overall, 1 in 40 items defective ($p = 1/40$), the customer being able to claim a refund if any box has more than two items defective. The checking of each item is a repeated experiment with two outcomes: defective or otherwise. Other applications include probability distributions for number of customers paying by credit card, insurance claims paid or not paid, consumers who can or cannot recognize a particular brand in blind tests, customers who default on payment, etc. All these can be looked at as repeated experiments with only two possible outcomes, the outcome in one experiment being (roughly) independent of another.

**How to apply it**  Having recognized the problem situation, how can we determine the probability distribution? The distribution is given by:

$$P(X = x) = \frac{n!}{(n-x)!x!} p^x (1-p)^{n-x} \tag{10-6}$$

The lower-case (small) $x$ denotes the specific value we want to find the probability of. The exclamation marks (factorial signs) were considered in the previous chapter and are mathematical shorthand for:

$$n! = n(n-1)(n-2)(n-3)\ldots 1$$

The expression $n!/((n-x)!x!)$ in Eq. (10-6) is also denoted by $_nC_r$ on some calculators ($r$ being used instead of $x$), and can be derived directly. We know from the previous chapter that it is the number of combinations of choosing $x$ from $n$. It makes sense that this should help determine the probability of $x$ occurring. Applying Eq. (10-6) to Problem I, where $n = 20$; $p = 0.1$:

$$P(X = 5) = \frac{20!}{(20-5)!5!} 0.1^5 (1-0.1)^{20-5}$$

$$= \frac{20!}{15!5!} 0.1^5 (0.9)^{15}$$

$$= \frac{20 \times 19 \times 18 \times 17 \times 16}{5 \times 4 \times 3 \times 2 \times 1} (0.00001)(0.20589)$$

$$= 0.0319, \quad \text{i.e. a very small chance}$$

Note how the 15! partially cancels out the 20! on moving to the third line of the calculation. In longhand the fraction in the calculation was worked out as

$$\frac{20 \times 19 \times 18 \times 17 \times 16 \times \cancel{15} \times \cancel{14} \times \cancel{13} \times \cancel{12} \times \cancel{11} \times \cancel{10} \times 9 \times 8 \times \cancel{7} \times 6 \times 5 \times \cancel{3} \times \cancel{2} \times \cancel{1}}{\cancel{15} \times \cancel{14} \times \cancel{13} \times \cancel{12} \times \cancel{11} \times \cancel{10} \times 9 \times 8 \times \cancel{7} \times 6 \times 5 \times \cancel{3} \times \cancel{2} \times \cancel{1}}$$

Note also that $0.9^{15}$ can be calculated by successive multiplication of 0.9, but when $n$ in Eq. (10-6) is very large this process is tedious and likely to result in errors. It is much better to use the $x^y$ facility on a calculator. Alternatively, those familiar with logarithms will know that if we want $a = x^y$, then $\log a = y \log x$; so for $0.9^{15}$ we find $\log(0.9)$, multiply it by 15, and then take the antilog of the result to get our answer. To make matters even easier, the calculation as a whole can be undertaken using binomial tables, available for a range of values of $n$ and $p$, and they yield the required probabilities. Often such tables are in a cumulative form giving the probabilities that $X$ is greater than or equal to a value. Probabilities that $X$ takes an individual value can be deducted by subtracting successive values, e.g. $P(X=3) = P(X \geqslant 3) - P(X \geqslant 4)$ (see Kmietowicz and Yannoulis (1988) for tables).

If we wanted to find the probability of making less than 2 sales in a day, using Eq. (10-6) we simply sum the probability of 0 and 1 sales, i.e. 0 OR 1 sales. If we wanted the probability of 3 or more sales we could use: $1 - [P(0) + P(1) + P(2)]$ since 1 is the sum of all probabilities. This would be easier than evaluating $P(3) + P(4) + P(5) + \ldots + P(20)$.

As an example of the success the binomial has in mapping out probabilities, W. F. R. Weldon went to the effort of throwing 12 dice 26 306 times, noting the values at each throw. The occurrence of a 5 or 6 was regarded as a 'success'. With $n = 12$ and $p = 0.3377$ (the dice were not perfect) the predicted number of times 0, 1, 2, 3, etc., successes occurred are given in Table 10-2, the binomial providing good predictions of what actually happened based on only two parameters, $n$ and $p$.

**Table 10-2** Frequency distribution of 26 306 throws of 12 dice, the occurrence of a 5 or 6 being counted as a success

| Number of successes | Observed frequency $O$ | Expected binomial frequency $E$ | $(O-E)^2/E$ |
|---|---|---|---|
| 0 | 185 | 187 | 0.021 |
| 1 | 1 149 | 1 146 | 0.008 |
| 2 | 3 265 | 3 215 | 0.778 |
| 3 | 5 475 | 5 465 | 0.018 |
| 4 | 6 114 | 6 269 | 3.832 |
| 5 | 5 194 | 5 115 | 1.220 |
| 6 | 3 067 | 3 043 | 0.189 |
| 7 | 1 331 | 1 330 | 0.001 |
| 8 | 403 | 424 | 1.040 |
| 9 | 105 | 96 | 0.844 |
| 10 and over | 18 | 16 | 0.250 |
| Total | 26 306 | 26 306 | 8.202 |

*Source*: Weldon in Kendall and Stuart (1969, p. 121).

Returning to Problem I, Table 10-1 shows the full probability distribution evaluated using Eq. (10-6) for different values of $X$. We generated the whole distribution just from a knowledge of the situation and the parameters $n$ and $p$.

**Determining its mean and standard deviation**   If we want to know the expected number and standard deviation of sales we might use the discrete version of Eqs (10-4) and (10-5) as evaluated in Table 10-1. Alternatively, it is the case that in a binomial situation:

$$\mu = E[X] = np \quad \text{and} \quad \sigma = \sqrt{np(1-p)} \tag{10-7}$$

i.e.

$$\mu = E[X] = 20(0.1) = 2 \quad \text{and} \quad \sigma = \sqrt{20(0.1)(1-0.1)} = 1.342$$

Finally, we have assumed that $p$ applies across any subset of the population. If, for example, our data were based on several salespersons all with different values of $p$ the binomial based on an overall $p$ may not provide a good fit.

### The Poisson distribution

**When to apply it**   The Poisson distribution applies to similar situations to the binomial, except that $p$ is very small and $n$ is very large. Indeed, it can be shown mathematically that if $p$ approaches 0 and $n$ becomes infinite in such a manner that $E[X] = np = \mu$ remains fixed, then the binomial distribution will approach the Poisson distribution with mean $\mu$ (Hoel, 1966). The Poisson distribution requires only one parameter, the expected or mean number of successes, $\mu$. In practice, Poisson provides an adequate approximation for most purposes when $n \geqslant 100$ and $p \leqslant 0.05$.

The Poisson comes into its own when our concern is with problems in which events of some kind occur over time, and we are concerned with the number of occurrences in some time interval. There is a sense in which, at each small period of time, an event—such as arrival of a shop's customer, airplane or 'phone call—can occur or not occur. Given that every fraction of a second provides an opportunity for an arrival, and that the actual probability of arriving in such a period can be quite small, this is like the binomial when $n$ is very large and $p$ very small. To divide time into small fractions of a second is awkward and rather arbitrary however, and so rather than use the binomial with large $n$ and small $p$, it is better to use the Poisson. The Poisson in such circumstances is based simply on the average number of events per unit of time. Further guidelines on the use of the Poisson distribution are given on page 176.

**How to use it**   Consider Problem II cited at the beginning of this section: a photocopier has a paperjam on average once every 2000 copies. The random variable $X$ is the number of jams every 2000 copies. We are required to determine $P(X > 2)$. The probabilities for the Poisson distribution are given by:

$$P(X = x) = \frac{e^{-\mu} \mu^x}{x!} \tag{10-8}$$

In this example, the mean or expected number, $\mu = 1$:

$$P(X = 0) = \frac{e^{-1} 1^0}{0!} = \frac{0.3679(1)}{1} = 0.3679$$

$$P(X = 1) = \frac{e^{-1} 1^1}{1!} = \frac{0.3679(1)}{1} = 0.3679$$

$$P(X=2)=\frac{e^{-1}1^2}{2\times 1}=\frac{0.3679(1)}{2}=0.1839$$

$$P(X>2)=1-[P(X=0)+P(X=1)+P(X=2)]$$

$$=1-[0.3679+0.3679+0.1839]=1-0.9197=0.0803$$

Note that 'e' is shorthand for the number 2.718281828 and $e^x$ or $e^{-x}$ is evaluated either through tables (often in books of logarithms) or by an appropriate facility on your calculator. Note also that anything to the power of zero is 1, and that 0! should be treated as equal to 1. Poisson probabilities can also be evaluated from ordinary or cumulative tables which, for given values of $\mu$ and $x$, allow the values to be read off directly (Kmietowicz and Yannoulis, 1988).

As a second example, consider that the demand for an item of stock is on average (mean) 4 per day. What is the probability that 6 items will be required on a single day?

$$P(X=6)=\frac{e^{-4}4^6}{6!}=\frac{0.0183(4096)}{720}=0.104$$

This helps to plan stock levels.

**Determining the mean and standard deviation and guidelines on when to use Poisson**    Poisson applies to discrete random variables and

$$E[X]=\mu \quad \text{and} \quad \sigma=\sqrt{\mu} \tag{10-9}$$

For example, Table 10-1, via Eqs (10-4) and (10-5), shows Problem I to not provide a good fit to the Poisson distribution since $E[X]=2.0002$, $\sigma=1.801$; thus $\sigma$ is not close to $\sqrt{\mu}=\sqrt{2.0002}=1.414$. This provides a rough mechanism for checking if Poisson is appropriate.

Consider the probability distribution of the number of accidents at work in a week, useful for planning health facilities. At first sight it is Poisson: however, it may be that the workforce can be divided into different groups with different accident-proneness (values of $\mu$). In such circumstances Poisson (based on an overall $\mu$) provides a poor fit and has to be evaluated differently (for details see Kendall and Stuart (1969, p. 129)).

### The normal distribution

**When to apply it**    Also called the Gaussian distribution, this applies in certain circumstances to continuous random variables though we shall see how its use may be modified to cope with the discrete case. The probability density function (PDF) is given by:

$$f(X)=\frac{1}{\sqrt{2\pi}\sigma}\exp\{-(X-\mu)^2/2\sigma^2\}\,dX \tag{10-10}$$

In Eq. (10-10) $\pi$ is a number (approximately 22/7), exp is 'the exponent of', i.e. 'e to the power of', and we use $f(X)$ instead of $P(X)$ since our probabilities will be made up from the area under $f(X)$, it being a continuous distribution. Note that the probabilities here depend on $\mu$ and $\sigma$, i.e. the normal distribution has two parameters, the mean and standard deviation. Just as the equation $Y=a+bX$ mapped out a straight line, Eq. (10-10) maps out the shape of the normal curve given in Fig. 10-2. The good news is that there is no reason for you to use Eq. (10-10) here since, as will be explained in the next section, tables of values of the areas under a normal curve have been prepared to save you the effort of using this equation directly. The normal distribution is often described as bell-shaped,

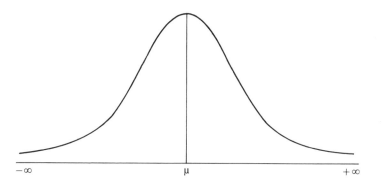

**Figure 10-2**  The normal distribution

and is perfectly symmetrical, the left-hand side of the centre being the mirror image of the right-hand side. The value of $X$ at the centre is $\mu$ which, as we learned from Chapter 4, is equal to the median and the mode for a symmetrical distribution. The values of $X$ extend (at least in principle) from minus to plus infinity and being a PDF, the area under the curve is equal to 1.

There are many applications of the normal distribution and Chapters 11 and 12 will develop these further in the context of inferential statistics. Consider for now some random variables: assume (this is fictitious) that 5000 students are studying annually for their MBA by a distance learning programme of the Open University. Courses include those in business statistics, economics and organizational behaviour (OB). The probability distribution of marks awarded in a statistics examination by 5000 students may be normally distributed with $\mu = 60$ and $\sigma = 10$, as in Fig. 10-3(a). Notice the symmetry, with a few students obtaining 10 percentage points above 60 per cent, and an equal few obtaining 10 percentage points below 60 per cent; likewise, for the very good and very bad (there are a few with 20 per cent above the mean, but these are counterbalanced by a few 20 per cent below $\mu$). The weight or size of a manufactured component, height of people, life of car tyres—all may be approximately normally distributed. Often when there are many variables, with each having a small effect on the value of a random variable, the outcome will be a normal distribution.

The decision that a random variable is approximately normally distributed may be one of judgement: you must ask yourself, if you were to map out the probability distribution, whether it would be bell-shaped. If there are any data with which to map out the shape, this would help with the decision and the coefficient of skewness outlined in Chapter 4 is a useful measure if such data are available. However, there is often an element of faith in the process. Once we assume the pattern to be normal, the rest is determined by its parameters. Given, in the above example, that examination marks are normally distributed, the mean tells us where the distribution is centred, and $\sigma$ its spread; $\mu$ and $\sigma$ allow any normal distribution to be described. Figure 10-3(a) shows marks in a Statistics examination while Fig. 10-3(b) show marks in an Economics examination and 10-3(c) marks in an Organizational Behaviour (OB) examination—all fictitious. Statistics and Economics have the same mean, but Statistics marks are more dispersed. OB marks have a lower mean, but very little dispersion. Given $\mu$, $\sigma$ and that the shape is normal, the full probability distribution can be evaluated; this is usually done with the help of tables as we shall now see.

**How to apply it**  Consider Problem III outlined earlier in which the mean life of a make and type of battery was 20 hours with $\sigma = 0.5$. We have to evaluate $P(X \geqslant 21)$. We recognize this to be a continuous random variable which is likely to be normally distributed since some batteries will last

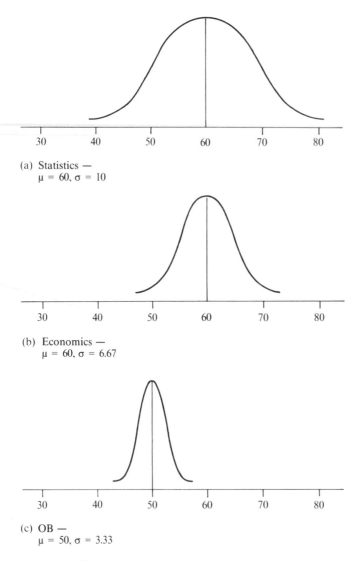

(a) Statistics —
    $\mu = 60, \sigma = 10$

(b) Economics —
    $\mu = 60, \sigma = 6.67$

(c) OB —
    $\mu = 50, \sigma = 3.33$

**Figure 10-3**   Examination marks

longer than 20 hours, but it is likely that these will be counterbalanced by a (roughly) equal number with shorter lifetimes. A few will last even longer, and a corresponding few even shorter, the effect being a bell-shaped pattern that is likely to be normally distributed. We now have two approaches to determining the probability: the first is the hard one based on Eq. (10-10). Those students familiar with the calculus will realize that 'all' they have to do is find the definite integral of the curve over the required range. There are approximations to this (see Kendall and Stuart, 1969, pp. 135–139), though the second approach is much easier and should invariably be used. This requires the use of tables of answers, which have already been worked out for us by someone else. The problem is that tables will be needed for all possible combinations of $\mu$ and $\sigma$, each covering a respectable range of $X$ (say $\mu \mp 3\sigma$). This is a lot of tables. The method used is to have available a table for a single combination of $\mu$ and $\sigma$, i.e. $\mu = 0$ and $\sigma = 1$, and then convert the $X$ random variable of the problem to (what is called) a $Z$ random variable of this special distribution and table. The special distribution is called the standardized normal distribution and $Z$-values have the unlikely name of standardized normal deviates.

The conversion from $X$ to $Z$ is undertaken using:

$$Z = \frac{X - \mu}{\sigma} \qquad (10\text{-}11)$$

For Problem III, assuming the lives of this make and type of battery are normally distributed, Fig. 10-4 provides a rough description of the problem. It is always useful to start with such a drawing. [To help: remember from Chapter 4 that for a normal distribution 99 per cent of observations lie within $\mu \mp 3\sigma$, i.e. $20 \mp 3(0.5)$, i.e. 18.5 to 21.5.] Probabilities are represented by areas; and we want the shaded area in Fig. 10-4 showing $P(X \geqslant 21)$. First convert this problem to the standardized normal distribution by transforming our $X$-value of 21 to its equivalent $Z$-value (which we shall call $Z^*$) *using Eq. (10-11)*:

$$Z^* = \frac{21 - 20}{0.5} = 2$$

Appendix 7 gives the areas under the normal distribution. We look down the row headings for 2.0, the column headings being used for the second decimal place, 0.00 in this case. The value from the tables can be seen to be 0.02275, i.e. the probability of the life of the battery being 21 hours or more.

What if our problem was the probability of the life being 19 hours or less (as in Fig. 10.5(a))? Then $Z^* = (19 - 20)/0.5 = -2$; there are no negative values for $Z$ in Appendix 7. However, since the normal distribution is symmetrical, the area to the right of $Z = 2$ is equivalent to the area to the left of $Z = -2$; thus, we do not need separate tables—the answer is 0.02275.

What if we wanted to determine the probability that the life of a battery lies between (and including) 19 and 20.85 hours (Fig. 10.5(b))? The area to the left of 19 is 0.02275. The area to the right of 20.85 is derived from $Z^* = (20.85 - 20)/0.5 = 0.17$; from the tables this yields an area of 0.43251. Since the total area under the curve is 1, our required area in Fig. 10.5(b) is $1 - [0.02275 + 0.43251] = 0.54474$, i.e. the probability that a battery will last between 19 and 20.85 hours.

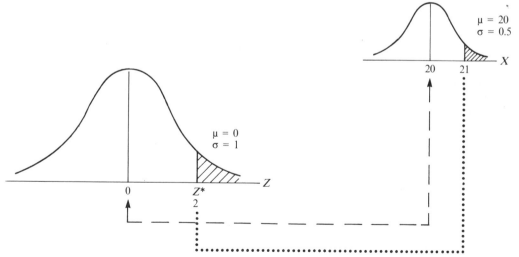

**Figure 10-4**  Life of batteries

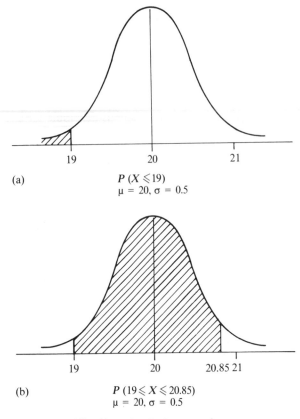

(a)  $P(X \leqslant 19)$
$\mu = 20, \sigma = 0.5$

(b)  $P(19 \leqslant X \leqslant 20.85)$
$\mu = 20, \sigma = 0.5$

**Figure 10-5**  Life of batteries: further example

So far we have rightly applied the normal distributions to continuous random variables. What if we had a *discrete random variable* that was normally distributed, say the marks in a statistics examination where the marker does not award fractions. Since, for example, a mark of 80 is the area directly above the point 80 this can only be represented in continuous space by an infinitely thin line, and the distribution by one such line for each mark on the scale—something like Fig. 10-6, except the lines will be too thin to see since they correspond only, for example, to 80, not to 79.9999999 or to 80.0000001. As such the total area under the curve, represented by these lines of infinitesimal width, will not sum to one. We require the area above each value to correspond to the probability of that value occurring, and these areas in total to represent the probabilities of all possible outcomes occurring, i.e. to sum to 1. To do this for discrete random variables: 80 becomes the area under the curve 79.5 to 80.5, 81 becomes the area under the curve 80.5 to 81.5, and so forth. The probability of a student scoring 40 or more when $\mu = 60$ and $\sigma = 10$ is the area to the right of 39.5 since 40 is 39.5 to 40.5. The probability of a student scoring 40 or less is the area to the left of 40.5 (Fig. 10-7). To determine these probabilities when $\mu = 60$ and $\sigma = 10$:

$P(X \geqslant 40)$
$Z^* = (39.5 - 60)/10 = -2.05$
$P(X \geqslant 40) = 1 - 0.02018$
$= 0.97982$

$P(X \leqslant 40)$
$Z^* = (40.5 - 60)/10 = -1.95$
$P(X \leqslant 40) = 0.02559$

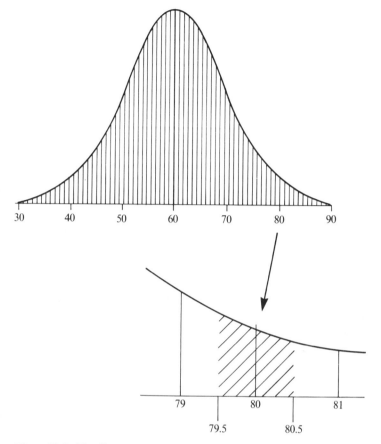

**Figure 10-6**   The discrete case for a normal distribution

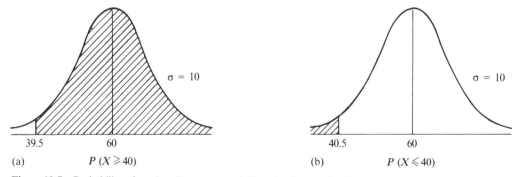

**Figure 10-7**   Probability of scoring 40 or more and 40 or less in examination

Note they do not sum to unity since they both include 40. $P(X = 40)$ is evaluated by working out the area to the left of 40.5, then to the left of 39.5, the difference yielding the required probability:

$P(X = 40)$

$$Z_1 = (40.5 - 60)/10 = 1.95 \qquad\qquad \text{Area} = 0.02559$$
$$Z_{11} = (39.5 - 60)/10 = 2.05 \qquad\qquad \text{Area} = 0.02018$$
$$P(X = 40) = 0.02559 - 0.02018 = 0.00541$$

We check our working:

$$P(X \geqslant 40) + P(X \leqslant 40) - P(X = 40) = 0.97982 + 0.02559 - 0.00541 = 1$$

The addition or subtraction of 0.5 is known as the *continuity correction*, and only applies in this form when the random variable is discrete in whole numbers (integers). If it was discrete in halves, the correction would involve the addition/subtraction of 0.25: 24.5 is really 24.25 to 24.75, and so forth.

### The normal approximation to the binomial

You may come across binomial problems that require the probability of $X$ taking a range of values. For example, for batches of 400 goods, what is the probability that 250 or more are red when they are packed at random and the overall proportion of red items is $p = 0.6$. For this problem we can:

(a) work out   $P(X = 250) + P(X = 251) + P(X = 252) + P(X = 253) + \ldots + P(X = 400)$,   against which there are better ways of spending a Sunday morning; or

(b) use comulative binomial probability tables which allow you to read off the probability that $X$ is greater/less than or equal to a value, except that only a limited range of values of $n$ and $p$ are usually available; or

(c) use the normal approximation to the binomial since the normal is tailor-made for finding probabilities greater/less than or equal to a value.

We shall look at this third approach.

It can be shown (e.g. Hoel, 1966, pp. 106–110) that as $n$ increases the approximation improves—though $p$ moving closer to 0.5 also helps matters. As a working rule the approximation is good for most purposes when $p$ is close to 0.5, or when $np > 5$ for problems in which $p \leqslant 0.5$, or $n(1 - p) > 5$ for problems in which $p > 0.5$. [Other working rules include, when $np^{3/2} > 1.07$, the error from using the approximation will never exceed 0.05 for any value of $X$ (Raff, 1956).]

In the above example $n = 400$, $p = 0.6$; since $400(1 - 0.6) = 160 > 5$ (or $400(0.6)^{3/2} = 185.9 > 1.07$), we can use the approximation. [*N.B.* To evaluate $0.6^{3/2}$, cube 0.6 then take the square root.]

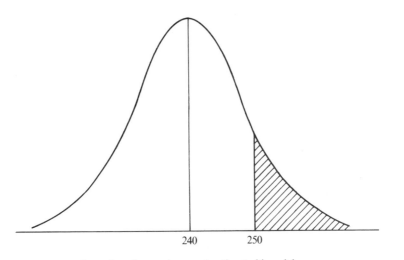

**Figure 10-8**   Illustration of normal approximation to binomial

For the normal distribution we need $\mu$ and $\sigma$: using Eq. (10-7) for the binomial, $\mu = np = 400(0.6) = 240$ and $\sigma = \sqrt{np(1-p)} = \sqrt{400(0.6)(0.4)} = 9.80$. Given $\mu = 240$, $\sigma = 9.8$ and a normal distribution we can now determine $P(X \geqslant 250)$ as illustrated in Fig. 10-8: applying the continuity correction we determine $P(X \geqslant 249.5)$. Note that since the binomial is applied to a discrete random variable we always need a continuity correction for the approximation.

$$Z^* = (249.5 - 240)/9.8 = 0.97$$

The corresponding area from tables and probability is 0.16602.

## GOODNESS OF FIT

Often we want to know if data on a random variable fit a particular distribution. If we have the data we do not need to apply a standard probability distribution since the probabilities can be generated directly from the relative frequencies. However, we may be interested in knowing if, for example, the binomial fits some data, so we can simulate what would happen under different values of $n$ and $p$, perhaps for a future period when we do not have values but can derive guesstimates of the new $n$ and $p$. Alternatively, it may simply be to develop an understanding of the processes by which the data were generated, e.g. repeated independent trials with two possible outcomes.

Table 10-2 shows some actual data and predicted values from a binomial distribution. To test whether the data provide a good fit, in the sense that differences between actual and expected values cannot be attributed to sampling error at the 5 per cent level, we use the chi-squared statistic ($\chi^2$) outlined in Chapter 6. The formula is given by:

$$\chi^2 = \Sigma (O_i - E_i)^2 / E_i \qquad (10\text{-}12)$$

From Table 10-2 we have $\chi^2 = 8.202$. Following the principles of Chapter 6, we now need to determine the degrees of freedom. Here we have $k = 11$ pairs of data. The degrees of freedom are $v = k - 2 - 1$ since these are two parameters for the binomial, i.e. $v = 8$. If any of the parameters are given, and not estimated from the data, we do not subtract these from the degrees of freedom. We set up the problem with $n$ known, not estimated from the data, therefore $v = 9$. However, $p$ was estimated from the data, revealing the dice to be possibly biased slightly. If we simply assumed that $p = 2/3$ then $v = 10$. However, in our case $v = 9$, and from the chi-squared tables in Appendix 5 we obtain a value, at the 5 per cent level, of 16.919. Since the calculated value, 8.202, is less than the value from the tables the difference between actual and predicted values can be seen to be not statistically significant at a 5 per cent level—in this sense the distribution fits the data.

Had we tested the normal distribution we would have used $v = k - 2 - 1$ where the two parameters $\mu$ and $\sigma$ are usually estimated from the data. If one or both take an 'assumed' value then $v = k - 2$ and $k - 1$ respectively. A similar principle applies to Poisson and its one parameter with $v = k - 1 - 1$.

## THE USE OF PROBABILITY DISTRIBUTIONS

Consider repeat-buying behaviour: the phenomenon of consumers remaining loyal to a brand, buying it more than once in a period, and continuing to buy it in the next period. One could list numerous factors that would determine the extent to which this occurs, including the merits of the product, pricing and advertising. Now it is important to consider why repeat-buying occurs and the impact of these factors. Yet as a separate exercise probability distributions have had a

**Table 10-3** Dirichlet model of toothpaste purchases over 48 weeks

| | | Number of purchases | | | | | | |
|---|---|---|---|---|---|---|---|---|
| | | 0 | 1 | 2 | 3 | 4 | 5 | 6+ |
| Maclean's | Observed | 67 | 13 | 6 | 4 | 2 | 2 | 5 |
| | Theoretical | 68 | 12 | 6 | 4 | 3 | 2 | 5 |
| Sainsbury's | Observed | 94 | 3 | 1 | 1 | 0.5 | 0.3 | 0.4 |
| | Theoretical | 94 | 3 | 1 | 1 | 0.4 | 0.2 | 0.6 |
| Average* | Observed | 81 | 8 | 4 | 2 | 1 | 1 | 3 |
| | Theoretical | 81 | 8 | 4 | 2 | 1 | 1 | 3 |

*Eight leading brands.

remarkable success for a wide range of product fields and brands in predicting repeat-buying in total ignorance of these factors. 'Of the thousand and one variables which might effect buyer behaviour, it is found that nine hundred and ninety nine usually do not matter. Many aspect of buyer behaviour can be predicted simply from the penetration and the average purchase frequency of the item, and even these two variables are interconnected' (Ehrenberg, 1988).

The probability distributions used are brought together as a Dirichlet model which covers brand and product purchase and includes some distributions not covered here, though the Poisson distribution is used to describe consumers' purchase of products. From only the sales level of each brand and two parameters we can generate the distribution of purchases over a period for individual brands and the product as a whole. Table 10-3 shows the 'observed' results based on a panel of 5240 continuously reporting households in a survey being conducted by a market research company called AGB Ltd their purchases of Sainsbury's and Maclean's toothpaste in 1973: 'theoretical' figures are derived from the model. The correspondence is very close: the model predicts that 68 per cent of households will not buy Maclean's in the period, with 12 per cent buying only once, 6 per cent twice, 4 per cent three times, etc., within the period—very close to what actually happened. Similar models have been successfully applied to a large number of products both in the USA and the UK and to store choice models (Wrigley, 1988), which predict loyalty to stores. The technical aspects of these models are outside the scope of this book, though the above illustrates one successful use of probability distributions.

## USING COMPUTERS

### Minitab

Minitab allows the probability distribution and the cumulative probability distributions to be generated using the commands PDF and CDF respectively for each of the binomial and Poisson distributions. For example, for binomial:

```
MTB  > PDF;
SUBC > BINOMIAL n=3, p=0.5.
BINOMIAL WITH n=3 p=0.500000
     K     P(X=K)
     0     0.1250
     1     0.3750
     2     0.3750
     3     0.1250
```

A range of distributions are included that will provide the required probabilities, given the name of the distribution and parameters in the subcommand, for a list of values of the random variable given in a column. For example, if we read the numbers 0, 1, 2, 3, 4, 5, 6 into C1, then the corresponding probabilities for a normal deviation distribution with mean 3 and standard deviation 1 is given in C3:

```
MTB  > PDF C1;
SUBC > NORMAL 3 1.
```

## Lotus 1-2-3

If you are using spreadsheets, the relevant formulae for binomial and Poisson can be entered directly. The Poisson would be given by:

$$+(@EXP(-\$B\$4)*\$B\$4\hat{\ }A2)/C2$$

where the mean is in B4, the dollar signs surrounding it holds it constant if the formula is copied. For values of $X = 0$, 1, etc., inserted in A2, A3, A4, etc., and in C2, zero; in C3, 1; in C4, (A4*A3); and C5, +(A5*C4); with subsequent values of C6, C7, C8 copied from C5 to represent the factorial $X$, we can generate Poisson values by copying the above formula downwards. Inserting different values of the mean in B4 generates different Poisson distributions to simulate what would happen if the mean changed, or to identify how sensitive the results are to an accurate estimate of the mean.

## EXERCISES

**10-1** You sell time-share by mail shots offering what appears to be valuable gifts to anyone who will attend a 'sales presentation'. Each day 15 people are booked to attend. The overall success rate is 0.15. However, you are badly in debt to some less than friendly loan sharks. Unless you pay them £1000 at the end of the day, the quality of your life will plunge. To achieve this sum you need commission on three or more sales. Assuming that commission is paid on the day, irrespective of whether the customers later withdraw in the cooling-off period, what is the probability of your legs being broken? Assuming that you have used 0.15 as $p$ in the above, explore how sensitive your results are to this value.

**10-2** You have a flock of 100 lambs and are concerned about the recent epidemic of 'mad-lamb' disease, which seemingly strikes lambs at random. The Ministry of Agriculture has found from random tests that as many as 4 per cent are affected. Lambs are tested for the disease before slaughter and, if affected, are not allowed to be sold and are destroyed by the Ministry with little compensation. What is the probability that five or more lambs will be destroyed? Comment on the validity of any assumptions made.

**10-3** Products are sold in batches of 40 and a penalty clause requires that, if any batch has three or more defectives, the customer does not have to pay for the batch. How likely is this to happen if the overall proportion of defectives is 0.02?

**10-4** A queue in a bank during lunchtime is, on average, three people long. The bank manager believes it to be unacceptable in terms of customer service if a queue becomes longer than five people. On what proportion of lunch hours is this likely?

**10-5** Pipes in 100 metre sections are tested for flaws. The results of recent tests on 200 pipes are: 30 pipes had no flaws; 50 pipes had 1 flaw; 56 pipes, 2 flaws; 37 pipes, 3 flaws; 17 pipes, 4 flaws; 9 pipes, 5 flaws; and 1 pipe, 6 flaws.
(a) Calculate the arithmetic mean of the flaws.
(b) Using this arithmetic mean for a Poisson distribution, predict the number of pipes out of a batch of 200 that would have 0, 1, 2, 3, etc., flaws.
(c) Compare the actual with the predicted results using the chi-squared test.
(d) Your senior manager believes there should never be more than eight flaws under normal operating conditions. Can you reassure her?

**10-6** The mean time it takes for a police vehicle to arrive following an emergency call in a particular region is 8 minutes, with a standard deviation of 6 minutes. What is the probability that a call will have to wait more than 25 minutes [data is fictitious]?

**10-7** A manufacturer produces widgets of mean size 0.8 cm with a standard deviation of 0.01 cm. To be accepted by the customer they have to be between 0.775 and 0.825 cm. What proportion of a 500 lot order will be rejected?

**10-8** Calculate the binomial probabilities for all values of $X$ for $n=5$, $p=0.3$. Repeat the exercise for $n=10$, $p=0.3$ and yet again for $n=20$, $p=0.3$. Draw all three probability distributions. What happens to the shape of the binomial if you increase $n$? [You may use a statistical package or spreadsheet.]

**10-9** Refer to Question 1: if the number of people booked to attend each day was 40, and the overall proportion 0.15, use the normal approximation to the binomial to determine the probability of 20 or more successes in a day.

**10-10** The proportion of eggs broken in a box of 6 in a supermarket was found to be 0.01. Calculate the probabilities of a box having 0, 1, 2, 3, 4, 5 and 6 eggs broken.

**10-11** Chess Pizzas deliver pizzas to your door on receipt of a telephone order. Their claim is that they will deliver within 20 minutes of the order, otherwise you get your order free. The mean delivery time for pizzas delivered in Cardiff is 15 minutes, with a standard deviation of 2 minutes. What is the probability of a customer receiving a 'free' order?

# ESTIMATION

Often our data do not comprise all members of the population, but a sample. For example, we may take a sample of television screens produced and test to see how strong they are; we would not take the population of all sets produced, since the test may involve breaking them and we would have none left to sell. Or we may take a sample of individuals in a survey of consumers rather than the population of all consumers because of time and cost constraints. The problem is: do we interpret the results of data from a sample differently to those from the general population? There is a sense in which results from a sample of, for example, 20 consumers with highly variable consumption patterns are less reliable than those from a sample of 200 consumers with similar consumption patterns. We need a mechanism to quantify how much faith we should have in such results. The principles involved will also be shown to be relevant to the determination of sample sizes, and be particularly applicable to quality control.

We shall assume that the sample data referred to is randomly selected—that is, each unit has the same probability of being drawn. We shall also assume that the method of choosing the sample from the population is *simple random sampling*; that is a process akin to putting all units into a very large hat, shaking it well and drawing the sample. Random number tables or generators on computers are the practical equivalent of this process. There are alternative ways of drawing samples—some more efficient, some less efficient, as discussed in Chapter 2— but the principles applied here apply to simple random sampling and we mention later how account can be taken of different sample designs.

Consider some data from a random sample of 100 consumers. We may find from the sample that average (arithmetic mean) expenditure on our product is £2 per month with a standard deviation of £0.10. But what we want to know is the mean and standard deviation expenditure *for the population*, for *all* consumers. Similarly, we may find that the proportion of consumers preferring our product to all others is 0.6, but this is for the sample and we want to know the population proportion. At this point common sense should take over. You should ask: How can we know the population value when we have only taken a sample? At first sight we should do as everyone reporting figures in the media does, and assume that the sample value provides a good indicator of the population value. When, for example, the results from political opinion polls report that 60 per cent of the electorate would vote Labour if there was a General Election tomorrow, we know their information is derived from a sample even if the result is phrased as if it is from a population. It is the accompanying error margins that concern us in this chapter.

Using the sample result for the mean and proportion as if they were the population result is known as a *point estimate*, and it can be shown that these sample values provide best unbiased estimates of their corresponding population values. The property of being a best unbiased estimator is important and its meaning will be considered later. However, we should point out that the best, unbiased estimator of the population variance is

$$s_{n-1}^2 = \frac{\Sigma(X_i - \bar{X})^2}{n-1} \tag{11-1}$$

Obviously, for small sample sizes ($n$) the sample and population formula can differ noticeably. Pocket calculators may well contain both $\sigma_n^2$ and $\sigma_{n-1}^2$, the latter referring to Eq. (11-1), and should be more properly labelled as $s_{n-1}^2$. So far we have said little that is not obvious: to estimate the mean and proportion for the population, use may be made of the sample values, though the variance point estimate of the population (and from it the standard deviation) should be based on Eq. (11-1).

However, these point estimates do not allow us insights into the confidence and error margins that should be applied to the result. All we know, for example, is that the average consumption of a product is estimated to be £2.00 per month irrespective of the size of the sample used and the inherent variability of the data. If a large sample size was used and there was little inherent variability we would have a good deal of faith in the result. But we know nothing of this from the point estimate. However, we can estimate, or make inferences about, the population values by using a second approach called *interval estimates* or *confidence intervals*, which provide the range within which the population value is expected to lie with a given probability or level of confidence. This approach is more appropriate since results based on small samples with a great deal of inherent variability are seen, therefore, to have wide ranges for the population value and/or low levels of confidence. Our result may be, for example, that we are only 90 per cent confident that the average consumption for the population lies in the range £0.50 to £3.50. This is not very accurate, but what do you expect from a small sample size with variable data? How do we derive and calculate these interval estimates? First, we must clarify the notation used so as not to confuse sample and population values:

| | | | |
|---|---|---|---|
| $\mu$ | population mean deviation | $\sigma$ | population standard |
| $\bar{X}$ | sample mean | $s$ | sample standard deviation |
| $\pi$ | population proportion | $N$ | population size |
| $p$ | sample proportion | $n$ | sample size |

We start by estimating the population mean.

## CONFIDENCE INTERVALS FOR MEANS

Consider the problem of determining the mean expenditure on a product. Let us, in theory (we do not do this in practice), take a random sample of 30 consumers, and find $\bar{X} = £2$. At the same time someone else might take another random sample of consumers and find $\bar{X} = £2.05$; and yet another random sample might yield $\bar{X} = £1.98$, with many more samples being taken. Figure 11-1 might well describe the outcome, being a frequency function of the arithmetic means from a very large number of separate random samples.

Most samples yield a value close to £2.00, with very few yielding as much as £2.04, and correspondingly few as low as £1.96. In this latter case, by chance, the consumers selected are relatively light users of the product, and, again by chance, in the former case relatively heavy users

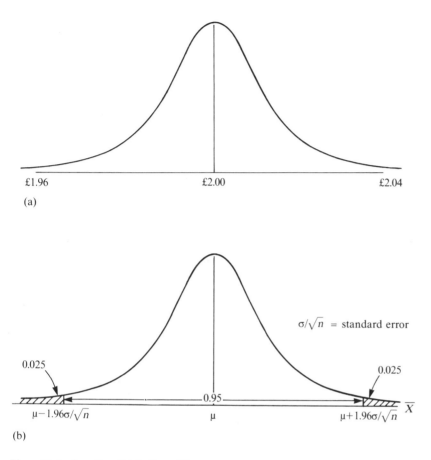

**Figure 11-1**   Sampling distribution of the means

have been included. This distribution is *not* of the actual purchases, but the arithmetic means from many separate random samples. The variability of actual purchases would be much greater. We call this distribution the *sampling distribution of the means*. An important result is that the mean of the sampling distribution of the means equals the population mean ($\mu$), and the standard deviation of this sampling distribution (called the standard error to avoid confusion with the standard deviation of the variable) is given by $\sigma/\sqrt{n}$. Now this is quite an important finding because, in practice, we do not know $\mu$, only the results from one sample, $\bar{X}$ and $s$. However, this result provides a link between $\bar{X}$ and $\mu$ by which we can estimate $\mu$.

We have drawn Fig. 11-1 as a normal distribution. *The Central Limit Theorem* demonstrates that as long as $n$ is large ($n \geqslant 30$ in most cases) the sampling distribution of the means ($\bar{X}$) *will be normal irrespective of the distribution of the underlying variable X.*

It should be stressed that the need for $n \geqslant 30$ is a rule of thumb, and smaller values of $n$ are permissible as the distribution of population values approximate to a normal distribution. Alternative, more general, procedures for dealing with $n < 30$ are given later in this chapter. The second part of Fig. 11-1 repeats a result from Chapters 4 and 10: the normal rule and tables told us that 95 per cent of observations will lie within $\mp 1.96$ standard deviations of the mean. Here our standard deviation (standard error) is $\sigma/\sqrt{n}$. Therefore, assuming normality via the Central Limit

Theorem for our sampling distribution, 95 per cent of values of $\bar{X}$ (sample means) will lie within $\mu \mp £1.96\sigma/\sqrt{n}$; or, put another way:

$$P\{\mu - 1.96\sigma/\sqrt{n} < \bar{X} < \mu + 1.96\sigma/\sqrt{n}\} = 0.95 \qquad (11\text{-}2)$$

i.e. the probability of $\bar{X}$ being in the range $\mu \mp 1.96\sigma/\sqrt{n}$ is 0.95.

Since $\mu - 1.96\sigma/\sqrt{n} < \bar{X}$ (change sign—change side) is the same as:

$$\mu < \bar{X} + 1.96\sigma/\sqrt{n}$$

and since

$$\bar{X} < \mu + 1.96\sigma/\sqrt{n}$$

is the same as

$$\bar{X} - 1.96\sigma/\sqrt{n} < \mu$$

we can rearrange Eq. (11-2) to become:

$$P\{\bar{X} - 1.96\sigma/\sqrt{n} < \mu < \bar{X} + 1.96\sigma/\sqrt{n}\} = 0.95 \qquad (11\text{-}3)$$

There is a probability of 0.95 that the population mean lies in the random interval $\bar{X} - 1.96\sigma/\sqrt{n}$ to $\bar{X} + 1.96\sigma/\sqrt{n}$.

We have the basis of a method of estimating the population mean from the results of one sample. However, Eq. (11-3) requires a knowledge of $\sigma$, which we do not have; we shall only know results from a sample, not the population, for that is the purpose of drawing a sample. However, we can show (Kendall and Stuart, 1969, p. 222) that when $n \geqslant 30$, $s$ provides a sufficiently good estimate of $\sigma$. Therefore, 95 per cent confidence intervals for means of large samples ($n \geqslant 30$ for the Central Limit Theorem) are given by:

$$\bar{X} \mp 1.96s/\sqrt{n} \qquad (11\text{-}4)$$

In our example a random sample of 30 consumers found average (mean) consumption to be £2.00 with a standard deviation of £0.10, i.e. $n = 30$, $\bar{X} = 2$, and $s = 0.10$. We are thus 95 per cent confident that the population mean $\mu$ lies in the random interval

$$2 \mp 1.96(0.10)/\sqrt{30} = 2 \mp 0.0358$$
$$= 2 - 0.0358 \text{ to } 2 + 0.0358$$
$$= £1.96 \text{ to } £2.04$$

By '95 per cent confident' we mean that if we took 100 samples from the same population and calculated the confidence intervals for each sample, then we would expect about 95 of these 100 intervals to contain the true value of $\mu$. In practice, we only take one sample and thus have one interval and do not know if ours is one of the 95 or of the 5; it is in this sense we use the expression that we are 95 per cent confident that the random interval contains $\mu$. We include the term 'random' because our interval is only one of many randomly chosen.

To confirm the principle of what we are doing it is worth considering what would happen if $\mu$ actually was £2.00 and, in the top half of Fig. 11-1, the random sample chosen was an extreme one, with $\bar{X}$ equal to the upper bound of the interval, i.e. £2.04. We would then have calculated our interval as:

$$2.04 \mp 1.96(0.1)/\sqrt{30} = £2.00 \text{ to } £2.08$$

i.e. we would have just included $\mu$. Likewise with the extreme lower bound of $\bar{X} = 1.96$. However, if we moved outside of these 95 per cent bounds and recalculated the intervals we would not include $\mu = £2.00$, what we are assuming to be the true population mean.

Consider a second example: the mean daily travelling time to and from work of a random sample of 50 workers in a region is 20 minutes with a standard deviation of 10 minutes. What can you say about the travelling time of all the workers (the population) in the region?

Since $\bar{X} = 20$, $s = 10$ and $n = 50$, our interval is

$$20 \mp 1.96(10/\sqrt{50}) = 20 \mp 2.77 = 17.23 \text{ to } 22.77 \text{ minutes}$$

We are 95 per cent confident (in the sense outlined above) that the mean daily travelling time of all workers in the region ($\mu$) lies in the random interval 17.23 to 22.77 minutes.

It is worth reflecting on our achievement. We choose a random sample that could contain results that are unrepresentatively high or low, or accurately reflect the population value; we simply have no way of knowing. Using a point estimate for the sample mean and proportion is not too bad an approach, since we can show that the expected value (means) of the sampling distribution equals the population value—this is what we understand by the sample value being an unbiased estimator. It is the best unbiased estimator if the dispersion or standard error of the sampling distribution is smaller than that of any other estimator. If we had a choice of two estimators, both of which were unbiased, we would choose the one with the least standard error since an 'extreme' sample result would be nearer the population mean for a best unbiased estimator. Our theory thus supports in a narrow sense the use of these point estimates.

However, the achievement of interval estimates is that they do not leave us with a single value which may be the population mean or an extreme value. The interval provides, in probabilistic terms, an interval in which the *population value* may be expected to lie with a given probability *from the results of a single sample*. The above theory has allowed us to say something about the population mean, proportion or whatever, when we do not know it. We use the sample value to make inferences about the population value—this branch of statistics being referred to as *inferential statistics*.

The size of the interval is the *sampling error* associated with the estimate. We mentioned in Chapter 2 that sampling errors were measurable; this is how we measure them. Sampling errors arise simply because we are taking a random sample of observations, and not the population of observations. The interval can be seen from expression (11-4) to be dependent on:

1. The sample size—the larger the sample size ($n$), the smaller the interval, as we would expect.
2. The variability in the actual data as estimated by $s$—the more variable the values of the observations, the larger the interval. If, for example, $s = 0$ so that there was no variability in results and each observation took the same value, then the interval would be very small (in fact zero) since a sample of 1 would yield a perfect estimate.
3. The level of confidence as given by $Z$ (more details in a forthcoming section). We decide, on the level of confidence we want to have, that the population parameter falls in the interval; higher levels of confidence (as we shall see) require larger intervals. So far we have used a 95 per cent level, represented by $Z = 1.96$.

Thus formula (11-4) allows us to calculate confidence intervals for the mean, given information on $\bar{X}$, $s$, $Z$ and $n$. Having established this basic formula we now develop the application further.

### Determining the level of confidence

In general, in the social sciences we use a 95 per cent level of confidence as an arbitrarily acceptable standard. In reporting the above result we might proclaim that the mean travelling time is 20 minutes, with an error margin of plus or minus 2.77 minutes—but we are only 95 per cent confident that this statement holds in the sense outlined above. For some purposes, e.g. medical research or major business decisions, 95 per cent confidence may not be sufficient and, for example, 99 per cent intervals might be required. In this case, in the lower half of Fig. 11-1 the shaded area on *each* side of the normal distribution should amount to 0.005. If you look in the body of the normal tables in Appendix 7 for 0.005, you will find the Z-value that corresponds to eliminating 0.005 in each tail of the distribution is (approximately) 2.58. Our general formula for confidence intervals for the means is:

$$\bar{X} \mp Zs/\sqrt{n} \tag{11-5}$$

where $Z$ is the standardized normal deviate for the appropriate level of confidence.

For our example on travelling times, where $\bar{X} = 20$, $s = 10$ and $n = 50$, at a 99 per cent level of confidence our interval is

$$20 \mp 2.58(10)/\sqrt{50} = 20 \mp 3.65$$

i.e. we are 99 per cent confident that $\mu$ lies in the random interval 16.35 to 23.65 minutes. Note that our increased level of confidence is at the cost of a wider interval ($\mp 3.65$ compared with $\mp 2.77$).

### The finite population correction

We have so far given the standard error for the mean as $\sigma/\sqrt{n}$. This, however, is only correct when infinite populations are considered *and/or* when drawing the sample, the unit (person) selected is replaced so that it might be drawn again in the next selection, i.e. sampling with replacement. However, in practice, sampling is generally without replacement (for example, we select Mrs Smith from the list at random, but we do not allow her to be chosen again) and from a finite population. For the case of sampling without replacement from a finite population, we need to multiply the standard error by the finite population correction (f.p.c.), i.e. by

$$\sqrt{\frac{N-n}{N-1}} \tag{11-6}$$

and confidence interval for the mean are calculated from

$$\bar{X} \mp Z \sqrt{\frac{N-n}{N-1}} \cdot \frac{s}{\sqrt{n}} \tag{11-7}$$

Obviously in many cases a finite $N$ will be very large with respect to $n$ and the correction will have little effect. A useful rule of thumb is to only use the f.p.c. when $n/N > 0.05$, i.e. when $n$ is more than 5 per cent of the population.

For example, a random sample of 60 operatives is taken from the 1000 operatives in a company and asked to rate the quality of their work environment on a 10-point scale (10 perfect, 0 terrible). The mean (assuming interval scale) was 6 and standard deviation 2.8. Construct a 95 per cent confidence interval for the population mean.

Since $n/N = 0.06 > 0.05$, we use formula (11-7) and not (11-5):

$$6 \mp 1.96 \sqrt{\frac{1000-60}{1000-1}} \frac{2.8}{\sqrt{60}}$$

$$= 6 \mp 1.96(0.97)0.361$$
$$= 6 \mp 0.686, \text{ i.e. } 5.3 \text{ to } 6.7$$

We are 95 per cent confident that $\mu$ lies in the random interval 5.3 to 6.7. Note the finite population adjustment of 0.97 is quite small, given that $n/N$ is very small and close to 0.05.

## Small samples

So far we have considered estimating $\mu$ for large samples with $n \geq 30$; in such circumstances the Central Limit Theorem allowed us to assume normality for the sampling distribution of the means, irrespective of the underlying distribution of $X$. We did *not* need to assume in any of the above examples that the variable was normally distributed.

However, what if $n < 30$? If the distribution of $X$ is normal we can obtain confidence intervals using a $t$-value from the tables of the $t$-distribution (Appendix 6), instead of a $Z$-value from the tables of normal distribution (Appendix 7). The $t$-distribution is symmetrical, like the normal distribution, but flatter. Its shape depends on the degrees of freedom given by $v = n - 1$; as $v$ increases, the $t$-distribution more closely approximates the normal distribution. Values of the $t$-distribution are given in Appendix 6. The distribution has a mean of zero and a standard deviation of $v/(v-2)$, where $v > 2$. To obtain confidence intervals (assuming $n/N \leq 0.05$ and thus no need for f.p.c.) we use:

$$\bar{X} \mp t(s_{n-1})/\sqrt{n} \tag{11-8}$$

It is particularly important that $s_{n-1}$, as opposed to $s$, is calculated; that is, the unbiased estimator in Eq. (11-1). You may wonder why $s_{n-1}$ as opposed to $s$ was not used in formula (11-5) for the confidence interval when $n \geq 30$ if, after all, the unbiased estimator is theoretically more sound and we previously made so much of this. The answer is that $s_{n-1}$ should be used throughout this and the next chapter (inferential statistics) irrespective of whether $n$ is large or small. It is just that when $n$ is large ($n \geq 30$) the difference between the formulae has very little effect on the results, and for inferential work the convention arose of using $s$ for large samples because it is easier to calculate. We continue with this convention, though we inform you that it is more acceptable to use $s_{n-1}$ as opposed to $s$ for large sample inferential work, and that $s_{n-1}$ *must* be used for the standard deviation for small sample inferential work.

For example, a random sample of $n = 5$ adult men found the mean shoe size to be 8 with an unbiased standard deviation of 3. The 95 per cent confidence intervals are:

$$8 \mp 2.78(3)/\sqrt{5} = 8 \mp 3.73, \text{ i.e. } 4.27 \text{ to } 11.73$$

This may seem to be a wide range of little use, but what do you expect from a sample size of 5? If you look at Appendix 6 we require the row corresponding to $v = n - 1 = 5 - 1 = 4$ and since we require a 95 per cent interval we need 5 per cent split between the two tails, i.e. 0.025 in each tail. The intersection of $v = 4$ (rows) and 0.025 (columns) should yield the appropriate figure.

Bear in mind that we need the underlying distribution of $X$ to be approximately normal if we are to use this technique for small samples (adult male shoe size might well be normally distributed). In practice, the distributions are unlikely to be perfectly normal but the methods are robust to reasonable approximations. Also, $s_{n-1}$ must be an unbiased estimator, which was held to be the case in the question. If it was an 'ordinary' standard deviation, we would square $s$, multiply the result by $n/(n-1)$, and then take the square root to yield Eq. (11-1); that is,

$$s = \sqrt{\frac{\Sigma(X - \bar{X})^2}{n}}; \qquad s^2 = \frac{\Sigma(X - \bar{X})^2}{n}$$

$$s^2 \frac{n}{n-1} = \frac{\Sigma(X - \bar{X})^2}{n} \frac{n}{n-1} = \frac{\Sigma(X - \bar{X})^2}{n-1} = s_{n-1}^2$$

$$s_{n-1} = \sqrt{\frac{\Sigma(X - \bar{X})^2}{n-1}} \tag{11-9}$$

### Determining the sample size

In undertaking sample surveys an essential decision is the size of the sample. We have seen that the size of the sample affects the sampling error associated with any estimate. The answer to 'What size of sample should I take?' is a reversal of formula (11-5). If we look at (11-5) we can see that the (sampling) error margin (e) on either side of an estimate is:

$$Z\frac{s}{\sqrt{n}}=e$$

$$\therefore \frac{Zs}{e}=\sqrt{n}$$

$$\therefore \frac{Z^2s^2}{e^2}=n \tag{11-10}$$

Thus, for example, when asked about the size of sample that should be taken for a survey to determine the mean expenditure by consumers of your product per month, we must in turn ask about the components of Eq. (11-10).

First, $e$, the error margin: 'If we provided the result as an interval, what range would be sufficiently accurate for your purposes? Perhaps plus or minus £1, or whatever?' For this, we need a value for $e$. 'Even if we provided you with an interval we cannot guarantee the average, for the population of consumers will lie within it. However, we can stipulate the level of confidence in which it would lie in the interval, in the sense that if the survey was repeated 100 times, the interval would contain the population parameter 95 per cent, 99 per cent or whatever of these. What level would be appropriate for your purpose?' For this, we need a value for $Z$. The sample size also depends on the variability in the data. We could draw a random sample of, say, 20 observations, and use it to estimate the required $s$. Alternatively, if you think the distribution of the variable is approximately normal, then 'What range of monthly expenditure values on your product would you expect 95 per cent of consumers of your product to lie within?' Since this is approximately $\mp2\sigma$, we get an estimate of $\sigma$ as an alternative to '$s$' in formula (11-4). If the replies were: an error margin of plus or minus £1 is acceptable, then $e=1$; with 95 per cent level of confidence, then $Z=1.96$; and if 95 per cent of expenditure values lie between £20 and £60 and are judged to be plus or minus £20 normally distributed (around a mean of £40) then $2\sigma=£20$, therefore $\sigma=£10=s$ (since $s$ approximates $\sigma$). Using Eq. (11-10):

$$n=(1.96)^2\frac{(10)^2}{1^2}=384.16, \text{ i.e. } n=385$$

If a sample size of 385 costs too much to undertake, then a smaller sample size must be traded off against less accuracy. If a 95 per cent confidence level was still required, but a sample size of only 200 could be afforded, then using Eq. (11-10):

$$200=\frac{(1.96)^2(10)^2}{e^2}$$

$$\therefore e^2=(1.96)^2(10)^2/200$$
$$\therefore e=1.39$$

i.e. an interval of $\mp£1.39$ results. Figure 11-2 shows different values of $e$ resulting from different values of $n$ from Eq. (11-10), holding $s$ and $Z$ constant at 10 and 1.96 respectively. As we would expect, larger sample sizes lead to lower error margins, but what is of particular interest is that the

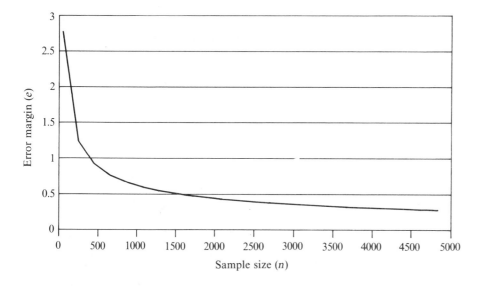

**Figure 11-2**   Sample size and error margins (95 per cent confidence: $s = 10$)

gains in accuracy (lower error margins) achieved by increasing sample sizes by a given amount are not constant; for smaller sample sizes, the reduction in sampling errors from a given increase in sample size are greater than when that same increase in sample size is applied to a large sample. Figure 11-2 shows, for example, a relatively large fall in sampling error if we increase the sample size by 500 when $n = 200$; but the fall is much less if we increase sample size by 500 when it is at 2000. This, in advising on sample size, is worth noting: very small error margins (unless $s$ is small and a low level of confidence is required) require disproportionately large sample sizes. For example, sample sizes of 5000 for individual results may well be a waste of time and money since they yield very little additional accuracy compared with a sample half this size. The theory helps to provide valuable lessons. Note also that as long as $n/N < 0.05$ it is the absolute size of the sample that counts. A sample of 1000 individuals from a relatively small city like Bath is as accurate in terms of these intervals as a sample of 1000 from London. Again theory teaches us valuable practical lessons.

In practice, the answers to the above questions on $e$, $Z$ and $s$—and thus the sample size required—will vary from question to question in a survey. It is usual to highlight the most important questions and desired 'accuracy' for these questions alone, since the sample size chosen will generally apply to all questions. However, it is possible to expand the sample size for selected important questions. In addition, the answers to many questions will be broken down by other variables—for example, the age and sex of the respondent. Since we shall quote results for, say, young females, we must ensure that the required sample size and accuracy are determined for each category. All too often impressive sample sizes are quoted for studies and then highly disaggregated results are provided on the basis of very small sample sizes.

So far we have looked at confidence intervals for the mean. By use of formula (11-5) we have a powerful method by which we can say something about the population mean. This is no small achievement: all we have in practice is the sample mean (and standard deviation) with no way of knowing if the sample mean is a good or a bad representation. Formula (11-5) gives us a link to the population mean. It is easy to calculate, though bear in mind the circumstances in which the finite population correction might be useful. Also note that we can vary the level of confidence. We also have to amend the approach for small samples ($n \geqslant 30$) and that given any three of $n$, $s$, $Z$ and $e$, we can derive the fourth—a special case being the derivation of the sample size. All of this is fine if we want to estimate the population mean. But what if our concern was with proportions; for example, the proportions of senior managers of small business against government economic policy, proportion of female customers, proportion of defective items produced, etc.?

## CONFIDENCE INTERVALS FOR PROPORTIONS

Fortunately, the derivation of such intervals involve similar issues to those considered for the mean. The expected value of the sampling distribution for sample *proportions* ($p$) is the population proportion ($\pi$), and the standard error is $\sqrt{\pi(1-\pi)/n}$. The sampling distribution for proportions is approximately normally distributed if $p=0.5$, or $np \geqslant 5$ for $p<0.5$, or $n(1-p) \geqslant 5$ for $p>0.5$. [However, as a rule of thumb, if $n \geqslant 30$, the normality assumption is usually justified.] This should be familiar being the same condition for the normal approximation of the binomial (Chapter 10). In fact the binomial distribution for proportions is the sampling distribution for $p$. The binomial was concerned with the number of successes, $X$; our concern is with the proportion, $X/n$. Remember that the expected value of $X$ for binomial was $n\pi$ and standard deviation, $\sqrt{n\pi(1-\pi)}$. Thus for $X/n$ we divide by $n$ to yield an expected value of $\pi$ and standard deviation of $\sqrt{n\pi(1-\pi)}/n = \sqrt{\pi(1-\pi)/n}$.

Our formula for the confidence interval for means was:

$$\bar{X} \mp Z\sigma/\sqrt{n}$$

By similar reasoning, instead of the standard error for means ($\sigma/\sqrt{n}$) we want the standard error for proportions ($\sqrt{\pi(1-\pi)/n}$) and instead of the sample mean ($\bar{X}$) we want the sample proportion $p$; the confidence interval for proportions is:

$$p \mp Z\sqrt{\pi(1-\pi)/n} \tag{11-11}$$

For the same reasons that we replaced $\sigma$ with $s$ in formula (11-4)—i.e. because we didn't know $\sigma$, a population value—we replace $\pi$ with its best unbiased estimate $p$; the more applied formula for confidence intervals for proportions is thus:

$$p \mp Z\sqrt{p(1-p)/n} \tag{11-12}$$

The finite population correction will have to be applied when necessary as discussed above; i.e. if $n/N > 0.05$, where $n$ and $N$ are the sample and population sizes respectively. We use:

$$p \mp Z\sqrt{p(1-p)/n} \ \sqrt{(N-n)/(N-1)} \tag{11-13}$$

For example, a survey of small businesses based on a random sample of 100 small businesses found 85 per cent of respondents (managing directors) to be against the government's current economic strategy. A 95 per cent confidence interval is applied; since $N$ is very large and $n/N$ is likely to be less than 0.05 we use formula (11-12). Our parameters are $p=0.85$, $n=100$, $Z=1.96$; N.B. $n(1-p)=15$ for $p>5$, i.e. normality assumptions acceptable:

$$0.85 \mp 1.96\sqrt{(0.85)(0.15)/100}$$
$$0.85 \mp 0.07$$

i.e. we are 95 per cent confident that the proportion of MDs of all small businesses against the government's current economic strategy is in the random interval 0.78 to 0.92.

Consider a survey of a random sample of $n=35$ members of a very large union showing 0.6 to be in favour of a work-to-rule. Using 95 per cent confidence intervals (normality assumption valid since $n(1-p) \geqslant 5$) we have:

$$n=35,\ p=0.6\ \text{and}\ Z=1.96$$
$$p \mp Z\sqrt{p(1-p)/n}$$
$$0.6 \mp 1.96\sqrt{0.6(0.4)/35}$$
$$0.6 \mp 0.16$$

We are 95 per cent confident that the proportion of *all* the union members in favour of the work-to-rule lies in the random interval 0.44 to 0.76, i.e. we cannot on the basis of these calculations say a majority of the members are in favour (at a 95 per cent level) even though 60 per cent of the sample said so. There is too much sampling error to allow this. The interval may seem wide, but this merely reflects the effect of the small sample size.

We could use expression (11-12) to determine the sample size necessary to achieve a given error margin. Since

$$e = Z\sqrt{p(1-p)/n}$$

then

$$e^2 = Z^2 p(1-p)/n$$
$$\therefore\ n = Z^2 p(1-p)/e^2 \qquad (11\text{-}14)$$

We need to know $p$ for the (most important) question at hand: a value of $p=0.5$ provides the largest possible sample size and is a cautious approach to take. Assume 95 per cent confidence and an acceptable error margin of plus or minus 3 per cent, then

$$p=0.5,\ Z=1.96,\ e=0.03$$
$$\therefore\ n = (1.96)^2 (0.5)(0.5)/(0.03)^2 = 1068$$

A sample size of 1068 is required for an error margin of plus or minus 3 per cent at a 95 per cent level of confidence.

## SUMMARY OF SOME POINTS RAISED

1. Our interest is with estimating population parameters—we have considered two parameters: the mean and proportion. We only have estimates based on a random sample; interval estimates of population parameters provide the random interval within which a population parameter lies with a given probability (level of confidence).
2. The formulae for means are (11-4) and (11-8), respectively, for large and small samples and (11-2) for proportions for large samples (there are problems with small sample estimates for proportions).
3. These formulae assume simple random sampling; if other random sampling schemes are used, such as stratified random sampling or multi-stage sampling, their standard errors have to be substituted into the equation for confidence intervals (see Cochran, 1966).
4. When $n/N < 0.05$ the finite population correction has to be used ((11-7) and (11-13)).
5. The error margin is given by the term following the $\mp$ signs in the confidence interval equations. The resulting formula can be used to determine the appropriate sample size to take for given levels of confidence, error margins and variability.

6. The level of confidence used (and error margins) depends on the needs of the user and thus the context of the problem, though higher levels of confidence lead to wider error margins, other things held constant.

## QUALITY CONTROL

Quality control provides a particularly useful application of the concepts considered in this chapter. Quality is often measured in terms of one or more characteristics of the product, such as durability, physical size or weight, or some operating characteristics, such as precision of a clock. It is often not possible to monitor all items produced, so random samples are taken.

### Means

Consider, for example, the production of a machine component that should be 3 cm long. Samples of 35 components are taken every hour and measured. Over the past few weeks the overall mean has been found to be 2.990 cm with a standard deviation of 0.01 cm. The results for the morning are 2.992, 2.986, 2.985 and 2.9855 cm. What can we say about the machine's performance?

First of all, over the past few weeks they have been taking several random samples each of size 35 and finding the mean of these individual sample means (which is equivalent to the overall average) to be 2.99 cm. We know from theory that this should be a best unbiased estimate of the population mean, and is slightly below the required 3 cm. The size of each component is not the same since the standard deviation is 0.01 cm. If we calculated 95 per cent confidence intervals for the mean we would find the range within which the results from the samples would be expected to lie. Using formula (11-5):

$$2.99 \mp 1.96(0.01)/\sqrt{35}$$
$$2.99 \mp 0.0033, \text{ i.e. } 2.9867 \text{ to } 2.9933$$

This, as can be seen does not include 3 cm, but may be within the customer's tolerance levels (i.e. close enough for the customer to not care), which we do not know. Figure 11-3 is a *control chart* or Shewhart diagram which shows the upper and lower intervals. Remember, if we took lots of samples of 35 and found their means, we would expect 95 out of 100 to lie within these bounds if $\mu = 2.99$ and $\sigma = 0.01$, i.e. if the machine performs in the same manner as it has in the past. We have four new values from successive recent samples of $n = 35$ which are plotted on Fig. 11-3 for the results of the morning work. The last three values are outside the lower boundary. We would expect 5 in every 100 to be outside, but 3 in succession suggests that the machine is moving out of control or out of its usual pattern of behaviour.

Our discussion has been in terms of confidence intervals leading on from the preceding work. However, our purpose here is not to estimate the population mean. We are using the features of the sampling distributions discussed earlier to build up boundaries or critical values against which we can judge in probabilistic terms if processes are going out of control. It has been outlined here using the formulae for confidence intervals for ease of exposition, though their use is not to estimate population values. We shall refer to them as (critical) boundaries or limits rather than intervals to make this distinction.

Limits of 95 per cent are referred to as warning limits since, if a single value falls outside, it may well be one of the expected 5 out of 100, but subsequent values should be closely monitored. Action bounds of 98 per cent or higher limits can also be imposed on the control chart in addition to the warning limits. Often a $Z$-value of 3 is used, which is equivalent to 99.73 per cent intervals. Here a

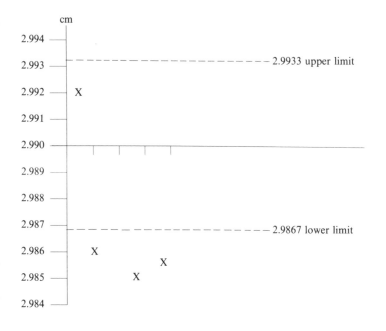

**Figure 11-3** Control chart for length of machine component

mean would fall out of the bounds 27 times in 10 000—thus one falling outside should be treated with suspicion.

A good chart should include both warning and *action* bounds such as these. In using control charts we must bear in mind that customers will have their own tolerance limits. If these are much wider than the control limits the machine going out of control need not mean we have to scrap some of the production, but it may indicate the beginnings of a drift towards that happening, which we would try and correct. So far we have looked at means or $\bar{X}$ *control charts*. Our measure of the quality characteristics was on an interval scale; products are often defective or not defective, and we are interested in controlling for the proportion of defective items, i.e. *p control charts*.

## Proportions

Consider a company producing battery-driven motors for toy cars. Over the last 10 hours they have taken a sample of 100 motors every hour, with the following results:

| Hour | 1 | 2 | 3 | 4 | 5 | 6 | 7 | 8 | 9 | 10 |
|---|---|---|---|---|---|---|---|---|---|---|
| Number defective | 6 | 2 | 7 | 5 | 3 | 5 | 5 | 4 | 6 | 8 |

The proportion of defectives is thus the total defectives $(6+2+7+5+\ldots+6+8=51)$ divided by the total tested $(10 \times 100 = 1000)$, i.e. $51/1000 = 0.051$. Using formula (11-12), 95 per cent warning intervals would be:

$$0.051 \mp 1.96\sqrt{0.051(0.949)/100}$$
$$0.051 \mp 0.043 = 0.008 \text{ to } 0.094$$

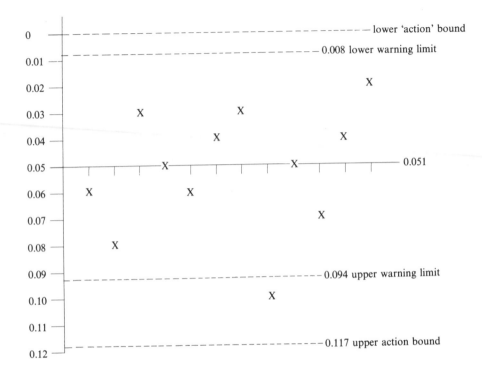

**Figure 11-4**  Control chart for proportions of defective motors

If we used $Z=3$ the interval would be:

$$0.051 \mp 3\sqrt{0.051(0.949)/100}$$
$$0.051 \mp 0.066 = 0 \text{ to } 0.117$$

The zero is an effective lower limit since negative values make no sense, but since the full range of this lower value is truncated, results of zero might be expected 98 per cent of the time, i.e. from a $Z$-value of 2.32 [try $Z=2.32$, which will yield a range starting at zero—the value of 2.32 was deduced by putting $Z\sqrt{p(1-p)/n}=0.051$.]

Figure 11-4 shows the warning limits and action bounds for the example. We have now set up the control chart for the manufacturer. They continue to manufacture, and if we assume that the last 10 hours was satisfactory, production is in control, and subsequent production is plotted on the graph. For example, if subsequent sample proportions from testing 100 motors were 0.06, 0.08, 0.03, 0.05, 0.06, 0.04, 0.03, 0.10, 0.05, 0.07, 0.04, 0.01 they would appear on Fig. 11-4 as plotted and the one figure outside the warning interval would not cause too much alarm since this would be expected in 5 out of every 95 tests.

**Range**

It may be that for a quality characteristic such as pressure before breaking (for the durability of the product) the average is under control, but the *dispersion* is increasing. This would have serious implications for quality control for our average durability would reassure us when in fact we are

**Table 11-1**   Constants for $R$-Charts

| | 95% | | 98% | |
|---|---|---|---|---|
| $n$ | $D_L$ | $D_U$ | $D_L$ | $D_U$ |
| 2 | 0.0393 | 2.8092 | 0.0016 | 4.1241 |
| 3 | 0.1791 | 2.1756 | 0.0356 | 2.9916 |
| 4 | 0.2888 | 1.9352 | 0.0969 | 2.5787 |
| 5 | 0.3653 | 1.8045 | 0.1580 | 2.3577 |
| 6 | 0.4206 | 1.7207 | 0.2110 | 2.2172 |
| 7 | 0.4624 | 1.6616 | 0.2556 | 2.1187 |
| 8 | 0.4952 | 1.6173 | 0.2932 | 2.0451 |
| 9 | 0.5218 | 1.5826 | 0.3251 | 1.9875 |
| 10 | 0.5438 | 1.5545 | 0.3524 | 1.9410 |
| 11 | 0.5624 | 1.5312 | 0.3761 | 1.9024 |
| 12 | 0.5783 | 1.5115 | 0.3969 | 1.8697 |
| 13 | 0.5922 | 1.4945 | 0.4152 | 1.8417 |
| 14 | 0.6044 | 1.4796 | 0.4316 | 1.8172 |
| 15 | 0.6153 | 1.4666 | 0.4463 | 1.7957 |
| 16 | 0.6250 | 1.4550 | 0.4596 | 1.7765 |
| 17 | 0.6338 | 1.4445 | 0.4711 | 1.7592 |
| 18 | 0.6417 | 1.4351 | 0.4827 | 1.7437 |
| 19 | 0.6490 | 1.4265 | 0.4928 | 1.7295 |
| 20 | 0.6557 | 1.4186 | 0.5022 | 1.7165 |

*Source*: H.R. Neave, *Statistical Tables*, George Allen and Unwin, 1978, Table 8.6.

**Table 11-2**   Pressure before breaking (kg/cm$^3$)

| | | | | | Sample number | | | | | |
|---|---|---|---|---|---|---|---|---|---|---|
| Item | 1 | 2 | 3 | 4 | 5 | 6 | 7 | 8 | 9 | 10 |
| 1 | 10.7 | 11.5 | 10.6 | 12.4 | 12.6 | 11.2 | 10.5 | 10.0 | 11.5 | 10.3 |
| 2 | 12.3 | 11.4 | 11.8 | 11.3 | 10.1 | 11.4 | 10.6 | 10.7 | 11.6 | 11.9 |
| 3 | 11.0 | 10.8 | 10.8 | 10.7 | 11.2 | 11.6 | 11.1 | 12.2 | 10.7 | 12.3 |
| 4 | 10.8 | 12.3 | 12.2 | 11.3 | 10.5 | 10.8 | 12.1 | 12.1 | 12.4 | 11.6 |
| 5 | 10.7 | 11.5 | 11.4 | 11.8 | 12.1 | 11.4 | 10.9 | 11.8 | 12.0 | 11.0 |
| Range | 1.6 | 1.5 | 1.4 | 1.7 | 2.5 | 0.8 | 1.6 | 2.2 | 1.7 | 2.0 |

producing some goods that can withstand a lot of pressure, while others can withstand only a little. Control charts for dispersion may be based on the standard deviation or the range, though common practice is to use the range. Such *R-charts* require use of the constants given in Table 11-1. Consider, from Table 11-2, random samples of 5 items taken on each of 10 occasions and tested to see how much pressure they can withstand before breaking.

The boundaries are given by:

$$D_L R \text{ lower limit and } D_U R \text{ upper limit} \tag{11-15}$$

$R$ is the sum of the range (the difference between the highest and lowest value) for each sample, divided by the number of samples:

$$R = \sum_{i=1}^{k} R_i/k \quad \text{for } i=1,\ldots,k \text{ samples} \tag{11-16}$$

In our case, from Table 11-2

$$R = (1.6+1.5+1.4+1.7+2.5+0.8+1.6+2.2+1.7+2.0)/10 = 1.7$$

Values of $D_L$ and $D_U$ are given in Table 11-1. The 95 per cent control limits are thus:

$$0.3653(1.7) \text{ to } 1.8045(1.7) = 0.621 \text{ to } 3.068 \text{ kg/cm}^3$$

and 98 per cent control bounds:

$$0.1580(1.7) \text{ to } 2.3577(1.7) = 0.269 \text{ to } 4.008 \text{ kg/cm}^3$$

The range of future samples of $n = 5$ can be plotted to see how they fall within these intervals, in a similar manner to the charts for means and proportions in Figs. 11-3 and 11-4 respectively.

## Specification and capability

There may also be a further requirement that needs to be applied to the control chart; i.e. that production satisfies some specification which should fall outside the warning and action lines. This may be one-sided—for example, a minimum strength—or two-sided following a customer's requirements or our own quality standards. The difference between what we expect from normal sampling variation and the specified limits is referred to as tolerance: the larger the tolerance, the better. Specification limits or requirements may be imposed by production managers; for example, that 99.73 per cent of products should satisfy the requirements. An index that measures the extent to which this is satisfied is a precision or capability index, given by:

$$C_p = \frac{S_U - S_L}{6s} \tag{11-17}$$

where $S_U$ and $S_L$ are upper and lower specified limits and $s$ is the standard deviation of the quality characteristic. If $C_p > 1$ then 99.73 per cent of products satisfy the requirement. The measure falls down if the process mean itself becomes variable, and to guard against this

$$C_{pk} = \text{minimum of } \frac{S_U - \bar{X}}{s}, \frac{\bar{X} - S_L}{s} \tag{11-18}$$

is used. $\bar{X}$ is a reliable measure of the process mean obtained from a current sample, when the process is known to be under control (Bissel, 1990).

## Total quality management and practice

There is, of course, much more to statistical quality control and Duncan (1986) and Oakland (1986) provide details. In particular, there has been extensive use of statistical techniques in production in Japan for many years and it is only recently that the UK is rediscovering them. The techniques extend beyond those discussed here and in any event are parts of a more general drive concerned with *Total Quality Management* (TQM). The philosophy was developed by Edward Deming and Joseph Juran with quality as a way of life, achieved with the help of statistical information systems and the motivation of employees (see Deming, 1986, and Kanji, 1990a, b). The theoretical foundations for the statistical control systems owed much to UK statisticians and while their practical realization in the methods proposed are not always robust, Japanese industry continues to flourish.

There is much in the above account that differs from standard practice, the purpose being in part to relate the quality control charts to the statistical theory derived earlier. In practice, about 20 samples of size 5 (per hour) may be initially taken to set up the guideline controls, the 20 samples being necessary to reflect the variability over a long enough time period. Sample sizes necessary for monitoring the production process were taken here to be 30 or more to use the normal distribution. In practice, they may be 4 or 5 an hour, depending on what is practical in the time available and the inherent variability in the process. In addition, while we have (rightly) used $s/\sqrt{n}$ as the standard error of the mean, in practice this is estimated by calculating the range and applying a value from specially prepared tables to act as an estimate (see Oakland, 1986). These tables simplify the calculations, though with computers and calculators there is little use for them. The approximation technique was used above for range control charts as opposed to standard deviation control charts. This was in part because the sampling distribution of standard deviations (which use the chi-squared distribution) were not covered in the previous chapter, though see Hoel (1966).

## CONCLUSIONS

In looking at confidence intervals in this chapter we have focused attention on means and proportions. Confidence intervals can be constructed for a number of statistics other than means and proportions, including trimmed means, medians and standard deviations. There are also alternative approaches to constructing such intervals (not considered here). These include *jack-knifing* in which a sample of $n$ observations are taken, the observations are dropped one by one, giving $n$ overlapping groups of $(n-1)$ observations. In the case of the mean, we would calculate the mean for each group which provides the basis for calculating the standard error and the confidence level. Alternatively, *bookstrapping* involves taking repeated samples of size $n$ with replacement; the average of these is the bookstrap estimate and their standard deviation is the bookstrap standard error.

## USING COMPUTERS

### Minitab

Confidence intervals are calculated via Minitab using one of the INTERVAL commands after the SET command has been used to read a single column of data.

```
MTB  > SET C1
DATA > 4.4  4.2  4.6  5.0  4.3  4.7  4.4  4.7  4.6
DATA > END
MTB  > ZINTERVAL  90  .3  C1
```

will yield a 90 per cent confidence interval for the sample data in column 1 if we have prior information that the standard deviation is 0.3. If we use the calculated standard deviation:

```
MTB > TINTERVAL 90 C1
```

will generate an appropriate interval which uses the unbiased standard deviation calculated from the data and also applies for $n \geqslant 30$ as an approximation to the normal.

Minitab has a number of commands to generate control charts directly.

```
MTB  > ICHART C1;
SUBC > MU=3;
SUBC > SIGMA=1.
```

will produce a control chart based on an upper control limit (UCL) and lower control limit (LCL) of plus and minus 3 standard deviations. The mean ($\mu$) and standard deviation ($\sigma$) are given by the user and values in C1 are plotted. Alternatively:

```
MTB > XBARCHART C1 10
```

produces a control chart for the data in C1 with the mean and standard deviation estimated from these data. The first 10 observations are treated as the results from the first random sample of 10; the next 10 observations as from the next sample of 10, etc. The means from each sample are plotted on the chart along with UCL and LCL based on 3 standard deviations. Subcommands include specifying a mean ($\mu = 3$) and standard deviation ($\sigma = 1$) and testing for patterns in the data (Nelson, 1984).

```
MTB > RCHART C1 10
```

produces a chart of sample ranges, a subcommand of SIGMA = 2 allowing you to impose a standard deviation of 2 here, this subcommand facility also applying for:

```
MTB > SCHART C1 10
```

which provides a control chart of standard deviations.

```
MTB > PCHART C1 30
```

provides control charts for proportions of, say, defective goods. If C1 contains 1, 3, 2, 4, 3 a control chart will be provided based on 5 samples of size 30 with the number of defective goods in each sample being given above in C1. The subcommand $p = 0.1$ allows you to impose an overall proportion, otherwise it is calculated from the data.

For each of the above the subcommand: SLIMITS 3 specifies the number (3) of standard deviation limits to use for UCL and LCL, the default is 3. HLINES 4.0 5.0 will draw 2 horizontal lines at 4.0 and 5.0 respectively to use as specification controls. ESTIMATE 10 : 22 25 only uses the results from samples 10 to 22 and 25 to estimate the mean and standard deviation. XSTART 5 10 plots results only for samples 5 to 10. YSTART 2 and YINC = 3 allow you to control the scaling, starting at 2 in increments of 3. There also exist labelling subcommands for titles and axes. The subcommand TEST allows you to test for patterns in the data.

## Lotus 1-2-3

Calculations for control charts can easily be devised using spreadsheet facilities, and the graphical facilities allow for relatively high quality control charts that can be regularly updated. /Graph Options Formats allows you to choose for each set of data 'lines' or 'symbols' or both, and /Graph Options Advanced Colours A–F Range allows symbols and lines or both to be depicted in different colours. The X-values are thus time (e.g. (day) 1, 2, 3, 4, ..., etc.), A and B may be lines, C and D action lines and E the actual data (symbols).

## EXERCISES

**11-1** The average (arithmetic mean) expenditure on books by a simple random sample of 100 first-year undergraduate management students is £70 with a standard deviation of £15. Construct 95 per cent confidence intervals for the average expenditure by all such students.

**11-2** A random sample of 50 employees is taken from a workforce of 500. Their arithmetic mean overtime worked per week was 5 hours with a standard deviation of 1 hour. Construct 99 per cent confidence intervals for the mean overtime worked per week by the whole workforce.

**11-3** A random sample of 20 pages typed by a central typing pool found a mean of 5 errors per page with a standard deviation of 1 error. Estimate, using both 95 per cent and 99 per cent levels of confidence, the population mean and comment on the differences in your results.

**11-4** Referring back to Question 11-1, where $s = 15$ and $n = 100$, plot a graph showing how the error margin $(Zs/\sqrt{n})$ varies with different values of $Z$ drawn up to correspond to 80, 90, 95 and 99 per cent levels of confidence.

**11-5** Again with Question 11-1 in mind, show how different values of $n$ will lead to different error margins at a 95 per cent level of confidence with $s = 15$. You should plot a graph showing the effects on the error margin of several values of $n$ in the range $n = 30$ and $n = 5000$.

**11-6** Recalculate the confidence interval from Question 11-1 using $s = 2$ instead of $s = 15$, and comment on how the interval changes.

**11-7** The proportion of workers in favour of a new incentive scheme was found to be 0.55 based on a random sample of 40 workers from a workforce of 600. Does this prove that a majority of workers are in favour of the scheme?

**11.8** A survey of consumers' attitudes to a new supermarket is being planned. There is particular interest in the answer to a question on whether petrol facilities should be provided. The belief is that around 20 per cent of shoppers will make use of the facility. The company wants error margins of no more than plus or minus 3 per cent to the response to the question, and are prepared to accept a confidence level of 95 per cent for their results. What size of sample will be necessary? One manager is arguing that a sample size of 500 has always been used. What error margin will this produce?

**11-9** A batch of 40 goods is taken at random every hour from a production process. After examining batches over the last few days 13 per cent have been found to be defective. Construct a 95 and 98 per cent control chart. If subsequent batches find 5, 6, 4, 7, 6, 8, 7 and 6 defectives, is the process out of control?

**11-10** Random samples of 6 batteries are taken regularly, tested, and the results from 7 samples are given in the table for their life in hours.

| Battery | Sample | | | | | | |
| | 1 | 2 | 3 | 4 | 5 | 6 | 7 |
| --- | --- | --- | --- | --- | --- | --- | --- |
| 1 | 25.1 | 25.0 | 25.9 | 25.0 | 25.5 | 26.2 | 25.0 |
| 2 | 24.8 | 25.7 | 25.7 | 26.1 | 25.4 | 25.1 | 25.9 |
| 3 | 26.1 | 25.6 | 25.5 | 24.9 | 25.6 | 25.2 | 25.3 |
| 4 | 25.4 | 24.9 | 25.3 | 25.4 | 25.8 | 25.6 | 25.7 |
| 5 | 25.2 | 26.0 | 25.2 | 25.9 | 24.8 | 25.7 | 25.5 |
| 6 | 25.3 | 26.1 | 25.8 | 25.7 | 24.9 | 25.6 | 25.4 |

Construct a control chart for the range. If two subsequent samples have values of 25.6, 26.2, 25.4, 25.9, 25.1 and 25.7 for the first sample and 25.1, 25.0, 26.2, 25.8, 25.9 and 25.7 for the second sample, is the range moving out of control?

**11-11** The mean number of matches in a box packed by machines has been found from experience to be 35, with a standard deviation of 1.1 match. Results from recent tests on batches of random samples of ten boxes show mean contents of 35.6, 35.0, 35.2, 34.89, 34.9, 35.1, 35.4, 34.85 and 34.9. Is there any evidence of the process moving out of control?

# 12

## TESTING HYPOTHESES

In this chapter we are concerned with assertions, claims or hypotheses: for example, it might be claimed that at least half of the workforce in your company are in favour of new working arrangements, or that a proportion of 0.02 of tools purchased by a company are defective, or that for a proportion of 0.5 of all households in your catchment area, inadequate parking is their main reason for not using your store. All these can be treated as hypotheses about proportions. Yet it is not enough just to make these claims or assertions—that is, to set up these hypotheses about proportions. If we are to act to make decisions, we have to test these hypotheses by turning to the empirical world to see if what is claimed is actually happening. We could test these hypotheses by balloting all your company's workers to see what proportion are in favour of the new working arrangements, by examining all tools to see what proportion are defective, and by surveying all households in the catchment area to discover their reasons for not using your store. The results from the empirical world can be used to test these hypotheses and appropriate decisions can then be made. All of this is straightforward: we set up a hypothesis, and test it to see if it is true. Why, then, do we need a chapter on the subject?

The problem arises when—due to the destructive nature of the testing procedure, or time and cost constraints—a *sample* of workers, tools or households is taken rather than the whole population. Our hypothesis is about the population proportion, $\pi$; our evidence is from a sample proportion, $p$. In the previous chapter we saw that by using random sampling methods the results of our sample proportion may be very close to $\pi$, but there again they may be a long way away from it. How can we refute a hypothesis about $\pi$ when we cannot be sure whether the sample proportion used to test it reflects $\pi$ accurately? The theory of the previous chapter on sampling distributions will obviously be of use here.

So far we have discussed the matter in terms of testing hypotheses about proportions. Yet hypotheses may be set up about arithmetic means: the mean time it takes to do a job, the mean area covered by a pot of paint, the mean number of purchases of an item by householders, etc. Hypotheses can also be tested about other statistics, some considered later in this chapter such as about correlation coefficient, the regression coefficients and the median. We shall also consider hypotheses about the *difference* between two proportions: for example, it may be claimed that there is no difference between the proportion of male and female workers in favour of new working arrangements; or no difference between the mean time taken to do a job by two different firms. Wherever the evidence used to test the hypotheses is based on a random sample, the principles and techniques developed in this chapter apply. We shall consider, in turn, how to set up our hypotheses and the types of errors involved; how to test hypotheses about individual means or proportions; the difference between two means, two variances or two proportions; and correlation and regression coefficients. Since we are using principles established in the previous chapter you should note that, as before:

- we assume simple random sampling; if other random sampling techniques are used, alternative formulae for the standard errors apply (given in Cochran, 1966)
- if $(n/N) > 0.05$ the standard error should be multiplied by the finite population correction.

## SETTING UP HYPOTHESES

Consider a company that undertakes laboratory tests on blood samples. Of critical importance in costing is the mean time taken to undertake the tests. A certain type of test has always been assumed to take 3 minutes. You want to test this hypothesis; you have no idea if the actual mean is more or less than 3 minutes. You start by setting up a *null hypothesis* that the mean time for the population of tests is 3 minutes, depicted by:

$$H_0: \mu = 3.00$$

We call this a *null* hypothesis $(H_0)$ since we are assuming there is *no* difference between what is being claimed and what actually happens. But to every null hypothesis there is an alternative hypothesis: in this case the alternative is that $\mu$ is more than or less than 3 minutes, or put another way:

$$H_1: \mu \neq 3.00$$

i.e. the alternative hypothesis $(H_1)$ of $\mu$ being not equal to 3 minutes. We call this a two-tailed test for reasons that will later become obvious. The alternative can fall on either side of the value given in the null hypothesis: it can be less than 3.00 or more than 3.00.

Consider the example of British Telecom (BT) who may make a claim that 95 per cent of their telephone boxes are always operational. The null hypothesis at first sight is, where $\pi$ is the proportion of BT boxes operational, that $H_0: \pi = 0.95$. But what are the other alternatives? They are that $\pi < 0.95$, which is a very real alternative; or that $\pi > 0.95$, but it is hardly likely that BT will understate their claim. In any event if $\pi > 0.95$ their claim still stands. This is a *one-tailed test* since the alternative hypothesis is in one direction. We can set up the hypothesis as:

$$H_0: \pi \geqslant 0.95$$
$$H_1: \pi < 0.95$$

Note that we set up the hypotheses not on the basis of whether the sample result is more or less than what is claimed, but prior to looking at any sample results. We ask ourselves *in theory* for the purpose of rejecting or otherwise the claim, whether the direction of the alternative is on one side (one-tailed test), or could be on both sides of what is being claimed (two-tailed test).

To better understand the tests we must be aware of possible types of errors. We start hypotheses tests by assuming $H_0$ is true, taking a sample of data and then identifying by test procedures (to be described) whether or not $H_0$ is rejected by the evidence of the data. However, two possible sources of errors may arise as illustrated in Table 12-1 and these are (imaginatively) called Type I and II errors.

A Type I error is when our null hypothesis, for example that 95 per cent or more of telephone

**Table 12-1**  Types of error

|  | Conclusion | |
| --- | --- | --- |
|  | Reject null hypothesis | Accept null hypothesis |
| Null hypothesis is true | Type I error <br> {$\alpha$: significance level} | No error <br> {$1-\alpha$} |
| Null hypothesis is false | No error <br> {$1-\beta$: power} | Type II error <br> {$\beta$} |

Figures in { ... } are probabilities: $\alpha$ is the probability of committing a type I error, i.e. rejecting the null hypothesis given it is true (this probability is called the level of significance); $\beta$ is the probability of committing a type II error, i.e. accepting the null hypothesis given it is false; $(1-\beta)$ is called the power.

As applied to production control:

|  | Process in control | Process out of control |
| --- | --- | --- |
| Stop production | Type I error | Correct decision |
| Continue production | Correct decision | Type II error |

boxes work is true, but on the basis of the sample data we reject it: i.e. Type I error arises when we reject a true null hypothesis. We denote the probability of committing such an error by $\alpha$—also called the significance level.

A Type II error is when the null hypothesis is false, i.e. less than 95 per cent of telephone boxes work, but on the basis of our sample data we conclude the hypothesis is true: i.e. we do not reject a false null hypothesis. We denote the probability of committing such an error by $\beta$. The value $1-\beta$ is called the power of the test.

Consider the example of a production process where the null hypothesis is that the process is working well and is in control. The alternative hypothesis is that it is out of control. We take samples of products and test their quality. The lower part of Table 12-1 illustrates the types of error: a type I error affects the producer by stopping the process unnecessarily; a type II error affects the consumer as the producer continues to make poor-quality goods.

Decision making invariably involves hypotheses being set up about the nature of things. We can aid the decision-making process by using results from sample data to test these hypotheses, but in doing so we must be aware of sampling errors.

## TESTING HYPOTHESES ABOUT AN INDIVIDUAL MEAN

### Large samples

Consider the hypothesis about the time taken to do a laboratory test mentioned earlier, i.e.:

$$H_0: \mu = 3.00, \quad H_1: \mu \neq 3.00$$

Now imagine we took a random sample of 35 tests and monitored the time taken to do them. Figure 12-1 shows how the sampling distribution of the mean might look *on the assumption that $H_0$ is true*. Now if $H_0$ is true it is possible that our random sample could take an extreme value of 2.95 or 3.05. It is more likely that it will take a value nearer $\mu = 3.00$ but it is possible using random techniques to pick a sample with unusually low or high values. However, being practical, if we found a sample mean of 35 minutes we would say that this is much too high to have come from a population with a mean of 3.00 minutes. The data would not appear to support the hypothesis.

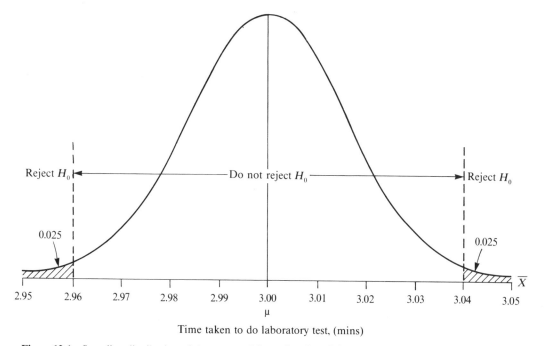

Time taken to do laboratory test, (mins)

**Figure 12-1** Sampling distribution of the means of time taken for a laboratory test (samples of $n = 35$)

Yet, given the sampling distribution in Fig. 12-1, a sample mean of 3.05 minutes might also be considered too high. It is possible, but unlikely, as is 3.03 minutes. So where do we draw the cut-off line? Where do we say that the result from the sample, while possible, is too extreme to be considered likely to have arisen from a distribution with $\mu = 3.00$?

Let us draw arbitrary cut-off lines which exclude 0.025 (2.5 per cent) of the distribution on each tail, i.e. a total of 0.05 (5 per cent). Via the Central Limit Theorem we know that the distribution of sample means is normal, and thus one side of the distribution is the mirror image of the other. Let us say the two lines drawn at 2.96 and 3.04 in Fig. 12-1 exclude to their left and right, respectively, 0.025 (2.5 per cent) of the distribution—i.e. a total of 0.05 (5 per cent). Now, if this is the case we could say that there is only a probability of 0.05 (5 per cent) of a sample mean being less than 2.96 or more than 3.04 if $\mu = 3.00$, i.e. if $H_0$ is true. Given that this is very unlikely, we shall reject the null hypothesis of $\mu = 3.00$ if the sample mean falls in these extreme areas. However, this is not foolproof; there is a 5 per cent chance that we are making a wrong decision; that $\mu$ really is 3.00 minutes and we are rejecting it because, owing to bad luck, we drew an extreme sample mean. This, of course, would be a type I error, of rejecting a null hypothesis that is true. The probability of our committing this error is $\alpha$, the significance level, which is 0.05.

Thus, if our sample mean fell in one of the extreme zones we would reject the null hypothesis *at a 5 per cent level of significance*. The difference between $\mu$ and $\bar{X}$ is too great to be attributed to sampling errors, though there is a 5 per cent chance that we are rejecting a hypothesis that is true. We might describe the difference between $\mu$ and $\bar{X}$ as being *statistically significant* at the 5 per cent level.

All well and good; but why did we choose 2.96 and 3.04 to be the appropriate cut-off points to eliminate 5 per cent of the area of the distribution? The answer is that we simply conjured them up to explain the principles. Then how do we know if a sample mean falls in the 'reject' or 'non-reject' area for a given level of significance? Answer: we employ the following approach.

We used the standardized normal distribution and tables in Appendix 7, since they allow us to determine the cut-off points by eliminating 0.025 from each tail. But this distribution is not of actual values; it is the standardized version of the sampling distribution. So our sample mean must be converted to a standardized $Z$ to enable us to compare it with the cut-off points.

Consider Fig. 12-2; in Chapter 10 we saw that to find areas under a normal distribution we have to convert the distribution in Fig. 12-1 to a standardized normal distribution and find the $Z$-value (standardized normal deviate) that corresponds to the $X$-value, using:

$$Z = (X - \mu)/\sigma$$

Here we are using a sampling distribution where our $\bar{X}$-value is equivalent to the $X$ and our estimate of the standard error $s/\sqrt{n}$ takes the place of $\sigma$ for reasons given in Chapter 11. As such, in Fig. 12-2:

$$Z = \frac{\bar{X} - \mu}{s/\sqrt{n}} \tag{12-1}$$

The 5 per cent cut-off points are found for Fig. 12-2 from the tables of the normal distribution in Appendix 7. We look in the body of the table for the area of 0.025 that falls outside of the corresponding $Z$-value: i.e. $Z = \mp 1.96$ excludes 0.025 on each side. The 0.025 excluded on each side is the reject area. What we must determine is whether the $Z$ value corresponding to the calculated $\bar{X}$ found from the sample falls in the 'reject' or 'non-reject' range of the distribution. Note: we have only moved from Fig. 12-1 to Fig. 12-2 because we need to obtain from the table of the standardized normal distribution, the cut-off values that exclude 5 per cent of the distribution (i.e. $\mp 1.96$).

Assume that our sample of $n = 35$ tests yielded $\bar{X} = 3.04$ minutes and $s = 0.11$ minutes. Is the difference between $\mu = 3.00$ (as claimed under $H_0$), and $\bar{X} = 3.04$ (the sample result) statistically significant at a 5 per cent level? Using Eq. (12-1):

$$Z = \frac{3.04 - 3.00}{0.11/\sqrt{35}} = \frac{0.04}{0.0186} = 2.15$$

This $Z$ value is in the reject area of Fig. 12-2. We thus reject the null hypothesis that the average time taken to undertake the test is 3.00 minutes ($\mu = 3.00$) at a 5 per cent level of significance (since $2.15 > 1.96$). It lies outside the cut-off point.

We can now see why the test was called a two-tailed test, since $H_0$ could be rejected by the $Z$-value falling in either tail of the distribution, outside the positive or negative cut-off. Before looking at a one-tailed test example it is worth summarizing the steps taken to undertake a significance test since they are quite straightforward in practice, the above (quite lengthy) account being to explain the principles upon which they are based.

- *Step 1*  Formulate the null and alternative hypotheses bearing in mind the need to decide at this stage whether a one-tailed or two-tailed test is appropriate.
- *Step 2*  Determine the level of significance to be used ($\alpha$); we shall see later how different levels can be determined.
- *Step 3*  Select the sample size ($n$) to be used for the study and the appropriate test—in our case (so far) a $Z$-test for a single mean, large sample using Eq. (12-1).
- *Step 4*  Determine the rejection rule—in our case (for a 5 per cent level, two-tailed $Z$-test) we reject if the result of Eq. (12-1), the test statistic $Z$, is $Z < -1.96$ or $Z > 1.96$. It is best to ignore the sign and see if the (modulus) of the test statistic exceeds the critical value from the tables in Appendix 7.

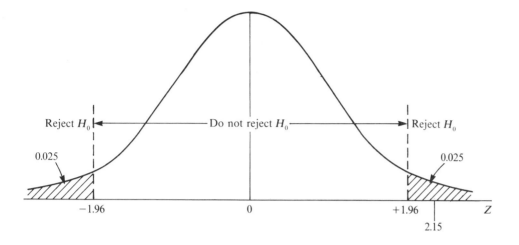

**Figure 12-2**  Standardized normal distribution for sampling distribution of time taken to undertake laboratory test

- *Step 5*  Collect the data using a simple random sample of size $n$ and calculate the appropriate sample values ($\bar{X}$ and $s$ in our case) to help determine $Z$, the test statistic.
- *Step 6*  Reject or do not reject $H_0$ at the chosen level of significance, depending on whether the test statistic ($Z$ in step 5) meets the rejection criteria (step 4).

Note that the test is set up in such a way that it is not influenced by the sample results: every decision on the nature of the test is made prior to the results being obtained.

Consider another example. You run a data entry department and your users claim gross inefficiency by your department due to high error rates—on average 10 errors per 200 successive figures entered.

- *Step 1*  $H_0: \mu \geq 10$,  $H_1: \mu < 10$, where $\mu$ is the overall mean number of errors per 200 entries. This is a one-tailed test: had the rate been higher than 10, this would have been claimed by your users, and for decision-making purposes $\mu > 10$ has the same implication as $\mu = 10$.
- *Step 2*  We shall use $\alpha = 0.01$ in this case, i.e. assume we want only a small chance of a type I error occurring so that we can refute the claim with confidence.
- *Step 3*  We shall choose $n = 100$ (100 sets of 200 entries) and a $Z$-test.
- *Step 4*  We need a $Z$-value from the tables in Appendix 7 which corresponds to an area of 0.01 in the body of the tables. Note: we do not divide this 0.01 by two as we would for a two-tailed test, since in step 1 we chose a one-tailed test. From Appendix 7, the appropriate value is 2.33. Therefore, if $Z < -2.33$ we reject $H_0$ at a 1 per cent level. Note that we expect $Z$ to be less than the critical value under $H_1$, so we use the lower tail of the distribution.
- *Step 5*  Assume we found $\bar{X} = 8$ and $s = 3$. By Eq. (12-1):

$$Z = \frac{8 - 10}{3/\sqrt{100}} = -6.667$$

- *Step 6*  Since $-6.667 < -2.33$ (or, ignoring signs, $6.667 > 2.33$) we reject the null hypothesis that the average number of errors per 200 entries is 10 ($\mu = 10$) at a 1 per cent level of significance.

### Small samples

The procedure adopted in Eq. (12-1) was to divide the difference between the sample and population mean by the standard error of the sampling distribution of the means. In the previous chapter we saw that for small samples, when $n < 30$, the resulting statistic will not follow a normal distribution. However, if the underlying distribution of the variable is normal, and if the unbiased estimator for the standard deviation, $s_{n-1}$, is used for $s$, as given by Eq. (11-1) then the sampling distribution follows a $t$-distribution with $v = n - 1$ degrees of freedom:

$$t = \frac{\bar{X} - \mu}{s_{n-1}/\sqrt{n}} \tag{12-2}$$

Consider a claim by a toilet roll salesperson that the rolls contain on average at least 240 sheets.

1. $H_0: \mu \geqslant 240$,  $H_1: \mu < 240$.
2. Assume that $\alpha = 0.05$ is a satisfactory level of significance for the test.
3. If a random sample of 20 rolls is taken, assuming number of sheets is normally distributed, a $t$-test is appropriate.
4. From Appendix 6, the $t$-table at $\alpha = 0.05$ for a one-tailed test and $v = 20 - 1 = 19$ is 1.7291, i.e. $t_{0.05, 19} = 1.7291$.
5. We draw the sample and find $\bar{X} = 239$ and $s = 3.1$. Since $s$ is not an unbiased estimate we need to convert $s$ to $s_{n-1}$ using the process outlined in Eq. (11-9). $s_{n-1} = \sqrt{(3.1)^2 20/19} = 3.1805$. From Eq. (12-2)

$$t = \frac{239 - 240}{3.1805/\sqrt{20}} = -1.406$$

6. Since (ignoring signs) $1.4061 < 1.7291$ we do not reject the null hypothesis that the mean number of sheets is at least 240 per roll at a 5 per cent level of significance.

It is worth developing a few general points here. First, the actual test is for $\mu = 240$, though we reject $H_0: \mu \geqslant 240$—if the test rejects the hypothesis that $\mu = 240$ it will also reject $\mu = 241$ or 242—so we include all of these values in $H_0$ automatically.

Second, we have demonstrated that the difference between what was claimed under $H_0$ and what was found by $\bar{X}$ is statistically significant at the 5 per cent level. It is in addition to what we would expect from sampling errors at this level of significance. There is a real difference, not one due to chance, at this level. This does not necessarily mean that the difference is important in a substantive or, in this case, commercial sense. A 95 per cent confidence interval for the mean would be (using formula (11-8)):

$$239 \mp 2.0930(3.1805)/\sqrt{20} = 237.5 \text{ to } 240.5 \text{ sheets}$$

The evidence does not reject the claim of an average of 240 sheets, and the $2\frac{1}{2}$ sheets possible shortfall may not be, at least in a commercial sense, critical. The tests identify for given $\alpha$ whether the data allow us to reject the null hypothesis, given the presence of sampling errors. If we do reject, it is then a separate question to ask if the difference is important. For large $n$ and small $s$, sampling errors are small so hypotheses may be rejected on the basis of quite small differences between $\bar{X}$ and the value of $\mu$ under $H_0$.

Third, there is an alternative way we can formulate these tests. We rejected the above test at a 5 per cent level. However, it might have been possible to reject it at a 4, 3, 2, 1, 0.1 per cent level, or whatever. The alternative approach is to find the margin or the lowest level of significance, a

$p$-value, at which we can reject it and then decide if this meets a (preferably) predetermined level. This is equivalent to the probability that the sample mean takes a value as (or more) extreme as was found if $H_0$ is true. Thus if, for example, a 5 per cent level was acceptable and we found the test had a $p$-value of a 3 per cent level, we would reject the hypothesis knowing it met our criterion (was significant at a 5 per cent level). If we found a $p$-value of (60 per cent) ($p=0.6$), this would show that we could not reject $H_0$ at any significance level below 60 per cent, which is unacceptably high. We can determine the marginal level or $p$-value (probability value) at which the hypothesis is rejected by using $t$ tables and our calculated $t$-value. In practice, we do not usually calculate $p$-values; they are generally available when tests are conducted using statistical packages on computers (see later) and we have thus given here an account of their interpretation.

## TESTING HYPOTHESES ABOUT A PROPORTION

Our tests in Eqs. (12-1) and (12-2) were based on dividing the difference between the sample mean and the population mean claimed under $H_0$ by the standard error of the sampling distribution of the means. For proportions we follow an equivalent procedure: the difference between the sample proportion $p$, and the population proportion $\pi$ claimed under $H_0$ divided by the standard error of the sampling distribution of proportions, i.e. $\sqrt{\pi(1-\pi)/n}$.

For $np \geqslant 5$ for $p \leqslant 0.5$ or $n(1-p) \geqslant 5$ for $p > 5$, or as a rule of thumb $n \geqslant 30$, the sampling distribution of proportions can be approximated by a normal distribution; thus the test statistic is given by:

$$Z = \frac{p - \pi}{\sqrt{\pi(1-\pi)/n}} \qquad (12\text{-}3)$$

Consider a claim by British Telecom that 95 per cent of their telephone boxes are operational at any given time. Assume that OFTEL (the telecommunications 'Watchdog') want to test the validity of this claim at a 5 per cent level of significance using a random sample of 100 boxes. Assume also that the result (all of this is fictitious) was that 85 per cent of boxes were operational, i.e. $p=0.85$.

1. $H_0$: $\pi \geqslant 0.95$
   $H_1$: $\pi < 0.95$
2. $\alpha = 0.05$.
3. $n = 100$; $Z$ test.
4. $Z$-value from Appendix 7 (since normally distributed) for one-tailed test: $Z_{0.05} = 1.64$. If (ignoring signs) calculated $Z$ is less than 1.64 we reject $H_0$ at a level of significance of 0.05.
5. From Eq. (12-3):

$$Z = \frac{0.85 - 0.95}{\sqrt{0.95(0.05)/100}} = \frac{-0.10}{0.06892} = -1.451$$

6. Since $1.451 < 1.64$ we do not reject the claim that 95 per cent of telephone boxes are operational at a 5 per cent level of significance. The difference between the sample result of 0.85 and claim of 0.95 is not statistically significant at this level and might be due to sampling errors.

## TESTING HYPOTHESES ABOUT THE DIFFERENCE BETWEEN MEANS : LARGE SAMPLES

So far our tests have been concerned with individual means and proportions—often referred to as *one-sample tests*. However, it may sometimes be claimed that there is no difference between the means or proportions of two groups. We thus need samples from each group: *two-sample tests*.

The test procedures are similar to those outlined above. We have two populations and are interested in testing claims as to a difference in their sample means. For example, the two populations may be male and female workers and there may be a claim that there is a difference in the mean minutes that males ($\mu_1$) and females ($\mu_2$) arrive late for work. We take random samples of size $n_1$ and $n_2$ and determine their sample means ($\bar{X}_1$) and ($\bar{X}_2$) along with unbiased sample standard deviations ($s_{n-1,1}$ and $s_{n-1,2}$) respectively. To undertake the test we need the standard error (SE) of the sample distribution of the difference between two means, which is divided into the difference between the population means subtracted from the difference between the sample means, i.e.:

One-sample

Two-sample

$$\frac{(\bar{X}-\mu)}{\text{SE means}} \qquad \frac{(\bar{X}_1-\bar{X}_2)-(\mu_1-\mu_2)}{\text{SE difference between means}} \qquad (12\text{-}4)$$

The form of the tests depend upon whether we can assume the variance (or standard deviation) is the same for each sample, and also depending on whether large or small samples are taken. We look at each case in turn: we use unbiased estimators of the standard deviation here throughout, though for large sample work, as noted before, they are not necessary.

### Testing $(\mu_1-\mu_2)=0$ when $\sigma_1=\sigma_2=\sigma$: large samples

If the test is to be valid, it is necessary that

- the two random samples are independently drawn
- the normality assumption for the large sample has *each* of $n_1$ and $n_2 \geqslant 30$.

The standard error of the difference between means is:

$$\text{SE}_{\bar{X}_1-\bar{X}_2}=\sqrt{(\sigma_1/\sqrt{n_1})^2+(\sigma_2/\sqrt{n_2})^2}=\sqrt{\sigma_1^2/n_1+\sigma_2^2/n_2}=\sqrt{\sigma^2[1/n_1+1/n_2]} \qquad (12\text{-}5)$$

The first expression shows the SE of the difference between means to be the square root of the sum of the squares of the SE for each population. The final expression is derived since $\sigma_1=\sigma_2=\sigma$. However, we do not know $\sigma_1$ or $\sigma_2$, but it can be shown that the best unbiased estimator of $\sigma$ is a *pooled estimator*, which is a weighted average of the unbiased estimators of the sample standard deviations, i.e.:

$$s_{\text{pooled}}^2=\frac{(n_1-1)s_{n-1,1}^2+(n_2-1)s_{n-1,2}^2}{n_1+n_2-2} \qquad (12\text{-}6)$$

where

$$s_{n-1,1}^2=\Sigma(X_i-\bar{X})^2/(n_1-1) \quad \text{for sample 1}$$

and

$$s_{n-1,2}^2=\Sigma(X_i-\bar{X})^2/(n_2-1) \quad \text{for sample 2}$$

Since Eq. (12-6) is a best unbiased estimator of $\sigma^2$ in Eq. (12-5):

$$SE_{\bar{X}_1-\bar{X}_2}=\sqrt{s^2_{pooled}[1/n_1+1/n_2]}$$

and the test is:

$$Z=\frac{(\bar{X}_1-\bar{X}_2)-(\mu_1-\mu_2)}{\sqrt{s^2_{pooled}[1/n_1+1/n_2]}} \tag{12-7}$$

The above may seem complex, but it is just the move from the one-sample to two-sample formulation in formula (12-4); in the one-sample case, $SE_{means}$ was $\sigma/\sqrt{n}$ and we used the best unbiased estimator of $s$ for $\sigma$: in the two-sample case we use $s^2_{pooled}$ for $\sigma^2$, and the denominator of Eq. (12-7) for the standard error.

Consider, for example, that the marketing department of an organization believes there to be no difference in the mean age of users of two brands of washing-up liquid. Random samples of $n_1=50$ and $n_2=35$ users of each of the two brands are selected to test if the average ages are equal, finding (in years): $\bar{X}_1=35$ with (unbiased) $s^2_{n-1,\,1}=10$ and $\bar{X}_2=38$ with $s^2_{n-1,\,2}=10.5$.

1. $H_0: \mu_1-\mu_2=0$, $H_1: \mu_1-\mu_2 \neq 0$. A one-tailed test is used since we have no idea if one group of users is older or younger than the other.
2. Assume $\alpha=0.05$.
3. $n_1=50$, $n_2=35$; Z-test.
4. Z-value from Appendix 7 (since normally distributed) for two-tailed test: $Z=1.96$—if calculated $Z$ (ignoring signs) is less than 1.96 we reject $H_0$ at a 5 per cent level of significance.
5. From Eqs (12-6) and (12-7), bearing in mind $(\mu_1-\mu_2)=0$ under $H_0$:

$$s^2_{pooled}=\frac{(50-1)10+(35-1)10.5}{50+35-2}=10.20$$

$$Z=\frac{(35-38)-0}{\sqrt{10.20[1/50+1/35]}}=\frac{3}{0.7040}=4.2612$$

6. We thus reject the null hypothesis of no difference between the mean ages of users of the two brands of washing-up liquid at a 5 per cent level of significance; the difference is statistically significant at this level and cannot be attributed to sampling errors.

### Testing $\mu_1-\mu_2=0$ when $\sigma_1 \neq \sigma_2$: large samples

The procedure is similar to that adopted above, but since we cannot assume $\sigma_1=\sigma_2=\sigma$ a pooled estimate of $\sigma$ cannot be used. The pooled approach is very slightly more powerful than the approach described here, but if the assumption of equal variances does not hold it can be very misleading. When in any doubt, this procedure is adopted. Since we cannot pool the estimated variance, the test statistic is:

$$Z=\frac{(\bar{X}_1-\bar{X}_2)-(\mu_1-\mu_2)}{\sqrt{s^2_{n-1,\,1}/n_1+s^2_{n-1,\,2}/n_2}} \tag{12-8}$$

with $s^2_{n-1,\,1}$ and $s^2_{n-1,\,2}$ being best unbiased estimators of $\sigma^2_1$ and $\sigma^2_2$ respectively for Eq. (12-5) inserted into the two-sample case of (12-4).

For example, male and female workers test and repair video-recorders and views have been expressed over the relative efficiency of each sex, though there is obviously no consensus as to which is more efficient. You monitor the time taken to repair a random sample of 80 videos. Some workers have argued that female workers are on average more efficient, but there is less variability in their performance, while the best male workers cannot be matched, but neither can the worst. While all you want to test is whether the means are the same you cannot choose a method that assumes equal variances. The resulting sample sizes are $n_f = 38$ and $n_m = 42$ with the time taken for the repairs of the different groups in minutes: $\bar{X}_f = 15$, $s^2_{n-1, f} = 8$, $\bar{X}_m = 14$, $s^2_{n-1, m} = 11$.

1. $H_0: \mu_f - \mu_m = 0$, $H_1: \mu_f - \mu_m \neq 0$, two-tailed test.
2. Assume $\alpha = 0.05$.
3. $n_f = 38$, $n_m = 42$; Z-test.
4. Z-values from Appendix 7 (normality) for two-tailed test—if (ignoring signs) calculated Z is greater than 1.96 we reject $H_0$ at a level of significance of 0.05.
5. From Eq. (12-8), bearing in mind $(\mu_f - \mu_m) = 0$ under $H_0$:

$$Z = \frac{(15 - 14) - 0}{\sqrt{8/38 + 11/42}} = \frac{1}{0.6873} = 1.4549$$

6. Since $1.4549 < 1.96$ we do not reject the null hypothesis of no difference between the mean male and female repair time at a 5 per cent level. The difference is not over and above what might be expected from sampling error (i.e. is not statistically significant) at this level.

## TESTING HYPOTHESES ABOUT THE EQUALITY OF VARIANCES

We might need to test hypotheses about the equality of variances between two groups, first, to let us know which of the two above tests to apply and, second, because we are interested in it *per se*. In the above example claims were made about the variability of performance of male workers. We discussed in Chapter 4 the importance of dispersion and often our interest is whether observations from one group are more dispersed than those from another.

A new distribution is used for this purpose: the *F*-distribution. The test requires that the observations from the population are normally distributed. It is quite straightforward to calculate:

$$F = s^2_{n-1, 1}/s^2_{n-1, 2} \tag{12-9}$$

To use *F*-tables we need to know the level of significance and the degrees of freedom associated with the sample variance in the numerator of Eq. (12-9), given by $v_1 = n_1 - 1$, and the degrees of freedom associated with the sample variance in the denominator of (12-9), given by $v_2 = n_2 - 1$; the sample variance, which is numerically largest, is designated $s^2_{n-1, 1}$ and is placed in the numerator.

For the above example on male and female efficiency, we might want to test if the (population) variances of time taken are the same.

1. $H_0: \sigma^2_f - \sigma^2_m = 0$, $H_1: \sigma^2_f - \sigma^2_m \neq 0$.
2. Assume $\alpha = 0.05$.
3. $n_f = 38$, $v_f = 38 - 1 = 37$; $n_m = 42$, $v_m = 42 - 1 = 41$; F-test.
4. F-value from Appendix 8: Since the male variance is the largest it is in the numerator and its degrees of freedom are designated $v_1 = 41$ in the tables while $v_2 = 37$, and at $\alpha = 0.05$ the F-value from the tables is between 1.832 ($v_1 = 50$, $v_2 = 40$) and 1.999 ($v_1 = 30$, $v_2 = 35$). Since exact figures do not exist, we could interpolate them or take a cautious view of the value from the F-tables being 1.832. The calculated value from Eq. (12-9) must exceed the value from the tables if we are to reject $H_0$. The placing of the larger variance in the numerator sets up the test as a one-tailed test, which is the way it should be.

5. From Eq. (12-9): $F = 11/8 = 1.375$.
6. Since $1.375 < 1.832$ we do not reject the null hypothesis of equal variances at a 5 per cent level of significance. The difference between the sample was due to sampling error and is not statistically significant at this level. We were thus overcautious to use a method for unequal variances and should have used Eq. (12-7). Had this been used:

$$s^2_{\text{pooled}} = \frac{(38-1)8 + (42-1)11}{38+42-2} = 9.5769$$

$$Z = \frac{(15-14)-0}{\sqrt{9.5769(1/38+1/42)}} = \frac{1}{0.69285} = 1.4433$$

Since $1.4433 < 1.96$ the outcome of the test has not changed, there being little difference in the calculated $Z$-values, though this need not always be the case.

## TESTING HYPOTHESES ABOUT DIFFERENCES BETWEEN MORE THAN TWO MEANS

This is beyond the scope of our text but the technique of analysis of variance (ANOVA) allows us to test hypotheses that the means of two or more groups are equal. For example, our hypothesis might be that the mean salaries for workers in several regions are the same. This would involve a one-way ANOVA; or we could extend the technique to multivariate analysis by classifying workers by region, occupation, industry, sex and ethnic origin and use five-way ANOVA to identify whether there are differences between mean salaries for each of these distinct variables, as well as interaction effects between the variables.

## TESTING HYPOTHESES ABOUT THE DIFFERENCE BETWEEN MEANS: SMALL SAMPLES

These are similar to the large sample tests except that, as well as requiring each sample to be drawn from independent random samples, the underlying distributions of the observations in each population must be normal. If this is the case the same formulae are adopted as above, except:

1. *Hypothesis concerning $\mu_1 - \mu_2$ for equal variances*
   Use Eqs (12-7) and (12-6), but instead of (12-7) following a normal distribution it follows a $t$-distribution with $n_1 + n_2 - 2$ degrees of freedom. The calculated value is compared with a value from $t$-tables (Appendix 6) based on the appropriate $\alpha$ and $v = n_1 + n_2 - 2$.

2. *Hypotheses concerning $\mu_1 - \mu_2$ for unequal variances*
   Use Eq. (12-8) but instead of it following a normal distribution, it follows a $t$-distribution with degrees of freedom given by:

$$v = \frac{(s^2_{n-1,\,1}/n_1 + s^2_{n-1,\,2}/n_2)^2}{[(s^2_{n-1,\,1}/n_1)^2/(n_1-1)] + [(s^2_{n-1,\,2}/n_2)^2/(n_2-1)]} \tag{12-10}$$

The calculated value from Eq. (12-8) is compared with a value from the $t$-tables (Appendix 6) based on the appropriate $\alpha$ and $v$ from Eq. (12-10).

## TESTING HYPOTHESES ABOUT PAIRED DIFFERENCES

The above tests concern observations randomly drawn from two independent populations. Yet it is often useful to design our experiments differently, and compare the effects of two different 'treatments' applied to the same objects or persons—a 'before' and 'after' type test. For example, we might consider the effect on sales of new packaging for the product, where the product is sold door-to-door. Taking, as before, two independent random samples of salespeople, one sample selling with the old packaging and one selling with the new, allows differences in average sales between the two groups to be attributed both to the new packaging and to the characteristics of the salesforce. However, here we are allowing each salesperson to sell the product first with the old packaging and then with the new packaging—so differences due to the personal characteristics of the salesperson are minimized. None of the preceding tests applies since they were concerned with independent random samples; here the choice of the 'after' sample is the same as the 'before', thus we cannot describe the two samples as independent.

It is only advantageous to use this approach to test differences between two means if variations between paired items are less than the variation between the sample items in the same population (sales for all persons) and the differences are assumed to be normally distributed. The appropriate test is:

$$t = \frac{\Sigma d_i/n}{s_d/\sqrt{n}} \tag{12-11}$$

where $d_i$ are the differences between the paired observations and $s_d$ is the unbiased standard deviation of the differences. For example, if we had six sales representatives whose average sales, based on a (randomly allocated) seven-day period using the new and old packaging, were:

| Sales representative: | A | B | C | D | E | F | |
|---|---|---|---|---|---|---|---|
| Old packaging (number sold): | 50 | 40 | 80 | 20 | 38 | 40 | |
| New packaging (number sold): | 60 | 45 | 78 | 20 | 40 | 45 | |
| $d_i$ | 10 | 5 | −2 | 0 | 2 | 5 | $\Sigma d_i = 20$ |
| $d_i^2$ | 100 | 25 | 4 | 0 | 4 | 25 | $\Sigma d_i^2 = 158$ |

1. $H_0: \mu_d \leq 0$, $H_1: \mu_d > 0$, one-tailed test assumes that new packaging is likely to be better than the old.
2. $\alpha = 0.05$.
3. $n = 6$, paired comparisons.
4. From Appendix 6, with $v = n - 1 = 6 - 1 = 5$ degrees of freedom for a one-tailed test at $\alpha = 0.05$, $t$ is 2.015.
5. $s_d = \sqrt{\Sigma(d-\bar{d})^2/(n-1)} = \sqrt{(\Sigma d^2 - (\Sigma d)^2/n)/(n-1)}$
   $= \sqrt{(158 - (20)^2/6)/5} = 4.274$.
   From Eq. (12-11)

$$t = \frac{20/6}{4.274/\sqrt{6}} = 1.910$$

6. We thus do not reject the hypothesis at 5 per cent level of significance that the average difference between sales using the two types of packaging is zero (since $1.910 < 2.015$).

This approach is the simplest form of an experimental design called *randomized block designs*, where a 'block' is each pair.

## TESTING HYPOTHESES ABOUT THE DIFFERENCES BETWEEN PROPORTIONS

Hypotheses about the difference between proportions may take the form of the difference in the proportion of male and female employees staying with the company for a year, difference between the proportion of companies in two industries going bankrupt, difference in proportion of 'young' or 'old' consumers satisfied with a product, etc. Consider the example of examining the difference in the proportion of car insurance policy holders renewing with your company if (at random) one group is offered more flexible payment arrangements. Our null hypothesis is that this has no difference in the proportions (i.e. the flexible payment system does not affect renewal rates for existing customers).

1. $H_0: \pi_1 - \pi_2 \leqslant 0$, $H_1: \pi_1 - \pi_2 > 0$, where $\pi_1$ is the proportion under the new payments scheme. This is a one-tailed test since the flexible payments should only help renewal rates.
2. $\alpha = 0.05$.
3. Assume random samples of 100 customers for each type of payment scheme, $n_1 = 100$ and $n_2 = 100$; a Z-test (normal) can be used as a rule of thumb, when $n_1 \geqslant 30$ and $n_2 \geqslant 30$. However, a more appropriate condition is to guess an average proportion from the two samples, say 0.8, which will be the overall proportion. If $n_1(1 - 0.8) \geqslant 5$ and $n_2(1 - 0.8) \geq 5$ the test can proceed.
4. The Z-value from Appendix 7, using a one-tailed test at $\alpha = 0.05$, is 1.64.
5. The calculated value takes a familiar form:

$$Z = \frac{(p_1 - p_2) - (\pi_1 - \pi_2)}{\sqrt{p_{\text{pooled}}(1 - p_{\text{pooled}})[1/n_1 + 1/n_2]}} \tag{12-12}$$

where

$$p_{\text{pooled}} = (n_1 p_1 + n_2 p_2)/(n_1 + n_2).$$

The numerator in Eq. (12-12) is the best unbiased estimator of the difference between proportions $(p_1 - p_2)$ which is compared with $(\pi_1 - \pi_2)$ which is, of course, zero under $H_0$. The denominator is the standard error of the sampling distribution of the difference between proportions. It is based on an unbiased estimate of $p$ since under $H_0$ we assume the proportions in the population to be the same.

If we found $p_1 = 0.85$ and $p_2 = 0.82$, then using Eq. (12-12):

$$p_{\text{pooled}} = \frac{100(0.85) + 100(0.82)}{100 + 100} = 0.835$$

and

$$Z = \frac{(0.85 - 0.82) - 0}{\sqrt{0.835(1 - 0.835)[1/100 + 1/100]}} = \frac{0.03}{0.05249} = 0.5715$$

6. We do not reject $H_0$ at a 5 per cent level of significance; the difference between the proportions renewing their policies under the two payment options is not statistically significant at this 5 per cent level of significance. There is thus no evidence (at least in terms of increased renewals) for the new flexible payments scheme. The difference between the two sample proportions may be attributed to sampling errors.

## TESTING HYPOTHESES ABOUT CORRELATION AND (REGRESSION) SLOPE COEFFICIENTS

In Chapters 6 and 7 we examined the statistical significance of the product moment correlation coefficient and the slopes of the regression equation. The data for these were considered to be taken from random samples and the principles of the tests explained on an intuitive level. We are now hopefully in a better position to understand the principles behind these tests. The null hypotheses were that the population correlation coefficient ($\rho$, called rho), and slope coefficient $\beta$ (distinguish from the probability of type II error—they both use the same symbol), were equal to zero—i.e. no association.

The alternative hypothesis depended in theory on whether the relationship could be on one side of zero (e.g. only positive or only negative—one-tailed test) or both sides (two-tailed test). For the product moment correlation coefficient we used specially designed tables to help judge if the difference between the calculated value from the sample and the hypothesized value of no linear association was statistically significant for a chosen level of significance, i.e. if it might be attributed to sampling errors. We might as well have conducted a formal test using:

$$t = \frac{r}{\sqrt{(1-r^2)/(n-2)}} \tag{12-13}$$

For example, if we took a random sample of 20 operatives and calculated the correlation coefficient from data on their ages and results from a computer aptitude test to find $r = 0.5$, then:

1. $H_0: \rho \leqslant 0$, $H_1: \rho > 0$, one-tailed test is likely to be a negative association.
2. $\alpha = 0.05$.
3. $n = 20$; using Eq. (12-13).
4. From the $t$-tables in Appendix 6, with $v = n - 2 = 20 - 2 = 18$ degrees of freedom, one-tailed test $t = 1.7341$.
5. Using Eq. (12-13):

$$t = \frac{-0.5}{\sqrt{(1-(0.5)^2)/18}} = \frac{-0.5}{0.20412} = -2.449$$

6. Since (ignoring signs) $2.449 > 1.7341$ we reject the hypothesis of no linear association between the two variables at a 5 per cent level of significance.

An equivalent test based on similar procedure for the slope coefficient for $H_0: \beta = 0$ is via:

$$t = b/\text{SE}_b \tag{12-14}$$

where $b$ is the sample slope coefficient and $\text{SE}_b$ the standard error of the sampling distribution of the slope coefficient where:

$$\text{SE}_b = \frac{S_{yx}}{S_x} = \frac{\Sigma e_i / n - 2}{\Sigma(X_i - \bar{X})^2 / n} \quad \text{(see Chapter 7)} \tag{12-15}$$

## DETERMINING THE PROBABILITY OF COMMITTING TYPE II ERRORS

At this point it is worth reflecting that we are able to cope with testing a variety of claims or hypotheses by recourse to data to see if they are rejected or not rejected by the data. If we reject we know this is at a predetermined level of significance, the probability of rejecting a true hypothesis given by $\alpha$, and we make our decisions based on this measured risk. But what if we do not reject? Often, in practice, the semantic difference between not rejecting and accepting is meaningless since we have to pursue policies as if we accepted the hypothesis. At the start of this chapter we explained the different types of errors by using an example of a production process that was hypothesized as being in control. If we do not reject this hypothesis on the basis of the quality of a sample of goods emanating from the process, then it continues to produce goods; we act as if we were accepting it. The reason why we were careful not to use the term 'accept' was because it too had errors; a type II error was accepting a false null hypothesis, and its probability was $\beta$. As we did not know how to measure $\beta$ we were worried about accepting a hypothesis; if, for example, $\beta$ was 0.95, such an acceptance would be less than helpful. To obtain a full picture of the decision-making process we need to measure $\beta$.

We considered an earlier example for the $t$-test for the average number of sheets in a toilet roll; $H_0: \mu \geqslant 240$, $H_1: \mu < 240$. If we modify the example to a $Z$-test for a random sample of $n = 30$ which yielded $\bar{X} = 239$ and $s = 41$, then applying Eq. (12-1)

$$Z = \frac{(239 - 240)}{4.1/\sqrt{30}} = \frac{-1}{0.7486} = -1.336$$

At $\alpha = 0.5$ (one-tailed test), $Z$ from tables $= -1.64$. Therefore, we do not reject $H_0$ at $\alpha = 0.05$.

We thus used Eq. (12-1) to test our hypotheses for a given $\alpha$ via:

$$Z = \frac{(\bar{X} - 240)}{4.1/\sqrt{30}}$$

If this calculated value was less than the critical value we found from $Z$-tables, i.e. $-1.64$, we would have rejected $H_0$ at $\alpha = 0.05$. The critical value of the sample mean for rejection can thus be determined as:

$$\frac{\bar{X} - 240}{4.1/\sqrt{30}} = -1.64.$$

$$\therefore \bar{X} - 240 = -1.64(4.1/\sqrt{30})$$
$$\therefore \bar{X} = 240 - 1.2276 = 238.77 \text{ sheets}$$

Thus a sample mean of 238.77 sheets is the borderline for testing $H_0: \mu \geqslant 240$ against $H_1: \mu < 240$ for $\alpha = 0.05$ one-tailed test. If the sample mean is less than 238.77 we reject $H_0$ in favour of $H_1$. All of this is simply an alternative and equivalent way of conducting our tests of hypotheses. However, it helps us to explain the measurement of type II errors. The top part of Fig. 12-3 illustrates this with the reject and (since we are testing with type II errors now) with the 'accept' areas marked in for the sampling distribution of the means for $\mu = 240$.

Consider now the second part of Fig. 12-3. Let us suppose that in reality the average number of sheets is an arbitrary 238, i.e. $\mu = 238$. The sampling distribution of the mean is drawn for $\mu = 238$. If we accepted $H_0: \mu \geqslant 240$ when in fact $\mu = 238$ we would be committing a type II error in accepting a false hypothesis. This is equivalent to saying, for the top part of Fig. 12-3, that the sampling distribution is set up for our hypothesis of $\mu = 240$. Since there are known sampling errors, values of sample means of 239.5 or 239, or as low as 238.77, will still be acceptable for our hypothesis, but anything less than this is unlikely ($\alpha = 0.05$) to be drawn from a population with $\mu = 240$ in this example. Yet, in the second part of the figure, when $\mu$ is actually 238, the possible range of values of $\bar{X}$ that might arise drifts into the acceptance area for $\mu = 240$, as shown by the shaded area. The

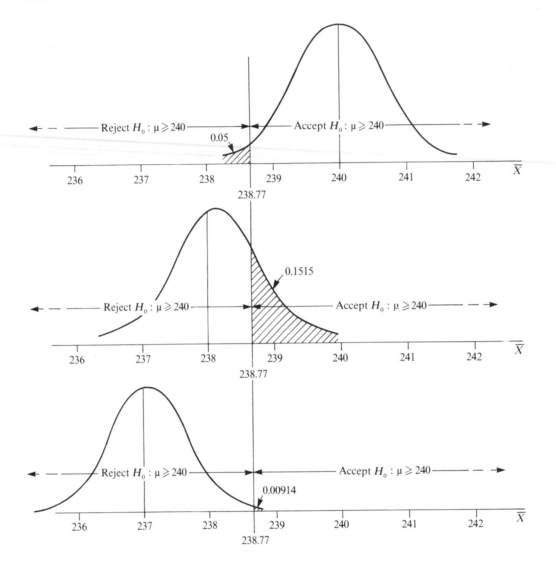

**Figure 12-3**  Sampling distribution of means for toilet roll example

probability of accepting $\mu \geqslant 240$ when $\mu = 238$, $\beta$, is given by the shaded area. How do we determine $\beta$? This is simply the area to the right of 238.77 on the distribution for $\mu = 238$ and a standard error (standard deviation for sampling distribution) of $s/\sqrt{n} = 4.1/\sqrt{30} = 0.7486$. To find this area we use the normal distribution: first, calculate a $Z$-value that corresponds to $\bar{X} = 238.77$, i.e.

$$Z = \frac{\bar{X} - \mu}{s/\sqrt{n}} = \frac{238.77 - 238}{4.1/\sqrt{30}} = \frac{0.77}{0.7486} = 1.0286$$

Second, from normal tables (Appendix 7) find the area to the right of 1.0286, i.e. 0.1515. Thus the probability of accepting $H_0 : \mu \geqslant 240$ when in fact it is not true, $\mu = 238$, is 0.1515, i.e. $\beta = 0.1515$.

At this point you should observe that all of this was worked out on the basis that, in reality,

$\mu = 238$. There are two problems with this. First, we do not know what $\mu$ is, so how can we calculate $\beta$? Second, had we chosen a different $\mu$, we would have obtained a different $\beta$. Both of these points are correct. $\beta$ will vary depending upon the actual value of $\mu$, which we do not know. What happens in practice is that we calculate several values of $\beta$ for different $\mu$ and this, as we shall see, helps us in decision making.

Consider the bottom part of Fig. 12-3. Here we assume that, in reality, $\mu = 237$ sheets: what is $\beta$ for this $\mu$? Adopting a similar procedure to that used above we want the area to the right of $\bar{X} = 238.77$; this is determined from:

$$Z = \frac{238.77 - 237}{4.1/\sqrt{30}} = \frac{1.77}{0.7486} = 2.3644$$

which, from tables, gives 0.00914, a much lower probability of committing a type II error. We would expect $\beta$ to be lower as the actual values assumed for $\mu$ move away from the hypothesized values for $\mu$. What we are saying is that the probability of wrongly accepting the mean number of sheets as 240, because in reality it is 237, is less than would be the case if in reality it was 238. As an extreme example, if in reality $\mu = 10$ sheets, the probability of wrongly accepting a hypothesis of $\mu \geqslant 240$ sheets is just about impossible, while if in reality $\mu = 399.99$ sheets, the probability of wrongly accepting a hypothesis of $\mu \geqslant 240$ is extremely likely.

Table 12-2 provides values of $\beta$ for a range of values of $\mu$ for a hypothesis of $H_0: \mu \geqslant 240$ against $H_1: \mu \geqslant 240$ at $\alpha = 0.05$. Note that the Z-values are negative when actual $\mu$ exceeds our critical value of 238.77, and that $\beta$ is calculated by finding the area to the left of the (negative) Z-value and taking this away from 1. The reason for this will be obvious if you mentally shift the lower two curves in Fig. 12-3 to the right to have a value of $\mu$ above 238.77. So what use are the data in Table 12-2? If we were a bulk purchaser of toilet rolls we would have to evaluate this brand against competing brands on price per roll, delivery, quality and, of course, average number of sheets. Now if in our evaluation the brand is on average a sheet lower than the claimed 240 sheets, there is a good chance (Table 12-2—probability $= 0.62171$) of our accepting the average as 240 or more when in fact it is 239. But if one sheet less is of little importance to our decision, then this does not matter. If a sheet was critical to our decision, then the fact that $\beta$ was high would be of concern. Alternatively, if being three sheets under on average was a serious cause for concern, i.e. if actual $\mu = 237$ when we accepted $H_0: \mu \geqslant 240$, Table 12-2 tells us not to worry since the probability of this occurring is very small, at $\beta = 0.00914$.

Actual $\mu$ (horizontal axis) and $\beta$ (vertical axis) are often graphed to show what is called an

**Table 12-2**  Probabilities of accepting and rejecting $H_0$ for a range of actual values for toilet roll example

| If actual $\mu$ is | $Z = \dfrac{238.77 - \mu}{4.1/\sqrt{30}}$ | Operating characteristic: probability of wrongly accepting $H_0$, $\beta$ | Power: probability of correctly rejecting $H_0$ |
|---|---|---|---|
| 237 | 2.36 | 0.00914 | 0.99086 |
| 237.5 | 1.70 | 0.04457 | 0.95543 |
| 238 | 1.03 | 0.15150 | 0.8485 |
| 238.5 | 0.36 | 0.35942 | 0.64058 |
| 239 | −0.31 | 0.62172 | 0.37828 |
| 239.5 | −0.73 | 0.76730 | 0.23270 |
| 240 | −1.64 | 0.9495 | 0.05050* |

*Probability of wrongly rejecting $H_0: \mu \geqslant 240$.

operating characteristic curve. We might also consider a power curve, which is a graph of $(1 - \beta)$ against actual $\mu$. The power figures are given in Table 12-2. $\beta$ is the probability of accepting $H_0$ when the actual $\mu$ are obviously outside $H_0$: $\mu \geqslant 240$ (i.e. it should not be accepted). The power figures are $(1 - \beta)$ and must be the probability of rejecting $H_0$ when the actual $\mu$ are obviously outside $H_0$: $\mu \geqslant 240$ (i.e. it should be rejected). The power of a test is the probability that a test will correctly reject a hypothesis for a different value of $\mu$, and statisticans compare the power efficiency of different tests to see which is most suitable. It is of interest that when actual $\mu$ is greater than or equal to 240, the power becomes the probability of rejecting $H_0$ when the actual $H_0$ is true, i.e. the probability of rejecting a true hypothesis is a type I error given by $\alpha$. We see from Table 12-2 that when $\mu = 240$, $\alpha = 0.0505$ or approximately a 5 per cent level of significance.

## SOME NON-PARAMETRIC TESTS

So far our tests have been concerned with statistics such as the mean, or standard deviation, or correlation coefficient, that have required an interval or ratio scale of measurement. For some tests assumptions of normality and equality of variances have been involved. As mentioned in Chapter 6, tests relying on an interval or ratio scale of measurement belong to a body of statistics called *parametric statistics*. However, for variables measured on an ordinal or nominal scale *non-parametric* statistical techniques are employed. No assumptions of normality are required for such methods and they are often referred to as *distribution-free* techniques. In Chapter 6 Spearman's correlation, Cramer's $V$, Kendall's tau, etc., were examples of non-parametric methods. We also employed some tests of hypotheses for association for variables on ordinal (Spearman's) and nominal (chi-squared—Cramer's $V$) scales of measurement. Non-parametric methods and tests are not new to us. However, while we covered measures of association in Chapter 6 (parametric and non-parametric), it seems appropriate to look at non-parametric tests here for measures of one-sample tests and comparisons between samples. First we look at central tendency as an illustration: that is, having looked at the parametric mean, we now turn to the non-parametric median, which only requires an ordinal scale of measurement.

### Testing hypotheses about a single median (Wilcoxon one-sample signed rank test and the sign test)

Consider a claim that if confidence in the managing director (MD) was scored on a 1 (very poor) to 10 (very good) scale by all employees of a large company, the median score would be less than or equal to 5. A random sample of 13 employees was taken and their scores were found to be: 8, 5, 4, 6, 3, 1, 7, 5, 5, 6, 2, 8, 6. The test is to be conducted at a 5 per cent level of significance and will be one-tailed since the claim is being made by a realistic supporter of the MD. If a higher claim was remotely feasible it would have been made. The value of the population median is denoted by the symbol $\eta$ (eta). The test assumes that the distribution of individual population values around the median is symmetrical (not *normal*, just symmetrical) as for example in Fig. 12-4. If it is not symmetrical the sign test is used, as discussed later.

1. $H_0$: $\eta \leqslant 5$,   $H_1$: $\eta > 5$.
2. $\alpha = 0.05$.
3. $n = 13$; Wilcoxon one-sample signed rank test.
4. The calculated value of the Wilcoxon statistic, $W$, is given by first subtracting the hypothesized value from the value of each observation; if any values are zero, eliminate them, i.e. subtracting

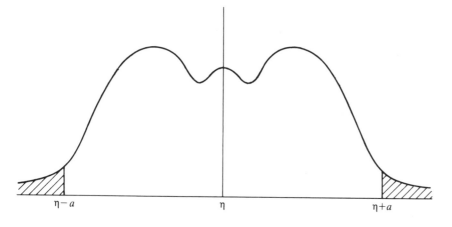

**Figure 12-4**  A symmetrical distribution

5 from each observation

$$3, 0, -1, 1, -2, -4, 2, 0, 0, 1, -3, 3, 1$$

eliminating the zeros:

$$3, -1, 1, -2, -4, 2, 1, -3, 3, 1$$

Arrange the resulting values in increasing order, *ignoring the signs on each value when determining the order*:

$$-1, 1, 1, 1, -2, 2, 3, -3, 3, -4$$

Set up a ranking scale of $1, 2, \ldots, n$: in this case $n = 10$. If there are tied values, use an average of the ranking as illustrated for Spearman's correlation in Chapter 6. For example, here the first four values are tied '1' (ignoring the signs), which would normally occupy places $1, 2, 3, 4$: since they are equal we say they are equivalent to $(1+2+3+4)/4 = 2.5$. Places 5 and 6 are occupied by two 2s (ignoring signs), giving them values of $(5+6)/2 = 5.5$ each; places 7, 8 and 9 are occupied by three 3s (ignoring signs), giving them places $(7+8+9)/3 = 24/3 = 8$ each; place 10 is occupied by a 4 (ignoring signs). We thus have:

$$2.5, 2.5, 2.5, 2.5, 5.5, 5.5, 8, 8, 8, 10$$

Needless to say, if tied values do not occur the process is much simpler. Now, having ignored the signs in the preceding step we replace them: the first was minus 1, so we start with minus 2.5; the second plus 1, we have plus 2.5, etc.:

$$-2.5 + 2.5 + 2.5 + 2.5 - 5.5 + 5.5 + 8 - 8 + 8 - 10 = 3$$

$W$ = the modulus of sum of the signed ranks = 3. Each individual $i = 1, 2, \ldots, n$ signed ranked observation is denoted by $R_i$ and

$$W = \Sigma R_i \tag{12-16}$$

For $n < 10$ there are special tables to test the statistical significance of the null hypotheses (Conover, 1980). However, for $n \geqslant 10$ the normal distribution provides a good approximation. (Note: we do need to assume that the results are normally distributed, we just use the tables.) The test statistic is given by:

$$\frac{\Sigma R_i}{\sqrt{\Sigma R_i^2}} = \frac{W}{\sqrt{\Sigma R_i^2}}$$

$$\Sigma R_i^2 = (-2.5)^2 + (2.5)^2 + (2.5)^2 + (2.5)^2 + (-5.5)^2 + (5.5)^2 + (8)^2$$
$$+ (-8)^2 + (8)^2 + (-10)^2 = 377.5.$$

The test statistic is thus:

$$\frac{3}{377.5} = 0.0079$$

We compare this with a 5 per cent level for a one-tailed test which, from Appendix 7, is 1.64. Since $0.0079 < 1.64$ we do not reject the hypotheses that the MD's confidence rating is 5 or less at a 5 per cent level of significance.

We should at this stage think back to an assumption of the method; that is, the population values can be assumed to be symmetric about the median. You may have good reason to believe this not to be the case. For example, some employees may have suffered particularly because of the MD's views or policies—this not being counterbalanced by an equal number having benefited particularly well. The sample data may give credence to this. An alternative test for the median is the *sign test*, which does not require the assumption of symmetry, but is less powerful than the Wilcoxon one-sample test. In our previous example, let us suppose that we have good reason to doubt the symmetry. Let us also assume that the data collected were for a random sample of 33 employees:

$$2, 4, 3, 8, 6, 7, 5, 4, 3, 10, 7, 4, 7, 6, 2, 1, 10, 6, 3, 4, 5, 3, 1, 7, 2, 6, 8, 4, 9, 3, 9, 2, 1$$

We can remove those observations that coincide with the critical value of 5. For the sign test we determine the proportion of observations in the sample above the claimed value in the hypothesis, i.e. there were 14 out of the remaining 31 observations above 5, i.e. $14/31 = 0.4516 = p$. Under our null hypothesis we would expect the proportion of observations above the median to be 0.5 by definition. We can use our test for proportions. We are now comparing a claimed proportion with an hypothesized one and we can use a Z-test if $np \geqslant 5$ for $p \leqslant 5$ ($np = 14$); the test statistic is given by:

$$Z = \frac{p - \pi}{\sqrt{\pi(1-\pi)/n}} = \frac{0.4355 - 0.5}{\sqrt{0.5(1-0.5)/31}} = -0.718$$

Before we continue with the test, we ask why 0.4516 has turned into 0.4355? This is because we are using a Z-test that is for a continuous normal distribution; our data are discrete so we need a continuity correction. If $p$ is greater than 0.5 the correction is to add 0.5 to the numerator of $p$; if it is less than 0.5 we subtract it. In our case $p = 14/31 = 0.4516$; therefore we use $p = (14-0.5)/31 = 0.4355$.

For a one-tailed test, where $Z = 1.64$ from Appendix 7 at a 0.05 level of significance, we do not reject the hypothesis that the median is less than or equal to 5 at a 5 per cent level. Note that while we have used the normal distribution the test itself is distribution free, requiring no assumption of anything following a normal distribution. The test is less sensitive to differences (a more 'conservative' test) though it is employed here because we have doubts about the symmetry. In fact, if we did not reject with the Wilcoxon test it is not likely that we would have done so with a more conservative test. However, there might be circumstances in which Wilcoxon wrongly applied to non-symmetric data would reject a hypothesis when the more appropriate sign test would not. Yet, given the conservative nature of the test for small samples, too much should not be read into a failure to reject. Small sample versions of the sign test procedure are given in Sprent (1990).

### Testing hypotheses about the differences between two populations: ordinal scale (Mann–Whitney test)

We have already considered testing the differences between two means where the variable is measured on an interval scale. But what if the scale is ordinal, or, for small samples, what if the normality assumptions or the equality of variance assumptions, or both, are not valid? We use the *Mann–Whitney test* (also called the *Wilcoxon rank-sum test*). The null hypothesis is that the two populations are identical, so rejection could be because either their means, variances or the shape of the distributions differ, or any combination of these. The test can be applied to quite small samples, that is, where both $n_1 > 10$ and $n_2 > 10$, where $n_1$ and $n_2$ are the respective sample sizes. The methodology and a copy of appropriate tables for critical values are given in Anderson *et al.* (1987). For larger sample sizes (either $n_1 > 20$ or $n_2 > 20$) the normal distribution can be used (though we need no assumption about normality).

Consider, for example, an interviewer's assessment of a particular skill for a random sample of two sets of applicants for a job, the first set without formal qualifications and the second with formal qualifications (the interviewer being unaware of this information). There are 21 applicants in the first set and 7 in the second, and the interviewer ranks them in order of merit (1 = best), the data being given in Table 12-3.

1. $H_0$: The two populations are identical with respect to the skill.
   $H_1$: The two populations are not identical with respect to the skill.
   The hypotheses are formulated for a two-tailed test, given no information on which set would be expected to perform better.
2. $\alpha = 0.05$.
3. $n_1 = 21$, $n_2 = 7$; large sample Mann–Whitney using $Z$-tables.
4. $Z$ from tables is $\mp 1.96$ for a two-tailed test, $\alpha = 0.05$.
5. We calculate the $T$-values by summing the ranks of the separate sets of applicants as in Table 12-3. Had any applicants been tied, the average of their rankings would have been used for each applicant. We use a normal distribution for the test where:

$$\mu = n_1(n_2)/2 = 21(7)/2 = 73.5$$

$$\sigma = \sqrt{((n_1 n_2)(n_1 + n_2 + 1))/12} = \sqrt{(21(7)(21 + 7 + 1))/12} = 18.848$$

$$U = T_2 - (n_2((n_2 + 1)/2)) = 96 - 7((7+1)/2) = 68$$

or $(T_1 - (n_1((n_1 + 1)/2)))$, whichever is the smaller (the sample with small ranked values or numbers of observations will yield the smallest $U$, i.e. using $T_2$ and $n_2$)

and

$$Z = \frac{U + 0.5 - \mu}{\sigma} = \frac{68 + 0.5 - 73.5}{18.848} = -0.265$$

Since $0.265 < 1.96$ (ignoring signs) we do not reject the hypothesis at a 5 per cent level that the two sets of applicants are drawn from the same population with regard to the skills considered. If there are many tied values a correction is necessary, though there were none in this case, but details of the correction are available in Sprent (1990).

**Table 12-3**  Mann–Whitney test

| Applicant | Ranking combined | Qualifications | Without qualifications | With qualifications |
|-----------|------------------|----------------|------------------------|---------------------|
| A | 1 | No | 1 | |
| B | 2 | Yes | | 2 |
| C | 3 | Yes | | 3 |
| D | 4 | No | 4 | |
| E | 5 | No | 5 | |
| F | 6 | No | 6 | |
| G | 7 | Yes | | 7 |
| H | 8 | No | 8 | |
| I | 9 | No | 9 | |
| J | 10 | No | 10 | |
| K | 11 | No | 11 | |
| L | 12 | No | 12 | |
| M | 13 | Yes | | 13 |
| N | 14 | No | 14 | |
| O | 15 | No | 15 | |
| P | 16 | No | 16 | |
| Q | 17 | No | 17 | |
| R | 18 | No | 18 | |
| S | 19 | No | 19 | |
| T | 20 | Yes | | 20 |
| U | 21 | No | 21 | |
| V | 22 | No | 22 | |
| W | 23 | No | 23 | |
| X | 24 | Yes | | 24 |
| Y | 25 | No | 25 | |
| Z | 26 | No | 26 | |
| AA | 27 | Yes | | 27 |
| AB | 28 | No | 28 | |
| | | | $T_1 = 310$ | $T_2 = 96$ |

Note that our test concerns whether or not the two populations differ; with the parametric tests our concern was with whether the means differ. The Mann–Whitney test is thus much more general, any difference found possibly being due to differences in the means, variances or shape of the distribution. It is of course preferable to test for these separately, so we gain greater insight into why the populations differ. However, for small samples this *may* require invalid assumptions and in any case interval scale data. Mann–Whitney is more general and less powerful in its conclusions, but more flexible in the circumstances in which it can be used.

### Testing techniques

As with parametric techniques, a host of non-parametric tests exist to cover a range of situations (see Neave and Worthington, 1988, and Sprent, 1990). We have already discussed parametric tests for matched paired comparisons, the non-parametric equivalent being the Wilcoxon signed-rank test, a variation of the one-sample test considered earlier. This test, unlike the parametric small sample equivalent, requires no assumptions of normality. Our non-parametric equivalent of ANOVA mentioned earlier for comparing means across more than two populations is the

Kruskal–Wallis test (for independent samples) or Friedman test (for matched dependent samples); and, of course, there are many more.

It thus becomes important to choose your test carefully. Identify what facet of the data you want to test—means, medians, variances or whatever. For the test, determine if the data are nominal, ordinal, or interval using the principles discussed in Chapter 6. These will help to guide you to the use of parametric or non-parametric tests. For parametric tests in particular, you have to consider if any assumptions they make are valid, and if not adopt non-parametric equivalents.

In all of this we should not lose sight of the nature of the exercise, which is to establish if claims about means, medians, differences between means, variances, populations, etc., can be supported by the data when account is taken of sampling error. For large samples, where there is little variability in values, as explained in Chapter 11, there is very little sampling error. The difference between what is claimed and what is found to be statistically significant at, say, the 5 per cent level may be of little interest, given that sampling errors are so small, and all that 'statistical significance' is concerned with is whether the difference between what is claimed and what is found is over and above that which may be due to sampling errors. We can make too much of statistical significance in such cases, and ignore the question as to whether the difference is large enough to have practical policy implications. Yet where sampling errors are of a magnitude likely to have a practical impact on what is being claimed, these tests are critical for we cannot allow claims to appear to be substantiated by results from samples that are swamped with sampling errors.

## USING COMPUTERS

### Lotus 1-2-3

There are no specific functions in Lotus 1-2-3 for these tests apart from those concerning the regression coefficient for which the coefficient and the standard error of each coefficient is provided; the former divided by the latter provides the calculated $t$-value to be compared with one from tables, all of which is described in Chapter 6. However, Lotus 1-2-3 is particularly useful with 'what if?' calculations. If a calculated $Z$-value is given by:

$$Z = (\bar{X} - \mu)/(s/\sqrt{n})$$

and we want to see how sensitive the results are to changes in $s$, a range of possible values for $s$ may be entered in A1..A8. The calculation (e.g. $\bar{X}=5$, $\mu=6$, $n=100$) is entered in B1 as $+(5-6)/(A1/10)$. The result is /Copy, copied for this entry to B2..B8 to yield the different values of $Z$ arising from the different values of $s$.

### Minitab

Tests of significance are provided for regression results including $p$-values as described in Chapter 6. In addition, a range of tests are provided:

```
MTB > Z TEST 4 3 C1
```

undertakes a $Z$-test on the data in C1 on the assumption it is a random sample to test the hypothesis that $\mu=4$ when $\sigma=3$. If only one figure is included (i.e. 4 is dropped) the test will assume the null hypothesis is that $\mu=0$. If you want to use the sample standard deviation this can be derived using DESCRIBE C1, before moving to the test. The output from ZTEST includes the sample size, mean and standard deviation of the sample, the standard error and the Z-value as well as a p-value. The p-value tells you the probability of obtaining from a normal distribution a value as extreme (as large in magnitude) as the Z-value, or more extreme. Thus, a p-value of 0.06 would tell you that a test at a 0.05 (5 per cent) level has been failed in the sense that we cannot reject the null hypothesis at this level.

```
MTB > TTEST 4 C1
```

performs a t-test using the data in C1 to test the null hypothesis that $\mu = 4$. The sample standard deviation is used for the test, and if the '4' is dropped, the test is for $\mu = 0$. The output is similar to that for ZTEST

```
MTB  > TWOSAMPLE 99 C1 C2;
SUB C > POOLED.
```

will undertake a two-sample (independent) t-test at a 1 per cent significance level (the default is 5 per cent) the inclusion of the POOLED subcommand being the assumption of equal population variances, its absence not requiring this assumption.

In *all* of the above tests a two-tailed test is carried out unless the subcommand ALTERNA-TIVE $= K$ is used. For a one-sample test if $K = -1$ (ALTERNATIVE $= -1$) the alternative hypothesis (for a hypothesized mean of 5) is $H_1: \mu < 5$ and for $K = +1$, $H_1: \mu > 5$. For two sample tests, $K = -1$ gives $H_1: \mu_1 < \mu_2$ and $K = +1$ gives $H_1: \mu_1 > \mu_2$.

Though only referred to in this text, but not covered, Minitab undertakes analysis of variance (ANOVA). It also contains a variety of non-parametric tests.

```
MTB  > WTEST 4 C1;
SUB C > ALTERNATIVE=+1.
```

undertakes a one-sample Wilcoxon signed-rank test for $H_0$: Median $< 4$ against $H_1$: Median $> 4$.

```
MTB  > STEST 4 C1;
SUB C > ALTERNATIVE=+1.
```

undertakes a sign test of the above hypothesis for the median.

```
MTB  > MANN-WHITNEY 99 C1 C2;
SUB C > ALTERNATIVE=-1.
```

does a two-sample rank test where the samples are independent, and while $H_0$, as described earlier, allows us to consider if they are drawn or not drawn from the same population, the formulation here is with regard to the median and the subcommand ALTERNATIVE $= -1$ allows an implicit alternative hypothesis for the medians of $\eta_1 < \eta_2$. The rankings are sorted for one sample in C1 and the other in C2 before the analysis.

Kruskal–Wallis test and the Friedman test referred to in the text can also be carried out on Minitab.

## EXERCISES

**12-1** The British judicial system is based on the principle of a person being innocent until proven guilty. In reaching a verdict what are the type I and type II errors associated with the verdict and the implications of these errors?

**12-2** Workers have been arriving late back from lunch, claiming it takes them at least 15 minutes on average to queue and be served in the canteen. Formulate null and alternative hypotheses to test this claim and describe how you would collect the necessary data. The canteen manager claims it only takes on average at most 10 minutes to queue and be served.

Formulate appropriate hypotheses to test this claim and reconcile this formulation with the formulation of the claim by the workers.

**12-3** A brand of correction fluid is labelled as containing 30 ml of fluid. Formulate appropriate hypotheses to test this claim, providing a justification for your use of either a one-tailed or two-tailed test as you deem appropriate. The contents of a random sample of 45 bottles were measured, finding a mean of 29.1 ml and a standard deviation of 0.5 ml. Test the manufacturer's claim at a 5 per cent level of significance.

**12-4** A car manufacturer produces a limited edition car (2000 cars only) with a petrol consumption claim of an average of 15 miles per litre (m.p.l.). You test a random sample of 10 of these cars and find $\bar{X} = 12$ with $s = 2$, where $s$ is calculated using $s^2 = \Sigma(X_i - \bar{X})^2/n$. Test the manufacturer's claim at a 1 per cent level of significance.

**12-5** Management have been claiming that bonuses paid to workers in a plant have averaged £1000. You take a random sample of 100 workers from the 1000 employed in the plant and find bonuses to average only £600, with a standard deviation of £100. Using a test at a 5 per cent level of significance comment on management's claim. Had 3000 people been employed and had the same sized sample been taken with the same results, would your conclusion be any different?

**12-6** You produce widgets which must be of a certain length and you know from past production that the standard deviation of the length of widgets is 0.005 inch. A customer has complained that a large consignment of widgets delivered are, on average, 5 inches long when they should be 4.95 inches. You take a random sample of 25 widgets from the consignments and, together with the customer, measure them to find a mean of 4.955 inches. Test the customer's claim at a 1 per cent level of significance.

**12-7** A nuclear waste disposal factory is planned to be set up near your back yard. The company claims that it has the support of the majority of the local community because of the jobs it will create in an area of high unemployment. You think otherwise, but they cite the results of a survey they conducted based on a random sample of 100 local residents, finding the proportion in favour of the new factory being set up to be 0.51. Have they proved their claim? Conduct your tests at both a 1 per cent and 5 per cent level of significance.

**12-8** A delivery company claims 95 per cent of their parcels under their 'special' service are delivered the same day in Britain if posted before 10 am. You post 50 parcels at randomly chosen posting points to regions randomly chosen in Britain. You find the proportion delivered the same day to be 0.92. Using tests at a 1 per cent level of significance, is their 'special' service as special as they claim? Could they claim your test is inappropriate because of your choice of posting points and destinations?

**12-9** Flowerpots are made in two (manufacturing) plants, known respectively as the Bill and Ben plants. The mean number of pots made per worker per day, with associated standard deviations based on the sample sizes given, are:

|       | $\bar{X}$ | $s$ | $n$ |
|-------|-----------|-----|-----|
| Bill  | 100       | 4   | 45  |
| Ben   | 105       | 4   | 60  |

Do you note any difference in the labour productivity of the two plants at a 5 per cent level of significance?

**12-10** A new type of storage unit is claimed to increase the average storage life of fruit sold, via a new type of cooling system. You randomly select 80 grade I items of a type of fruit, store 40 of them in the new and existing systems, and monitor their life until they can no longer be classified as grade I. For the new system the mean life was 30 days with $s = 1$ days compared with the old system which had a mean of 25 days with $s = 3$ days. Does the new system produce an improved average storage life at a 5 per cent level of significance?

**12-11** Under a training scheme the graduate intake are supposed to do better than the non-graduate intake in the final assessment. However, the non-graduate intake are claimed to have a lower variability in their assessment, the graduate intake being very variable and, in this sense, a less reliable bet. The variances of these marks for a random sample of 15 graduates and non-graduates are, respectively, 10 and 6 per cent. Is this evidence of a difference in variability at a 1 per cent level of significance?

**12-12** Five applicants for a job score the following marks on an assessment of their technical and personal skills. Is there any difference in the mean scores at a 1 per cent level of significance?

| Applicant | Personal skills (%) | Technical skills (%) |
|-----------|---------------------|----------------------|
| A         | 20                  | 35                   |
| B         | 50                  | 48                   |
| C         | 60                  | 70                   |
| D         | 65                  | 68                   |
| E         | 70                  | 78                   |

**12-13** Two brands of the same product are test marketed with the proportion of males preferring brand X over brand Y, being 0.6 compared with 0.55 for females, based on random samples of 200 males and 150 females. Is there any difference in the views of the different sexes on the two brands at a 5 per cent level of significance?

**12-14** You manufacture screws and a large DIY chain buy large quantities of your $3\frac{1}{2}$-inch brass variety. From past trials you know the standard deviation of the length is 0.01 inch. You plan to take random samples of 40 screws to test this hypothesis about the size of the screws, since the DIY store has expressed concern that the screws are, on average, a little on the short side. If your random sample yielded a mean of 3.49 inches does this support your claim that the mean length is $3\frac{1}{2}$ inches at a 5 per cent level of significance? Derive a table of the operating characteristics of the test, yielding values of $\beta$ for a range of actual $\mu$.

# PART
# TWO

## TEST YOURSELF

# 13

## WORKED EXAMPLES

# QUESTIONS

### CHAPTER 1—OBTAINING DATA: SECONDARY SOURCES

**1-1** The Research Department of a dairy products processing company for which you work has come up with, what to your mind, is a breakthrough—powdered eggs that taste like the real thing. The Marketing Department is reporting back on their hall tests. These involved renting a hall in Birmingham City Centre and asking passers-by if they would be willing to take part in a test for 10 minutes for market research, for a fee of £5.00. The report found that the blind tests were quite favourable with regard to taste, *but even given this*, as the Marketing Manager emphasized, 80 per cent stated they would not buy the product instead of fresh eggs. When you queried the composition of the sample you were told it was composed of 60 women. The marketing manager advises you to drop the project on the basis of these results. What concerns might you have over the validity of the results?

### CHAPTER 2—OBTAINING DATA: PRIMARY SOURCES AND SURVEY METHODOLOGY

**2-1** You are President of the Institute of Chartered Charterers with 31 215 full members and 1383 student members. To become a full member you have to pass a difficult set of examinations after which, as long as you pay an annual fee, you are eligible to practice. There are then many opportunities for lucrative work. The Royal Society of Charterers is a less formal body primarily made of academics researching in the area and a few practitioners (who are always Institute members) who have an interest in, what appears to most Institute members to be, the esoteric side of Charterism. There are talks underway of merging the two bodies and you want to survey your members (including the students) as to their views. You think a sample of 1000 members is appropriate and have collected the information given in the table since you believe views may vary according to age, sex and type of membership.

| Membership and sex | Age band | | | | | |
| | Under 25 | 25–34 | 35–44 | 45–54 | 55–64 | Total |
|---|---|---|---|---|---|---|
| Full member | | | | | | |
| Male | 1 972 | 6 430 | 5 335 | 4 019 | 3 698 | 21 454 |
| Female | 1 254 | 4 862 | 3 010 | 625 | 10 | 9 761 |
| Student member | | | | | | |
| Male | 642 | 25 | 6 | 0 | 0 | 673 |
| Female | 649 | 31 | 25 | 5 | 0 | 710 |
| Total | 4 517 | 11 348 | 8 376 | 4 649 | 3 708 | 32 598 |

The committee has voted to put aside sufficient funds to allow for a sample of 1400 members to be surveyed by post and the results analysed, and have designed a simple questionnaire which meets their aims and objectives. How would you select the composition of your sample and what contingency plans might you make for non-response error?

2-2 Your company has a showroom for Rover cars. You are thinking of using an advertising board alongside a very busy road to advertise the Metro. This road is the main artery for just about all traffic into the city where your dealership is located and you are more generally interested in the type of cars driven along this road as an indicator of your local market. To determine if it is worthwhile advertising you need an idea as to how much of the 'right type' of traffic goes by. How would you find this out?

## CHAPTER 3—PRESENTING NUMERICAL INFORMATION

3-1 The table below shows changes in trade union membership in Great Britain for male and female employees and self-employed for 1989 and 1990. You are required to draw up a single chart to broadly indicate to the lay public changes between 1989 and 1990 in trade union membership for employees and self-employed of each sex.

Trade union membership*

| | | 1989 | | 1990† | |
| | | TU member | Not TU member | TU member | Not TU member |
|---|---|---|---|---|---|
| Employees: | Men | 5217 | 6649 | 5152 | 6788 |
| | Women | 3351 | 6838 | 3303 | 7008 |
| Self-employed: | Men | 256 | 2351 | 261 | 2366 |
| | Women | 59 | 760 | 68 | 776 |

*Includes staff associations.
†Preliminary estimates at time of writing.
*Source*: Central Statistical Office, *Employment Gazette*, April 1991, Table 15.

3-2 The data in the table show the highest and lowest share prices achieved by the 10 water companies in England and Wales between 1 January 1991 and 31 July 1991. Analysts are interested in how the range between high and low prices has varied between companies. Portray the data in an easy-to-read, visually attractive form.

| Company | High | Low | Company | High | Low |
|---------|------|-----|---------|------|-----|
| Anglia | 383 | 331 | Southern | 397 | 293 |
| North West | 387 | 322 | Thames | 394 | 323 |
| Northumbria | 406 | 327 | Welsh | 422 | 341 |
| Severn Trent | 370 | 300 | Wessex | 456 | 325 |
| South West | 392 | 308 | Yorkshire | 401 | 335 |

## CHAPTER 4—SUMMARY MEASURES

**4-1**  The following table shows the number of unemployed in Great Britain in Spring 1990 according to their age band for men and women.

| Age (years) | Number of unemployed (thousands)* | |
|-------------|------|-------|
| | Men | Women |
| 16–19 | 144 | 105 |
| 20–24 | 194 | 132 |
| 25–34 | 278 | 222 |
| 35–49 | 227 | 217 |
| 50–59 | 162 | 85 |
| 60–64 | 67 | † |
| All aged 16 and over † | 1073 | 761 |

*Estimated from Labour Force Survey using International Labour Office's definition of unemployment as described in source. Figures are preliminary estimates.

†Includes here only those prior to pensionable age, 60 for women, 65 for men.

*Source*: Central Statistical Office, *Employment Gazette*, April 1991, Table 16, p. 190.

(a) Calculate the (arithmetic) mean, median and standard deviation ages of male and of female unemployed using the above data.

(b) Interpret your results, drawing attention to differences in the ages of male and female unemployed.

**4-2**  You run management training courses in London, one of which is aimed at teaching managers how to use spreadsheets. Each course involves 20 managers and lasts for two days. Over the last two weeks you have run three such courses, each course being run by a different lecturer. At the end of each course the managers are asked to rate the overall performance of the lecturer on a 1 (useless) to 10 (perfect) scale. The ratings for each of the lecturers by their 20 managers are given below:

| | | | | | | | | | | | | | | | | | | | | |
|--|--|--|--|--|--|--|--|--|--|--|--|--|--|--|--|--|--|--|--|--|
| Lecturer A: | 8 | 9 | 4 | 5 | 8 | 7 | 4 | 8 | 8 | 5 | 10 | 7 | 6 | 8 | 9 | 7 | 8 | 8 | 5 | 4 |
| Lecturer B: | 6 | 7 | 8 | 9 | 6 | 8 | 9 | 6 | 7 | 6 | 7 | 7 | 8 | 6 | 6 | 5 | 7 | 8 | 6 | 7 |
| Lecturer C: | 5 | 6 | 5 | 5 | 5 | 6 | 7 | 10 | 6 | 5 | 5 | 6 | 7 | 5 | 5 | 9 | 6 | 6 | 5 | 5 |

Summarize the data on each lecturer to facilitate comparisons between their overall performance.

## CHAPTER 5—INDEX NUMBERS

**5-1** Your company, Aussie Toys Ltd, manufactures and sells two products for the UK market, 'stuffed kangaroos' and 'cuddly wombats'. The price ($P$), quantity sold ($Q$) and sales value ($V$) are given below for 1990 to 1992.

|  | 1990 | | | 1991 | | | 1992 | | |
|---|---|---|---|---|---|---|---|---|---|
| Product | $P$ | $Q$ | $V$ | $P$ | $Q$ | $V$ | $P$ | $Q$ | $V$ |
| Stuffed kangaroo | 8 | 6.40 | 51.2 | 10 | 6.5 | 65.0 | 9 | 5.3 | 47.7 |
| Cuddly wombat | 10 | 10.08 | 100.8 | 12 | 9.5 | 114.0 | 11 | 6.9 | 75.9 |

(a) Calculate: (i) Laspeyres price index, (ii) Paasche price index and (iii) Fisher's 'ideal' price index for the overall sales of the company.

(b) Calculate: (i) Laspeyres quantity index, (ii) Paasche quantity index and (iii) Fisher's 'ideal' quantity index for the overall sales of the company.

(c) Comment on the results for (a) and (b), paying particular attention to any differences between the results for the different formulae.

**5-2** The average earnings index for employees working in education and health services is given below along with the Retail Prices Index for 1988 to 1990. How has the earnings of these employees changed in real terms?

|  | Average earnings index, education and health services (1988 = 100) | Retail Prices Index, all items (13 Jan. 1987 = 100) |
|---|---|---|
| 1988 | 100.0 | 106.9 |
| 1989 | 108.6 | 115.2 |
| 1990 | 118.0 | 126.1 |

All indices are annual averages, with the exception of the reference period for the RPI which is 13 January 1987.
*Source*: Central Statistical Office, *Employment Gazette*, July 1991, Tables 5.3 and 6.4.

## CHAPTER 6—MEASURES OF ASSOCIATION

**6-1** You sell single long-stemmed, boxed, red roses that are sent by post to loved ones for only £9.99, including post and packaging. You advertise in a number of newspapers and magazines and, while the response is very good, you are unsure as to whether sales are sensitive to price. Recently you have experimented by varying the price for a week at a time to see the extent to which price and sales are associated. The results are given in the first two columns of the table. [The data on advertising will be used in the Questions in Chapter 7.]

| Price (£) | Sales (number sold) | Advertising (£) |
|---|---|---|
| 8.99 | 496 | 1 795 |
| 9.50 | 465 | 1 756 |
| 9.99 | 482 | 2 805 |
| 10.50 | 459 | 2 218 |
| 10.99 | 408 | 1 965 |
| 11.50 | 382 | 2 285 |
| 11.99 | 315 | 1 089 |
| 12.50 | 363 | 1 888 |
| 12.99 | 309 | 1 430 |

Draw a scatter diagram and calculate the product moment correlation coefficient for the above variables. Specific attention should be devoted to the interpretation of your results and making clear any assumptions implicit in your study.

6-2 You have eight trainees who, as part of their in-house training, have each completed a project. These have been sent to the Managing Director who has ranked them in order of merit (1 = best).

You are interested in whether variation in this ranking is associated with variation in their academic background. Using the data given in the table, is there an association?

| Trainee | MD ranking | Qualifications |
|---|---|---|
| A | 1 | BSc 2(i) |
| B | 2 | 3 'A' level GCEs grade A, C, D |
| C | 3 | 3 'A' level GCEs grade A, A, C |
| D | 4 | OND (BTEC) |
| E | 5 | BSc 2(ii) |
| F | 6 | OND (BTEC) |
| G | 7 | MSc |
| H | 8 | 3 'A' level GCEs grade C, C, D |

6-3 The following data show trade union membership in (Spring) 1990 for the 22.251 million employees by sex. Are sex and trade union membership independent?

|  | Men | Women | Total |
|---|---|---|---|
| Member of trade union* | 5 152 | 3 303 | 8 455 |
| Not a member* | 6 788 | 7 008 | 13 796 |
| Total* | 11 940 | 10 311 | 22 251 |

*Includes staff associations.

*Source*: Central Statistical Office, *Employment Gazette*, April 1991, Table 15, from CSO, Labour Force Survey time series estimates.

## CHAPTER 7—REGRESSION ANALYSIS

7-1 Using the data on sales of roses and prices given in Question 6-1, estimate an appropriate regression equation and interpret your answer.

**7-2** Using again the data in Question 6-1, but this time also including the data on advertising expenditure, estimate, using either Lotus 1-2-3 or Minitab, a multiple regression of sales on prices and advertising expenditure. Interpret your answer.

## CHAPTER 8—TIME SERIES AND FORECASTING

**8-1** You have discovered that some rich, middle-aged people seem to enjoy spending at least some of their vacations in remote places in uncomfortable conditions and are willing to pay a lot for such 'holidays'. You have formed a company called Adventure Holidays Co. Ltd and since 1987 have traded quite handsomely. Indeed, the more you cut costs, making the conditions unpleasant, the more they seem to enjoy it. You have noticed a strong seasonality to your growing company and wish to establish its nature and extent. Using Classical Decomposition, provide estimates of the trend, seasonality and residuals of the following data, commenting on how satisfactorily the data fit your model.

| Date | No. of holidays taken | Date | No. of holidays taken |
|------|------|------|------|
| 1987: Q1 | 12 | 1990: Q1 | 30 |
| Q2 | 25 | Q2 | 65 |
| Q3 | 56 | Q3 | 160 |
| Q4 | 33 | Q4 | 50 |
| 1988: Q1 | 16 | 1991: Q1 | 38 |
| Q2 | 40 | Q2 | 75 |
| Q3 | 82 | Q3 | 175 |
| Q4 | 37 | Q4 | 63 |
| 1989: Q1 | 28 | 1992: Q1 | 45 |
| Q2 | 58 | Q2 | 77 |
| Q3 | 102 | Q3 | 209 |
| Q4 | 41 | Q4 | 82 |

**8-2** Using the above data and suitable software, such as Lotus 1-2-3 or Minitab, derive the multiple regression equation of number of holidays on time trend (1, 2, 3, ..., 24), and three seasonal dummies for each of Q1, Q2 and Q3 (e.g. D1 = 1 if Q1, 0 otherwise). Using this model, derive predicted (ex-post) values for the period 1987: Q1 to 1992: Q4 and graphically compare these predictions with your results from Question 8-1. Forecast the number of holidays for 1993.

## CHAPTER 9—PROBABILITY

**9-1** Customers of A Company Ltd have a choice to settle their accounts on an annual or biannual basis. The payment method varies between credit card, cheque and cash. A breakdown of the current payment methods is given below:

| Number of customers settling accounts | Payment | | | |
|------|------|------|------|------|
| | Credit card | Cheque | Cash | Total |
| Annually | 15 | 52 | 10 | 77 |
| Biannually | 18 | 108 | 20 | 146 |
| Total | 33 | 160 | 30 | 223 |

Find the probability that a randomly selected customer:
(a) pays either by credit card or biannually;
(b) pays both by credit card and biannually;
(c) pays annually by cheque or annually by cash or biannually by credit card.

**9-2** You organize open-air concerts. The probability that it will rain on your concert in two days time is, from past patterns, 0.3. A private company is selling forecasts based on sunspot activity. They claim their forecasts of rain are correct in 80 per cent of cases, and forecast of 'no rain' correct in 70 per cent of cases. If they forecast it will rain, what is the probability that it will (assuming you believe in the use of sunspot activity for this purpose)?

**9-3** (a) You have two alternatives, established, investment opportunities you can buy into: the first is a rock concert at Wembley Stadium, London for a (yet another) final concert by an established rock band. The arrangements have been made by accident to coincide with the day of the Final of the World Cup football match and it is considered that England has a 1 in 5 chance of getting through to the Final. An additional complication is that there is considered to be a probability of 0.1 that it might be discovered that the lead singer of the band has for years donated money to Conservative Party funds and invested in South Africa and (what were) Brazilian rain forests. If this is discovered ticket sales for the concert would plummet. If England don't get through to the Final the return on the investment would be £20 000 compared with £10 000 if they do. If the truth about the lead singer is revealed the return will be £2000 if England don't get through, and £1200 if England do. Alternatively, you can invest in 'official' England World Cup souvenirs which are believed will yield (for the same sum invested) £3000 if England don't win through to the Final, but £30 000 if they do. It is thought that any revelations about the lead singer will have hardly any effect on souvenir sales. What should you do?

(b) If the story about the lead singer was discovered by a journalist prior to your investment decision, how much would you be prepared to contribute to bribe the reporter not to publish the story? You should for the purpose of this question leave aside ethical issues or concerns about being found out.

## CHAPTER 10—PROBABILITY DISTRIBUTIONS

**10-1** As the manager of an up-market shoe shop you find that a profitable aspect of the business is to sell shoe care kits alongside the sale of the shoes '. . . to keep your new shoes in good condition'. For every 10 customers, 5 will buy the kit. You have left the shop in the control of a new assistant for a short period and on your return check the purchase patterns of the last 10 customers who bought shoes, only to find no sales of the shoe care kit. The assistant insists that all refused. What do you think?

**10-2** You sell computer software by direct mail from a specialized mailing list of potential customers. Each week 400 letters and brochures are sent out and, on average, 26 respond favourably with a purchase. If purchases drop to 18 or less you do not cover the costs of mailing and make a loss. What is the probability of this occurring?

**10-3** There are a large number of Personal Computers (PCs) in your organization, mainly of the same type. Experience from PCs of the same make, model, age and specification is that the average annual number of faults to expect is 0.08. If a model is selected at random, what is the probability that it will not develop a fault in the forthcoming year?

**10-4** There are a large number of sales representatives in your organization, all of whom have their own car. They all undertake substantial mileage on the same make and model of company car. The miles per gallon (m.p.g.) varies depending on, among other things, the style of driving, condition of the car, and type of route taken. Past experience shows the distribution of average m.p.g. for your drivers to be normally distributed. The latest figures show a mean of 32.15 m.p.g. and a standard deviation of 1.1 m.p.g.
(a) What is the probability of a driver averaging 28 m.p.g. or less?
(b) Within what range of m.p.g. would you expect the middle 95 per cent of your drivers to fall?

## CHAPTER 11—ESTIMATION

**11-1** A survey of household expenditure on newspapers has been conducted for a town in the UK. The survey results were based on a simple random sample of 100 households and found the mean annual expenditure per household to be £70.2 and the standard deviation £20.2. What statement can you make about the mean expenditure of all households in the region on newspapers using (a) a 95 per cent confidence interval and (b) a 99 per cent confidence interval?

**11-2** A credit card company is to undertake a sample survey of the average (mean) time between receipt of a payment and it being processed. The survey is to be conducted over the next month. It receives about a million payments a year. A previous study found a standard deviation of 4 hours. An estimate at a 95 per cent level of confidence is required. The company has in mind an acceptable error margin for the results of plus or minus 15 minutes, but would like to see something of the trade-off between the increased costs of a larger sample and the decrease in the error margin arising from it. The fixed costs for the survey are £2000, there being an additional cost of £2 per payment sampled. Advise the company on sample size.

**11-3** You have started a new airline service and you conduct a simple random sample of 35 of your 120 passengers as to their views of the service. One question relates simply to whether they would use the service again, 'yes or no'; and 40 per cent said 'yes'. Using 95 per cent confidence intervals what can you say about the proportion of passengers who might say 'yes'.

**11-4** A routine task is performed hundreds of times by each of your 200 workers every day. One day you take a simple random sample of 25 tasks and find the mean time taken for the task to be 1.12 minutes with an (unbiased) standard deviation of 0.1 minute. What can you say with 95 per cent confidence about the average time taken of all tasks during that day?

**11-5** On a production line, 50 ml bottles are filled with ink. Every hour a sample (35 bottles) is taken and the volume of ink measured. Over the past weeks these measures have been relatively stable, with a mean of 49.001 ml and a standard deviation of 0.0042. Your most recent results for the last six hours are, in turn: 49.0010, 49.0015, 48.9975, 49.0020, 48.9972. Have you cause for concern?

## CHAPTER 12—TESTING HYPOTHESES

12-1  You are trying to sell your products via direct mail and have bought a list of names and addresses of prospective customers from a list brokerage. They inform you that, at most, 2 per cent of your mailing will be returned 'not known at this address' or 'address unknown', or whatever. You start your mailing on a trial basis with a simple random sample of only 40 addresses and find 3 returned on the above basis. What can you conclude about the above claim by the list brokerage that, at most, only 2 per cent will be returned?

12-2  You are responsible for a museum in the UK which depicts how people lived in American history, each room showing a different scene. You have always preferred rooms relating to native American Indians and have asked your senior staff to consider having a further such room to replace the eighteenth-century Virginian living room. Your senior staff are quite annoyed by such an idea and insist that visitors spend on average at least 3.5 minutes in the room, which is quite impressive by the standards of this museum. You monitor a simple random sample of 25 visitors and find a mean of 2.9 minutes with an unbiased standard deviation of 1 minute. Do the results of your sample support the claim by the senior staff?

12-3  Range Chickens Ltd is a major manufacturer of processed chickens. They have decided to explore the introduction of an additive into the feed to increase water retention, and thus weight, and thus profits. The additive was given to half of the chickens on a random basis. All chickens live and die under the same regime except insofar as some have the additive and some do not. A simple random sample of 75 chickens is examined after processing and 31 are traced to having had the additive while the remaining 44 did not. Those with the additive have a mean weight of 3.4 lb and unbiased standard deviation of 0.4 lb, while those without have a mean of 3.01 lb with an unbiased standard deviation of 0.35 lb. Are chickens reared with the additive heavier?

12-4  You are supplied with a large number of components made to an identical specification. You may notice from the prefix to the serial number that some of the components are produced by the supplier's plant in Cardiff, and some by the plant in Leeds. You suspect the proportion of defective components to be higher for those produced in Leeds as compared with Cardiff. A simple random sample of 600 components from Cardiff are identified and tested and are found to have a rejection rate ($p_1$) of 0.015 compared with $p_2 = 0.017$ for an equal sample of 600 components tested from Leeds. Is the difference between these rejection rates statistically significant at a 1 per cent level?

# ANSWERS

## CHAPTER 1—OBTAINING DATA: SECONDARY SOURCES

1-1  The answer will pay attention to the potential sources of error in survey design followed by the interpretation and conclusion reached by the marketing manager on the basis of the figures.

  *Sampling error*  For the project to go ahead the 80 per cent unfavourable response was deemed too high, suggesting that a lower percentage would have made the project viable. It is necessary to be aware of what that lower percentage is to enable us to test whether the difference between the 80 per cent found and the actual percentage needed for the project to be viable has resulted from sampling error. The formal methods by which this can be judged are given in Chapter 12. For our purpose we bear in mind that, with a sample of 60, there may be a relatively high margin of sampling error.

*Non-response error*   The non-respondents (those who refuse to take part) are likely to be in a rush (lunch break) or better-off (the financial incentive not being sufficient). We need to know the extent of the non-response and then make a judgement as to the nature of the bias. Those in a rush may have a stronger preference for the product than those who participated because of the convenience nature of the product. However, this might be counterbalanced by the richer people preferring the real thing.

*Response error*   We know little of the phrasing of the question and the context in which it was asked. The respondents were aware that the new product was being tested and thus might have been more favourably predisposed to the product in order to 'help out'. Alternatively, it might be that they were unwilling to admit that they would buy a down-market product such as powdered eggs, when in fact it would be quite suitable for their needs, and they would.

*Design error*   The sampling frame used was everyone who passed the hall at the time of the test. Shoppers in Birmingham may well have different preferences from the rest of the country. The time of day the test was conducted might also affect the result, depending on whether it includes lunch hours with office workers having a preference for convenience foods relative to those not in paid employment. The selection of only women from the frame is curious, especially since men may well have stronger preferences for convenience foods. The age composition of the sample would be critical since older women with memories of powdered eggs from the Second World War will have quite different views from younger people brought up on the concept of convenience foods. We need to have much more information on the selection process.

*Interpretation of results*   The decision not to continue because 80 per cent would not buy the product instead of fresh eggs needs comment. First, we know little of the views of the remaining 20 per cent. If there are no 'don't knows' and 20 per cent would switch, given the size of the market this represents a potentially highly successful product. Second, the product may extend to those who said they would not switch, for use as a back-up to fresh eggs. Third, the effect of marketing has yet to play a role with, possibly, the product being given a more up-market image. More generally the conclusions arrived at extend beyond what the results of the data permit. We have no knowledge of user patterns in that the sample may have been biased towards light, medium or heavy users of eggs. It might be the case that the 20 per cent willing to switch to powdered eggs are heavy users of eggs; indeed, their heavy usage is one reason why they prefer the powdered variety. Again, we have no idea as to the reasons why most would not switch. They would have no knowledge of whether the product was cheaper than fresh eggs, though this would be assumed to be the case.

*Summary*   The above is indicative of the lines along which answers should proceed. A lot of the analysis incorporates a subjective component. However, this is the reality of challenging results of other people's surveys and ascertaining bias. Your answer might include quite different facets from the above or interpret some of the above differently. The moral is that when undertaking market research you should start by trying to identify possible sources of error and design the survey to minimize the effects of such errors. There are many other factors that would normally be part of such research to give further insights into the market. Such hall tests remain a major part of market research in the UK and elsewhere.

## CHAPTER 2—OBTAINING DATA: PRIMARY SOURCES AND SURVEY METHODOLOGY

2-1    It is reasonable to assume that the Institute has a mailing list of its members which is quite up to date since membership fees are necessary for eligibility to practice. The President believes that views will vary according to age, sex and membership status. If this were so the sample of 1000 would be distributed as follows (where, for example, full member, male under $25 = (1972/32\,598) \times 1000 = 60$):

|  | Age band | | | | | |
|  | Under 25 | 25–34 | 35–44 | 45–54 | 55–64 | Total |
|---|---|---|---|---|---|---|
| Full member |  |  |  |  |  |  |
| Male | 60 | 197 | 164 | 123 | 113 | 658 |
| Female | 38 | 149 | 92 | 19 | 0 | 299 |
| Student member |  |  |  |  |  |  |
| Male | 20 | 1 | 0 | 0 | 0 | 21 |
| Female | 20 | 1 | 1 | 0 | 0 | 22 |
| Total | 139 | 348 | 257 | 143 | 114 | 1000 |

Points to note:

- Use stratified random sampling, selection of the sample within each strata being by simple random sampling.
- The sampling frame must have information on sex, age, and type of membership.
- If information on differential variability of views is available, we may use Neyman allocation, which draws proportionately larger samples from strata in which views are more variable.
- We should seek information as to whether views are likely to vary between all strata unless the above categorization does not involve too much administrative work.
- A pilot survey may be necessary to check the questionnaire and possibly help with above two points.
- The results for individual strata will be based on small sample sizes and are likely to suffer from severe sampling error, especially those relating to student members and some age categories of female full members. If the views of student members are considered important and are believed to be quite variable, a disproportionately large sample might be required, the results for each strata then being appropriately weighted.
- Allowance has to be made for a non-response rate and sending out a proportionately larger sample may not be an adequate solution, since non-respondents may be indifferent to merger and the results that ignored non-respondents would be distorted. Estimates of non-respondent rates would be necessary and a smaller sample size than 1000 should be used since resources would be necessary for follow-up letters and telephone calls. The views from the responding follow-ups should be monitored and allowed to represent the views of all non-respondents in a particular strata.

2-2    There may be more than one acceptable approach to this question. Certain factors need to be taken into account.

- The type and method of collecting data. This involves devising a classification scheme for the 'right' type of cars (which models of which makes), details of age of car, number plate and model (different), sex of driver, etc. The method of collecting data may involve a camera or person for each side of the road. If it is a person, data entry may be directly into electronic form via a remote device, or manually on pre-prepared coded sheets to facilitate subsequent entry onto a computer. If it is via camera, the data will be transcribed from the video playback. For detailed information on a busy road, cameras mounted in appropriate positions might be the only reliable method that has the advantage of being able to be checked for validity.

- The number and type of car used will vary according to the time of day, day of week, and week. Indeed, not all weeks can be analysed due to time constraints and guesstimates for seasonal variations will be necessary. Depending on resources and time available, a design has to be set up which allows data to be representative. For example, you might decide patterns of traffic to be similar on Tuesdays and Wednesdays and Thursdays, and randomly select a morning, afternoon and evening from these days, while monitoring all of Monday, Friday, and the weekend. You will also have to consider if the particular week chosen is likely to have unusually heavy or light traffic flows.
- The use of the data for market analysis should bear in mind that some of the traffic will not comprise residents of your catchment area. Your advertising will then put sales into other Rover dealers' pockets and your analysis possibly misrepresent the market if, for example, sales in neighbouring catchment areas (possibly due to inferior Rover dealers) are biased away from your cars.

More formally the sampling frame is 'all periods of time in, say, the forthcoming year'. The sample design involves choosing periods from the frame and the sample size is the number of periods chosen. Each observation is of very short duration and with manual collection, a feature of the design is that a random sample of, for example, ten second periods cannot be chosen, it being more economical to employ someone to monitor traffic for discrete long periods. This way we obtain large samples, but in discrete blocks. If a camera was mounted to continuously monitor traffic for a year (without supervision), the message being sent to a separate recording facility, then a mechanism could be developed to stop the play at randomly selected intervals, and record the composition of traffic.

Alternatively, a random sample of residents could answer a survey question that included information about their car, the route taken, and many more salient issues, which would probably be much more satisfactory.

## CHAPTER 3—PRESENTING NUMERICAL INFORMATION

3-1   There are a number of acceptable approaches to this question, some not outlined here, and there is a judgemental element governing their choice. However, bar charts are preferred to line charts because of the discrete nature of the categories, and pie diagrams are not used since it is easier to compare the length of lines to areas. The change over time is the feature of interest. As such, comparisons for each category are made with 1989 alongside the corresponding bar for 1990, as shown in Fig. 13-1. Alternatively, we might not have dealt with the absolute figures, but percentage trade union membership in each category, thus removing the need for stacked bars. Yet again we might decide that interest really lies in the percentage change in the membership between 1989 and 1990, with eight bars, one for each combination of sex, employment status and trade union membership.

Figure 13-1 shows very little change between 1989 and 1990 in any of the categories, which

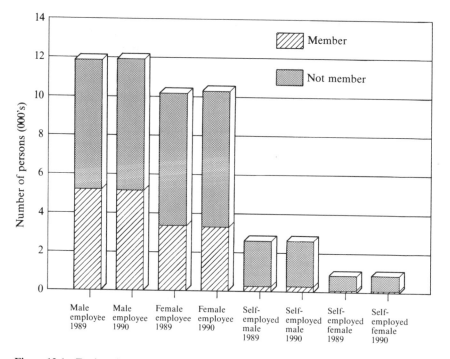

**Figure 13-1**  Trade union membership in Great Britain 1989 and 1990

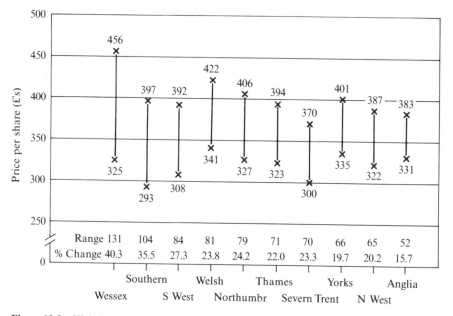

**Figure 13-2**  High–low water share prices

is an accurate reflection of the data. The dispirit sizes of the categories are shown, which some of the alternative measures discussed above would not.

**3-2**  Figure 13-2 is again but one of a number of ways of displaying the data. The companies are ordered along the horizontal axis according to the width of the range. Exact information might be required, and to aid the analysis the range (High minus Low) and percentage change $(((\text{High}-\text{Low})/\text{Low})\times100)$ from the Low is given along with the individual prices. Since our interest lies in how the range of prices varies between companies, we use an artificial starting point to the scale of 250. High–low (close-open) charts of a technical nature are used by financial analysts and are available in Lotus 1-2-3, though we assume here that these are *not* required.

## CHAPTER 4—SUMMARY MEASURES

**4-1**  (a) Working out the mid-points for age bands is a little awkward. For example, 16–19 includes all of 16, 17, 18 and 19:

|  | start | start | start | start | end |
|---|---|---|---|---|---|
|  | 16 | 17 | 18 | 19 | 19 |

The start of 18 is the mid-point.

| Mid-point $X$ | Men $f_m$ | Women $f_w$ | $f_m X$ | $f_w X$ | $f_m X^2$ | $f_w X^2$ |
|---|---|---|---|---|---|---|
| 18 | 144 | 105 | 2 592.0 | 1 890.0 | 46 656.00 | 34 020.00 |
| 22.5 | 194 | 132 | 4 365.0 | 2 970.0 | 98 212.50 | 66 825.00 |
| 30 | 278 | 222 | 8 340.0 | 6 660.0 | 250 200.00 | 199 800.00 |
| 42.5 | 227 | 217 | 9 647.5 | 9 222.5 | 410 018.75 | 391 956.25 |
| 55 | 162 | 85 | 8 910.0 | 4 675.0 | 490 050.00 | 257 125.00 |
| 62.5 | 67 |  | 4 187.5 |  | 261 718.75 |  |
| Total | 1 072 | 761 | 38 042.0 | 25 417.5 | 1 556 856.00 | 949 726.25 |

*For men*:

Mean $=\Sigma f_m X/\Sigma f_m=(38\,042/1072)=35.49$ years.

$$\text{Standard deviation} \quad =\sqrt{\frac{\Sigma f_m X^2}{\Sigma f_m}-\left(\frac{\Sigma f_m X}{\Sigma f_m}\right)^2}$$

$$=\sqrt{\frac{1\,556\,856}{1072}-\frac{38\,042}{1072}}=13.89 \text{ years.}$$

Median: Median class interval is one which contains the $((n+1)/2)$th observation, i.e. $1073/2=536.5$th observation, i.e. 25–34.

$$\text{Median} \quad =L_m+C_m\left[\frac{(n+1)/2-F_{m-1}}{f_m}\right]$$

$$=25+10\left[\frac{1073/2-338}{278}\right]=32.14 \text{ years}$$

where $F_m - 1$ is the cumulative frequency of the interval before the median class interval (144 + 194); $L_m$, $C_m$, $F_m$ are the lower value, width and frequency of the median class interval.

Results for women are given below, calculated in the same way.

|  | Men | Women |
|---|---|---|
| Mean | 35.49 | 33.40 |
| Median | 32.14 | 31.51 |
| Standard deviation | 13.89 | 11.51 |

(b) The mean age of unemployed men is higher than that for women, though not substantially so, and there is hardly any difference in the median ages, though these are lower at 32.14 and 31.51 years respectively. The differences between the means and medians reflect a positive skewness, the extent of the skewness being greater for men than women, possibly reflecting the effect on the figures of differential pensionable ages (Pearson's coefficient of skewness, 0.72 and 0.49 for men and women respectively). The skewness reflects the absence of extremely young unemployed (less than 16) due to school requirements, not matched by older unemployed who may find it difficult because of their age to obtain employment. Ages of unemployed women are less dispersed than those of men, again in part reflecting the inclusion of 60–64-year-old men (if they were excluded the standard deviation would be 12.41).

**4-2** There are a number of approaches to this question, some of which are given below:

| | Number of ratings | | |
|---|---|---|---|
| Ratings | Lecturer A | Lecturer B | Lecturer C |
| 4 | 3 | | |
| 5 | 3 | 1 | 10 |
| 6 | 1 | 7 | 6 |
| 7 | 3 | 6 | 2 |
| 8 | 7 | 4 | |
| 9 | 2 | 2 | 1 |
| 10 | 1 | | 1 |

(a) *Frequency tables* The method clearly summarizes the patterns without loss of information and allows comparisons between lecturers with respect to central tendency, dispersion and skewness, though these are not accurately determined. For example, the average will obviously be lowest for Lecturer C, but it is not immediately apparent how A and B will compare on average. The dispersion of A's ratings are the highest with B less so, and C's managers are relatively consistent, though positively skewed. The method readily allows identification of outliers, a couple of managers really rated C. Thus, while A may score well on average, the wide dispersion suggests that he or she is leaving some people behind. B's more consistent record might be preferred, and C's position is less attractive.

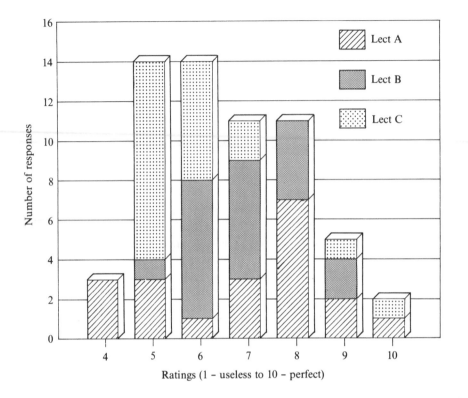

**Figure 13-3**  Ratings of lecturers

(b) *Stacked-bar chart*  The data in the frequency table can be presented as a stacked-bar chart depending on the need for visual impact and the type of audience. The stacked-bar chart, shown in Fig. 13-3 is but one of a number of graphical methods discussed in Chapter 3, an alternative being a multiple bar chart.

(c) *Box plots*  The box plots in Fig. 13-4 are produced by Minitab. The crosses are the medians showing Lecturer A to have the highest median, closely followed by B with C having a very poor median (5.5). The edges of the boxes (I) are the hinges and are normally equivalent to the quartiles. The narrow spread of rating for Lecturer C is conspicuous, as is the dispersed rating for A. The dashed lines of whiskers show the data extending from the quartiles quite substantially for Lecturer A, less so for B and only slightly for higher values (positive skew) for C. The * and O represent possible and probable outliers respectively. The box plots capture the features of the frequency table in a more visually identifiable form, though it is based on summary measures such as the median and hinges which, rather than display the actual data, summarize its features.

(d) *Summary measures*  Here we use a more extensive range of actual summary measures than in box plots, and because we use the measures rather than read them off the box plot (which Minitab labels poorly), comparisons are more accurate, though less visually attractive. The results are given in the table.

LECTURER

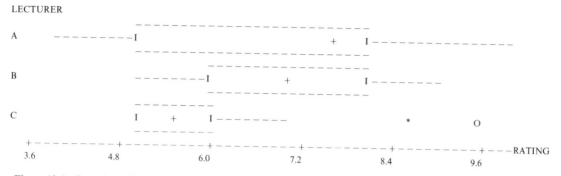

**Figure 13-4**  Box plots of lecturers' ratings

|  | Lecturer A | Lecturer B | Lecturer C |
|---|---|---|---|
| Arithmetic mean | 6.9 | 6.95 | 5.95 |
| Median | 7.5 | 7.00 | 5.50 |
| Standard deviation | 1.786 | 1.0712 | 1.359 |
| First quartile (Q1) | 5 | 6 | 5 |
| Third quartile (Q3) | 8 | 8 | 6 |
| Minimum | 4 | 5 | 5 |
| Maximum | 10 | 9 | 10 |

The above patterns can be identified from the table: the positive skewness of C by the mean being pulled above the median, though for B the distribution is symmetrical, while for A there is a clear negative skew. As noted above, the ratings for A are more dispersed than C, which in turn is more dispersed than B according to the standard deviation, though $(Q3-Q1)/2$ shows C's rating to be less dispersed than B's once we discount the extreme 25 per cent at each end. Thus, while on the median (given the only slight differences between A's and B's mean ratings) we would consider A the best lecturer, the high dispersion of results suggests that there is a tail of dissatisfied customers (albeit counterbalanced by highly satisfied ones). Lecturer B is the softer bet, and C the worst.

The calculations can be illustrated in Table 13-1. The ratings have been ranked and the value of the $((n+1)/2)$th $= (20+1)/2 = 10.5$th observation is the median; for Lecturer A, between 7 and 8, i.e. 7.5, for Lecturers B and C the result is 7 and 5.5 respectively.

The mean is derived by summing the observations (summing the ranked observations gives the same results) to yield for A, 138; B, 139; and C, 111, and then dividing by the number of observations.

$$\frac{\Sigma X_A}{n} = \frac{138}{20} = 6.9$$

$$\frac{\Sigma X_B}{n} = \frac{139}{20} = 6.95$$

**Table 13-1**  Ranked and squared values for lecturers' ratings

| Row | Rank A | Rank B | Rank C | $A^2$ | $B^2$ | $C^2$ |
|-----|--------|--------|--------|-------|-------|-------|
| 1 | 4 | 5 | 5 | 16 | 25 | 25 |
| 2 | 4 | 6 | 5 | 16 | 36 | 25 |
| 3 | 4 | 6 | 5 | 16 | 36 | 25 |
| 4 | 5 | 6 | 5 | 25 | 36 | 25 |
| 5 | 5 }Q1 | 6 | 5 | 25 | 36 | 25 |
| 6 | 5 | 6 | 5 | 25 | 36 | 25 |
| 7 | 6 | 6 | 5 | 36 | 36 | 25 |
| 8 | 7 | 6 | 5 | 49 | 36 | 25 |
| 9 | 7 | 7 | 5 | 49 | 49 | 25 |
| 10 | 7 }Median | 7 | 5 | 49 | 49 | 25 |
| 11 | 8 | 7 | 6 | 64 | 49 | 36 |
| 12 | 8 | 7 | 6 | 64 | 49 | 36 |
| 13 | 8 | 7 | 6 | 64 | 49 | 36 |
| 14 | 8 | 7 | 6 | 64 | 49 | 36 |
| 15 | 8 }Q3 | 8 | 6 | 64 | 64 | 36 |
| 16 | 8 | 8 | 6 | 64 | 64 | 36 |
| 17 | 8 | 8 | 7 | 64 | 64 | 49 |
| 18 | 9 | 8 | 7 | 81 | 64 | 49 |
| 19 | 9 | 9 | 9 | 81 | 81 | 81 |
| 20 | 10 | 9 | 10 | 100 | 81 | 100 |
| | 138 | 139 | 119 | 1016 | 989 | 745 |
| | $=\Sigma X_A$ | $=\Sigma X_B$ | $=\Sigma X_C$ | $=\Sigma X_A^2$ | $=\Sigma X_B^2$ | $=\Sigma X_C^2$ |

$$\frac{\Sigma X_C}{n} = \frac{119}{20} = 5.95$$

$$s_A = \sqrt{\frac{\Sigma X_A^2}{n} - \left(\frac{\Sigma X_A}{n}\right)^2} = \sqrt{\frac{1016}{20} - \left(\frac{138}{20}\right)^2} = 1.786$$

$s_B$ and $s_C$ are calculated in a similar manner.

Q1$_A$ is the value of the $((n+1)/4)$th observation, i.e. $(20+1)/4 = 5.25$th, a quarter of the way along the interval 5 to 5, which is of course 5. Q1$_B$ and Q1$_C$ are calculated in a similar manner. Q3$_A$ is the value of the $(3(n+1)/4)$th observation, i.e. $3(20+1)/4 = 15.75$th, three-quarters of the way along the interval 8 to 8, again easy to calculate, in this case, 8. Q3$_B$ and Q3$_C$ are calculated in a similar manner.

## CHAPTER 5—INDEX NUMBERS

5-1  (a) For price indices the aggregative formulae are:

Laspeyres

$$L_{b,c} = \frac{\Sigma P_c Q_b}{\Sigma P_b Q_b} \times 100$$

Paasche

$$P_{b,c} = \frac{\Sigma P_c Q_c}{\Sigma P_b Q_c} \times 100$$

Fisher's 'ideal'

$$F_{b,c} = \sqrt{L_{b,c} \times P_{b,c}}$$

(i) Laspeyres price

$$L_{90,\,91} = \frac{10(6.40) + 12(10.08)}{51.2 + 100.8} \times 100 = 121.68$$

$$L_{90,\,92} = \frac{9(6.40) + 11(10.08)}{51.2 + 100.08} \times 100 = 110.84$$

(ii) Paasche price

$$P_{90,\,91} = \frac{65.0 + 114.0}{8(6.5) + 10(9.5)} \times 100 = 121.77$$

$$P_{90,\,92} = \frac{47.7 + 75.9}{8(5.3) + 10(6.9)} \times 100 = 110.95$$

(iii) Fisher's 'ideal' price

$$F_{90,\,91} = \sqrt{121.68 \times 121.77} = 121.72$$
$$F_{90,\,92} = \sqrt{110.84 \times 110.95} = 110.89$$

(b) For quantity indices the formulae are:

| Laspeyres | Paasche | Fisher's 'ideal' |
|---|---|---|
| $L_{b,\,c} = \dfrac{\Sigma P_b Q_c}{\Sigma P_b Q_b} \times 100$ | $P_{b,\,c} = \dfrac{\Sigma P_c Q_c}{\Sigma P_c Q_b} \times 100$ | $F_{b,\,c} = \sqrt{L_{b,\,c} \times P_{b,\,c}}$ |

(i) Laspeyres quantity

$$L_{90,\,91} = \frac{8(6.5) + 10(9.5)}{51.2 + 100.8} \times 100 = 96.71$$

$$L_{90,\,92} = \frac{8(5.3) + 10(6.9)}{51.2 + 100.8} \times 100 = 73.29$$

(ii) Paasche quantity

$$P_{90,\,91} = \frac{65.0 + 114.0}{10(6.4) + 12(10.08)} \times 100 = 96.78$$

$$P_{90,\,92} = \frac{47.7 + 75.9}{9(6.4) + 11(10.08)} \times 100 = 73.36$$

(iii) Fisher's 'ideal'

$$F_{90,\,91} = \sqrt{96.71 \times 96.78} = 96.74$$
$$F_{90,\,92} = \sqrt{73.29 \times 73.36} = 73.32$$

Note that $IV = IP \times IQ$ and that:

Laspeyres price × Paasche quantity = Value index

OR

Laspeyres quantity × Paasche price = Value index

Summary table

|  | 1990 | 1991 | 1992 |
|---|---|---|---|
| Laspeyres price | 100.00 | 121.68 | 110.84 |
| Paasche price | 100.00 | 121.77 | 110.95 |
| Fisher's price | 100.00 | 121.72 | 110.89 |
| Laspeyres quantity | 100.00 | 96.71 | 73.29 |
| Paasche quantity | 100.00 | 96.78 | 73.36 |
| Fisher's quantity | 100.00 | 96.74 | 73.32 |
| Value index | 100.00 | 117.76* | 81.32† |

$*(65.0 + 114.0)/(51.2 + 100.8) \times 100$
$†(47.7 + 75.9)/(51.2 + 100.8) \times 100.$

The value index is the total value in the current period divided by the total value in 1990 multiplied by 100, given in the summary table. As such we could have eased our calculations by using the above relationships in that the answers for this part would be:

Quantity: $L_{90, 91} = (117.76/121.77)100 = 96.71$ {Value/Paasche price}
Quantity: $L_{90, 92} = (81.32/110.95)100 = 73.29$ {Value/Paasche price}
Quantity: $P_{90, 91} = (117.76/121.68)100 = 96.78$ {Value/Laspeyres price}
Quantity: $P_{90, 92} = (81.32/110.84)100 = 73.37$ {Value/Laspeyres price}.

Making use of the factor reversal test we can simplify the burden of the calculations. The same principles could have been applied to the results for Fisher's 'ideal' index since it satisfies the test: Fisher $P \times$ Fisher $Q =$ Value (try it). Thus, to simplify calculations, calculate part (a) as above, calculate the value index, and use the above relationships to deduce the results for (b). Either the approach initially used or this short-cut approach yields the correct answers and may be used to gain full marks.

(c) The summary table above shows the value of sales to have increased by 17.76 per cent in 1991 compared with 1990, but fallen by 18.68 per cent in 1992 compared with 1990, or fallen by $(1 - (81.32/117.76)100)$ approximately 31 per cent in 1992 compared with 1991. The increase in 1991 is due to an approximately 20 per cent increase in the volume sold, with prices falling slightly in the period. The substantial fall in the value of sales in 1992 has arisen in spite of an increase of nearly 11 per cent in prices (compared with 1990). The increase in prices may well have led to the over 25 per cent fall in quantity sold, which underpins the poor sales value figures for 1992.

The difference between the results of Laspeyres and Paasche is relatively small for 1991 and more apparent for 1992. Laspeyres is base period weighted (1991) and Paasche is current period weighted. For 1990 the weight or relative importance of Kangaroos was $(51.2/(100.8 + 52.2))100 = 34$ per cent of sales, the weight for 1991 was 36 per cent for 1992, 38.65 per cent. The price and quantity changes of each product were in any event similar, so even if the weights have shifted, they would be applied to similar price or quantity changes. We thus do *not* expect Laspeyres to differ much from Paasche in these circumstances, and this is what we found.

5-2 The question requires us to remove the effects of inflation from the changes in earnings to provide a measure of the changes in the purchasing power of the earnings. We can see that average earnings increased by 18 per cent between 1988 and 1990; however, because prices were also rising sharply we wish to remove the effects of inflation from (deflate) the earnings index to arrive at an index of the real (quantity) of purchasing power.

Since $I$Value $= I$Price $\times I$Quantity
$I$Quantity $= I$Value $\div I$Price.

|  | Earnings | RPI | Real earnings | RPI (1988 = 100) |
|---|---|---|---|---|
| 1988 | 100.0 | 106.9 | 100.00 | 100.00 |
| 1989 | 108.6 | 115.2 | 100.78* | 107.76 |
| 1990 | 118.0 | 126.1 | 100.03† | 117.96 |

*[(108.6/100) ÷ (115.2/106.9)]100
†[(118.0/100.0) ÷ (126.1/106.9)]100.

It seems that average real earnings have hardly changed.

It is worth noting that the RPI can be given as averages for a year as well as at a particular date in a month. In this case our reference period was for a particular date (13 January 1987 = 100), but this did not affect the calculation. We could have assigned the value of 100.0 to any date for reference. A useful date would be 1988 = 100.0 so we can easily compare the RPI with the earnings index, and this is provided as the last column of our earnings/RPI table {(115.2/106.9 = 107.76); (126.1/106.9 = 117.96)}. Real earnings could then be calculated, as before, using this new index, but since we would cancel the 100.0s, the calculation would be:

1989: (108.6/107.76)100 = 100.78
1990: (118.0/117.96)100 = 100.03 as before.

## CHAPTER 6—MEASURES OF ASSOCIATION

6-1   Theoretically we would expect a negative correlation with higher prices, leading to less sales. The correlation would be expected to be strong since flower shops may offer a similar service and customers may have more trust in them than in an anonymous advertisement. As prices increase customers may go to shops or substitute alternative gifts for the rose, such as chocolates. We would thus expect sales to be highly sensitive to price changes.

The scatter diagram is shown in Fig. 13-5. Since sales depend on price we label sales as the $Y$ variable on the vertical axis and price as the $X$ variable on the horizontal axis. The labelling does not affect the result of the correlation coefficient, but it does affect the results of the regression analysis. For our purpose it is appropriate to ignore the convention used by economists of labelling these axes otherwise. The relationship is approximately linear and negative, as expected. There are no apparent outliers. We have no reason to doubt the accuracy of the data. The design of the experiment may need further consideration since some weeks may 'naturally' have more sales than others, the extreme example being Valentine's day, though marriages (and thus anniversaries) and birthdays have seasonal patterns. This may distort the results if, for example, a decrease in price coincided with a seasonal upswing, leading us to believe that sales were more price sensitive than they are. We are not asked to take account of advertising expenditure and if, for example, this increases when price increases, it may mask the effect of the price increase leading us to underestimate the degree of association between price and sales. Both variables are measured on interval scales so we can use the product moment correlation coefficient, given by:

$$r = \frac{n\Sigma XY - \Sigma X \Sigma Y}{\sqrt{[n\Sigma X^2 - (\Sigma X)^2][n\Sigma Y - (\Sigma Y)^2]}}$$

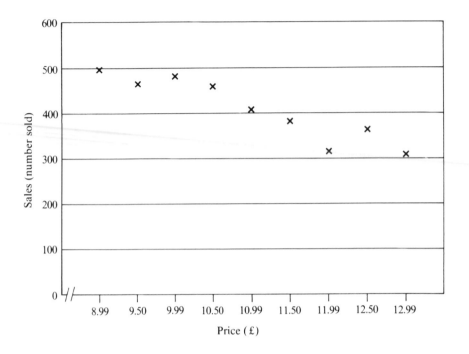

**Figure 13-5** Scatter diagram: sales on price of red roses

**Table 13-2** Calculations for examples on roses

| Prices X | Sales Y | XY | $X^2$ | $Y^2$ |
|---|---|---|---|---|
| 8.99 | 496 | 4459.04 | 80.82 | 246016 |
| 9.50 | 465 | 4417.50 | 90.25 | 216225 |
| 9.99 | 482 | 4815.18 | 99.80 | 232324 |
| 10.50 | 459 | 4819.50 | 110.25 | 210681 |
| 10.99 | 408 | 4483.92 | 120.78 | 166464 |
| 11.50 | 382 | 4393.00 | 132.25 | 145924 |
| 11.99 | 315 | 3776.85 | 143.76 | 99225 |
| 12.50 | 363 | 4537.50 | 156.25 | 131769 |
| 12.99 | 309 | 4013.91 | 168.74 | 95481 |
| 98.95 | 3679 | 39716.40 | 1102.90 | 1544.109 |

From the calculations in Table 13-2

$$r = \frac{9(39\,716.4) - 98.95(3679)}{\sqrt{[9(1102.9) - (98.95)^2][9(1\,544\,109) - (3679)^2]}}$$

$$= \frac{-6589.45}{\sqrt{(134.9975)(361\,940)}} = -0.94$$

The correlation is negative, higher prices being associated with lower sales, and vice versa. The association is also very strong. Using Table 6-3 in Chapter 6 we test if the coefficient is statistically significant at a 5 per cent level using a one-tailed test (since in theory we expected only a negative association). The critical value from Table 6-3 for $v = n - 2 = 9 - 2 = 7$ degrees of freedom for $\alpha = 0.05$ is 0.5822. Since (ignoring the sign) the calculated value $0.94 > 0.5822$ (the critical value from Table 6-3) the difference between the coefficient and zero (no association) is deemed statistically significant at a 5 per cent level.

**6-2**  We assume that data are accurate. Since the variables are measured on an ordinal (ranked) scale we use Spearman's correlation coefficient. We would in theory expect a positive association, as better projects arise from better academic education, but the nature of the projects and judgement of the MD may not guarantee this. Indeed, the scatter diagram shows little association, in particular the trainee with the MSc being judged poorly.

  We rank the qualifications as to their academic strength to yield the following ranking under 'Qualifications'. D and F are joint 7th, i.e. they are jointly allocated 7.5 instead of 7 and 8.

| Trainee | MD ranking $Y$ | Qualifications $X$ | $D^2 = (Y - X)^2$ |
|---------|----------------|--------------------|-------------------|
| A | 1 | 2 | 1.00 |
| B | 2 | 5 | 9.00 |
| C | 3 | 4 | 1.00 |
| D | 4 | 7.5 | 12.25 |
| E | 5 | 3 | 4.00 |
| F | 6 | 7.5 | 2.25 |
| G | 7 | 1 | 36.00 |
| H | 8 | 6 | 4.00 |
| Total | | | 69.50 |

Using Spearman's correlation

$$r_s = 1 - [6\Sigma D^2/(n^3 - n)]$$
$$= 1 - [6(69.50)/(8^3 - 8)]$$
$$= 1 - 0.827 = 0.17$$

We have a very weak, positive association between the two variables. However, given the small sample size the difference between the low value for Spearman's correlation coefficient and zero (no association) may not be statistically significant. Testing at the 5 per cent level, one-tailed (two-tailed only if we assume good academic ability may be a hindrance to the projects set or the bias of MD) the value from tables (Appendix 4) is 0.6190. Since this exceeds 0.17 the difference between 0.17 and zero (no association) is not statistically significant at a 5 per cent level. The data thus give no evidence of an association between the two variables.

**6-3**  The origin of the data is the Central Statistical Office's *Labour Force Survey*, the results given being preliminary estimates. There are a number of issues that would need to be investigated, including the methodology of the survey, the methods of estimation, treatment of part-time workers (included), etc., to see if there was anything in the nature of the survey that might mislead (details are given in the actual survey). In theory, membership of a trade union will vary according to type of work, with industries such as the retail trade having particularly low membership and women dominating this industry. In this case it might be argued that women are not less likely to join unions because they are women, but because they work in jobs where union participation is relatively low. Thus, an association may arise from 'third' variable effects, including earnings, skill, age, type of work, expected duration of work period. Some of these factors might be argued to lead to their being more likely to join (e.g. earnings being lower), while others less (e.g. duration of work if some plan to leave work after having children). The results by themselves of this exercise will not allow us to distinguish between these theories, and while it is beyond the scope of this book, data would need to be collected on a range of variables and membership/non-membership of a union regressed (see Chapter 7) on these variables using logit or probit models. For now we use chi-squared to test for independence between sex and trade union membership. We calculate expected values as

(Row total × Column total)/Grand total, given by the figures in brackets

|  | Men | Women | Total |
|---|---|---|---|
| Trade union member | 5 152 (4 537) | 3 303 (3 918) | 8 455 |
| Not member | 6 788 (7 403) | 7 008 (6 393) | 13 796 |
| Total | 11 940 | 10 311 | 22 251 |

$$\text{Chi-squared} = \frac{\Sigma(|O-E|-0.5)^2}{E} \text{ including Yates' correction}$$

| $O$ | $E$ | $(|O-E|-0.5)^2/E$ |
|---|---|---|
| 5152 | 4537 | 83.23 |
| 6788 | 7403 | 51.01 |
| 3303 | 3918 | 96.38 |
| 7008 | 6393 | 59.07 |
| Total |  | 289.69 |

With a 5 per cent level of significance and $(2-1)(2-1)=1$ degree of freedom the critical value from tables (Appendix 5) is 3.841. Since (the calculated value) $286.69 > 3.841$ (the critical value from tables) the difference between the calculated value of chi-squared and zero (independence) is over and above that due to sampling error. Trade union membership and sex are not independent at the 5 per cent level. As regards the strength of the association (in terms of departure from independence),

$$\text{Cramer's } V = \sqrt{\frac{\chi^2}{n(m-1)}}$$

where $n$ is the number of observations and $m$ the minimum of the number of rows ($r$) or columns ($c$); both are 2 in this case, so $m=1$ and $n=22\,251$. Thus,

$$V = \sqrt{\frac{289.69}{22\,251(1)}} = 0.11$$

A weak positive association.

This should have been apparent from the relatively low discrepancies between the observed and expected values.

## CHAPTER 7—REGRESSION ANALYSIS

**7-1**   Bearing in mind the comments made in the answers to Question 6-1, we move to the calculation:

$$b = \frac{n\Sigma XY - \Sigma X \Sigma Y}{n\Sigma X^2 - (\Sigma X)^2}$$

$$a = \frac{\Sigma Y - b\Sigma X}{n}$$

$$b = \frac{-6589.45}{134.9975} = -48.8116$$

The calculation is eased by noting that the numerator and denominator have already been calculated as major components of the calculation of the correlation coefficient.

$$a = \frac{3679 - (-48.8116(98.95))}{9} = 945.43$$

The regression equation is

$$Y = 945.43 - 48.81X$$

The intercept tells us that if the price was zero, sales would be 945, the model not providing a good forecast at this extreme point. It is better looked at as a base line level of sales against which the effects of increasing prices will have some effect. The slope coefficient is the unit change in sales that arises from a unit change in prices. If we increase prices by £1, sales will fall (negative sign) by approximately 49. This effect will occur throughout the range of the data since we assume a linear relationship which has a constant slope. If we knew something of the cost of the additional roses we could advise on the price to charge to profit maximize. The correlation coefficient of $-0.94$ deduced in the previous section gives us reason for confidence in our estimate; indeed, the coefficient of determination is $R^2 = r^2 = (-0.94)^2 = 0.8836$; i.e. 88 per cent of variation in $Y$ can be explained by variation in $X$. The results are given in Table 13.3 from Lotus 1-2-3 and give the standard error of the slope coefficient as 6.531. To test if the difference between the slope coefficient and zero (no effect) is statistically significant we calculate

$$t = b/\mathrm{SE}_b = -48.8116/6.531 = 7.47$$

The critical $t$-value from tables at $\alpha = 0.05$ for a one-sided test and $v = n - 2 = 9 - 2 = 7$ degrees of freedom is $-1.895$. Since the calculated value of 7.47 exceeds the critical value (ignoring signs) from the table of 1.895, the difference between zero and the calculated value is statistically significant at a 5 per cent level.

**Table 13-3** Lotus output on roses examples

Sales on price:
Regression Output:

| | | |
|---|---|---|
| Constant | | 945.4168 |
| Std Err of Y Est | | 25.29472 |
| R Squared | | 0.888631 |
| No. of Observations | | 9 |
| Degrees of Freedom | | 7 |
| | | |
| X Coefficient(s) | −48.81 | |
| Std Err of Coef | 6.531019 | |

Sales on advertising and price:

Regression Output:

| | | |
|---|---|---|
| Constant | | 795.4283 |
| Std Err of Y Est | | 15.7928 |
| R Squared | | 0.962789 |
| No. of Observations | | 9 |
| Degrees of Freedom | | 6 |
| X Coefficient(s) | 0.04244 | −42.5583 |
| Std Err of Coef | 0.012273 | 4.46048 |

**7-2** The results using Lotus 1-2-3 for regressing sales on price *and* advertising expenditure are also given in Table 13-3. The inclusion of advertising increases the $R^2$ from 0.8886 to 0.9628. The signs of the coefficient are what we would expect: positive for advertising expenditure as more advertising should result in more sales, and negative for price as discussed previously. The calculated $t$-values for advertising expenditure and price (ignoring signs) are $(0.04244/0.012273) = 3.458$ and $(42.5583/4.46048) = 9.541$ respectively. For the critical value at $\alpha = 0.05$, $v = 9 - 3 = 6$ degrees of freedom and a one-tailed test, we have, from Appendix 6, 1.943. Since both calculated values exceed the critical value the difference between our coefficients and zero are statistically significant at a 5 per cent level.

Note that the coefficient for price has changed slightly from the value found in Question 7-1. This reflects some multicollinearity between price and advertising, but not a serious level. Indicative of this (though by no means a good test) is that the correlation coefficient between price and advertising expenditure (not calculated here) is only 0.405. The coefficient for advertising is 0.04244 and provides an estimate that an increase of £1 on advertising expenditure will lead to an increase of 0.04244 in sales; an increase of £100 leading to an increase of 4.244 sales. Thus, while in our test of statistical significance we have found that the association between advertising expenditure and sales in this model cannot be attributed to a sampling error at a 5 per cent level, this statistical significance does not mean it is having a substantive effect. Indeed, the evidence is that although it is having an effect, commercially it is not worth the expenditure. One problem with the analysis is our lack of information on advertising expenditure. It may be that the relationship is poor because increases in advertising expenditure are spent on different forms of advertising that are relatively ineffective. The increases in expenditure may arise from increasing the size of the advertisement, the range of newspapers covered, exposure in other media, etc. More information on this will help to distinguish why the advertising expenditure is not effective.

## CHAPTER 8—TIME SERIES AND FORECASTING

**8-1**  Table 13-4 shows the results of the decomposition. Note that the figures presented have been rounded to 2 decimal places, the actual calculations being to many more places. The data on

**Table 13-4**  Decomposition of time series on holidays

| Date | No. of holidays taken ($Y$) | Moving average | Centred moving average ($T$) | De-trended ($Y/T$) | Seasonal ($S$) | Residual $Y/(T \times S)$ |
|---|---|---|---|---|---|---|
| 1987:Q1 | 12 | | | | | |
| Q2 | 25 | | | | | |
| | | 31.50 | | | | |
| Q3 | 56 | | 32.00 | 1.75 | 1.89 | 0.93 |
| | | 32.50 | | | | |
| Q4 | 33 | | 34.38 | 0.96 | 0.75 | 1.27 |
| | | 36.25 | | | | |
| 1988:Q1 | 16 | | 39.50 | 0.41 | 0.47 | 0.87 |
| | | 42.75 | | | | |
| Q2 | 40 | | 43.25 | 0.92 | 0.89 | 1.03 |
| | | 43.75 | | | | |
| Q3 | 82 | | 45.25 | 1.81 | 1.89 | 0.96 |
| | | 46.75 | | | | |
| Q4 | 37 | | 49.00 | 0.76 | 0.75 | 1.00 |
| | | 51.25 | | | | |
| 1989:Q1 | 28 | | 53.75 | 0.52 | 0.47 | 1.12 |
| | | 56.25 | | | | |
| Q2 | 58 | | 56.75 | 1.02 | 0.89 | 1.14 |
| | | 57.25 | | | | |
| Q3 | 102 | | 57.50 | 1.77 | 1.89 | 0.94 |
| | | 57.75 | | | | |
| Q4 | 41 | | 58.63 | 0.70 | 0.75 | 0.93 |
| | | 59.50 | | | | |
| 1990:Q1 | 30 | | 66.75 | 0.45 | 0.47 | 0.97 |
| | | 74.00 | | | | |
| Q2 | 65 | | 75.13 | 0.87 | 0.89 | 0.97 |
| | | 76.25 | | | | |
| Q3 | 160 | | 77.25 | 2.07 | 1.89 | 1.10 |
| | | 78.25 | | | | |
| Q4 | 50 | | 79.50 | 0.63 | 0.75 | 0.83 |
| | | 80.75 | | | | |
| 1991:Q1 | 38 | | 82.63 | 0.46 | 0.47 | 0.99 |
| | | 84.50 | | | | |
| Q2 | 75 | | 86.13 | 0.87 | 0.89 | 0.97 |
| | | 87.75 | | | | |
| Q3 | 175 | | 88.63 | 1.97 | 1.89 | 1.05 |
| | | 89.50 | | | | |
| Q4 | 63 | | 89.75 | 0.70 | 0.75 | 0.93 |
| | | 90.00 | | | | |
| 1992:Q1 | 45 | | 94.25 | 0.48 | 0.47 | 1.03 |
| | | 98.50 | | | | |
| Q2 | 77 | | 100.88 | 0.76 | 0.89 | 0.85 |
| | | 103.25 | | | | |
| Q3 | 209 | | | | | |
| Q4 | 82 | | | | | |

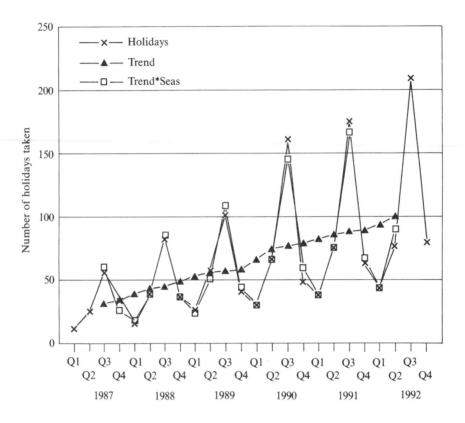

**Figure 13-6** Number of holidays taken

holidays is plotted in Fig. 13-6 and shows a multiplicative model in which the amplitude increases with the increasing trend. A 4-point moving average is appropriate, given in theory that we expect patterns to vary with each quarter, and in practice the graph shows distinct 4-period regular fluctuations. The moving average is given in Table 13-4 (e.g. $(12 + 25 + 56 + 33)/4 = 31.50$), which is centred (e.g. $(31.50 + 32.50)/2 = 32.00$) to provide the trend. The de-trended series is $Y/T$ and, since a multiplicative model is used, this leaves the seasonal elements and the residuals, i.e.

$$Y = T \times S \times R$$
$$Y/T = S \times R$$

Table 13-5 is used to derive the seasonal components by first listing in this new format, i.e. by year and quarter, the de-trended values. Unity denotes no deviation from the trend; Q1 shows an average (mean) of 0.47, a substantial fall-off in holidays in the first quarter, picking up but still below the trend in Q2 at 0.89 with Easter and early summer, and for Q3 a substantial increase above the trend near doubling the trend value at 1.89, reflecting the summer holidays, falling off again from the trend in Q4 (0.75), not to the depth of Q1, benefiting from late summer and maybe Christmas holidays. Note that all seasons are below the trend except for Q3. The average (mean) of the figures for any one quarter over a few years summarizes the patterns. However, they also serve as an estimate of the seasonal

**Table 13-5** Derivation of seasonality

|  | Q1 | Q2 | Q3 | Q4 |  |
|---|---|---|---|---|---|
| 1987 |  |  | 1.750000 | 0.960000 |  |
| 1988 | 0.405063 | 0.924855 | 1.812155 | 0.755102 |  |
| 1989 | 0.520930 | 1.022026 | 1.773913 | 0.699360 |  |
| 1990 | 0.449438 | 0.865225 | 2.071197 | 0.628931 |  |
| 1991 | 0.459909 | 0.870827 | 1.974612 | 0.701950 |  |
| 1992 | 0.477454 | 0.763321 |  |  |  |
| Sum | 2.312795 | 4.446255 | 9.381877 | 3.745343 |  |
| Mean | 0.462559 | 0.889251 | 1.876375 | 0.749069 | Total = 3.977254 |
| Adj. mean* | 0.465204 | 0.894337 | 1.887107 | 0.753353 | Total = 4.000000 |

*The adjusted means are the means multiplied by 4/3.977254. The adjustment ensures that the sum of the seasonal factors is 4. The adjusted means are the seasonal factors.

component for that quarter since the random component is to a large extent removed by averaging over the years. The means should sum to 4 (if they were on the trend they would each be unity). The difference between 3.977254 and 4 is distributed evenly between the quarters to allow for this, the adjusted means being the seasonal components. Seasonality reduces the trend of holidays by $(1 - 0.465)$, 54 per cent in Q1, 11 per cent in Q2, increases it by 89 per cent above the trend in Q3 and reduces it by 25 per cent below trend in Q4.

Table 13-4 shows the seasonal elements and the residual component, the latter being relatively small (close to unity), showing a good fit of the model to the data and showing no pattern, thus reflecting an appropriate model.

Figure 13-6 shows the series on holidays, trend and the trend multiplied by the seasonal component. As can be seen, the model fits the data very well, the random components (difference between actual and predicted) being very slight.

**8-2** The estimated multiple regression equation is given below, the output from Lotus 1-2-3 being in Table 13-6, where the exogenous (independent) variables are, in turn: T, time trend; D1 = 1 for Q1, 0 otherwise; D2 = 1 for Q2, 0 otherwise; D3 = 1 for Q3, 0 otherwise.

$$\text{HOLIDAYS} = 0.025 + 3.641T - 11.910D1 + 12.949D2 + 83.308D3$$
$$(6.133) \quad (-1.026) \quad (1.123) \quad (7.253)$$

The (adjusted) $R^2$ is 0.87, i.e. 87 per cent of variations in the number of holidays can be accounted for by the model, i.e. by trend and seasonality. The bracketed figures under the coefficients are calculated $t$-values, i.e. Coefficient ÷ Standard error from Table 13-6. The

**Table 13-6** Regression output, holidays on time and seasonal dummies

| Regression Output: |  |  |  |  |
|---|---|---|---|---|
| Constant |  | 0.025 |  |  |
| Std Err of Y Est |  | 19.86694 |  |  |
| R Squared |  | 0.870457 |  |  |
| No. of Observations |  | 24 |  |  |
| Degrees of Freedom |  | 19 |  |  |
| X Coefficient(s) | 3.641071 | −11.9101 | 12.94881 | 83.30774 |
| Std Err of Coef | 0.593638 | 11.60762 | 11.53147 | 11.48553 |

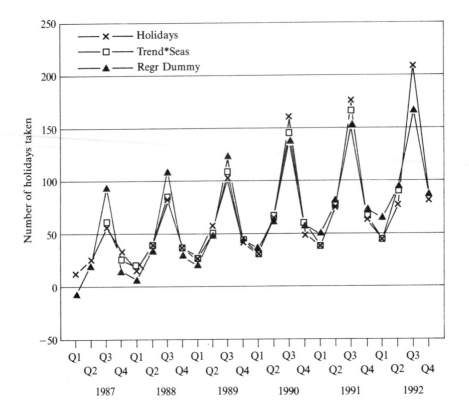

**Figure 13-7**  Number of holidays taken

critical values from Appendix 6 for $v = n - k - 1$, where $k$ is the number of exogenous variables ($v = 24 - 4 - 1 = 19$) at a 5 per cent level for a two-tailed test is 2.093. If we felt confident in theory that a one-tailed test was sufficient, the critical $t$-value is 1.729. Either way only the coefficients on T and D3 are statistically significantly different from zero (no affect) at a 5 per cent level. The signs are appropriate, increasing trend and summer increase. We cannot comment on the validity of the signs on the other coefficients since they may have arisen from sampling error. Re-estimating the model with Q1 and Q2 excluded does not improve the fit. The coefficient on T shows as a trend, that as every quarter goes by, holidays increase by about 3.6 holidays. However, the seasonal effect of moving into Q3 is to increase the number of holidays by 83 over and above what might be expected from the trend. Figure 13-7 shows the results and, as should be anticipated by the adjusted $R^2$, gives a good fit. The estimates appear to fall below actual values for Q1, Q2 and Q4, but above actual values in Q3 in the early years, the position being reversed in the later years, the model not capturing the multiplicative, non-linearity of the relationship, which is a major defect. Forecasts for 1993 are given below. [D1 and D2, though not significant, are included for illustration].
For 1993: Q1, we insert 25 for T, 1 for D1 and 0 for D2 and D3:

$$\text{HOLIDAYS} = 0.025 + 3.641(25) - 11.910(1) = 79.14.$$

For 1993:Q2, we insert 26 for T, 1 for D2 and 0 for D1 and D3:

$$\text{HOLIDAYS} = 0.025 + 3.641(26) + 12.949(1) = 107.64$$

For 1993:Q3, we insert 27 for T, 1 for D3 and 0 for D1 and D2:

$$\text{HOLIDAYS} = 0.025 + 3.641(27) + 83.308(1) = 181.64$$

For 1993:Q4, we insert 28 for T, for D1, D2 and D3:

$$\text{HOLIDAYS} = 0.025 + 3.641(28) = 101.973$$

For 1993:Q1   79 holidays
         Q2  108 holidays
         Q3  182 holidays
         Q4  102 holidays

Note from Fig. 13-7 that the forecasts would still underplay continuation of the Q3 seasonality, which is what we would expect in this case from imposing an additive linear regression model on multiplicative trend and seasonal interaction.

## CHAPTER 9—PROBABILITY

**9-1** (a) Let the event 'pay by credit card' be designated as $A$, and 'biannually' by $B$.
We want the addition (OR) rule and since $A$ and $B$ are *not mutually exclusive* (there are outcomes in common—you can pay by credit card annually) we use;

$$P(A \text{ or } B) = P(A) + P(B) - P(A \text{ and } B)$$

From the table in Question 9-1,

$$P(A) + P(B) = 33/223 + 146/223: \quad P(A \text{ and } B) = 18/223$$
$$P(A \text{ or } B) = 33/223 + 146/223 - 18/223 = 161/223 = 0.72$$

Note that the 18 customers paying biannually by credit are included in both P(A) and $P(B)$, and it is this double-counting which makes us subtract it in the third term of the formula.

(b) We want the multiplication (AND) rule and since $A$ and $B$ are *not independent* (knowing that one has occurred changes the probability of the other event occurring—for example, knowing that a person pays by credit card makes it more likely he or she will pay annually, as is obvious from the data) we use:

$$P(A \text{ and } B) = P(A) \times P(B|A)$$

From the table,

$$P(A) = 33/223; \quad P(B|A) = 18/33$$
$$P(A \text{ and } B) = (33/223) \times (18/33) = 18/223 = 0.08$$

This could have been deduced immediately from the table as 18 who satisfied the condition out of 223, the above formula illustrating the principles.

(c) $P(A \text{ or } B \text{ or } C) = P(A) + (B) + P(C)$ since mutually exclusive where $A$ is annually by cheque, $B$ is annually by cash and $C$ is biannually by credit card:

$$P(A) \text{ or } P(B) \text{ or } P(C) = (52/223) + (10/223) + (18/223) = 80/223 = 0.36$$

**9-2**    A tree diagram helps to map out the problem.

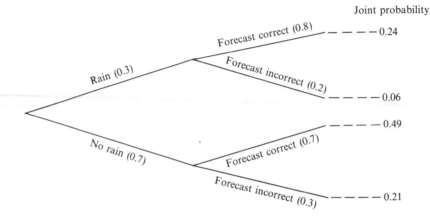

Figure 9-1 **Answer**    A tree diagram

[Check that joint probabilities sum to 1, all possible outcomes.]
    Using Bayes' theorem

$$P(A_1|B) = \frac{P(A_1) \times P(B|A_1)}{(P(A_1) \times P(B|A_1)) + (P(A_2) \times P(B|A_2))}$$

In our case, event $A_1$ is that it will rain, and $B$ that the forecast is correct. $P(A_1|B)$ is the *posterior probability*, your view of $P(A_1)$—the *prior probability*—after the information in event $B$ is taken into account:

$$P(A_1|B) = \frac{0.3 \times 0.8}{(0.3 \times 0.8) + (0.7 \times 0.7)} = \frac{0.24}{0.73} = 0.33$$

The effect of the company's forecast is to revise our prior probability of 0.3 slightly upwards. That the modification is slight reflects the less than accurate past performance.

**9-3**    (a) Basing your answer on expected values, a decision tree is useful.

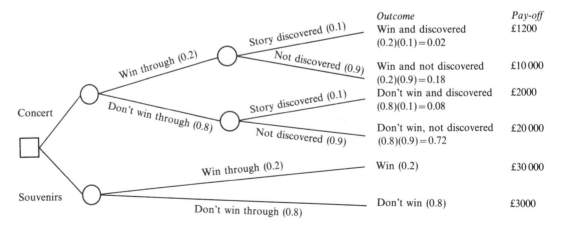

Figure 9-2 **Answer**    A decision tree

The expected return from investing in the concert is the individual probabilities of each outcome multiplied by their respective pay-offs, and summed:

$$0.02(1200)+0.18(10\,000)+0.08(2000)+0.72(20\,000)=£16\,384.$$

The expected return from investing in souvenirs is:

$$0.2(30\,000)+0.8(3000)=£8400.$$

The concert provides a much more attractive investment. Though this is based on *expected* returns, it is a type of average which takes into account the different probabilities of achieving different pay-offs. £16 384 will never be earned. It helps to provide a guide as to overall attractiveness of the project. In spite of the higher expected return from the concert, it is quite possible to have a return of £1200 or £2000 from investing in the concert, lower than the worst outcome from investing in souvenirs. Investors need not use the highest expected (discounted) income as a criterion, but may, for example, choose projects that give the highest (maximum) of the worst (minimum) outcomes (maximin criterion). In this case souvenirs would be attractive.

(b) From the tree diagram in 9-3(a) we can deduce that if we ignored the issue of whether or not the story was discovered (because we bribe the reporter) we would have two outcomes for the concert: 'win through' and 'don't win through' with their respective pay-offs and probabilities which yield an expected value of:

$$0.2(10\,000)+0.8(20\,000)=£18\,000.$$

The difference of $(18\,000-16\,384)=£1616$ is available and even if £1615 was paid towards a bribe we would still be £1 better off compared with not bribing the reporter. In addition, we would be removing the possibility of the very low incomes of £1200 and £2000 being paid, making the concert also attractive on maximin criterion.

# CHAPTER 10—PROBABILITY DISTRIBUTIONS

10-1 The random variable is the number of shoe care kits sold $(X_i)$, where $X_i=0,\ldots,10$. It can be considered to approximate a binomial distribution since the experiment of trying to sell the kit has two outcomes, and is repeated, the outcome of one not affecting the outcome of the other. It is likely that the experiments are not perfectly identical and the outcomes are not independent in that the phrasing and context of the attempt to sell will vary, and it may be that a customer seeing one being sold will affect their decision. We bear in mind that the binomial fit will not be perfectly accurate, but experience shows a good approximation can be expected.

Applying the binomial for $n=10$, $p=0.5$ for no sales $(X=0)$:

$$P(X=x)=\frac{n!}{(n-x)!x!}p^x(1-p)^{n-x}$$

$$P(X=0)=\frac{10!}{(10-0)!0!}0.5^0(1-0.5)^{10-0}$$

Since $0!=1$ and $0.5^0=1$,

$$P(X=0)=\frac{10!}{10!}0.5^{10}=0.5^{10}=0.00098$$

It seems most unlikely (though it is possible) that no sales of the kit would be made. This suggests that the assistant forgot to try to sell the kit or $p=0.5$ does not apply to the new assistant, given his (lack of) sales ability. For example, if his ability was such that overall his personal $p=0.2$, $P(X=0)=0.107$. Thus, a possible explanation is that he is not at all good at selling the kits, but he did try.

**10-2**  The random variable is the number of respondents purchasing something, $X=0, 1, \ldots, 400$. The binomial distribution will approximate since there are two possible outcomes (purchasing or otherwise) with each trial being identically repeated and independent. To apply the binomial our parameters are $n=400$ and $p=(26/400)=0.065$. Since we need to work out $P(X=0)$, $P(X=1)$, $P(X=2), \ldots, P(X=18)$ and sum these, and as this is a time-consuming task, we instead apply the normal approximation to the binomial to save on the laborious calculations. To use the normal here $np \geqslant 55$; in this case $np=26$. We thus adopt the normal for which:

$$\mu = np = 400(0.065) = 26$$
$$\sigma = \sqrt{np(1-p)} = \sqrt{400(0.065)(1-0.065)} = 4.9305$$

Applying the continuity correction since the random variable is a discrete integer and the normal is a continuous distribution, our concern is with $P(X \leqslant 18.5)$.

$$Z = \frac{18.5 - 26}{4.9305} = -1.52$$

From the tables of normal distribution in Appendix 7,

$$P(X \leqslant 18.5) = 0.0643$$

Thus, the probability of your not covering the costs by having purchases drop to 18 or less is quite low, at about 0.06.

**10-3**  The random variable is the number of faults that will develop in the year. At first sight binomial might be applied since we have only two possible outcomes, fault or no fault, and at each interval in time the experiment is repeated on a more or less identically independent basis. However, instead of the binomial the Poisson distribution is appropriate since the sampling interval is over time and there are, in theory, an infinite number of opportunities for failure to occur $(n)$ and thus $p$ can be regarded as being very close to zero.

$$P(X=x) = \frac{e^{-\mu}\mu^x}{x!}$$

$$P(X=0) = \frac{e^{-0.08} 0.08^0}{0!} = e^{-0.08} = 0.923$$

It seems quite likely that no fault will develop and this might be borne in mind in deciding on whether to purchase a warranty. Care should be exercised that the 0.08 applies to machines that are identical to yours. The 0.08 has arisen from machines that are a year older than yours, since your concern is with what happens in the forthcoming year. In practice, an estimate of $\mu$ might need to be used.

**10-4**  (a) $\mu=32.15$, $\sigma=1.10$. To find $P(X \geqslant 28)$ we apply the normal distribution. Note: we do not apply the continuity correction since data appear to be collected at 2 decimal places. The correction would be to add or deduct (as appropriate) 0.005, which is unlikely to affect the desired level of accuracy. If the raw data were integers we would be adding or deducting 0.5, which would have a more substantial affect.

$$Z = \frac{28 - 32.15}{1.10} = -3.77$$

From the tables of normal distribution in Appendix 7 the probability is very small, at around 1 in 10 000 (0.0001).

(b) We require an area of 5 per cent to be excluded, that is, 2.5 per cent or 0.025 from either tail of the distribution. We look to the body of the tables of normal distribution in Appendix 7 to find the equivalent $Z$-values to be plus or minus 1.96. The $Z$-value is:

$$Z = \frac{X - \mu}{\sigma}$$

$$\therefore \ 1.96 = \frac{X - 32.15}{1.1}$$

$$\therefore \ 1.96(1.1) + 32.15 = X$$
$$\therefore \ 34.306 = X$$

The $X$-value equivalent of $-1.96$ is deduced as

$$-1.96 = \frac{X - 32.15}{1.1}$$

$$\therefore \ -1.96(1.1) + 32.15 = X$$
$$\therefore \ 29.994 = X$$

Thus we would expect the middle 95 per cent of drivers to report average m.p.g. in the range 30.00 to 34.31 m.p.g.

## CHAPTER 11—ESTIMATION

**11-1** Confidence intervals for the mean using $Z$-values are given by:

$$\bar{X} \mp Z(s/\sqrt{n})$$

where $Z = 1.96$ for 95 per cent confidence and $Z = 2.58$ for 99 per cent confidence. We do not use the finite population correction (f.p.c.) since $n/N$ is unlikely to exceed 0.05.

(a) $70.2 \mp 1.96\left(\dfrac{20.2}{\sqrt{100}}\right) = 70.2 \mp 3.96$, i.e. £66.24 to £74.16.

We are 95 per cent confident that that the mean annual expenditure on newspapers by households in this town lies in the random interval £66.24 to £74.16.

(b) $70.2 \mp 2.58\left(\dfrac{20.2}{\sqrt{100}}\right) = 70.2 \mp 5.21$, i.e. £64.99 to £75.41.

We are 99 per cent confident that the mean annual expenditure on newspapers by households in this town lies in the random interval £64.99 to £75.41. Note how the error margin of 5.21 has increased (from 3.96) to take account of the increased confidence (99 per cent) in the interval containing the population value.

**11-2** Using $Z$-values, assuming simple random sampling, where $e$ is the error margin:

$$e = Z\left(\frac{s}{\sqrt{n}}\right) \quad \text{and} \quad n = \left(\frac{Zs}{e}\right)^2$$

$$= \left(1.96\frac{4(60)}{15}\right)^2 = 984 \text{ [the 60 is to keep the units in minutes]}$$

The magnitude of the sample size is such that there is no need to rework the estimate to see if a f.p.c. correction is necessary or if a $t$-distribution should have been used. For one month $N$ is 83 333, $n$ is 984, thus, $n/N \leqslant 0.05$.

There is a fixed cost of £2000 and a current cost (in practice we would 'round up' to 1000) of $1000(2) = £2000$; i.e. total costs $= £4000$. Further possibilities at a 95 per cent level are given below:

| Sample size (n) | Cost (£) | Error margin, e (mins) |
|---|---|---|
| 200 | 2 400 | 33 |
| 400 | 2 800 | 23 |
| 600 | 3 200 | 19.2 |
| 800 | 3 600 | 16.6 |
| 1 000 | 4 000 | 14.9 |
| 1 200 | 4 400 | 13.6 |
| 1 400 | 4 800 | 12.6 |
| 1 600 | 5 200 | 11.76 |
| 2 000 | 6 000 | 10.52 |
| 4 000 | 10 000 | 7.44 |

The error margin required depends on the purpose to which the arithmetic mean is to be used. We know nothing of this, only that 15 minutes is 'acceptable'. We would need to find out more about the purpose if we are to advise on sample size. Note how costs do not decline linearly with error margins. We would advise the company of this using the above data for illustration. Note how the reduction of the error margin by 10 minutes from 33 to 23 minutes costs an estimated £400, while at higher sample sizes the £400 spent increasing the cost from £4800 to £5200 only achieved a 0.84 minute reduction.

**11-3** Since $n/N > 0.05$ $(35/120 = 0.29)$ we use f.p.c.

$$p \mp Z\sqrt{\frac{p(1-p)}{n}}\sqrt{\frac{N-n}{N-1}} = 0.4 \mp 1.96\sqrt{\frac{(0.4)(0.6)}{35}}\sqrt{\frac{120-35}{120-1}}$$

$$= 0.4 \mp 1.96(0.0828)(0.8452)$$
$$= 0.4 \mp 0.137, \text{ i.e. } 0.263 \rightarrow 0.537$$

We are 95 per cent confident that the proportion of all passengers who answered 'yes' to using the service again was in the random interval 0.26 to 0.54.

**11-4** Using a $t$-distribution; assume that the time taken to undertake a task is approximately normally distributed—some will take longer, a corresponding number will be quicker, etc. There is no need for the f.p.c. and the standard deviation is an unbiased estimate.

$$\bar{X} \mp t\left(\frac{S_{n-1}}{\sqrt{n}}\right) = 1.12 \mp 2.064\left(\frac{0.1}{\sqrt{25}}\right)$$

$$= 1.12 \mp 0.04, \text{ i.e. } 1.08 \rightarrow 1.16 \text{ minutes}$$

We are 95 per cent confident that the average time taken to undertake the task on that day lies in the random interval 1.08 to 1.16 minutes.

**11-5** Use 95 per cent confidence intervals, $Z$-values and no need for the f.p.c., and assume simple random sampling for selection within the hour. Note that since selection is hourly we are stratifying the selection which ensures that a representative sample is taken with regard to the hour in which production occurred. Since our method assumes simple random sampling the intervals will be slightly wider than necessary. It is beyond the scope of this text to correct for this.

$$\bar{X} \mp Z\left(\frac{s}{\sqrt{n}}\right) = 49.001 \mp 1.96\left(\frac{0.0042}{\sqrt{35}}\right)$$

$$= 49.001 \mp 0.00139, \text{ i.e. } 48.9996 \rightarrow 49.00239$$
$$\text{(warning interval)}$$

Using $Z = 3$:

$$\bar{X} \mp Z\left(\frac{s}{\sqrt{n}}\right) = 49.001 \mp 3\left(\frac{0.0042}{\sqrt{35}}\right)$$

$$= 49.001 \mp 0.0021297, \text{ i.e. } 48.99887 \rightarrow 49.00313$$
$$\text{(action interval)}$$

The control diagram (Fig. 11-1 Ans) provides cause for concern, the tendency being to underfill.

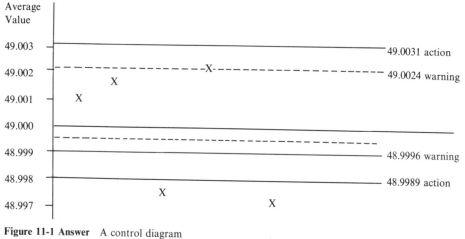

**Figure 11-1 Answer** A control diagram

## CHAPTER 12—TESTING HYPOTHESES

**12-1** 1. $H_0: \pi \leqslant 0.02$, $H_1: \pi > 0.02$.

The null hypothesis is that there is no difference between what is claimed and what will happen. It is a one-tailed test since if less than 2 per cent were returned, this would have been claimed and this is incorporated into the null hypothesis.

2. Use $\alpha = 0.05$.
3. $n = 40$, Z-test.
4. Critical Z-value from tables in Appendix 7 for normal distribution, one-tailed test, is 1.64.
5. Calculated Z-value:

$$Z = \frac{P - \pi}{\sqrt{\pi(1 - \pi)/n}} = \frac{3/40 - 0.02}{\sqrt{0.02(0.98)/40}}$$

$$= 2.48$$

6. Since calculated Z-value < critical Z-value (2.48 > 1.64) we should reject the null hypothesis at a 5 per cent level. The data does allow us to reject the claim at a 5 per cent level that, at most, 2 per cent will be returned. The difference between what we found from the data and what was claimed is over and above that expected from sampling errors at this level of significance.

**12-2**  1. $H_0: \mu \geq 3.5$,   $H_1: \mu < 3.5$.

The test is one-tailed since, if visitors spend on average more than 3.5 minutes, this would have been claimed.

2. Use $\alpha = 0.05$; assume that time spent for the population is roughly normal distribution.
3. $n = 25$, t-test.
4. Critical t-value from tables in Appendix 6 for one-tailed test, then for $25 - 1 = 24$ degrees of freedom $t = -1.7109$.
5. Calculated t-value is:

$$t = \frac{\bar{X} - \mu}{s/\sqrt{n}} = \frac{2.9 - 3.5}{1/5} = -3$$

6. Since (ignoring signs) calculated t-value > critical t-value (3 > 1.711) we reject the hypothesis at a 5 per cent level that visitors spend on average at least 3.5 minutes in the eighteenth-century Virginian living room. The difference between the claimed mean of 3.5 minutes and the observed mean of 2.9 minutes cannot be attributed to sampling error at a 5 per cent level of significance.

**12-3**  1. $H_0: \mu_1 \geq \mu_2$,   $H_1: \mu_1 < \mu_2$,

where $\mu_1$ and $\mu_2$ are mean weights of chickens with the additive and without the additive, respectively, we have a one-tailed test as we do not have reason to believe the additive will lead to a weight loss.

2. Use $\alpha = 0.05$, Z-test for difference between means. Do we use the equal variances formula? An F-test for the difference variances is given by:

$$H_0: \sigma_1^2 = \sigma_2^2, \quad H_1: \sigma_1^2 \neq \sigma_2^2$$

$$F = \frac{s_{n-1,1}^2}{s_{n-1,2}^2} = \frac{0.4^2}{0.35^2} = 1.3061$$

3. The critical Z-value from Appendix 8, at a 5 per cent level, one-tailed (always one-tailed

since the higher $s_{n-1}^2$ is always in the numerator) for $v_1 = n_1 - 1 = 30$ degrees of freedom and $v_2 = n_2 - 1 = 43$ degrees of freedom, is (using $v_2 = 40$ as approximation) 1.744. Since calculated value < critical value (1.3061 < 1.744) we do not reject the null hypothesis of equality of variances at a 5 per cent level and can proceed with the test.

The test requires that the samples are independent and random. There is nothing in the question to lead us to doubt this. The population values should be normally distributed and again we have no reason to doubt this.

4. Critical value from Appendix 7 for a one-tailed Z-test at a 5 per cent level is 1.64.
5. Calculated Z-value is:

$$Z = \frac{(\bar{X}_1 - \bar{X}_2) - (\mu_1 - \mu_2)}{\sqrt{s_{pooled}^2 (1/n_1 + 1/n_2)}}$$

where

$$s_{pooled}^2 = \frac{(n_1 - 1)s_{n-1,\,1}^2 + (n_2 - 1)s_{n-1,\,2}^2}{n_1 + n_2 - 2}$$

$$= \frac{(31 - 1)0.4 + (44 - 1)0.35}{31 + 44 - 2} = 0.3705$$

therefore,

$$Z = \frac{3.40 - 3.01}{\sqrt{0.3705(1/31 + 1/46)}} = 2.7573$$

6. Since calculated Z-value > critical Z-value (2.7573 > 1.64) we reject the null hypothesis at a 5 per cent level. The larger difference between the weights of the chickens with additives, compared with those without, is over and above what we would expect from sampling errors at a 5 per cent level.

It is worth noting two points:
(a) The fact that the difference is statistically significant at this level supports the view that the additive is having an effect. The test does not tell you to go ahead with the additive. Other considerations need be considered, such as the effect on the flavour of the chicken, whether the difference in weight is substantial given the cost of the additive, etc.
(b) The simple sampling random selection of 75 chickens found 31 with the additive and 46 without. Since simple random sampling was used we would expect roughly 50 per cent to have the additive; instead only $(31/75)100 = 41.3$ per cent did. It might be that one effect of the additive is to increase the mortality rate, thus leading to less chickens with the additive being traced than expected. We might test this as a hypothesis between the proportion selected with the additive ($\pi_1$) assuming mortality is not increased and the actual proportion of 0.413. In this case we would not reject $H_0$: $\pi_1 \geqslant 0.5$ against $H_1$: $\pi_1 < 0.5$ for $\alpha = 0.05$ using a Z-test where calculated $Z = -1.51$ does not fall outside the critical $Z = -1.64$.

**12-4** 1. $H_0: \pi_1 \leqslant \pi_2$,  $H_0: \pi_1 > \pi_2$

where $\pi_1$ are the proportion defective from Leeds and $\pi_2$ from Cardiff.
2. $\alpha = 0.01$, both sample sizes can be deemed to be large since $n_1 p_{pooled}(1 - p_{pooled}) \geqslant 5$ and similarly $n_2 p_{pooled}(1 - p_{pooled}) \geqslant 5$, where $p_{pooled}$ is defined and calculated below.

3. $n_1 = 600$, $n_2 = 600$, Z-test.
4. Critical Z-value from tables in Appendix 7, $Z = -2.33$
5. Calculated Z-value is:

$$Z = \frac{(p_1 - p_2) - (\pi_1 - \pi_2)}{\sqrt{p_{\text{pooled}}(1 - p_{\text{pooled}})(1/n_1 + 1/n_2)}}$$

where

$$p_{\text{pooled}} = \frac{n_1 p_1 + n_2 p_2}{n_1 + n_2}$$

$$= \frac{600(0.015) + 600(0.017)}{600 + 600} = 0.016$$

$$Z = \frac{0.015 - 0.017}{\sqrt{0.016(0.984)(1/600 + 1/600)}} = -0.276$$

6. Since the calculated Z-value does not fall outside the critical Z-value we do not reject the hypothesis that there is no difference in the rejection rates at a 5 per cent level.

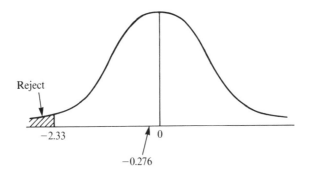

Reject

$-2.33$

$0$

$-0.276$

**Figure 12-1 Answer**

# THREE

APPENDICES

*1*

# BASIC MATHEMATICS

This text requires *very little* preliminary knowledge of mathematics. However, what is little to some readers is quite frightening to others. Undergraduate students, who almost always possess a pass in GCSE mathematics, should find this appendix insultingly easy. However, more mature MBA arts-based students will be approaching it with some concern. In Sections 1–5 inclusive are the main arithmetical tools needed for the text. Sections 6 and 7 are included in case other courses such as Operations Management and Managerial Economics require a little more mathematics. This appendix is made up of seven sections, the Diagnostic Test being in Section 8. Any readers in the slightest doubt should attempt the diagnostic test *now*, before reading the text. Answers to the test are given at the end of Section A. If you have any problems you can cross-reference to the appropriate section. At worst you waste some time and boost your confidence; at best you learn the basic tools needed for this and other subjects.

## 1 THE NUMBERING SYSTEM AND BASIC OPERATIONS

**1-1 Integers** We refer to whole (or natural) numbers as integers which possess the characteristic of being able to be listed endlessly in succession, namely:

$$1, 2, 3, 4, 5, 6, 7, 8, 9, 10, 11, 12, \ldots$$

Integers provide for the process of counting (referred to as their ordinal aspect) and allow us to designate the quantity of, say, items in a collection (referred to as their cardinal aspect), for example, 5 books and 5 university lecturers.

**1-2 Rational numbers** Integers can be added, subtracted and multiplied together and will always result in an integer answer. However, when two integers are divided a whole number (integer) may not result. For example, 3 divided into 10 goes 3 times with a remainder of $\frac{1}{3}$. When the process of division of integers does not result in an integer, the resulting expression may be expressed as a fraction $\frac{10}{3}$ or the sum of an integer and a fraction (written as $3\frac{1}{3}$ denoting 3 plus $\frac{1}{3}$, three plus one-third of a whole (or 3 into one)). Integers and fractions make up the system of rational numbers. Such a system does not describe all types of numbers and irrational and imaginary or complex numbers will be mentioned later. An alternative representation of rational numbers uses decimal notation. The decimal notation is based on what is referred to as a 'base' of 10 and the reason for this should become apparent.

**1-3  Decimal system**   A rational number expressed in a decimal form possesses a decimal point (full stop) and numbers to the left and right of it. Numbers to the left of the point are integers and numbers to the right of the point together express the fraction or remainder term. Thus: 5.0 denotes an integer value of 5 with no remainder fraction. The first number to the right of the point denotes a value 'out of' 10. Thus: 5.5 denotes 5 plus (and) $\frac{5}{10}$ (5 over, divided by, or out of, 10). Since $\frac{5}{10}$ is the same as a half: $5.5 = 5\frac{1}{2}$. The second number to the right of the decimal point denotes a value 'out of' 100; thus $5.51 = 5\frac{51}{100}$ or 5 and $\frac{5}{10}$ and $\frac{1}{100} = 5$ and $\frac{50}{100}$ and $\frac{1}{100} = 5\frac{51}{100}$.

Similarly:

$$5.511 = 5\tfrac{511}{1000}; \qquad 5.5111 = 5\tfrac{5111}{10000};$$

$$8.25 = 8\tfrac{25}{100}; \qquad 6.735 = 6\tfrac{735}{1000}$$

Multiplication, division, addition and subtraction of decimals is readily achieved through the use of electronic calculators. Several years ago multiplication and division of higher integer values or 'long' decimal terms required the use of logarithms. With electronic calculators a fraction, say, $\frac{29}{5}$, may be converted into a decimal (either by dividing on a calculator 29 by 5 or appreciating that $\frac{29}{5} = 5$ remainder $\frac{4}{5}$ which is the same as 5 remainder $\frac{8}{10}$, i.e. 5.8) and multiplied/divided by further numbers.

**1-4  Fractions: addition, subtraction, multiplication, division**   For some purposes it is useful to deal in fractions for exact decimal equivalents do not exist. For example, $10 \div 3$ is equal to $3\frac{1}{3} = 3.333\dot{3}$, etc.; in fact the threes continue ad infinitum and it is common practice to put a dot above the last 3 to show the approximate nature of the answer and the recurring last number or pattern of last numbers. Fractions are also useful when electronic calculators are not at hand, and, more importantly, the rules for conducting arithmetical operations on rational numbers also apply to algebraic expressions and it is with this purpose in mind that we consider such operations to apply them later to algebraic expressions.

First, we note that if the top number of a fraction, the numerator, and the bottom number, the denominator, are divided or multiplied by the same number (note this does NOT hold for addition or subtraction by the same number), the fraction takes the same value. For example, $\frac{50}{100}$ (numerator (50) and denominator (100) divided by 10) $= \frac{5}{10}$; (dividing by 5) $= \frac{1}{2}$. Similarly $\frac{9}{3} = \frac{3}{1} = 3$ (dividing by 3); $\frac{3}{4} = \frac{15}{20}$ (multiplying by 5).

**1-4-1  Multiplication**   To multiply two fractions together (i) the numerators are multiplied together to yield a value (ii) the denominators are multiplied together to yield a value, and (iii) the answer is the value resulting from (i) divided by the value resulting from (ii), for example:

$$\frac{15}{21} \times \frac{7}{5} = \frac{15 \times 7}{21 \times 5} = \frac{105}{105} = 1 \quad \text{(dividing numerator and denominator by 105)}$$

The problem could have been simplified by reducing $\frac{15}{21}$ (dividing by 3) to $\frac{5}{7}$ and then conducting the above process or extending our rule for dividing the numerator and denominator by a common number to encompass the numerator or denominator of any of the two fractions multiplied together. Thus the numerator of the first fraction and the denominator of the second may be divided by 5 to yield:

$$\frac{3}{21} \times \frac{7}{1}$$

and the denominator of the first fraction and the numerator of the second divided by 7 to yield:

$$\frac{3}{3} \times \frac{1}{1} = 1$$

Such a procedure much simplifies multiplication of fractions and is usually not undertaken in stages but by crossing out original numbers and inserting new ones after each operation, for example:

$$\frac{\overset{1}{\cancel{8}}}{\underset{1}{\cancel{10}}} \times \frac{\overset{\overset{1}{\cancel{2}}}{\cancel{20}}}{\underset{\underset{4}{\cancel{8}}}{\cancel{64}}} = \frac{1}{4}$$

**1-4-2 Division**   Division is accomplished by simply interchanging the numerator for the denominator in the fraction which is being divided into the other fraction, and then multiplying this new resulting fraction by the other fraction, for example:

$$\frac{\left(\dfrac{27}{9}\right)}{\left(\dfrac{13}{3}\right)} = \frac{27}{9} \times \frac{3}{13} = \frac{\overset{9}{\cancel{27}}}{\underset{3}{\cancel{9}}} \times \frac{\overset{1}{\cancel{3}}}{13} = \frac{9}{13}$$

$$\text{Try:} \quad \left(\frac{14}{5}\right) \div \left(\frac{7}{10}\right)$$

The answer is: 4.

The number of times a half goes into 4 is eight times because each of the four units is being split into (multiplied by) two. Thus:

$$\frac{4}{\left(\dfrac{1}{2}\right)} = \frac{\left(\dfrac{4}{1}\right)}{\left(\dfrac{1}{2}\right)} = \frac{4}{1} \times \frac{2}{1} = 8$$

**1-4-3 Addition**

$$\frac{3}{8} + \frac{2}{8} = \frac{5}{8}$$

This can be verified by splitting a square into eight equal parts; three of the parts plus two of the parts = 5 of the parts.

$$\frac{3}{7} + \frac{2}{3}$$

presents problems since unlike our previous example the denominators of each of the fractions are not the same (or common). Thus by multiplying one or both of the denominators (and the numerators to ensure the value of each fraction is not changed) by an appropriate number a common denominator may be achieved. A common (integer) denominator may be found by multiplying the two denominators together, i.e. $7 \times 3 = 21$. The first fraction, $\frac{3}{7}$, is converted to a denominator of 21 by multiplying by 3: $\frac{3}{7}$ becomes $\frac{9}{21}$; the second fraction is converted to a denominator of 21 by multiplying by 7, i.e. $\frac{2}{3}$ becomes $\frac{14}{21}$. Thus:

$$\frac{3}{7} + \frac{2}{3} = \frac{9}{21} + \frac{14}{21} = \frac{23}{21}$$

i.e. we can add numerators together since there exists a common denominator.

A popular framework for this type of problem is to draw a line below the fractions under which the lowest common denominator is placed:

$$\frac{3}{4} + \frac{1}{2}$$

$$\overline{\phantom{xx}4\phantom{xx}}$$

note that 8 would be a common denominator but both denominators can be divided into 4 to yield integer values and the calculation is eased if the lowest common value is used.

Our next step is to divide the denominator of the first fraction into the common denominator and multiply the result by the numerator of the first fraction, i.e. $(4 \div 4) \times 3 = 3$ and insert the answer as indicated below; a similar procedure being undertaken for the second fraction $(4 \div 2) \times 1 = 2$, the value being inserted below as indicated:

$$\frac{3}{4} + \frac{1}{2}$$

$$\frac{3+2}{4}$$

The addition sign is then inserted and the bottom half of the expression taken to be the answer, i.e.

$$\frac{3+2}{4} = \frac{5}{4} (= 1.25).$$

**1-4-4 Subtraction** The procedure for addition is followed but the values in the final numerator are subtracted, for example:

$$\frac{3}{4} - \frac{1}{2} = \frac{3-2}{4} = \frac{1}{4} = (0.25)$$

$$\frac{3-2}{4}$$

## 2 SIGNS, POWERS, ROOTS, INEQUALITIES AND ORDERING OF OPERATIONS

**2-1 Signs** The numbering system referred to so far has a major defect in that it cannot always allow subtraction to occur. We have only considered a positive range of numbers and, to deal with subtracting, say, 3 from 2, a negative scale is required. We can include such a negative scale by constructing a continuous sequence of numbers, with zero as its central value; that is:

$$\ldots -5, -4, -3, -2, -1, 0, 1, 2, 3, 4, 5 \ldots$$

**2-1-1**   The numbering system extends from minus infinity through zero to plus infinity and includes positive and negative integers and fractions. Note how the scale of numbers allows us to determine $2-3$:

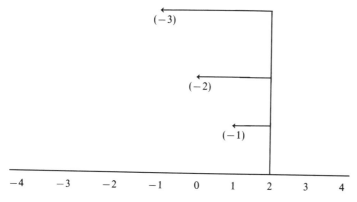

**Figure A1-1**

the answer being: $-1$.

For similar reasons $4-6=-2$; $8-16=-8$; $4-4=0$, etc.

Note that, for example, $-2-4=-6$ as we move further along the negative scale towards minus infinity and $-3+8=5$ as we move from the negative scale through zero to the positive scale. For example, if a country's value of merchandise exports is £500 bn and imports £600 bn, the balance of merchandise trade is £500 bn $-$ £600 bn $= -$£100 bn (a £100 bn deficit). The terms loss, deficit, debit, all refer to the negative sequence of numbers.

**2-1-2**   When numbers are multiplied or divided, not only are the numbers multiplied together or divided by each other, but also the signs attached to the numbers, for $-5$ denotes quite a different point on our scale to $+5$. The rules for multiplying and dividing positive and negative numbers are:

$+$ multiplied (divided) by $+ = +$     e.g. $(+2)\times(+4)=+8$
$-$ multiplied (divided) by $- = +$     e.g. $(-2)\times(-4)=+8$
$-$ multiplied (divided) by $+ = -$     e.g. $(-2)\times(+4)=-8$
$+$ multiplied (divided) by $- = -$     e.g. $(+2)\times(-4)=-8$

If a number has no sign attached it is conventional to take it to represent a positive number: for example, $8\div(-2)=-4$. Our only problem lies with dividing any value by zero, though we shall ignore this problem. The money analogy helps in explaining the above rules; in the second case we are taking away 2 lots of a negative amount (debt) of 4 resulting in a positive gain of 8. In the third case we have 4 lots of a negative amount (debt) of 2 resulting in a negative amount (debt) of 8; in the final case we have 2 lots of a negative amount (debt) of 4 resulting in a negative amount (debt) of 8. The second case is remembered as the double negative being positive, for example, your progress so far is not unsatisfactory—that is, it is satisfactory.

**2-2 Powers**   At this stage it is necessary to consider a valuable notation or shorthand used in mathematics referred to as powers or exponents. Consider multiplying 2 by itself 6 times, i.e.:

$$2\times2\times2\times2\times2\times2$$

To save us writing this out in length (imagine doing so for 2 multiplied by itself 100 times!), we adopt the notation:

$$2^6 \text{ read as '2 to the power of 6'—the number two being called the}$$
$$\text{base and 6 the power or exponent.}$$

Thus:

$$4 \times 4 \times 4 = 4^3 \text{ (sometimes read as '4 cubed')}$$

and

$$4 \times 4 = 4^2 \text{ (sometimes read as '4 squared')}$$

Consider:

$$4 \times 4 \times 4 \times 4 \times 4 \text{—this is the same as:}$$

$$4^3 \times 4^2 = 4^5$$

Note we have a first power rule here, namely: when expressions to the same base are multiplied together we add powers (exponents) (since the powers $3 + 2 = 5$). Thus:

$$5^8 \times 5^7 = 5^{15}$$

Consider:

$$\frac{3 \times 3 \times 3 \times 3 \times 3}{3 \times 3} = \frac{3^5}{3^2}$$

Dividing the numerator and denominator by $3 \times 3$ designated by 'crossing out' as noted in Section 1:

$$\frac{3 \times 3 \times 3 \times \cancel{3} \times \cancel{3}}{\cancel{3} \times \cancel{3}} = 3 \times 3 \times 3 = 3^3$$

Thus $\frac{3^5}{3^2} = 3^3$ providing an insight into a second rule, namely: when expressions to the same base are divided we subtract the power (exponent) of the denominator from the numerator (since the powers $5 - 2 = 3$). Thus:

$$\frac{8^7}{8^4} = 8^3$$

If this rule is doubted evaluate, using a calculator, 8 multiplied by itself 7 times, then 8 multiplied by itself 4 times, divide the latter into the former and the result should be 8 multiplied by itself 3 times.

Consider:

$$\frac{4^3}{4^4} = \frac{\cancel{4} \times \cancel{4} \times \cancel{4}}{4 \times \cancel{4} \times \cancel{4} \times \cancel{4}} = \frac{1}{4}$$

By subtracting exponents or powers our answer is $4^{-1}$, thus a negative power or exponent is a natural extension of our notation to represent the reciprocal of a number, i.e. the number placed in the denominator of a fraction when the numerator is 1.

$$\frac{4^5}{4^7}=\frac{\cancel{4}\times\cancel{4}\times\cancel{4}\times\cancel{4}\times\cancel{4}}{4\times4\times\cancel{4}\times\cancel{4}\times\cancel{4}\times\cancel{4}\times\cancel{4}}=\frac{1}{4\times4}=\frac{1}{4^2}=4^{-2}$$

$$4^{-3}=\frac{1}{4^3}$$

the negative sign denoting: the expression should be placed in the denominator of a fraction.

$$3^{-8}=\frac{1}{3^8}$$

The above notation is often (but not always) employed in electronic calculators. Try dividing 10 by 300 000 using a calculator. Your calculator's display may be composed of two parts, say, 3.3333333 and $-05$. This should be read as multiplying the first figure (though in some calculators the order may be reversed) by the second figure as a power of 10, that is:

$$3.3333333\times10^{-5}$$

(the zero is ignored in 05 simply representing the place where a number greater than 9 but less than 100 would occupy)

this is equal to:

$$3.3333333\times\frac{1}{10^5}=\frac{3.3333333}{100\,000}=0.00003333333\dot{3}$$

**2-3 Roots**   An extension of the powers notation allows us to consider the 'root' of a number. The square root of a number is another value, which when multiplied by itself (squared) is equal to the original number. The square root of 4, denoted by $\sqrt{4}$, is equal to 2 since $2\times2=4$. An alternative answer to the expression $\sqrt{4}$, is $-2$, since we noted in Sec. 2-1-2 that $-2\times-2=+4$. Thus, $\sqrt{4}=\mp2$ (read as plus or minus 2). Similarly, $\sqrt{16}=\mp4$; $\sqrt{64}=\mp8$ and $\sqrt{100}=\mp10$. The cube root of a number is another value, which when multiplied by itself three times (cubed) is equal to the original number; for example, the cube root of 8, denoted by $\sqrt[3]{8}=2$ since $2\times2\times2=8$, though negative solutions will not exist. Similar definitions exist for the fourth $(\mp)$, fifth $(+)$, sixth $(\mp)$, seventh $(+)$, eighth $(\mp)$ root, etc.

It is now necessary to provide a uniform notation which includes both powers and roots and this is accomplished by expressing roots as powers or exponents of the number. We noted previously that:

$$4^1=4$$
$$4^2=4\times4$$
$$4^3=4\times4\times4$$

To express roots as a series of powers the square root, cubed root, fourth root, fifth root, etc., must follow a sequence that declines in value, is less than unity and corresponds to the start of the power sequence. Such a sequence is obtained by using fractions whereby the denominator shows the value of the root (square, cubed, fourth, etc.) and the numerator is 1. Thus:

$$4^{\frac{1}{2}}=\sqrt{4}=\mp2$$

$$8^{\frac{1}{3}}=\sqrt[3]{8}=2$$

$$16^{\frac{1}{4}}=\sqrt[4]{16}=\mp2$$

$$64^{\frac{1}{2}}=\sqrt{64}=\mp8$$

Our notation is now complete and we can amalgamate our power and roots notation into a general system of power (exponent) notation. Note how $4^{\frac{3}{2}}=8$ is composed of:

$$4^{3 \times \frac{1}{2}}=\sqrt{4^3}=\sqrt{64}=\mp 8$$

Examples given above have all yielded 'perfect squares'; for example: $4^{\frac{1}{2}}=\mp 2$; $11.56^{\frac{1}{2}}=\mp 3.4$; $81^{\frac{1}{2}}=\mp 9$, etc. Yet the square roots of 2, 3, 5 and 8, for example, do not yield perfect rational numbers (calculators only yield approximate answers, stopping after 6 or 8 or whatever decimal places). The square roots of such numbers are examples of irrational numbers which cannot be exactly given but do form part of our numbering system and thus, together with rational numbers, form what is referred to as the real number system.

A more complex expression worth considering takes the form of an exponent which is a negative fraction. In Sec. 2-2 it was noted that a negative sign in an exponent denotes that the expression should be placed in the denominator of a fraction. Thus:

$$6^{-\frac{3}{2}}=\frac{1}{6^{\frac{3}{2}}}=\frac{1}{\sqrt{6^3}}=\frac{1}{\sqrt{216}}=\frac{1}{\mp 14.697}$$

$$=\mp 0.068$$

A final point of concern is the determination of the square or fourth, sixth, eighth, root, etc., of a negative number. For example, consider $\sqrt{-4}$. Neither $+2$ $((+2)\times(+2)=+4)$ nor $-2$ $((-2)\times(-2)=+4)$ give a solution and, in fact, a solution cannot be found in the real number system, the answer being phrased in terms of an imaginary (or complex) numbering system (see Section 7.5).

*Note*: *Any* expression that has a power exponent of zero is equal to 1; $2^0=1$, $50\,000^0=1$. This arises from the notation $10^6 \div 10^6=10^{6-6}=10^0=1$.

**2-4 Inequalities**   At this stage it is necessary to ensure that the reader is familiar with some further symbols or notation used in mathematics. Part of any problem for students unfamiliar with mathematics is being faced with symbols that are adopted simply to denote often used expressions of which they are unaware:

| | |
|---|---|
| $=$ | What is on the left of the sign is equal to what is on the right of the sign $(6=6)$. |
| $\simeq$ or $\approx$ | What is on the left of the sign is approximately equal to what is on the right of the sign $(6 \simeq 5.9999)$. |
| $>$ | What is on the left of the sign (the wider part) is greater than what is on the right of the sign (the narrower part) $(8>5)$. |
| $<$ | What is on the left of the sign is less than what is on the right of the sign $(5<8)$. |
| $\geqslant$ | What is on the left of the sign is greater than or equal to what is on the right of the sign. |
| $\leqslant$ | What is on the left of the sign is less than or equal to what is on the right of the sign. |
| $\equiv$ | What is on the left of the sign is identical to what is on the right of the sign. Such an expression is often referred to as an identity. |
| $\neq$ | What is on the left of the sign is not equal to what is on the right of the sign. |

Some of the above symbols are often combined to show the range within which a variable (explained later) may lie; for example:

$$0<x\leqslant 100$$

denotes that the variable $x$ may be greater than zero (not equal to it) but less than or equal to 100.

**2-5 Ordering of operations**    The language of mathematics needs to be very precise for it involves, through the use of symbols, a notation which allows us to carry out particular calculations. As such there must be no confusion as to the interpretation of this notation. For example: $2+4 \times 3$ may mean: first of all we add 2 and 4 together and multiply the result by $3(=18)$ or we multiply $4 \times 3$ and then add 2 to the result $(=14)$. The ordering of operations in mathematics tells us the latter process is correct, the former being described by $(2+4)3$. The ordering of operations is best explained through the mnemonic BEDMAS.

B—Brackets: which 'protect' a set of operations. All workings in brackets should be undertaken first. If there is more than one set of brackets the innermost brackets should be evaluated first, working through to the outermost brackets.

The sequence of operations for working within brackets and out of brackets is:

E—Exponents, D—Division, M—Multiplication, A—Addition and finally S—Subtraction.

Multiplication may be denoted by a number (including its sign) touching a bracket, that is:

$$2 \times 3 = 2(3) = 6$$

Applying BEDMAS:

$$3+4(8+2) = 3+4(10) \quad \text{brackets first}$$
$$= 3+40 \quad \text{then multiplication}$$
$$= 43 \quad \text{then addition}$$

i.e. we have 3, plus 4 lots of (multiplied by) $(8+2)$ NOT $3+4=7$ lots of (multiplied by) $(8+2)$. The latter would be denoted by $=(3+4)(8+2)=70$.

Consider:

$$2[3-2(2^2-40 \times 0.5)] \qquad \text{innermost brackets first: and then exponents}$$
$$= 2[3-2(4-40 \times 0.5)] \qquad \text{first}$$

$$= 2[3-2(4-20)] \qquad \text{innermost brackets: multiplication next}$$
$$= 2[3-2(-16)] \qquad \text{innermost brackets: subtraction next}$$
$$= 2[3+32] \qquad \text{Outermost brackets: multiplication first (minus 2 multiplied by minus 16—note in the numbering sequence the sign and number designate a particular value)}$$
$$= 2[35] \qquad \text{outermost brackets: addition next}$$
$$= 70$$

Try:

$$-5\left[2^3 + 3\left(\frac{2+4}{3} - 1\right)\right]$$

The answer is: $-5[2^3 + 3] = -55$.

# 1  VARIABLES

**3-1**    The principles established above concerning numbers can be generalized to include variables, thus developing algebraic concepts and principles from arithmetical concepts and principles.

Variables are usually denoted by letters from the Roman alphabet, for example, $x$, $y$, $z$, and can take any value from a 'pool' of real numbers. The sequence of real numbers contained within the pool is called the range of the variable. Examples of variables, or 'things' which take variable real number values, are the annual sales value of a company over time, the number of students in a lecture theatre in different time periods, the ages of different students on single honours undergraduate management courses at a university in the academic year 1992–1993 within a particular lecture theatre each day. We adopt a form of shorthand to save us writing this latter example out in full by calling this variable $x$. The range of the variable, or pool of real numbers it can be drawn from in the sequence, is $0 \leqslant x \leqslant 160$ (there being assumed to be 160 such students). Variables thus can take a range of values and we are usually interested in ascertaining a particular value(s) of the variable which meets certain conditions. Before considering this process in further detail it is necessary to reconsider the previously discussed arithmetical operations as applied to variables.

**3-2**  Consider two distinct variables, labelled as $x$ and $y$. Note our notation for multiplication may be written as:

$$2 \text{ multiplied by } x = 2 \times x = 2(x) = 2.x = 2x$$
$$x \text{ multiplied by } y = x \times y = x(y) = x.y = xy$$

Thus

$$2x \ (2 \text{ 'lots' of } x) \text{ plus } 5x \ (5 \text{ 'lots' of } x) = 7x$$

i.e.

$$2x + 5x = 7x$$

Similarly:

$$6x - 8x = -2x$$

If $x$ is the number of male students and $y$ the number of female students in the UK, we cannot add the two together to result in a 'new' expression (unless we define $z$ to be the total number of UK students $x + y = z$).

$$3x + 2y = 3x + 2y$$

We cannot (and would not want to) add the two variables together to make some form of jointly integrated male/female student—the two variables being quite distinct.

**3-3**  We note that:

$$x \times x \times x = x^3$$
$$x^3 \times x^2 = x^5$$
$$\frac{y^6}{y^4} = y^2$$

simply applying our arithmetical operations to the variables.

**3-4**  Given an expression such as:

$$(x+4)(x-2)$$

we first evaluate the expression within each bracket. In this case $(x+4)$ and $(x-2)$ cannot be reduced to any further form—we simply have a variable $x$ plus 4 and a variable $x$ minus 2. Yet we note that anything touching a bracket, namely every individual 'item' in the first brackets, should, in turn, be multiplied by every individual 'item' in the second brackets. Consider:

$$(2+3)(4+5)$$

Instead of adding together the numbers in each bracket we can multiply the 2 by 4 and then by 5, followed by the 3 by 4 and then by 5, i.e.:

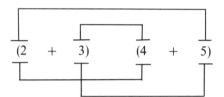

**Figure A1-2**

$$=2(4)+2(5)+3(4)+3(5)=45 \quad (\text{i.e. } 5(9)=45)$$

Thus:

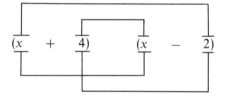

**Figure A1-3**

$$=x(x)+x(-2)+4(x)+4(-2)$$
$$=x^2-2x+4x-8$$
$$=x^2+2x-8$$

(note how the minus sign is attached to the number designating a separate part of the real numbering sequence)

**3-5**   Consider:

$$x[y+x(2-x)-y(2+y)+x^2]$$

Remembering BEDMAS—first innermost brackets: no further work can be done in these brackets; next no evaluation of exponents or division; next multiplication of terms touching brackets:

$$=x[y+2x-x^2-2y-y^2+x^2]$$

working in outermost brackets: addition and subtraction

$$=x[2x-y-y^2]$$

multiplying terms in brackets by $x$:

$$= 2x^2 - xy - xy^2$$

Try:

$$9x^2 - 3x(x + 2 + 2x)$$

The answer is: $-6x$.

**3-6** Given an expression such as:

$$\frac{x^2 + 2x}{x}$$

both the terms in the numerator, i.e. $x^2$ and $2x$, are divided by $x$, thus:

$$\frac{x^2 + 2x}{x} = \frac{x^2}{x} + \frac{2x}{x} = x + 2$$

we are simply dividing the numerator and denominator of a fraction by the same value (or in this case) variable.

Compare the above example with:

$$\frac{4 + 8}{2} = \frac{4}{2} + \frac{8}{2} = 6 \quad \text{or} \quad \frac{12}{2} = 6$$

or dividing each term in the numerator and denominator by 2:

$$\frac{4 + 8}{2} = \frac{2 + 4}{1} = 6$$

The operations for numbered fractions can be seen to apply for variables in fractions:

$$\frac{\left(\dfrac{2x}{y}\right)}{\left(\dfrac{x}{y}\right)} = \frac{2x}{y} \div \frac{x}{y} = \frac{2x}{y} \times \frac{y}{x} = \frac{2\cancel{x}}{\cancel{y}} \times \frac{\cancel{y}}{\cancel{x}} = 2$$

**3-7** Consider:

$$\frac{x^2}{(x+2)} - \frac{2}{(x-1)}$$

Applying the principles for subtraction of fractions, a common denominator can be found by multiplying the denominators of each fraction together, i.e. $(x+2)(x-1)$. By adopting the framework and operations for addition/subtraction of fractions given in Sec. 1:

$$\frac{\dfrac{x^2}{(x+2)} - \dfrac{2}{(x-1)}}{(x+2)(x-1)}$$

$$= \frac{x^2(x-1) - 2(x+2)}{(x+2)(x-1)}$$

since $(x+2)$ divided into $(x+2)(x-1)$ yields $(x-1)$; and $(x-1)$ divided into $(x+2)(x-1)$ yields $(x+2)$

$$= \frac{x^3 - x^2 - 2x - 4}{(x+2)(x-1)}$$

## 4 FUNCTIONS AND THEIR GRAPHICAL REPRESENTATION

**4-1**   Functions are concerned with relationships between two or more variables. We write, for example, $y = f(x)$, that is, $y$ is a function of $x$, or $y$ depends for its values on values of $x$. The letters $y$ and $x$ are variables; they denote 'things' which vary in magnitude from observation to observation. The letters $y$ and $x$ are usually utilized as a form of shorthand by which we save effort in not having to constantly write down a full description of the variable. For example, the percentage mark a student is assessed by for a subject, denoted by $y$, may be made up from a percentage coursework mark, and a percentage mark from an examination, $z$. The respective weighting or relative importance of coursework and examination is $40:60$. The relationship between the total assessment mark, $y$, and the coursework and examination, $x$ and $z$, is given by the equation:

$$y = 0.4x + 0.6z$$

Thus, if a student scores a mark of 40 per cent on the coursework and 80 per cent in the examination, the final assessment mark is:

$$y = 0.4(40) + 0.6(80)$$
$$= 16 + 48$$
$$= 64 \text{ per cent}$$

**4-2**   Now this equation is but one form of a function. It relates one variable ($y$) to two variables, $x$ and $z$. Consider the following example expressing a relationship between two variables. A householder's consumption, $C$, is related to the earned disposable income available to the household, $I$. Consumption depends on (or is a function of) income ($C = f(I)$). The more income a household receives, other things being equal, the more consumption one would expect to take place. Not all of any changes in income will be reflected in changes in consumption since some of the income will be saved. This relationship may be translated into an algebraic form, say:

$$C = 100 + 0.75I$$

We shall consider some of the features of this relationship in the next section. For the moment the function can be seen to describe the relationship between $C$ and $I$; for given values of income, $I$, corresponding values of $C$ may be determined. The equation is some sort of mechanism representing reality by which income values put into the mechanism are converted into corresponding consumption patterns in a manner that is supposed to model the real life relationship. Such functions are often referred to as *mathematical models*. Thus if the relationship above pertains to monthly income and consumption by the household, an income of £200 per month, i.e. $I = 200$, will lead to consumption of:

$$C = 100 + 0.75I$$

where $I = 200$. Substitute 200 for $I$ in the above equation, therefore:

$$C = 100 + 0.75(200)$$
$$= 100 + 150 = 250$$

Consumption is higher than earned, disposable income in this case as the social welfare services intercede. Let us increase the income to £300.
   For $I = 300$:

$$C = 100 + 0.75(300)$$
$$= 100 + 225 = 325$$

For $I = 400$:

$$C = 100 + 0.75(400)$$
$$= 100 + 300 = 400$$

For $I = 500$:

$$C = 100 + 0.75(500)$$
$$= 100 + 375 = 475$$

For $I = 600$:

$$C = 100 + 0.75(600)$$
$$= 100 + 450 = 550$$

The above (fictitious) relationship thus 'maps out' values of $C$ which correspond to values of $I$. Having outlined the principles of algebraic representation of functions and noted that this will be considered in further detail in the next section, it is of interest to consider the graphical representation of such functions.

4-3  If required to represent the relationship between two variables an initial step may be to consider a graphical method. For example, a study of the number of employees in a company over time may have as its starting point a graph of such a relationship with number of employees on the vertical axis, and time on the horizontal axis. Figure A1-4 based on data given in Table A1-1, shows such a relationship over the period 1986 to 1992. The underlying pattern or relationship over this period between the two variables, number of manufacturing employees and time, can be seen to be one of decline, number of manufacturing employees decreasing as time increases.

4-4  Note in graphing such a relationship (though see Chapter 3 for details):

1. The graph should be titled and, if more than one graph is given, numbered sequentially in order to facilitate easy reference.
2. A vertical and horizontal axis should be drawn and a sensible scale clearly marked. Note how in Fig. A1-4 the vertical scale is broken by wavy lines. This shows the scale not to be started from zero at the origin (intersection of the two axes) but from 6800. Were a scale starting from zero to be used we would be left with a large blank at the bottom of the graph which is not appropriate for this purpose, the pertinent features of the graph being squeezed together closely at the top, between 6800 and 7900. A starting point to deciding on the scale to use is to pick out the highest and lowest figures to be plotted against each axis, and use these as upper and lower bounds on the axis. If the lower bound is close to zero (i.e. a large blank would not ensue by starting the scale from zero) then zero is preferable as the lower bound to the scale. In general, whenever possible zero should be the natural starting point for both axes. However, Chapter 3 provides further details on this issue relating it to the purpose of the graph.
3. Having assigned a sensible scale to both axes, label each axis with a title. Further explanatory notes on the definition of each label may be stated in a footnote below or, reference given to the table (with notes) from which the graph was derived if published with the graph. Similarly, a source should be given.
4. Each value of a particular variable, together with the corresponding value of the other variables, should be taken to represent a data plot on the graph. For example, the first cross or plot working from the left of Fig. A1-4 denotes, for 1986, the number of manufacturing employees, 7873—the cross being marked at the intersection of 1986 and 7873. Similarly, for each pair of values given in Table A1-4 a cross is marked.

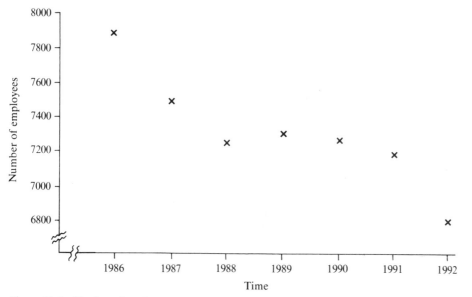

**Figure A1-4**   Number of employees

**Table A1-1**   Number of employees

| Year* | Number of employees |
|-------|---------------------|
| 1986 | 7873 |
| 1987 | 7490 |
| 1988 | 7246 |
| 1989 | 7292 |
| 1990 | 7257 |
| 1991 | 7176 |
| 1992 | 6807 |

*Average of each respective year.

**4-5**   The above example was concerned with the graphical representation of two related variables. However, if the relationship between three variables is required to be represented graphically, for example, for the function:

$$y = 0.4x + 0.6z$$

given in Section 4.1, then the graph should be drawn with three axes (for $y$, $x$ and $z$); that is, in three dimensions. The graphical representation of relationships between more than three variables is in practice impossible, requiring venturing into, for example, eight-dimensional hyperspace. For relationships involving more than three dimensions we shall content ourselves with their algebraic representation.

**4-6**   Having noted that relationships may be expressed graphically or algebraically, two questions should be considered. First, given data of the form shown in Table A1-1, having graphically represented such data, how can we determine its algebraic formulation? Such a formulation is derived using a method called regression analysis, the exposition of which is given in Chapter 7 of this book. Second, given an algebraic representation, how can we represent it graphically? The answer is to convert it into a series of corresponding pairs of data for each variable, as given in Table A1-1. Consider the function relating household consumer expenditure to income outlined in Sec. 4.2, that is:

$$C = 100 + 0.75I$$

**4-7**   In Sec. 4-2 values of $C$ were derived which corresponded to particular values of $I$ and these may be expressed in a tabular form, namely:

| $I = 200$ | 300 | 400 | 500 | 600 |
|-----------|-----|-----|-----|-----|
| $C = 250$ | 325 | 400 | 475 | 550 |

The range of values and number of data points considered to be relevant in general depends on the range of values and number of points and accuracy in which the user is interested.

**4-8**   The pairs of figures tabulated above are plotted in Fig. A1-5. It is apparent from this figure that no need existed to plot each individual pair of points. Strictly speaking only two points require plotting, the remaining ones being derived from a straight line drawn to connect these points. In this particular case the functional relationship possessed the characteristic of taking the form of a straight line when graphed. This is a particular type of functional form known as a linear form and its features will be described later. Readers familiar with this form would have recognized it from the format of the equation:

$$C = 100 + 0.75I$$

They would have known no need existed to plot more than three points (two for forming the line, and one to check) to yield its graphical representation. The means by which different functions can be recognized as belonging to particular typological groups will be outlined in Sec. 5.

**4-9**   Reference should be made to the predictive use of graphs. Say, only the first and last pairs of values in the table in Sec. 4-7 were known; that is, when $I = 200$, $C = 250$ and when $I = 600$, $C = 550$. These may be plotted on Fig. A1-5 (these crosses are encircled). From this graph on the assumption that the relationship is linear between the range $I = 200$ and $600$ intermediate values may be determined. For example, when $I = 400$, the corresponding value of $C$ would be derived by drawing a vertical line up from the horizontal axis at 400 to the line (given by the vertical broken line). The value of the vertical axis yields the value of $C$ corresponding to $I = 400$, namely $C = 400$, by coincidence. This procedure is the graphical equivalent of the more accurate algebraic process:

when $\qquad\qquad\qquad\qquad\qquad I = 400$

$$C = 100 + 0.75I$$
$$= 100 + 0.75(400) = 400$$

**4-10**   If our function is recognizable as being non-linear (see Sec. 5) then joining two points to yield all intermediate values (and external values within the relevant range) is not feasible for the patterns between (and outside of) these points will not be linear. As such, a range of particular values of one variable must be considered and the corresponding values of the other variable derived. These resulting pairs of values are then plotted. A problem arises in ensuring that the

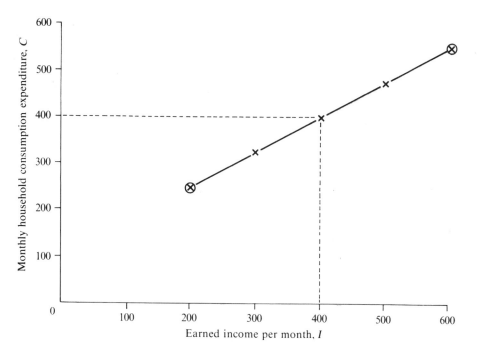

**Figure A1-5**  Household consumption function

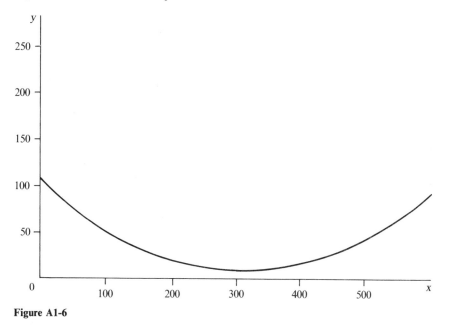

**Figure A1-6**

range of values chosen includes the features of the function pertinent to the analysis. In some cases the investigation will be directed to particular values of one variable that are of interest and no problem exists in this case. However, in other cases a function may, say, take the form of that graphed in Fig. A1-6 and graphing the function over the range of, say, $x = 0$ to $x = 5$ will do little to feature all the characteristics of the relationship.

**4-11**   The problem of determining the range of a function that contains its pertinent features is best approached through an identification of the types of forms of alternative functions and a knowledge of differential calculus. For example, the determination of a relevant range over which to graph the function $y = x^2 - 4x + 2$ would take into account a knowledge that the form of this equation is quadratic and, as such, it possesses a single point at which it turns, being symmetrical to either side of this 'turning point'. Differential calculus enables the determination of this point, i.e. at $x = 2$, and the 'nature' of the turning point, the $y$-value is a minimum. As such, a range may be devised which encloses the major characteristics of the function. For now readers must content themselves with a trial-and-error process based on features of curves briefly outlined in Sec. 5.

**4-12**   Having derived a sensible scale the function may be represented graphically. Consider the function $y = x^2 - 4x + 2$. First a table of values is formed over a range of values of $x$:

when $x = +5$;

$$y = x^2 - 4x + 2$$
$$= (5) - 4(5) + 2$$
$$= 25 - 20 + 2 = +7$$

when $x = +4$;

$$y = x^2 - 4x + 2$$
$$= (4)^2 - 4(4) + 2$$
$$= 16 - 16 + 2 = +2$$

when $x = +3$;

$$y = x^2 - 4x + 2$$
$$= (3)^2 - 4(3) + 2$$
$$= 9 - 12 + 2 = -1$$

when $x = +2$;

$$y = x^2 - 4x + 2$$
$$= (2)^2 - 4(2) + 2$$
$$= 4 - 8 + 2 = -2$$

when $x = +1$;

$$y = x^2 - 4x + 2$$
$$= (1)^2 - 4(1) + 2$$
$$= 1 - 4 + 2 = -1$$

when $x = 0$;

$$y = x^2 - 4x + 2$$
$$= (0)^2 - 4(0) + 2$$
$$= 0 - 0 + 2 = +2$$

when $x = -1$;

$$y = x^2 - 4x + 2$$
$$= (-1)^2 - 4(-1) + 2$$
$$= 1 + 4 + 2 = +7$$

which, summarized, yields:

| $x$ | $-1$ | 0 | 1 | 2 | 3 | 4 | 5 |
|---|---|---|---|---|---|---|---|
| $y$ | 7 | 2 | $-1$ | $-2$ | $-1$ | 2 | 7 |

Values of $x$ and their corresponding values of $y$ have been plotted on Fig. A1-7. The points have been joined to yield the (non-linear) graphical representation of the function $y = x^2 - 4x + 2$.

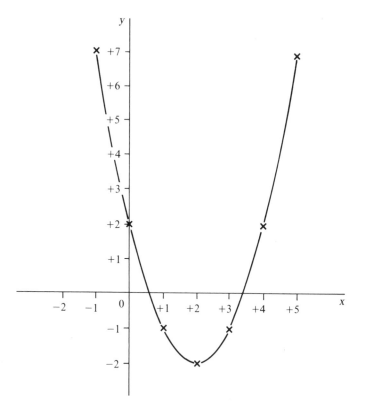

**Figure A1-7**   Graphical presentation of $y = x^2 - 4x + 2$

# 5 'TYPES' OF FUNCTIONS AND THEIR INTERPRETATION

**5-1**   If algebra is a language, then functions are the way of expressing relationships between two or more variables. In algebra we find that relationships among variables differ and this is necessary if they are to model the different types of relationship between variables occurring in everyday life. For instance, the function relating consumption to income (see Sec. 4-2) may well have a very different form from the function which might be expected to link the sales of ice-cream and the temperature. In this latter case an increase in temperature from 0 °C to 10 °C is unlikely to cause a large rise in sales, but if the temperature rises from 20 °C to 30 °C then very much more ice-cream is likely to be sold; the change in temperature was the same in each case, but the effect on ice-cream sales might be very different.

   In this section a few of the more common types of functions will be discussed. Functional relationships between two variables, that is of the form $y = f(x)$, can be categorized into two types: linear and non-linear. By definition linear functions can have only one 'structural' form—they can be represented on a graph only as a straight line. Non-linear functions can take a large variety of forms: only the simplest will be discussed in any detail here. Brief mention will also be made of functions with more than two variables.

**5-2 Linear functions**  In Sec. 4-2 the reader was introduced to a simple 'consumption' function in which the level of a household's consumption ($C$) was shown to vary directly with its income ($I$) according to the function:

$$C = 100 + 0.75I \tag{5-1}$$

It was seen in Fig. A1-5 that this function is represented on a graph by a straight line. Hence this type of relationship is referred to as a linear function. As previously noted, $C$ and $I$ are variables in this function. In any one function there are also constants, referred to as *parameters*, which tell us the way in which the two variables are related. In this case these constants or parameters are 100 and 0.75, and the meaning of these is discussed below.

Instead of $C$ and $I$, we can use the more conventional variables $y$ and $x$ in the following examples of linear functions:

$$y = 1 + 2x \tag{5-2}$$
$$y = 5x - 3 \tag{5-3}$$
$$y = 13 - 7x \tag{5-4}$$
$$y = 4x \text{ (which could be written } y = 0 + 4x) \tag{5-5}$$
$$y = -x \text{ (which could be written } y = 0 - x) \tag{5-6}$$
$$y = 2 \text{ (which could be written } y = 2 + 0(x)) \tag{5-7}$$

A linear function can be written in the general form:

$$y = a + bx \tag{5-8}$$

where $a$ and $b$ are used to represent the numerical parameters or constants. So, in any one function $a$ and $b$ will have fixed or constant values, while $y$ and $x$ may be varied. Thus in Eq. (5-2) $a = 1$ and $b = 2$; in Eq. (5-3) $a = -3$ and $b = 5$, and so on; in Eq. (5-7) $a = 2$ and $b = 0$. It is stressed that the sign ($-$ or $+$) is part of the parameter or constant term and must not be ignored (see Sec. 2).

Equation (5-7) is a very special case where $y$ is not influenced by changes in the value of $x$, and so $y$ takes a constant value of 2, and it would be represented on a graph by a straight line parallel to the horizontal or $x$-axis. The reader is invited to 'map' or 'plot' the functions (5-2) to (5-6) using the principles of Sec. 4.

In all cases it will be found that the functions are represented by a straight line since they are linear functions. Another way of establishing that a function is linear is by noting that in each case the variable $x$ (or $I$ in Eq. (5-1)) has a power of 1; for instance, we could write Eq. (5-4) as:

$$y = 13 - 7x^1$$

(If this is not clear the reader should refer to Secs 2-2 and 2-3.) For this reason linear functions are also referred to as first-degree functions. The degree of a function is the highest power of the '$x$-variable' which appears in the equation.

**5-2-1 The meaning of $a$ and $b$**  Consider again Eq. (5-1), which may be interpreted as follows. It has already been established that it means that a household's consumption, $C$, is a (linear) function of its income, $I$. The functional relationship of (5-1) contains more information. It may be interpreted as saying that consumption consists of two components. First, consider the situation when $I = 0$ and therefore $C = 100$. In other words, household consumption is £100 even if there is no income at all; in practice this would mean that the household is running down its savings—something which obviously could not continue indefinitely. In terms of a graphical presentation, point $a$ in Fig. A1-8 (which is an extended version of Fig. A1-5) is the one at which income is zero; $I = 0$, and $C = 100$. This point $a$ is where the graph of the function (5-1) crosses the vertical axis; it is for this reason that the parameter or constant term ($a$ in $y = a + bx$) is referred to as the intercept.

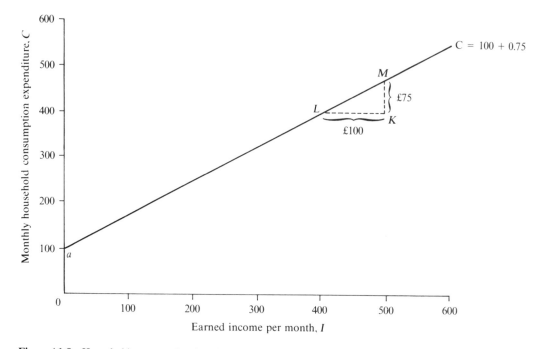

**Figure A1-8**  Household consumption function illustrating the parameters of a linear function

The second component of consumption is that which relates it directly or proportionally to income. Thus, Eq. (5-1) tells us that 0.75 (or 75 per cent) of income will be devoted to consumption in addition to the £100 which is consumed independent of income. The slope coefficient $b$ may also be interpreted as showing that if income changes by £100 then consumption will change by £75. Consider again Fig. A1-8 where income rises from £400 to £500—that is, by an amount equal to the distance $LK$ (i.e. between points $L$ and $K$)—while consumption rises by an amount represented by $KM$. We can now define the gradient or slope of the function as:

$$\frac{\text{Increase in consumption}}{\text{Increase in income}} = \frac{KM}{LK} = \frac{75}{100} = 0.75$$

The slope is the number of units by which consumption increases if income increases by one unit. In linear functions the slope is constant; thus, wherever on the graph it is measured, the slope is always the same. (This is different from non-linear functions—see Sec. 5-3 below.)

Applying these principles to the general form of a linear function given by Eq. (5-8), then $a$ is the intercept (the value of $y$ if $x=0$) and $b$ is the slope (the amount by which $y$ changes if $x$ changes by one unit). It should be noted that both $a$ and $b$ can be either positive or negative. If the slope, $b$, is positive (as in Eq. (5-2) for instance) then the graph of the function slopes upwards from left to right as $x$ increases; and conversely, if the slope is negative (as in Eq. (5-4)), then the graph will slope downwards from left to right as $x$ increases. It is most important that the sign of this slope should be established firmly before attempting to interpret any function.

In general it is possible to find the slope of a linear function if two points are known. Take the points $L$ and $M$ in Fig. A1-9. $L$ has an $x$-value of $x_1$, and a corresponding $y$-value of $y_1$. The $x$-value rises to $x_2$, that is the change is $(x_2 - x_1)$. Similarly the $y$-value rises to $y_2$, a change of $(y_2 - y_1)$.

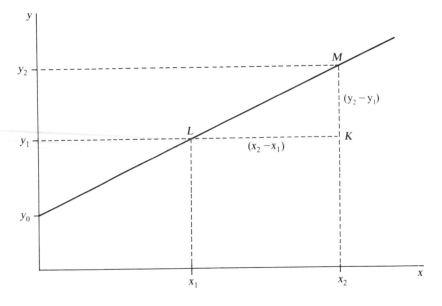

**Figure A1-9**

Then the slope of the function is:

$$\frac{\text{Change in } y}{\text{Change in } x} = \frac{y_2 - y_1}{x_2 - x_1} \tag{5-9}$$

When using this method be particularly careful to make sure the signs of the top (numerator) and bottom lines (denominator) are correct. Finding the intercept is, of course, much easier; it is simply the value of $y$ when $x$ is zero. Thus in Fig. A1-9 the intercept is $y_0$.

### 5-3 Non-linear functions

**5-3-1 Quadratic (second degree) functions**   Such functions are ones in which, for $y = f(x)$, the highest exponent of $x$ is 2. Examples of such functions were encountered in previous sections (see Sec. 4-10 where the expression $y = x^2 - 4x + 2$ was used in Fig. A1-7). Remember from Sec. 5-2 above that the degree of a function is the highest power of the $x$-variable which is present so a quadratic or second-degree function must have a term in $x^2$ and no term with a higher power of $x$.

   Some examples of quadratic functions are:

$$y = 3x^2 + 2x + 1 \tag{5-10}$$
$$y = 5x^2 - 3x + 2 \tag{5-11}$$
$$y = -x^2 + 8x - 3 \tag{5-12}$$
$$y = x^2 - 4 \tag{5-13}$$
$$y = x(x - 1) + 2 \text{ (which could be written: } y = x^2 - x + 2) \tag{5-14}$$
$$y = -5x^2 \text{ (which could be written: } y = 5x^2 + 0(x) + 0) \tag{5-15}$$

So a general form of the quadratic function is:

$$y = ax^2 + bx + c \tag{5-16}$$

As explained in Sec. 5-2, the variables are $y$ and $x$; $a, b, c$ represent the constants or parameters. For instance, in (5-11) above $a = 5, b = -3$ and $c = 2$; in (5-15) $a = -5, b = 0$ and $c = 0$. It is not necessary for a term in $x$ or for a constant term to be present for a function to be quadratic or second order, as long as there is a term in $x^2$.

The graphical representation in Fig. A1-7 of the function $y = x^2 - 4x + 2$, suggests that when plotted over an appropriate range of values of $x$, quadratic functions are very distinctly non-linear. Usually they have a distinct 'U' (or valley) or inverted 'U' (or hill) shape as a result of a distinct bend or 'turning point'. The shape of the function is determined by the sign of $a$ in (5-16). If $a$ is positive the curve will be U-shaped; if $a$ is negative it will be in the form of an inverted 'U'.

As with linear functions, the constant term is the intercept or the point of intersection of the curve with the vertical or $y$-axis. In Fig. A1-7 the intercept is 2, in Eq. (5-10) it is 1, in Eq. (5-13) it is $-4$, and in the general form of Eq. (5-16) the intercept is $c$.

The most marked difference between the linear and non-linear cases is that in non-linear functions the slope is not constant; in fact the slope is always changing, and it is this feature which gives the graphs of such functions their curved appearance. Although it is possible to make a rough estimate of the slope for small changes over a short range of values using the method contained in Eq. (5-9), this is by no means accurate and could at times be highly misleading (for instance, in the function $y = x^2 - 4x + 2$ or Fig. A1-7)), the true value of the slope is $-4$ when $x = 0$ and $+4$ when $x = 4$. If the method given by Eq. (5-9) had been used this would have given a slope of zero if the same two values of $x$ had been used.

This method of calculating the slope for non-linear equations is not recommended except in certain limited circumstances and only very small changes in $x$ should be used (e.g. 0.1 or less). The correct method involves the use of differential calculus, which is beyond the scope of this text.

**5-3-2 Other non-linear functions**  While a quadratic (second-degree) function has one 'bend' or turning point, functions of higher degrees have more such bends though they are not always very pronounced. so, for instance, a cubic (or third-degree) function will have two turning points, a fourth-degree function three turning points, and so on. An example of a cubic (or third-degree) function is:

$$y = 2x^3 + 4x^2 - 5x + 10$$

that is, it has a term in $x^3$ but no higher power of $x$ is present.

There are other types of functions that have distinctly different properties to those above, and details will be found in more advanced textbooks. Examples are exponential, logarithmic and power functions.

**5-4 Functions of two or more variables**  The discussion above has concerned different forms of relationships between the variables $y$ and $x$, which are formally expressed as:

$$y = f(x)$$

It is possible, and often more realistic, to suggest that the variable $y$ is affected by several variables. For example, returning to the consumption function in Eq. (5-1), it may be that a household's consumption is determined not only by its income, but by the number of individuals within the family ($N$), and the average age of its members ($A$). So instead of saying that $C$ is a function of $I$ (i.e. $C = f(I)$), it is now being suggested that $C$ is a function of $I$, $N$ and $A$, that is:

$$C = f(I, N, A)$$

Returning to the $y$ and $x$ notation, it is possible that $y$ is influenced not just by $x$, but by $v$, $w$ and $z$ as well, that is:

$$y = f(v, w, x, z)$$

An example of this was introduced in Sec. 4-5:

$$y = 0.4x + 0.6z \qquad (5\text{-}17)$$

where $y$ was a student's final overall mark, $x$ was the coursework mark and $z$ was the examination mark.

Incidentally it is of interest to note that this relationship can be manipulated in various ways. At the end of the year the examiner knows $x$ and $z$ and so can work out $y$, the final mark. But the student can use the equation too. He or she knows that the pass mark is 50 (for example), and that in the coursework a mark of 40 was obtained. The problem is how well does he or she have to do in the examinations in order to pass? This can be restated in algebra as follows: given the relationship (5-17) and knowing that $y = 50$ and $x = 40$, what is the value of $z$?

Substituting $y = 50$ and $x = 40$ in (5-17) gives:

$$50 = 0.4(40) + 0.6z$$

therefore

$$50 = 16 + 0.6z$$

At this stage it is necessary to become familiar with some principles of algebraic/numerical manipulation. We know that: $50 = 16 + 0.6z$. However, our aim is to determine the value of $z$. Since we have an equation with one 'unknown' it is (generally) possible to solve the equation to determine its value (this principle will be extended in Sec. 6-2). Since the aim of the exercise is to determine $z$, we need to isolate $z$ on one side of the 'equals' sign so that something is equal to $z$ ($z$ on the left-hand side (LHS) of the 'equals' sign) or $z$ is equal to something ($z$ on the right-hand side (RHS) of the 'equals' sign)—for this example the former process will be adopted.

| | |
|---|---|
| $50 = 16 + 0.6z$ | transfer the '16' to the LHS by subtracting '16' from both sides |
| $50 - 16 = 16 + 0.6z - 16$ | |
| $50 - 16 = 0.6z$ | transfer the '0.6' to the LHS by dividing both sides by 0.6 |
| $\dfrac{50 - 16}{0.6} = \dfrac{0.6z}{0.6}$ | |
| $\therefore \dfrac{50 - 16}{0.6} = z$ | evaluate LHS |
| $\therefore 56.66 = z$ | |

The student needs to score 57 per cent in the examination to ensure that the exam is passed. Note that in each of the above steps the same operation was conducted on both sides of the equation to maintain the logic of the relationship. For example, if $x$ is the price of a colour television in £s and 2 colour televisions cost £600:

$$2x = 600$$

By dividing both sides by 2:

$$x = 300$$

the logic of the relationship is maintained.

Functions in which $y$ is determined by more than one variable can be divided into linear and non-linear types, although it is not so easy to identify these by means of graphical techniques (see Sec. 4-5). Some examples are given below of different forms of the functional relationship:

$$y=f(x,z)$$

(a) Linear (first degree):

$$y=4+2x+3z$$
$$y=3x-17z$$
$$y=4x-z-2$$
$$y=ax+bz+c$$

(b) Non-linear (higher degree)

$$y=4+2x^2+z$$
$$y=8+2x^2z+z-x$$
$$y=x(x^2-z)$$
$$\text{which could also be written } y=x^3-xz$$

**5-5 Dependent and independent variables**　In all the functions discussed so far it has been said that $y$ is a function of $x$ (and perhaps $z$, $w$, etc.). Another way of expressing this is to say that $y$ is determined by, or is dependent on, $x$ (and $z$, $w$, etc.). It is usual to refer to $y$ as the dependent variable, and $x$ (and $z$, $w$, etc.) as the independent variable(s), signifying that the latter are not determined by any variable within the system. It is conventional to write the dependent variable on the left-hand side of a function, and to plot it on the vertical axis of a graph, with the independent variables on the right-hand side, and on the horizontal axis (in the case of one independent variable). The notation $y=f(x)$ implies the dependence of $y$ on $x$, though on occasions where no straightforward dependence can be discerned, variables are interdependent, and the notation $f(x,y)$ is used.

# 6 SOLUTION OF SIMULTANEOUS EQUATIONS: GRAPHICAL AND ALGEBRAIC

**6-1 Introduction**　Readers will no doubt have seen brainteasers like this:

Ten years ago a father was twice as old as his daughter is now. The sum of their present ages is 70. What are their present ages?

The solution to this is very simple if a little algebra is used. Let the father's present age be denoted by $f$, and the daughter's age by $d$. We know that the sum of their present ages is 70, so:

$$f+d=70 \tag{6-1}$$

Now the father's age 10 years ago was $(f-10)$ and that is two times his daughter's present age, so:

$$f-10=2d$$

This can be rearranged to give:

$$f-2d=10 \tag{6-2}$$

Equation (6-1), $f+d=70$, does not have a unique solution. Indeed any number of combinations of $f$ and $d$ would satisfy this: for instance, $f=1$ and $d=69$ would be algebraically correct, but in the context of the question is nonsense, since it would mean that the daughter was 68 years older than her father! Furthermore, these values would not simultaneously satisfy Eq. (6-2). Similarly, if we took Eq. (6-2), we would find that $f=12$ and $d=1$ provide a possible 'solution'. But then this would not meet the requirement of Eq. (6-1) that the sum of their ages is 70 (not to mention the biological problems!).

If the two equations ((6-1) and (6-2)) are each considered separately they will not provide an easy answer—except through a laborious process of 'trial and error', that is seeing whether a 'solution' for (6-1) satisfied (6-2), and so on until both equations were solved. Instead of this it is possible to solve both equations at the same time and equations (I) and (II) constitute a system of simultaneous equations. A method of solving these is described below.

**6-2 Some conditions for a solution**  An essential condition for a unique solution (that is one in which $x$, $y$, $z$, etc., each have one numerical solution) is that the number of variables (or 'unknowns') in the system should be equal to the number of equations. This does not, however, mean that each variable must appear in each equation. So the following three equations constitute a system of simultaneous equations:

$$2x+y+z = 11$$
$$y+4z = 17$$
$$7x+4y-3z = 13$$

In principle, there is no limit to the size of a system of simultaneous equations, subject to the condition that the number of variables is equal to the number of equations.

There is another condition for a complete solution: *no equation should be an exact multiple of another*. For instance, the following is not a true system of simultaneous equations:

$$3x+6y=15$$

$$2x+4y=10$$

because if each of the terms of the second equation are multiplied by 1.5 the two equations become identical, and no solution will be found. The two original equations in effect are simply two ways of saying the same thing.

**6-3 An economic example**  Simultaneous equations describe several sets of relationships that are true at the same time. To illustrate this principle and the solution an economic example is used: that of the relationship between supply and demand.

A demand function relates the quantity demanded, $q$, to the price, $p$, of the good in question. The demand function is likely to be represented by a downward sloping curve (that is, a negative slope coefficient) because it is to be expected that the higher the price, the smaller will be the demand (and vice versa). As an example, consider the demand for bars of chocolate which is (fictionally) given by the linear demand function:

$$q_D = 100 - 2p$$

where $q_D$ is the quantity demanded (in million bars of chocolate per year) and $p$ is the price in pence per bar. This is plotted in Fig. A1-10 as the curve *DD*. By similar reasoning, a supply function describes the varying quantity produced by manufacturers of chocolate in response to different prices. The supply function is likely to have a positive slope coefficient, because the higher the price, the larger is the level of production likely to be. So the supply function will be upward sloping, as illustrated, by the line *SS* in Fig. A1-11, which is the graphical representation of the hypothetical linear supply function:

$$q_S = 25 + 3p$$

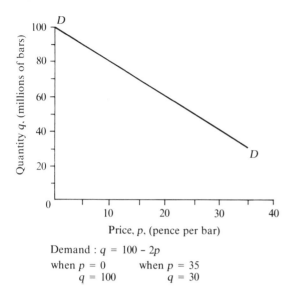

Demand : $q = 100 - 2p$
when $p = 0$     when $p = 35$
     $q = 100$       $q = 30$

**Figure A1-10**   Demand for chocolate

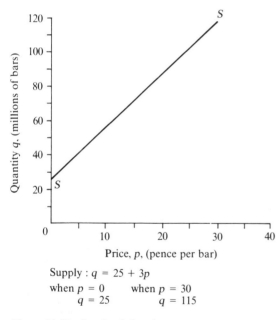

Supply : $q = 25 + 3p$
when $p = 0$     when $p = 30$
     $q = 25$         $q = 115$

**Figure A1-11**   Supply of chocolate

The problem is to determine the price at which quantity demanded will equal quantity supplied, i.e. $q_D = q_S = q$. The two equations, now given by:

$$q = 100 - 2p \quad \text{and} \quad q = 25 + 3p$$

may be solved for values of $p$ and $q$.

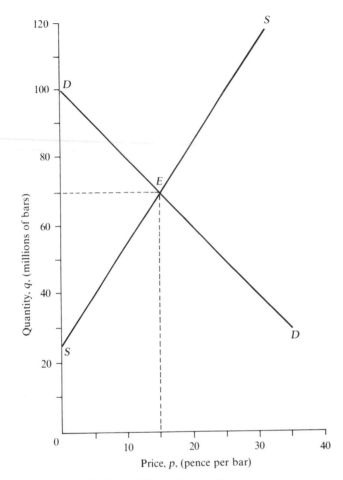

**Figure A1-12**  Market equilibrium for chocolate

**6-4  A graphical solution**  It is clear from Figs A1-10 and A1-11, which show a range of quantities demanded and supplied at corresponding prices, that there is no way of finding out from just one curve which quantity/price combination will actually exist, since it is supposed that only one price can exist. This 'equilibrium' quantity/price combination will exist where the two lines intersect, that is when the quantity yielded by the supply function and the demand function is the same in each case. A graphical solution can be obtained by plotting both functions on the same graph and reading off the values of $q$ and $p$ at their point of intersection. This has been done in Fig. A1-12 and the 'equilibrium' is found at point $E$ where the price, $p$, is 15, and the quantity (demanded and supplied), $q$, is 70.

This method should be used only to provide an approximate answer; it is in any case not suitable for a system with three or more variables because of the problems in constructing three-dimensional graphs, and the impossibility of drawing four-(or more)-dimensional graphs. A much more satisfactory (and less time-consuming) method is the following algebraic solution.

**6-5  Algebraic solutions**

**6-5-1  Supply and demand**  The most general method is a process of elimination in which one variable is removed from the system, so that the second variable can be calculated and then in turn this value is used to obtain the value taken by the first variable. There are two fundamental rules:

*Rule 1*   An equation may be multiplied or divided throughout (i.e. on both sides) by a constant (number).

*Rule 2*   An equation (or any multiple of it) may be added to or subtracted from any other equation in the system.

The correct application of these rules will always lead to the solution, if one exists.
    Consider again the supply and demand equations above:

$$\text{Demand}: q = 100 - 2p$$
$$\text{Supply}: \quad q = 25 + 3p$$

'Rearrange' them to bring the 'unknowns' to the left-hand side and the constants to the right-hand side; that is, add $2p$ to each side of the demand equation and subtract $3p$ from each side of the supply equation:

$$q + 2p = 100 \tag{6-3}$$
$$q - 3p = 25 \tag{6-4}$$

We now proceed with the elimination method which, in this case, is quite straightforward. It is easily seen that if Eq. (6-4) is subtracted term by term from Eq. (6-3) (using Rule 2), $q$ is eliminated.

Subtract (6-4) from (6-3):     $(q - q) + (2p - (-3p)) = 100 - 25$
(and be very careful about signs)
$$5p = 75$$
Divide both sides by 5:     $p = 15$

So the equilibrium price, $p$, is 15. We can now substitute $p = 15$ in either of Eqs (6-3) or (6-4) to obtain the equilibrium value of $q$, and then check by substituting the values of $p$ and $q$ in whichever equation was not used.

Substitute $p = 15$ in (6-3):     $q + 2(15) = 100$
$$q + 30 \quad = 100$$
$$q \qquad = 100 - 30$$
$$q \qquad = 70$$

Checking by substituting:

$$p = 15 \text{ and } q = 70 \text{ in } (6\text{-}4): 70 - 3(15) = 70 - 45 = 25$$

Therefore, the solution is $p = 15$ and $q = 70$.
    In this (rather special) case a slightly quicker method would have been to notice that the original demand and supply equations both had $q$ on the left-hand side. It would have been legitimate to write:

$$100 - 2p = 25 + 3p$$

then to solve for $p$ and substitute back into one of the equations to calculate $q$, checking as before.

**6-5-2 A further example**   The solution outlined in detail was very simply reached because the variable $q$ had a coefficient of 1 in each case. It is rare to find such an obliging system of equations.
    Consider the following system:

$$3x + 7y = 88 \tag{6-5a}$$
$$8x - 11y = 27 \tag{6-6a}$$

There is no obvious choice as to which to eliminate first; $x$ is chosen since the magnitudes are slightly smaller. In such a case multiply the first equation by the coefficient of $x$ (the variable to be eliminated) in the second equation and vice versa.

Multiply each term in (6-5a) by 8: $\quad 24x + 56y = 704$ (Rule 2) $\qquad\qquad\qquad$ (6-5b)

Multiply each term in (6-6a) by 3: $\quad 24x - 33y = \phantom{0}81$ (Rule 2) $\qquad\qquad\qquad$ (6-6b)

Subtract (6-6b) from (6-5b):
$$(24x - 24x) + (56y - (-33y)) = 704 - 81 \text{ (Rule 1)}$$
$$0 + 56y + 33y = 623$$
$$89y = 623$$
$$y = 7$$

Substitute $y = 7$ in (6-5a):
$$3x + 7(7) = 88$$
$$3x + 49 = 88$$
$$3x = 39$$
$$x = 13$$

Check by substitution of $x$ and $y$ in (6-6a): $8(13) - 11(7) = 104 - 77 = 27$.

There are no general rules about which variable to eliminate first; this is something of an acquired knack and the only answer is practice.

**6-5-3 A solution by substitution**  In some simpler systems of equations the method of elimination may prove rather laborious, although it will always give a result. In some cases it may be quicker to use the substitution method. This is demonstrated by using the example given in Sec. 6-1 concerning the ages of father and daughter. The equations obtained were:

$$f + d = 70 \qquad\qquad\qquad (6\text{-}1)$$
$$f - 2d = 10 \qquad\qquad\qquad (6\text{-}2)$$

Add $2d$ to both sides of (6-2):

$$f = 10 + 2d \qquad\qquad\qquad (6\text{-}7)$$

Substitute this expression of $f$ into (6-1):

$$(10 + 2d) + d = 70$$
$$10 + 2d + d = 70$$
$$10 + 3d = 70$$
$$3d = 70 - 10$$
$$3d = 60$$
$$d = \frac{60}{3} = 20$$

Substitute $d = 20$ in (6-1):

$$f + 20 = 70$$
$$f = 50$$

Check by substituting $f = 50$ and $d = 20$ in (6-2):

$$50 - 2(20) = 50 - 40 = 10$$

So the father is 50 and his daughter is 20.

The method therefore consists of using one equation (in this case (6-2)) to express one variable in terms of the other (i.e. $f$ in terms of $d$) and then using the resulting expression in the remaining equation.

**6-6 Systems of more than two equations**   In principle the numerical solutions described above (particularly the method of elimination) can be extended to systems with any number of equations, but for more than three equations the solutions become very cumbersome. An alternative is to use matrix algebra. [This section is beyond the needs of the text].

It must suffice here to provide an example of the solution of a system of three equations in three variables $x$, $y$ and $z$. The method consists of first eliminating one variable to give two equations in two 'unknowns' and then solving as in Sec. 6-5. Consider:

$$x+y-z=0 \tag{6-8a}$$
$$2x+y+4z=16 \tag{6-9}$$
$$-x-2y+3z=4 \tag{6-10}$$

First eliminate $x$.

Add (6-8a) to (6-10):

$$0-y+2z=4 \tag{6-11}$$

Bring down (6-9) for next operation:

$$2x+y+z=16 \tag{6-9}$$

Multiply (6-8a) by 2:

$$2x+2y-2z=0 \tag{6-8b}$$

Subtract (6-8b) from (6-9):

$$0-y+6z=16 \tag{6-12}$$

Equations (6-11) and (6-12) may now be solved as a pair of equations in $y$ and $z$:

$$-y+2z=4 \tag{6-11}$$
$$-y+6z=16 \tag{6-12}$$

Subtract (6-11) from (6-12):

$$\begin{aligned}(-y-(-y))+(6z-2z)&=16-4\\ 0+4z&=12\\ z&=3\end{aligned}$$

Substitute $z=3$ in (6-11):

$$\begin{aligned}-y+2(3)&=4\\ -y+6&=4\\ -y&=4-6=-2\\ y&=2\end{aligned}$$

Check by substitution of $y$ and $z$ in (6-12).
Substitute $y=2$ and $z=3$ in (6-8a) to obtain $x$:

$$\begin{aligned}x+2-3&=0\\ x&=-2+3\\ x&=1\end{aligned}$$

Check by substitution in (6-9) (or (6-10)):

$$2(1)+2+4(3)=2+2+12=16$$

The solution is $x=1$; $y=2$; $z=3$.

# 7 'SOLUTION' OF QUADRATIC EQUATIONS: GRAPHICAL AND ALGEBRAIC

**7-1 Introduction**   Previous sections have outlined the 'solution' of single equations (e.g. $3x+8=0$) and systems of simultaneous equations with two or more variables (e.g. $x+y=3$; $x-y=1$). In both cases these have been equations of the first degree. This section introduced some of the methods of 'solving' equations of the second degree, otherwise called quadratic equations.

In Sec. 5 a general form of a quadratic equation was said to be:

$$y=ax^2+bx+c$$

where $x$ and $y$ are variables, and, $b$ and $c$ stand for constants. A specific example (where $a=2$, $b=3$ and $c=1$) is:

$$y=2x^2+3x+1$$

We have repeatedly said that one equation with two variables or 'unknowns' does not have a unique solution. However, suppose that we know (or assume) that $y=0$, then the equation above becomes (after rearrangement):

$$2x^2+3x+1=0$$

This equation has only one 'unknown' and can in principle be solved. Three methods for solving such equations will be discussed in this section:

(a) by graphical means
(b) by factorization
(c) by using a formula.

Before proceeding to solutions various points should be made. First, the values of $x$ which satisfy a quadratic equation with zero on the right-hand side are referred to as the roots of the equation. Second, if the product of two or more unknowns is zero, than at least one of the unknowns must be zero; for example, if

$$K \times L \times M \times N = 0$$

then at least one of $K$, $L$, $M$ or $N$ is also zero. This is because the product of zero and any other number is zero. It is thus true that if

$$(x+2)(x-1)=0$$

then either $(x+2)=0$ or $(x-1)=0$ or both are equal to zero.

Consider a very simple quadratic function, whose roots can be seen intuitively:

$$y=x^2-1$$

Set $y=0$ to find the roots of the quadratic equation $x^2-1=0$.

If $x^2-1=0$ then, subtracting 1 from both sides, $x^2=1$.

The solution here can be found by asking 'what value of $x$ when squared gives the answer 1?'; in other words find the square root of 1, which is $+1$ or $-1$. That is:

$$\text{If } x^2=1 \text{ then } either \; x=1 \; or \; x=-1.$$

The roots of the equation $x^2 - 1 = 0$ are 1 and $-1$. In such cases where the absolute value is the same we can write $x = \mp 1$ (read as '$x$ is equal to plus or minus one').

**7-2 A graphical solution**  Consider the quadratic function:

$$y = x^2 + 2x - 5$$

In order to find its roots it is necessary that $y = 0$. In terms of a graphical presentation this is the point (or points) at which the curve crosses the $x$-axis (the value of $y$ at all points on the horizontal or $x$-axis is zero). Thus the 'solution' consists of identifying the point or points at which the curve intersects the $x$-axis; the values of $x$ at these points are the roots of the equation. In Fig. A1-13 the

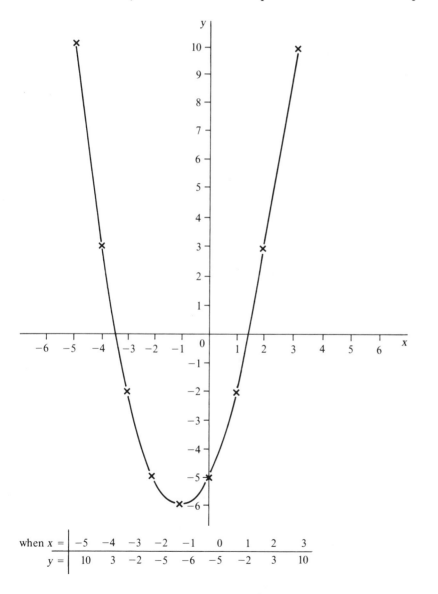

| when $x =$ | $-5$ | $-4$ | $-3$ | $-2$ | $-1$ | 0 | 1 | 2 | 3 |
|---|---|---|---|---|---|---|---|---|---|
| $y =$ | 10 | 3 | $-2$ | $-5$ | $-6$ | $-5$ | $-2$ | 3 | 10 |

**Figure A1-13**  Graph of the quadratic function $y = x^2 + 2x - 5$ over the range $x = -5$ to $x = 3$

above function intersects the $x$-axis at the points where $x = -3.5$ and $x = 1.5$ approximately. These two values provide rough estimates of roots of the equation.

It must be stressed that graphical solutions provide only approximate answers, owing to inaccuracies in drawing graphs and reading values from them. Wherever possible algebraic solutions should be sought.

When the quadratic function is plotted as a graph the curve may not touch or intersect the $x$-axis at all. An example of such a function is:

$$y = x^2 + x + 1$$

It will also be seen in the following sections that no numerical solution (using the basic techniques) exists. In these cases the equation does not have 'real' roots (see later for a further explanation).

**7-3 Solution by factorization** Factorization consists of attempting to break the quadratic expression $ax^2 + bx + c$ into two terms of the form $(fx + d)$ and $(gx + e)$ whose product is equal to the original quadratic expression (once again the letters $a, b, c, d, e, f$ and $g$ stand for constants). For instance, it can be shown that the expression $x^2 + 3x + 2$ can be broken into the factors $(x + 1)$ and $(x + 2)$ where $f = g = 1$. That is:

$$x^2 + 3x + 2 = (x + 1)(x + 2)$$

Before proceeding to the method of factorization we shall see how the factors are used to solve a quadratic equation. In order to find the roots of the quadratic

$$x^2 + 3x + 2 = 0$$

the left-hand side is factorized:

$$(x + 1)(x + 2) = 0$$

Then it must be true that:

$$\text{either} \quad (x + 1) = 0$$
$$x = -1$$
$$\text{or} \quad (x + 2) = 0$$
$$x = -2$$

Therefore, the roots of the equation are $-1$ and $-2$. This can be checked by calculating the value of $y$ in the functional relationship $y = x^2 + 3x + 2$ when $x = -1$ and $x = -2$:

when $x = -1$; 
$$y = (-1)^2 + 3(-1) + 2$$
$$= 1 - 3 + 2$$
$$= 0$$

when $x = -2$; 
$$y = (-2)^2 + 3(-2) + 2$$
$$= 4 - 6 + 2$$
$$= 0$$

This was based on our definition of the roots of an equation as being the values of $x$ for which $y$ is zero.

**7-3-1 The methods of factorization** Factorization is the reverse of the process described in Section 3 (see Sec. 3-4 in particular) for multiplying together two expressions like $(x - 1)$ and $(6x - 4)$. Each item in the first brackets is multiplied in turn by each term in the second brackets, thus:

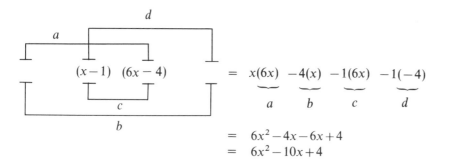

$$= x(6x) \; -4(x) \; -1(6x) \; -1(-4)$$

$$\underbrace{\phantom{x(6x)}}_{a} \quad \underbrace{\phantom{-4(x)}}_{b} \quad \underbrace{\phantom{-1(6x)}}_{c} \quad \underbrace{\phantom{-1(-4)}}_{d}$$

$$= 6x^2 - 4x - 6x + 4$$
$$= 6x^2 - 10x + 4$$

In the above example $(x-1)(6x-4)$ was reduced to the quadratic $6x^2 - 10x + 4$. The problem we now turn to is given a quadratic how do we convert it into two expressions multiplied together (or two factors). This is the process of *factorization*. Consider:

$$4x^2 + 4x - 8 = y$$

our answer through factorization is:

$$(4x - 4)(x + 2) = y$$

This was obtained by taking the item with the highest power first $(4x^2)$ and choosing two items which, when multiplied together, yield $4x^2$; for example, $4x$ and $x$. These are placed as the first entry in each set of brackets, i.e.:

$$(4x \qquad)(x \qquad) = y$$

The number (or constant) value in the quadratic is chosen next $(-8)$ and two items which, when multiplied together, yield $-8$ are chosen, $-4$ and $+2$, and inserted as the last items in each of the brackets, i.e.:

$$(4x - 4)(x + 2) = y$$

The remaining steps designated above are multiplied out and the middle term $(+4x)$ results. Now the choice of items has been fortunate; however, in practice we may have initially chosen $2x$ and $2x$ as the first entries to yield $4x^2$ and the middle terms would not have multiplied out to yield $+4x$. Alternatively, we could have used $-8$ and $+1$ to yield $-8$, and again the process would not have been successful. Even if the values chosen to yield $-8$ were correct, by inserting $+2$ in the brackets containing $4x$ and $-4$ in the brackets containing $x$ the middle term would not have been forthcoming. In reality a series of possible combinations must be tried until a correct answer results. Practice on a large number of problems is suggested (try making up a few quadratic expressions and factorizing them). It should be pointed out that many expressions will not yield any possible factors (at least in real numbers) and the meaning of and reason for this will now be discussed, as will an alternative approach to this problem.

By 'solution' of a quadratic equation we mean the values of $x$ where the function crosses the $x$-axis; that is, when $y=0$. Thus, in Fig. A1-13 the solutions of the quadratic equation $y = x^2 + 2x - 5$ can be seen to be $x = -3.5$ and $x = 1.5$. Such solutions are called *roots* of the equation. They are the values of the variable which makes the function have the value zero.

Figure A1-14 shows three quadratic functions; the function graphed in (a) has two roots ($x = 2$ and $x = 4$); the function graphed in (b) has two roots yet these coincide to yield only one value of

(a) $y = x^2 - 6x + 8$

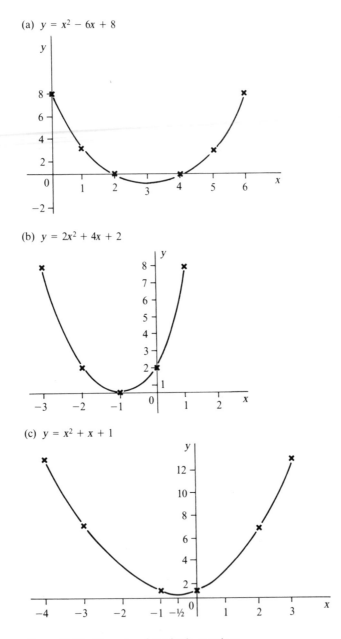

(b) $y = 2x^2 + 4x + 2$

(c) $y = x^2 + x + 1$

**Figure A1-14** Examples of quadratic equations

$x$ ($x = -1$) which solves the equation; the function graphed in (c) does not touch or cut the $x$-axis and has no *real* roots. There does exist a solution in terms of what are known as *imaginary* or *complex* numbers (as opposed to *real* numbers) but this involves a new field of mathematics, and is beyond the scope of this book.

Thus, given an equation, say:

$$y = x^2 - 6x + 8$$

the equation may be solved for where the function cuts the x-axis; that is, $y=0$, and values of $x$ which satisfy:

$$x^2 - 6x + 8 = 0$$

determined by graphing the function. The answer can be checked out by inserting each of the x-values ($x=2$ and $x=4$) back into the equation given above and identifying whether the result is equal to zero.

However, a precise and quicker algebraic solution may be obtained by factorizing the quadratic and putting each factor equal to zero, for example,

$$\begin{aligned}
x^2 - 6x + 8 &= 0 \\
(x-4)(x-2) &= 0 \\
(x-4) &= 0 \qquad\qquad (x-2) = 0 \\
\therefore\; x &= 4 \qquad\qquad \therefore\; x = 2
\end{aligned}$$

as given by Fig. A1-14(a).

If the function cannot be factorized it has no real roots. Try $2x^2 + 4x + 2 = 0$ and $x^2 + x + 1 = 0$ and check with Fig. A1-14(b) and (c); the former has one real root, the latter none.

**7-4 The formula method**   More generally, by using the following formula the roots may readily be determined:

$$x = \frac{-b \mp \sqrt{b^2 - 4ac}}{2a}$$

where $a$, $b$ and $c$ are the values given by the quadratic of the form $ax^2 + bx + c = 0$. Thus, for $x^2 - 6x + 8 = 0$, $a=1$, $b=-6$ and $c=+8$. Therefore:

$$x = \frac{-(-6) \mp \sqrt{(-6)^2 - 4(1)(8)}}{2(1)}$$

$$= \frac{6 \mp \sqrt{36 - 32}}{2} = \frac{6 \mp 2}{2}$$

The roots are obtained by first considering the $+$ sign in the $\mp$ part of the expression, and then the minus sign. For instance:

$$\frac{6+2}{2} = 4; \qquad \frac{6-2}{2} = 2$$

the roots of the equation being $x=4$ and $x=2$.

If the equation has one root (that is, two coincidental roots) then:

$$\sqrt{b^2 - 4ac} = 0 \quad \text{(try } 2x^2 + 4x + 2 = 0\text{)}$$

If the equation has no real roots, then $\sqrt{b^2 - 4ac}$ is negative—there being no real number equivalent of the square root of a minus number.

*Example*   The quantity demanded of a good, $D$, is related to the price of the good, $p$, as given by $D = 100 - p^2$, and the quantity supplied of the same good, $S$, is related to price, $p$, by the equation $S = 50 + 2p$. Determine the equilibrium price under which quantity demanded is equal to quantity supplied.

Equilibrium is where $D=S$:

$$D = 100 - p^2; \qquad S = 50 + 2p$$

where $D=S$

$$100 - p^2 = 50 + 2p \quad \text{(i.e. } 0 = p^2 + 2p - 50\text{)}$$

$$p = \frac{-2 \mp \sqrt{4 - 4(1)(-50)}}{2} = \frac{-2 \mp \sqrt{204}}{2}$$

$$= \frac{-2 \mp 14.28}{2}$$

Therefore $p = -8.14$ or $6.14$.

The former price is meaningless and we should, of course, have outlined the meaningful range for our function at the start of the problem. The latter price of 6.14 is the equilibrium price.

As a second example consider:

$$14x^2 + 22x - 12 = 0 \quad \text{(i.e. } a = 14, \ b = 22, \ c = -12\text{)}$$

Substituting:

$$x = \frac{-22 \mp \sqrt{(22)^2 - 4(14)(-12)}}{2(14)}$$

$$= \frac{-22 \mp \sqrt{484 + 672}}{28} = \frac{-22 \mp \sqrt{1156}}{28}$$

$$= \frac{-22 \mp 34}{28}$$

$$= \frac{-56}{28} \ \text{or} \ \frac{12}{28}$$

$$= -2 \ \text{or} \ \frac{3}{7}$$

**7-5 Quadratic equations without roots?**  In Sec. 7-3 a particular type of quadratic equation was mentioned which, when plotted on to a graph, was found not to touch or intersect the $x$-axis. An example is plotted in Fig. A1-14(c) and is seen not to touch the $x$-axis, i.e. $y$ is always positive (never zero). Let us now see what happens when we apply the 'solution' by formula (Sec. 7-4) to try to find its roots:

$$x^2 + x + 1 = 0 \quad (a = 1, \ b = 1, \ c = 1)$$

then

$$x = \frac{-1 + \sqrt{1 - 4(1)(1)}}{2(1)} = \frac{-1 + \sqrt{1 - 4}}{2}$$

$$= \frac{-1 + \sqrt{-3}}{2}$$

We have the apparently 'insoluble' problem of trying to find the square root of a negative number (see Sec. 2-3). In fact there is a 'solution' which involves the use of what are called *imaginary* or *complex* numbers, but that lies outside the scope of an introductory text. Let it suffice to say that the basic building block of the system of imaginary or complex numbers is the square root of $-1$, $\sqrt{-1}$, which is denoted by 'i'. It obeys many of the rules of ordinary algebra but there are, of course, some exceptions.

## 8 DIAGNOSTIC TEST

### QUESTIONS

#### Section 1: Elementary operations: arithmetical

1. $6(2) =$
2. $\frac{6}{5} \times \frac{3}{2} =$
3. $\frac{3}{2} \times 6 =$
4. $\frac{3}{4} \div \frac{1}{4} =$

5. $\frac{6}{2} \div 3 =$
6. $\frac{3}{2} + \frac{4}{2} =$
7. $\frac{4}{3} + \frac{1}{12} =$
8. $\frac{5}{100} - \frac{2}{100} =$

9. $\frac{6}{10} - \frac{1}{5} =$
10. $-6(-12) =$
11. $-3 + 2 =$
12. $\frac{4}{12} - \frac{5}{12} =$

#### Section 2: Powers and roots

1. $2^2 =$
2. $3^3 =$
3. $4^2 \times 4^3 =$
4. $3^4 \div 3^2 =$

5. $x^3 \times x^4 =$
6. $x^4 \div x =$
7. $10^0 =$
8. $x^0 =$

9. $2^{-1} =$
10. If $x = 3$ then $x^{-2} =$
11. $4^{-\frac{1}{2}} =$
12. If $x = 4$ then $x^{-\frac{3}{2}} =$

13. $\sqrt{16} =$
14. $49^{\frac{1}{2}} =$
15. $\sqrt{49} =$
16. $\sqrt[3]{125} =$

17. $(-3)^{-2} =$
18. $x^{-5} \times x^8 =$
19. $x^2 + x^3 =$
20. $3x^2 - 2x^2 + 6x =$

*Order of evaluation of basic mathematical operations*

1. $2 + 3(2 + 4) =$
2. $3 - 2(2^2 + 4 + 2) =$
3. $6(3 - 4) =$
4. $(6 - 2)(3 - 4) =$

5. $(x + 2)(x - 2) =$
6. $x + \dfrac{(2 - 6x)}{2} =$
7. $x^3 - x^2(x^3) =$

*Mathematical notation*

$NB$ = equals
  < less than
  > greater than

  ⩽ less than or equal to
  ⩾ greater than or equal to
  ≠ not equal to

Which of the following are correct?

1. $6 = 4$
2. $8 > 7$
3. $6 \geqslant 8$
4. $7 \neq 2$
5. $3 < 2 < 1$
6. $4 \geqslant 4 \geqslant 5$

#### Section 3: Elementary operations: algebraic

1. $x + x =$
2. $2x - x =$
3. $3x + 2y - x =$
4. $\dfrac{3x}{2x} \times \dfrac{1}{3x} =$
5. $\dfrac{1}{2x} \div \dfrac{1}{2x} =$
6. $\dfrac{2}{3x} + \dfrac{5}{2x} =$

**7.** Multiply out $(6x+2)(3x-1)$     **8.** Multiply out $(4x+2)(3x+1)$

## Section 4: Graphical representation of functions

Plot the following functions:

**1.** $y=6x+4$              **2.** $y=6x+8$              **3.** $y=-6x+8$
**4.** $y=12x+8$             **5.** $y=2x^2+4x+4$         **6.** $y=2+4x-x^2$
**7.** Shade the area denoted by $y\geqslant 6x+8$

## Section 5: Algebraic representation of functions

Which of the following functions are linear and which are quadratic?

**1.** $8=y-6x$             **2.** $y=-3x$             **3.** $y=4x^2-8x+2$
**4.** $y=3x-4$            **5.** $y=x^2+8$           **6.** $y=6x+4x-8$

For the equation $y=4-6x$ which of the following statements are correct?

**7.** The slope or gradient of the line is $-6$.     **8.** The intercept of the line is 4.
**9.** The line passes through the point $(0,2)$—i.e. $x=0$, $y=2$.
**10.** The line passes through the point $(2,-8)$  **11.** If $x=-2$, then $y=16$.

Evaluate $y$ for the following:

**12.** $y=6x^2-2x+8$; if $x=1$ then $y=$        **13.** $y=2x^2-8$; if $x=-1$ then $y=$
**14.** $y=2x^3-2x+8$; if $x=-2$ then $y=$       **15.** $y+5=2y+2$; therefore $y=$

**16.** $\dfrac{(20-y)}{2}=10$; therefore $y=$

## Section 6: Simultaneous equations

Determine the values of $x$ and $y$ for:

**1.** $6x+2y=10$          $x=$
    $3x+2y=7$          $y=$

**2.** $2x-4y=-6$         $x=$
    $3x-2y=-1$         $y=$

**3.** $B$ is the price of a pint of beer and $W$ is the price of a single whisky. Determine $B$ and $W$ given that 4 pints of beer and 8 whiskies cost £16.80 and 10 pints of beer and 4 whiskies cost £18.00.
    $B=$          $W=$

## Section 7: Quadratic equations

Using either factorization or the formula:

$$x=\frac{-b\mp\sqrt{b^2-4ac}}{2a} \quad \text{for } y=ax^2+bx+c$$

Solve where possible the following equations for real values of $x$ where $y=0$.

1. $y=x^2+4x+4$        $x=$
2. $y=2x^2+4x+2$       $x=$
3. $y=3x^2+10x-8$      $x=$
4. $y=3x^2+4x+2$       $x=$
5. Which of the above equations (1, 2, 3 or 4) has no real solution, that is the equation when graphed does not cut or touch the $x$-axis $(y=0)$?
6. Which of the above equations (1, 2, 3 or 4) has only one real solution, that is the equation when graphed touches the $x$-axis at only one point?
7. Which of the above equations (1, 2, 3 or 4) has two real solutions, that is the equation when graphed touches the $x$-axis at two points?

## ANSWERS

### Section 1: Elementary operations: arithmetical

1. 12      2. $\frac{18}{10}=\frac{9}{5}=1.8$      3. $\frac{18}{2}=9$      4. 3

5. 1      6. $\frac{7}{2}=3.5$      7. $\frac{17}{12}=1.42$      8. $\frac{3}{100}=0.03$

9. $\frac{4}{10}=0.4$      10. 72      11. $-1$      12. $-\frac{1}{12}$

### Section 2: Powers and roots

1. 4      2. 27      3. $4^5=1024$      4. $3^2=9$

5. $x^7$      6. $x^3$      7. 1      8. 1

9. $\frac{1}{2}=0.5$      10. $\frac{1}{9}$      11. $\frac{1}{2}=0.5$      12. $\frac{1}{8}$

13. 4      14. 7      15. 7      16. 5

17. $\frac{1}{9}$      18. $x^3$      19. $x^2+x^3$      20. $x^2+6x$

*Order of evaluation of basic mathematical operations*

1. 20      2. $-17$      3. $-6$      4. $-4$
5. $x^2-4$      6. $1-2x$      7. $x^3-x^5$

*Mathematical notation*
*Correct*: Questions 2 and 4.

### Section 3: Elementary operations: algebraic

1. $2x$      2. $x$      3. $2x+2y$      4. $\dfrac{1}{2x}$

5. 1      6. $\dfrac{19}{6x}$      7. $18x^2-2$      8. $12x^2+10x+2$

## Section 4: Graphical representation of functions

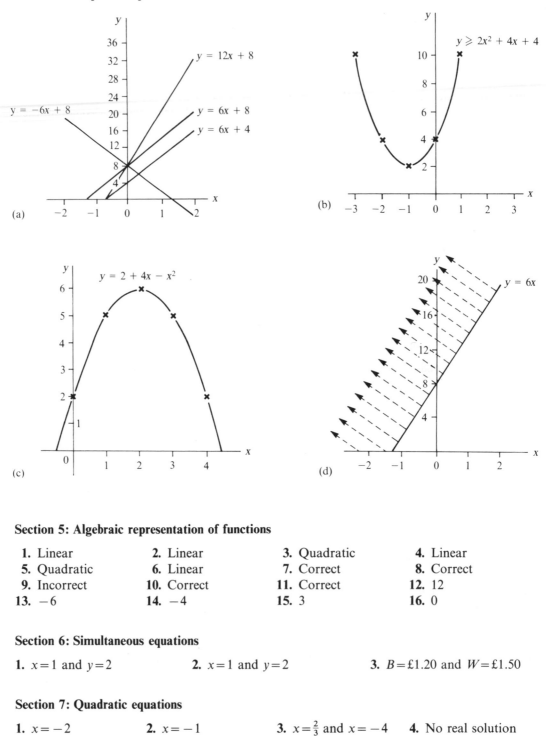

(a)

(b)

(c)

(d)

## Section 5: Algebraic representation of functions

| | | | |
|---|---|---|---|
| **1.** Linear | **2.** Linear | **3.** Quadratic | **4.** Linear |
| **5.** Quadratic | **6.** Linear | **7.** Correct | **8.** Correct |
| **9.** Incorrect | **10.** Correct | **11.** Correct | **12.** 12 |
| **13.** $-6$ | **14.** $-4$ | **15.** 3 | **16.** 0 |

## Section 6: Simultaneous equations

**1.** $x=1$ and $y=2$  **2.** $x=1$ and $y=2$  **3.** $B=£1.20$ and $W=£1.50$

## Section 7: Quadratic equations

**1.** $x=-2$  **2.** $x=-1$  **3.** $x=\frac{2}{3}$ and $x=-4$  **4.** No real solution

**5.** Equation 4  **6.** Equations 1 and 2  **7.** Equation 3

# 2

# MINITAB QUICK REFERENCE

This appendix* summarizes all Minitab commands in Release 7. Commands are flush left, subcommands are indented.

## NOTATION

**K** denotes a constant such as 8.3 or K14,
**C** denotes a column, such as C12 or 'Height'.
**E** denotes either a constant or column.
**M** denotes a matrix, such as M5.
[] encloses an optional argument.

## App. 2-1   GENERAL INFORMATION

**HELP**             explains Minitab commands, can be a command or a subcommand
**INFO** [C ... C]   gives the status of worksheet
**STOP**             ends the current session

## App. 2-2   INPUT AND OUTPUT OF DATA

**READ**             the following data      into **C ... C**
**READ**             data [from **'filename'**] into **C ... C**
**SET**              the following data      into **C**
**SET**              data [from **'filename'**] into **C**
**INSERT**           data [from **'filename'**] between rows **K** and **K** of **C ... C**
**INSERT**           data [from **'filename'**] at the end          of **C ... C**

    **READ, SET,** and **INSERT** all have the subcommands
    **FORMAT** (Fortran format)
    **NOBS** = **K**

*Reproduced with permission from Minitab *Reference Manual Release* 7, Penn: Minitab Inc., 1989.

| | |
|---|---|
| **END** | of data (optional) |
| **NAME** | for **C** is **'name'**, for **C** is **'name'** . . . for **C** is **'name'** |
| **PRINT** | the data in **E . . . E** |
| **WRITE** | [to **'filename'**] the data in **C . . . C** |

    **PRINT** and **WRITE** have the subcommand
    **FORMAT (Fortran format)**

| | |
|---|---|
| **SAVE** | [in **'filename'**] a copy of the worksheet |
|   **PORTABLE** | |
| **RETRIEVE** | the Minitab saved worksheet [from **'filename'**] |
|   **PORTABLE** | |

## App. 2-3   EDITING AND MANIPULATING DATA

| | |
|---|---|
| **LET C(K) = K** | #changes the number in row **K** of **C** |
| **DELETE** | rows **K . . . K** of **C . . . C** |
| **INSERT** | (see Input and Output of data) |
| **COPY** | **C**     into **K . . . K** |
| **COPY** | **C . . . C** into **C . . . C** |

    **USE**   rows **K . . . K**
    **USE**   rows where **C = K . . . K**
    **OMIT** rows **K . . . K**
    **OMIT** rows where **C = K . . . K**

| | |
|---|---|
| **COPY** | **K . . . K** into **C** |
| **CODE** | **(K . . . K)** to **K . . . (K . . . K)** to **K** for **C . . . C**, store in **C . . . C** |
| **STACK** | **(E . . . E)** . . . on **(E . . . E)**, store in **(C . . . C)** |
|   **SUBSCRIPTS** into **C** | |
| **UNSTACK** | **(C . . . C)** into **(E . . . E)** . . . **(E . . . E)** |
|   **SUBSCRIPTS** are in **C** | |
| **CONVERT** | using table in **C C**, the data in **C**, and store in **C** |
| **CONCATENATE** | **C . . . C** put in **C** |
| **ALPHA** | **C . . . C** |

## App. 2-4   ARITHMETIC

**LET** = expression

Expressions may use arithmetic operators $+ - * / **$ (exponentiation), comparison operators $=$ $\sim= < > <= >=$ or the letter equivalents EQ NE LT GT LE GE, logical operators $\& \mid \sim$ or the letter equivalents AND OR NOT, and any of the following: ABSOLUTE, SQRT, LOG-TEN, LOGE, EXPO, ANTILOG, ROUND, SIN, COS, TAN, ASIN, ACOS, ATAN, SIGNS, NSCORE, PARSUMS, PARPRODUCTS, COUNT, N, NMISS, SUM, MEAN, STDEV,

MEDIAN, MIN, MAX, SSQ, SORT, RANK, LAG. You can use subscripts to access individual numbers, for example;

LET C2 = SQRT(C1 − MIN(C1))
LET C3(5) = 4.5

### App. 2-4-1   Simple arithmetic operations

| | | |
|---|---|---|
| **ADD** | E to E . . . to | E, put into E |
| **SUBTRACT** | E from | E, put into E |
| **MULTIPLY** | E by E . . . by | E, put into E |
| **DIVIDE** | E by | E, put into E |
| **RAISE** | E to the power | E, put into E |

### App. 2-4-2   Columnwise functions

| | |
|---|---|
| **ABSOLUTE** value | of E, put into E |
| **SQRT** | of E, put into E |
| **LOGE** | of E, put into E |
| **LOGTEN** | of E, put into E |
| **EXPONENTIATE** | E, put into E |
| **ANTILOG** | of E, put into E |
| **ROUND** to integer | E, put into E |
| **SIN** | of E, put into E |
| **COS** | of E, put into E |
| **TAN** | of E, put into E |
| **ASIN** | of E, put into E |
| **ACOS** | of E, put into E |
| **ATAN** | of E, put into E |
| **SIGNS** | of E, put into E |
| **PARSUMS** | of C, put into C |
| **PARPRODUCTS** | of C, put into C |
| **NSCORES** (normal scores) | of C, put into C |

### App. 2-4-3   Columnwise statistics

| | |
|---|---|
| **COUNT** the number of values | in C [put into K] |
| **N** (number of non-missing values) | in C [put into K] |
| **NMISS** (number of missing values) | in C [put into K] |
| **SUM** of the values | in C [put into K] |
| **MEAN** of the values | in C [put into K] |
| **STDEV** of the values | in C [put into K] |
| **MEDIAN** of the values | in C [put into K] |
| **MINIMUM** of the values | in C [put into K] |
| **MAXIMUM** of the values | in C [put into K] |
| **SSQ** (uncorrected sum of squares) | for C [put into K] |

### App. 2-4-4   Rowwise statistics

| | |
|---|---|
| **RCOUNT** | of E . . . E put into C |
| **RN** | of E . . . E put into C |
| **RNMISS** | of E . . . E put into C |
| **RSUM** | of E . . . E put into C |
| **RMEAN** | of E . . . E put into C |
| **RSTDEV** | of E . . . E put into C |
| **RMEDIAN** | of E . . . E put into C |
| **RMINIMUM** | of E . . . E put into C |
| **RMAXIMUM** | of E . . . E put into C |
| **RSSQ** | of E . . . E put into C |

### Indicator variables

INDICATOR variables for subscripts in **C**, put into **C** . . . **C**

### App. 2-5   PLOTTING DATA

| | |
|---|---|
| **HISTOGRAM** | C . . . C |
| **DOTPLOT** | C . . . C |

HISTOGRAM and DOTPLOT have the subcommands
**INCREMENT = K**
**START**     at K [end at K]
**BY C**
**SAME scales for all columns**

| | |
|---|---|
| **PLOT** | C vs C |

   **SYMBOL** = 'symbol'

| | |
|---|---|
| **MPLOT** | C vs C, and C vs C, and . . . C vs C |
| **LPLOT** | C vs C using tags in C |
| **TPLOT** | C vs C vs C |

PLOT, MPLOT, LPLOT and TPLOT have the subcommands

| | |
|---|---|
| **TITLE** | = 'text' |
| **FOOTNOTE** | = 'text' |
| **YLABEL** | = 'text' |
| **XLABEL** | = 'text' |
| **YINCREMENT** | = K |
| **YSTART** | at K [end at K] |
| **XINCREMENT** | = K |
| **XSTART** | at K [end at K] |

**TSPLOT** [period **K**] of **C**
**MTSPLOT** [period **K**] of **C** . . . **C**
   **ORIGIN** = **K** for **C** . . . **C**, . . ., origin = **K** for **C** . . . **C**

TSPLOT and MTSPLOT have the subcommands
**INCREMENT** = **K**

| | | |
|---|---|---|
| **START** | at **K** [end at **K**] | |
| **ORIGIN** | = **K** | |
| **TSTART** | at **K** [end at **K**] | |

**GRID**      **C** [**K** to **K**] **C** [**K** to **K**]
**CONTOUR**   **C** vs **C** and **C**
   **BLANK** bands between letters
   **YSTART**        = **K** [up to **K**]
   **YINCREMENT** = **K**

**WIDTH**  of all plots that follow is **K** spaces
**HEIGHT** of all plots that follow is **K** lines

**App. 2-5-1   High resolution graphics**

**GOPTIONS**
   **\*DEVICE** = 'device'
   **HEIGHT** = **K** inches
   WIDTH  = **K** inches

**GHISTOGRAM C . . . C**
   **INCREMENT** = **K**
   **START**        at **K** [end at **K**]
   **BY C**
   **SAME** scales for all columns

**GPLOT**     **C** vs **C**
   **SYMBOL** = 'symbol'
**GMPLOT**   **C** vs **C**, and **C** vs **C**, and . . . **C** vs **C**
**GLPLOT**   **C** vs **C** using tags in **C**
**GTPLOT**   **C** vs **C** vs **C**

   GPLOT, GMPLOT, GLPLOT and GTPLOT have the subcommands
   **TITLE**            = 'text'
   **FOOTNOTE**    = 'text'
   **YLABEL**         = 'text'
   **XLABEL**         = 'text'
   **YINCREMENT** = **K**
   **YSTART**          at **K** [end at **K**]
   **XINCREMENT** = **K**
   **XSTART**          at **K** [end at **K**]
   **LINES** [style **K** [color **K**]] connecting points in **C C**
   **COLOR C**

All high resolution graphics commands have the subcommand

   **FILE 'filename'** to store graphics output

\*Not implemented in the DOS microcomputer version.

**App. 2-6   BASIC STATISTICS**

**DESCRIBE C . . . C**
   **BY C**

**ZINTERVAL**  [**K**% confidence] assuming sigma = **K** for **C . . . C**
**ZTEST**      [of mu = **K**]   assuming sigma = **K** for **C . . . C**
   **ALTERNATIVE = K**
**TINTERVAL**  [**K**% confidence] for data in **C . . . C**
**TTEST**      [of mu = **K**]    on data in **C . . . C**
   **ALTERNATIVE = K**

**TWOSAMPLE** test and c.i. [**K**% confidence] samples in **C C**
   **ALTERNATIVE = K**
   **POOLED** procedure

**TWOT** test and c.i. [**K**% confidence] data in **C**, groups in **C**
   **ALTERNATIVE = K**
   **POOLED** procedure

**CORRELATION** between **C . . . C** [put into **M**]
**COVARIANCE**  between **C . . . C** [put into **M**]

**CENTER** the data in **C . . . C** put into **C . . . C**
   **LOCATION** [subtracting **K . . . K**]
   **SCALE**     [dividing by **K . . . K**]
   **MINMAX**   [with **K** as min and **K** as max]

**App. 2-7   REGRESSION**

**REGRESS C** on **K** predictors **C . . . C** [store st. resids in **C** [fits in **C**]]
   **NOCONSTANT**   in equation
   **WEIGHTS**       are in   **C**
   **MSE**            put into **K**
   **COEFFICIENTS**  put into **C**
   **XPXINV**       put into **M**
   **RMATRIX**      put into **M**
   **HI**             put into **C** (leverage)
   **RESIDUALS**     put into **C** (observed - fit)
   **TRESIDUALS**    put into **C** (deleted studentized)
   **COOKD**        put into **C** (Cook's distance)
   **DFITS**         put into **C**
   **PREDICT**      for **E . . . E**
   **VIF**             (variance inflation factors)
   **DW**             (Durbin-Watson statistic)
   **PURE**          (pure error lack-of-fit test)
   **XLOF**         (experimental lack-of-fit test)
   **TOLERANCE**    **K** [**K**]

**STEPWISE** regression of **C** on the predictors **C** . . . **C**
    **FENTER**   = **K**  (default is four)
    **FREMOVE** = **K**  (default is four)
    **FORCE**    **C** . . . **C**
    **ENTER**    **C** . . . **C**
    **REMOVE**  **C** . . . **C**
    **BEST K** alternative predictors (default is zero)
    **STEPS** = **K** (default depends on output width)

**BREG C** on predictors **C** . . . **C**
    **INCLUDE** predictors **C** . . . **C**
    **BEST K** models
    **NVARS K [K]**
    **NOCONSTANT** in equation

**NOCONSTANT**  in all REGRESS, STEPWISE and BREG commands that follow
**CONSTANT**       fit a constant in all STEPWISE, REGRESS and BREG that follow


**App. 2-8**  **ANALYSIS OF VARIANCE**

**AOVONEWAY**  aov, for samples in **C** . . . **C**
**ONEWAY**      aov, data in **C**, subscripts in **C**   [store resids in **C** [fits in **C**]]
**TWOWAY**      aov, data in **C**, subscripts in **C C** [store resids in **C** [fits in **C**]]
    **ADDITIVE** model
    **MEANS** for the factors **C [C]**

**ANOVA model**
    **RANDOM factorlist**
    **EMS**
    **FITS**           put into **C** . . . **C**
    **RESIDUALS**    put into **C** . . . **C**
    **MEANS**       for **termlist**
    **TEST**         for **termlist / errorterm**
    **RESTRICT**

**ANCOVA model**
    **COVARIATES**   are in   **C** . . . **C**
    **FITS**           put into **C** . . . **C**
    **RESIDUALS**    put into **C** . . . **C**
    **MEANS**       for **termlist**
    **TEST**         for **termlist / errorterm**

**GLM model**
    **COVARIATES**   are in   **C** . . . **C**
    **WEIGHTS**     are in   **C**
    **FITS**           put into **C** . . . **C**
    **RESIDUALS**    put into **C** . . . **C**
    **SRESIDS**      put into **C** . . . **C**
    **TRESIDS**      put into **C** . . . **C**

| HI | put into **C** |
|---|---|
| **COOKD** | put into **C** ... **C** |
| **DFITS** | put into **C** ... **C** |
| **XMATRIX** | put into **M** |
| **COEFFICIENTS** | put into **C** ... **C** |
| **MEANS** | for **termlist** |
| **TEST** | for **termlist** / **errorterm** |
| **BRIEF** | **K** |
| **TOLERANCE** | **K** [**K**] |

## App. 2-9   MULTI-VARIATE ANALYSIS

**PCA** principal component analysis of **C** ... **C**
    **COVARIANCE** matrix
    **NCOMP**   = **K** (number of components)
    **COEF**    put into **C** ... **C**
    **SCORES**   put into **C** ... **C**

**DISCRIMINANT** groups in **C**, predictors in **C** ... **C**
    **QUADRATIC**  discrimination
    **PRIORS**    are in **K** ... **K**
    **LDF** coef   put in **C** ... **C**
    **FITS**     put in **C** [**C**]
    **XVAL**    cross validation
    **PREDICT**  for **E** ... **E**
    **BRIEF**    **K**

## App. 2-10   NON-PARAMETRICS

| **RUNS** | test [above and below **K**] for **C** | |
|---|---|---|
| **STEST** | sign test [median = **K**] for **C** ... **C** | |
|    **ALTERNATIVE** = **K** | | |

| **SINTERVAL** | sign confidence interval | [**K**% confidence] for **C** ... **C** |
|---|---|---|
| **WTEST** | Wilcoxon one-sample rank test [median = **K**] | for **C** ... **C** |
|    **ALTERNATIVE** = **K** | | |

| **WINTERVAL** | Wilcoxon confidence interval | [**K**% confidence] for **C** ... **C** |
|---|---|---|
| **MANN-WHITNEY** | test and confidence interval | [**K**% confidence] on **C C** |
|    **ALTERNATIVE** = **K** | | |

| **KRUSKAL-WALLIS** | test, data in **C**, subscripts in **C** |
|---|---|
| **MOOD** | median test, data in **C**, subscripts in **C** [put resids in **C** [fits in **C**]] |
| **FRIEDMAN** | data in **C**, treatment in **C**, blocks in **C** [put resids in **C** [fits in **C**]] |

| **WALSH** | averages for **C**, put into **C** [indices into **C C**] |
|---|---|
| **WDIFF** | for **C** and **C**, put into **C** [indices into **C C**] |
| **WSLOPE** | y in **C**, x in **C**, put into **C** [indices into **C C**] |

**App. 2-11   TABLES**

**TALLY** the data in **C . . . C**
    **COUNTS**
    **PERCENTS**
    **CUMCOUNTS**      cumulative counts
    **CUMPERCENTS**   cumulative percents
    **ALL**              four statistics above

**CHISQUARE** test on table stored in **C . . . C**

**TABLE** the data classified by **C . . . C**
    **MEANS**        for **C . . . C**
    **MEDIANS**      for **C . . . C**
    **SUMS**          for **C . . . C**
    **MINIMUMS** for **C . . . C**
    **MAXIMUMS** for **C . . . C**
    **STDEV**         for **C . . . C**
    **STATS**         for **C . . . C**
    **DATA**          for **C . . . C**
    **N**              for **C . . . C**
    **NMISS**         for **C . . . C**
    **PROPORTION** of cases = **K** [thru **K**] in **C . . . C**
    **COUNTS**
    **ROWPERCENTS**
    **COLPERCENTS**
    **TOTPERCENTS**
    **CHISQUARE**    analysis [output code = **K**]
    **MISSING**      level for classification variable **C . . . C**
    **NOALL**        in margins
    **ALL**           for **C . . . C**
    **FREQUENCIES** are in **C**
    **LAYOUT**       **K** rows by **K** columns

**App. 2-12   TIME SERIES**

**ACF**            [with up to **K** lags] for series in **C** [put into **C**]
**PACF**          [with up to **K** lags] for series in **C** [put into **C**]
**CCF**            [with up to **K** lags] between series in **C** and **C**
**DIFFERENCES**  [of lag **K**] for data in **C**, put into **C**
**LAG**            [by **K**]     for data in **C**, put into **C**

**ARIMA**  p = **K** d = **K** q = **K**, data in **C** [put resids in **C** [preds in **C** [coefs in **C**]]]
**ARIMA**  p = **K** d = **K** q = **K** P = **K** D = **K** Q = **K** S = **K**, data in **C** [**C** [**C** [**C**]]]
    **CONSTANT**     term in model
    **NOCONSTANT**  term in model
    **STARTING**     values are in **C**
    **FORECAST**     [origin = **K**] up to **K** leads [put in **C** [limits in **C C**]]

## App. 2-13   STATISTICAL PROCESS CONTROL

**XBARCHART**     for C . . . C, subgroups are in **E**
**GXBARCHART**  for C . . . C, subgroups are in **E**
    **MU**          = **K**
    **SIGMA**      = **K**
    **RSPAN**      = **K**
    **TEST**        **K . . . K**
    **SUBGROUP** size is **E**
    (Subcommands used in all control charts)

**RCHART**     for C . . . C, subgroups are in **E**
**GRCHART**  for C . . . C, subgroups are in **E**
    **SIGMA**       = **K**
    **SUBGROUP**  size is **E**
    (Subcommands used in all control charts)

**SCHART**     for C . . . C, subgroups are in **E**
**GSCHART**  for C . . . C, subgroups are in **E**
    **SIGMA**       = **K**
    **SUBGROUP**  size is **E**
    (Subcommands used in all control charts)

**ICHART**     for C . . . C
**GICHART**  for C . . . C
    **MU**          = **K**
    **SIGMA**      = **K**
    **RSPAN**      = **K**
    **TEST**        **K . . . K**
    (Subcommands used in all control charts)

**MACHART**     for C . . . C, subgroups are in **E**
**GMACHART**  for C . . . C, subgroups are in **E**
    **MU**            = **K**
    **SIGMA**         = **K**
    **SPAN**          = **K**
    **RSPAN**        = **K**
    **SUBGROUP**  size is **E**
    (Subcommands used in all control charts)

**EWMACHART**     for C . . . C, subgroups are in **E**
**GEWMACHART**  for C . . . C, subgroups are in **E**
    **MU**            = **K**
    **SIGMA**         = **K**
    **WEIGHT**       = **K**
    **RSPAN**        = **K**
    **SUBGROUP**    size is **E**
    (Subcommands used in all control charts)

**MRCHART**     for C . . . C
**GMRCHART**  for C . . . C

**SIGMA** = **K**
**RSPAN** = **K**
(Subcommands used in all control charts)


**PCHART**   number of non-conformities are in **C** ... **C**, sample size = **E**
**GPCHART**   number of non-conformities are in **C** ... **C**, sample size = **E**
  **P**       = **K**
  **TEST**    **K** ... **K**
  **SUBGROUP**   size is **E**
(Subcommands used in all control charts)


**NPCHART**   number of non-conformities are in **C** ... **C**, sample size = **E**
**GNPCHART**   number of non-conformities are in **C** ... **C**, sample size = **E**
  **P**       = **K**
  **TEST**    **K** ... **K**
  **SUBGROUP**   size is **E**
(Subcommands used in all control charts)


**CCHART**   number of non-conformities are in **C** ... **C**
**GCCHART**   number of non-conformities are in **C** ... **C**
  **MU**   = **K**
  **TEST**   **K** ... **K**
(Subcommands used in all control charts)


**UCHART**   number of non-conformities are in **C** ... **C**, sample size = **E**
**GUCHART**   number of non-conformities are in **C** ... **C**, sample size = **E**
  **MU**       = **K**
  **TEST**    **K** ... **K**
  **SUBGROUP**   size is **E**
(Subcommands used in all control charts)


All statistical process control charts have the subcommands

  **SLIMITS**     are **K** ... **K**
  **HLINES**      at **E** ... **E**
  **ESTIMATE**    using just samples **K** ... **K**
  **TITLE**       = 'text'
  **FOOTNOTE**    = 'text'
  **YLABEL**      = 'text'
  **XLABEL**      = 'text'
  **YINCREMENT** = **K**
  **YSTART**      at **K** [end at **K**]
  **XSTART**      at **K** [end at **K**]


All high resolution charts have the subcommand

  **FILE** 'filename' to store graphics output

**App. 2-14  EXPLORATORY DATA ANALYSIS**

**STEM-AND-LEAF** display of C . . . C
    **TRIM**          outliers
    **INCREMENT** = K
    **BY** C

**BOXPLOT**    for C
**GBOXPLOT**    for C (high resolution version)

        BOXPLOT, GBOXPLOT have the subcommands
    **INCREMENT**  = K
    **START**        at K [end at K]
    **BY** C
    **LINES**        = K
    **NOTCH** [K% confidence] sign c.i.
    **LEVELS**      K . . . K
    **FILE 'filename'** to store GBOXPLOT output

**LVALS**  of C [put lvals in C [mids in C [spreads in C]]]
**MPOLISH** C, levels in C C [put residuals in C [fits in C]]
    **COLUMNS**        (start iteration with column medians)
    **ITERATIONS**     = K
    **EFFECTS**        put common into K, rows into C, cols into C
    **COMPARISONS**  values, put into C

**RLINE** y in C, x in C [put residuals in C [fits in C [coefs in C]]]
    **MAXITER** = K (maximum number of iterations)

**RSMOOTH** C, put rough into C, smooth into C
    **SMOOTH** by 3RSSH, twice

**CPLOT** (condensed plot) C vs C
    **LINES**         = K
    **CHARACTERS** = K
    **XBOUNDS**    = from K to K
    **YBOUNDS**    = from K to K

**CTABLE** (coded table) data in C, row C, column C
    **MAXIMUM**   value in each cell should be coded
    **MINIMUM**    value in each cell should be coded

**ROOTOGRAM** data in C [use bin boundaries in C]
    **BOUNDARIES**    store them in C
    **DRRS**          store them in C
    **FITTED** values    store them in C
    **COUNTS**        store them in C
    **FREQUENCIES**    are in C [bin boundaries are in C]
    **MEAN**          = K
    **STDEV**        = K

**App. 2-15    DISTRIBUTIONS AND RANDOM DATA**

**RANDOM K** observations into **C . . . C**
    **BERNOULLI** trials p = **K**

| | |
|---|---|
| **PDF** | for values in **E** [store results in **E**] |
| **CDF** | for values in **E** [store results in **E**] |
| **INVCDF** | for values in **E** [store results in **E**] |

    RANDOM, PDF, CDF, INVCDF have the subcommands

| | |
|---|---|
| **BINOMIAL** | n = **K** p = **K** |
| **POISSON** | mu = **K** |
| **INTEGER** | discrete uniform on integers **K** to **K** |
| **DISCRETE** | distribution with values in **C** and probabilities in **C** |
| **NORMAL** | [mu = **K** [sigma = **K**]] |
| **UNIFORM** | continuous on the interval **K** to **K** |
| **T** | degrees of freedom = **K** |
| **F** | df numerator = **K**, df denominator = **K** |

Additional subcommands are

    **CAUCHY, LAPLACE, LOGISTIC, LOGNORMAL, CHISQUARE, EXPONENTIAL, GAMMA, WEIBULL, BETA**

| | |
|---|---|
| **SAMPLE** | **K** rows from **C . . . C** put into **C . . . C** |
| **REPLACE** | (sample with replacement) |
| **BASE** | for random number generator = **K** |

**App. 2-16    SORTING**

**SORT**   **C** [carry along **C . . . C**] put into **C** [and **C . . . C**]
    **BY**                 **C . . . C**
    **DESCENDING**   **C . . . C**
**RANK**   the values in **C**, put ranks into **C**

**App. 2-17    MATRICES**

| | |
|---|---|
| **READ** | [from '**filename**'] into a **K** by **K** matrix **M** |
| **PRINT** | **M . . . M** |
| **TRANSPOSE** | **M** into **M** |
| **INVERT** | **M** into **M** |
| **DEFINE** | **K** into **K** by **K** matrix **M** |
| **DIAGONAL** | is **C**, form into **M** |
| **DIAGONAL** | of **M**, put into **C** |

| | |
|---|---|
| **COPY C . . .C** | into **M** |
| **COPY M** | into **C . . . C** |
| **COPY M** | into **M** |
|     **USE** | rows **K . . . K** |
|     **OMIT** | rows **K . . . K** |

**EIGEN**   for **M** put values into **C** [vectors into **M**]

In the following commands **E** can be either **C**, **K** or **M**

| | | |
|---|---|---|
| **ADD** | **E** to | **E**, put into **E** |
| **SUBTRACT** | **E** from | **E**, put into **E** |
| **MULTIPLY** | **E** by | **E**, put into **E** |

## App. 2-18   MISCELLANEOUS

**ERASE**   **E . . . E**

| | |
|---|---|
| **OUTFILE**  'filename' | put all output in file |
| **OW = K** | output width of file |
| **OH = K** | output height of file |
| **NOTERM** | no output to terminal |
| **NOOUTFILE** | output to terminal only |
| | |
| **PAPER** | output to printer |
| **OW = K** | output width of printer |
| **OH = K** | output height of printer |
| **NOTERM** | no output to terminal |
| **NOPAPER** | output to terminal only |
| | |
| **JOURNAL** ['filename'] | record Minitab commands in this file |
| **NOJOURNAL** | cancels JOURNAL |

| | |
|---|---|
| **NOTE** | comments may be put here |
| **NEWPAGE** | start next output on a new page |
| **UC** | use only upper case letters on output |
| **LC** | use mixed case letters on output |
| **OW**   = **K** | number of spaces for width of output |
| **OH**   = **K** | number of lines for height of one page (or screen) of output |
| **IW**   = **K** | number of spaces for width of input |
| **BRIEF** = **K** | controls amount of output from REGRESS GLM DISCRIM ARIMA RLINE |

| | |
|---|---|
| **RESTART** | begin fresh Minitab session |
| **SYSTEM** | provides access to operating system commands |
| **TSHARE** | interactive or timesharing mode |
| **BATCH** | batch mode |

## App. 2-19   STORED COMMANDS AND LOOPS

The commands STORE and EXECUTE provide the capability for simple macros (stored command files) and loops.

| | |
|---|---|
| **EXECUTE** | 'filename' [K times] |
| **STORE** | [in 'filename'] the following commands |
| | (Minitab commands go here) |
| **END** | of storing commands |

**NOECHO**    the commands that follow
**ECHO**    the commands that follow
**YESNO**    **K**

**The CK capability.** The integer part of a column number may be replaced by a stored constant.

Example       LET K1 = 5
              PRINT C1 - CK1

since K1 = 5, this prints C1 through C5.

## App. 2-20   SYMBOLS

\*   **Missing Value Symbol.** An * can be used as data in READ, SET and INSERT and in data files. Enclose the * in single quotes in commands and subcommands.

Example   CODE (-99) to '*' in C1, put into C3
Example   COPY C6 INTO C7;
                   OMIT C6 = '*'.

\#   **Comment Symbol.** The symbol # anywhere on a line tells Minitab to ignore the rest of the line.
&   **Continuation Symbol.** To continue a command onto another line, end the first line with the symbol &. You can use + + as a synonym for &.

## App. 2-21   WORKSHEET AND COMMANDS

Minitab consists of a worksheet for data and over 200 commands. The worksheet contains columns of data denoted by C1, C2, C3 ..., stored constants denoted by K1, K2, K3 ..., and matrices denoted by M1, M2, M3, ....

A column may be given a name with the command NAME (see Input and output of data). A name may be up to 8 characters long, with any characters except apostrophes and # Names may be used in place of column numbers. When a name is used, it must be enclosed in apostrophes (single quotes).

Example:   PLOT 'INCOME' vs 'AGE'

Each command starts with a command word and is usually followed by a list of arguments. An argument is a number, a column, a stored constant, a matrix or a file name. Only the command word and arguments are needed. All other text is for the readers' information.

## App. 2-22   SUBCOMMANDS

Some Minitab commands have subcommands. To use a subcommand, put a semicolon at the end of the main command line. Then type the subcommands. Start each on a new line, then end it with a semicolon. When you are done, end the last subcommand with a period [full stop].

The subcommand ABORT cancels the whole command.

# 3

# LOTUS 1-2-3 QUICK REFERENCE

**TASK SUMMARY\***

This summary describes 1-2-3 tasks and lists the commands you use to complete them. It is organized by category, with the tasks listed alphabetically on the left and the 1-2-3 commands you use to accomplish the tasks, or a reference to a specific part of the 1-2-3 documentation, on the right. Throughout this appendix, *Reference* refers to *Lotus 1-2-3 Release 3.1 Reference*, Cambridge, Lotus Development Corporation, 1990. Use this summary to help you identify a specific command for completing a task, and then refer to the description of the command in Chapter 2 of *Reference* for specific procedures.

Although this summary includes many tasks you can accomplish using 1-2-3 commands, it is not a comprehensive list of commands. The 1-2-3 menu trees (Figs A3-1 to A3-6) included at the end of *Quick Reference*, provide a graphic representation of all the 1-2-3 commands.

The information in this summary is divided among the following sections. Note also that as this is a reproduction of the original, American terms and spelling have been retained.

- Annotating data
- Controlling worksheet appearance
- Converting formulas to values
- Copying data
- Data analysis
- Database tables
- Defining and using ranges
- Editing data
- Entering labels, numbers and formulas
- Erasing data
- Fixing mistakes
- Graphing data
- Listing information
- Moving data and the cell pointer

---

\*Reproduced with permission from *Lotus 1-2-3 Release 3.1 Quick Reference*, Cambridge: Lotus Development Corporation, 1990.

- Printing data and graphs
- Protecting data and files
- Returning 1-2-3 to the operating system
- Using files
- Using macros

## ANNOTATING DATA

◆ Attach notes to formulas or values        See 'Working with Formulas' in
                                             Chapter 1 of *Reference*

◆ Create, list, and delete notes for range   /Range Name Note
  names

## CONTROLLING WORKSHEET APPEARANCE

When you turn GROUP mode on with /Worksheet Global Group Enable, any changes you make to cell formats and settings in the current worksheet affect the corresponding area of every worksheet in the current file. The following commands work in GROUP mode: /Range Format; /Range Label; /Range Prot; /Range Unprot; /Worksheet Column; /Worksheet Global Col-Width, Format, Label, Prot, and Zero; and /Worksheet Titles.

  Worksheet Global Format commands and Range Format commands provide the same formatting options. /Worksheet Global Format affects an entire worksheet. /Range Format affects the area (range) you choose and overrides /Worksheet Global Format.

### Changing text display

Rearrange a column of labels to fit in a      /Range Justify
specified range

Reset the label alignment (left, right, or    /Range Label
center) in a range after you enter labels

Set the label alignment (left, right, or center)   /Worksheet Global Label
for the current worksheet before you enter
labels

### Controlling columns, rows, and worksheets

Change the width of all columns in a          /Worksheet Global Col-Width
worksheet

Change the width of one column or a range     /Worksheet Column
of columns

Fix rows or columns so they remain in view    /Worksheet Titles
when you scroll through a worksheet

◆ Insert blank columns, rows, and worksheets  /Worksheet Insert
  in the current file

◆ Remove columns, rows, and worksheets from   /Worksheet Delete
  the current file

### Displaying numbers and formulas in different formats

| | |
|---|---|
| Control how 1-2-3 displays data | /Worksheet Global Format /Range Format |
| Display actual formulas, not the results | /Worksheet Global Format Text /Range Format Text |
| ◆ Display blank cells or a label instead of zeros | /Worksheet Global Zero |
| ◆ Display negative values in a different color (color monitors) or intensity (monochrome monitors) | /Worksheet Global Format Other Color /Range Format Other Color |
| ◆ Format cells to display numbers automatically in Date, Time, Percent, Fixed, Sci (Scientific), Currency, or , (Comma), format | /Worksheet Global Format Other Automatic /Range Format Other Automatic |
| Reset a range to the global cell format | /Range Format Reset |
| ◆ Set formats for international currency, date, and time | /Worksheet Global Default Other International |
| Widen a column to display values instead of asterisks | /Worksheet Column Set-Width |

### Hiding data

| | |
|---|---|
| Hide or redisplay columns | /Worksheet Column |
| Hide or redisplay ranges | /Range Format Hidden and /Range Format Reset |
| ◆ Hide or redisplay values equal to zero | /Worksheet Global Zero |
| ◆ Hide or redisplay worksheets | /Worksheet Hide |

### Using Windows

| | |
|---|---|
| Display different parts of a worksheet or file by splitting the screen into two windows | /Worksheet Window Horizontal or Vertical |
| ◆ Display three consecutive worksheets at once | /Worksheet Window Perspective |
| Synchronize and unsynchronize window scrolling | /Worksheet Window Sync or Unsync |
| ◆ View data in the worksheet by displaying symbols for labels, numbers, and formulas | /Worksheet Window Map |
| ◆ View the current graph in a window to the right of the current worksheet | /Worksheet Window Graph |

## CONVERTING FORMULAS TO VALUES

| | |
|---|---|
| Convert a range of formulas to values | /Range Value |

| Convert the formula in the current cell to a value | Press EDIT (F2) then CALC (F9) then ENTER |
| Copy a range, switching columns, rows, or worksheets and converting all formulas to values | /Range Trans |
| Save a range from the current file in a new file, converting formulas to values in the new file | /File Xtract Values |

## COPYING DATA

| Copy a range, switching columns, rows, or worksheets and converting all formulas to values | /Range Trans |
| Copy data from one worksheet or file to another worksheet or file | /Copy |

## DATA ANALYSIS

| Create a frequency distribution of values in a range | /Data Distribution |
| Invert a matrix formed by rows and columns of data | /Data Matrix Invert |
| Multiply two matrices | /Data Matrix Multiply |
| ◆ Perform customized what-if analysis and enter results in a table | /Data Table Labeled |
| Perform linear regression analysis (calculate the relationships between independent and dependent variables) | /Data Regression |
| ◆ Perform what-if analysis or cross-tabulate information and enter the results in a table | /Data Table 1, 2, or 3 |

## DATABASE TABLES

### Using 1-2-3 database tables

| Create a 1-2-3 database table | See 'Database Tables' in 'Data Commands' in chapter 2 of *Reference* |
| ◆ Delete, extract, find, or modify records in a database table | /Data Query |
| Sort records in a database table | /Data Sort |

**Using 1-2-3 with external database tables**

◆ Connect 1-2-3 to external tables, such as dBASE® III tables, so you can manipulate data in the tables /Data External Use

◆ Create a new table in an external database /Data External Create

◆ List the names of tables in an external database or list the fields in a table /Data External List Tables or Fields

◆ Remove a table from an external database /Data External Delete

◆ Translate data created using foreign language character sets in an external database /Data External Other Translation

## DEFINING AND USING RANGES

Assign a name to a range of cells /Range Name Create

◆ Cancel the association between a range name and its range address /Range Name Undefine

◆ Create, edit, and delete notes for range names /Range Name Note

Delete all range names and notes /Range Name Reset

Delete one range name /Range Name Delete

Indicate a range in a worksheet See 'Working with Ranges' in Chapter 1 of *Reference*

Use a label entered in one cell as the range name for an adjacent cell /Range Name Labels

## EDITING DATA

Edit data in one cell Press EDIT (F2) See 'Entering Data' in Chapter 1 of *Reference*

◆ Find and replace text in formulas or labels in the current file /Range Search

## ENTERING LABELS, NUMBERS, AND FORMULAS

Enter a character that is not on the keyboard See 'Displaying Characters' in Appendix 2 of *Reference*

◆ Enter a sequence of numbers, dates, or times /Data Fill

Enter formulas See 'Working with Formulas' in Chapter 1 of *Reference*

◆ Enter formulas that link to data in other files See 'Linking Files with Formulas' in Chapter 1 of *Reference*

| | |
|---|---|
| Enter labels and numbers in a worksheet | See 'Entering Data' in Chapter 1 of *Reference* |
| ◆ Enter numbers as labels | /Range Format Other Label<br>Type a label prefix before a number and press ENTER |

## ERASING DATA

| | |
|---|---|
| Erase data in one or more cells | /Range Erase |
| ◆ Remove all active worksheets and files from memory and replace them with one blank worksheet | /Worksheet Erase Yes |
| ◆ Remove one file from memory | /Worksheet Delete File |
| ◆ Remove one or more columns, rows, or worksheets from the current file | /Worksheet Delete |

## FIXING MISTAKES

| | |
|---|---|
| Edit data in one cell | Press EDIT (F2)<br>See 'Entering Data' in Chapter 1 of *Reference* |
| Erase data | /Range Erase |
| List error messages, causes, and possible solutions | Press HELP (F1) and select Error Message Index from the Help Index |
| Locate a circular reference in a file | /Worksheet Status |
| ◆ Use undo to cancel a mistake in the worksheet | Press UNDO (ALT-F4)<br>See Appendix 8 of *Reference* |

## GRAPHING DATA

### Creating graphs

| | |
|---|---|
| ◆ Clear some or all of the current graph settings | /Graph Reset |
| ◆ Create a graph by assigning all data ranges at once when data is located in consecutive columns or rows | /Graph Group |
| Create a graph by selecting individual data ranges | See 'Creating a Graph' in 'Graph Commands' in Chapter 2 of *Reference* |
| ◆ Create a second y-axis | /Graph Type Features 2Y-Ranges |
| Select color or black and white for displaying and printing graphs | /Graph Options Color or B&W |
| Select the kind of graph you want to display or print | /Graph Type |

◆ Set whether 1-2-3 uses rows or columns to create automatic graphs

/Worksheet Global Default Graph Columnwise or Rowwise

### Displaying graphs

Display a named graph on the full screen

/Graph Name Use

◆ Display the current graph in a graph window to the right of the current worksheet

/Worksheet Window Graph

Display the current graph on the full screen

/Graph View or press GRAPH (F10)

### Enhancing graphs

Add horizontal and/or vertical grid lines

/Graph Options Grid

◆ Change the way 1-2-3 displays numbers along an axis

/Graph Options Scale [Y-Scale, X-Scale, 2Y-Scale] Format

◆ Graph data ranges as a percentage of the total value in line, bar, mixed, stacked bar, and XY graphs

/Graph Type Features 100%

◆ Hide a pie slice in a pie chart

/Graph Type Pie and /Graph B with a negative number in the B data range

◆ Remove the percent labels from a pie chart

/Graph Type Pie and /Graph C with the C data range containing zero

◆ Rotate the x-axis 90° so it is vertical rather than horizontal

/Graph Type Features Vertical

◆ Select the colors or hatch patterns for the data in a graph

/Graph Options Advanced Colors or Hatches

Separate one or more slices in a pie chart

/Graph Type Pie and /Graph B with values equal to or greater than 100 in the B data range

Set the appearance of lines in line, mixed, HLCO, and XY graphs

/Graph Options Format

Set the axis scaling

/Graph Options Scale

◆ Set the colors or hatch pattern of each slice in a pie chart

/Graph Type Pie and /Graph B with the B data range containing 1 to 16 (for colors) if the display is set to color or 1 to 14 (for hatch patterns) if the display is set to black and white

◆ Stack the values in the data ranges in line, bar, and mixed graphs

/Graph Type Features Stacked

### Labeling data in graphs

◆ Add graph titles, axis titles, and notes

/Graph Options Titles

Add text below a graph to label the data ranges represented by each symbol, color, or hatch pattern

/Graph Options Legend

| | |
|---|---|
| Create labels for the x-axis in line, bar, stacked bar, mixed, and HLCO graphs or label the slices in a pie chart | /Graph X |
| Label the points or bars in a graph | /Graph Options Data-Labels |
| ◆ Set font, size, and color of text in a graph | /Graph Options Advanced Text |
| Set the number of labels displayed along the x-axis | /Graph Options Scale Skip |

**Saving graphs**

| | |
|---|---|
| Name a graph and save it with a file so you can view the graph again when you use the file | /Graph Name Create and then /File Save |
| Save a graph in a graph file for use with other programs | /Graph Save |
| ◆ Set the type of graph file (graphic metafile or picture) 1-2-3 creates when you use /Graph Save | /Worksheet Global Default Graph |

## LISTING INFORMATION

| | |
|---|---|
| ◆ Display a list of active files, files on disk, or files linked to the current file | /File List |
| ◆ Display a list of advanced macro commands and enter a command in a macro | Type {, press NAME (F3) twice, highlight a macro command, and press ENTER |
| ◆ Display a list of file, graph, range, or print settings names when 1-2-3 is in the middle of a command | Press NAME (F3) after selecting any command that lists names of files, graphs, ranges, or print settings |
| ◆ Display a list of @functions and enter an @function in a formula | Type @, press NAME (F3) twice, highlight an @function, and press ENTER |
| Display a list of range names | Press GOTO (F5) once and press NAME (F3) |
| Display global default settings | /Worksheet Global Default Status |
| Display information about memory use, hardware, and global settings | /Worksheet Status |
| In the current worksheet, list defined range names | /Range Name Table |
| ◆ In the current worksheet, list information about active files, files on disk, or files linked to active files | /File Admin Table |

◆ In the current worksheet, list named graphs  /Graph Name Table

◆ In the current worksheet, list named print  /Print [E,F,P] Options Name Table
settings

◆ In the current worksheet, list notes attached  /Range Name Note Table
to range names

## MOVING DATA AND THE CELL POINTER

Move data within the same file  /Move

◆ Move the cell pointer between active files  See 'Working with Multiple Files' in
Chapter 1 of *Reference*

◆ Move the cell pointer between worksheets in  See 'Using Multiple-Sheet Files' in
a file  Chapter 1 of *Reference*

Move the cell pointer within a  See 'The 1-2-3 Screen' in Chapter 1 of
worksheet  *Reference*

## PRINTING DATA AND GRAPHS

You must select a printer when you install 1-2-3 in order to print worksheet data or graphs. See Chapter 3 of *Setting Up 1-2-3* for information on selecting a printer.

**Note:** /Print [E,F,P] means /Print [Encoded, File, Printer] for the Print commands listed below.

### Selecting data and graphs for printing

◆ Select a graph you want to print  /Print [E,P] Image

Select a range of data you want to print  /Print [E,F,P] Range

◆ Select nonadjacent columns and rows to print  /Print [E,F,P] Range and enter each
one after the other  range separated by a comma

◆ Select text and a named graph you want to  /Print [E,P] Range and enter the
print on the same page  range for text, a comma, an asterisk,
and then the graph name

### Selecting options for printing data and graphs

◆ Advance the paper one line or insert one  /Print [E,F,P] Line
blank line in a text or encoded file

◆ Advance the paper to the next page or insert  /Print [E,F,P] Page
blank lines in a text or encoded file

◆ Control margins, borders, page length, headers, footers, and setup strings for the current session

/Print [E,F,P] Options

Eliminate page breaks, headers, footers, and top and bottom margins when you print the range

/Print [E,F,P] Options Other Unformatted

◆ Eliminate the blank lines 1-2-3 leaves at the top and bottom of a printed page

/Print [E,F,P] Options Other Blank-Header Suppress

Print contents of each cell in the print range including the cell address, format, and protection status

/Print [E,F,P] Options Other Cell-Formulas

◆ Print worksheet frame with each print range

/Print [E,F,P] Options Borders Frame

◆ Select a color for a print range

/Print [E,P] Options Advanced Color

◆ Select fonts for the border, frame, header/footer, or print range

/Print [E,P] Options Advanced Fonts

◆ Select line spacing, orientation, and pitch

/Print [E,P] Options Advanced Layout

◆ Select the colors or hatch patterns for the data in a graph

/Graph Options Advanced Colors or Hatches

◆ Select the density, size, and orientation of a printed graph

/Print [E,P] Options Advanced Image

◆ Select the font, size, and color for the text in a graph

/Graph Options Advanced Text

◆ Set the order in which 1-2-3 prints each print job

/Print [P] Options Advanced Priority

Tell 1-2-3 where to start printing a new page

/Worksheet Page

### Setting up 1-2-3 to work with a printer

◆ Select a printer for the current print job if you do not want to use the default printer

/Print Printer Options Advanced Device Name

Select the default printer you want 1-2-3 to use from a list of printers you selected in Install

/Worksheet Global Default Printer Name

◆ Set the connection between your computer and your printer (parallel, serial, or output device) if different from the default setting

/Print Printer Options Advanced Device Interface

Set the default connection between your computer and your printer (parallel, serial, or output device)

/Worksheet Global Default Printer Interface

### Starting and stopping printing

◆ Cancel all 1-2-3 print jobs /Print Cancel

End the print job by closing the file if printing to a text or encoded file on disk /Print [E,F] Quit

◆ Leave the /Print menu and return 1-2-3 to READY mode without closing the current print job so you can make changes to the worksheet and then continue the print job /Print [E,F,P] Hold

Print worksheets and graphs on a printer you selected in the Install program /Print Printer Go

◆ Save data, graphs, and formatting codes in an encoded file to print later /Print Encoded Go

Save data in a text file for use with programs that can read text files /Print File Go

◆ Temporarily halt and then resume printing /Print Suspend and then /Print Resume

### Viewing and changing print settings

Change the default print settings that 1-2-3 automatically uses when you start 1-2-3 /Worksheet Global Default Printer

◆ Create, select, modify, and delete print settings names /Print [E,F,P] Options Name

Display a list of the default print settings that 1-2-3 automatically uses when you start 1-2-3 /Worksheet Global Default Status

◆ Print a sample page that shows you the current print settings and your printer's capabilities /Print [E,F,P] Sample

Reset some or all of the current print settings to the default print settings /Print [E,F,P] Clear

Reset the page counter to one and tell 1-2-3 to begin printing at the top of a page /Print [E,F,P] Align

## PROTECTING DATA AND FILES

### Protecting data

When a file is in GROUP mode, /Worksheet Global Prot, /Range Prot, and /Range Unprot affect all worksheets in the file.

Display worksheet protection status /Worksheet Status

Prevent or allow changes to data in a worksheet /Worksheet Global Prot

Protect or unprotect cells in a range /Range Prot or Unprot

Restrict cell-pointer movement to unprotected cells for data entry /Range Input

**Protecting files**

◆ Allow a user to read a file into memory but prevent changes to some graph, print, range, worksheet, and reservation settings

/File Admin Seal

◆ Prevent more than one person from simultaneously saving changes to a shared file

/File Admin Reservation
See 'Using Data Files on a Network' in Appendix 5 of *Reference*

Save a worksheet file with a password

See /File Save in 'File Commands' in Chapter 2 of *Reference*

## RETURNING 1-2-3 TO THE OPERATING SYSTEM

End a 1-2-3 session                                    /Quit
Suspend 1-2-3 to use the operating system              /System

## USING FILES

**Copying data between files**

Add numbers from a worksheet file on disk to numbers in the current file

/File Combine Add

Copy data from a worksheet file on disk to the current file

/File Combine Copy

Copy data from one worksheet or file to another worksheet or file

/Copy

Subtract numbers in a worksheet file on disk from numbers in the current file

/File Combine Subtract

◆ Write formulas that refer to data in other files (link files)

See 'Linking Files with Formulas' in Chapter 1 of *Reference*

**Erasing files**

◆ Delete one file from memory                          /Worksheet Delete File
  Erase a file on disk                                 /File Erase
◆ Remove all active worksheets and files from memory and replace them with one blank worksheet

/Worksheet Erase Yes

Replace the current file with a file from disk         /File Retrieve

**Reading files from disk into memory**

Change the current directory that 1-2-3 uses when you save, read, or list files

/File Dir

◆ Read a file from disk into memory before or after the current file

/File Open

Read data from a text file into separate cells in the current worksheet

/File Import Numbers with a delimited text file or /File Import Text and then /Data Parse

Read data from a text file into the current worksheet

/File Import

Replace the current file with a file from disk

/File Retrieve

Set the default directory that 1-2-3 automatically uses to save, read, and list files when you begin a session

/Worksheet Global Default Dir

**Saving files on disk**

Save a graph in a file to use with another program

/Graph Save

Save a range of data, converting formulas to values, in a worksheet file on disk

/File Xtract Values

Save a range of data, including formulas, in a worksheet file on disk

/File Xtract Formulas

Save a worksheet file with a password

See /File Save in Chapter 2 of *Reference*

◆ Save data, graphs, and formatting codes in an encoded file

/Print Encoded Go

Save data in a text file

/Print File Go

Save modified active files in files on disk

/File Save

**Starting a new file**

◆ Create a new worksheet file in memory

/File New

**Transferring data between 1-2-3 and other programs**

Read data from a text file into separate cells in the current worksheet

/File Import Numbers with a delimited text file or /File Import Text and then /Data Parse

Save data in a text file for use with programs that can read text files

/Print File Go

Translate files with other file formats to and from 1-2-3 Release 3.1 format

See 'Available Translation' in Appendix 1 of *Reference*

**Using multiple-sheet files**

◆ Delete one or more worksheets from the current file

/Worksheet Delete Sheet

◆ Insert one or more worksheets in a file          /Worksheet Insert Sheet

◆ View three worksheets at one time               /Worksheet Window Perspective

## USING MACROS

Create a macro to perform 1-2-3 tasks          See 'Creating a Macro' in Chapter 4
                                                of *Reference*

◆ Record 1-2-3 keystrokes to create a macro     See 'Using the Record Feature for
                                                Macros' in Chapter 4 of *Reference*

◆ Run a macro as soon as 1-2-3 reads the file    /Worksheet Global Default Autoexec
   that contains the macro into memory

◆ Use the sample macro library                   See 'Sample Macros' in Chapter 4 in
                                                *Reference*

## MENU TREES

This section contains menu trees for the Data, File, Graph, Print, Range, and Worksheet
commands.

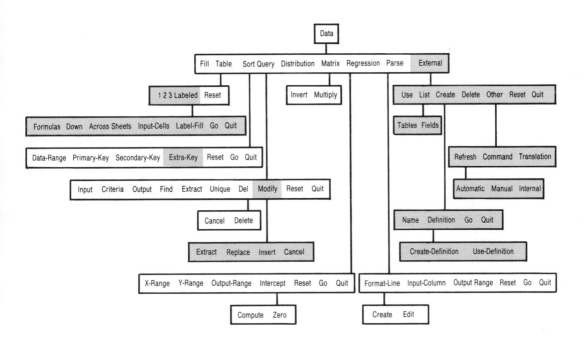

**Figure A3-1**   Data commands

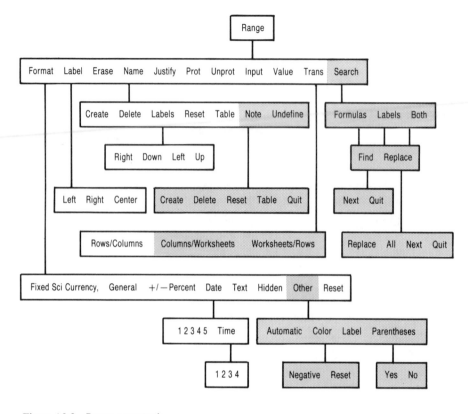

**Figure A3-2**  Range commands

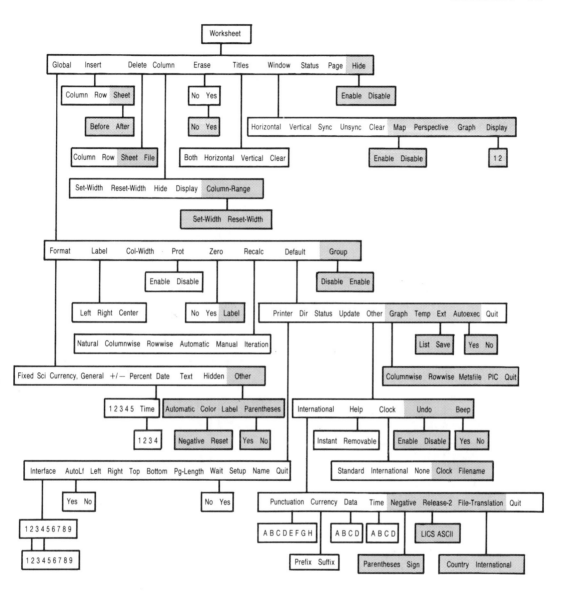

**Figure A3-3**   Worksheet commands

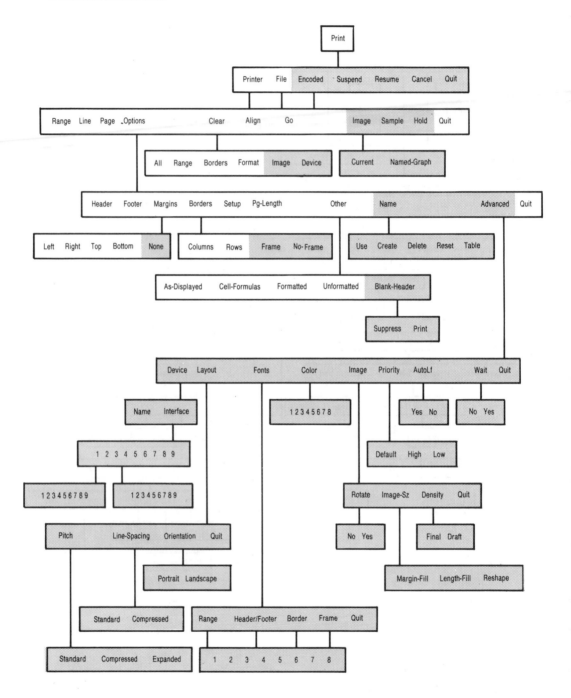

**Figure A3-4** Print commands

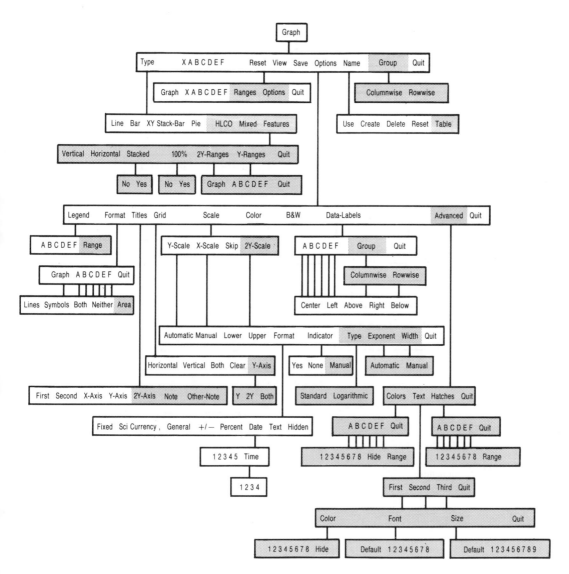

**Figure A3-5**   Graph commands

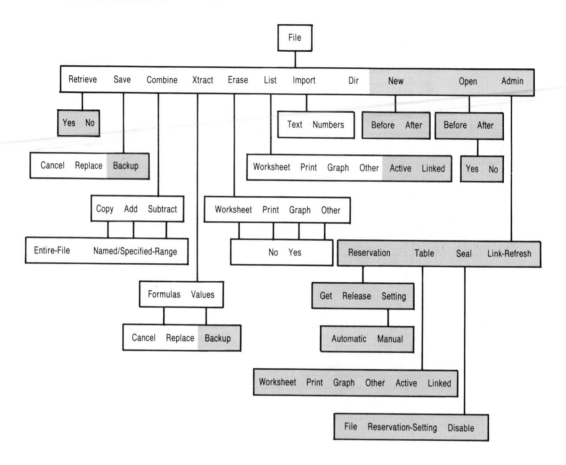

**Figure A3-6**   File commands

# 4

# SIGNIFICANCE OF RANK (SPEARMAN)· CORRELATION COEFFICIENT

Critical values of the coefficient $r_s = 1 - \left[ 6 \sum_{i=1}^{n} d_i^2 / n(n^2 - 1) \right]$, where $d =$ difference between ranks, for different values of $n =$ sample size and $\alpha =$ significance level (one tail). Example: If a random sample of 10 observations yields $r_s = 0.56$, the hypothesis that $\rho_s = 0$ in the population may be rejected at 5 per cent significance level (one-tail test) as $0.56 > 0.5515 = r_s(\alpha = 0.05)$. When $r_s$ is negative, ignore the sign and test as above. When ranks are tied, both observations are given the rank equal to the average of the two ranks, e.g. if two observations are ranked equal third, they are both given the rank of $3\frac{1}{2}$.

| $n$ \ $\alpha$ | .100 | .050 | .025 | .010 | .005 | .001 |
|---|---|---|---|---|---|---|
| 4 | .8000 | .8000 | | | | |
| 5 | .7000 | .8000 | .9000 | .9000 | | |
| 6 | .6000 | .7714 | .8286 | .8857 | .9429 | |
| 7 | .5357 | .6786 | .7450 | .8571 | .8929 | .9643 |
| 8 | .5000 | .6190 | .7143 | .8095 | .8571 | .9286 |
| 9 | .4667 | .5833 | .6833 | .7667 | .8167 | .9000 |
| 10 | .4424 | .5515 | .6364 | .7333 | .7818 | .8667 |
| 11 | .4182 | .5273 | .6091 | .7000 | .7455 | .8364 |
| 12 | .3986 | .4965 | .5804 | .6713 | .7273 | .8182 |
| 13 | .3791 | .4780 | .5549 | .6429 | .6978 | .7912 |
| 14 | .3626 | .4593 | .5341 | .6220 | .6747 | .7670 |
| 15 | .3500 | .4429 | .5179 | .6000 | .6536 | .7464 |
| 16 | .3382 | .4265 | .5000 | .5824 | .6324 | .7265 |
| 17 | .3260 | .4118 | .4853 | .5637 | .6152 | .7083 |
| 18 | .3148 | .3994 | .4716 | .5480 | .5975 | .6904 |
| 19 | .3070 | .3895 | .4579 | .5333 | .5825 | .6737 |

*continued*

| n \ α | .100 | .050 | .025 | .010 | .005 | .001 |
|---|---|---|---|---|---|---|
| 20 | .2977 | .3789 | .4451 | .5203 | .5684 | .6586 |
| 21 | .2909 | .3688 | .4351 | .5078 | .5545 | .6455 |
| 22 | .2829 | .3597 | .4241 | .4963 | .5426 | .6318 |
| 23 | .2767 | .3518 | .4150 | .4852 | .5306 | .6186 |
| 24 | .2704 | .3435 | .4061 | .4748 | .5200 | .6070 |
| 25 | .2646 | .3362 | .3977 | .4654 | .5100 | .5962 |
| 26 | .2588 | .3299 | .3894 | .4564 | .5002 | .5856 |
| 27 | .2540 | .3236 | .3822 | .4481 | .4915 | .5757 |
| 28 | .2490 | .3175 | .3749 | .4401 | .4828 | .5660 |
| 29 | .2443 | .3113 | .3685 | .4320 | .4744 | .5567 |
| 30 | .2400 | .3059 | .3620 | .4251 | .4665 | .5479 |

Reproduced from Z. W. Kmietowicz and Y. Yannoulis (1988) *Statistical Tables for Economic, Business and Social Studies*, Harlow: Longman with permission. Original sources is G. J. Glasser and R. Winter, 'Critical values of the coefficient of rank correlation for testing the hypothesis of independence', *Biometrika*, vol. 48, 1961 with permission of the publishers.

When $n > 30$, use Appendix Table 7 as an approximation.

# 5

# $\chi^2$ (CHI-SQUARED)-DISTRIBUTION

Values of $\chi^2_\alpha$ giving area $(\alpha)$ in the right-hand tail for different number of degrees of freedom $(v)$. Example: For $v = 15$ area beyond $\chi^2_{0.95} = 7.261$ is 0.950 and beyond $\chi^2_{0.10} = 22.307$ is 0.100.

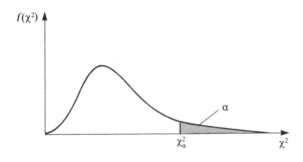

Chi-square distribution critical values table.

| ν \ α | 0.995 | 0.990 | 0.975 | 0.950 | 0.900 | 0.750 | 0.500 | 0.250 | 0.100 | 0.050 | 0.025 | 0.010 | 0.005 |
|---|---|---|---|---|---|---|---|---|---|---|---|---|---|
| 1 | $0.0^4 3927^*$ | $0.0^3 1571^*$ | $0.0^3 9821^*$ | $0.0^3 3932^*$ | 0.01579 | 0.1015 | 0.4549 | 1.323 | 2.706 | 3.841 | 5.024 | 6.635 | 7.879 |
| 2 | 0.01003 | 0.02010 | 0.05065 | 0.1026 | 0.2107 | 0.5754 | 1.386 | 2.773 | 4.605 | 5.991 | 7.378 | 9.210 | 10.597 |
| 3 | 0.07172 | 0.1148 | 0.2158 | 0.3518 | 0.5844 | 1.213 | 2.366 | 4.108 | 6.251 | 7.815 | 9.348 | 11.345 | 12.838 |
| 4 | 0.2070 | 0.2971 | 0.4844 | 0.7107 | 1.064 | 1.923 | 3.357 | 5.385 | 7.779 | 9.488 | 11.143 | 13.277 | 14.860 |
| 5 | 0.4117 | 0.5543 | 0.8312 | 1.145 | 1.610 | 2.675 | 4.351 | 6.626 | 9.236 | 11.070 | 12.833 | 15.086 | 16.750 |
| 6 | 0.6757 | 0.8721 | 1.237 | 1.635 | 2.204 | 3.455 | 5.348 | 7.841 | 10.645 | 12.592 | 14.449 | 16.812 | 18.548 |
| 7 | 0.9893 | 1.239 | 1.690 | 2.167 | 2.833 | 4.255 | 6.346 | 9.037 | 12.017 | 14.067 | 16.013 | 18.475 | 20.278 |
| 8 | 1.344 | 1.646 | 2.180 | 2.733 | 3.490 | 5.071 | 7.344 | 10.219 | 13.362 | 15.507 | 17.535 | 20.090 | 21.955 |
| 9 | 1.735 | 2.088 | 2.700 | 3.325 | 4.168 | 5.899 | 8.343 | 11.389 | 14.684 | 16.919 | 19.023 | 21.666 | 23.589 |
| 10 | 2.156 | 2.558 | 3.247 | 3.940 | 4.865 | 6.737 | 9.342 | 12.549 | 15.987 | 18.307 | 20.483 | 23.209 | 25.188 |
| 11 | 2.603 | 3.053 | 3.816 | 4.575 | 5.578 | 7.584 | 10.341 | 13.701 | 17.275 | 19.675 | 21.920 | 24.725 | 26.757 |
| 12 | 3.074 | 3.571 | 4.404 | 5.226 | 6.304 | 8.438 | 11.340 | 14.845 | 18.549 | 21.026 | 23.337 | 26.217 | 28.300 |
| 13 | 3.565 | 4.107 | 5.009 | 5.892 | 7.041 | 9.299 | 12.340 | 15.984 | 19.812 | 22.362 | 24.736 | 27.688 | 29.819 |
| 14 | 4.075 | 4.660 | 5.629 | 6.571 | 7.790 | 10.165 | 13.339 | 17.117 | 21.064 | 23.685 | 26.119 | 29.141 | 31.319 |
| 15 | 4.601 | 5.229 | 6.262 | 7.261 | 8.547 | 11.036 | 14.339 | 18.245 | 22.307 | 24.996 | 27.488 | 30.578 | 32.801 |
| 16 | 5.142 | 5.812 | 6.908 | 7.962 | 9.312 | 11.912 | 15.338 | 19.369 | 23.542 | 26.296 | 28.845 | 32.000 | 34.267 |
| 17 | 5.697 | 6.408 | 7.564 | 8.672 | 10.085 | 12.792 | 16.338 | 20.489 | 24.769 | 27.587 | 30.191 | 33.409 | 35.718 |
| 18 | 6.265 | 7.015 | 8.231 | 9.390 | 10.865 | 13.675 | 17.338 | 21.605 | 25.989 | 28.869 | 31.526 | 34.805 | 37.156 |
| 19 | 6.844 | 7.633 | 8.907 | 10.117 | 11.651 | 14.562 | 18.338 | 22.718 | 27.204 | 30.143 | 32.852 | 36.191 | 38.582 |
| 20 | 7.434 | 8.260 | 9.591 | 10.851 | 12.443 | 15.452 | 19.337 | 23.828 | 28.412 | 31.410 | 34.170 | 37.566 | 39.997 |
| 21 | 8.034 | 8.897 | 10.283 | 11.591 | 13.240 | 16.344 | 20.337 | 24.935 | 29.615 | 32.670 | 35.479 | 38.932 | 41.401 |
| 22 | 8.643 | 9.542 | 10.982 | 12.338 | 14.041 | 17.240 | 21.337 | 26.039 | 30.813 | 33.924 | 36.781 | 40.289 | 42.796 |
| 23 | 9.260 | 10.196 | 11.688 | 13.090 | 14.848 | 18.137 | 22.337 | 27.141 | 32.007 | 35.172 | 38.076 | 41.638 | 44.181 |
| 24 | 9.886 | 10.856 | 12.401 | 13.848 | 15.659 | 19.037 | 23.337 | 28.241 | 33.196 | 36.415 | 39.364 | 42.080 | 45.558 |
| 25 | 10.520 | 11.524 | 13.120 | 14.611 | 16.473 | 19.939 | 24.337 | 29.339 | 34.382 | 37.652 | 40.646 | 44.314 | 46.928 |
| 26 | 11.160 | 12.198 | 13.844 | 15.379 | 17.292 | 20.843 | 25.336 | 30.434 | 35.563 | 38.885 | 41.923 | 45.642 | 48.290 |
| 27 | 11.808 | 12.879 | 14.573 | 16.151 | 18.114 | 21.749 | 26.336 | 31.528 | 36.741 | 40.113 | 43.194 | 46.963 | 49.645 |
| 28 | 12.461 | 13.565 | 15.308 | 16.928 | 18.939 | 22.657 | 27.336 | 32.620 | 37.916 | 41.337 | 44.461 | 48.278 | 50.993 |
| 29 | 13.121 | 14.256 | 16.047 | 17.708 | 19.768 | 23.567 | 28.336 | 33.711 | 39.087 | 42.557 | 45.722 | 49.588 | 52.336 |
| 30 | 13.787 | 14.954 | 16.791 | 18.493 | 20.599 | 24.478 | 29.336 | 34.800 | 40.256 | 43.773 | 46.979 | 50.892 | 53.672 |
| 35 | 17.192 | 18.509 | 20.569 | 22.465 | 24.797 | 29.054 | 34.336 | 40.223 | 46.059 | 49.802 | 53.203 | 57.342 | 60.275 |
| 40 | 20.707 | 22.164 | 24.433 | 26.509 | 29.050 | 33.660 | 39.335 | 45.616 | 51.805 | 55.758 | 59.342 | 63.691 | 66.766 |
| 45 | 24.311 | 25.901 | 28.366 | 30.612 | 33.350 | 38.291 | 44.335 | 50.985 | 57.505 | 61.656 | 65.410 | 69.957 | 73.166 |
| 50 | 27.991 | 29.707 | 32.357 | 34.764 | 37.689 | 42.942 | 49.335 | 56.334 | 63.167 | 67.505 | 71.420 | 76.154 | 79.490 |

| | $-2.5758$ | $-2.3263$ | $-1.9600$ | $-1.6449$ | $-1.2816$ | $-0.6745$ | 0.0000 | 0.6745 | 1.2816 | 1.6449 | 1.9600 | 2.3263 | 2.5758 |
|---|---|---|---|---|---|---|---|---|---|---|---|---|---|
| 55 | 31.735 | 33.571 | 36.398 | 38.958 | 42.060 | 47.611 | 54.335 | 61.665 | 68.796 | 73.311 | 77.381 | 82.292 | 85.749 |
| 60 | 35.535 | 37.485 | 40.482 | 43.188 | 46.459 | 52.294 | 59.335 | 66.981 | 74.397 | 79.082 | 83.298 | 88.379 | 91.952 |
| 70 | 43.275 | 45.442 | 48.758 | 51.739 | 55.329 | 61.698 | 69.334 | 77.577 | 85.527 | 90.531 | 95.023 | 100.425 | 104.215 |
| 80 | 51.172 | 53.540 | 57.153 | 60.391 | 64.278 | 71.144 | 79.334 | 88.130 | 96.578 | 101.879 | 106.629 | 112.329 | 116.321 |
| 90 | 59.196 | 61.754 | 65.647 | 69.126 | 73.291 | 80.625 | 89.334 | 98.650 | 107.565 | 113.145 | 118.136 | 124.116 | 128.299 |
| 100 | 67.328 | 70.065 | 74.222 | 77.929 | 82.358 | 90.133 | 99.334 | 109.141 | 118.498 | 124.342 | 129.561 | 135.807 | 140.169 |
| 120 | 83.829 | 86.909 | 91.568 | 95.705 | 100.627 | 109.224 | 119.335 | 130.051 | 140.228 | 146.565 | 152.214 | 158.963 | 163.670 |
| 150 | 109.122 | 112.655 | 117.980 | 122.692 | 126.278 | 137.987 | 149.334 | 161.288 | 172.577 | 179.579 | 185.803 | 193.219 | 198.380 |
| 200 | 152.224 | 156.421 | 162.724 | 168.279 | 174.828 | 186.175 | 199.334 | 213.099 | 226.018 | 233.993 | 241.060 | 249.455 | 255.281 |
| 250 | 196.145 | 200.929 | 208.095 | 214.392 | 221.809 | 234.580 | 249.334 | 264.694 | 279.947 | 287.889 | 295.691 | 304.948 | 311.361 |
| $z_\alpha$ | $-2.5758$ | $-2.3263$ | $-1.9600$ | $-1.6449$ | $-1.2816$ | $-0.6745$ | 0.0000 | 0.6745 | 1.2816 | 1.6449 | 1.9600 | 2.3263 | 2.5758 |

*E.g. $0.0^43927 = 0.00003927$.

Interpolation: For $v > 100$, $\chi_\alpha^2 = \frac{1}{2}(z_\alpha + \sqrt{2v-1})^2$ where $z_\alpha$ is the standardized normal variable shown in the bottom line of the table.

Reproduced from Z. W. Kmietowicz and Y. Yannoulis (1988) *Statistical Tables for Economic, Business and Social Studies*, Harlow: Longman, with permission.

# 6

# *t*-DISTRIBUTION

Critical points $(t_\alpha)$ for different probability levels $(\alpha)$ and different number of degrees of freedom $(v)$. Example: For $v = 19$, $P(t > 2.0930) = 0.025$ and $P(|t| > 2.0930) = 0.05$.

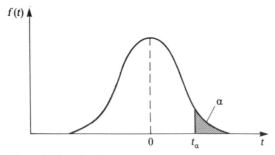

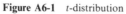

**Figure A6-1**   *t*-distribution

| $\alpha$ / $v$ | 0.4 | 0.25 | 0.15 | 0.1 | 0.05 | 0.025 | 0.01 | 0.005 | 0.001 | 0.0005 |
|---|---|---|---|---|---|---|---|---|---|---|
| 1 | 0.3249 | 1.0000 | 1.9626 | 3.0777 | 6.3138 | 12.7062 | 31.8205 | 63.6567 | 318.3087 | 636.6189 |
| 2 | 0.2887 | 0.8165 | 1.3862 | 1.8856 | 2.9200 | 4.3027 | 6.9646 | 9.9248 | 22.3271 | 31.5991 |
| 3 | 0.2767 | 0.7649 | 1.2498 | 1.6377 | 2.3534 | 3.1824 | 4.5407 | 5.8409 | 10.2145 | 12.9240 |
| 4 | 0.2707 | 0.7407 | 1.1896 | 1.5332 | 2.1318 | 2.7764 | 3.7469 | 4.6041 | 7.1732 | 8.6103 |
| 5 | 0.2672 | 0.7267 | 1.1558 | 1.4759 | 2.0150 | 2.5706 | 3.3649 | 4.0321 | 5.8934 | 6.8688 |
| 6 | 0.2648 | 0.7176 | 1.1342 | 1.4398 | 1.9432 | 2.4469 | 3.1427 | 3.7074 | 5.2076 | 5.9588 |
| 7 | 0.2632 | 0.7111 | 1.1192 | 1.4149 | 1.8946 | 2.3646 | 2.9980 | 3.4995 | 4.7853 | 5.4079 |
| 8 | 0.2619 | 0.7064 | 1.1081 | 1.3968 | 1.8595 | 2.3060 | 2.8965 | 3.3554 | 4.5008 | 5.0413 |
| 9 | 0.2610 | 0.7027 | 1.0997 | 1.3830 | 1.8331 | 2.2622 | 2.8214 | 3.2498 | 4.2968 | 4.7809 |
| 10 | 0.2602 | 0.6998 | 1.0931 | 1.3722 | 1.8125 | 2.2281 | 2.7638 | 3.1693 | 4.1437 | 4.5869 |
| 11 | 0.2596 | 0.6974 | 1.0877 | 1.3634 | 1.7959 | 2.2010 | 2.7181 | 3.1058 | 4.0247 | 4.4370 |
| 12 | 0.2590 | 0.6955 | 1.0832 | 1.3562 | 1.7823 | 2.1788 | 2.6810 | 3.0545 | 3.9296 | 4.3178 |
| 13 | 0.2586 | 0.6938 | 1.0795 | 1.3502 | 1.7709 | 2.1604 | 2.6503 | 3.0123 | 3.8520 | 4.2208 |
| 14 | 0.2582 | 0.6924 | 1.0763 | 1.3450 | 1.7613 | 2.1448 | 2.6245 | 2.9768 | 3.7874 | 4.1405 |

| α / ν | 0.4 | 0.25 | 0.15 | 0.1 | 0.05 | 0.025 | 0.01 | 0.005 | 0.001 | 0.0005 |
|---|---|---|---|---|---|---|---|---|---|---|
| 15 | 0.2579 | 0.6912 | 1.0735 | 1.3406 | 1.7531 | 2.1314 | 2.6025 | 2.9467 | 3.7328 | 4.0728 |
| 16 | 0.2576 | 0.6901 | 1.0711 | 1.3368 | 1.7459 | 2.1199 | 2.5835 | 2.9208 | 3.6862 | 4.0150 |
| 17 | 0.2573 | 0.6892 | 1.0690 | 1.3334 | 1.7396 | 2.1098 | 2.5669 | 2.8982 | 3.6458 | 3.9651 |
| 18 | 0.2571 | 0.6884 | 1.0672 | 1.3304 | 1.7341 | 2.1009 | 2.5524 | 2.8784 | 3.6105 | 3.9216 |
| 19 | 0.2569 | 0.6876 | 1.0655 | 1.3277 | 1.7291 | 2.0930 | 2.5395 | 2.8609 | 3.5794 | 3.8834 |
| 20 | 0.2567 | 0.6870 | 1.0640 | 1.3253 | 1.7247 | 2.0860 | 2.5280 | 2.8453 | 3.5518 | 3.8495 |
| 21 | 0.2566 | 0.6864 | 1.0627 | 1.3232 | 1.7207 | 2.0796 | 2.5176 | 2.8314 | 3.5272 | 3.8193 |
| 22 | 0.2564 | 0.6858 | 1.0614 | 1.3212 | 1.7171 | 2.0739 | 2.5083 | 2.8188 | 3.5050 | 3.7921 |
| 23 | 0.2563 | 0.6853 | 1.0603 | 1.3195 | 1.7139 | 2.0687 | 2.4999 | 2.8073 | 3.4850 | 3.7676 |
| 24 | 0.2562 | 0.6848 | 1.0593 | 1.3178 | 1.7109 | 2.0639 | 2.4922 | 2.7969 | 3.4668 | 3.7454 |
| 25 | 0.2561 | 0.6844 | 1.0584 | 1.3163 | 1.7081 | 2.0595 | 2.4851 | 2.7874 | 3.4502 | 3.7251 |
| 26 | 0.2560 | 0.6840 | 1.0575 | 1.3150 | 1.7056 | 2.0555 | 2.4786 | 2.7787 | 3.4350 | 3.7066 |
| 27 | 0.2559 | 0.6837 | 1.0567 | 1.3137 | 1.7033 | 2.0518 | 2.4727 | 2.7707 | 3.4210 | 3.6896 |
| 28 | 0.2558 | 0.6834 | 1.0560 | 1.3125 | 1.7011 | 2.0484 | 2.4671 | 2.7633 | 3.4082 | 3.6739 |
| 29 | 0.2557 | 0.6830 | 1.0553 | 1.3114 | 1.6991 | 2.0452 | 2.4620 | 2.7564 | 3.3962 | 3.6594 |
| 30 | 0.2556 | 0.6828 | 1.0547 | 1.3104 | 1.6973 | 2.0423 | 2.4573 | 2.7500 | 3.3852 | 3.6460 |
| 35 | 0.2553 | 0.6816 | 1.0520 | 1.3062 | 1.6896 | 2.0301 | 2.4377 | 2.7238 | 3.3400 | 3.5911 |
| 40 | 0.2550 | 0.6807 | 1.0500 | 1.3031 | 1.6839 | 2.0211 | 2.4233 | 2.7045 | 3.3069 | 3.5510 |
| 45 | 0.2549 | 0.6800 | 1.0485 | 1.3006 | 1.6794 | 2.0141 | 2.4121 | 2.6896 | 3.2815 | 3.5203 |
| 50 | 0.2547 | 0.6794 | 1.0473 | 1.2987 | 1.6759 | 2.0086 | 2.4033 | 2.6778 | 3.2614 | 3.4960 |
| 60 | 0.2545 | 0.6786 | 1.0455 | 1.2958 | 1.6706 | 2.0003 | 2.3901 | 2.6603 | 3.2317 | 3.4602 |
| 70 | 0.2543 | 0.6780 | 1.0442 | 1.2938 | 1.6669 | 1.9944 | 2.3808 | 2.6479 | 3.2108 | 3.4350 |
| 80 | 0.2542 | 0.6776 | 1.0432 | 1.2922 | 1.6641 | 1.9901 | 2.3739 | 2.6387 | 3.1953 | 3.4163 |
| 90 | 0.2541 | 0.6772 | 1.0424 | 1.2910 | 1.6620 | 1.9867 | 2.3685 | 2.6316 | 3.1833 | 3.4019 |
| 100 | 0.2540 | 0.6770 | 1.0418 | 1.2901 | 1.6602 | 1.9840 | 2.3642 | 2.6259 | 3.1737 | 3.3905 |
| 120 | 0.2539 | 0.6765 | 1.0409 | 1.2886 | 1.6577 | 1.9799 | 2.3578 | 2.6174 | 3.1595 | 3.3735 |
| 150 | 0.2538 | 0.6761 | 1.0400 | 1.2872 | 1.6551 | 1.9759 | 2.3515 | 2.6090 | 3.1455 | 3.3566 |
| 200 | 0.2537 | 0.6757 | 1.0391 | 1.2858 | 1.6525 | 1.9719 | 2.3451 | 2.6006 | 3.1315 | 3.3398 |
| 300 | 0.2536 | 0.6753 | 1.0382 | 1.2844 | 1.6499 | 1.9679 | 2.3388 | 2.5923 | 3.1176 | 3.3233 |
| ∞ | 0.2533 | 0.6745 | 1.0364 | 1.2816 | 1.6449 | 1.9600 | 2.3263 | 2.5758 | 3.0902 | 3.2905 |

Reproduced from Z. W. Kmietowicz and Y. Yannoulis (1988) *Statistical Tables for Economics, Business and Social Studies*, Harlow: Longman, with permission.

# NORMAL DISTRIBUTION (AREAS)

Area ($\alpha$) in the tail of the standardized normal curve, $N(0,1)$, for different values of $z$. Example: Area beyond $z = 1.96$ (or below $z = -1.96$) is $\alpha = 0.02500$. For Normal curve with $\mu = 10$ and $\sigma = 2$, area beyond $x = 12$, say, is the same as area beyond $z = \dfrac{x-\mu}{\sigma} = \dfrac{12-10}{2} = 1$, i.e. $\alpha = 0.15866$.

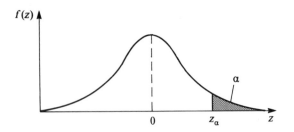

**Figure A7-1** Normal distribution

| $z$ | 0.00 | 0.01 | 0.02 | 0.03 | 0.04 | 0.05 | 0.06 | 0.07 | 0.08 | 0.09 |
|---|---|---|---|---|---|---|---|---|---|---|
| 0.0 | .50000 | .49601 | .49202 | .48803 | .48405 | .48006 | .47608 | .47210 | .46812 | .46414 |
| 0.1 | .46017 | .45620 | .45224 | .44828 | .44433 | .44038 | .43644 | .43251 | .42858 | .42465 |
| 0.2 | .42074 | .41683 | .41294 | .40905 | .40517 | .40129 | .39743 | .39358 | .38974 | .38591 |
| 0.3 | .38209 | .37828 | .37448 | .37070 | .36693 | .36317 | .35942 | .35569 | .35197 | .34827 |
| 0.4 | .34458 | .34090 | .33724 | .33360 | .32997 | .32636 | .32276 | .31918 | .31561 | .31207 |
| 0.5 | .30854 | .30503 | .30153 | .29806 | .29460 | .29116 | .28774 | .28434 | .28096 | .27760 |
| 0.6 | .27425 | .27093 | .26763 | .26435 | .26109 | .25785 | .25463 | .25143 | .24825 | .24510 |
| 0.7 | .24196 | .23885 | .23576 | .23270 | .22965 | .22663 | .22363 | .22065 | .21770 | .21476 |
| 0.8 | .21186 | .20897 | .20611 | .20327 | .20045 | .19766 | .19489 | .19215 | .18943 | .18673 |
| 0.9 | .18406 | .18141 | .17879 | .17619 | .17361 | .17106 | .16853 | .16602 | .16354 | .16109 |

| z \ z | 0.00 | 0.01 | 0.02 | 0.03 | 0.04 | 0.05 | 0.06 | 0.07 | 0.08 | 0.09 |
|---|---|---|---|---|---|---|---|---|---|---|
| 1.0 | .15866 | .15625 | .15386 | .15150 | .14917 | .14686 | .14457 | .14231 | .14007 | .13786 |
| 1.1 | .13567 | .13350 | .13136 | .12924 | .12714 | .12507 | .12302 | .12100 | .11900 | .11702 |
| 1.2 | .11507 | .11314 | .11123 | .10935 | .10749 | .10565 | .10383 | .10204 | .10027 | .09853 |
| 1.3 | .09680 | .09510 | .09342 | .09176 | .09012 | .08851 | .08692 | .08534 | .08379 | .08226 |
| 1.4 | .08076 | .07927 | .07780 | .07636 | .07493 | .07353 | .07214 | .07078 | .06944 | .06811 |
| 1.5 | .06681 | .06552 | .06426 | .06301 | .06178 | .06057 | .05938 | .05821 | .05705 | .05592 |
| 1.6 | .05480 | .05370 | .05262 | .05155 | .05050 | .04947 | .04846 | .04746 | .04648 | .04551 |
| 1.7 | .04457 | .04363 | .04272 | .04182 | .04093 | .04006 | .03920 | .03836 | .03754 | .03673 |
| 1.8 | .03593 | .03515 | .03438 | .03362 | .03288 | .03216 | .03144 | .03074 | .03005 | .02938 |
| 1.9 | .02872 | .02807 | .02743 | .02680 | .02619 | .02559 | .02500 | .02442 | .02385 | .02330 |
| 2.0 | .02275 | .02222 | .02169 | .02118 | .02068 | .02018 | .01970 | .01923 | .01876 | .01831 |
| 2.1 | .01786 | .01743 | .01700 | .01659 | .01618 | .01578 | .01539 | .01500 | .01463 | .01426 |
| 2.2 | .01390 | .01355 | .01321 | .01287 | .01254 | .01222 | .01191 | .01160 | .01130 | .01101 |
| 2.3 | .01072 | .01044 | .01017 | .00990 | .00964 | .00939 | .00914 | .00889 | .00866 | .00842 |
| 2.4 | .00820 | .00798 | .00776 | .00755 | .00734 | .00714 | .00695 | .00676 | .00657 | .00639 |
| 2.5 | .00621 | .00604 | .00587 | .00570 | .00554 | .00539 | .00523 | .00509 | .00494 | .00480 |
| 2.6 | .00466 | .00453 | .00440 | .00427 | .00415 | .00403 | .00391 | .00379 | .00368 | .00357 |
| 2.7 | .00347 | .00336 | .00326 | .00317 | .00307 | .00298 | .00289 | .00280 | .00272 | .00263 |
| 2.8 | .00256 | .00248 | .00240 | .00233 | .00226 | .00219 | .00212 | .00205 | .00199 | .00193 |
| 2.9 | .00187 | .00181 | .00175 | .00169 | .00164 | .00159 | .00154 | .00149 | .00144 | .00139 |
| 3.0 | .00135 | .00131 | .00126 | .00122 | .00118 | .00114 | .00111 | .00107 | .00104 | .00100 |
| 3.1 | .00097 | .00094 | .00090 | .00087 | .00085 | .00082 | .00079 | .00076 | .00074 | .00071 |
| 3.2 | .00069 | .00066 | .00064 | .00062 | .00060 | .00058 | .00056 | .00054 | .00052 | .00050 |
| 3.3 | .00048 | .00047 | .00045 | .00043 | .00042 | .00040 | .00039 | .00038 | .00036 | .00035 |
| 3.4 | .00034 | .00032 | .00031 | .00030 | .00029 | .00028 | .00027 | .00026 | .00025 | .00024 |
| 3.5 | .00023 | .00022 | .00022 | .00021 | .00020 | .00019 | .00019 | .00018 | .00017 | .00017 |
| 3.6 | .00016 | .00015 | .00015 | .00014 | .00014 | .00013 | .00013 | .00012 | .00012 | .00011 |
| 3.7 | .00011 | .00010 | .00010 | .00010 | .00009 | .00009 | .00009 | .00008 | .00008 | .00008 |
| 3.8 | .00007 | .00007 | .00007 | .00006 | .00006 | .00006 | .00006 | .00005 | .00005 | .00005 |
| 3.9 | .00005 | .00005 | .00004 | .00004 | .00004 | .00004 | .00004 | .00004 | .00004 | .00003 |
| 4.0 | .00003 | .00003 | .00003 | .00003 | .00003 | .00002 | .00002 | .00002 | .00002 | .00002 |

| $\alpha$ | 0.4 | 0.25 | 0.2 | 0.15 | 0.1 | 0.05 | 0.025 | 0.01 | 0.005 | 0.001 |
|---|---|---|---|---|---|---|---|---|---|---|
| $z_\alpha$ | .2533 | .6745 | .8416 | 1.0364 | 1.2816 | 1.6449 | 1.9600 | 2.3263 | 2.5758 | 3.0902 |

$8$

# $F$-DISTRIBUTION

Values of $F_\alpha$ ($\alpha = 0.1$, $0.05$ and $0.01$) for different combinations of degrees of freedom in the numerator, $v_1$, and denominator, $v_2$. Example: When $v_1 = 10$ and $v_2 = 20$ area ($\alpha$) to the right of $F_{0.05} = 2.348$ is $0.05$. To find $F_{1-\alpha}$, leaving an area $\alpha$ in the left-hand tail, use the relation: $F_{1-\alpha}(v_1, v_2) = 1/F_\alpha(v_2, v_1)$. Example: $F_{0.95}(20, 10) = 1/F_{0.05}(10, 20) = 1/2.348 = 0.4259$.

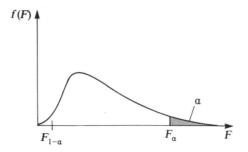

**Figure A8-1** $F$-distribution

| $v_2$ | $\alpha$ | 1 | 2 | 3 | 4 | 5 | 6 | 7 | 8 | 9 | 10 | 12 | 15 | 20 | 25 | 30 | 50 | 100 | $\infty$ |
|---|---|---|---|---|---|---|---|---|---|---|---|---|---|---|---|---|---|---|---|
| 1 | 0.10 | 39.86 | 49.50 | 53.59 | 55.83 | 57.24 | 58.20 | 58.91 | 59.44 | 59.86 | 60.19 | 60.71 | 61.22 | 61.74 | 62.05 | 62.26 | 62.69 | 63.01 | 63.33 |
|  | 0.05 | 161.4 | 199.5 | 215.7 | 224.6 | 230.2 | 234.0 | 236.8 | 238.9 | 240.5 | 241.9 | 243.9 | 245.9 | 248.0 | 249.3 | 250.1 | 251.8 | 253.0 | 254.3 |
|  | 0.01 | 4052 | 4999 | 5403 | 5625 | 5764 | 5859 | 5928 | 5981 | 6022 | 6056 | 6106 | 6157 | 6209 | 6240 | 6261 | 6303 | 6334 | 6366 |
| 2 | 0.10 | 8.526 | 9.000 | 9.162 | 9.243 | 9.293 | 9.326 | 9.349 | 9.367 | 9.381 | 9.392 | 9.408 | 9.425 | 9.441 | 9.451 | 9.458 | 9.471 | 9.481 | 9.491 |
|  | 0.05 | 18.51 | 19.00 | 19.16 | 19.25 | 19.30 | 19.33 | 19.35 | 19.37 | 19.38 | 19.40 | 19.41 | 19.43 | 19.45 | 19.46 | 19.46 | 19.48 | 19.49 | 19.50 |
|  | 0.01 | 98.50 | 99.00 | 99.17 | 99.25 | 99.30 | 99.33 | 99.36 | 99.37 | 99.39 | 99.40 | 99.42 | 99.43 | 99.45 | 99.46 | 99.47 | 99.48 | 99.49 | 99.50 |
| 3 | 0.10 | 5.538 | 5.462 | 5.391 | 5.343 | 5.309 | 5.285 | 5.266 | 5.252 | 5.240 | 5.230 | 5.216 | 5.200 | 5.184 | 5.175 | 5.168 | 5.155 | 5.144 | 5.134 |
|  | 0.05 | 10.13 | 9.552 | 9.277 | 9.117 | 9.013 | 8.941 | 8.887 | 8.845 | 8.812 | 8.786 | 8.745 | 8.703 | 8.660 | 8.634 | 8.617 | 8.581 | 8.554 | 8.526 |
|  | 0.01 | 34.12 | 30.82 | 29.46 | 28.71 | 28.24 | 27.91 | 27.67 | 27.49 | 27.35 | 27.23 | 27.05 | 26.87 | 26.69 | 26.58 | 26.50 | 26.35 | 26.24 | 26.13 |
| 4 | 0.10 | 4.545 | 4.325 | 4.191 | 4.107 | 4.051 | 4.010 | 3.979 | 3.955 | 3.936 | 3.920 | 3.896 | 3.870 | 3.844 | 3.828 | 3.817 | 3.795 | 3.778 | 3.761 |
|  | 0.05 | 7.709 | 6.944 | 6.591 | 6.388 | 6.256 | 6.163 | 6.094 | 6.041 | 5.999 | 5.964 | 5.912 | 5.858 | 5.803 | 5.769 | 5.746 | 5.699 | 5.664 | 5.628 |
|  | 0.01 | 21.20 | 18.00 | 16.69 | 15.98 | 15.52 | 15.21 | 14.98 | 14.80 | 14.66 | 14.55 | 14.37 | 14.20 | 14.02 | 13.91 | 13.84 | 13.69 | 13.58 | 13.46 |
| 5 | 0.10 | 4.060 | 3.780 | 3.619 | 3.520 | 3.453 | 3.405 | 3.368 | 3.339 | 3.316 | 3.297 | 3.268 | 3.238 | 3.207 | 3.187 | 3.174 | 3.147 | 3.126 | 3.105 |
|  | 0.05 | 6.608 | 5.786 | 5.409 | 5.192 | 5.050 | 4.950 | 4.876 | 4.818 | 4.772 | 4.735 | 4.678 | 4.619 | 4.558 | 4.521 | 4.496 | 4.444 | 4.405 | 4.365 |
|  | 0.01 | 16.26 | 13.27 | 12.06 | 11.39 | 10.97 | 10.67 | 10.46 | 10.29 | 10.16 | 10.05 | 9.888 | 9.722 | 9.553 | 9.449 | 9.379 | 9.238 | 9.130 | 9.020 |
| 6 | 0.10 | 3.776 | 3.463 | 3.289 | 3.181 | 3.108 | 3.055 | 3.014 | 2.983 | 2.958 | 2.937 | 2.905 | 2.871 | 2.836 | 2.815 | 2.800 | 2.770 | 2.746 | 2.722 |
|  | 0.05 | 5.987 | 5.143 | 4.757 | 4.534 | 4.387 | 4.284 | 4.207 | 4.147 | 4.099 | 4.060 | 4.000 | 3.938 | 3.874 | 3.835 | 3.808 | 3.754 | 3.712 | 3.669 |
|  | 0.01 | 13.75 | 10.92 | 9.780 | 9.148 | 8.746 | 8.466 | 8.260 | 8.102 | 7.976 | 7.874 | 7.718 | 7.559 | 7.396 | 7.296 | 7.229 | 7.091 | 6.987 | 6.880 |
| 7 | 0.10 | 3.589 | 3.257 | 3.074 | 2.961 | 2.883 | 2.827 | 2.785 | 2.752 | 2.725 | 2.703 | 2.668 | 2.632 | 2.595 | 2.571 | 2.555 | 2.523 | 2.497 | 2.471 |
|  | 0.05 | 5.591 | 4.737 | 4.347 | 4.120 | 3.972 | 3.866 | 3.787 | 3.726 | 3.677 | 3.637 | 3.575 | 3.511 | 3.445 | 3.404 | 3.376 | 3.319 | 3.275 | 3.230 |
|  | 0.01 | 12.25 | 9.547 | 8.451 | 7.847 | 7.460 | 7.191 | 6.993 | 6.840 | 6.719 | 6.620 | 6.469 | 6.314 | 6.155 | 6.058 | 5.992 | 5.858 | 5.755 | 5.650 |
| 8 | 0.10 | 3.458 | 3.113 | 2.924 | 2.806 | 2.726 | 2.668 | 2.624 | 2.589 | 2.561 | 2.538 | 2.502 | 2.464 | 2.425 | 2.400 | 2.383 | 2.348 | 2.321 | 2.293 |
|  | 0.05 | 5.318 | 4.459 | 4.066 | 3.838 | 3.687 | 3.581 | 3.500 | 3.438 | 3.388 | 3.347 | 3.284 | 3.218 | 3.150 | 3.108 | 3.079 | 3.020 | 2.975 | 2.928 |
|  | 0.01 | 11.26 | 8.649 | 7.591 | 7.006 | 6.632 | 6.371 | 6.178 | 6.029 | 5.911 | 5.814 | 5.667 | 5.515 | 5.359 | 5.263 | 5.198 | 5.065 | 4.963 | 4.859 |
| 9 | 0.10 | 3.360 | 3.006 | 2.813 | 2.693 | 2.611 | 2.551 | 2.505 | 2.469 | 2.440 | 2.416 | 2.379 | 2.340 | 2.298 | 2.272 | 2.255 | 2.218 | 2.189 | 2.159 |
|  | 0.05 | 5.117 | 4.256 | 3.863 | 3.633 | 3.482 | 3.374 | 3.293 | 3.230 | 3.179 | 3.137 | 3.073 | 3.006 | 2.936 | 2.893 | 2.864 | 2.803 | 2.756 | 2.707 |
|  | 0.01 | 10.56 | 8.022 | 6.992 | 6.422 | 6.057 | 5.802 | 5.613 | 5.467 | 5.351 | 5.257 | 5.111 | 4.962 | 4.808 | 4.713 | 4.649 | 4.517 | 4.415 | 4.311 |
| 10 | 0.10 | 3.285 | 2.924 | 2.728 | 2.605 | 2.522 | 2.461 | 2.414 | 2.377 | 2.347 | 2.323 | 2.284 | 2.244 | 2.201 | 2.174 | 2.155 | 2.117 | 2.087 | 2.055 |
|  | 0.05 | 4.965 | 4.103 | 3.708 | 3.478 | 3.326 | 3.217 | 3.135 | 3.072 | 3.020 | 2.978 | 2.913 | 2.845 | 2.774 | 2.730 | 2.700 | 2.637 | 2.588 | 2.538 |
|  | 0.01 | 10.04 | 7.559 | 6.552 | 5.994 | 5.636 | 5.386 | 5.200 | 5.057 | 4.942 | 4.849 | 4.706 | 4.558 | 4.405 | 4.311 | 4.247 | 4.115 | 4.014 | 3.909 |
| 11 | 0.10 | 3.225 | 2.860 | 2.660 | 2.536 | 2.451 | 2.389 | 2.342 | 2.304 | 2.274 | 2.248 | 2.209 | 2.167 | 2.123 | 2.095 | 2.076 | 2.036 | 2.005 | 1.972 |
|  | 0.05 | 4.844 | 3.982 | 3.587 | 3.357 | 3.204 | 3.095 | 3.012 | 2.948 | 2.896 | 2.854 | 2.788 | 2.719 | 2.646 | 2.601 | 2.570 | 2.507 | 2.457 | 2.404 |
|  | 0.01 | 9.646 | 7.206 | 6.217 | 5.668 | 5.316 | 5.069 | 4.886 | 4.744 | 4.632 | 4.539 | 4.397 | 4.251 | 4.099 | 4.005 | 3.941 | 3.810 | 3.708 | 3.602 |
| 12 | 0.10 | 3.177 | 2.807 | 2.606 | 2.480 | 2.394 | 2.331 | 2.283 | 2.245 | 2.214 | 2.188 | 2.147 | 2.105 | 2.060 | 2.031 | 2.011 | 1.970 | 1.938 | 1.904 |
|  | 0.05 | 4.747 | 3.885 | 3.490 | 3.259 | 3.106 | 2.996 | 2.913 | 2.849 | 2.796 | 2.753 | 2.687 | 2.617 | 2.544 | 2.498 | 2.466 | 2.401 | 2.350 | 2.296 |
|  | 0.01 | 9.330 | 6.927 | 5.953 | 5.412 | 5.064 | 4.821 | 4.640 | 4.499 | 4.388 | 4.296 | 4.155 | 4.010 | 3.858 | 3.765 | 3.701 | 3.569 | 3.467 | 3.361 |
| 13 | 0.10 | 3.136 | 2.763 | 2.560 | 2.434 | 2.347 | 2.283 | 2.234 | 2.195 | 2.164 | 2.138 | 2.097 | 2.053 | 2.007 | 1.978 | 1.958 | 1.915 | 1.882 | 1.846 |
|  | 0.05 | 4.667 | 3.806 | 3.411 | 3.179 | 3.025 | 2.915 | 2.832 | 2.767 | 2.714 | 2.671 | 2.604 | 2.533 | 2.459 | 2.412 | 2.380 | 2.314 | 2.261 | 2.206 |
|  | 0.01 | 9.074 | 6.701 | 5.739 | 5.205 | 4.862 | 4.620 | 4.441 | 4.302 | 4.191 | 4.100 | 3.960 | 3.815 | 3.665 | 3.571 | 3.507 | 3.375 | 3.272 | 3.165 |

*continued*

| $v_2$ | $\alpha$ | 1 | 2 | 3 | 4 | 5 | 6 | 7 | 8 | 9 | 10 | 12 | 15 | 20 | 25 | 30 | 50 | 100 | $\infty$ |
|---|---|---|---|---|---|---|---|---|---|---|---|---|---|---|---|---|---|---|---|
| 14 | 0.10 | 3.102 | 2.726 | 2.522 | 2.395 | 2.307 | 2.243 | 2.193 | 2.154 | 2.122 | 2.095 | 2.054 | 2.010 | 1.962 | 1.933 | 1.912 | 1.869 | 1.834 | 1.797 |
|  | 0.05 | 4.600 | 3.739 | 3.344 | 3.112 | 2.958 | 2.848 | 2.764 | 2.699 | 2.646 | 2.602 | 2.534 | 2.463 | 2.388 | 2.341 | 2.308 | 2.241 | 2.187 | 2.131 |
|  | 0.01 | 8.862 | 6.515 | 5.564 | 5.035 | 4.695 | 4.456 | 4.278 | 4.140 | 4.030 | 3.939 | 3.800 | 3.656 | 3.505 | 3.412 | 3.348 | 3.215 | 3.112 | 3.004 |
| 15 | 0.10 | 3.073 | 2.695 | 2.490 | 2.361 | 2.273 | 2.208 | 2.158 | 2.119 | 2.086 | 2.059 | 2.017 | 1.972 | 1.924 | 1.894 | 1.873 | 1.828 | 1.793 | 1.755 |
|  | 0.05 | 4.543 | 3.682 | 3.287 | 3.056 | 2.901 | 2.790 | 2.707 | 2.641 | 2.588 | 2.544 | 2.475 | 2.403 | 2.328 | 2.280 | 2.247 | 2.178 | 2.123 | 2.066 |
|  | 0.01 | 8.683 | 6.359 | 5.417 | 4.893 | 4.556 | 4.318 | 4.142 | 4.004 | 3.895 | 3.805 | 3.666 | 3.522 | 3.372 | 3.278 | 3.214 | 3.081 | 2.977 | 2.868 |
| 16 | 0.10 | 3.048 | 2.668 | 2.462 | 2.333 | 2.244 | 2.178 | 2.128 | 2.088 | 2.055 | 2.028 | 1.985 | 1.940 | 1.891 | 1.860 | 1.839 | 1.793 | 1.757 | 1.718 |
|  | 0.05 | 4.494 | 3.634 | 3.239 | 3.007 | 2.852 | 2.741 | 2.657 | 2.591 | 2.538 | 2.494 | 2.425 | 2.352 | 2.276 | 2.227 | 2.194 | 2.124 | 2.068 | 2.010 |
|  | 0.01 | 8.531 | 6.226 | 5.292 | 4.773 | 4.437 | 4.202 | 4.026 | 3.890 | 3.780 | 3.691 | 3.553 | 3.409 | 3.259 | 3.165 | 3.101 | 2.967 | 2.863 | 2.753 |
| 17 | 0.10 | 3.026 | 2.645 | 2.437 | 2.308 | 2.218 | 2.152 | 2.102 | 2.061 | 2.028 | 2.001 | 1.958 | 1.912 | 1.862 | 1.831 | 1.809 | 1.763 | 1.726 | 1.686 |
|  | 0.05 | 4.451 | 3.592 | 3.197 | 2.965 | 2.810 | 2.699 | 2.614 | 2.548 | 2.494 | 2.450 | 2.381 | 2.308 | 2.230 | 2.181 | 2.148 | 2.077 | 2.020 | 1.960 |
|  | 0.01 | 8.400 | 6.112 | 5.185 | 4.669 | 4.336 | 4.102 | 3.927 | 3.791 | 3.682 | 3.593 | 3.455 | 3.312 | 3.162 | 3.068 | 3.003 | 2.869 | 2.764 | 2.653 |
| 18 | 0.10 | 3.007 | 2.624 | 2.416 | 2.286 | 2.196 | 2.130 | 2.079 | 2.038 | 2.005 | 1.997 | 1.933 | 1.887 | 1.837 | 1.805 | 1.783 | 1.736 | 1.698 | 1.657 |
|  | 0.05 | 4.414 | 3.555 | 3.160 | 2.928 | 2.773 | 2.661 | 2.577 | 2.510 | 2.456 | 2.412 | 2.342 | 2.269 | 2.191 | 2.141 | 2.107 | 2.035 | 1.978 | 1.917 |
|  | 0.01 | 8.285 | 6.013 | 5.092 | 4.579 | 4.248 | 4.015 | 3.841 | 3.705 | 3.597 | 3.508 | 3.371 | 3.227 | 3.077 | 2.983 | 2.919 | 2.784 | 2.678 | 2.566 |
| 19 | 0.10 | 2.990 | 2.606 | 2.397 | 2.266 | 2.176 | 2.109 | 2.058 | 2.017 | 1.984 | 1.956 | 1.912 | 1.865 | 1.814 | 1.782 | 1.759 | 1.711 | 1.673 | 1.631 |
|  | 0.05 | 4.381 | 3.522 | 3.127 | 2.895 | 2.740 | 2.628 | 2.544 | 2.477 | 2.423 | 2.378 | 2.308 | 2.234 | 2.155 | 2.106 | 2.071 | 1.999 | 1.940 | 1.878 |
|  | 0.01 | 8.185 | 5.926 | 5.010 | 4.500 | 4.171 | 3.939 | 3.765 | 3.631 | 3.523 | 3.434 | 3.297 | 3.153 | 3.003 | 2.909 | 2.844 | 2.709 | 2.602 | 2.489 |
| 20 | 0.10 | 2.975 | 2.589 | 2.380 | 2.249 | 2.158 | 2.091 | 2.040 | 1.999 | 1.965 | 1.937 | 1.892 | 1.845 | 1.794 | 1.761 | 1.738 | 1.690 | 1.650 | 1.607 |
|  | 0.05 | 4.351 | 3.493 | 3.098 | 2.866 | 2.711 | 2.599 | 2.514 | 2.447 | 2.393 | 2.348 | 2.278 | 2.203 | 2.124 | 2.074 | 2.039 | 1.966 | 1.907 | 1.843 |
|  | 0.01 | 8.096 | 5.849 | 4.938 | 4.431 | 4.103 | 3.871 | 3.699 | 3.564 | 3.457 | 3.368 | 3.231 | 3.088 | 2.938 | 2.843 | 2.778 | 2.643 | 2.535 | 2.421 |
| 21 | 0.10 | 2.961 | 2.575 | 2.365 | 2.233 | 2.142 | 2.075 | 2.023 | 1.982 | 1.948 | 1.920 | 1.875 | 1.827 | 1.776 | 1.742 | 1.719 | 1.670 | 1.630 | 1.586 |
|  | 0.05 | 4.325 | 3.467 | 3.072 | 2.840 | 2.685 | 2.573 | 2.488 | 2.420 | 2.366 | 2.321 | 2.250 | 2.176 | 2.096 | 2.045 | 2.010 | 1.936 | 1.876 | 1.812 |
|  | 0.01 | 8.017 | 5.780 | 4.874 | 4.369 | 4.042 | 3.812 | 3.640 | 3.506 | 3.398 | 3.310 | 3.173 | 3.030 | 2.880 | 2.785 | 2.720 | 2.584 | 2.475 | 2.360 |
| 22 | 0.10 | 2.949 | 2.561 | 2.351 | 2.219 | 2.128 | 2.060 | 2.008 | 1.967 | 1.933 | 1.904 | 1.859 | 1.811 | 1.759 | 1.726 | 1.702 | 1.652 | 1.611 | 1.567 |
|  | 0.05 | 4.301 | 3.443 | 3.049 | 2.817 | 2.661 | 2.549 | 2.464 | 2.397 | 2.342 | 2.297 | 2.226 | 2.151 | 2.071 | 2.020 | 1.984 | 1.909 | 1.849 | 1.783 |
|  | 0.01 | 7.945 | 5.719 | 4.817 | 4.313 | 3.988 | 3.758 | 3.587 | 3.453 | 3.346 | 3.258 | 3.121 | 2.978 | 2.827 | 2.733 | 2.667 | 2.531 | 2.422 | 2.305 |
| 23 | 0.10 | 2.937 | 2.549 | 2.339 | 2.207 | 2.115 | 2.047 | 1.995 | 1.953 | 1.919 | 1.890 | 1.845 | 1.796 | 1.744 | 1.710 | 1.686 | 1.636 | 1.594 | 1.549 |
|  | 0.05 | 4.279 | 3.422 | 3.028 | 2.796 | 2.640 | 2.528 | 2.442 | 2.375 | 2.320 | 2.275 | 2.204 | 2.128 | 2.048 | 1.996 | 1.961 | 1.885 | 1.823 | 1.757 |
|  | 0.01 | 7.881 | 5.664 | 4.765 | 4.264 | 3.939 | 3.710 | 3.539 | 3.406 | 3.299 | 3.211 | 3.074 | 2.931 | 2.781 | 2.686 | 2.620 | 2.483 | 2.373 | 2.256 |
| 24 | 0.10 | 2.927 | 2.538 | 2.327 | 2.195 | 2.103 | 2.035 | 1.983 | 1.941 | 1.906 | 1.877 | 1.832 | 1.783 | 1.730 | 1.696 | 1.672 | 1.621 | 1.579 | 1.533 |
|  | 0.05 | 4.260 | 3.403 | 3.009 | 2.776 | 2.621 | 2.508 | 2.423 | 2.355 | 2.300 | 2.255 | 2.183 | 2.108 | 2.027 | 1.975 | 1.939 | 1.863 | 1.800 | 1.733 |
|  | 0.01 | 7.823 | 5.614 | 4.718 | 4.218 | 3.895 | 3.667 | 3.496 | 3.363 | 3.256 | 3.168 | 3.032 | 2.889 | 2.738 | 2.643 | 2.577 | 2.440 | 2.329 | 2.211 |
| 25 | 0.10 | 2.918 | 2.528 | 2.317 | 2.184 | 2.092 | 2.024 | 1.971 | 1.929 | 1.895 | 1.866 | 1.820 | 1.771 | 1.718 | 1.683 | 1.659 | 1.607 | 1.565 | 1.518 |
|  | 0.05 | 4.242 | 3.385 | 2.991 | 2.759 | 2.603 | 2.490 | 2.405 | 2.337 | 2.282 | 2.236 | 2.165 | 2.089 | 2.007 | 1.955 | 1.919 | 1.842 | 1.779 | 1.711 |
|  | 0.01 | 7.770 | 5.568 | 4.675 | 4.177 | 3.855 | 3.627 | 3.457 | 3.324 | 3.217 | 3.129 | 2.993 | 2.850 | 2.699 | 2.604 | 2.538 | 2.400 | 2.289 | 2.169 |
| 26 | 0.10 | 2.909 | 2.519 | 2.307 | 2.174 | 2.082 | 2.014 | 1.961 | 1.919 | 1.884 | 1.855 | 1.809 | 1.760 | 1.706 | 1.671 | 1.647 | 1.594 | 1.551 | 1.504 |
|  | 0.05 | 4.225 | 3.369 | 2.975 | 2.743 | 2.587 | 2.474 | 2.388 | 2.321 | 2.265 | 2.220 | 2.148 | 2.072 | 1.990 | 1.938 | 1.901 | 1.823 | 1.760 | 1.691 |
|  | 0.01 | 7.721 | 5.526 | 4.637 | 4.140 | 3.818 | 3.591 | 3.421 | 3.288 | 3.182 | 3.094 | 2.958 | 2.815 | 2.664 | 2.569 | 2.503 | 2.364 | 2.252 | 2.131 |

| df | α | | | | | | | | | | | | | | | | | | |
|---|---|---|---|---|---|---|---|---|---|---|---|---|---|---|---|---|---|---|---|
| 27 | 0.10 | 2.901 | 2.511 | 2.299 | 2.165 | 2.073 | 2.005 | 1.952 | 1.909 | 1.874 | 1.845 | 1.799 | 1.749 | 1.695 | 1.660 | 1.636 | 1.583 | 1.539 | 1.491 |
|  | 0.05 | 4.210 | 3.354 | 2.960 | 2.728 | 2.572 | 2.459 | 2.373 | 2.305 | 2.250 | 2.204 | 2.132 | 2.056 | 1.974 | 1.921 | 1.884 | 1.806 | 1.742 | 1.672 |
|  | 0.01 | 7.677 | 5.488 | 4.601 | 4.106 | 3.785 | 3.558 | 3.388 | 3.256 | 3.149 | 3.062 | 2.926 | 2.783 | 2.632 | 2.536 | 2.470 | 2.330 | 2.218 | 2.097 |
| 28 | 0.10 | 2.894 | 2.503 | 2.291 | 2.157 | 2.064 | 1.996 | 1.943 | 1.900 | 1.865 | 1.836 | 1.790 | 1.740 | 1.685 | 1.650 | 1.625 | 1.572 | 1.528 | 1.478 |
|  | 0.05 | 4.196 | 3.340 | 2.947 | 2.714 | 2.558 | 2.445 | 2.359 | 2.291 | 2.236 | 2.190 | 2.118 | 2.041 | 1.959 | 1.906 | 1.869 | 1.790 | 1.725 | 1.654 |
|  | 0.01 | 7.636 | 5.453 | 4.568 | 4.074 | 3.754 | 3.528 | 3.358 | 3.226 | 3.120 | 3.032 | 2.896 | 2.753 | 2.602 | 2.506 | 2.440 | 2.300 | 2.187 | 2.064 |
| 29 | 0.10 | 2.887 | 2.495 | 2.283 | 2.149 | 2.057 | 1.988 | 1.935 | 1.892 | 1.857 | 1.827 | 1.781 | 1.731 | 1.676 | 1.640 | 1.616 | 1.562 | 1.517 | 1.467 |
|  | 0.05 | 4.183 | 3.328 | 2.934 | 2.701 | 2.545 | 2.432 | 2.346 | 2.278 | 2.223 | 2.177 | 2.104 | 2.027 | 1.945 | 1.891 | 1.854 | 1.775 | 1.710 | 1.638 |
|  | 0.01 | 7.598 | 5.420 | 4.538 | 4.045 | 3.725 | 3.499 | 3.330 | 3.198 | 3.092 | 3.005 | 2.868 | 2.726 | 2.574 | 2.478 | 2.412 | 2.271 | 2.158 | 2.034 |
| 30 | 0.10 | 2.881 | 2.489 | 2.276 | 2.142 | 2.049 | 1.980 | 1.927 | 1.884 | 1.849 | 1.819 | 1.773 | 1.722 | 1.667 | 1.632 | 1.606 | 1.552 | 1.507 | 1.456 |
|  | 0.05 | 4.171 | 3.316 | 2.922 | 2.690 | 2.534 | 2.421 | 2.334 | 2.266 | 2.211 | 2.165 | 2.092 | 2.015 | 1.932 | 1.878 | 1.841 | 1.761 | 1.695 | 1.622 |
|  | 0.01 | 7.562 | 5.390 | 4.510 | 4.018 | 3.699 | 3.473 | 3.304 | 3.173 | 3.067 | 2.979 | 2.843 | 2.700 | 2.549 | 2.453 | 2.386 | 2.245 | 2.131 | 2.006 |
| 35 | 0.10 | 2.855 | 2.461 | 2.247 | 2.113 | 2.019 | 1.950 | 1.896 | 1.852 | 1.817 | 1.787 | 1.739 | 1.688 | 1.632 | 1.595 | 1.569 | 1.513 | 1.465 | 1.411 |
|  | 0.05 | 4.121 | 3.267 | 2.874 | 2.641 | 2.485 | 2.372 | 2.285 | 2.217 | 2.161 | 2.114 | 2.041 | 1.963 | 1.878 | 1.824 | 1.786 | 1.703 | 1.635 | 1.558 |
|  | 0.01 | 7.419 | 5.268 | 4.396 | 3.908 | 3.592 | 3.368 | 3.200 | 3.069 | 2.963 | 2.876 | 2.740 | 2.597 | 2.445 | 2.348 | 2.281 | 2.137 | 2.020 | 1.891 |
| 40 | 0.10 | 2.835 | 2.440 | 2.226 | 2.091 | 1.997 | 1.927 | 1.873 | 1.829 | 1.793 | 1.763 | 1.715 | 1.662 | 1.605 | 1.568 | 1.541 | 1.483 | 1.434 | 1.377 |
|  | 0.05 | 4.085 | 3.232 | 2.839 | 2.606 | 2.449 | 2.336 | 2.249 | 2.180 | 2.124 | 2.077 | 2.003 | 1.924 | 1.839 | 1.783 | 1.744 | 1.660 | 1.589 | 1.509 |
|  | 0.01 | 7.314 | 5.170 | 4.313 | 3.828 | 3.514 | 3.291 | 3.124 | 2.993 | 2.888 | 2.801 | 2.665 | 2.522 | 2.369 | 2.271 | 2.203 | 2.058 | 1.938 | 1.805 |
| 45 | 0.10 | 2.820 | 2.425 | 2.210 | 2.074 | 1.980 | 1.909 | 1.855 | 1.811 | 1.774 | 1.744 | 1.695 | 1.643 | 1.585 | 1.546 | 1.519 | 1.460 | 1.409 | 1.349 |
|  | 0.05 | 4.057 | 3.204 | 2.812 | 2.579 | 2.422 | 2.308 | 2.221 | 2.152 | 2.096 | 2.049 | 1.974 | 1.895 | 1.808 | 1.752 | 1.713 | 1.626 | 1.554 | 1.470 |
|  | 0.01 | 7.234 | 5.110 | 4.249 | 3.767 | 3.454 | 3.232 | 3.066 | 2.935 | 2.830 | 2.743 | 2.608 | 2.464 | 2.311 | 2.213 | 2.144 | 1.997 | 1.875 | 1.737 |
| 50 | 0.10 | 2.809 | 2.412 | 2.197 | 2.061 | 1.966 | 1.895 | 1.840 | 1.796 | 1.760 | 1.729 | 1.680 | 1.627 | 1.568 | 1.529 | 1.502 | 1.441 | 1.388 | 1.327 |
|  | 0.05 | 4.034 | 3.183 | 2.790 | 2.557 | 2.400 | 2.286 | 2.199 | 2.130 | 2.073 | 2.026 | 1.952 | 1.871 | 1.784 | 1.727 | 1.687 | 1.599 | 1.525 | 1.438 |
|  | 0.01 | 7.171 | 5.057 | 4.199 | 3.720 | 3.408 | 3.186 | 3.020 | 2.890 | 2.785 | 2.698 | 2.562 | 2.419 | 2.265 | 2.167 | 2.098 | 1.949 | 1.825 | 1.683 |
| 60 | 0.10 | 2.791 | 2.393 | 2.177 | 2.041 | 1.946 | 1.875 | 1.819 | 1.775 | 1.738 | 1.707 | 1.657 | 1.603 | 1.543 | 1.504 | 1.476 | 1.413 | 1.358 | 1.291 |
|  | 0.05 | 4.001 | 3.150 | 2.758 | 2.525 | 2.368 | 2.254 | 2.167 | 2.097 | 2.040 | 1.993 | 1.917 | 1.836 | 1.748 | 1.690 | 1.649 | 1.559 | 1.481 | 1.389 |
|  | 0.01 | 7.077 | 4.977 | 4.126 | 3.649 | 3.339 | 3.119 | 2.953 | 2.823 | 2.718 | 2.632 | 2.496 | 2.352 | 2.198 | 2.098 | 2.028 | 1.877 | 1.749 | 1.601 |
| 70 | 0.10 | 2.779 | 2.380 | 2.164 | 2.027 | 1.931 | 1.860 | 1.804 | 1.760 | 1.723 | 1.691 | 1.641 | 1.587 | 1.526 | 1.486 | 1.457 | 1.392 | 1.335 | 1.265 |
|  | 0.05 | 3.978 | 3.128 | 2.736 | 2.503 | 2.346 | 2.231 | 2.143 | 2.074 | 2.017 | 1.969 | 1.893 | 1.812 | 1.722 | 1.664 | 1.622 | 1.530 | 1.450 | 1.353 |
|  | 0.01 | 7.011 | 4.922 | 4.074 | 3.600 | 3.291 | 3.071 | 2.906 | 2.777 | 2.672 | 2.585 | 2.450 | 2.306 | 2.150 | 2.050 | 1.980 | 1.826 | 1.695 | 1.540 |
| 80 | 0.10 | 2.769 | 2.370 | 2.154 | 2.016 | 1.921 | 1.849 | 1.793 | 1.748 | 1.711 | 1.680 | 1.629 | 1.574 | 1.513 | 1.472 | 1.443 | 1.377 | 1.318 | 1.245 |
|  | 0.05 | 3.960 | 3.111 | 2.719 | 2.486 | 2.329 | 2.214 | 2.126 | 2.056 | 1.999 | 1.951 | 1.875 | 1.793 | 1.703 | 1.644 | 1.602 | 1.508 | 1.426 | 1.325 |
|  | 0.01 | 6.963 | 4.881 | 4.036 | 3.563 | 3.255 | 3.036 | 2.871 | 2.742 | 2.637 | 2.551 | 2.415 | 2.271 | 2.115 | 2.015 | 1.944 | 1.788 | 1.655 | 1.494 |
| 90 | 0.10 | 2.762 | 2.363 | 2.146 | 2.008 | 1.912 | 1.841 | 1.785 | 1.739 | 1.702 | 1.670 | 1.620 | 1.564 | 1.503 | 1.461 | 1.432 | 1.365 | 1.304 | 1.228 |
|  | 0.05 | 3.947 | 3.098 | 2.706 | 2.473 | 2.316 | 2.201 | 2.113 | 2.043 | 1.986 | 1.938 | 1.861 | 1.779 | 1.688 | 1.629 | 1.586 | 1.491 | 1.407 | 1.302 |
|  | 0.01 | 6.925 | 4.849 | 4.007 | 3.535 | 3.228 | 3.009 | 2.845 | 2.715 | 2.611 | 2.524 | 2.389 | 2.244 | 2.088 | 1.987 | 1.916 | 1.759 | 1.623 | 1.457 |
| 100 | 0.10 | 2.756 | 2.356 | 2.139 | 2.002 | 1.906 | 1.834 | 1.778 | 1.732 | 1.695 | 1.663 | 1.612 | 1.557 | 1.494 | 1.453 | 1.423 | 1.355 | 1.293 | 1.214 |
|  | 0.05 | 3.936 | 3.087 | 2.696 | 2.463 | 2.305 | 2.191 | 2.103 | 2.032 | 1.975 | 1.927 | 1.850 | 1.768 | 1.676 | 1.616 | 1.573 | 1.477 | 1.392 | 1.283 |
|  | 0.01 | 6.895 | 4.824 | 3.984 | 3.513 | 3.206 | 2.988 | 2.823 | 2.694 | 2.590 | 2.503 | 2.368 | 2.223 | 2.067 | 1.965 | 1.893 | 1.735 | 1.598 | 1.427 |
| 120 | 0.10 | 2.748 | 2.347 | 2.130 | 1.992 | 1.896 | 1.824 | 1.767 | 1.722 | 1.684 | 1.652 | 1.601 | 1.545 | 1.482 | 1.440 | 1.409 | 1.340 | 1.277 | 1.193 |
|  | 0.05 | 3.920 | 3.072 | 2.680 | 2.447 | 2.290 | 2.175 | 2.087 | 2.016 | 1.959 | 1.910 | 1.834 | 1.750 | 1.659 | 1.598 | 1.554 | 1.457 | 1.369 | 1.254 |
|  | 0.01 | 6.851 | 4.787 | 3.949 | 3.480 | 3.174 | 2.956 | 2.792 | 2.663 | 2.559 | 2.472 | 2.336 | 2.192 | 2.035 | 1.932 | 1.860 | 1.700 | 1.559 | 1.381 |

*continued*

| $v_2$ | $\alpha$ | 1 | 2 | 3 | 4 | 5 | 6 | 7 | 8 | 9 | 10 | 12 | 15 | 20 | 25 | 30 | 50 | 100 | $\infty$ |
|---|---|---|---|---|---|---|---|---|---|---|---|---|---|---|---|---|---|---|---|
| 150 | 0.10 | 2.739 | 2.338 | 2.121 | 1.983 | 1.886 | 1.814 | 1.757 | 1.712 | 1.674 | 1.642 | 1.590 | 1.533 | 1.470 | 1.427 | 1.396 | 1.325 | 1.259 | 1.169 |
|  | 0.05 | 3.904 | 3.056 | 2.665 | 2.432 | 2.274 | 2.160 | 2.071 | 2.001 | 1.943 | 1.894 | 1.817 | 1.734 | 1.641 | 1.580 | 1.535 | 1.436 | 1.345 | 1.223 |
|  | 0.01 | 6.807 | 4.749 | 3.915 | 3.447 | 3.142 | 2.924 | 2.761 | 2.632 | 2.528 | 2.441 | 2.305 | 2.160 | 2.003 | 1.900 | 1.827 | 1.665 | 1.520 | 1.331 |
| 200 | 0.10 | 2.731 | 2.329 | 2.111 | 1.973 | 1.876 | 1.804 | 1.747 | 1.701 | 1.663 | 1.631 | 1.579 | 1.522 | 1.458 | 1.414 | 1.383 | 1.310 | 1.242 | 1.144 |
|  | 0.05 | 3.888 | 3.041 | 2.650 | 2.417 | 2.259 | 2.144 | 2.056 | 1.985 | 1.927 | 1.878 | 1.801 | 1.717 | 1.623 | 1.561 | 1.516 | 1.415 | 1.321 | 1.189 |
|  | 0.01 | 6.763 | 4.713 | 3.881 | 3.414 | 3.110 | 2.893 | 2.730 | 2.601 | 2.497 | 2.411 | 2.275 | 2.129 | 1.971 | 1.868 | 1.794 | 1.629 | 1.481 | 1.279 |
| 500 | 0.10 | 2.716 | 2.313 | 2.095 | 1.956 | 1.859 | 1.786 | 1.729 | 1.683 | 1.644 | 1.612 | 1.559 | 1.501 | 1.435 | 1.391 | 1.358 | 1.282 | 1.209 | 1.087 |
|  | 0.05 | 3.860 | 3.014 | 2.623 | 2.390 | 2.232 | 2.117 | 2.028 | 1.957 | 1.899 | 1.850 | 1.772 | 1.686 | 1.592 | 1.528 | 1.482 | 1.376 | 1.275 | 1.113 |
|  | 0.01 | 6.686 | 4.648 | 3.821 | 3.357 | 3.054 | 2.838 | 2.675 | 2.547 | 2.443 | 2.356 | 2.220 | 2.075 | 1.915 | 1.810 | 1.735 | 1.566 | 1.408 | 1.164 |
| 1000 | 0.10 | 2.711 | 2.308 | 2.089 | 1.950 | 1.853 | 1.780 | 1.723 | 1.676 | 1.638 | 1.605 | 1.552 | 1.494 | 1.428 | 1.383 | 1.350 | 1.273 | 1.197 | 1.060 |
|  | 0.05 | 3.851 | 3.005 | 2.614 | 2.381 | 2.223 | 2.108 | 2.019 | 1.948 | 1.889 | 1.840 | 1.762 | 1.676 | 1.581 | 1.517 | 1.471 | 1.363 | 1.260 | 1.078 |
|  | 0.01 | 6.660 | 4.625 | 3.801 | 3.338 | 3.036 | 2.820 | 2.657 | 2.529 | 2.425 | 2.339 | 2.203 | 2.056 | 1.897 | 1.791 | 1.716 | 1.544 | 1.383 | 1.112 |
| $\infty$ | 0.10 | 2.706 | 2.303 | 2.084 | 1.945 | 1.847 | 1.774 | 1.717 | 1.670 | 1.632 | 1.599 | 1.546 | 1.487 | 1.421 | 1.375 | 1.342 | 1.263 | 1.185 | 1.000 |
|  | 0.05 | 3.841 | 2.996 | 2.605 | 2.372 | 2.214 | 2.099 | 2.010 | 1.938 | 1.880 | 1.831 | 1.752 | 1.666 | 1.571 | 1.506 | 1.459 | 1.350 | 1.243 | 1.000 |
|  | 0.01 | 6.635 | 4.605 | 3.782 | 3.319 | 3.017 | 2.802 | 2.639 | 2.511 | 2.407 | 2.321 | 2.185 | 2.039 | 1.878 | 1.773 | 1.696 | 1.523 | 1.358 | 1.000 |

# BIBLIOGRAPHY

Allen, R. G. D. (1975) *Index Numbers in Theory and Practice*, London: Macmillan.

Anderson, D. R., Sweeney, D. J. and Williams, T. A. (1987) *Statistics for Business and Economics* (3rd edn), New York: West Publishing Co.

Auerbach, R. D. and Rutner, J. L. (1978) The misspecification of a nonseasonal cycle as a seasonal cycle by the X-11 seasonal adjustment program, *The Review of Economics and Statistics*, **60**, (November), 601–603.

Ball, S. (1989) *Directory of International Sources of Business Information*, London: Pitman Publishing.

Barker, R. L. (1990) SPC and total quality management, *Total Quality Management*, **1** (2), 183–196.

Bartlett, M. S. (1990) Chance or chaos? (with discussion), *Journal of the Royal Statistical Society*, Series A, **153** (Part 3), 321–348.

Bissel, A. F. (1990) Control charts and cusums for high precision processes, *Total Quality Management*, **1** (2), 221–228.

Bond, K. and Scott, J. P. (1988) *Essential Business Statistics: A Minitab Framework*, Boston: PWS-Kent Publishing Co.

British Overseas Trade Board (annual) *Directory of Published International Market Research*, London: BOTB and Arlington Management Publications.

Bryant, C. G. E. and Daniel, D. L. (1989) The effect of rebasing on the estimates of Gross Domestic Product, *Economic Trends*, No. 423, January, pp. 118–129.

Bunn, D. (1989) and other papers in: Special issue on combining forecasts, *Journal of Forecasting*, **8** (3).

Business Information Associates (1990) *International Directory of Non-official Statistical Sources*, London: Euromonitor.

Cannell, C. F., Miller, P. V. and Oksenberg, L. (1981) Research on interviewing techniques, in S. Leinhardt (ed.) *Sociological Methodology 1981*, San Francisco: Jossey-Bass, pp. 389–437.

Carruthers, A. G., Sellwood, D. J. and Ward, P. (1980) Recent developments in the Retail Prices Index, *The Statistician*, **29** (1), 1–32.

Central Statistical Office (CSO) (1989) The rebased index of production, *Economic Trends*, 424, February, London: HMSO.

Central Statistical Office (CSO) (1990) *Family Expenditure Survey: Report for 1988 Giving the Results for the United Kingdom*, London: HMSO.

Chapman, M. (1986) in collaboration with Basil Mahon, *Plain Figures*, Cabinet Office (Management and Personnel Office) Civil Service College, London: HMSO.

Chatfield, C. (1985) The initial examination of data (with discussion), *Journal of the Royal Statistical Society*, Series A, **148**, 214–253.

Chatfield, C. (1988a) *Problem Solving: A Statistician's Guide*, London: Chapman and Hall.

Chatfield, C. (1988b) What is the 'best' method of forecasting?, *Journal of Applied Statistics*, **15** (1), 17–36.

Chisnall, P. (1986) *Marketing Research* (3rd edn), London: McGraw-Hill.

Chung, K. L. (1979) *Elementary Probability Theory with Stochastic Processes*, New York: Springer-Verlag.

Cleveland, W. S. and McGill, N. (1985) Graphical perception and graphical methods for analysing and presenting scientific data, *Science*, **229**, 828–833.

Cleveland, W. S. and McGill, R. (1987) Graphical perception: the visual decoding of quantitative information on graphical displays of data (with discussion), *Journal of the Royal Statistical Society*, Series A, **150** (3), 192–229.

Cochran, W. G. (1966) *Sampling Techniques* (2nd edn), London: Wiley.

Collins, M. and Sykes, W. (1987) The problems of non-coverage and unlisted numbers in telephone surveys in Britain. *Journal of the Royal Statistical Society, Series A*, **150** (Part 3), 241–253.

Comptroller and Auditor General (1990) *The Retail Prices Index: Report*, London: HMSO.

Conover, W. J. (1980) *Practical Nonparametric Statistics* (2nd edn), New York: Wiley.

Croxton, F. E., Crowden, D. J. and Klein, S. (1968) *Applied General Statistics*, London: Pitman.

Culbertson, H. M. and Powers, R. D. (1959) A study of graph comprehension difficulties, *Audio Visual Communication Review*, **17**, 97–110.

Day, D. J. and Dunn, J. E. (1969) Estimating the audience for advertising on the outside of London buses, *Applied Statistics, Journal of the Royal Statistical Society, Series C*, **18** (3).

Day, S. (1987) Clover New Product Development, in U. Bradley (ed.) *Applied Marketing and Social Research* (2nd edn), Chichester: Wiley.

Deaton, A. and Muellbauer, J. (1980) *Economics and Consumer Behaviour*, Cambridge: Cambridge University Press.

Deming, W. E. (1986) *Out of the Crisis*, Cambridge, Mass.: MIT Press.

Department of Employment (1975) *Housing Costs, Weighting and Other Matters Affecting the Retail Prices Index*, Report of the Retail Prices Index Advisory Committee, London: HMSO.

Department of Employment (1987a) *Retail Prices Indices 1914–1986*, Government Statistical Services, London: HMSO.

Department of Employment (1987b) A short guide to the Retail Prices Index, *Employment Gazette*, **95** (8; August), 395–406.

Department of Employment (1988), Retail Prices Index: revision of weights, *Employment Gazette*, 96, 4, 199–258.

Dickens, J. (1987) The fresh cream cake market: The use of qualitative research as part of a consumer research programme, in U. Bradley (ed.) *Applied Marketing and Social Research* (2nd edn), Chichester: J. Wiley.

Dickinson, G. C. (1977) *Statistical Mapping and the Presentation of Statistics* (2nd edn), London: Edward Arnold.

Drake, M. (1987) A cost effective use of research to evaluate sales promotions, in U. Bradley (ed.) *Applied Marketing and Social Research* (2nd edn), Chichester: Wiley.

Duncan, A. J. (1986) *Quality Control and Industrial Statistics* (5th edn), Homewood, Ill.: Irwin.

Durbin, J. (1987) Statistics and statistical science: The Address of the President, *Journal of the Royal Statistical Society, Series A*, **150** (Part 3), 177–191.

Durlacher, J. (ed.) (intermittent), *Direct Mail Databook*, Aldershot: Gower.

Ehrenberg, A. S. C. (1975) *Data Reduction: Analysing and Interpreting Statistical Data*, London: Wiley.

Ehrenberg, A. S. C. (1977) Rudiments of numeracy (with discussion), *Journal of the Royal Statistical Society, Series A*, **140**, 277–297.

Ehrenberg, A. S. C. (1978) Graphs or tables?, *The Statistician*, **27** (2), 87–96.

Ehrenberg, A. S. C. (1988) *Repeat-Buying: Facts, Theory and Applications* (2nd edn), London: Griffin.

Eichhorn, W. and Vveller, J. (1983) Axiomatic foundation of price indexes and purchasing power parties, in W. E. Diewert and C. Montmarquette (eds) *Price Level Measurement*, Proceedings of a conference sponsored by Statistics, Canada, Ottawa: Ministry of Supply and Services, Canada, pp. 411–454.

Evans, M. K. (1969) *Macroeconomic activity: Theory Forecasting and Control*, New York: Harper & Row.

Flaxen, D. W. (1980) *The Tax and Price Index*, edited version of Proceedings of the General Meeting of the Royal Statistical Society, London: Royal Statistical Society.

Fisher, F. M. (1960) *The Identification Problem in Econometrics*, New York: McGraw-Hill.

Fletcher, J. (1983) *How to Write a Report*, London: Institute of Personnel Management.

Forsyth, F. G. and Fowler, R. F. (1981) The theory and practice of chain price index numbers, *Journal of the Royal Statistical Society, Series A*, **144** (2), 224–247.

Fowler, R. F. (1970) Some problems of index number construction, *Studies in Official Statistics, Research Series*, No. 3, London: HMSO.

Frude, N. (1987) *A Guide to SPSS – PC +*, Basingstoke: Macmillan.

Fry, V. and Pashardes, P. (1986) *The RPI and the Cost of Living*, The Institute for Fiscal Studies (IFS) Report Series, No. 22, London: IFS.

Gaito, J. (1980) Measurement scales and statistics: resurgence of an old misconception, *Psychological Bulletin*, **87**, 564–567.

Gardner, E. S. (1985) Exponential smoothing: The state of the art, *Journal of Forecasting*, **4** (1), 1–28.

Gilchrist, W. (1976) *Statistical Forecasting*, London: Wiley.

Glaser, B. G. and Strauss, A. L. (1967) *The Discovery Of Grounded Theory: Strategies for Qualitative Research*, New York: Aldine Publishing Co.

Gorham, K. D. (1990) *Personal Productivity with Lotus 1-2-3: version 2.01 primer*, Oxford: WCB Publishers International.

Gowers, Sir E. (1973) *The Complete Plain Words*, revised by Sir Bruce Fraser, London: HMSO.

Granger, C. W. J. and Newbold, P. (1974) Spurious regressions in econometrics, *Journal of Econometrics*, **2**, 111–120.

Hawkins, D. I. and Coney, K. A. (1981) Uniformed response error in survey research, *Journal of Marketing Research*, August, 373.

Hibbert, J. (1990) Public Confidence in the integrity and validity of official statistics (with discussion), *Journal of the Royal Statistical Society, Series A*, **153** (Part 2), 121–150.

Hite, S. (1988) *Women and Love: A Cultural Revolution in Progress*, New York: Knopf.

Hoaglin, D. C., Mosteller, F. and Tukey, J. W. (1983) *Understanding Robust and Exploratory Data Analysis*, New York: Wiley.

Hoel, P. (1966) *Introduction to Mathematical Statistics* (3rd edn), London: Wiley.

Hunt, S. D., Sparkman, R. D. Jr and Wilcox, J. B. (1982) The pretest in survey research: issues and preliminary findings, *Journal of Marketing Research*, May, 269–273.

Huff, D. (1965) *How to Lie with Statistics*, Harmondsworth: Penguin.

International Labour Office (annual), *Nineteenth International Conference of Labour Statisticians: Report on Consumer Price Indices*, Geneva: ILO.

Jenkins, G. M. (1982) Some practical aspects of forecasting in organisations, *Journal of Forecasting*, **1** (1), 3–22.

Judge, G. (1990) *Quantitative Analysis for Economic and Business using Lotus 1-2-3*, London: Harvester Wheatsheaf.

Kalton, G. and Schuman, H. (1982) The effect of the question on survey responses: a review, *Journal of the Royal Statistical Society, Series A*, **145** (Part 1), 42–73.

Kalton, G., Collins, M. and Brook, L. (1978) Experiments in wording opinion questions, *Applied Statistics: Journal of the Royal Statistical Society, Series C*, **27**, 149–161.

Kanji, G. K. (1990a) Total Quality Management: the second industrial revolution, *Total Quality Management*, **1** (1), 3–12.

Kanji, G. K. (1990b) Total Quality Management: myth or miracle, *Total Quality Management*, **1** (2), 163–167.

Kazmier, L. J. (1988) *Business Statistics* (2nd edn), Schaum's Outline Series in Business, London: McGraw-Hill.

Kemsley, W. F. F., Redpath, R. U. and Holmes, M. (1980) *Family Expenditure Survey Handbook*, Office of Population and Censuses, Social Survey Division, London: HMSO.

Kendall, M. G. (1962) *Rank Correlation Methods*, London: Griffin.

Kendall, M. G. and Stuart, A. (1969) *The Advanced Theory of Statistics*, London: Griffin.

Kennedy, P. (1985) *A Guide to Econometrics*, Oxford: Blackwell.

Kenny, P. B. and Durbin, J. (1982) 'Local trend estimation and seasonal adjustments of economic and social time series', *Journal of the Royal Statistical Society*, Series A, 145, 1.

Kmietowicz, Z. W. and Yannoulis, Y. (1988) *Statistical Tables for Economic, Business and Social Studies*, Harlow: Longman.

Koutsoyiannis, A. (1977) *A Theory of Econometrics*, An Introductory Exposition of Econometric Methods, London: Macmillan.

Lawal, H. B. (1980) Tables of percentage points of Pearson's goodness-of-fit statistic for use with small expectations, *Journal of the Royal Statistical Society, Series C, Applied Statistics*, **29** (3), 292–298.

Lehmann, E. L. (1975), *Non-Parametrics: Statistical Methods Based on Ranks*, San Francisco: Holden Day.

Lewis, C. (1989) *Business Forecasting in a Lotus 1-2-3 Environment*, Chichester: Wiley.

Maddala, G. S. (1977) *Econometrics*, Tokyo: McGraw-Hill.

Mahmoud, E. (1984) Accuracy in forecasting, *Journal of Forecasting*, **3**, 139–159.

Majani, B. E. (1983) Decomposition methods for medium-term planning and budgeting, in Makridakis and Wheelwright (eds).

Makridakis, S. (1986) The art and science of forecasting, *International Journal of Forecasting*, **2**, 15–34.

Makridakis, S., Anderson, A., Carbone, R. *et al.* (1984) *The Forecasting Accuracy of Major Time Series Methods*, New York: Wiley.

Makridakis, S. and Wheelwright, S. C. (eds) (1983) *The Handbook of Forecasting*, New York: Wiley.

Makridakis, S., Wheelwright, S. C. and McGee, V. (1980) *Forecasting Methods for Management* (3rd edn), New York: Wiley.

Manly, B. F. J. (1986) *Multivariate Statistical Methods*, London: Chapman and Hall.

Meade, N. (1984) The use of growth curves in forecasting market development—a review and appraisal, *Journal of Forecasting*, **3** (4), 429–451.

Meddis, R. (1984) *Statistics Using Ranks: A Unified Approach*, London: Blackwell.

Meihofer, H. J. (1973) The visual perception of the circle in thematic maps: experimental results, *Canadian Cartographer*, **10**, 63–84.

Mellis, C., Meen, G., Pain, N. and Whittaker, R. (1989) *The New Treasury Model Project, Government Economic Service Working Paper*, No. 106, (*Treasury Working Paper No. 54*), London: Treasury.

Miller, R. B. (1988) *Minitab Handbook for Business and Economics*, Boston: Duxburg Press.

Minitab (1989) *Reference Manual*, Release 7, State College, Pennsylvania: Minitab Inc.

Moore, P. G. (1990) The skills and challenge of the nineties (the Address of the President), *Journal of the Royal Statistical Society*, Series A, 153, 3, 265–285

Monopolies and Mergers Commission (1989) *The Supply Of Beer: A Report on the Supply of Beer for retail sale in the United Kingdom*, Cm. 651, London: HMSO, March.

Moroney, M. J. (1965) *Facts from Figures*, Harmondsworth: Penguin.

Moser, C. A. and Kalton, G. (1985) *Survey Methods in Social Investigation*, London: Heinemann.

Neave, H. R. and Worthington, P. L. (1988) *Distribution-Free Tests*, London: Unwin Hyman.

Nelson, L. (1984) The Shewhart control chart—Tests for special causes, *Journal of Quality Technology*, **16**, 237–239.

*News and Notes*, The Royal Statistical Society, March 1991.

Norusis, M. J. (1985) *SPSS-X Advanced Statistics Guide*, New York: McGraw-Hill.

Norusis, M. J. (1987) *The SPSS Guide to Data Analysis for SPSS-X with Additional Instructions for SPSS/PC +*, Chicago, Ill.: SPSS.

Norusis, M. J. (1988a) *SPSS/PC + Version 2.0 Base Manual for the IBM PC/XT/AT and PS/2*, Chicago, Ill.: SPSS.

Norusis, M. J. (1988b) *SPSS/PC + Advanced Statistics Version 2.0 for the IBM PC/XT/AT and PS/2*, Chicago, Ill.: SPSS.

Norusis, M. J. (1988c) *SPSS/PC + Version 3.0 Update Manual for the IBM PC/XT/AT and PS/2*, Chicago, Ill.: SPSS.

O'Donovan, T. M. (1983) *Short Term Forecasting: An Introduction to the Box-Jenkins Approach*, Chichester: Wiley.

Oakland, J. S. (1986) *Statistical Processes Control, A Practical Guide*, London: Heinemann.

Owen, F. and Jones, R. (1982) *Statistics*, Stockport, Lancashire: Polytech Publishers.

Raff, M. S. (1956) On approximating the point binomial, *Journal of the American Statistical Association*, **51**, 293.

Raveh, A. (1984) Comments on some properties of X-11, *The Review of Economics and Statistics*, **66**, 343–348.

Ross, S. C. (1987) *Understanding and Using Lotus 1-2-3, Release 2*, St Paul: West Publishing.

Ryan, B. F., Joiner, B. L. and Ryan, T. A. (1985) *Minitab Handbook* (2nd edn), Boston: PWS-Kent Publishing Co.

Saren, M. A. and Brownlie, D. T. (1983) A review of technological forecasting techniques, *Management Bibliographies and Reviews*, **9** (4).

Schmid, C. F. (1985) *Statistical Graphics*, London: Wiley.

Schuman, H. and Presser, S. (1979) The open and closed question, *American Sociological Review*, **44**, 692–712.

Scott, E. L. (1979) Correlation and suggestions of causality: spurious correlation, in L. Orloci, C. R. Rao and W. M. Stiteler (eds) *Multivariate Methods in Ecological Work*, Fairland, Maryland: International Cooperative Publishing House, pp. 237–251.

Shiskin, J., Young, A. H. and Musgrave, J. C. (1967) United States Bureau of the Census, the X-11 variant of the census method, II. Seasonal adjustment program, *Bureau of the Census, Technical Paper*, No. 15, Washington DC: Department of Commerce.

Shultz, R. Z. (1984) The implementation of forecasting models, *Journal of Forecasting*, **3**, 43–45.

Silver, M. S. (1984) Criteria for choosing between alternative consumer price index number formulae with special reference to chained indices, *The Statistician*, **33**, 224–237.

Silver, M. (1989) Sampling frames and non-response problems in surveys of United Kingdom companies: A case study of the ESRC/DTI survey of management training, *The Statistician*, **38** (1), 47–60.

Silver, M. S. and Goode, M. (1990) Econometric forecasting model for rents in the British retail property market, *OMEGA, The International Journal of Management Science*, **18** (5), 529–539.

Silver, M. and Mahdavy, K. (1989) The measurements of a nation's terms of trade effect and real national disposable income within a national accounting framework, *Journal of the Royal Statistical Society*, Series A, **152** (Part 1), 87–107.

Smith, H. A. (1987) Assessing what is being measured by a readership survey, in U. Bradley (ed.) *Applied Marketing and Social Research* (2nd edn), Chichester: Wiley.

Spiegel, M. R. (1988) *Statistics* (2nd edn), Schaum's Outline Series in Mathematics, London: McGraw-Hill.

Sprent, P. (1990) *Applied Nonparametric Statistical Methods*, London: Chapman and Hall.

SPSS (Statistical Package for the Social Scientist) (1988) *SPSS-X Users Guide* (3rd edn) Chicago, Ill.: SPSS.

Stewart, I. (1989) *Does God Play Dice? The Mathematics of Chaos*, Oxford: Blackwell.

Stuvel, G. (1986) *National Accounts Analysis*, London: Macmillan.

Sudman, S., Finn, A. and Lannom, L. (1984) The use of bounded recall procedures in single interviews, *Public Opinion Quarterly*, Summer, 520–524.

Sykes, W. (1990) Validity and reliability in qualitative market research: A review of the literature, *Journal of the Market Research Society*, **32** (3; July).

Szulc, B. J. (1983) Linking price index numbers, in W. E. Diewert and C. Montmarquette (eds) *Price Level Measurement*, Proceedings from a conference sponsored by Statistics, Canada, Ottawa: Ministry of Supply and Services, Canada, pp. 527–598.

Tufte, E. R. (1983) *The Visual Display of Quantitative Information*, Cheshire, Conn.: Graphics Press.

Tukey, J. U. (1977) *Exploratory Data Analysis*, Reading, Mass.: Addison-Wesley.

Tull, D. S. and Hawkins, D. I. (1987) *Marketing Research, Measurement and Method*, New York: Macmillan.

United Nations (1977) Guidelines on principles of a system of price and quantity statistics, *Statistical Papers*, Series M, No. 59, United Nations: New York.

United Nations (1979) Manual on National Accounts at constant prices, *Statistical Papers*, Series M, No. 64, New York: United Nations.

Upton, G. J. G. (1982) A comparison of alternative tests for the $2 \times 2$ comparative trial, *Journal of the Royal Statistical Society*, **145** (Part 1), 86–105.

Velleman, P. F. and Hoaglin, D. C. (1981) *Applications, Business and Computing of Exploratory Data Analysis*, Boston: Duxburg Press.

Vernon, K. D. C. (ed.) (1984) *Information Sources in Management and Business* (2nd edn), London: Butterworth.

Wallace, T. D. and Silver, J. L. (1988) *Econometrics: An Introduction*, Reading, Mass.: Addison-Wesley.

Wallis, K. F. (1974) Seasonal adjustment and the relations between variables, *Journal of the American Statistical Association*, **69**, 318–322.

Wilson, J. H. and Keating, B. (1990) *Business Forecasting*, Homewood, Ill.: Irwin.

Wilson, P. R. and Elliott, D. J. (1987) An evaluation of the postcode address file as a sampling frame and its use within OPCS, *Journal of the Royal Statistical Society, Series A*, **150** (Part 3), 230–240.

Winkler, R. L. and Makridakis, S. (1983) The combination of forecasts, *Journal of the Royal Statistical Society*, Series A, **146** (Part 2), 150–157.

Wright, G. and Ayton, P. (1987) *Judgemental Forecasting*, New York: Wiley.

Wright, P. and Fox, K. (1970) Presenting information in tables, *Applied Ergonomics*, **1** (4), 234–242.

Wrigley, N. (ed.) (1988) *Store Choice, Store Location and Market Analysis*, London: Routledge.

Yates, F. (1984) Tests of significance for $2 \times 2$ contingency tables (with discussion), *Journal of the Royal Statistical Society, Series A*, **147** (Part 3), 426–463.

Yule, G. U. (1971) Why do we sometimes get nonsense correlations between time-series? A study in sampling and the nature of time-series, in A. Stuart and M. G. Kendall (eds) *Statistical Papers of George Udny Yule*, London: Griffin, p. 326; reprinted from the *Journal of the Royal Statistical Society*, **89** (1926), 1–64.

# INDEX